STREE'

Tyne & Wear

First published in 2001 as
Tyne & Wear Northumberland by

Philip's, a division of
Octopus Publishing Group Ltd
2-4 Heron Quays, London E14 4JP

First edition 2005
First impression 2005

ISBN-10   0-540-08753-X (pocket)
ISBN-13   978-0-540-08753-2 (pocket)

© Philip's 2005

OS Ordnance Survey®

This product includes mapping data licensed from
Ordnance Survey® with the permission of the
Controller of Her Majesty's Stationery Office.
© Crown copyright 2005. All rights reserved.
Licence number 100011710.

Printed and bound in Spain
by Cayfosa-Quebecor

Contents

III **Key to map symbols**

IV **Key to map pages**

VI **Route planning**

VIII **Administrative and Postcode boundaries**

1 **Street maps** at 2⅔ inches to 1 mile

98 **Street maps of Newcastle upon Tyne and Sunderland city centres** at 5⅓ inches to 1 mile

104 **Index** of towns and villages

106 **Index** of streets, hospitals, industrial estates, railway stations, schools, shopping centres, universities and places of interest

Digital Data

The exceptionally high-quality mapping found in this atlas is available as digital data in TIFF format, which is easily convertible to other bitmapped (raster) image formats.

The index is also available in digital form as a standard database table. It contains all the details found in the printed index together with the National Grid reference for the map square in which each entry is named.

For further information and to discuss your requirements, please contact Philip's on 020 7644 6932 or james.mann@philips-maps.co.uk

Motorway with junction number	Ambulance station
Primary route – dual/single carriageway	Coastguard station
A road – dual/single carriageway	Fire station
B road – dual/single carriageway	Police station
Minor road – dual/single carriageway	Accident and Emergency entrance to hospital
Other minor road – dual/single carriageway	Hospital
Road under construction	Place of worship
Tunnel, covered road	Information Centre (open all year)
Rural track, private road or narrow road in urban area	Shopping Centre
Gate or obstruction to traffic (restrictions may not apply at all times or to all vehicles)	Parking, Park and Ride
Path, bridleway, byway open to all traffic, road used as a public path	Post Office
Pedestrianised area	Camping site, caravan site
Postcode boundaries	Golf course, picnic site
County and unitary authority boundaries	Important buildings, schools, colleges, universities and hospitals
Railway, tunnel, railway under construction	Built up area
Tramway, tramway under construction	Woods
Miniature railway	Water name
Railway station	River, weir, stream
Private railway station	Canal, lock, tunnel
Metro station	Water
Tram stop, tram stop under construction	Tidal water
Bus, coach station	Non-Roman antiquity
	Roman antiquity

DY7

Walsall

South Shields

Prim Sch

River Medway

Church

ROMAN FORT

Adjoining page indicators and overlap bands
The colour of the arrow and the band indicates the scale of the adjoining or overlapping page (see scales below)

Acad	Academy	Inst	Institute
Allot Gdns	Allotments	Ct	Law Court
Cemy	Cemetery	L Ctr	Leisure Centre
C Ctr	Civic Centre	LC	Level Crossing
CH	Club House	Liby	Library
Coll	College	Mkt	Market
Crem	Crematorium	Meml	Memorial
Ent	Enterprise	Mon	Monument
Ex H	Exhibition Hall	Mus	Museum
Ind Est	Industrial Estate	Obsy	Observatory
IRB Sta	Inshore Rescue	Pal	Royal Palace
	Boat Station	PH	Public House

Recn Gd	Recreation Ground
Resr	Reservoir
Ret Pk	Retail Park
Sch	School
Sh Ctr	Shopping Centre
TH	Town Hall/House
Trad Est	Trading Estate
Univ	University
W Twr	Water Tower
Wks	Works
YH	Youth Hostel

■ The small numbers around the edges of the maps identify the 1 kilometre National Grid lines
■ The dark grey border on the inside edge of some pages indicates that the mapping does not continue onto the adjacent page

Enlarged mapping only

Railway or bus station building

Place of interest

Parkland

The scale of the maps on the pages numbered in blue is 4.2 cm to 1 km • 2⅔ inches to 1 mile • 1: 23810

0	¼	½	¾	1 mile
0	250 m	500 m	750 m	1 kilometre

The scale of the maps on pages numbered in red is 8.4 cm to 1 km • 5⅓ inches to 1 mile • 1: 11900

0	220 yards	440 yards	660 yards	½ mile
0	125 m	250 m	375 m	½ kilometre

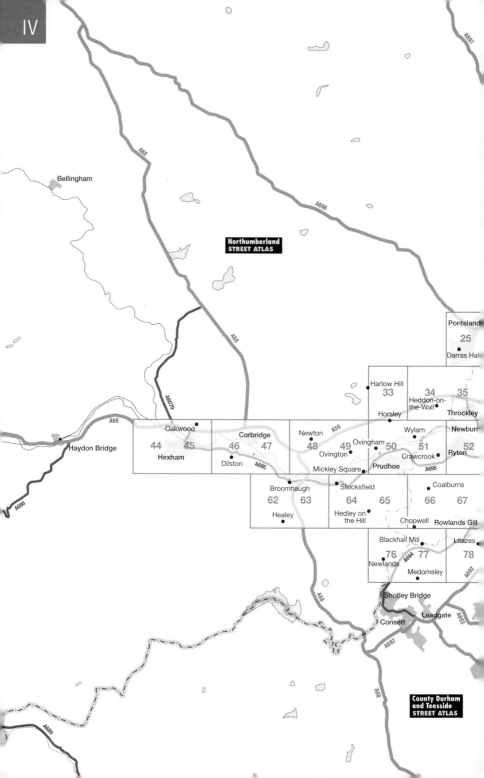

Key to map pages

| 1 | Map pages at 2⅔ inches to 1 mile |

| 98 | Map pages at 5⅓ inches to 1 mile |

Scale

0   5   10 km
0   1   2   3   4   5 miles

A1

A1068

Cresswell

1 Ellington   **2** Lynemouth

A189

A1068

Hebron   Longhirst

3 Fair Moor   **4** Pegswood   **5**   **6** Ashington   **7** Newbiggin-by-the-Sea

A197   A192

Morpeth

8 Hepscott   **9**   Guide Post **10**   Stakeford **11**   **12** Cambois

A1068

Bedlington

A192

Nedderton   A193   Blyth

13 Saltwick   **14**   **15**   **16**   **17**   **18**

Stannington   A192   East Hartford   A1061   A193

A1

New Hartley

Cramlington   **22**   **23** Seaton Delaval   **24** Hartley   Seaton Sluice

19 Berwick Hill   **20** Brenkley   **21** Seaton Burn   A190

A1

Dudley

Prestwick   Dinnington   **28** Wide Open   **29**   Backworth **30**   Earsdon **31**   Whitley Bay **32**

26   **27**

Newcastle International

Killingworth   Shiremoor   A191   Cullercoats

Longbenton

Gosforth

36 Westerhope   **37** Kenton   **38**   **39**   **40**   North Shields **41**   **42**   Tynemouth **43**

A1058   Wallsend   South Shields

West Jesmond

A19

98 99

Newcastle upon Tyne   Byker   A185   Jarrow   Marsden

53 Blaydon   **54** Dunston   **55**   **56**   **57** Hebburn   **58** Hedworth A1300 **59**   **60**   **61** Whitburn Colliery

100 101 Teams   Gateshead   Whiteleas   A183

Winlaton Mill   A1   A1018

Whickham   Felling   New Town   Boldon   Whitburn

68   **69**   **70**   **71**   **72**   A184 **73**   **74**   **75**

Sunniside   Chowdene   Wrekenton   Usworth   Southwick   Monkwearmouth

A1   A19

A1231   A690

Byermoor   Kibblesworth   Washington   South Hylton   **102 103**

79   **80**   **81**   **82** Birtley **83**   **84**   **85** Pennywell   **Sunderland**   Hendon

Tanfield   Urpeth   Fatfield   A183   **86**   **87**

Beamish   A6076   A6127   A1018

A693   Penshaw   Ryhope

Stanley   Shiney Row   **90**   **91** Doxford Park   **92**   **93**

Annfield Plain   **88**   **89** Bournmoor   Newbottle   Burdon   A19

A6076   Chester-le-Street

Houghton-le-Spring   Seaham

94   **95** Hetton-le-Hole   A19   A182

Manchester   Sacriston   A167   A1(M)   A690   West Rainton   Murton   A182   Easington Colliery

A691   Framwellgate Moor   High Pittington   Easington

Langley Park   **96**   **97** Haswell   A1086

Ushaw Moor   Durham   A19

Esh Winning   A177   A181   Peterlee

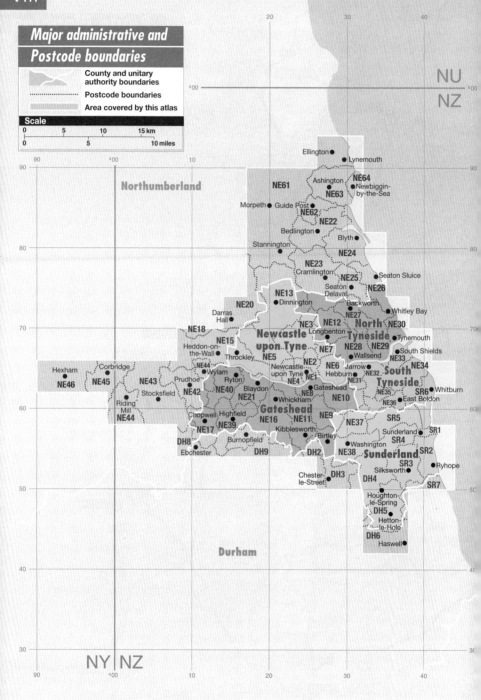

Major administrative and Postcode boundaries

County and unitary authority boundaries
.... Postcode boundaries
Area covered by this atlas

Scale
0   5   10   15 km
0   5   10 miles

NU
NZ

Ellington
Lynemouth

Northumberland

NE61
Ashington
NE64
Newbiggin-
by-the-Sea
NE63
Morpeth   Guide Post
NE62
NE22
Bedlington
Blyth
Stannington
NE24
NE23
Cramlington
Seaton
Delaval
Seaton Sluice
NE25
NE26
NE13
Dinnington
Backworth
NE20
Whitley Bay
Darras
Hall
NE12
NE3
Longbenton
North
Tyneside
NE30
NE18
Newcastle
upon Tyne
NE27
NE28
NE29
Tynemouth
NE15
NE7
Wallsend
South Shields
Heddon-on-
the-Wall
Throckley
NE5
NE6
Jarrow
NE33
NE34
Hexham
Corbridge
NE44
Wylam
Newcastle
upon Tyne
NE2
Hebburn
NE32
South
Tyneside
NE46
NE45
NE43
Prudhoe
Ryton
NE4
NE31
Stocksfield
NE42
NE40
Blaydon
Gateshead
NE35
SR6
Whitburn
NE21
NE8
NE36
East Boldon
Riding
Mill
NE44
Whickham
NE10
Chopwell
Highfield
Gateshead
NE9
SR5
NE17
NE16
NE39
Kibblesworth
Birtley
NE37
Sunderland
SR1
DH8
Burnopfield
Sunderland
SR4
SR2
Ebchester
DH9
DH2
NE38
SR3
Ryhope
Chester-
le-Street
DH3
DH4
Silksworth
SR7
Houghton-
le-Spring
DH5
Hetton-
le-Hole
DH6
Haswell

Durham

NU
NZ

NY   NZ

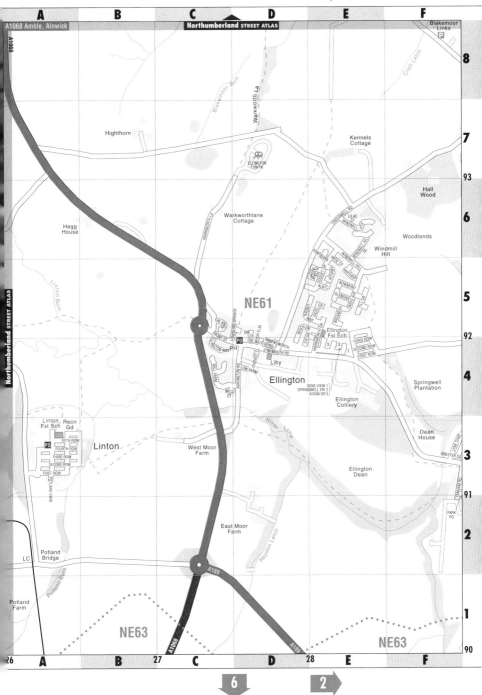

9

Northumberland STREET ATLAS

Cresswell

NE61

Sea Lodge

SOUTH SIDE

ST BARTHOLOMEWS CL

Caravan Site

Snab Point

Cresswell Home Farm

CRESSWELL HOME FARM COTTS

Chugdon Wood

Bewick Drift

River Lyne

CHESTER SQ
JUBILEE COTTS
CORONATION COTTS
RIVER VIEW
EDEN TERR
DUNLIN CL
DALTON AVE
INGLEBY TERR
ALBION TERR
GUILDFORD SQ
HENLEY SQ
JERSEY SQ
QUEEN ST
MATLOCK SQ 1
NEVILLE SQ 2
PARK VIEW
PARK RD

Lynemouth Fst Sch
Liby
CHURCH SQ

Lynemouth

MARKET SQ

Sewage Works

Lyne Hill

Cemy

Works

Power Station

NE63

Lyne Sands

Works

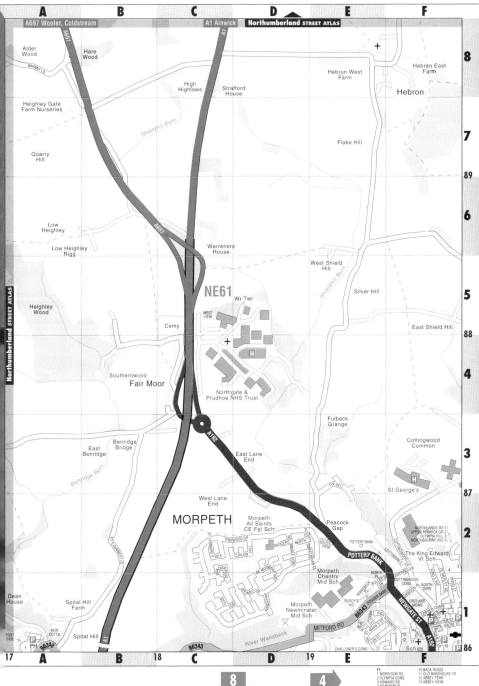

A1 Alnwick
A697 Wooler, Coldstream
Northumberland STREET ATLAS

Northumberland STREET ATLAS

Alder Wood
Hare Wood
WHINNY LA
A697

Hebron West Farm
Hebron East Farm
Hebron

8

High Highlaws
Strafford House

Heighley Gate Farm Nurseries
Shieldhill Burn

Flake Hill

7

89

Quarry Hill

Low Heighley

A697

Low Heighley Rigg

Warreners House

West Shield Hill
Shieldhill Burn

Silver Hill

6

5

88

NE61
Wr Twr
WEST VIEW

Heighley Wood

Cemy
H

East Shield Hill

Southernwood
Fair Moor

Northgate & Prudhoe NHS Trust

4

A192

Fulbeck Grange

Cottingwood Common

3

East Benridge
Benridge Bridge

East Lane End

87

Benridge Burn

West Lane End
TYNE DELL

St George's
H

NORTHLANDS RD 1
UPPER FENWICK GR 2
OLYMPIA HILL 3
NORTHBOURNE AVE 4

2

MORPETH

Morpeth All Saints CE Fst Sch

Peacock Gap

POTTERY BANK

The King Edward VI Sch

Morpeth Chantry Mid Sch

Morpeth Newminster Mid Sch

NEWGATE ST

ORCHARD MEWS

1

Dean House

Spital Hill Farm

NEW COTTS

Spital Hill

B6343

MITFORD RD
River Wansbeck

CHALLONER'S GDNS

A192

86

FONT SIDE
PH
B6343

17
A
18
B
C
18
D
19
E
F

8

4

F1
1 MORRISON RD
2 OLYMPIA GDNS
3 HOWARD RD
4 MARITIME PL
5 GREYSTOKE GDNS
6 HOWARD TERR
7 ST JAMES TERR
8 WELLWAY CT
9 CORPORATION YD

10 BACK RIGGS
11 OLD BAKEHOUSE YD
12 ABBEY TERR
13 ABBEY VIEW

Northumberland STREET ATLAS

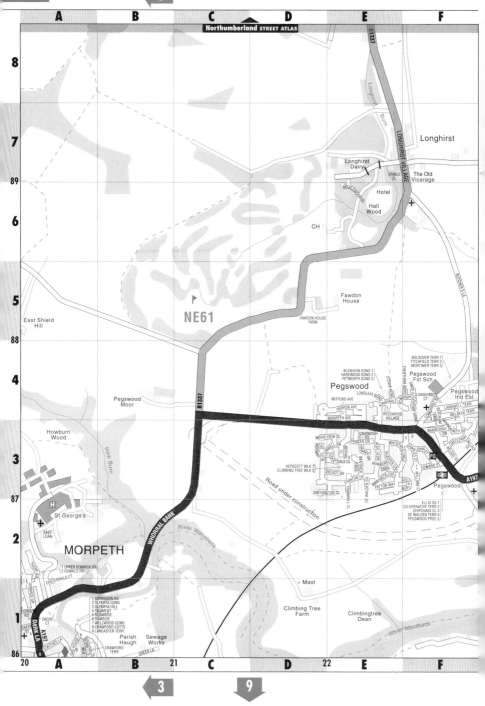

Longhirst

Longhirst Dairy

The Old Vicarage

STABLE CL

Hotel

MICKLEWOOD CL

Hall Wood

CH

Fawdon House

NE61

FAWDON HOUSE FARM

East Shield Hill

BOLSOVER TERR 1
TITCHFIELD TERR 2
MORTIMER TERR 3

Pegswood Fst Sch

Pegswood Ind Est

BLENHEIM GDNS 1
HAREWOOD GDNS 2
PETWORTH GDNS 3

LANGWELL TERR
WELBECK TERR

Pegswood

Pegswood Moor

LONGLEAT AVE
MITFORD AVE
HEBRON AVE
MORPETH AVE

PEGSWOOD VILLAGE

BAMBURGH

Howburn Wood

MOOR VIEW CL
SPENCER DR

CAVENDISH SQ

WHITEFIELD CRES

CHAS JOHN ST

CASTLE

PO

HEPSCOTT WLK 1
CLIMBING TREE WLK 2

BEATTOCK CRES

CHEVIOT GR

STANTON DR

FARWELL CL

PATTON WAY

WILLIAM ST

Pegswood

A197

CHEVINGTON CL

ELLIS SQ 1
CO-OPERATIVE TERR 2
CHIPCHASE CL 3
DE WALDEN TERR 4
PEGSWOOD PREC 5

Road under construction

St George's

EAST LOAN

MORPETH

WHORRAL BANK

How Burn

River Wansbeck

1 UPPER FENWICK GR
2 OSWALD RD

EASTERFIELD CT

DACRE CT

1 MORRISON RD
2 OLYMPIA GDNS
3 OLYMPIA HILL
4 SILVAS ST
5 BURNSIDE
6 DAMSIDE
7 WELLWOOD GDNS
8 CRAWFORD COTTS
9 LANCASTER TERR

Mast

Climbing Tree Farm

Climbingtree Dean

River Wansbeck

DARK LA

A197

HOWARD RD

STAITHES LA

CRAWFORD TERR

Parish Haugh

Sewage Works

GREEN LA

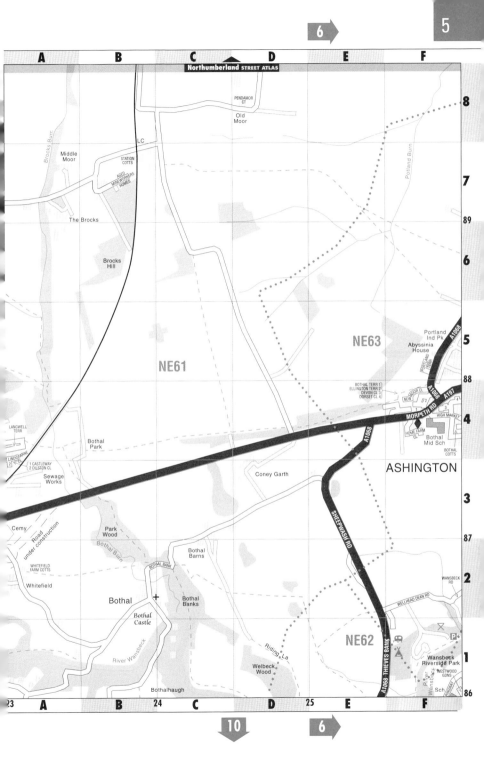

5 | 1

A B C D E F

NE61 NE61

8

New Moor
Cottages

LC

Whinny
Plantation

Haydon Letch

7

Hotel

P

89

Third House
Farm

A189

6

Queen
Elizabeth II
Country
Park

Hawthorn
Cottage

Woodhorn Colliery
Mus

A1068

NE63

WOODHORN COTTS 1
AGED MINERS' HOMES 2
ST CHRISTOPHERS CL 3

5

LC

A197

Works

Wansbeck
Bsns Pk

LINTONVILLE
PARKWAY

Northumbria
Ctr For Ent

LC Lintonville
Ent Pk

WOODHORN
VILLAS

ST
PAUL'S CL

1 DUKE ST
2 CHARLTON ST
3 COUNCIL TERR
4 CRESSWELL TERR
5 WANSBECK SQ
6 GREENSIDE
7 HILLSIDE

CHEVIOT VIEW

88

A197 MORPETH RD

EL EVENTH
ROW

ROTARY PARKWAY

Woodhorn
Pk

Wansbeck
General

H

4

HIGH MARKET

WELLHEAD TERR

NINTH ROW

EIGHTH ROW

SEVENTH ROW

HALTONE ST.

STATION RD

LANGWELL
CRES

NORTH
VIEW

SOUTH VIEW

Liby

P

Ashington
Mid Sch

1 ESLINGTON MEWS
2 KIDLAND CL

BOTHAL
CNTS

AGED
MINERS'
HOMES

FIRST ROW 1
NORFOLK CL 2
SUFFOLK CL 3
SURREY CL 4

HENDON
RD

PARK VIEW

PARK
VILLAS

DARNLEY RD

ASHBOURNE CRES

RIDSDALE
SQ

Sch

1 MOORHOUSE CL
2 FONTBURN CRES
3 HEBRON PL

Ashington
Alexandra
Fst Sch

Ashington
Wansbeck
Fst Sch

CTR

INSTITUTE
CT

CHURCH
MEWS

1 MORVEN TERR
2 MOREN PL

ARUNDEL
SQ

H

1 HOLLY ST
2 BOLSOVER TERR
3 CAVENDISH GDNS
4 BERTRAM TERR
5 ACACIA TERR

St Benedict's
RC Mid Sch

ASHINGTON

Ashington
Com High Sch

LAWN
CT

ELSDON DR

KIELDER
DR

COUPLAND
RD

Sch

GARDEN
CITY VILLAS

Hirst

Hirst
High
Sch

Liby

87

Ashington
Farm

SHIRE FARM GR

THE
STEADINGS

GREEN LA

A J COOK

Senet
Enterprise
Workshops

GREENCROFT

TITCHFIELD TERR 1
BOWMAN SQ 2
FELTON TERR 3

WELBECK RD

FARNE AVE

WELBECK AVE

2

BARRASFORD

HENSHAW CT 1
BELLSBURN CT 2
SHOTLEY GT 3
HOUNDSLOW DR 4

P P Wansbeck
Riverside Pk

Wellhead Dean

WEST PASTURES

EAST
PASTURES

FALLOWFIELD WAY

CHELTENHAM

3 OATFIELD CL
6 RYEDALE CL
7 LINNET CL

ORCHID

GOODWOOD

1 ORPINE CT
2 SHALLON CT

SEVENTH AVE

Coll

NELSON CL 1
COLLEGE PL 2
GREENLEE 3
BEECH TERR 4
CEDAR TERR 5

Sch

MONKSEATON TERR

NEWBIGGIN RD

B1334

1

NE62

River Wansbeck

CELANDINE CT 1
BURNET CT 2
PRIMROSE CT 3
CRANEMARSH CL 4

Jubilee
Ind Est

5 JASMINE CT
6 LILAC CT
7 LARCHWOOD DR

Schs

NEWBIGGIN RD

1 SWALLOW CL
2 SANDPIPER WAY
3 WATERFORD GN

North
Seaton
Ind Est

1 PERCY GDNS
2 FARNDALE AVE
3 WESTWOOD GDNS

A196 B1334

LC BLACKCLOSE
EST

BLACKCLOSE BANK

NORTH SEATON RD

B C D E F

27 C 28 E

5 | 11

F2
1 LINSHIELS GDNS
2 SIMONBURN LA
3 CALLERTON CL
4 HESLEYSIDE
5 ALWINTON SQ
6 WINCHESTER CL
7 SALISBURY CL

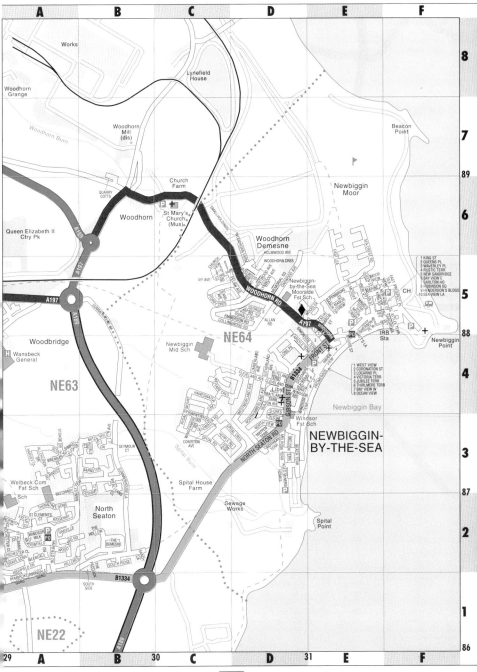

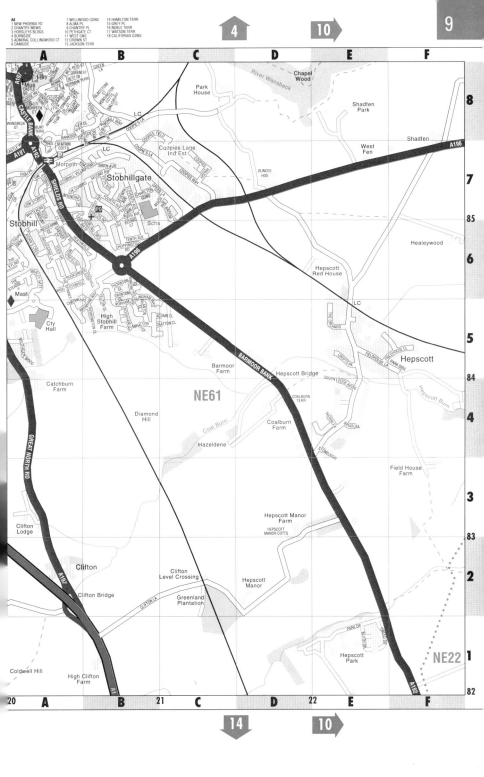

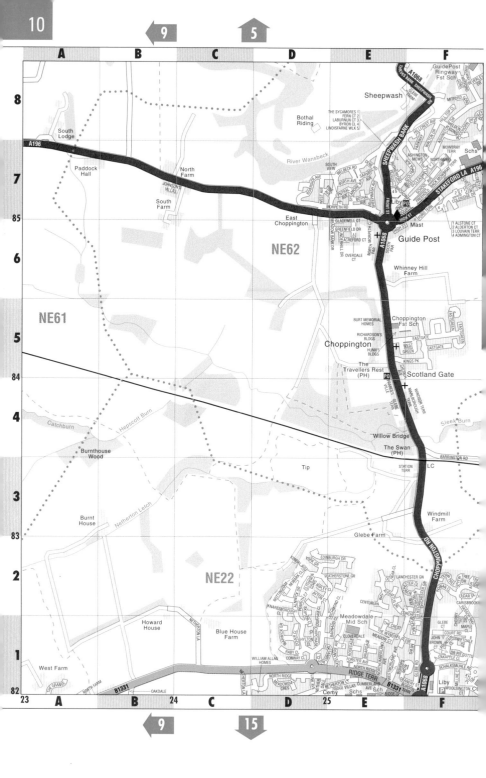

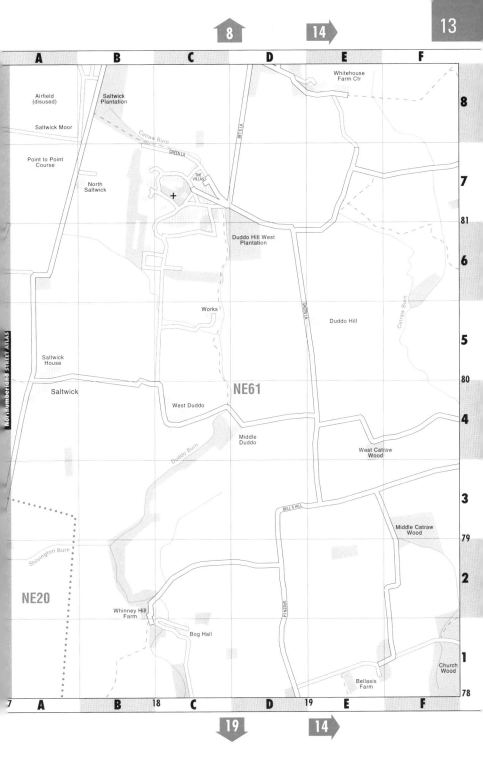

Airfield
(disused)

Saltwick Moor

Point to Point
Course

North
Saltwick

Saltwick
Plantation

Whitehouse
Farm Ctr

Catraw Burn

GREEN LA

THE
VILLAS

Duddo Hill West
Plantation

Works

Duddo Hill

GREEN LA

Catraw Burn

Saltwick
House

Saltwick

NE61

West Duddo

Middle
Duddo

West Catraw
Wood

Duddo Burn

BELL'S HILL

Middle Catraw
Wood

Shilvington Burn

NE20

GREEN LA

Whinney Hill
Farm

Bog Hall

Church
Wood

Bellasis
Farm

13
9

A
B
C
D
E
F
8
7
81
6
5
80
4
3
79
2
1
78
20
21
22
A1
A192
B1331
Netherton Letch
Moor Farm Estate
LC
STANNINGTON STATION RD
Works
Pegwhistle Burn
Netherton Wood
NE22
Dovecote Farm
Moor Farm
MOOR LA
Netherton Park Farm
Mast
Buckie's Bridge
Lough House
Netherton Park
THE DRIVE
Low Middle Moor
East Moor
NE61
West House Farm
Catraw Valley North
THE BEECHES
GREEN CL
Stannington Fst Sch
THE GLEBE
BEECH LEA
PH
THE CLOSE
Briery Hill
Stannington
Catraw
CHURCH RD
PO
P
Catraw Valley South
Town Farm
THE LIMES
BRIERY HILL LA
Catraw Burn
Swan Farm
Fox Hill
Stannington Vale
Plessey Hall Farm
Sewage Works
Plessey Wood
NE23
Stottford Dene
Stannington Banks
Greensfield Plantation
Catraw Plantation
Victoria Plantation
River Blyth
STANNINGTON VALE
Stannington Bridge
Mill Banks
Scroggy Plantation
Ewe Hill Plantation
Burntland Plantation
NE13
Shotton North Farm
SHOTTON LA

13
20

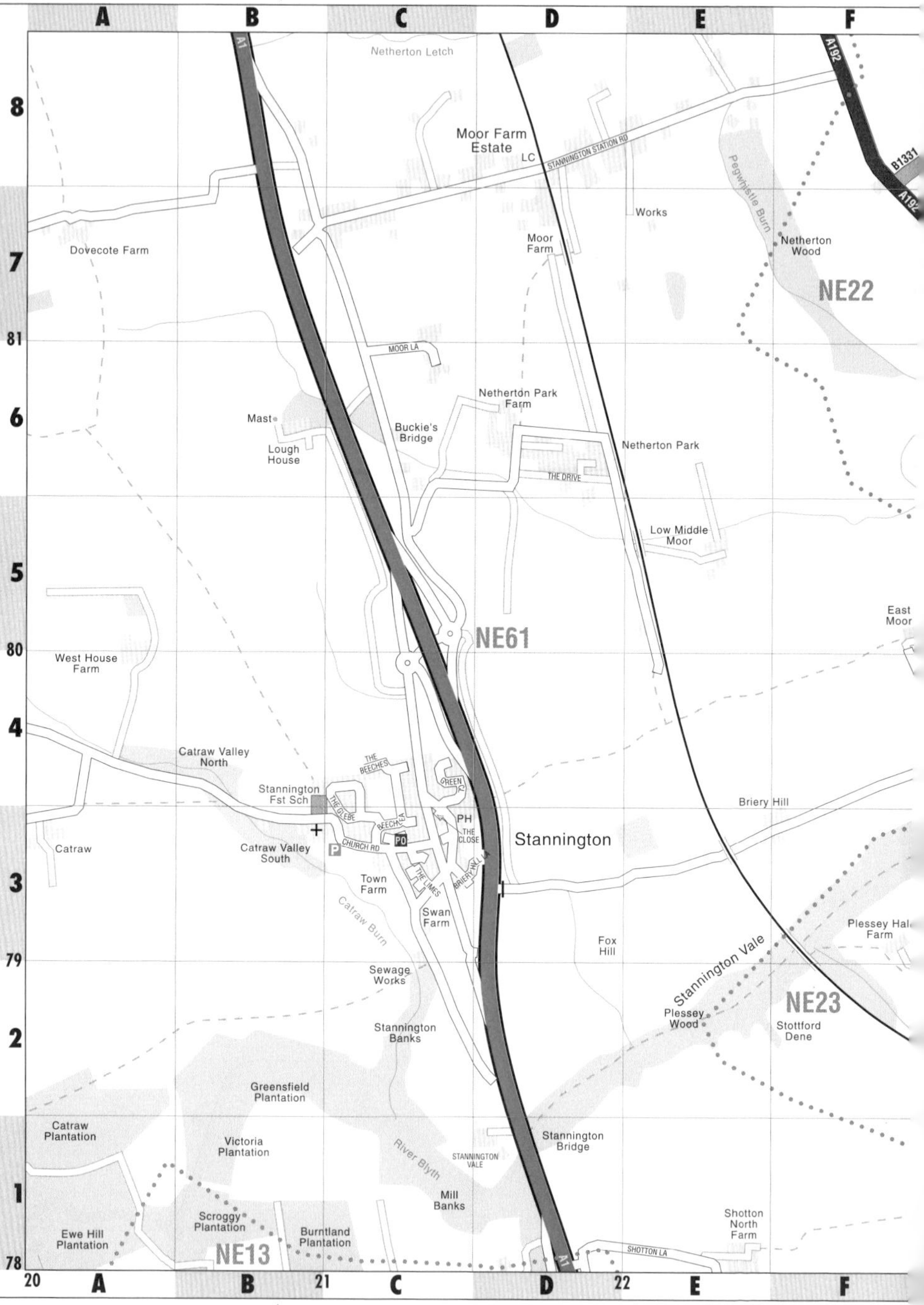

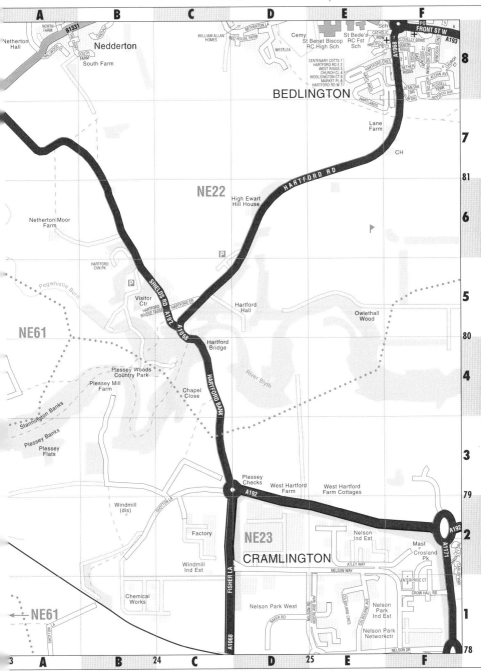

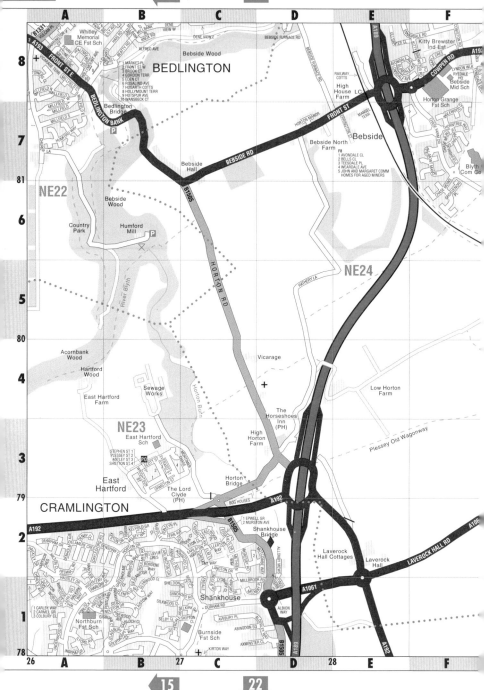

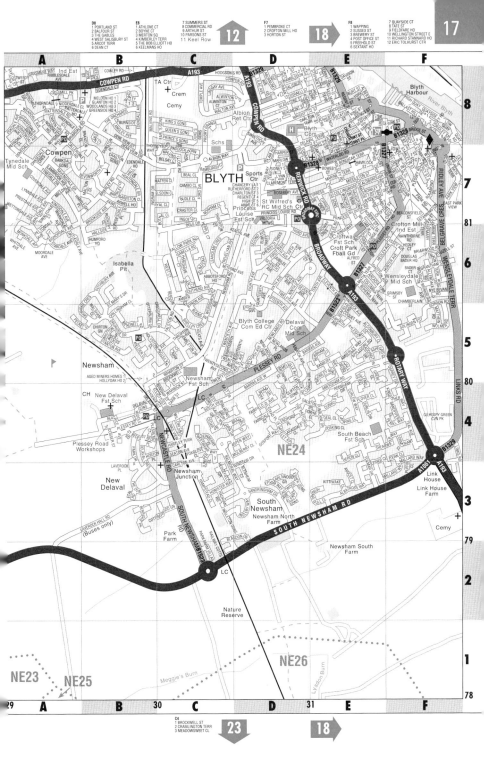

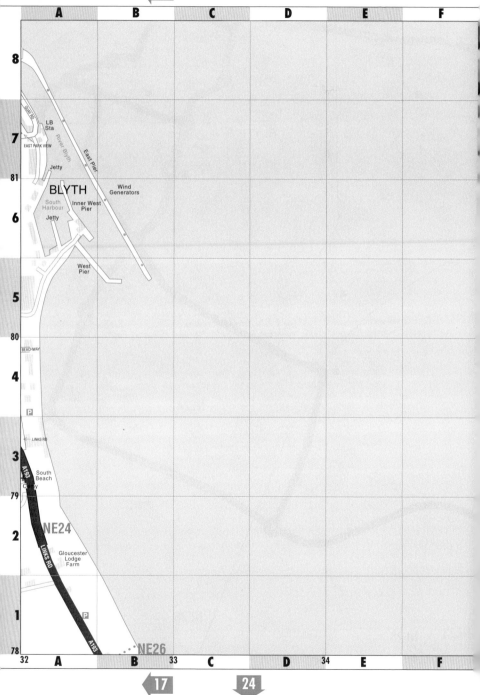

A B C D E F

8

QUAY RD

LB Sta

7

EAST PARK VIEW

River Blyth

East Pier

Jetty

81

BLYTH

Wind Generators

South Harbour

Inner West Pier

6

Jetty

West Pier

5

80

BEACHWAY

P

LINKS RD

3

A193

South Beach Cvny

79

NE24

2

LINKS RD

Gloucester Lodge Farm

1

P

78

A193

NE26

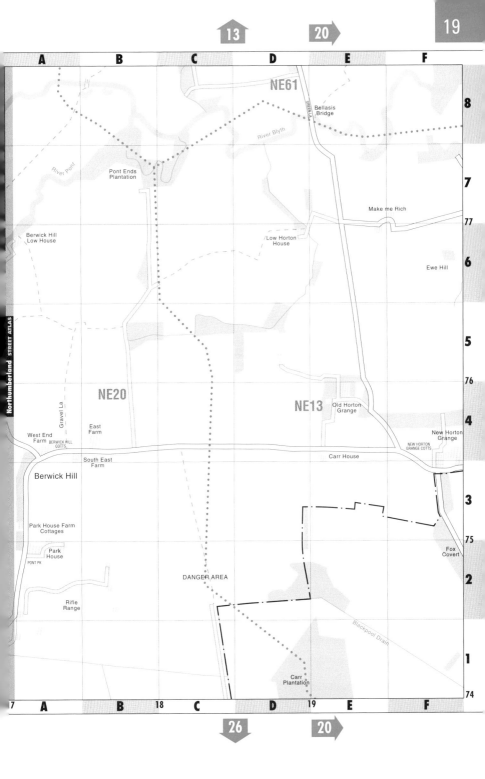

A B C D E F

8

NE61

Ewe Hill

Blagdon Lake

Lake Plantation

New Kennels

Election Plantation

Home Farm

New Cottages

Shotton

Shotton South Farm

NE61

SHOTTON LA

SHOTTON LA

A1

Lake Wiseman

Old Kennels

Cascade Dene

Coal Wood

7

Twist Plantation

Bog House

North Wood

Shotton Edge

Snitter Burn

77

Blagdon Hall

Grove Pond

North Wood

Fusilier Plantation

6

Deer Park Wood

Blagdon Park

LEDGES DR

SOUTH DR

Thornhill Cottage

Shotton Grange

Park House

5

Milkhope Plantation

MILKHOPE CTR

NE13

Hoys Wood

Shotton Edge South

76

4

Brenkley

North Farm

South Brenkley

East Brenkley Farm

Crow Wood

Seven Mile House

3

75

Trinidad Plantation

2

Gardener's Houses Farm

Carr Grange Farm

PRESTWICK CARR RD

1

74

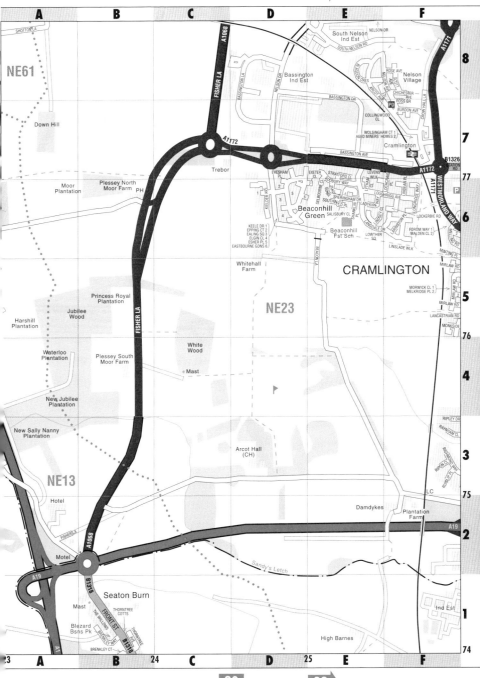

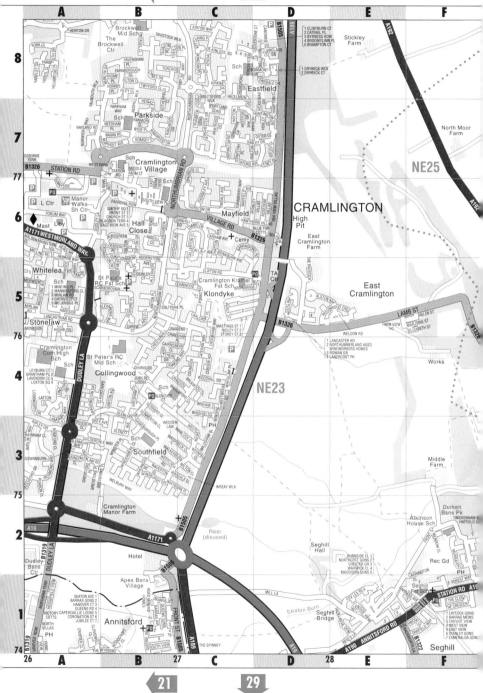

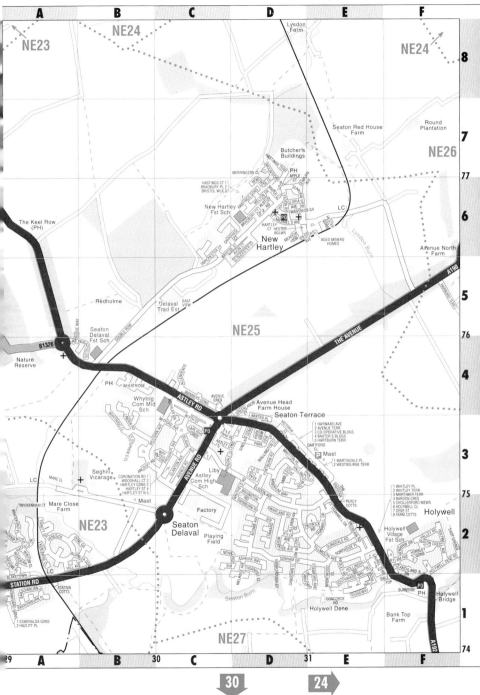

A B C D E F

NE24

Mile Hill

8

Hartley Links

LINKS RD

A193

7

Seaton Sluice
Mid Sch

ASTLEY
VILLAS

Astley Arms
Hotel
(PH)

CONWAY
ALSTON

BENFIELD GR

DENWAY GR

FRANKLYN AVE

MARDEN
CT

NAYLOR PL

ASTLEY GR

DERWENT RD

BADMINTON
PARK

ASTLEY RD

77

DERWENT RD

A190

The Sumps

Rocky
Island

6

Lookout Farm

THE AVENUE

HALL GDNS

A190

FOUNTAIN HEAD BANK

GREENRIGG

FERRYBANK

THE COPPICE

PASTFIELD RD

CROSSBERY AVE

THE
LINKS

THE SHERRIA

Seaton
Lodge

LINKS RD

OCHILTREE

WATERFORD CL

WEST TERR

Sandy
Island

Kings Arms
Hotel
(PH)

Seaton Delaval
Hall

Mausoleum

Seaton Lodge
Farm

Seaton Sluice

Holywell Dene

PO

BELL CL

SOUTHWAY

COLLYWELL CT

Liby

COLLYWELL BAY RD

Collywell Bay

5

Seaton Village Farm

MILLFIELD

LYNE CL

Sch

GRANGE

MELTON CRES

BERESFORD RD

Crag Point

76

Obelisk
Plantation

Obelisk

NE26

Starlight
Castle

MILLFIELD
CT

EDGEWORTH

ELSDONHALE

SIMONSIDE

SUMMERSIDE

THE RISE

ST MARY'S
WYND

THE CROSS

WEST END

Fort
House

Cvn. Pk.

EAST END

THE
STEADINGS

4

B1325

Hartley

Masts

3

Hartley West
Farm

Dark
Plantation

BLYTH RD

75

NE25

Holywell Dene

Seaton Burn

HARTLEY LA

2

Crow Hall
Farm

Cemy

WHITLEY
BAY

GERARDO RD

GARSDALE RD

CHARNWOOD AVE

WESTLEY CL

WESTLEY AVE

GORSDENE RD

ASTLEY

BEAMISH

THE LINKS

A193

HASTINGS

1

Brier Dene
Farm

B1325

74

32 A B 33 C D 34 E F

NE26 (inset)

2

75

1

F 35 G

Visitor Ctr

St Mary's or
Bait Island

Causeway

NE26

F

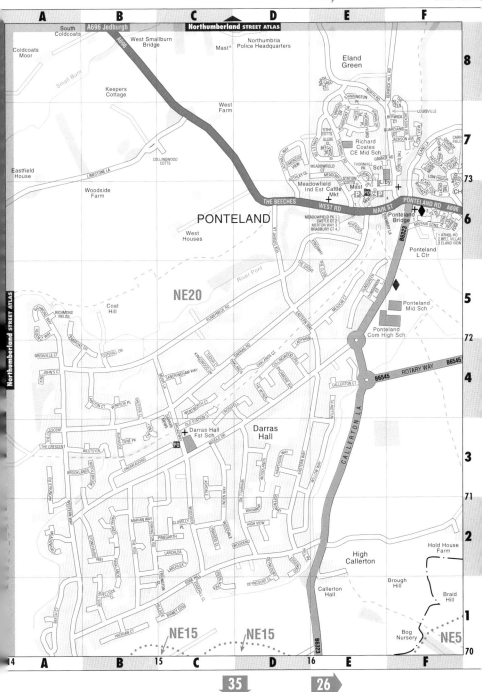

25 19

	A	B	C	D	E	F

8

Prestwick Mill Farm

DANGER AREA

Prestwick Carr

7

Eland Hall

ELAND LA

Moory Spot Cottages

CARR FIELD

73

Moory Spot

6

A696

CLICKEMIN

NE20

Prestwick Whins

PONTELAND RD

RUSSELL DR

RUSSELL CL

CHEVIOT VIEW

ELM RD

East Farm

West Farm

The Martins

Prestwick

Prestwick Hall

THE SQUARE

5

Prestwick Hall Farm

Street Houses

72

B6545

ROTARY WAY

Cemy

4

P P P

Hotel

P

3

B6918

Hotel

PRESTWICK TERR

Airport

Newcastle International Airport

NE13

71

Hold House Farm

Black Callerton Hill

Woolsington Hall

2

AIRPORT FREIGHTWAY

MIDDLE DR

Wheatsheaf Hotel (PH)

Callerton Station House

LC

P&R Callerton Parkway

1

NE5

Low Luddick

A696

B6918

70

17	A	B	18	C	D	19	E	F

25 36

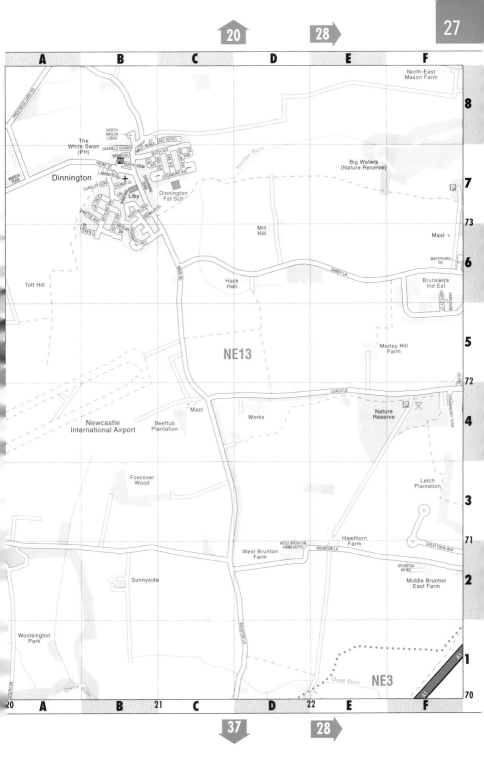

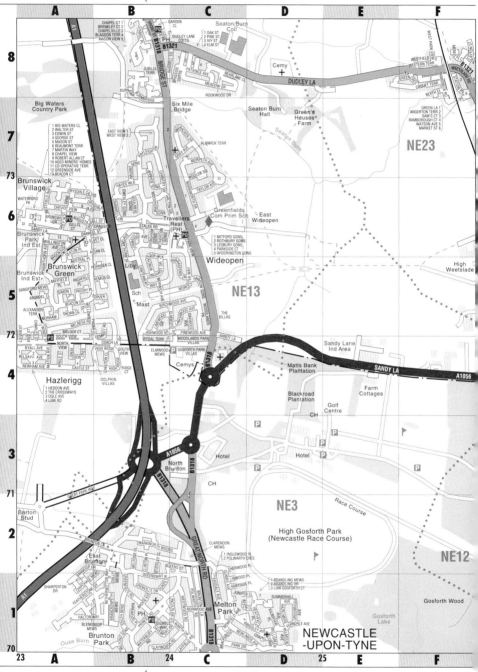

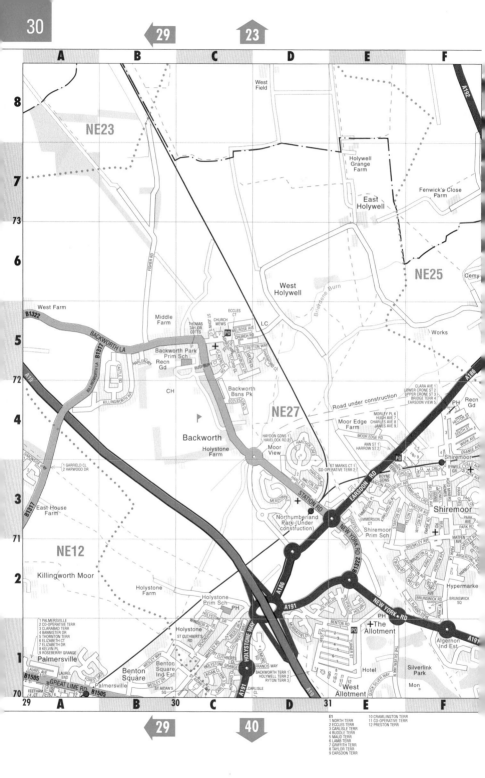

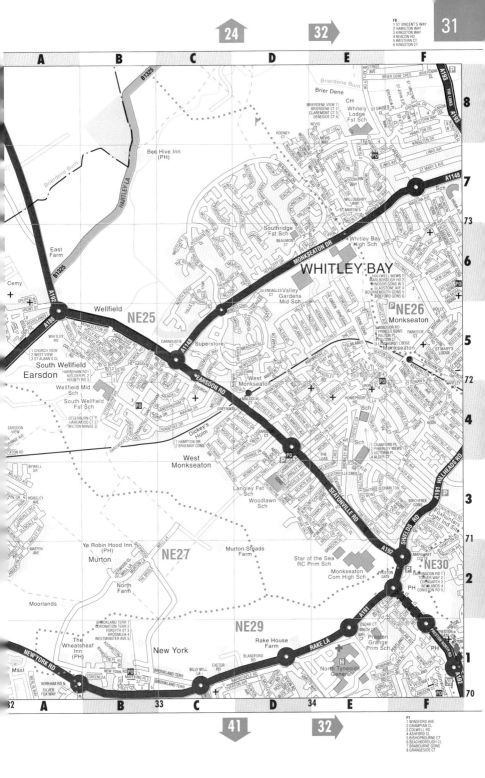

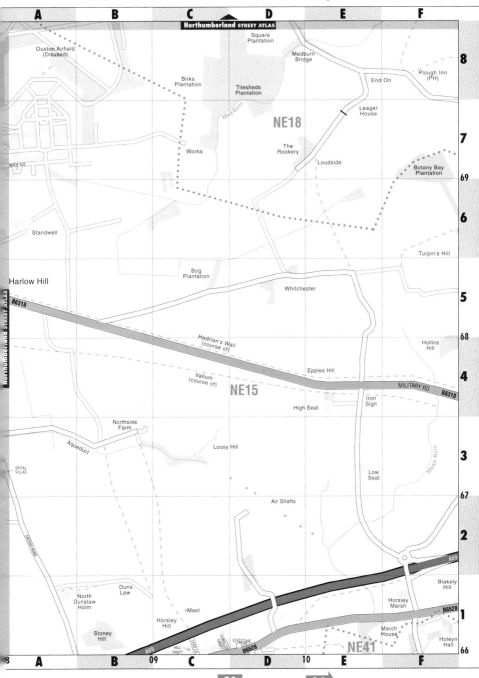

8

Ouston Airfield
(Disused)

Square
Plantation

Medburn
Bridge

Plough Inn
(PH)

Birks
Plantation

End On

Tilesheds
Plantation

Mud Burn

NE18

Leager
House

7

WADE AVE

Works

The
Rookery

Loudside

Botany Bay
Plantation

69

Standwell

6

Turpin's Hill

Harlow Hill

B6318

Bog
Plantation

Whitchester

5

Hadrian's Wall
(course of)

Hollins
Hill

68

Vallum
(course of)

Eppies Hill

MILITARY RD

B6318

NE15

4

High Seat

Iron
Sign

Northside
Farm

Aqueduct

Lousy Hill

Low
Seat

March Burn

3

SPITAL
VILLAS

Air Shafts

67

OUSTON PARK

2

A69

Duns
Law

Blakely
Hill

North
Dunslaw
Holm

Mast

Horsley
Marsh

B6528

Horsley
Hill

March
House

1

Stoney
Hill

A69

HILL
CROFT

LEALTA

DUNSTON
CROFT

STONEGATE

B6528

NE41

Holeyn
Hall

66

NORTHUMBERLAND STREET ATLAS

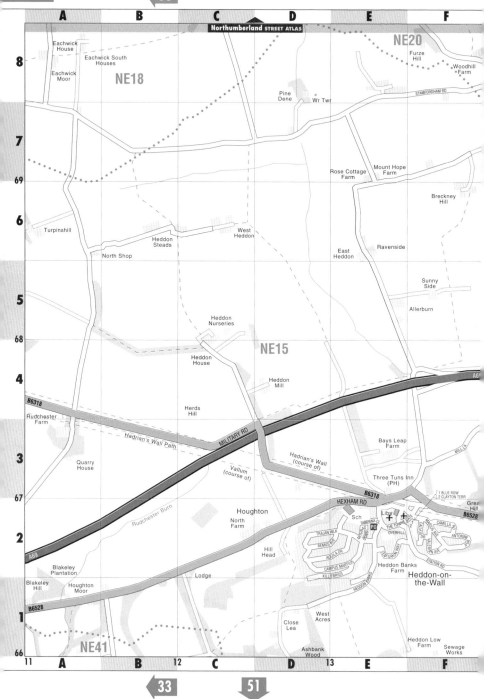

Northumberland STREET ATLAS

NE20

NE18

NE15

NE41

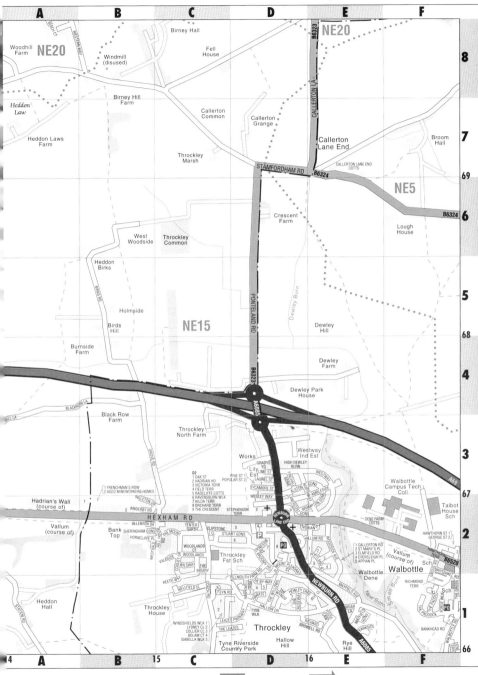

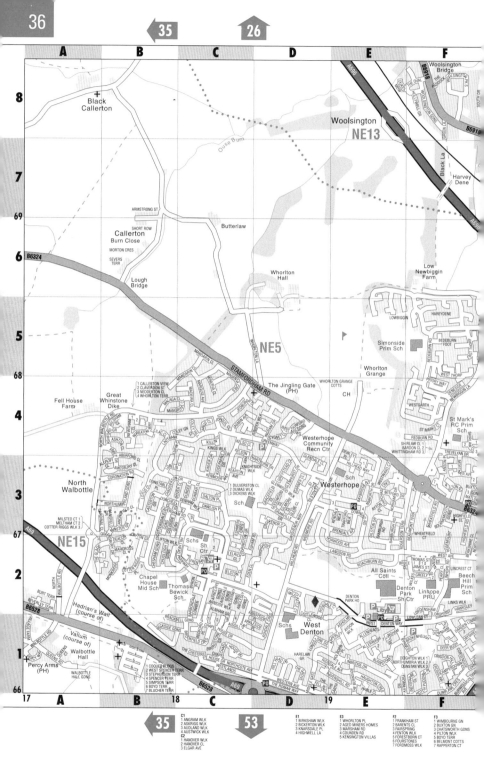

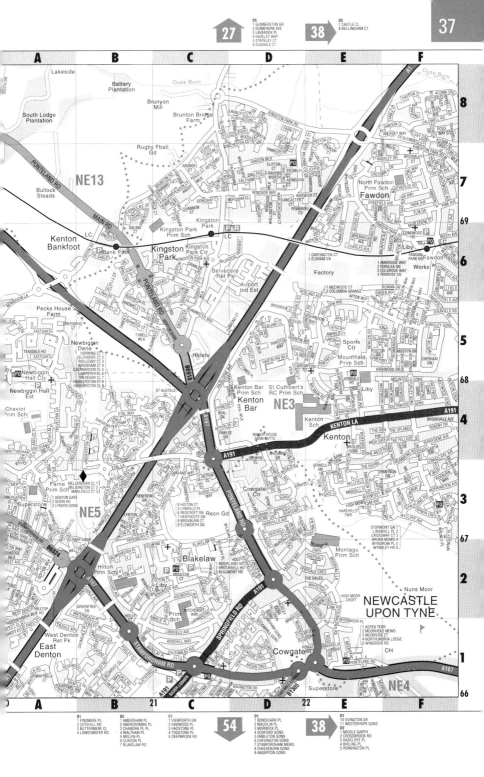

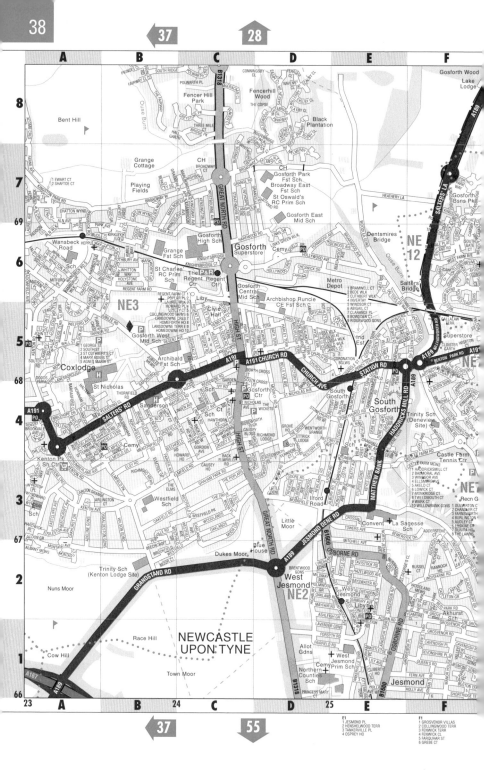

A6
1 STONELEIGH PL
2 SANDRINGHAM AVE
3 ST CLEMENTS CT

29

D8
1 WILSON TERR
2 BURN AVE
3 FAIRFIELD AVE
4 NORTH VIEW
5 WEST VIEW
6 WHITFIELD RD

40

D8
7 IRVINE HO
8 LANGLEY MERE

| A | B | C | D | E | F |

NE3

Factory

Fir Tree Farm

The Letch

LONGBENTON

Longbenton Com Coll

Longbenton North Farm

Balliol Bsns Pk

Gosforth Bsns Pk

St Stephen's RC Prim Sch

Benton North Farm

Percy Hedley Sch Cemy

Forest Hall

North Tyne Ind Est

NE12

Bellway Ind Est

Benton

Goathland Prim Sch

Four Lane Ends

St Bartholomew's CE Prim Sch

FRONT ST

Whitley Rd

Benton Quarry Bridge

East Benton Farm

East Benton Cotts

BENTON PARK RD

St Mary's RC Comp Sch

NE3

Govt Bldgs (DWP)

Benton Park Prim Sch

Tyneview Pk (DWP)

St Andrew's Ct

Redesdale Prim Sch

Brooksmead

Allot Gdns

NE28

Govt Bldgs (DWP)

Freeman

Northumbria Univ Coach Lane Campus

NE7

Cochrane Pk (Sp Gd)

Henderson Hall

Cragside Prim Sch

High Heaton

Cemy

Heaton Manor Sch

Bigges Main

WALLSEND

Wallsend Sp Ctr

CH

Jesmond Dene

Ouse Burn

Ravenswood Prim Sch

TA Ctr

Benfield Sch

NE6

Welburn Pk

Armstrong Bridge

NE2

Rokeby

Sp Gd

Walkerville

Walkergate

Churchill Gdns

**1 THE TERRACE
2 CAROLYN CL
3 CARVED VIEW
4 ST MARGARETS AVE
5 LINDEN TERR
6 CRAGMONT CT
7 THE BEECHES
8 NORWOOD CT
9 ENNISMORE CT
10 WHINSTONE MEWS**

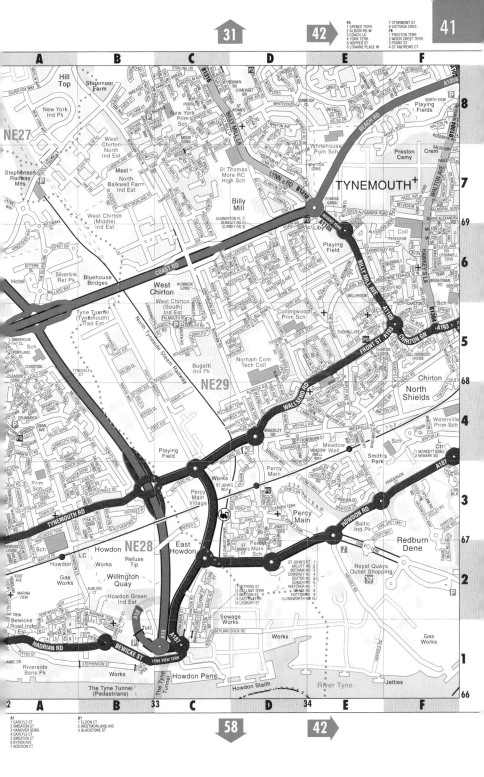

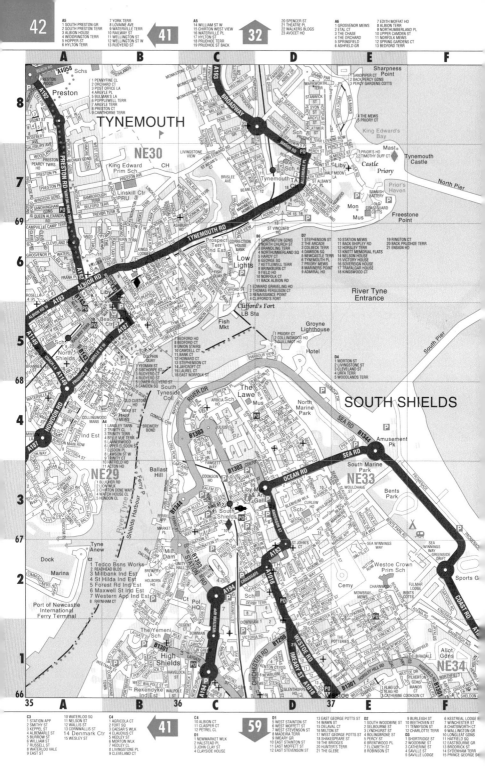

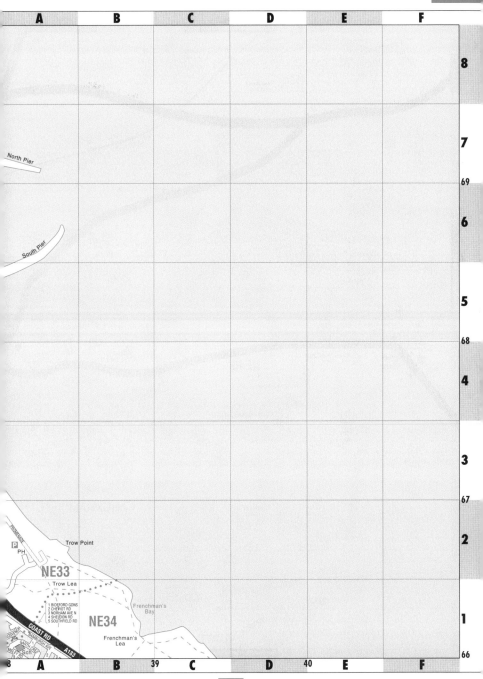

North Pier

South Pier

PROMENADE

P
PH

Trow Point

NE33

Trow Lea

1 BIDEFORD GDNS
2 CHEVIOT RD
3 NORHAM AVE N
4 SHELDON RD
5 SOUTHFIELD RD

NE34

Frenchman's
Bay

Frenchman's
Lea

COAST RD

A183

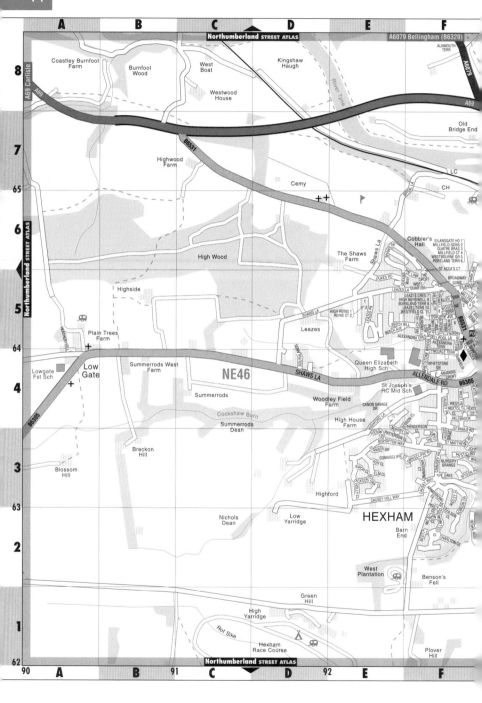

A6079 Bellingham (B6320)

A6079

ALNMOUTH TERR

A69 Carlisle

Northumberland STREET ATLAS

Coastley Burnfoot Farm

Burnfoot Wood

West Boat

Kingshaw Haugh

River Tyne

Westwood House

Old Bridge End

B6531

Highwood Farm

LC

Cemy

CH

High Wood

The Shaws Farm

Shaws La

Cobbler's Hall

EILANSGATE HO 1
MILLFIELD GDNS 2
QUATRE BRAS 3
MILLFIELD CT 4
WESTBOURNE GR 5
PORTLAND TERR 6

ST ACCA'S CT

THE LINK
DUKES RD
THE CROFT
WEST QUARTER

BROADWAY

EILANSGATE

Highside

LEAZES

LEAZES CRES 7
HIGH BURSWELL 8
BURLAND TERR 9
LEAZES TERR 10
WESTFIELD CT 11

GLEN TERR
WOODBINE TERR
OSBORNE TERR

SHAWS LA

HIGH REINS 1
REINS CT 2

BEECH HILL

Leazes

BEECH AVE

ALEXANDRA CRES

ALEXANDRA TERR

WHETSTONE GN

TYNEDALE TERR

Plain Trees Farm

HEATHERY HILL

Low Gate

NE46

Summerrods West Farm

SHAWS LA

Queen Elizabeth High Sch

ALLENDALE RD

Lowgate Fst Sch

Summerrods

Woodley Field Farm

St Joseph's RC Mid Sch

B6305

CANON SAVAGE DR

WEST HEXTOL

VALEBROOK

ST PAUL'S RD

B6305

Cockshaw Burn

Summerrods Dean

High House Farm

HENDERSON

DERBEY DR

BISHOPTON WAY

ST MATTHEW

Breckon Hill

CONISCLIFFE CL

CONISCLIFFE RD

FRONKHOLME

NURSERY GRANGE

Blossom Hill

BIRCH CL

ASH CL

ELM CL

DICKSON CL

HOLLY CL

THE OAKS

WYCOM CT

Highford

CAUSEY HILL WAY

ARMSTRONG

Nichols Dean

Low Yarridge

HEXHAM

Barn End

CHARLTON CL

West Plantation

Benson's Fell

Green Hill

High Yarridge

Rot Sike

Hexham Race Course

Plover Hill

90 A B 91 C D 92 E F

A5
1 PEARSON'S TERR
2 MILLFIELD TERR
3 WESTBOURNE GR
4 FENWICK GR
5 KINGSGATE
6 DUNWOODIE TERR

7 COCKSHAW CT
8 GIBSON PL
9 COCKSHAW TERR
10 TANNERS ROW
11 HOLY ISLAND
12 ALEXANDER PL
13 GILES PL

14 GLOVERS PL
15 STEPHENSON HO
16 GILESGATE CT

B5
1 CHURCH ROW
2 MARKET PL

3 PUDDING MEWS
4 ORCHARD TERR
5 ABBEY CT
6 CHISHOLM PL
7 MEAL MKT
8 ST MARY'S WYND
9 ST MARY'S CHARE

A4
1 WEST END TERR
2 ETHEL TERR
3 SEAL TERR
4 HENCOTES MEWS
5 SELE CT
6 ST CUTHBERT'S TERR
7 HENCOTES CT
8 GIBSON HO
9 ST WILFRID'S CT

10 BURNCROFT
11 LONGLANDS
12 PRIESTLANDS AVE
13 CROFT TERR
14 ST OSWALD'S RD

B4
1 STAINTHORPE CT
2 NEWMAN'S WAY
3 JUBILEE BLDGS
4 COMMERCIAL PL
5 DIAMOND SQ
6 SEZZE BLDG
7 PESCOTT CT
8 BRAMLEY CT
9 HIGH GABLES

A68 Jedburgh

Beaufront Castle Flats
Beaufront Castle
The Park
Knoll Hill

Hampstead House

8

CORCHESTER LA

Cor Burn

7

Beaufront Red House
Red House Plantation

A69

Corbridge Mid Sch

65

Prior Thorns

Redhouse Burn

Corchester Twrs

Leazes Terr
Corchester Terr

NE46

Redhouse Haughs

Corbridge Roman Site

CORCHESTER TERR 1
CORCHESTER AVE 2
TRINITY CT 3

Trinity Terr
Prior Terr
Cockson Cl
West Terr
Prince

6

River Tyne

Orchard View
Well Bank

St Helen's La
Middle St
Front St

Widehaugh Nursery
Wide Haugh

Dilston Haughs

Tynedale Mews
Market Pl

Corbridge Bridge

5

Sam's Island LC

Cemy

Corbridge

64

A695

Dilston Plains

DILSTON HAUGH COTTS
B6321
LC

Station Rd
Tinkler's

4

Dilston Park

NE45

Corbridge

Dilston Haugh Farm
Dilston Mill

B6307

The Scrogs

Bowlingally Hill

Dilston

Scurl Hill

3

Dilston South Park
Dilston Hall

High Town

Ladycutters La
Roecliff Lodge

63

Dilston Park
East Haugh
Devil's Water
DILSTON WEST COTTS

West Fell

2

Park Wood

Birchside Wood

Snokoehill Plantation

Snokoe Hill

Quarry Cottage Belt

West Haugh

1

Swallowship Wood
Swallowship Hill

Birchy Sike

B6307

Birchy Wood

Temperley Grange Farm

62

A 97 B C D 98 E F

Northumberland STREET ATLAS

Car Burn

Gallow Hill
Gallowhill

Thornbrough High Barns

Thornbrough Kiln House

AYDON RD

Aydon Grange

Piperclose House

Quarry Wood

Linn Burn Wood

Corbridge CE Fst Sch

NE45

1 CHANTRY EST
2 ST HELEN'S ST
3 ST WILFREDS CT
4 WINDSOR CT
5 AYDON GR
6 AYDON RD EST
7 AYDON WAY

Crooks Hill

Corbridge

Howden Dene Farm

Thornbrough

PRINCESS ST

Cricket Plantation

Thornbrough Buildings

MAIN ST B6530 NEWCASTLE RD

STABLE BLOCK

Sidle Hill

Howden Dene

Gallow Hill

Thornbrough Haugh

East Lodge

Brocks Bushes

A69

B6530

Eales

Tynedale Park

Thornbrough Wood

Styford Toll Bar

Styford Lodge

Gravel Pit

River Tyne

Farnley Haughs

Farnley Grange

Gravel Pit

NE43

High Barns

Whinney Corner

LC

Farnley Gate

Styford Cottages

Grey Court

Abbeybank Wood

NE44

Prospect Hill

Riding Hills

Styford Park

Styford Hall

Mast

A695

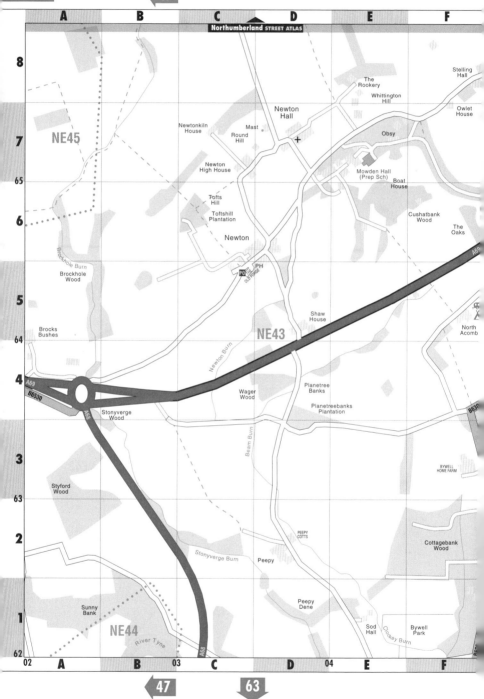

A B C D E F

8

7

NE45

65

6

Stelling
Hall

The
Rookery

Whittington
Hill

Owlet
House

Newton
Hall

Newtonkiln
House

Mast

Round
Hill

Obsy

Newton
High House

Mowden Hall
(Prep Sch)

Boat
House

Tofts
Hill

Toftshill
Plantation

Cushatbank
Wood

The
Oaks

Newton

Brockhole Burn

Brockhole
Wood

PO THE
OLD FORGE

PH

5

Shaw
House

North
Acomb

Brocks
Bushes

NE43

64

A69

B6530

Wager
Wood

Planetree
Banks

4

A68

Stonyverge
Wood

Planetreebanks
Plantation

B6309

Beam Burn

3

BYWELL
HOME FARM

Styford
Wood

63

PEEPY
COTTS

Cottagebank
Wood

2

Stonyverge Burn

Peepy

Sunny
Bank

Peepy
Dene

NE44

River Tyne

A68

Sod
Hall

Bywell
Park

Cloxey Burn

1

62

02 A 03 B C 03 D 04 E F

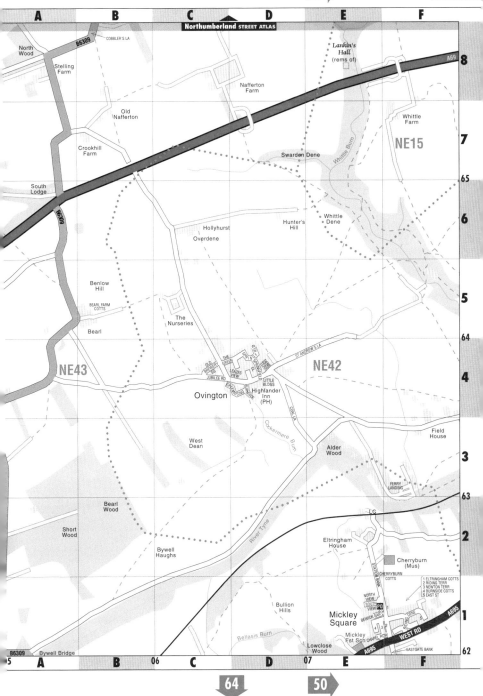

B6309
North Wood
Stelling Farm
COBBLER'S LA
Old Nafferton
Nafferton Farm
Lankin's Hall (rems of)
A69
Whittle Farm
Crookhill Farm
Swarden Dene
NE15
Whittle Burn
South Lodge
Whittle Dene
Hollyhurst
Hunter's Hill
Overdene
Benlow Hill
BEARL FARM COTTS
The Nurseries
Bearl
St Andrew's La
NE42
NE43
OLD BREWERY RD
THE GREEN
LEAZES VIEW
JUBILEE RD
BACKRIGG LA
BURNSIDE
LITTLE BLDGS
Highlander Inn (PH)
Ovington
Cockermere Burn
OAK LA
West Dean
Alder Wood
Field House
FERRY LANDING
Bearl Wood
Short Wood
River Tyne
Bywell Haughs
Eltringham House
Cherryburn (Mus)
CHERRYBURN COTTS
1 ELTRINGHAM COTTS
2 RIDING TERR
3 NEWTON TERR
4 BURNSIDE COTTS
5 EAST ST
STATION BANK
NORTH VIEW
SOUTH VIEW
PO
Bullion Hills
Mickley Square
BEWICK GDNS
CEDE
A695
WEST RD
Mickley Fst Sch
CHAPEL ROW
Bellasis Burn
Lowclose Wood
EASTGATE BANK
B6309
Bywell Bridge

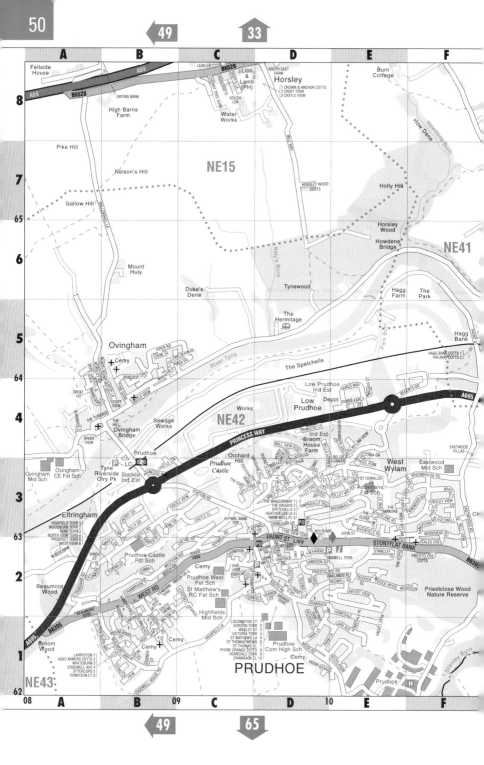

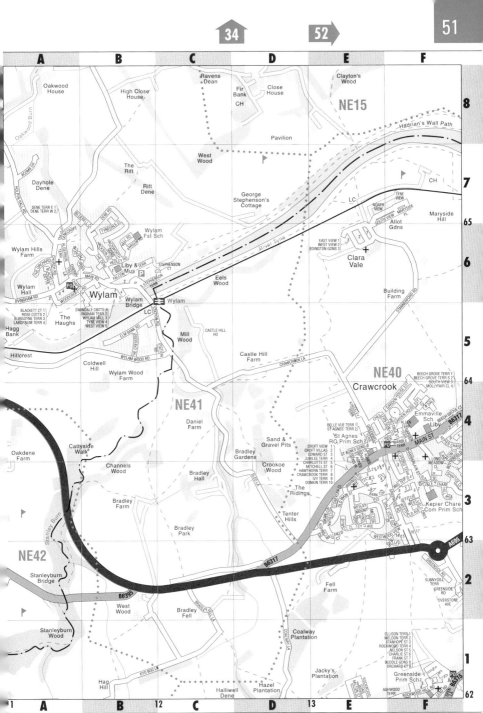

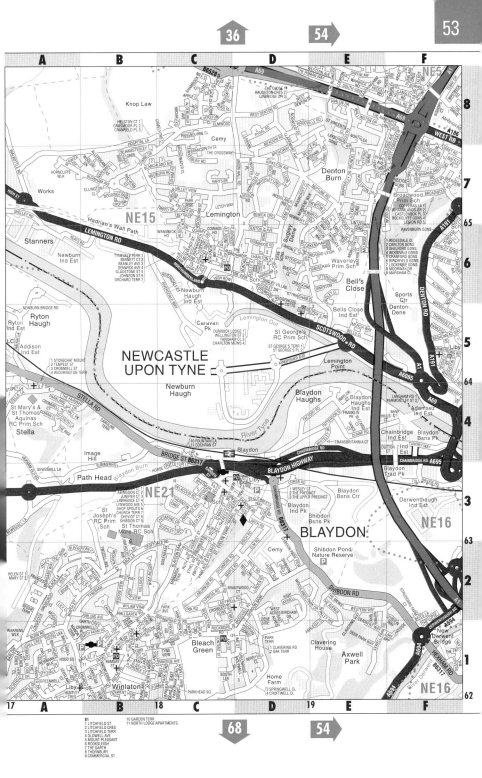

NE5

NE15

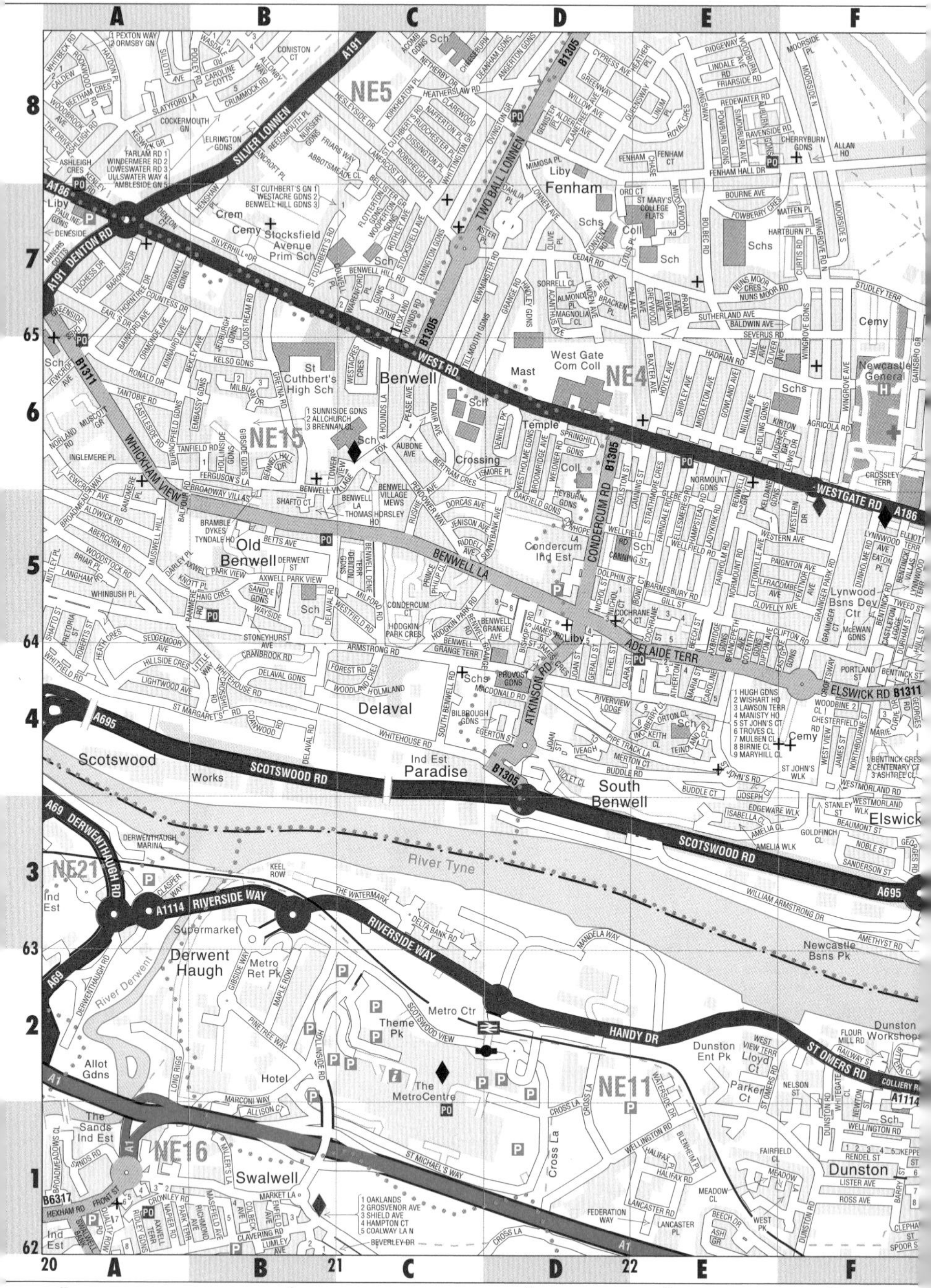

NE4

Fenham

Liby

Benwell

Old Benwell

Delaval

Scotswood

Paradise

South Benwell

Elswick

River Tyne

Derwent Haugh

The MetroCentre

NE21

NE16

Swalwell

NE11

Dunston

St Cuthbert's High Sch

West Gate Com Coll

Newcastle General H

A191 DENTON RD

SILVER LONNEN

TWO BALL LONNEN

WEST RD

WESTGATE RD A186

WHICKHAM VIEW

BENWELL LA

CONDERCUM RD B1305

ADELAIDE TERR

ELSWICK RD B1311

SCOTSWOOD RD

A695

A69 DERWENTHAUGH RD

A1114 RIVERSIDE WAY

RIVERSIDE WAY

HANDY DR

ST OMERS RD A1114

Metro Ctr

Dunston Workshops

River Derwent

A1

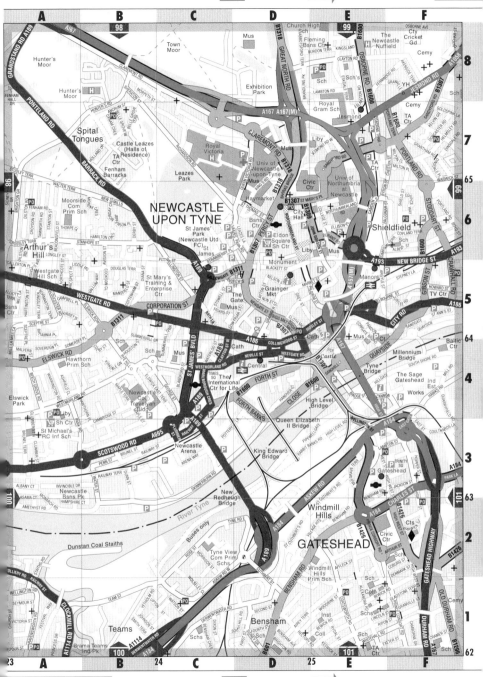

For full street detail of the
highlighted area see pages
98, 99, 100 and 101.

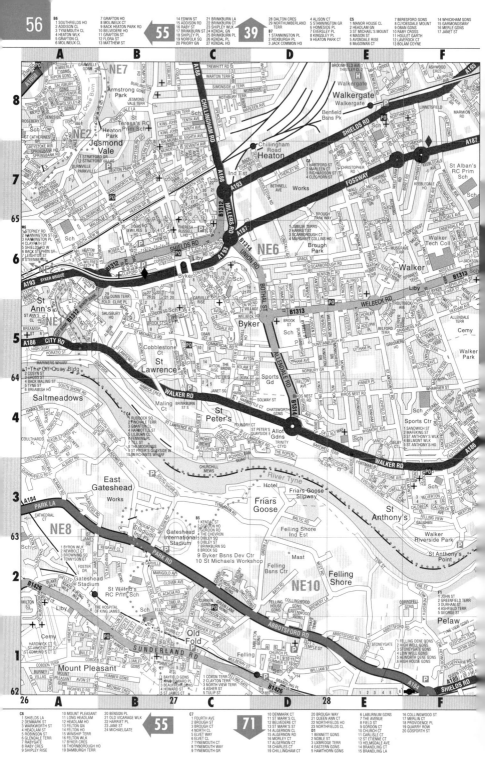

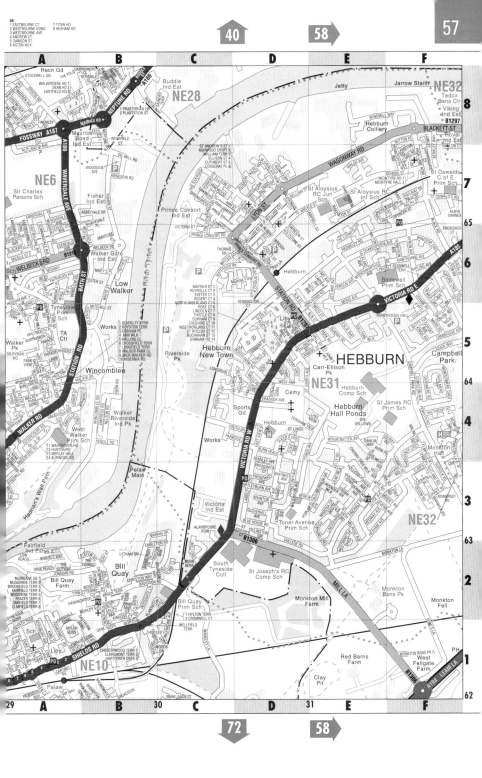

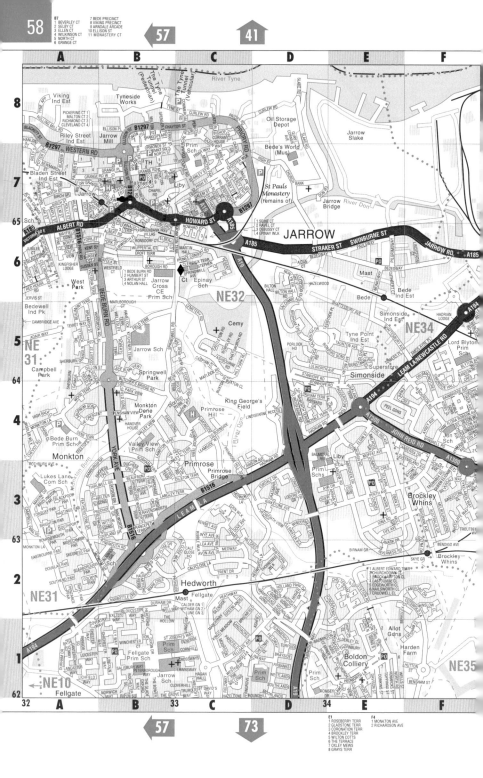

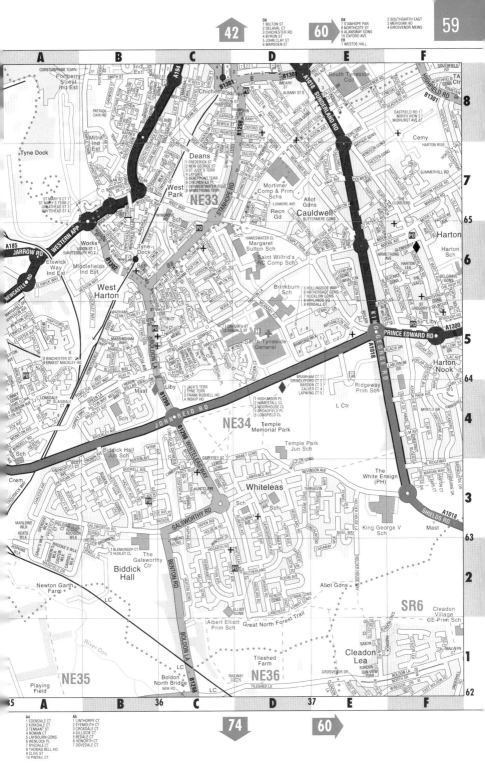

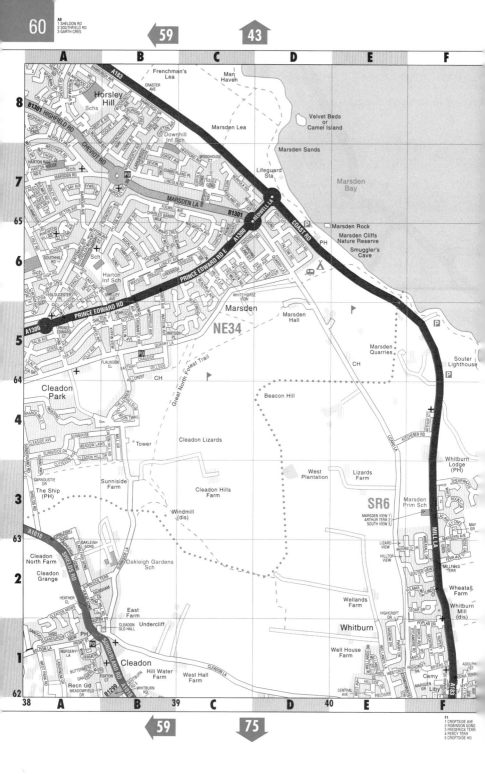

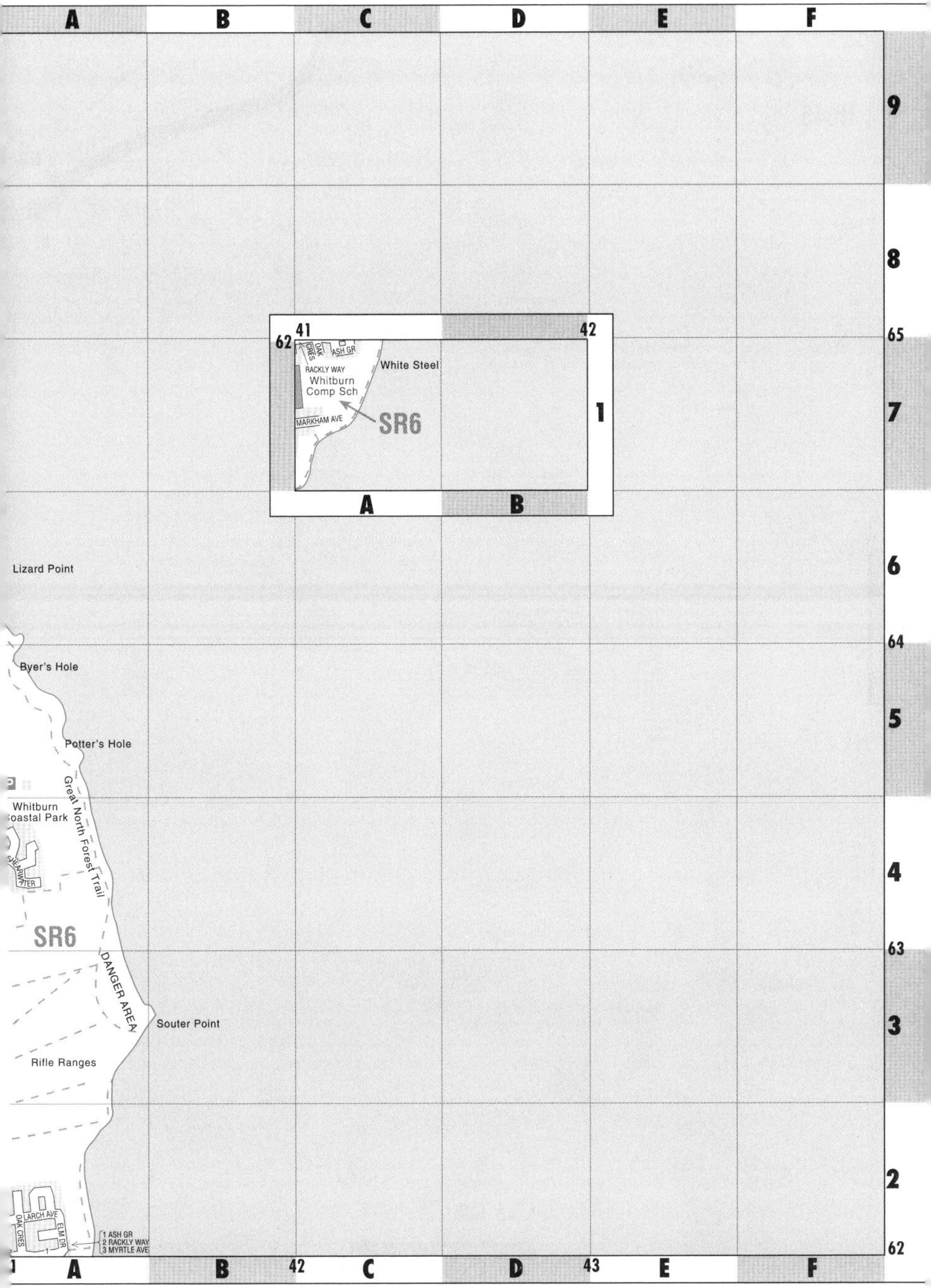

A B C D E F

9

8

65

62 **41** **42**

ASH GR

RACKLY WAY
Whitburn
Comp Sch

White Steel

1

MARKHAM AVE **SR6**

7

A **B**

Lizard Point

6

64

Byer's Hole

5

Potter's Hole

Whitburn
Coastal Park

Great North Forest Trail

SR6

DANGER AREA

Souter Point

4

63

3

Rifle Ranges

2

LARCH AVE

ELM GR

OAK CRES

1 ASH GR
2 RACKLY WAY
3 MYRTLE AVE

62

A **B** **42** **C** **D** **43** **E** **F**

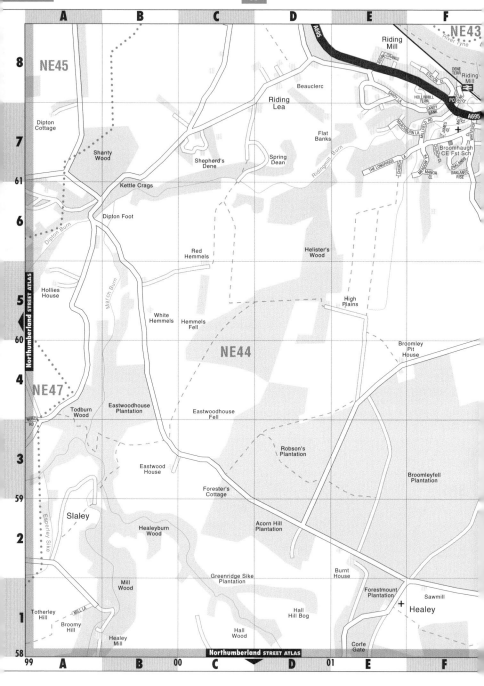

NE43

River Tyne

Riding Mill

A695

NE45

Beauclerc

Riding Lea

Dipton Cottage

Shanty Wood

Shepherd's Dene

Spring Dean

Flat Banks

Kettle Crags

Dipton Foot

Dipton Burn

Red Hemmels

Helister's Wood

Hollies House

March Burn

White Hemmels

Hemmels Fell

NE44

High Plains

Broomley Pit House

NE47

Todburn Wood

Eastwoodhouse Plantation

Eastwoodhouse Fell

NORTH RD

Eastwood House

Robson's Plantation

Broomleyfell Plantation

Forester's Cottage

Slaley

Esperley Sike

Healeyburn Wood

Acorn Hill Plantation

Greenridge Sike Plantation

Burnt House

Mill Wood

MILL LA

Totherley Hill

Broomy Hill

Healey Mill

Hall Wood

Hall Hill Bog

Forestmount Plantation

Sawmill

Healey

Corfe Gate

Riding Mill

RIDING GRANGE

DENE TERR

STATION CL

SANDY LA

HOLLINHILL TERR

SANDY BANK

Riding Mill

PO

A695

MARCHBURN LA

MILLFIELD RD

ST JAMES

CHURCH

THE LONGRIGGS

CHURCH LA

Broomhaugh CE Fst Sch

OAKLANDS

NEW MANOR CL

OAKLANDS RISE

WHITE SIDE

99   A   B   00   C   D   01   E   F

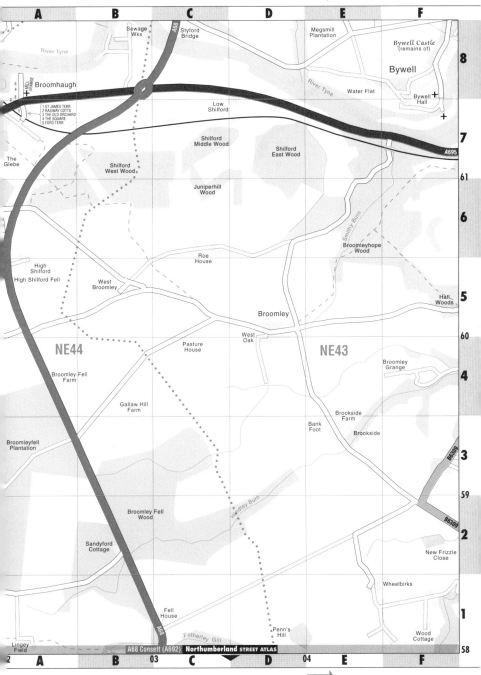

8

7

61

6

5

60

4

3

59

2

1

58

Sewage Wks

River Tyne

Styford Bridge

Megsmill Plantation

Bywell Castle (remains of)

Bywell

Water Flat

River Tyne

Bywell Hall

Broomhaugh

MILL GRANGE

1 ST JAMES TERR
2 RAILWAY COTTS
3 THE OLD ORCHARD
4 THE SQUARE
5 FORD TERR

Low Shilford

Shilford Middle Wood

Shilford East Wood

A695

The Glebe

Shilford West Wood

Juniperhill Wood

Smithy Burn

Broomleyhope Wood

High Shilford

High Shilford Fell

West Broomley

Roe House

Hall Woods

Broomley

NE44

Pasture House

West Oak

NE43

Broomley Grange

Broomley Fell Farm

Gallaw Hill Farm

Brookside Farm

Bank Foot

Brookside

Broomleyfell Plantation

B6309

Broomley Fell Wood

Hedley Burn

B6309

Sandyford Cottage

New Frizzle Close

Wheelbirks

Fell House

Wood Cottage

Lingey Field

Fotherley Gill

Penn's Hill

A68

03

04

64

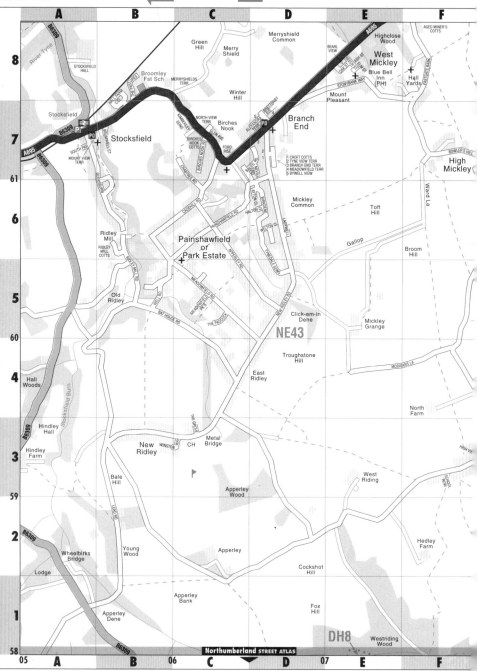

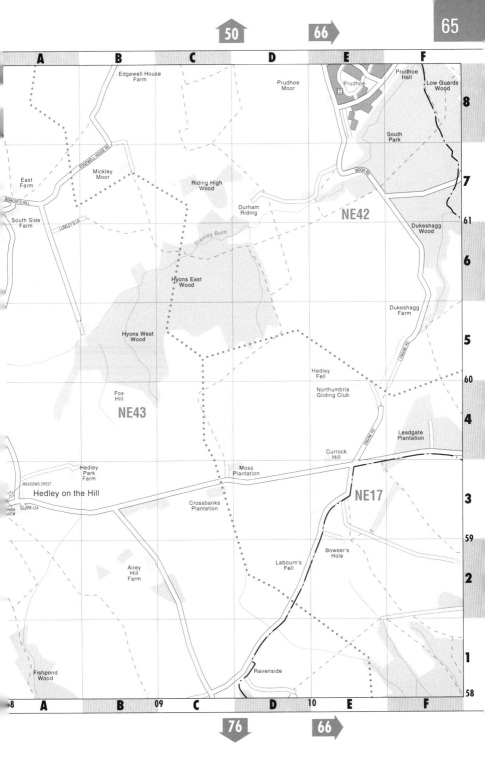

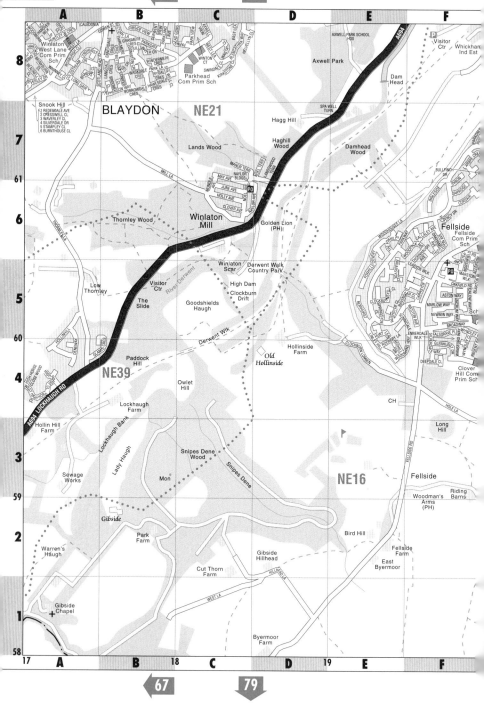

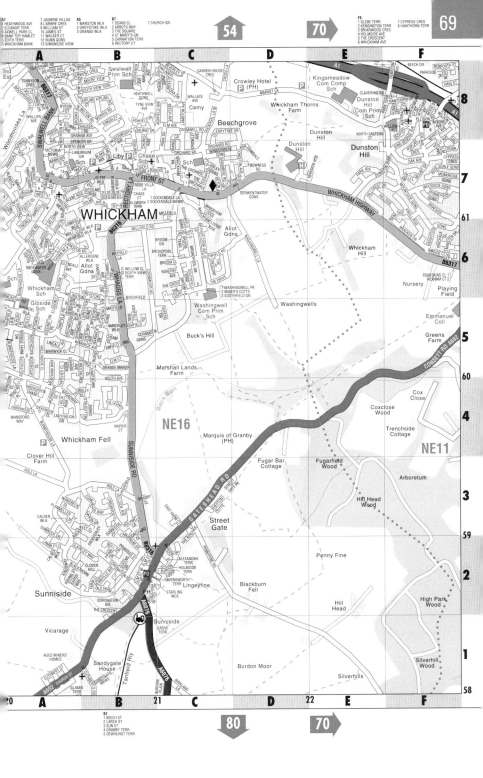

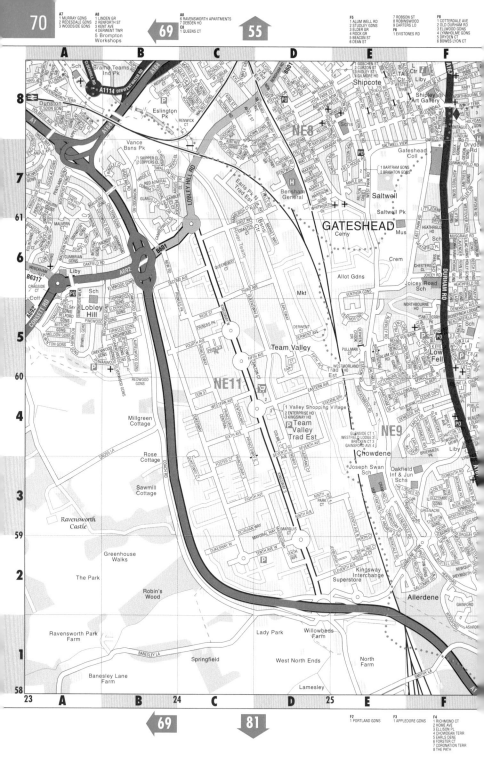

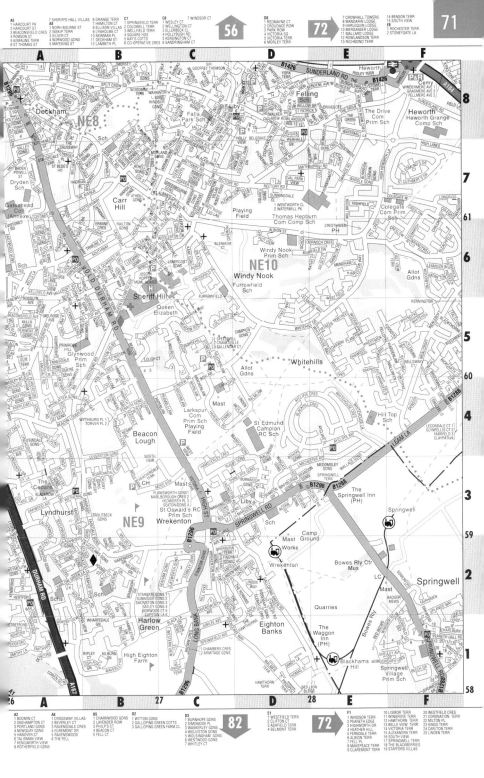

A5
1 HARCOURT PK
2 HARCOURT ST
3 BEACONSFIELD CRES
4 ROBSON ST
5 KINFAUNS TERR
6 ST THOMAS ST

A6
1 NORH BOURNE ST
2 INSKIP TERR
3 SILVER ST
4 NORWOOD GDNS
5 MAFEKING ST

7 SHERIFFS HALL VILLAS
6 HAMILTON PL
7 ELLISON VILLAS
8 LYNHOLME CT
9 LYNHOLME CT
10 NEWMAN PL
11 DECKHAM ST
12 LAMBETH PL

C7
1 SPRINGFIELD TERR
2 COLDWELL ST
3 WELLFIELD TERR
4 SQUARE HOS
5 KAY'S COTTS
6 CO-OPERATIVE CRES

C8
1 WESLEY CT
2 WELLINGTON CT
3 ELLERBECK CL
4 HOLLYBUSH RD
5 KENSINGTON CT
6 SANDRINGHAM CT

7 WINDSOR CT

D8
1 REDMAYNE CT
2 CROUDACE ROW
3 PARK ROW
4 VICTORIA SQ
5 VICTORIA TERR
6 MORLEY TERR

7 CROWHALL TOWERS
8 MANDARIN LODGE
9 HARLEQUIN LODGE
10 MERGANSER LODGE
11 MALLARD LODGE
12 ROWLANDSON TERR
13 RICHMOND TERR

14 BENSON TERR
15 SOUTH VIEW

E9
1 ROCHESTER TERR
2 STONEYGATE LA

A2
1 BODMIN CT
2 OKEHAMPTON CT
3 PORTLAND GDNS
4 NEWQUAY GDNS
5 HANOVER CT
6 TALISMAN VIEW
7 KENILWORTH VIEW
8 ROTHERFIELD GDNS

A6
1 CROSSWAY VILLAS
2 BEVERLEY CT
3 RAVENSDALE CRES
4 EGREMONT DR
5 RAVENSWOOD
6 THE FELL

B5
1 CHARNWOOD GDNS
2 LAVENDER ROW
3 PHILPS CT
4 BEACON CT
5 FELL CT

D2
1 WITTON GDNS

2 GALLOPING GREEN COTTS
3 GALLOPING GREEN FARM CL

D3
1 BURNHOPE GDNS
2 SIMONSIDE PL
3 WASKERLEY GDNS
4 WOLLISTON GDNS
5 WOLSINGHAM GDNS
6 WESTWOOD GDNS
7 WHITLEY CT

E1
1 WESTFIELD TERR
2 CLIFTON CT
3 ASHFIELD TERR
4 BELMONT TERR

F1
1 WINDSOR TERR
2 PEARETH EDGE
3 HIGHWORTH DR
4 HEATHER HILL
5 FERNDALE TERR
6 ALBION TERR
7 FELL PL
8 MAKEPEACE TERR
9 CLAREMONT TERR

10 LISMOR TERR
11 WINDGOVE TERR
12 HAWTHORN TERR
13 BELLE VIEW TERR
14 VICTORIA TERR
15 ALEXANDRA TERR
16 SOUTH VIEW
17 SPRINGWELL TERR
18 THE BLACKBERRIES
19 STAFFORD VILLAS

20 WESTFIELD CRES
21 CORONATION TERR
22 MERLIN PL
23 KINGS TERR
24 CARLTON TERR
25 LINDEN TERR

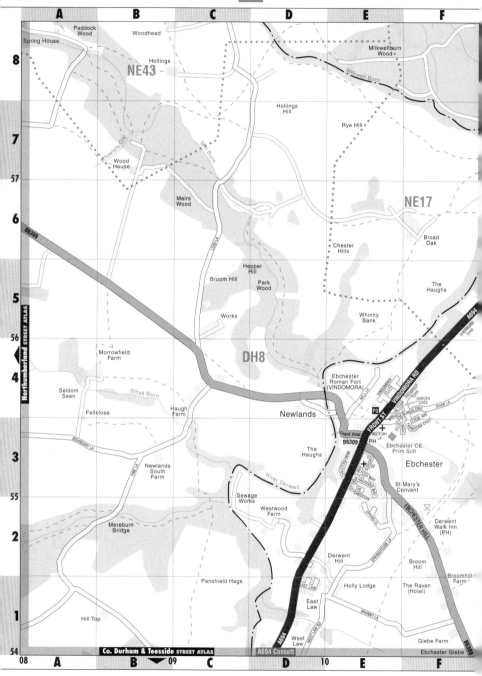

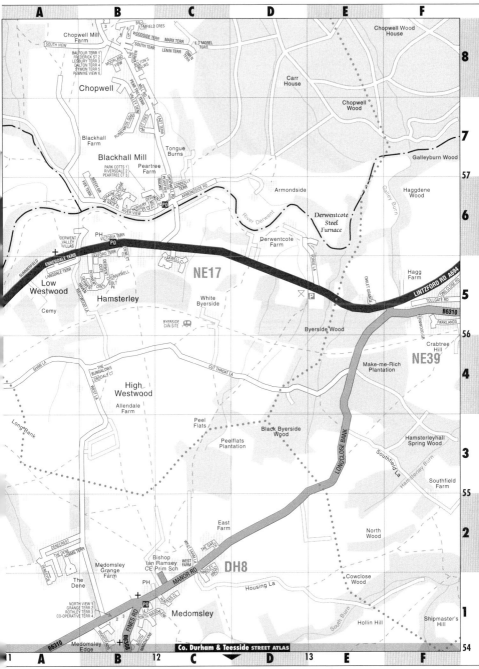

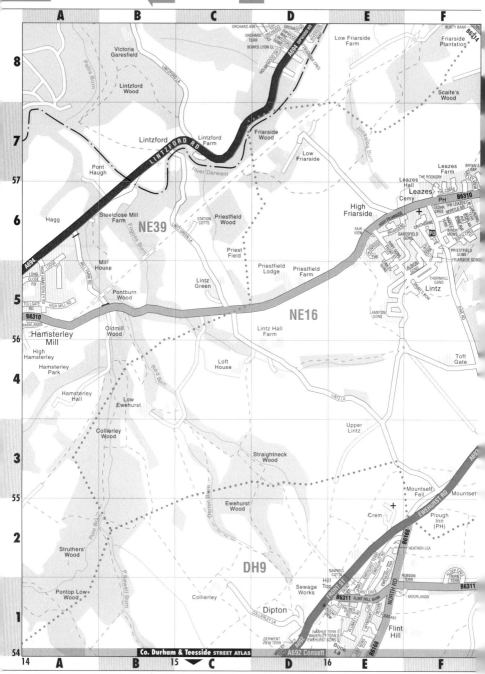

A   B   C   D   E   F

8

7

57

6

5

56

4

55

3

2

1

54

ORCHARD AVE
ORCHARD
ORCHARD TERR
BOWES LYON CL
HOLMWOOD CL

Low Friarside Farm

BUSTY BANK
Friarside Plantation
B6314

Scaife's Wood

Victoria Garesfield

Lintzford Wood

Pallis Burn

LINTZFORD LA

Lintzford Farm

Friarside Wood

Leazes Farm
Bryan's Leap
THE ROOKERY

Leazes Hall
Leazes
B6310

Lintzford
LINTZFORD RD

Pont Haugh

Low Friarside

Jockeys Burn

High Friarside

Cemy
PH
CEDAR CRES
MYRTLE GR
THE LEAZES
BIRCH AV

Hagg

Steelclose Mill Farm

NE39

STATION COTTS

Priestfield Wood

Priest Field

FAIR VIEW

HIGH FRIARSIDE

CRATHORNE
GARESFIELD GDNS
PO
PRIESTFIELD GDNS
FRIARSIDE GDNS

Mill House

MILL FARM RD

Pontburn Wood

LINTZ GREEN LA

Lintz Green

Priestfield Lodge

Priestfield Farm

ALBION GDNS
THORNHILL GDNS

Lintz

A694
LONG CLOSE RD
HIGH HAMSTERLEY RD

TOLLGATE RD
HIGH MILL RD

Priest Field

LAMBTON GDNS

SYKE RD

B6310
PARKLANDS

Hamsterley Mill

Oldmill Wood

Red Burn

Lintz Hall Farm

NE16

Toft Gate

High Hamsterley

Hamsterley Park

Loft House

Hamsterley Hall

Low Ewehurst

Collierley Wood

Straightneck Wood

LINTZ LA

Upper Lintz

A692

Ewehurst Wood

Mountsett Fell

Mountset

Pont Burn

Oldpit Burn

Crem

EWEHURST RD

Plough Inn (PH)

Struthers' Wood

B6168

HEATHER LEA

ROBSON TERR
ALDER CLOSE

Pontop Low Wood

P Hewell Burn

Collierley

DH9

Sewage Works

Dipton

COLLIERLEY LA

Hill Top
SAWMILL COTTS
FRONT ST
FIRST CRES
B6311
FLINT HILL BANK
PALMER

MOORLANDS
B6311

NORTH RD

IVANHOE TERR
WAVERLEY TERR
EWEHURST GDNS
PLEASANT

Flint Hill

DERWENT VIEW TERR
Bone La
B6168
A692 Consett

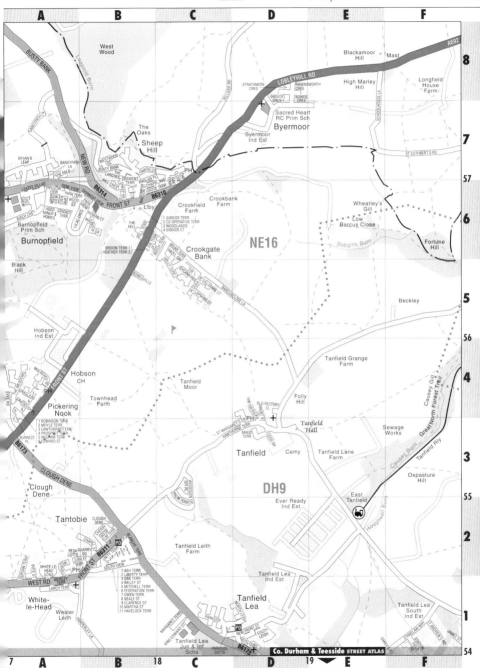

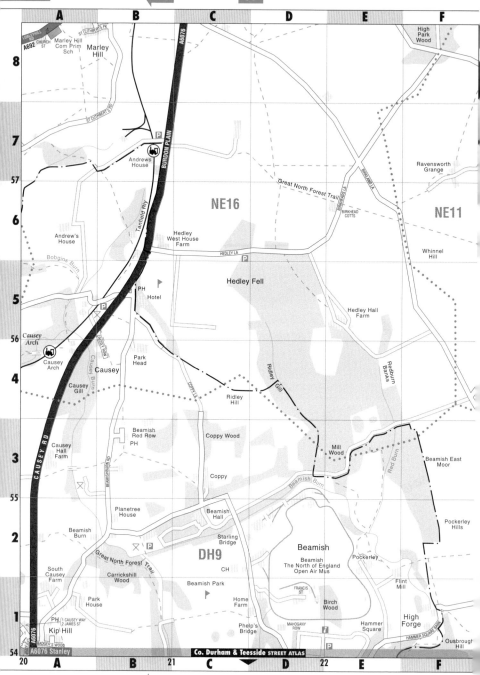

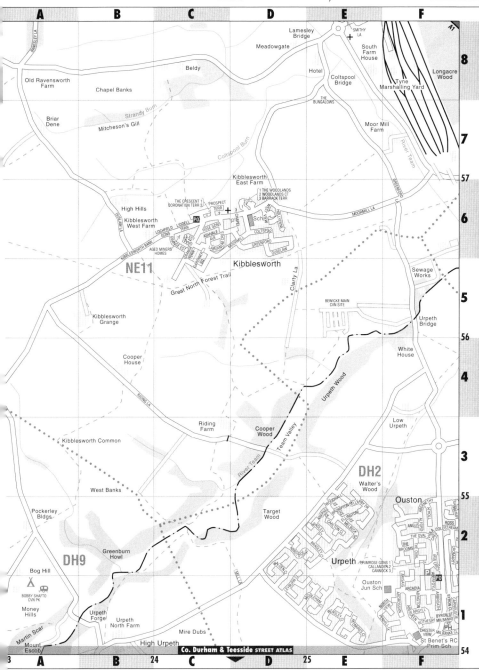

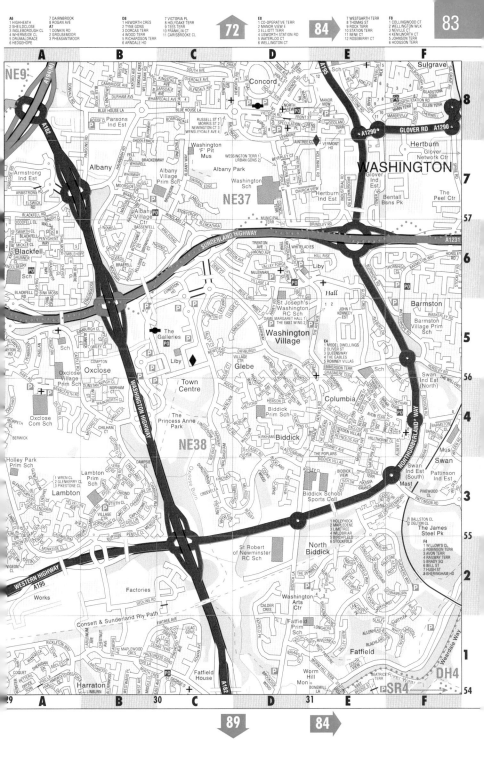

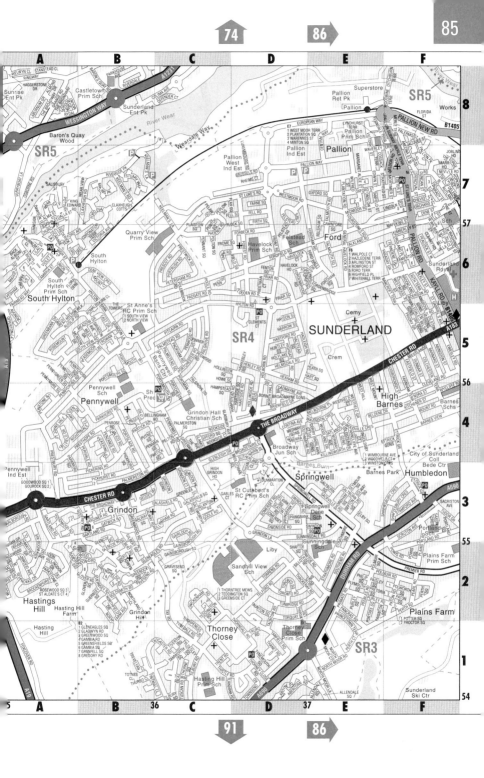

85 75

| | A | B | C | D | E | F |

8

Queen Alexandra Bridge
Works
River Wear
Deptford Works
B1405
Ayre's Quay
Millfield Works
Deptford
Stadium of Light (Sunderland FC)
Quay
Dame Dorothy Prim Sch
National Glass Ctr (Mus)
Sunderland Harbour

7

Neville Rd
Treby St
St Joseph's RC Prim Sch
Millfield
Millfield
Bishopwearmouth
Wearmouth Bridge
WEST WEAR ST
Univ of Sunderland St Peter's Campus
St John & St Patrick's Church Sch
B1293

57

102
Crowtree L Ctr
Univ of Sunderland
Univ University
Mkt
Sunderland
B1204
BOROUGH RD
103

6

Sunderland Royal
CHESTER RD
NEW DURHAM RD A690
Univ University
Park Lane
Univ
SUNDERLAND
Mus & Art Gall
Hudson Road Prim Sch
Mowbray Park
WHITE HOUSE RD
Hendon

5

A183
B1405
ORMONDE ST
HUTTON ST
St Anthony's RC Girls Sch
Coll
Ashbrooke
Coll Schs
PARK RD
Univ of Sunderland Bede Tower
Sunderland High Sch
Univ of Sunderland

56

102
Thornhill Sch
The Limes Jun Sch
Liby
103
Liby
Sp Ctr
Valley Road Com Prim Sch
Robinson Terr

4

SR4
BARNES PARK RD B1405
Prim Sch
Barbara Priestman Sch
St Mary's RC Prim Sch
MEADOW VALE
Univ of Sunderland Ashburne Ho (School of Arts, Design & Media)
Backhouse Park
Liby
Allot Gdns
Mast
PROMENADE

3

Humbledon Hill
B1405
St Aidan's RC Comp Sch
Ashbrooke Cross
Southmoor Com Sch
Sunderland Eye
SR2
Grangetown Prim Sch
Works

55

2

Superstore
The Precinct
Elstob House
Tunstall Hills
Maiden Paps
Hillview
Hill View Inf Sch
Hill View Jun Sch
WROXHAM CT
B1405
B1522
Cemy Grangetown

1

Low Newport Farm
AGED MINERS HOMES
SR3
Tunstall Hills East
Tunstall Hope Rd
Hypermarket
Leechmere Ind Est
Nunthorpe Ave

54

| 38 | A | B | 39 | C | D | 40 | E | F |

For full street detail of the highlighted area see pages 102 and 103.

B3
1 HEATHERLEA GDNS
2 GREENRIGG GDNS
3 PEMBERTON GDNS
4 PINESWAY

C4
1 AVENUE TERR
2 BROOKSIDE TERR
3 BROOK SIDE LODGE
4 BROOKSIDE GDNS
5 HUMBLEDON VIEW
6 ASHBROOKE MOUNT
7 WILLOW GN
8 PEARTREE MEWS

E4
1 TOWER PL
2 HENDON BURN AVE W
3 ATHOL PK
4 BEAUMONT LODGE
5 JUNIPER CL
6 VILLETTE BROOK ST
7 HENDON VALLEY CT
8 ERNEST ST
9 ROWLANDSON TERR

10 TAYLOR GDNS
F2
1 WESTHOLME TERR
2 HOLYROOD RD
3 WINDSOR TERR
4 WESTMINSTER TERR
5 RYHOPE ST
6 OCEAN RD N
7 OCEAN RD S
8 STOCKTON TERR

9 HEMMING ST
10 GARNEGIE ST
11 OSWALD TERR
12 ALDERLEY CL
D4
1 ASHBROOKE HALL
2 WESTBROOKE
3 ASHBURNE CT
4 ASHBROOKE CRES

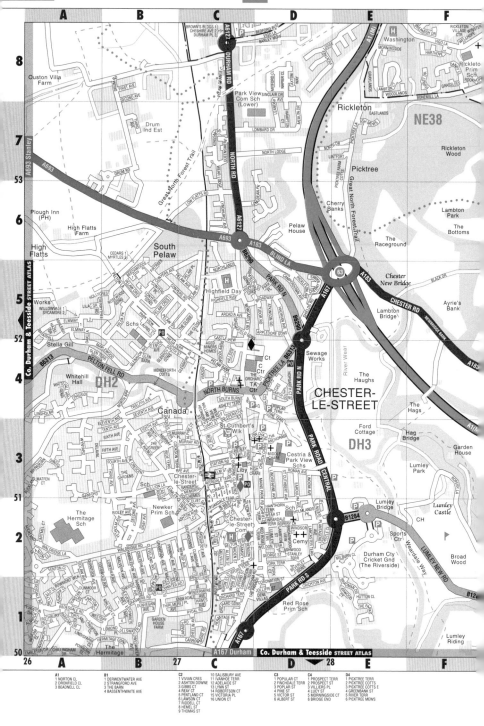

A167 Durham
Co. Durham & Teesside STREET ATLAS

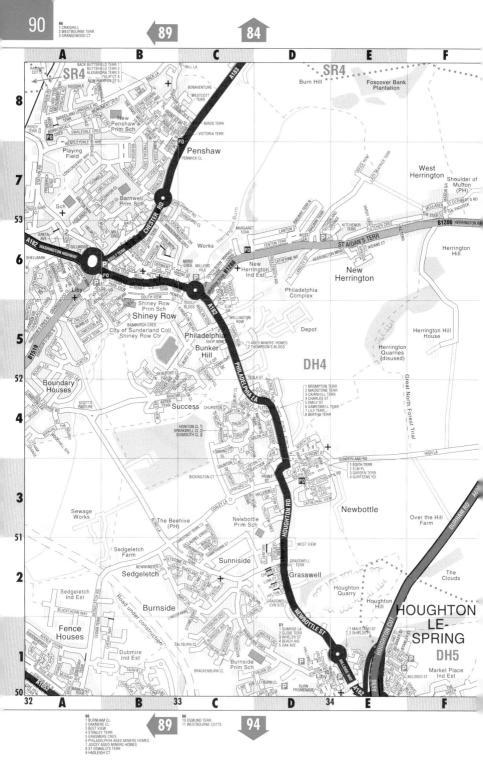

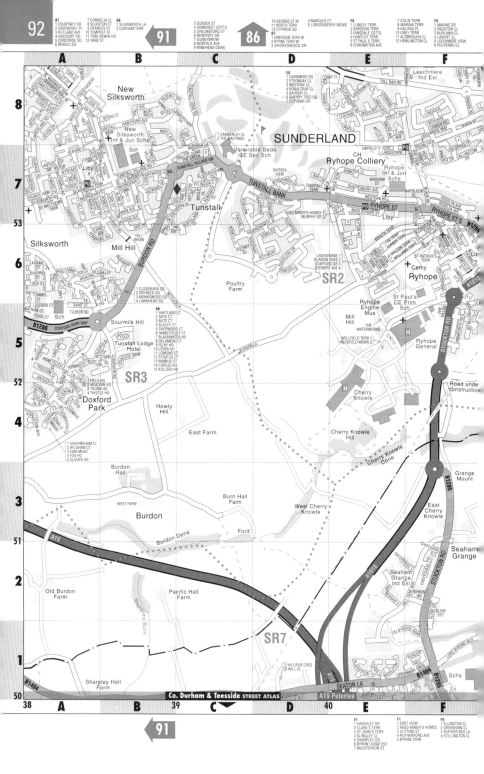

A7
1 COURTNEY DR
2 CAVENDISH PL
3 RUTLAND AVE
4 VISCOUNT RD
5 CONCORDE SQ
6 BEAGLE SQ

7 CORNELIA CL
8 SILKSTUN CT
9 FRANCES ST
10 TEMPEST ST
11 TOM URWIN HO
12 VANE ST

A8
1 SILKSWORTH LA
2 DURHAM TERR

3 SUSSEX ST
4 SOMERSET COTTS
5 CHELMSFORD ST
6 NEWPORT GR
7 SUNNYBROW
8 NORFOLK AVE
9 MINEHEAD GDNS

10 GEORGE ST W
11 NORTH TERR
12 CYPRESS SQ
B7
1 EMERSON TERR W
2 BYRNE TERR W
3 SHORESWOOD DR

4 MARQUIS CT
5 LONDONDERRY MEWS

F6
1 LUMLEY TERR
2 EARSDON TERR
3 DINSDALE COTTS
4 HUNTLEY TERR
5 ST PAUL'S TERR
6 CORONATION AVE

7 COLIN TERR
8 MARINA TERR
9 HALIFAX PL
10 GREY TERR
11 ALDBROUGH CL
12 HEMLINGTON CL

F8
1 MARINE DR
2 PADSTOW CL
3 BURLAWN CL
4 LANIVET CL
5 LEECHMERE VIEW
6 POLPERRO CL

E1
1 HAVERLEY DR
2 CLARK S TERR
3 ST JOHN'S TERR
4 SLINGLEY CL
5 SHARPLEY DR
6 BYRON LODGE EST
7 McCUTCHEON ST

F1
1 EAST VIEW
2 AGED MINER'S HOMES
3 CUTTING ST
4 RUTHERFORD AVE
5 BYRON TERR

F5
1 ELLINGTON CL
2 GREENHOW CL
3 FEATHER BED LA
4 STILLINGTON CL

A   B   C   D   E   F

8

7

53

6

5

52

4

3

51

2

1

50

A4016

PALTERDEN RD

SALTERDEN LA

Ryhope
Nook

RYHOPE RD

1 TOLLBAR RD
2 MARINE DR
3 TOLLBAR RD
4 LEECHMERE WAY
5 QUEEN ST
6 LADOCK CL
7 POLPERRO CL

Maiden's
Flat

CLIFF
VIEW

BYRON TERR

PO VILLAGE

THE VILLAGE

B1287

STATION RD

Halliwell Banks

1 FLORALIA AVE
2 GREY TERR
3 GORDON TERR
4 KILBURN CL
5 SOUTH FARM
6 ERNEST TERR
7 RICHARDSON TERR
8 FAWCETT TERR
9 THOMPSON TERR
10 CRANSTON PL
11 ROBSON PL
12 ARTHUR ST
13 MOIR TERR
14 CHARLES ST
15 JOHN ST

SR2

Pincushion

Road under construction

Ryhope Dene
House
(Convent)

Ryhope Dene

Road under construction

SR7

Hall
Farm

Seaham
Hall

BYRON'S
CT

LC

LORD BYRONS WLK

Seaham Dene

NEW DR

1 BURNWAY
2 NEWLANDS RD W
3 NEWARK CRES
4 NAVENBY CL

SEAHAM

PROMENADE

B1287

NORTH RD

P

1 SUTHERLAND ST
2 EMBANKMENT RD

STONEYCROFT WAY 1
ROCKINGHAM CL 2

THE
CASTLEREAGH
HOMES

Seaham
Sch

Northlea

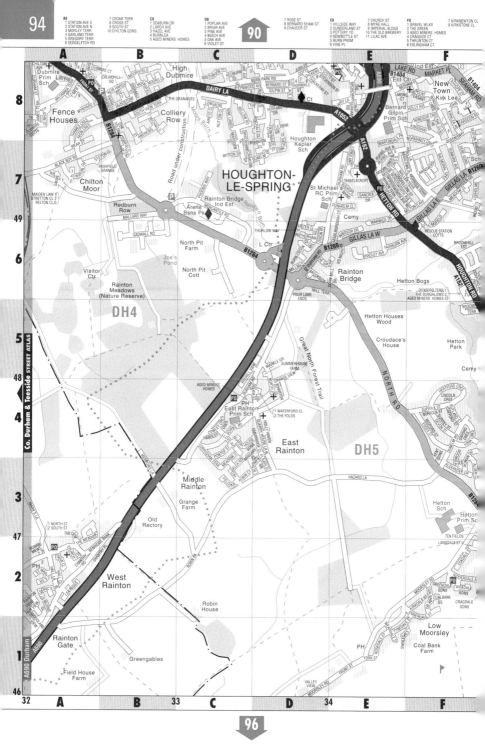

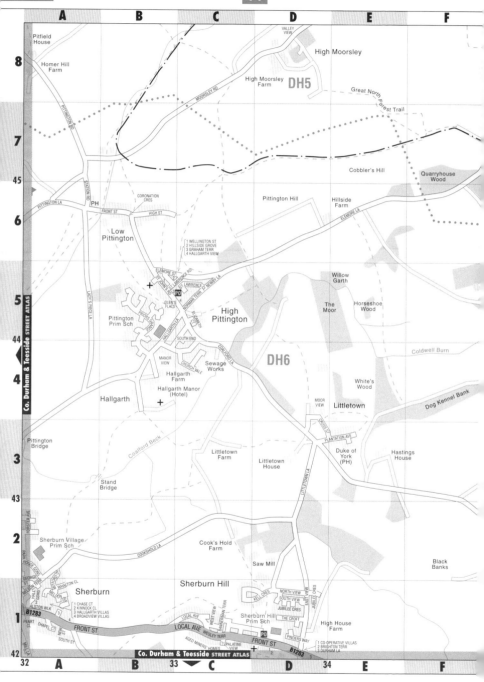

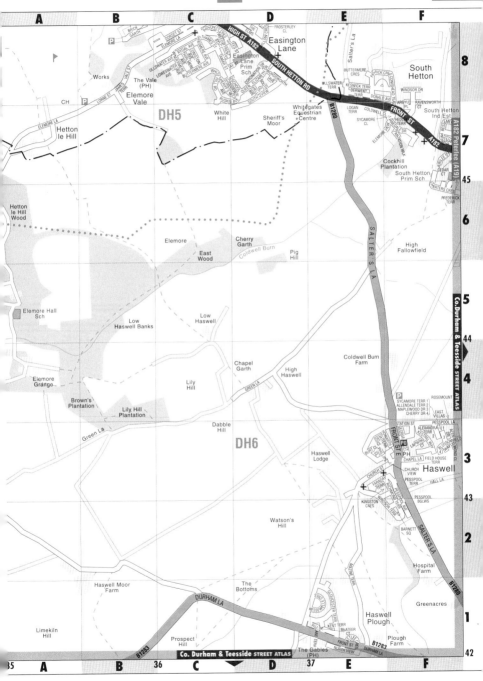

DH5

Easington Lane

South Hetton

Hetton le Hill

Elemore Vale

The Vale (PH)

Works

White Hill

Sheriff's Moor

Whitegates Equestrian Centre

South Hetton Ind Est

Cockhill Plantation

South Hetton Prim Sch

Hetton le Hill Wood

Elemore

Cherry Garth

East Wood

Pig Hill

High Fallowfield

Coldwell Burn

Elemore Hall Sch

Low Haswell Banks

Low Haswell

Coldwell Burn Farm

Chapel Garth

High Haswell

Elemore Grange

Lily Hill

Brown's Plantation

Lily Hill Plantation

Dabble Hill

DH6

Haswell Lodge

Haswell

Watson's Hill

Hospital Farm

Haswell Moor Farm

The Bottoms

Greenacres

Limekiln Hill

Prospect Hill

Haswell Plough

Plough Farm

The Gables (PH)

Co. Durham & Teesside STREET ATLAS

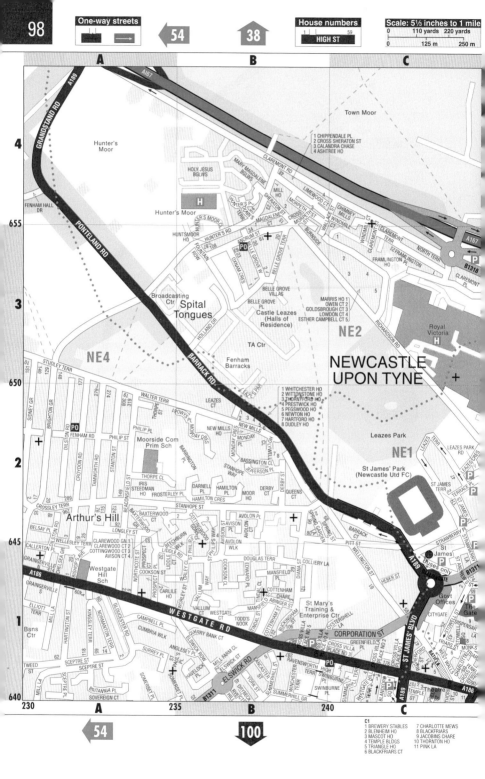

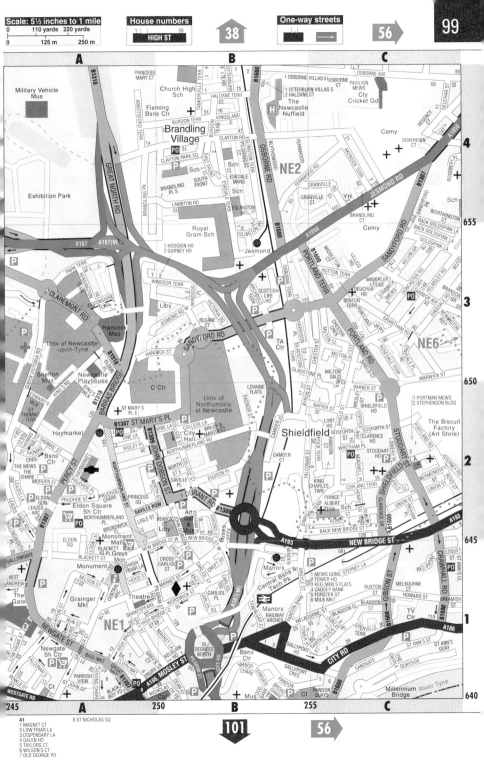

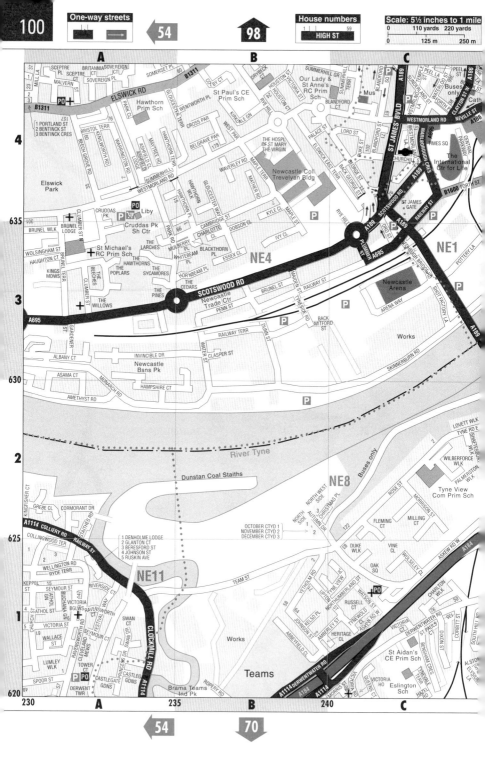

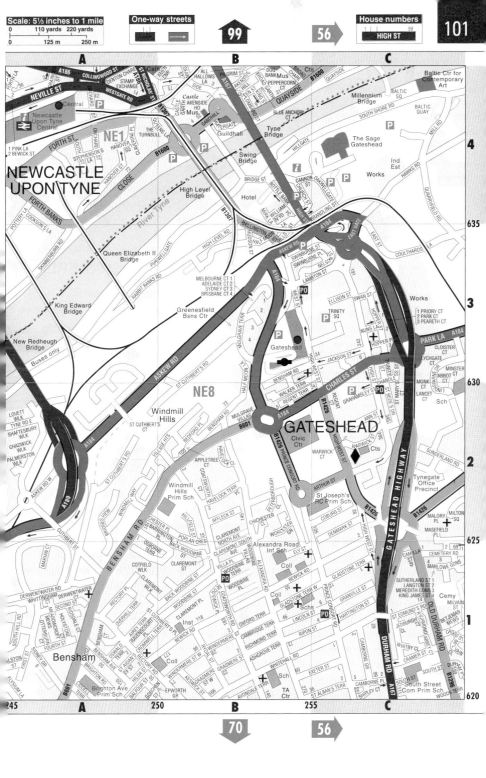

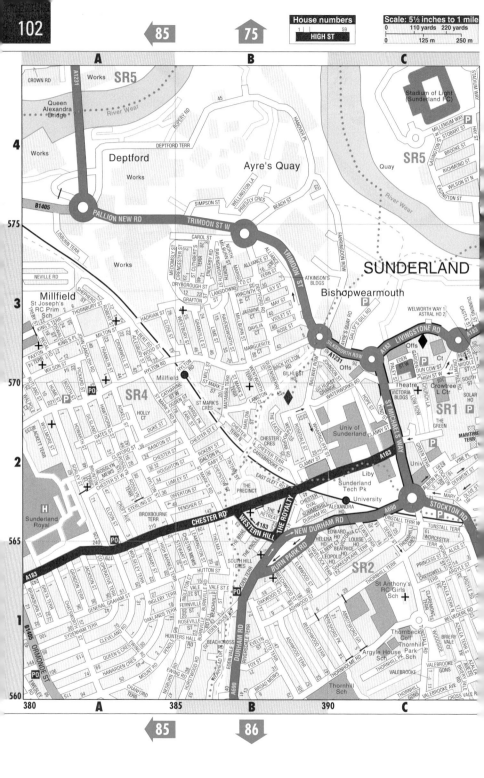

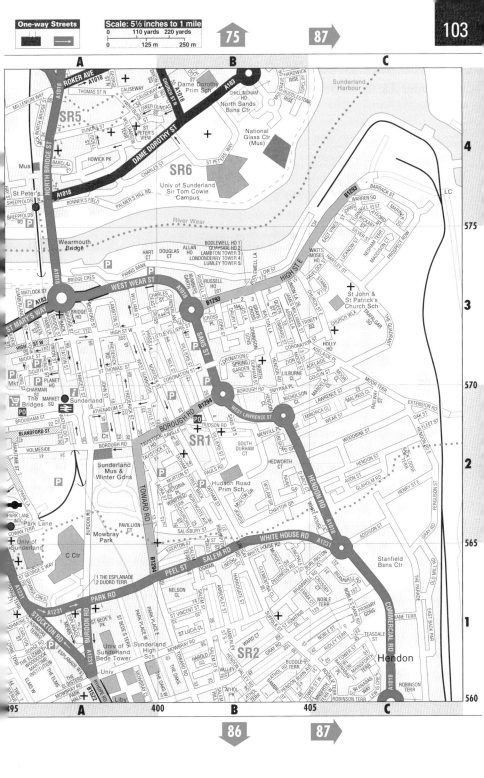

Index

Church Rd **6** Beckenham BR2......... **53** C6

Place name	Location number	Locality, town or village	Postcode district	Page and grid square
May be abbreviated on the map	Present when a number indicates the place's position in a crowded area of mapping	Shown when more than one place has the same name	District for the indexed place	Page number and grid reference for the standard mapping

Public and commercial buildings are highlighted in magenta   **Places of interest** are highlighted in blue with a star★

Abbreviations used in the index

Acad	**Academy**	Comm	**Common**	Gd	**Ground**	L	**Leisure**	Prom	**Promenade**
App	**Approach**	Cott	**Cottage**	Gdn	**Garden**	La	**Lane**	Rd	**Road**
Arc	**Arcade**	Cres	**Crescent**	Gn	**Green**	Liby	**Library**	Rcn	**Recreation**
Ave	**Avenue**	Cswy	**Causeway**	Gr	**Grove**	Mdw	**Meadow**	Ret	**Retail**
Bglw	**Bungalow**	Ct	**Court**	H	**Hall**	Meml	**Memorial**	Sh	**Shopping**
Bldg	**Building**	Ctr	**Centre**	Ho	**House**	Mkt	**Market**	Sq	**Square**
Bsns, Bus	**Business**	Ctry	**Country**	Hospl	**Hospital**	Mus	**Museum**	St	**Street**
Bvd	**Boulevard**	Cty	**County**	HQ	**Headquarters**	Orch	**Orchard**	Sta	**Station**
Cath	**Cathedral**	Dr	**Drive**	Hts	**Heights**	Pal	**Palace**	Terr	**Terrace**
Cir	**Circus**	Dro	**Drove**	Ind	**Industrial**	Par	**Parade**	TH	**Town Hall**
Cl	**Close**	Ed	**Education**	Inst	**Institute**	Pas	**Passage**	Univ	**University**
Cnr	**Corner**	Emb	**Embankment**	Int	**International**	Pk	**Park**	Wk, Wlk	**Walk**
Coll	**College**	Est	**Estate**	Intc	**Interchange**	Pl	**Place**	Wr	**Water**
Com	**Community**	Ex	**Exhibition**	Junc	**Junction**	Prec	**Precinct**	Yd	**Yard**

Index of localities, towns and villages

A

Addison 52 F5
Albany 83 B7
Allerdene 70 F2
Anick 45 F8
Annitsford 22 B1
Arthur's Hill 98 A2
Ashbrooke 86 C5
Ashington 6 B3
Axwell Park 53 E1
Ayre's Quay 102 B4
Ayton 82 F2

B

Backworth 30 C4
Barley Mow 82 C2
Barlow 67 C6
Bar Moor 52 A5
Barmston 83 F5
Beaconhill Green 21 E6
Beacon Lough 71 B4
Beamish 80 D2
Bebside 16 E7
Bedlington 11 A1
Bedlington Station 11 B3
Beechgrove 69 C8
Bell's Close 53 E6
Bensham 101 A1
Benton Square 30 B1
Benwell 54 C6
Berwick Hill 19 A3
Biddick 83 D4
Biddick Hall 59 B2
Bill Quay 57 B2
Billy Mill 41 D7

Birtley 82 C3
Bishopwearmouth 102 C3
Black Callerton 36 A8
Blackfell 83 A6
Blackhall Mill 77 B7
Blakelaw 37 C2
Blaydon 53 E3
Blaydon Burn 52 E1
Blaydon Haughs 53 E4
Bleach Green 53 C1
Blyth 17 C7
Boldon 74 A8
Boldon Colliery 58 E1
Bomarsund 11 C6
Bothal 5 B2
Boundary Houses 90 A4
Bournmoor 89 D3
Branch End 64 D7
Brandling Village 99 B4
Brenkley 20 D3
Bridge End 45 C6
Brockley Whins 58 F3
Broomhaugh 63 A8
Broom Hill 95 A6
Broomley 63 D5
Brunswick Green 28 A5
Brunswick Village 28 A6
Brunton Park 28 B1
Bunker Hill 90 C5
Burdon 92 B3
Burnopfield 79 A6
Burnside 90 B2
Burradon 29 C6
Byermoor 79 D7
Byker 56 C5
Bywell 63 F8

C

Callerton 36 B6
Callerton Lane End 35 E7
Cambois 12 C5
Campbell Park 57 F5
Camperdown 29 C5
Canada 88 B4
Carley Hill 75 A4
Carr Hill 71 B7
Castletown 74 B1
Cauldwell 59 E7
Causey 80 C4
Chester-le-Street 88 E4
Chilton Moor 94 A7
Chirton 41 F5
Choppington 10 E5
Chopwell 66 B1
Chowdene 70 E4
Clara Vale 51 E6
Cleadon 60 B1
Cleadon Lea 59 E1
Cleadon Park 60 A4
Clifton 9 A2
Coalburns 66 D7
Colliery Row 94 B8
Collingwood 22 B4
Columbia 83 E4
Concord 83 D8
Corbridge 47 B5
Cowgate 37 D1
Cowpen 17 A7
Cramlington 21 F5
Cramlington Village ...22 B7
Crawcrook 51 E4
Cresswell 2 A7
Crookgate Bank 79 C6

Crookhill 52 D5
Cullercoats 32 D3

D

Darras Hall 25 D3
Deans 59 C7
Deckham 71 A8
Delaval 54 C4
Denton Burn 53 E7
Deptford 102 A4
Derwent Haugh 54 B2
Dilston 46 D3
Dinnington 27 A7
Dipton 78 D1
Donwell 72 B1
Downhill 74 B4
Doxford Park 91 E6
Dudley 29 A7
Dunston 54 F1
Dunston Hill 69 E7

E

Earsdon 31 A5
Easington Lane 97 D8
East Boldon 74 D7
East Cramlington 22 E5
East Denton 37 A1
Eastfield 22 D8
East Gateshead 56 B3
East Herrington 91 C6
East Holywell 30 E7
East Howdon 41 C2
East Rainton 94 D4

East...

East Sleekburn 12
Ebchester 76
Eighton Banks 71
Eland Green 25
Elemore Vale 97
Ellington 1
Elswick 54
Eltringham 50

F

Fair Moor 3
Farringdon 91
Fatfield 83
Fawdon 37
Felling 71
Felling Shore 56
Fellside 68
Fence Houses 94
Fenham 54
Flint Hill 78
Follingsby 72
Ford 85
Fordley 29
Forest Hall 39
Friars Goose 56
Fulwell 75

G

Gateshead 55
Glebe 83
Gosforth 38
Grangetown 86
Grasswell 90
Great Lumley 89

5

55 Degrees N NE1 . . . .**.99** B1

A

A J Cook Ct NE63 . . . .**.6** C3
A J Cook's Cotts NE39 . . . . . .**.67** B2
Abbay St SR5 . . . .**.75** A1
Abbey Cl Washington NE38 .**.83** D5
  Whitley Bay NE25 . . . .**.31** D4
Abbey Ct Gateshead NE8 .**.101** C1
  5 Hexham NE46 . . . .**.45** B5
Abbey Dr Burnside DH4 . . . . .**.90** C2
  Jarrow NE32 . . . .**.58** C7
  Newcastle-u-T NE5 . . . .**.36** B4
  Tynemouth NE30 . . . .**.42** D8
Abbey Gate NE61 . . . .**.8** D7
Abbey Mdws NE61 . . . .**.8** D7
Abbey Rd NE38 . . . .**.83** D5
Abbey Terr
  12 Morpeth NE61 . . . .**.3** F1
  Shiremoor NE27 . . . .**.30** E3
Abbey View Hexham NE46 . .**.45** C4
  3 Morpeth NE61 . . . .**.3** F1
Abbeyfield Cl NE8 . . . .**.100** B1
Abbeyfields Fst Sch NE61 . .**.8** E8
Abbeyvale Dr NE46 . . . .**.57** B7
Abbie Ct NE24 . . . .**.17** D7
Abbot Cl NE8 . . . .**.101** C3
Abbot's Way NE61 . . . .**.8** E8
Abbots Cl NE62 . . . .**.11** B8
Abbots Way
  Tynemouth NE29 . . . .**.41** E8
  2 Whickham NE16 . . . .**.69** B7
Abbotsfield Cl SR3 . . . .**.91** F5
Abbotsford Gr SR2 . . . .**.102** C1
Abbotsford Ho NE24 . . . .**.17** C6
Abbotsford Pk NE25 . . . .**.31** F4
Abbotsford Rd NE10 . . . .**.56** D1
Abbotsford Terr NE2 . . . .**.99** A4
Abbotside Cl DH2 . . . .**.81** D2
Abbotside Pl NE5 . . . .**.36** D2
Abbotsmeade Cl NE5 . . . . . .**.54** C8
Abbs St SR5 . . . .**.75** D1
Abercorn Pl NE28 . . . .**.40** E6
Abercorn Rd
  Newcastle-u-T NE15 . . . .**.54** A5
  Sunderland SR3 . . . .**.91** D8
Abercrombie Pl **2** NE5 . . . .**.37** B2
Aberdare Rd SR3 . . . .**.91** E7
Aberdeen DH2 . . . .**.81** F1
Aberdeen Ct NE3 . . . .**.37** D8
Aberdeen Dr NE32 . . . .**.58** E3
Aberdeen Twr SR3 . . . .**.91** E8
Aberford Cl NE5 . . . .**.36** B3
Aberfoyle NE11 . . . .**.88** A6
Abernethy DH2 . . . .**.81** F2
Abigail Cl NE3 . . . .**.38** E5
Abingdon Ct
  Blaydon NE21 . . . .**.53** C3
  Newcastle-u-T NE3 . . . .**.37** D7
Abingdon Rd NE6 . . . .**.57** B7
Abingdon Sq NE23 . . . .**.16** C1
Abingdon St SR4 . . . .**.85** F5
Abingdon Way NE35 . . . .**.73** E7
Abinger St NE4 . . . .**.98** B1
Abington DH2 . . . .**.81** F1
Aboyne Sq SR3 . . . .**.85** D1
Acacia Ave NE34 . . . .**.90** A1
Acacia Gr Hebburn NE31 . . . .**.57** E4
  South Shields NE34 . . . .**.59** F5
Acacia Rd NE10 . . . .**.56** B2
Acacia Terr NE31 . . . .**.6** D3
Acanthus Ave NE4 . . . .**.54** D7
Acer Ct SR2 . . . .**.86** D4
Acer Dr DH6 . . . .**.97** F3
Acklam Ave SR2 . . . .**.87** A1
Acomb Ave
  Seaton Delaval NE25 . . . .**.23** D2
  Wallsend NE28 . . . .**.40** D7
Acomb Cl NE61 . . . .**.9** C5
Acomb Cres NE3 . . . .**.38** A8
Acomb Ct Bedlington NE22 . .**.11** A1
  Gateshead NE9 . . . .**.71** B2
  Killingworth NE12 . . . .**.29** D3
  Sunderland SR2 . . . .**.86** F1
Acomb Dr NE41 . . . .**.51** A7
Acomb Gdns NE5 . . . .**.37** C1
Acorn Ave Bedlington NE22 .**.15** F8
  Gateshead NE8 . . . .**.70** C8
Acorn Cl NE9 . . . .**.71** D3
Acorn Rd NE2 . . . .**.38** E2
Acorn Sq NE42 . . . .**.50** D2
Acreford Ct NE62 . . . .**.10** E6
Acton Dr NE29 . . . .**.41** D8
Acton Ho **11** NE29 . . . .**.42** A4
Acton Pl NE7 . . . .**.39** B2
Acton Rd NE5 . . . .**.53** F8
Ada St Newcastle-u-T NE6 . .**.56** E6
  South Shields NE33 . . . .**.42** D1
Adair Ave NE15 . . . .**.54** C6
Adair Way NE31 . . . .**.58** A5
Adams Terr DH8 . . . .**.77** A2
Adamsez Ind Est NE15 . . . . .**.53** F4
Adderlane Fst Sch NE42 . . . .**.50** E3
Adderlane Rd NE42 . . . .**.50** E3
Adderstone Ave NE23 . . . . . .**.22** B5
Adderstone Cres NE2 . . . . . .**.38** F2
Adderstone Ct NE2 . . . .**.38** F2
Adderstone Gdns NE29 . . . . .**.31** B1
Addington Cres NE29 . . . .**.41** E6

Addington Dr Blyth NE24 . .**.17** E5
  Wallsend NE28 . . . .**.40** D7
Addison Cl **2** NE6 . . . .**.56** B6
Addison Ct Ryton NE40 . . . .**.52** B5
  7 Wallsend NE28 . . . .**.41** A1
Addison Gdns NE10 . . . .**.72** B8
Addison Ind Est
  Ryton NE40 . . . .**.52** F5
  Ryton NE21 . . . .**.52** A5
Addison Rd
  15 Newcastle-u-T NE6 . . . . .**.56** B6
  Newcastle-u-T,Lemington
  NE15 . . . .**.53** D7
  West Boldon NE36 . . . .**.74** A7
Addison St
  North Shields NE29 . . . .**.42** A4
  Sunderland SR2 . . . .**.103** C2
Addison Wlk NE34 . . . .**.59** A3
Addycombe Terr NE6 . . . .**.39** C1
Adelaide Cl SR1 . . . .**.103** C3
Adelaide Ct NE8 . . . .**.101** B3
Adelaide Ctr The **5** NE4 . . .**.54** E5
Adelaide Ho **8** NE4 . . . .**.54** E5
Adelaide Pl SR1 . . . .**.103** C3
Adelaide St **12** DH3 . . . .**.88** C2
Adelaide Terr NE4 . . . .**.54** E4
Adeline Gdns NE3 . . . .**.38** A3
Adelphi Cl NE29 . . . .**.41** C8
Adelphi Pl NE6 . . . .**.56** C5
Aden Twr SR3 . . . .**.91** E8
Admington Ct NE62 . . . .**.10** F7
Admiral Collingwood Ct **5**
  NE61 . . . .**.9** A8
Admiral Ho **9** NE30 . . . .**.42** D7
Admiral Way SR3 . . . .**.91** C5
Adolphus St SR6 . . . .**.60** F1
Affleck St NE8 . . . .**.70** C7
Afton Ct NE34 . . . .**.59** C5
Afton Way NE3 . . . .**.37** E6
Agar Rd SR3 . . . .**.91** D8
Aged Miner's Cotts NE43 .**.64** F8
Aged Miner's Homes
  Boldon Colliery NE35 . . . .**.58** D1
  Burnopfield NE16 . . . .**.79** A6
  Hetton le H DH5 . . . .**.95** A2
  3 Houghton-le-S,New Town
  DH5 . . . .**.94** F8
  Ryhope SR2 . . . .**.92** E7
  2 Seaham SR2 . . . .**.92** F1
Aged Miners Cotts NE42 . .**.50** B1
Aged Miners Homes
  Blyth NE24 . . . .**.17** E8
  Cambois NE24 . . . .**.12** D4
  Chester le S DH2 . . . .**.88** C4
  Newbiggin-by-t-S NE64 . . . .**.7** D3
  2 Newcastle-u-T NE5 . . . . . .**.36** E3
Aged Miners' Homes
  Annitsford NE23 . . . .**.22** B1
  Ashington NE63 . . . .**.6** F4
  Ashington,Woodhorn NE63 . . .**.6** F5
  3 Hebburn NE31 . . . .**.57** D6
  Rowlands Gill NE39 . . . .**.67** A1
Aged Miners' Homes
  DH4 . . . .**.89** C2
Aged Miners' Homes
  Brunswick Village NE13 . . . . .**.28** A6
  Cramlington NE23 . . . .**.21** F7
  Dudley NE23 . . . .**.29** A6
  East Rainton DH5 . . . .**.94** C4
Aged Miners' Homes
  DH3 . . . .**.89** B1
Aged Miners' Homes
  DH5 . . . .**.94** F6
Aged Miners' Homes
  NE39 . . . .**.67** A4
Aged Miners' Homes **5**
  DH4 . . . .**.89** B1
Aged Miners' Homes
  NE11 . . . .**.81** C6
Aged Miners' Homes
  New Hartley NE25 . . . .**.23** E6
  New Silksworth SR3 . . . .**.86** A1
Aged Miners' Homes
  NE39 . . . .**.67** A4
Aged Miners' Homes
  NE40 . . . .**.52** E4
Aged Miners' Homes
  Sherburn Hill DH6 . . . .**.96** C1
  Shiney Row DH4 . . . .**.90** C5
  South Shields NE34 . . . .**.60** A7
Aged Miners' Homes
  Stakeford NE62 . . . .**.11** C8
  Sunderland SR5 . . . .**.74** E2
Aged Miners' Homes
  NE16 . . . .**.69** A1
Aged Miners' Homes
  NE27 . . . .**.30** F3
Aged Mineworkers Homes
  Longhirst NE61 . . . .**.5** B7
  Throckley NE15 . . . .**.35** B2
Agincourt Hebburn NE31 . . .**.57** D7
  Killingworth NE12 . . . .**.29** D4
Agnes Maria St NE3 . . . .**.38** A5
Agricola Ct **11** NE33 . . . .**.42** C4
Agricola Gdns NE28 . . . .**.40** D7
Agricola Rd NE4 . . . .**.54** F6
Aidan Ave NE26 . . . .**.24** B6
Aidan Cl
  Brunswick Village NE13 . . . . .**.28** A6
  Wallsend NE27 . . . .**.30** C1
Aidan Ct Jarrow NE32 . . . .**.58** B6
  Longbenton NE7 . . . .**.39** C5
Aidan Gr NE61 . . . .**.1** E4
Aidan Wlk NE3 . . . .**.38** E5
Aiden Way DH5 . . . .**.95** A5
Ailesbury St SR4 . . . .**.102** A3
Ainderby Rd NE15 . . . .**.35** B2
Ainsdale Gdns NE5 . . . .**.36** C2
Ainslie Pl NE5 . . . .**.37** C2
Ainsworth Ave NE34 . . . .**.59** A3

Ainthorpe Cl SR3 . . . .**.92** B7
Ainthorpe Gdns NE7 . . . .**.39** C4
Aintree Cl Ashington NE43 . . .**.6** C2
  Washington NE37 . . . .**.83** D7
Aintree Gdns NE8 . . . .**.70** C7
Aintree Rd SR3 . . . .**.91** D8
Airedale NE28 . . . .**.39** F5
Airedale Gdns DH5 . . . .**.94** F2
Airey Terr
  Gateshead NE8 . . . .**.101** A1
  Newcastle-u-T NE6 . . . .**.57** A5
Aireys Cl DH4 . . . .**.94** C8
Airport Freightway NE13 . .**.26** E2
Airport Ind Est NE3 . . . .**.37** D6
Airport Sta NE13 . . . .**.26** D3
Airville Mount SR3 . . . .**.92** A4
Aisgill Cl NE23 . . . .**.22** B6
Aisgill Dr NE5 . . . .**.36** C1
Aiskell St SR4 . . . .**.102** A2
Akeld Cl NE23 . . . .**.22** B5
Akeld Ct NE3 . . . .**.38** E1
Akeld Mews **7** SR6 . . . .**.75** E1
Akenside Hill NE1 . . . .**.101** B4
Akenside Ho NE1 . . . .**.101** B4
Akenside Terr NE2 . . . .**.99** C4
Akhurst Sch NE2 . . . .**.38** F2
Alamein Ave DH5 . . . .**.94** F8
Alanbrooke Row NE31 . . . . . .**.57** C3
Alansway Gdns **9** NE33 . . . .**.59** C8
Alansway Ave NE12 . . . .**.39** D7
Albany Cl NE4 . . . .**.100** A3
Albany Gdns **2** NE26 . . . . . .**.32** B4
Albany Ho SR5 . . . .**.75** C1
Albany Mews NE3 . . . .**.38** A2
Albany Rd NE8 . . . .**.56** A3
Albany St E NE33 . . . .**.59** D8
Albany St W NE33 . . . .**.59** D8
Albany Village Ctr NE37 . . .**.83** B7
Albany Village Prim Sch
  NE37 . . . .**.83** C7
Albany Way NE37 . . . .**.83** C7
Albatross Way NE17 . . . .**.33** B3
Albemarle Ave NE2 . . . .**.38** D3
Albemarle St **4** NE33 . . . . . .**.42** C3
Albert Ave **9** NE28 . . . .**.40** B2
Albert Cl SR2 . . . .**.102** B1
Albert Dr NE9 . . . .**.70** F4
Albert Edward Terr SR5 . . .**.58** E2
Albert Elliott Prim Sch
  NE34 . . . .**.59** C4
Albert Pl Gateshead NE9 . . . .**.70** C2
  Washington NE38 . . . .**.83** F4
Albert Rd Bedlington NE22 . . .**.11** A1
  Jarrow NE32 . . . .**.58** A6
  Jarrow NE32 . . . .**.58** B6
  Seaton Sluice NE26 . . . .**.24** D6
  Sunderland SR4 . . . .**.102** A3
Albert St Blyth NE24 . . . .**.17** E8
  6 Chester le S DH3 . . . .**.88** C3
  Hebburn NE31 . . . .**.57** D6
  Newcastle-u-T NE2 . . . .**.99** C2
  Rowlands Gill NE39 . . . .**.67** A1
Albert Terr
  Longbenton NE12 . . . .**.29** C1
  5 Whitley Bay NE26 . . . .**.32** B4
Albion Ct
  Newcastle-u-T NE6 . . . .**.56** B5
  South Shields NE33 . . . .**.42** C4
Albion Gdns NE16 . . . .**.78** F5
Albion Ho NE8 . . . .**.42** A5
Albion Pl SR1 . . . .**.102** C2
Albion Rd NE29,NE30 . . . .**.42** A6
Albion Rd W NE29 . . . .**.42** A5
Albion Ret Ctr NE24 . . . .**.17** D8
Albion Row
  Newcastle-u-T NE6 . . . .**.56** B6
  Newcastle-u-T,St Lawrence
  NE6 . . . .**.56** B5
Albion St Gateshead NE8 . . .**.71** D6
  Sunderland SR4 . . . .**.85** A6
Albion Terr
  6 Gateshead NE9 . . . .**.71** F1
  Hexham NE46 . . . .**.45** A5
  2 North Shields NE29 . . . .**.2** A3
  6 North Shields NE29 . . . . . .**.42** A6
Albion Way Blyth NE24 . . . . . .**.17** C7
  Cramlington NE23 . . . .**.16** D1
Albury Park Rd NE30 . . . .**.42** C7
Albury Pl NE16 . . . .**.69** A5
Albury Rd NE2 . . . .**.38** E3
Albyn Gdns SR3 . . . .**.86** A3
Alcester Cl NE62 . . . .**.10** F7
Alconbury Cl NE24 . . . .**.17** E6
Alcroft Cl NE5 . . . .**.36** B3
Aldborough St NE24 . . . .**.17** E7
Aldbrough Cl **11** SR2 . . . .**.92** F6
Aldbrough St NE34 . . . .**.59** A5
Aldeburgh Ave NE15 . . . .**.53** C8
Aldenham Gdns NE30 . . . . . .**.32** C1
Aldenham Rd SR3 . . . .**.91** E8
Aldenham Twr SR3 . . . .**.91** E8
Alder Ave NE4 . . . .**.54** D8
Alder Cl Hetton le H DH5 . . . .**.94** F3
  Morpeth NE61 . . . .**.9** A8
Alder Cres DH9 . . . .**.78** F2
Alder Ct NE25 . . . .**.31** E4
Alder Gr NE25 . . . .**.31** E4
Alder Rd Shiremoor NE27 . . . .**.41** B7
  Wallsend NE28 . . . .**.40** C6
Alder St SR5 . . . .**.74** B1
Alder Way NE12 . . . .**.29** C4
Alderley Cl
  Boldon Colliery NE35 . . . .**.58** E1
  12 Sunderland SR2 . . . .**.86** F2
Alderley Dr NE12 . . . .**.29** F4
Alderley Rd NE9 . . . .**.70** E5
Alderley Way NE23 . . . .**.16** D1
Alderney Gdns NE5 . . . .**.36** C2

Aldershot Rd SR3 . . . .**.91** D7
Aldershot Sq SR3 . . . .**.91** D7
Alderton Ct NE62 . . . .**.10** F7
Alderwood Ashington NE63 . .**.6** C2
  Washington NE38 . . . .**.89** B8
Aldesam Ct NE6 . . . .**.39** F1
Alderwyk NE10 . . . .**.72** B6
Aldsworth Cl NE9 . . . .**.72** A1
Aldwick Rd NE15 . . . .**.54** A5
Aldwych Dr NE29 . . . .**.41** B7
Aldwych Ho NE33 . . . .**.42** B2
Aldwych Rd SR3 . . . .**.91** D7
Aldwych Sq SR3 . . . .**.91** D6
Aldwych St NE33 . . . .**.42** E2
Alemouth Rd NE46 . . . .**.45** B5
Alexander Dr DH5 . . . .**.94** F3
Alexander Pl **12** NE46 . . . . .**.45** A5
Alexander Terr
  Hazlerigg NE13 . . . .**.28** A5
  Sunderland SR6 . . . .**.75** D3
Alexandra Ave SR5 . . . .**.74** F1
Alexandra Cres NE46 . . . .**.44** F5
Alexandra Dr NE16 . . . .**.69** C8
Alexandra Rd
  Ashington NE63 . . . .**.6** F3
  Gateshead NE8 . . . .**.101** B1
  Morpeth NE61 . . . .**.9** A8
  Newcastle-u-T NE6 . . . .**.39** B1
Alexandra Road Inf Sch
  NE8 . . . .**.101** B1
Alexandra St
  Rowlands Gill NE39 . . . .**.67** A1
  Wallsend NE28 . . . .**.40** C2
Alexandra Terr
  Bedlington NE22 . . . .**.11** B1
  Haswell DH6 . . . .**.97** F3
  Hexham NE46 . . . .**.44** F5
  Penshaw DH4 . . . .**.90** B8
  15 Springwell NE9 . . . .**.71** F1
  Stocksfield NE43 . . . .**.64** A7
  Sunnyside NE16 . . . .**.69** C2
  4 Whitley Bay NE26 . . . .**.32** B4
Alexandra Way NE23 . . . .**.22** B5
Alford DH2 . . . .**.81** F2
Alford Gn NE12 . . . .**.39** C7
Alfred Ave NE22 . . . .**.11** B1
Alfred St Blyth NE24 . . . .**.17** E6
  Hebburn NE31 . . . .**.57** D6
  Newcastle-u-T NE6 . . . .**.56** E6
  South Shields NE33 . . . .**.59** B8
Algernon NE12 . . . .**.29** D5
Algernon Cl **14** NE6 . . . .**.56** C7
Algernon Ct **17** NE6 . . . .**.56** C7
Algernon Ind Est NE27 . . . . . .**.30** F1
Algernon Pl NE26 . . . .**.32** B4
Algernon Rd
  16 Newcastle-u-T,Heaton
  NE6 . . . .**.56** C7
  Newcastle-u-T,Lemington
  NE15 . . . .**.53** C6
Algernon Terr
  Tynemouth NE30 . . . .**.42** C8
  Wylam NE41 . . . .**.51** A6
Algiers Rd SR3 . . . .**.91** C7
Alice St Blaydon NE21 . . . .**.53** B1
  South Shields NE33 . . . .**.59** C8
  Sunderland SR2 . . . .**.102** C1
Alice Well Villas SR4 . . . .**.84** B3
Aline St SR3 . . . .**.92** B7
Alison Ct **4** NE6 . . . .**.56** B7
Alison Dr NE36 . . . .**.74** D7
All Hallows La NE1 . . . .**.101** B4
All Saints Bsns Ctr NE1 . . .**.99** B1
All Saints CE Prim Sch
  NE34 . . . .**.59** B4
All Saints Coll NE5 . . . .**.36** C2
All Saints Ct
  North Shields NE29 . . . .**.41** D6
  Sunderland SR6 . . . .**.75** D1
All Saints Dr DH5 . . . .**.95** A5
All Saints Ho **6** SR6 . . . .**.75** D1
Alan Ho
  Newcastle-u-T NE4 . . . .**.54** F8
  Sunderland SR1 . . . .**.103** B3
Allan Rd NE43 . . . .**.7** D5
Allandale Ave NE12 . . . .**.39** D7
Allanville NE12 . . . .**.29** C5
Allchurch NE15 . . . .**.54** B6
Allchurch Dr NE63 . . . .**.7** A3
Allen Ave NE11 . . . .**.70** D7
Allen Dr NE46 . . . .**.45** B4
Allen St DH3 . . . .**.88** C2
Allen Terr NE40 . . . .**.51** F4
Allendale Ave NE28 . . . .**.40** B4
Allendale Cres
  Penshaw DH4 . . . .**.90** B8
  Shiremoor NE27 . . . .**.31** A3
  Stakeford NE62 . . . .**.6** A1
Allendale Dr NE34 . . . .**.60** A8
Allendale Pl NE30 . . . .**.42** D7
Allendale Rd Blyth NE24 . . . .**.17** F6
  Hexham NE46 . . . .**.44** F4
  Newcastle-u-T NE6 . . . .**.56** D5
  Sunderland SR3 . . . .**.91** D8
Allendale Sq SR3 . . . .**.91** E8
Allendale St DH5 . . . .**.95** A2
Allendale Terr
  Haswell DH6 . . . .**.97** F3
  Newcastle-u-T NE6 . . . .**.56** F5
Allenhead NE38 . . . .**.83** E1
Allenheads
  Newcastle-u-T NE5 . . . .**.36** E1
  Seaton Delaval NE25 . . . .**.23** C4
Allensgreen NE23 . . . .**.22** B6

Allerdean Cl
  Newcastle-u-T NE15 . . . .**.53** B7
  Seaton Delaval NE25 . . . .**.23** D2
Allerdene Wlk NE16 . . . .**.69** B6
Allerhope NE23 . . . .**.22** B5
Allerton Cl NE15 . . . .**.39** D2
Allerton Pl NE16 . . . .**.68** F5
Allerwash NE5 . . . .**.36** E1
Allery Banks NE61 . . . .**.9** A8
Allgood Terr NE22 . . . .**.11** B1
Allhusen Terr NE8 . . . .**.56** B1
Alliance Pl SR4 . . . .**.102** B3
Alliance St SR4 . . . .**.102** B3
Allingham Cl NE7 . . . .**.39** E3
Allison Ct NE16 . . . .**.54** B1
Alloa Rd SR3 . . . .**.91** D8
Allonby Mews NE23 . . . .**.16** C2
Allonby Way NE5 . . . .**.54** B8
Alloy Terr NE39 . . . .**.67** C1
Allwork Terr NE16 . . . .**.69** A7
Alma Pl **8** Morpeth NE61 . . . .**.9** A8
  North Shields NE29 . . . .**.42** A6
  Whitley Bay NE26 . . . .**.32** A6
Alma St SR4 . . . .**.85** A3
Alma Terr NE40 . . . .**.52** C2
Almond Cl DH6 . . . .**.97** F3
Almond Cres NE8 . . . .**.70** C8
Almond Dr SR5 . . . .**.85** A6
Almond Gr NE24 . . . .**.17** C4
Almond Pl NE4 . . . .**.54** D2
Almshouses NE15 . . . .**.52** F7
Aln Ave NE3 . . . .**.38** A7
Aln Cres NE3 . . . .**.38** A7
Aln Ct Ellington NE61 . . . .**.1** E7
  Newcastle-u-T NE15 . . . .**.53** C6
Aln Gr NE15 . . . .**.53** C7
Aln St Ashington NE63 . . . .**.6** F4
  Hebburn NE31 . . . .**.57** D6
Aln Wlk NE3 . . . .**.38** A7
Alnham Ct NE3 . . . .**.37** E1
Alnham Gr NE5 . . . .**.36** C2
Alnmouth Ave NE29 . . . .**.41** D6
Alnmouth Dr NE3 . . . .**.38** E4
Alnmouth Terr NE46 . . . .**.44** F4
Alnwick Ave
  North Shields NE29 . . . .**.41** D6
  Whitley Bay NE26 . . . .**.32** B4
Alnwick Cl
  Chester le S DH2 . . . .**.88** A1
  Whickham NE16 . . . .**.54** A1
Alnwick Ct NE38 . . . .**.83** B1
Alnwick Dr NE22 . . . .**.10** D1
Alnwick Rd
  South Shields NE34 . . . .**.59** C6
  Sunderland SR3 . . . .**.91** E8
Alnwick Sq SR3 . . . .**.91** E7
Alnwick St Newburn NE15 . .**.52** F7
  Wallsend NE28 . . . .**.40** C1
Alnwick Terr NE13 . . . .**.28** C
Alpine Ct DH4 . . . .**.89** F
Alpine Gr NE36 . . . .**.74** D
Alpine Way SR3 . . . .**.86** A
Alresford NE12 . . . .**.29** D
Alston Ave
  East Cramlington NE23 . . . . . .**.22** D
  Newcastle-u-T NE6 . . . .**.56** E
Alston Cl Tynemouth NE29 . . .**.41** A
  Wallsend NE28 . . . .**.41** A
Alston Cres SR6 . . . .**.75** C
Alston Gdns NE15 . . . .**.35** D
Alston Gr NE26 . . . .**.24** B
Alston Rd
  New Hartley NE25 . . . .**.23** D
  Washington NE38 . . . .**.84** B
Alston St NE8 . . . .**.101** A
Alston Wlk DH6 . . . .**.96** F
Alstone Cl NE62 . . . .**.10** F
Altan Pl NE12 . . . .**.29** B
Altree Grange SR5 . . . .**.75** C
Altrincham Twr SR3 . . . .**.91** E
Alum Well Rd
  Gateshead NE9 . . . .**.70** F
  1 Gateshead,Low Fell NE9 .**.70** F
Alverston Cl NE15 . . . .**.53** C
Alverstone Ave NE9 . . . .**.70** F
Alverstone Rd SR3 . . . .**.91** D
Alverthorpe St NE33 . . . .**.59** D
Alveston Cl NE62 . . . .**.10** F
Alwin NE38 . . . .**.83** A
Alwin Grange
  Hebburn NE31 . . . .**.57** F
  Jarrow NE32 . . . .**.58** D
Alwinton Ave NE29 . . . .**.41** D
Alwinton Cl Blyth NE24 . . . . .**.17** C
  Newcastle-u-T NE5 . . . .**.37** B
Alwinton Ct NE63 . . . .**.6** C
Alwinton Dr DH2 . . . .**.88** A
Alwinton Gdns NE11 . . . .**.70** A
Alwinton Rd NE27 . . . .**.30** E
Alwinton Sq **5** NE63 . . . .**.6** C
Alwinton Terr NE3 . . . .**.38** B
Alwyn Cl DH4 . . . .**.89** E
Amalfi Twr SR3 . . . .**.91** E
Amara Sq SR3 . . . .**.91** E
Ambassadors Way NE29 . . .**.41** C
Amber Ct NE42 . . . .**.17** C
Ambergate Cl NE5 . . . .**.37** A
Amberley Chase NE12 . . . . . .**.29** F
Amberley Ct NE24 . . . .**.17** C
Amberley Gdns NE7 . . . .**.39** C
Amberley Prim Sch NE12 . .**.29** F
Amberley St
  Gateshead NE8 . . . .**.100** C
  Sunderland SR2 . . . .**.103** A
Amberley St S SR2 . . . .**.103** A
Amberley Way NE24 . . . .**.17**

Amberley Wlk NE16 ....69 B5
Amberly Ct NE3 ....69 A5
Amble Ave
  South Shields NE34 ....60 B8
  Whitley Bay NE25 ....32 B4
Amble Cl Blyth NE24 ....17 C5
  North Shields NE29 ....41 E4
Amble Gr NE2 ....56 A7
Amble Pl NE1 ....29 F1
Amble Twr SR3 ....91 E8
Amble Way NE3 ....38 B6
Ambleside NE15 ....35 E3
Ambleside Ave NE34 ....59 E6
Ambleside Cl NE25 ....23 D3
Ambleside Gdns NE9 ....71 A4
Ambleside Sch NE5 ....54 B8
Ambleside Terr SR6 ....75 C4
Ambridge Way
  Newcastle-u-T NE3 ....37 F5
  Seaton Delaval NE25 ....23 A4
Ambrose Ct NE21 ....53 B1
Ambrose Ho NE33 ....57 B6
Ambrose Rd SR3 ....91 D8
Amec Dr NE28 ....41 A1
Amec Way NE28 ....40 E1
Amelia Cl NE4 ....54 E3
Amelia Gdns SR3 ....91 C7
Amelia Wlk NE4 ....54 E3
Amen Cnr NE1 ....101 B4
Amersham Pl NE1 ....37 B2
Amersham Rd NE24 ....17 E4
Amesbury Cl NE5 ....36 B3
Amethyst NE4 ....100 A1
Amethyst St NE4 ....85 F7
Amherst Rd NE3 ....37 E6
Amos Ayre Pl NE34 ....58 F5
Amsterdam Rd SR3 ....91 E8
Amy St SR5 ....75 B2
Ancaster Ave NE12 ....39 B6
Ancaster Rd NE16 ....68 F6
Anchorage The
  Chester le S DH3 ....88 B7
  Penshaw DH4 ....90 B6
Ancona St SR4 ....85 F7
Ancroft Ave NE29 ....41 F7
Ancroft Pl Ashington NE63 ....6 F1
  Newcastle-u-T NE5 ....54 B8
Ancroft Rd NE25 ....23 B3
Ancroft Way NE3 ....37 F8
Ancrum St NE2 ....98 B3
Ancrum Way NE16 ....68 F5
Anderson St NE33 ....42 D3
Andover Pl NE28 ....40 E6
Andrew Cl NE6 ....57 A6
Andrew Rd SR3 ....91 D7
Andrews House Sta*
  NE16 ....80 B7
Anfield Ct NE3 ....37 E5
Anfield Rd NE3 ....37 E5
Angel of the North* NE9 ....82 A8
Angerton Ave
  Shiremoor NE27 ....30 F2
  Tynemouth NE30 ....32 A1
Angerton Gdns NE5 ....54 D8
Angerton Terr NE23 ....28 F8
Angle Terr NE28 ....40 F2
Anglesey Gdns NE5 ....36 C2
Anglesey Pl NE4 ....98 B1
Anglesey Rd SR3 ....91 D7
Anglesey Sq SR3 ....91 D7
Angram Dr SR2 ....87 A1
Angram Wlk NE5 ....36 C1
Angrove Gdns SR4 ....85 F5
Angus DH2 ....81 F2
Angus Cl NE12 ....29 C3
Angus Cres NE29 ....41 D3
Angus Rd NE30 ....70 C8
Angus Sq SR3 ....91 D7
Ann St Blaydon NE21 ....53 C3
  Gateshead NE8 ....101 C2
  Hebburn NE31 ....57 C7
  Shiremoor NE27 ....30 E4
Ann Wlk NE6 ....57 A4
Ann's Row NE24 ....12 E1
Anne Dr NE12 ....40 A8
Annfield Rd NE23 ....16 B2
Annie St SR6 ....75 E4
Annitsford Dr NE23 ....29 B8
Annitsford Rd NE23 ....22 E1
Annville Cres NE6 ....57 A4
Anscomb Gdns NE7 ....39 A2
Anson Cl NE33 ....59 B8
Anson Pl NE5 ....36 F3
Anstead Cl NE23 ....22 B6
Anthony Rd SR3 ....91 D8
Anton Pl NE23 ....22 B5
Antonine Wlk NE15 ....34 F2
Antrim Cl NE5 ....37 C3
Antwerp Rd SR3 ....91 C7
Apex Bsns Village NE23 ....22 B1
Apperley NE5 ....36 E1
Apperley Ave NE3 ....37 C4
Apperley Rd NE43 ....64 C6
Appian Pl Gateshead NE9 ....71 B7
  Throckley NE15 ....35 E2
Apple Cl NE15 ....53 C8
Apple Ct NE25 ....23 D6
Appleby Ct
  Bournmoor DH4 ....89 D1
  Longbenton NE12 ....39 B6
  North Shields NE29 ....41 F5
Appleby Gdns
  Gateshead NE9 ....71 A3
  Wallsend NE28 ....41 A4
Appleby Pk NE29 ....41 F6
Appleby Rd SR3 ....91 D7
Appleby Sq SR3 ....91 D7
Appleby St NE29 ....42 A4

Appledore Cl NE40 ....66 E8
Appledore Gdns
  Chester le S DH3 ....88 D5
  Gateshead NE9 ....70 F3
Appledore Rd NE24 ....17 E5
Appleforth Ave SR2 ....87 A1
Appletree Cl NE11 ....70 A8
Appletree Ct NE8 ....101 B2
Appletree Gardens Fst Sch
  NE25 ....31 E4
Appletree Gdns
  Newcastle-u-T NE6 ....39 F1
  Whitley Bay NE25 ....31 E3
Appletree La NE45 ....47 A5
Appletree Rise NE45 ....47 A5
Applewood NE12 ....29 F3
Appley Terr SR6 ....75 E2
Apsley Cres NE3 ....37 E5
Aqua Terr NE64 ....7 D4
Aquila Dr NE15 ....34 E2
Arbeia Ho NE33 ....42 C4
Arbeia Roman Fort Mus*
  NE33 ....42 C4
Arbroath DH2 ....81 F1
Arbroath Rd SR3 ....91 D8
Arcade The NE30 ....42 D7
Arcadia DH2 ....81 F1
Arcadia Ave DH3 ....88 C5
Arcadia Terr NE24 ....17 E6
Archbishop Runcie CE Fst
  Sch NE3 ....38 D5
Archbold Terr NE2 ....99 B3
Archer Rd SR3 ....91 D8
Archer Sq SR3 ....91 D8
Archer St NE28 ....40 E3
Archer Villas NE28 ....40 D3
Archibald Fst Sch NE3 ....38 C5
Archibald St NE3 ....38 C5
Arcot Ave
  Cramlington NE23 ....21 E8
  Whitley Bay NE25 ....31 E3
Arcot Dr
  Newcastle-u-T NE5 ....53 F8
  Whitley Bay NE25 ....31 E3
Arcot Terr NE5 ....17 D8
Arden Ave NE3 ....28 B1
Arden Cl NE28 ....40 D7
Arden Cres NE5 ....37 D1
Arden Sq SR3 ....91 E8
Ardrossan DH2 ....81 F1
Ardrossan Rd SR3 ....91 D7
Arena Bsns Pk DH4 ....94 F7
Arena Way NE4 ....100 C3
Argus Cl NE11 ....70 B7
Argyle Ct NE3 ....81 F1
Ariel St NE63 ....6 E3
Arisaig DH2 ....81 F1
Arkle Rd SR3 ....91 D7
Arkle St Gateshead NE8 ....70 C8
  Hazlerigg NE13 ....28 A4
Arklecrag NE37 ....83 C6
Arkleside Pl NE5 ....36 C2
Arkwright St NE8 ....70 D7
Arlington Ave NE3 ....37 F3
Arlington Cl DH4 ....89 E3
Arlington Ct NE3 ....38 A3
Arlington Gr
  Cramlington NE23 ....16 B2
  Whickham NE16 ....69 A6
Arlington Rd NE31 ....57 F4
Arlington St NE4 ....54 F6
Arlott Ho NE29 ....41 D3
Armitage Gdns NE9 ....71 C1
Armondside Rd NE17 ....77 C6
Armstrong Ave
  Newcastle-u-T NE6 ....39 B1
  South Shields NE34 ....59 E6
Armstrong Cl NE46 ....44 B3
Armstrong Ind Est NE37 ....83 A7
Armstrong Rd
  Newcastle-u-T NE15,NE4 ....54 C4
  Wallsend NE28 ....41 A1
  Washington NE37 ....83 A7
Armstrong St
  Gateshead NE8 ....70 D7
  Woolsington NE5 ....36 B7
Armstrong Terr
  Morpeth NE61 ....9 A8
  South Shields NE33 ....59 C8
Arncliffe Ave SR4 ....85 E4
Arncliffe Gdns NE16 ....36 C2
Arndale Arc NE32 ....58 B7
Arndale Ho Birtley DH3 ....82 C5
  Newcastle-u-T NE5 ....37 E5
  Washington NE37 ....83 D8
Arndale Sq NE12 ....39 D3
Arnold Rd SR3 ....91 D8
Arnold St NE35 ....73 F8
Arnside Wlk NE5 ....36 C2
Arran Ct SR3 ....92 A6
Arran Dr NE32 ....58 E3
Arran Gdns NE10 ....71 C7

Arran Pl NE29 ....41 C8
Arras La SR1 ....103 B3
Arrol Pk SR4 ....102 B2
Arrow Cl NE12 ....29 B2
Arthington Way NE34 ....59 E5
Arthur Ave SR2 ....93 A6
Arthur Cook Ave NE16 ....69 C6
Arthur St Blyth NE24 ....17 E8
  Gateshead NE8 ....101 C2
  Jarrow NE32 ....58 B6
  Ryhope SR2 ....93 A6
  Whitburn SR6 ....60 F4
Arundel Ct SR2 ....60 F3
Arundel Cl
  Bedlington NE22 ....11 C3
  Brunswick Village NE13 ....28 A5
Arundel Dr
  Whitley Bay NE25 ....31 C4
Arundel Gdns
  Gateshead NE9 ....71 A5
  Sunderland SR3 ....91 C7
Arundel Rd SR3 ....91 D8
Arundel Sq NE63 ....6 B5
Arundel Wlk NF16 ....69 A5
Ascham House Sch NE3 ....38 C4
Ascot Cl NE28 ....40 D6
Ascot Ct SR3 ....70 C7
Ascot Ct
  Newcastle-u-T NE5 ....53 E7
  Sunderland SR3 ....91 D7
  West Boldon NE36 ....73 F6
Ascot Gdns NE34 ....59 D7
Ascot Gdns NE8 ....6 D2
Ascot Wlk NE3 ....37 C7
Ascott Ct NE12 ....39 B6
Ash Ave NE13 ....27 C7
Ash Banks NE61 ....9 A7
Ash Cl NE46 ....44 E3
Ash Ct NE29 ....31 E1
Ash Gr Dunston NE11 ....54 E1
  Morpeth NE61 ....8 E7
  Ryton NE40 ....52 C6
  Wallsend NE28 ....40 D1
  Whitburn SR6 ....61 A2
Ash Mdws NE38 ....88 E7
Ash Sq NE38 ....83 E4
Ash St Blaydon NE21 ....53 C1
  Mickley Square NE43 ....64 E8
Ash Terr Ryhope SR2 ....79 F2
Ash Tree Dr NE22 ....10 F2
Ashberry Gr SR6 ....75 D1
Ashbourne Ave NE6 ....56 F6
Ashbourne Cl NE27 ....30 C5
Ashbourne Cres NE63 ....6 C3
Ashbourne Rd NE32 ....58 C5
Ashbrooke NE25 ....31 E5
Ashbrooke Cres NE6 ....31 E5
Ashbrooke Cl NE25 ....86 D4
Ashbrooke Cross SR2 ....86 C3
Ashbrooke Dr NE20 ....25 E7
Ashbrooke Gdns NE28 ....40 E3
Ashbrooke Hall SR2 ....86 D4
Ashbrooke Mount
  SR2 ....86 C4
Ashbrooke Range SR2 ....86 D3
Ashbrooke Rd SR2 ....86 C4
Ashbrooke St NE3 ....37 E3
Ashbrooke Terr SR2 ....86 D3
Ashburn Rd NE28 ....40 E6
Ashburne Ct SR2 ....86 D3
Ashburton Rd NE3 ....38 A4
Ashby St SR2 ....86 F3
Ashcroft Dr NE12 ....39 E7
Ashdale Penshaw DH4 ....89 E8
  Ponteland NE20 ....25 C3
Ashdale Cres NE5 ....36 D1
Ashdale Ct SR5 ....75 E2
Ashdown Cl NE12 ....39 B7
Ashdown Rd SR3 ....91 D7
Ashdown Way NE12 ....39 B7
Asher St NE10 ....56 C1
Ashfield NE32 ....58 D2
Ashfield Ave NE16 ....69 C8
Ashfield Cl NE4 ....100 A4
Ashfield Ct
  North Shields NE29 ....42 A6
  Whitley Bay NE25 ....32 A7
Ashfield Gr
  Newcastle-u-T NE3 ....38 A4
  Whickham NE16 ....69 B5
Ashfield Lodge NE4 ....100 A4
Ashfield PN NE16 ....69 B8
Ashfield Rd
  Newcastle-u-T NE3 ....38 A4
  Whickham NE16 ....69 B5
Ashfield Rise NE16 ....69 B5
Ashfield Terr
  Chester le S DH3 ....88 D2
  Gateshead NE10 ....56 F1
  Ryton NE40 ....61 C1
  Springwell NE9 ....71 E1
Ashford NE9 ....71 A1
Ashford Dr SR3 ....91 D7
Ashford Gr NE5 ....36 B4
Ashford Rd SR3 ....91 D7
Ashgill NE37 ....83 B6
Ashgrove Ave NE34 ....59 D6
Ashgrove Terr Birtley DH3 ....82 B5
  Gateshead NE8 ....101 B1

Ashill Ct SR2 ....86 D4
Ashington Alexandra Fst Sch
  NE63 ....6 F3
Ashington Alexandra Mid Sch
  NE63 ....6 E4
Ashington Central Fst Sch
  NE63 ....6 D3
Ashington Com High Sch
  NE63 ....6 D3
Ashington Dr NE62 ....11 A8
Ashington Hirst Park Mid Sch
  NE63 ....6 E4
Ashington Hospl 6 C3
Ashington Mews NE62 ....10 F7
Ashington Rd NE61 ....1 D4
Ashington Wansbeck Fst Sch
  NE63 ....6 A4
Ashkirk Dudley NE23 ....29 A8
  Sunderland SR3 ....91 E8
Ashkirk Cl DH2 ....88 A1
Ashkirk Way NE25 ....23 D2
Ashleigh DH2 ....88 A5
Ashleigh Cl NE21 ....53 E1
Ashleigh Cres NE5 ....54 A8
Ashleigh Gdns SR6 ....60 A2
Ashleigh Gr
  Longbenton NE12 ....39 D7
  Newcastle-u-T NE2 ....38 D2
  Sunderland SR6 ....75 E4
  Tynemouth NE30 ....32 B2
Ashleigh Rd NE5 ....54 A8
Ashleigh Sch NE30 ....42 B5
Ashleigh Special Sch
  NE30 ....42 A6
Ashleigh Terr SR6 ....75 E4
Ashleigh Villas NE36 ....74 D7
Ashley Cl Killingworth NE12 ....29 F4
  Washington NE38 ....83 D3
Ashley Gdns NE62 ....11 A8
Ashley Prim Sch NE34 ....59 C6
Ashley Rd NE34 ....59 C6
Ashmead Cl NE12 ....39 C6
Ashmore Ho SR6 ....75 F4
Ashmore St SR2 ....103 A1
Ashmore Terr SR2 ....103 A1
Asholme NE5 ....36 E1
Ashridge Cl NE34 ....60 C5
Ashridge Ct NE10 ....72 C7
Ashton Cl NE5 ....36 B4
Ashton Ct NE40 ....52 D4
Ashton Downe NE2 DH2 ....88 C2
Ashton Rise DH4 ....88 C2
Ashton Way
  Sunderland SR3 ....91 C6
  Whitley Bay NE26 ....31 E7
Ashtree Cl
  Newcastle-u-T NE4 ....54 F4
  Rowlands Gill NE39 ....67 F7
Ashtree Gdns NE25 ....31 E3
Ashtree Ho NE2 ....98 B4
Ashtree La NE21,NE39 ....67 B5
Ashtrees Gdns NE9 ....70 F4
Ashvale Ave NE11 ....41 C1
Ashwell Rd SR3 ....91 D7
Ashwood Cl
  Cramlington NE23 ....16 C2
  Longbenton NE12 ....39 E8
Ashwood Cres NE6 ....57 D7
Ashwood Croft NE31 ....57 D7
Ashwood Gdns NE9 ....71 A2
Ashwood Gr
  Greenside NE40 ....51 F1
  Sunderland SR5 ....102 B1
Askern Ave SR2 ....87 A1
Askew Rd NE8 ....101 B3
Askew Rd W NE8 ....100 C1
Askrigg Ave
  Sunderland SR5 ....74 B1
  Wallsend NE28 ....40 D7
Askrigg Cl DH2 ....81 E2
Askrigg Wlk NE5 ....36 C1
Aspen Cl DH4 ....89 F5
Aspen Ct NE5 ....91 E6
Aspen Terr NE63 ....37 E1
Aspen Way NE24 ....17 D4
Aspenlaw NE9 ....71 C4
Aspley Cl SR3 ....92 A6
Association Rd SR6 ....75 E2
Astbury Cl NE38 ....89 B8
Aster Pl NE4 ....54 C7
Aster Terr DH4 ....90 B4
Astley Com High Sch
  NE25 ....23 C3
Astley Ct NE12 ....29 D3
Astley Dr NE26 ....31 E8
Astley Gdns
  Seaton Delaval NE25 ....23 C3
  Seaton Sluice NE26 ....24 B7
Astley Gr NE25 ....24 B7
Astley Rd NE25 ....23 C4
Astley St SR3 ....16 B3
Aston Sq SR3 ....91 D7
Aston St NE33 ....59 D7
Aston Way NE10 ....68 F5
Aston Wlk NE6 ....57 A4
Astral Ho SR1 ....104 C3
Athelhampton NE38 ....84 A5
Athelstan Rigg SR2 ....93 A7

Athenaeum St SR1 ....103 A2
Atherton Dr
  Fence Houses DH4 ....94 A4
  Newcastle-u-T NE3 ....54 E4
Athlone Ct NE24 ....17 E8
Athlone Pl DH3 ....82 D1
Athol Gdns Ryhope SR2 ....93 A6
  Whitley Bay NE25 ....31 D3
Athol Gr NE11 ....100 A1
Athol Gr SR3 ....92 A7
Athol Ho NE20 ....25 F6
Athol Pk SR2 ....86 F4
Athol Rd SR2 ....103 B1
Athol St NE11 ....100 A1
Athol Terr SR2 ....103 B1
Atholl DH2 ....81 F2
Atkin Pl NE11 ....11 B7
Atkin St NE12 ....29 B5
Atkinson Gdns NE29 ....42 A3
Atkinson House Sch
  NE23 ....22 F7
Atkinson Rd
  Chester le S DH3 ....88 D5
  Newcastle-u-T NE4 ....54 D4
  Sunderland SR6 ....75 E4
Atkinson Road Prim Sch
  NE4 ....54 D4
Atkinson St NE28 ....40 B1
Atkinson Terr
  Newcastle-u-T NE4 ....54 D5
  Wallsend NE28 ....40 B1
Atkinson's Bldgs SR4 ....102 B3
Atlantis Rd SR3 ....91 C8
Atley Way NE23 ....15 E2
Atmel Way NE28 ....41 A7
Attlee Cl NE23 ....29 B5
Attlee Cres DH6 ....97 E1
Attlee Gr SR2 ....92 E8
Attlee Terr NE64 ....7 F5
Attwood Gr SR5 ....75 B2
Auburn Cl NE15 ....54 C6
Auburn Ct NE28 ....41 A2
Auburn Ct NE28 ....41 B2
Auburn Gdns NE4 ....54 E8
Auburn Pl NE61 ....1 A8
Auckland DH2 ....88 A3
Auckland Ave NE34 ....60 B6
Auckland Rd NE31 ....57 F7
Auckland Rd SR3 ....58 E4
Auden Gr NE4 ....54 C6
Audland Wlk NE5 ....36 C1
Audley Ct NE2 ....38 F2
Audley Gdns SR3 ....86 B3
Audley Rd NE3 ....38 E4
Audouins Row NE8 ....70 B8
August Pl NE33 ....42 D1
Augusta Ct NE13 ....28 A6
Augusta St NE28 ....40 A6
Augusta Sq SR3 ....91 D7
Augustus Dr NE22 ....10 E2
Austen Ave NE34 ....59 B4
Austin Sq SR5 ....75 B2
Austral Pl NE13 ....28 A5
Australia Gr NE34 ....58 F3
Australia Twr SR3 ....91 B8
Austwick Wlk NE5 ....36 C1
Autumn Cl NE38 ....83 D6
Autumn Dr NE8 ....100 B2
Avalon Dr NE15 ....53 E8
Avalon Rd SR3 ....91 D8
Avebury Ave NE62 ....11 A7
Avebury Dr NE38 ....83 E5
Avebury Pl NE23 ....16 C1
Avenue Cres NE25 ....23 C4
Avenue Rd Gateshead NE8 ....70 D8
  Seaton Delaval NE25 ....23 D3
Avenue Terr
  Seaton Delaval NE25 ....23 D3
  Sunderland SR2 ....103 A1
Avenue The Birtley DH3 ....82 C4
  Blaydon NE21 ....53 E2
  Bournmoor DH4 ....89 E6
  Chester le S DH2 ....88 B3
  Corbridge NE45 ....46 F4
  Gateshead,Carr Hill NE9 ....71 B7
  Gateshead,Felling NE10 ....56 F1
  Hetton le H DH5 ....95 B4
  Morpeth NE61 ....9 B8
  Rowlands Gill NE39 ....67 F1
  Seaton Delaval NE25,NE26 ....23 E5
  Seaton Sluice NE26 ....24 C5
  Sunderland SR2 ....103 A1
  Wallsend NE28 ....40 B2
  Washington NE38 ....83 E5
  Whitley Bay NE26 ....32 A5
Avenue Vivian
  Fence Houses DH4 ....90 A1
  Great Lumley DH4 ....89 F1
Aviemore Rd NE36 ....74 B7
Avis Ave NE4 ....54 C6
Avison Ct NE4 ....98 B2
Avison Pl NE4 ....98 B2
Avison St NE4 ....98 B2
Avocet Cl NE24 ....17 C3
Avocet Ho NE2 ....42 A5
Avolon Ct NE4 ....98 B2
Avolon Pl NE4 ....98 B2
Avolon Wlk NE4 ....98 B2
Avon Ave Hedworth NE32 ....58 C2
  North Shields NE29 ....41 E4
Avon Cl Rowlands Gill NE39 ....78 D6
  Wallsend NE28 ....40 D6
Avon Cres DH4 ....94 A8
Avon Ct NE25 ....23 D6
Avon Rd NE31 ....57 F4

Avon St Gateshead NE8 ......**56** A1
Avon St Sunderland SR2 ......**103** C2
Avon Terr
Washington NE38 ....**83** F4
3 Washington NE38 .....**83** F4
Avondale SR4 ....**85** A5
Avondale Ave Blyth NE24 ..**16** E8
Longbenton NE12 ....**39** D8
Penshaw DH4 ....**90** B7
Avondale Cl 1 NE24 ......**16** F8
Avondale Ct NE3 ....**38** D4
Avondale Gdns
Ashington NE63 ....**7** A2
West Boldon NE36 ....**74** A7
Avondale Rd
Newcastle-u-T NE6 ......**56** C5
Ponteland NE20 ....**25** A2
Avondale Rise 5 NE6 ....**56** C5
Avonlea Way NE5 ....**37** C3
Avonmouth Rd SR3 ......**91** D7
Avonmouth Sq SR3 ......**91** D7
Awnless Ct NE34 ....**59** C5
Axbridge Cl NE62 ....**11** A7
Axbridge Gdns NE4 ......**54** E5
Axford Terr NE17 ....**77** B6
Axminster Cl NE23 ......**16** D1
Axwell Dr NE24 ....**17** D7
Axwell Ho NE24 ....**17** B7
Axwell Park Cl 3 NE16 ..**69** A7
Axwell Park Rd NE21 ....**53** E1
Axwell Park School Hos
NE21 ....**68** C8
Axwell Park View NE15 ..**54** B5
Axwell Terr NE16 ....**54** A1
Axwell View Blaydon NE21 .**53** C1
Whickham NE16 ....**69** A7
Aycliffe Ave NE9 ....**71** D4
Aycliffe Cres NE9 ....**71** D4
Aycliffe Pl NE9 ....**71** E4
Aydon Ave NE45 ....**47** A6
Aydon Cl NE30 ....**32** C1
Aydon Cres NE45 ....**47** B6
Aydon Dr NE45 ....**47** A6
Aydon Gdns
Corbridge NE45 ....**47** A6
Longbenton NE12 ....**38** F6
Aydon Gr Corbridge NE45 ..**47** A6
Jarrow NE32 ....**58** B3
Aydon Ho SR3 ....**91** E7
Aydon Rd NE45 ....**47** C7
Aydon Rd Est NE45 .....**47** A6
Aydon Way NE45 ....**47** B6
Aydon Wlk NE5 ....**36** E1
Aylesbury Dr SR3 ....**92** A5
Aylesbury Pl NE12 ....**39** B7
Aylesford Mews SR2 .....**86** E2
Aylesford Sq NE24 ......**17** E5
Aylsham Cl NE5 ....**36** B4
Aylsham Ct SR3 ....**92** A4
Aylyth Pl NE3 ....**37** F3
Ayr Dr NE32 ....**58** E3
Ayre's Quay Rd SR1 ....**102** C3
Ayre's Terr NE29 ....**42** A6
Ayrey Ave NE34 ....**58** F4
Aysgarth Ave
Sunderland SR2 ....**86** F2
Wallsend NE28 ....**40** D7
Aysgarth Gn NE3 ....**37** F4
Aytoun Ave SR2 ....**87** A1
Ayton Cl
Newcastle-u-T NE5 ......**36** E3
Stocksfield NE43 ....**64** D6
Ayton Ct NE62 ....**11** A7
Ayton Prim Sch NE38 ....**82** F3
Ayton Rd NE38 ....**82** F4
Ayton Rise NE6 ....**56** D5
Ayton St NE6 ....**56** D5
Azalea Ave SR2 ....**102** C1
Azalea Terr N SR2 .....**102** C1
Azalea Terr S SR2 .....**102** C1
Azalea Way NE15 ....**52** E8

B

Back Albion St 11 NE30 ..**42** B6
Back Albion St SR4 ......**85** A6
Back Beaumont Terr
NE3 ....**38** D5
Back Bridge St SR1 .....**103** A3
Back Buttsfield Terr DH4 .**90** B8
Back Chapman St NE6 ...**56** C7
Back Coronation Terr
DH5 ....**95** A2
Back Croft Rd NE24 .....**17** E7
Back Elmfield Rd NE3 ...**38** C4
Back George St NE4 ....**100** C4
Back Goldspink La NE2 ..**99** C4
Back Hawthorn Rd W
NE3 ....**38** C4
Back Heaton Park Rd 9
NE6 ....**56** B6
Back High St NE3 ....**38** C4
Back Hylton Rd SR4 ....**102** B3
Back La Blaydon NE21 ....**53** B2
Great Lumley DH3 ....**89** A1
Penshaw DH4 ....**90** B8
Whitley Bay NE25 ....**31** E5
Back Lodge Terr SR1 ...**103** C2
Back Maling St NE6 .....**56** A5
Back Mitford St NE4 ....**100** B3

Back Mowbray Terr NE62 .**10** F7
Back New Bridge St NE1,
NE2 ....**99** C2
Back North Bridge St
SR5 ....**103** A4
Back Percy Gdns NE30 ...**42** D8
Back Prudhoe Terr 20
NE30 ....**42** D7
Back Riggs 10 NE61 ....**3** F1
Back Row Hexham NE46 ...**45** B5
Whickham NE16 ....**69** B7
Back Ryhope St SR2 .....**92** E7
Back Shipley Rd 11 NE30 .**42** D7
Back St NE21 ....**53** A2
Back Stephen St 6 NE6 .**56** A6
Back Walker Rd NE6 .....**57** A4
Back Woodbine St NE8 ..**101** B1
Backworth Bsns Pk NE27 ..**30** C4
Backworth La NE23,NE27 ..**29** C7
Backworth Park Prim Sch
NE27 ....**29** C7
Backworth Terr NE27 ....**30** D1
Baden Cres SR5 ....**74** A3
Baden Powell St NE9 ....**71** A7
Baden St DH3 ....**88** C2
Bader Ct NE24 ....**17** F6
Badger Cl SR3 ....**92** A5
Badger Mews NE9 ....**71** F2
Badger's Wood DH9 .....**80** A1
Badgers Gn NE61 ....**3** D2
Badminton Cl NE35 .....**58** E1
Baffin Ct SR3 ....**91** F6
Baildon Cl NE28 ....**40** C4
Bailey Green Prim Sch
NE12 ....**29** C4
Bailey Sq SR5 ....**74** A4
Bailey St DH9 ....**79** B2
Bailey Way DH5 ....**95** B2
Bainbridge Ave
South Shields NE34 ......**58** F4
Sunderland SR3 ....**86** B3
Bainbridge Holme Cl
SR3 ....**86** C3
Bainbridge Holme Rd
SR3 ....**86** C3
Bainford Ave NE15 .....**54** A7
Baird Ave NE28 ....**41** C2
Baird Cl NE37 ....**72** E2
Baird St NE8 ....**56** B1
Baird St SR5 ....**74** A3
Baker Gdns
1 Dunston NE11 ......**54** F1
Gateshead NE10 ....**72** B8
Baker Sq SR5 ....**74** A3
Baker St
Houghton-le-S DH5 ....**90** E1
Sunderland SR5 ....**74** A3
Bakewell Terr NE6 ......**56** D4
Baldersdale Gdns SR2 ...**86** B2
Baldwin Ave Cleadon NE36 .**74** E8
Newcastle-u-T NE4 ....**54** F7
Balfour Rd NE15 ....**54** A6
Balfour St 2 Blyth NE24 ..**17** D8
Gateshead NE8 ....**101** A1
Houghton-le-S DH5 ....**90** E1
Balfour Terr NE17 ......**66** B1
Balgonie Cotts NE40 ....**52** C5
Baliol Rd NE42 ....**64** D7
Balkwell Ave NE29 ......**41** D5
Balkwell Gn NE29 ....**41** E6
Ballast Hill NE24 ....**17** B8
Ballast Hill Rd NE29 ....**42** A3
Balliol Ave NE12 ....**29** C1
Balliol Bsns Pk NE12 ....**39** A7
Balliol Gdns NE7 ....**39** B5
Balliol Prim Sch NE12 ...**39** B6
Ballston Cl NE38 ....**83** E3
Balmain Rd NE5 ....**37** C4
Balmlaw NE9 ....**71** D4
Balmoral Ave
Brockley Whins NE32 .....**58** D3
Newcastle-u-T NE3 ....**38** C4
Balmoral Cl NE22 ....**11** C2
Balmoral Cres DH5 ......**94** F7
Balmoral Ct 5 SR5 ......**74** A3
Balmoral Dr NE10 ....**71** C8
Balmoral Gdns
Tynemouth NE29 ....**41** F7
Whitley Bay NE26 ....**31** F6
Balmoral Terr
Newcastle-u-T,Heaton NE6 ..**56** B8
Newcastle-u-T,South Gosforth
NE3 ....**38** E4
Sunderland,East Herrington
SR3 ....**91** C7
Sunderland,Grangetown
5 ....**91** E3
Balmoral Way Hexham NE46 .**17** C3
Gateshead NE10 ....**71** C8
Balroy Ct NE12 ....**39** E7
Baltic Ct NE33 ....**42** E2
Baltic Ctr for Contemporary
Art* NE8 ....**101** C4
Baltic Ind Pk NE28 ......**41** E3
Baltic Quay NE8 ....**101** C4
Baltic Rd NE10 ....**56** F2
Baltic Sq NE8 ....**101** C4
Baltimore Ave SR5 ......**73** E3
Baltimore Ct NE37 ......**83** C8
Baltimore Sq SR5 ....**73** F3
Bamborough Ct NE23 ....**29** A8
Bamborough Terr NE30 ..**42** C7
Bambro' St SR2 ....**103** B1
Bamburgh Ave NE33,
NE34 ....**43** A1
Bamburgh Cl Blyth NE24 ..**17** C7

Bamburgh Cl continued
Washington NE38 ....**83** B5
Bamburgh Cres
Shiney Row DH4 ....**90** B5
Shiremoor NE27 ....**30** F3
Bamburgh Ct
Gateshead NE8 ....**70** C7
Newcastle-u-T NE7 ......**38** F5
Bamburgh Dr
Gateshead NE10 ....**57** B2
Pegswood NE61 ....**4** F3
Wallsend NE28 ....**40** F2
Bamburgh Gdns SR3 .....**86** B3
Bamburgh Gr
Jarrow NE32 ....**58** A3
South Shields NE34 ......**60** B8
Bamburgh Ho NE5 ......**36** B3
Bamburgh Rd
Longbenton NE12 ....**29** F1
Newcastle-u-T NE5 ......**36** E3
Bamburgh Sch NE34 ....**60** A8
Bamburgh Terr
Ashington NE63 ....**6** C3
10 Newcastle-u-T NE6 ..**56** C6
Bamford Wlk NE3 ....**38** A6
Bamford Wlk NE34 .....**59** D5
Bampton Ave SR6 ......**75** C1
Banbury NE37 ....**83** E8
Banbury Ave SR5 ....**74** A4
Banbury Rd NE3 ....**37** C3
Banbury Gdns NE28 ....**40** D5
Banbury Terr NE33,NE34 .**59** D8
Banbury Way Blyth NE24 ..**17** E5
North Shields NE29 ......**41** D4
Bancroft Terr SR4 ......**85** F6
Banesley La NE11 ....**70** B1
Banff St SR5 ....**74** A4
Bangor Sq NE32 ....**58** A1
Bank Ave NE16 ....**69** A7
Bank Ct Blaydon NE21 ...**53** F4
North Shields NE30 ......**42** B5
Bank Foot Sta NE13 .....**37** B6
Bank Head NE46 ....**45** B5
Bank Top Crawcrook NE40 .**51** E3
Greenside NE40 ....**52** B3
Tynemouth NE30 ....**32** C3
Bank Top Hamlet 4
NE16 ....**69** A7
Bankdale Gdns NE24 ....**17** A7
Bankhead Rd NE15 ......**35** F1
Bankhead Terr DH4 .....**94** A8
Bankside NE61 ....**8** B8
Bankside Ct SR2 ....**92** E7
Bankside La NE34 ......**59** C5
Bankside Rd NE15 ......**53** F5
Bankside Wlk NE62 .....**11** B8
Bankwell La NE8 ....**101** B4
Bannerman Terr DH6 ....**96** C1
Bannister Dr NE12 ......**40** A8
Bannockburn NE12 ......**29** C4
Barbara Priestman Sch
SR2 ....**86** B4
Barbara St SR2 ....**86** F2
Barbary Dr SR6 ....**75** F2
Barbondale Lonnen NE5 .**36** C2
Barbour Ave NE34 ......**60** A7
Barclay Pl NE5 ....**37** B1
Barclay St SR6 ....**103** A4
Barcusclose La DH9,NE16 ..**79** D1
Bardolph Rd NE29 ......**41** D6
Bardon Cl NE5 ....**36** F4
Bardon Cres NE25 ......**23** F2
Bardsey Pl NE12 ....**39** B7
Barehirst St NE33 ......**59** B7
Barents Ct 2 NE5 ....**36** B4
Baret Rd
Newcastle-u-T,Walker NE6 ..**56** F7
Newcastle-u-T,Walkergate
NE6 ....**56** E8
Barford Ct NE9 ....**71** A2
Barford Dr DH2 ....**88** A1
Baring St NE33 ....**42** F4
Barker St NE2 ....**99** C2
Barking Cres SR5 ....**73** F3
Barking Sq SR5 ....**73** F3
Barkwood Rd NE39 ......**67** D2
Barley Mow DH3 ....**88** D8
Barley Mow Prim Sch
DH3 ....**82** D1
Barlow Cres NE21 ......**67** C8
Barlow Fell Rd NE21 ....**67** C5
Barlow La NE21 ....**67** E7
Barlow Rd NE21 ....**67** C6
Barlowfield Cl NE21 ....**68** A8
Barmoor Bank NE61 .....**9** D5
Barmoor Dr NE3 ....**28** A2
Barmoor La NE40 ......**52** B5
Barmoor Pl NE40 ....**52** B5
Barmoor Terr NE40 .....**52** A5
Barmouth Cl NE28 ......**40** D5
Barmouth Way NE29 ....**41** C5
Barmston Cl NE38 ......**83** B4
Barmston Cnr NE38 .....**83** F4
Barmston La NE38 ......**84** C6
Barmston Rd NE38 ......**83** C8
Barmston Village Prim Sch
NE38 ....**83** F5
Barmston Way NE38 ....**83** F6
Barn The 3 DH2 ....**88** B1
Barnabas Pl SR2 ......**103** C1
Barnard Cl NE38 ....**82** F5
Barnard Cres NE31 .....**57** E2
Barnard Ct DH4 ....**89** D1
Barnard Gn NE32 ....**58** D3
Barnard Gr NE32 ....**58** D4
Barnard Pk DH5 ....**95** A4

Barnard St Blyth NE24 ...**17** E7
Sunderland SR4 ....**85** F5
Barnes Jun & Inf Schs
SR4 ....**85** F4
Barnes Park Rd SR4 .....**86** A4
Barnes St DH5 ....**95** A4
Barnes View SR4 ....**85** F4
Barnes' Rd NE33 ....**59** B8
Barnesbury Rd NE4 .....**54** E5
Barnett Ct SR5 ....**75** B2
Barnett Sq DH6 ....**97** F2
Barningham NE38 ......**84** A5
Barningham Cl SR3 .....**86** B2
Barns Cl NE22 ....**58** A4
Barnstaple Cl NE28 .....**40** C5
Barnstaple Rd NE29 ....**31** D1
Barnston NE63 ....**7** B3
Barnton Rd NE10 ....**71** E6
Barnwell Prim Sch NE8 .**90** B7
Barnwood Cl NE28 ......**40** C5
Baron's Quay Rd SR5 ...**35** B8
Baroness Dr NE15 ......**54** A7
Baronswood NE3 ....**38** B5
Barr Cl NE28 ....**40** E5
Barrack Ct NE4 ....**98** C2
Barrack Rd NE2,NE4 ....**98** B3
Barrack Row DH4 ....**90** A6
Barrack Terr NE11 .....**81** D6
Barras Ave
Annitsford NE23 ....**22** B1
Blyth NE24 ....**17** E5
Barras Ave W NE24 .....**17** D5
Barras Bridge NE1 ......**99** A2
Barras Dr SR3 ....**86** B3
Barras Gdns NE23 ......**22** B1
Barras Mews NE23 .....**22** F1
Barrasford Cl
Ashington NE63 ....**6** A2
Newcastle-u-T NE3 ......**38** A4
Barrasford Dr NE13 .....**28** C5
Barrasford Rd NE23 ....**22** C6
Barrasford St NE28 .....**41** C1
Barrass Ave NE23 ......**22** F1
Barrie Sq SR5 ....**75** B2
Barrington Ave NE30 ...**31** F2
Barrington Ct
Bedlington NE22 ....**16** A8
Hetton le H DH5 ....**95** A4
Barrington Dr NE38 .....**83** D4
Barrington Ind Est NE22 .**11** A4
Barrington Pk NE22 .....**11** F3
Barrington Pl
Gateshead NE8 ....**101** A2
Newcastle-u-T NE4 ....**98** B2
Barrington Rd NE22 ....**11** B3
Barrington St NE33 .....**42** C3
Barron St S SR5 ....**74** C1
Barron St SR5 ....**73** F4
Barrowburn Pl NE23 ....**23** A1
Barry St Dunston NE11 ..**54** F1
Gateshead NE8 ....**70** D7
Barton Cl Tynemouth NE30 .**32** B1
Wallsend NE28 ....**40** D5
Washington NE37 ....**72** F2
Barton Ct SR6 ....**75** C5
Barton Dr NE22 ....**10** F1
Barton Pk NE29 ....**70** E7
Bartram Gdns NE8 .....**70** C7
Bartram St SR5 ....**75** D3
Barwell Cl NE28 ....**40** D5
Barwell Rd NE7 ....**39** E3
Basil Way NE34 ....**59** E3
Basildon Gdns NE28 ....**40** C5
Basingstoke Pl NE12 ....**39** C7
Baslow Gdns SR3 ......**86** B3
Bassenfell Ct NE37 .....**83** B6
Bassenthwaite Ave 4
DH2 ....**88** B1
Bassington Ave NE23 ...**21** E7
Bassington Cl NE23 .....**21** E8
Bassington Dr NE23 ....**21** E8
Bassington Ind Est NE23 .**21** D8
Bassington La NE23 .....**21** D8
Bat House Rd NE43 .....**64** F5
Bates La NE21 ....**53** F2
Bath Cl NE28 ....**40** E5
Bath La Blyth NE24 .....**17** F7
Newcastle-u-T NE1,NE4 ...**98** C1
Bath Rd Gateshead NE10 .**56** D2
Hebburn NE31 ....**57** E3
Bath Sq NE32 ....**58** B1
Bath St NE6 ....**57** B6
Bath Terr Blyth NE24 ....**17** F7
Newcastle-u-T NE3 ......**38** D5
Tynemouth NE30 ....**42** D7
Bathgate Ave SR5 ......**73** F3
Bathgate Cl NE28 ......**40** E5
Bathgate Sq SR5 ....**73** F3
Batley St SR5 ....**74** C1
Battle Hill NE46 ....**45** B4
Battle Hill Dr NE28 .....**40** D4
Battle Hill Prim Sch
NE28 ....**40** D5
Baugh Cl NE37 ....**83** A7
Baulkham Hills DH4 .....**90** B7
Bavington NE10 ....**72** A5
Bavington Dr NE5 ......**37** D1
Bavington Gdns NE30 ...**32** B1
Bavington Rd NE25 .....**23** D2
Bawtry Cl NE28 ....**40** C5
Bawtry Gr NE29 ....**41** E5
Baxter Ave NE4 ....**54** E6
Baxter Pl NE25 ....**23** D3
Baxter Rd SR5 ....**73** F4
Baxter Sq SR5 ....**73** F3
Baxter's Bldgs NE25 ....**23** D3
Baxterwood Ct NE4 .....**98** A2

Baxterwood Gr NE4 .....**98** A2
Bay View E NE64 ....**7** E1
Bay View W NE64 ....**7** E4
Baybridge Rd NE5 ......**36** E3
Bayfield Gdns NE8 ......**56** B7
Baysdale DH4 ....**89** E8
Bayswater Ave SR5 .....**74** A3
Bayswater Rd
Gateshead NE8 ....**71** B8
Newcastle-u-T NE2 ......**38** C2
Bayswater Sq 1 SR5 ....**74** A3
Baytree Gdns NE25 .....**31** F7
Baywood Gr NE28 ......**40** C5
Beach Ave
Whitley Bay NE26 ....**32** A3
4 Whitley Bay NE26 ..**90** D7
Beach Croft Ave NE30 ..**32** B2
Beach Rd
South Shields NE33 ......**42** E4
Tynemouth NE29 ....**42** A4
Newcastle-u-T NE3 ......**102** B8
Beach Terr NE64 ....**7** F2
Beach Way NE30 ....**32** A4
Beachborough Cl 6
NE29 ....**31** F6
Beachcross Rd NE4 ....**102** B6
Beaches The NE4 ......**100** A4
Beachville St SR4 ......**102** B8
Beachway NE4 ....**18** A4
Beacon Ct
Brunswick Village NE13 ..**28** A8
4 Newcastle-u-T NE9 ..**71** B8
Beacon Dr
Brunswick Village NE13 ..**28** A4
Sunderland SR5 ....**75** F1
Beacon Glade NE34 .....**60** C7
Beacon Ho NE26 ....**31** F7
Beacon La NE23 ....**21** E7
Beacon Lough Rd NE9 ..**71** B8
Beacon Rise NE9 ....**71** B8
Beacon St Gateshead NE9 .**71** A7
North Shields NE30 ......**42** C7
South Shields NE33 ......**42** D4
Beaconsfield Ave NE9 ...**71** A4
Beaconsfield Cl NE25 ....**31** B5
Beaconsfield Cres 3
NE9 ....**71** A4
Beaconsfield Rd NE9 ....**70** F4
Beaconsfield St
Blyth NE24 ....**17** F7
Newcastle-u-T NE4 ......**98** A1
Beaconsfield Terr
Birtley DH3 ....**82** B6
Chopwell NE17 ....**66** E1
Beaconside NE34 ....**60** C7
Beadling Gdns NE4 .....**54** E7
Beadnell Cl Blaydon NE21 .**68** A8
3 Chester le S DH2 ....**88** A1
Beadnell Gr NE27 ....**30** E1
Beadnell Pl NE2 ....**99** C4
Beadnell Rd Blyth NE24 ..**17** B8
Beadnell Way NE3 ......**38** A4
Beagle Sq 6 SR3 ....**92** A5
Beal Cl NE24 ....**17** C4
Beal Dr NE12 ....**29** F8
Beal Gdns NE28 ....**40** F3
Beal Gn NE5 ....**37** C4
Beal Rd NE27 ....**30** E2
Beal Terr NE6 ....**56** F7
Beal Way NE3 ....**38** B8
Beamfleet Way NE3 ....**37** C3
Beamish Cl NE28 ....**40** C4
Beamish Ct NE25 ....**31** E3
Beamish La NE16,DH9 ...**80** F6
Beamish The North of
England Open Air Mus*
DH9 ....**80** D1
Beamish View DH3 .....**82** B3
Beamishburn Rd DH9,
NE16 ....**80** B6
Beamsley Terr NE63 .....**6** C2
Beamsley Ave
Hebburn NE31 ....**57** F1
Newcastle-u-T NE15 .....**53** C6
Beanley Cres NE30 .....**42** C1
Beanley Pl NE7 ....**39** B4
Bearl Farm Cotts NE43 ..**49** A3
Bearl View NE43 ....**64** A1
Beatrice Ave NE24 ......**17** A8
Beatrice Gdns
7 East Boldon NE36 ...**74** D7
South Shields NE34 ......**59** F6
Beatrice Ho SR2 ....**92** F8
Beatrice Rd NE6 ....**39** F1
Beatrice St Ashington NE63 .**6** D3
Sunderland SR6 ....**75** E1
Beatrice Terr
Penshaw DH4 ....**90** B8
Shiney Row DH4 ....**90** B8
Beattie St NE34 ....**59** D4
Beatty Ave
Newcastle-u-T NE2 ......**38** F1
Sunderland SR5 ....**73** F1
Beatty Rd NE22 ....**16** B3
Beaufort Cl
Newcastle-u-T NE5 ......**37** B1
Shiney Row DH4 ....**90** B8
Beaufort Gdns NE28 ....**40** D5
Beaufront Ave NE46 ....**45** B5
Beaufront Castle Flats
NE46 ....**46** F1
Beaufront Cl NE10 ......**72** A7
Beaufront Gdns
Gateshead NE8 ....**56** B1
Newcastle-u-T NE5 ......**37** B1

Beaufront Terr
Jarrow NE32 .58 B3
South Shields NE33 .59 C8
Beauly NE38 .83 D3
Beaumaris DH4 .89 D3
Beaumaris Ct NE12 .39 A6
Beaumaris Gdns SR3 .91 C7
Beaumaris Way NE5 .37 B4
Beaumont Ct NE25 .31 D6
Beaumont Dr
Washington NE38 .83 D5
Whitley Bay NE25 .31 D7
Beaumont Ho NE5 .37 C2
Beaumont Lodge 4 SR2 .86 E4
Beaumont Manor NE24 .16 F7
Beaumont St Blyth NE24 .17 D8
Hexham NE46 .45 B5
Newcastle-u-T NE4 .54 F3
North Shields NE29 .42 A5
Sunderland,Hendon SR2 .86 E4
Sunderland,Southwick SR5 .75 A2
Beaumont Terr
Brunswick Village NE13 .28 A6
Jarrow NE32 .58 A5
Newcastle-u-T NE5 .36 F3
Newcastle-u-T,Gosforth NE3 .38 D5
Prudhoe NE42 .50 A2
Beaumont Way NE42 .50 B1
Bebdon Ct NE24 .17 C6
Bebside Furnace Rd NE24 .16 D8
Bebside Mid Sch NE24 .16 F8
Bebside Rd NE24 .16 C7
Beckenham Ave NE36 .74 D8
Beckenham Cl NE36 .74 E8
Beckenham Gdns NE28 .40 C4
Beckett St NE8 .56 A4
Beckfoot Cl NE5 .37 B1
Beckford NE38 .84 A4
Beckford Cl NE28 .40 C5
Beckside Gdns NE5 .36 B1
Beckwith Rd SR3 .91 C8
Beda Cotts DH9 .79 A2
eda Hill NE21 .53 C3
edale Cl NE28 .40 C5
edale Cres SR5 .74 A3
edale Ct Gateshead NE9 .71 B2
5 South Shields NE34 .59 A5
edale Dr NE25 .31 F3
edale Gn NE5 .37 D3
edale St DH5 .95 A2
edburn NE38 .82 F1
edburn Ave SR5 .74 C2
ede Burn Prim Sch NE32 .58 A4
ede Burn Rd NE32 .58 B5
ede Burn View NE32 .58 B5
ede Cl NE12 .40 C8
ede Com Prim Sch NE10 .56 B2
ede Cres Wallsend NE28 .40 E3
Washington NE38 .83 D6
ede Ct Chester le S DH3 .88 C3
Gateshead NE8 .56 A2
Tynemouth NE30 .32 C3
ede Ho 9 SR3 .91 D7
ede Ind Est NE32 .58 E6
ede Prec 7 NE32 .58 B7
ede St SR6 .75 E2
ede Sta NE32 .58 E6
ede Terr
Chester le S DH2 .88 B3
East Boldon NE36 .74 E7
Jarrow NE32 .58 C5
ede Wlk Hebburn NE31 .57 F5
Newcastle-u-T NE3 .38 E5
ede's World (Mus)* NE32 .58 D7
edeburn Foot NE5 .36 F5
edeburn Rd NE5 .36 F5
edesway NE32 .58 E6
edewell Ind Pk NE31 .58 A5
edewell Prim Sch NE31 .57 F6
edford Ave Birtley DH3 .82 D1
Chester le S DH3 .88 D8
South Shields NE33 .42 C1
Wallsend NE28 .40 A3
edford Ct NE30 .42 B5
edford Ho NE30 .42 B5
edford Pl
Gateshead NE8 .101 B2
New Silksworth SR3 .92 A8
Newcastle-u-T NE5 .36 C1
edford St
Hetton le H DH5 .94 F4
North Shields NE29,NE30 .42 B5
Sunderland SR1 .103 A3
edford Terr 13 NE29 .42 A6
edford Way NE29 .42 B5
edlington Bank NE22, NE24 .16 A7
edlington West End Fst Sch NE22 .10 E1
edlingtonshire Com High Sch NE22 .11 D2
eech Ave
Cramlington NE23 .22 D5
Dinnington NE13 .27 B7
Hexham NE46 .44 E5
4 Houghton-le-S DH4 .94 D8
Morpeth NE61 .9 C7
Newcastle-u-T NE3 .37 F6
Whickham NE16 .69 C8
Whitburn SR6 .60 F1
eech Cl NE3 .28 C1
eech Ct
Newcastle-u-T NE3 .38 C4
Beech Ct continued
North Shields NE29 .41 F6
Ponteland NE20 .25 A1
Tynemouth NE29 .31 E1
Beech Dr Corbridge NE45 .47 B6
Dunston NE11 .54 E1
Ellington NE61 .1 D5
Beech Gdns NE9 .70 F6
Beech Gr Bedlington NE22 .11 A1
Blackhall Mill NE17 .77 B6
Longbenton NE12 .39 D6
Prudhoe NE42 .50 B2
South Shields NE34 .59 F4
Springwell NE9 .71 F1
Wallsend NE28 .40 B2
Whitley Bay NE26 .31 F5
Beech Gr S NE42 .50 B2
Beech Grove Ct NE40 .51 F4
Beech Grove Rd NE4 .100 A4
Beech Grove Terr NE40 .51 F4
Beech Grove Terr S NE40 .51 F4
Beech Hill NE46 .44 E5
Beech Hill Prim Sch NE5 .36 F2
Beech Sq NE38 .83 E4
Beech St Gateshead NE8 .56 B1
Jarrow NE32 .58 A7
Mickley Square NE43 .64 E8
Newcastle-u-T NE4 .54 E5
1 Sunniside NE16 .69 B2
Beech Terr Ashington NE63 .6 E2
Blaydon NE21 .53 C2
Burnopfield NE16 .79 C6
Beech Way NE12 .29 C4
Beechbrooke SR2 .92 F6
Beechburn Wlk NE4 .98 A1
Beechcroft
Newcastle-u-T NE3 .38 B2
Washington NE37 .72 B2
Beechcroft Ave NE3 .38 A3
Beecher St NE24 .17 B8
Beeches The
Longbenton NE12 .39 D6
Ponteland NE20 .25 D6
Stannington NE61 .14 C4
Beechfield Gdns NE28 .40 A3
Beechfield Rd NE3 .38 B4
Beechlea NE61 .14 C3
Beecholm Ct SR2 .86 D3
Beechway Ashington NE63 .7 A3
Gateshead NE10 .71 F5
Beechwood NE39 .67 A2
Beechwood Ave
Gateshead NE9 .71 A3
Newcastle-u-T NE3 .38 E6
Ryton NE40 .52 C5
Stakeford NE62 .11 A8
Whitley Bay NE25 .31 D4
Beechwood Cl NE32 .58 D6
Beechwood Cres SR5 .74 F2
Beechwood Gdns NE11 .70 B5
Beechwood Ho NE7 .39 A4
Beechwood Pl NE20 .25 E7
Beechwood St SR2 .102 B1
Beechwood Terr
Burnside DH4 .90 C2
Sunderland SR2 .102 B1
Beechwoods DH2 .88 B5
Beeston Ave SR5 .73 F3
Beetham Cres NE5 .54 A8
Beethoven St 10 NE33 .42 D2
Begonia Cl NE31 .57 E3
Beldene Dr SR4 .85 E4
Belford Ave NE27 .30 F3
Belford Cl Sunderland SR2 .86 D3
Wallsend NE28 .40 D5
Belford Gdns NE11 .70 A5
Belford Rd SR2 .86 E3
Belford Terr
Newcastle-u-T NE6 .56 E5
Sunderland SR2 .86 E3
Tynemouth NE30 .42 A7
Belfry The DH4 .90 A4
Belgrade Cres SR5 .73 F4
Belgrade Sq SR5 .73 F3
Belgrave Cres NE24 .17 F6
Belgrave Ct NE10 .71 D8
Belgrave Gdns
Ashington NE63 .7 A2
South Shields NE34 .59 F6
Belgrave Par NE4 .100 B4
Belgrave Terr
Gateshead NE10 .71 D7
South Shields NE33 .42 D3
Bell Gr NE12 .29 B4
Bell House Rd SR5 .75 A5
Bell Rd NE41 .51 B6
Bell St Hebburn NE31 .57 D6
North Shields NE30 .42 B5
Penshaw DH4 .90 B8
Sunderland SR4 .85 F6
6 Washington NE38 .83 F4
Bell View NE42 .50 F3
Bell Villas NE20 .25 F6
Bell's Cotts NE40 .52 A1
Bell's Hill NE61 .13 D3
Bell's Pl NE22 .16 A8
Bellamy Cres SR5 .73 F3
Bellburn Ct NE23 .22 D8
Belle Grove Pl NE2 .98 B3
Belle Grove Terr NE2 .98 B3
Belle Grove Villas NE2 .98 B3
Belle Grove W NE2 .98 B3
Belle View Terr 13 NE9 .71 F1
Belle Vue NE39 .66 F5
Belle Vue Ave NE3 .38 D5
Belle Vue Bank NE9 .70 E5
Belle Vue Cres
South Shields NE33 .59 B6
Belle Vue Cres continued
Sunderland SR2 .86 C4
Belle Vue Dr SR2 .86 C4
Belle Vue Gr NE9 .70 F5
Belle Vue Pk SR2 .86 C4
Belle Vue Pk W SR2 .86 C4
Belle Vue Rd SR2 .86 C4
Belle Vue St NE30 .32 C3
Belle Vue Terr
Crawcrook NE40 .51 F4
Gateshead NE9 .70 E5
4 North Shields NE29 .42 A4
Belle Vue Villas NE36 .74 C7
Bellerby Dr DH2 .81 E2
Bellevue Cres NE23 .16 B2
Bellfield Ave NE3 .37 F6
Bellgreen Ave NE3 .28 D1
Bellingham Cl NE28 .40 D4
Bellingham Ct
Bedlington NE22 .11 A1
8 Newcastle-u-T NE3 .37 D5
Bellingham Dr NE12 .40 A8
Bellingham Ho SR4 .85 B4
Bellister Gr NE5 .54 C7
Bellister Rd NE29 .41 D6
Belloc Ave NE34 .59 B3
Bells Cl 2 Blyth NE24 .16 F8
Newcastle-u-T NE15 .53 E5
Bells Close Ind Est NE15 .53 E5
Bells Lonnen NE42 .50 D4
Bellsburn Ct NE63 .6 B2
Bellshill Cl NE28 .40 E6
Bellway Ind Est NE12 .39 F7
Belmont NE10 .72 A5
Belmont Ave NE25 .31 D4
Belmont Cl NE28 .40 E5
Belmont Cotts 6 NE5 .36 F3
Belmont Rd SR4 .85 F5
Belmont Rise DH5 .95 A1
Belmont St NE6 .56 F3
Belmont Terr 4 NE9 .71 E1
Belmont Wlk NE6 .56 F3
Belmount Ave NE3 .28 D1
Belper Cl NE28 .40 C5
Belsay NE38 .82 F4
Belsay Ave Hazlerigg NE13 .28 A4
South Shields NE34 .60 A7
Whitley Bay NE25 .32 B4
Belsay Cl Pegswood NE61 .4 F3
Wallsend NE28 .40 C5
Belsay Ct NE24 .17 C7
Belsay Gdns
Dunston NE11 .70 A5
Newcastle-u-T NE3 .37 F8
Sunderland SR4 .85 F5
Belsay Gr NE22 .11 C3
Belsay Ho 7 SR3 .91 D7
Belsay Pl NE4 .98 A2
Belsfield Gdns NE32 .58 B4
Belsize Pl NE6 .56 F8
Beltingham NE5 .36 E1
Belvedere NE29 .41 F7
Belvedere Ave NE25 .31 F4
Belvedere Ct 12 NE6 .56 C7
Belvedere Gdns NE12 .39 D6
Belvedere Ho 10 NE6 .56 B6
Belvedere Parkway NE3 .37 D6
Belvedere Rd SR2 .102 C1
Belvedere Ret Pk NE3 .37 C6
Bemersyde Dr NE2 .38 E3
Benbrake Ave NE29 .31 E1
Bendigo Ave NE34 .58 F3
Benedict Biscop CE Prim Sch SR3 .91 D5
Benedict Rd SR6 .75 F2
Benfield Bsns Pk NE6 .56 E8
Benfield Gr NE26 .24 B7
Benfield Rd NE6 .39 E1
Benfield Sch NE6 .39 E1
Benfleet Ave SR5 .73 F3
Benjamin Rd NE28 .41 A3
Benjamin St 11 NE40 .51 F3
Bennett Ct
Newcastle-u-T NE15 .53 C6
Sunderland SR2 .86 E3
Bennett Gdns 1 NE10 .56 D1
Bennett's Wlk NE61 .9 A8
Benridge Bank DH4 .94 A2
Benridge Pk NE24 .17 B3
Bensham Ave NE8 .101 A1
Bensham Cres NE8 .100 C1
Bensham Ct
Gateshead NE8 .101 A1
South Shields NE34 .59 C5
Bensham General Hospl NE8 .70 D7
Bensham Rd
Gateshead NE8 .101 B3
Gateshead,Bensham NE8 .101 A1
Gateshead,Windmill Hills NE8 .101 B2
Bensham St NE35 .58 F1
Bensham Trad Est NE8 .70 D8
Benson Cl NE46 .44 E4
Benson Pl 20 NE6 .56 C6
Benson Rd NE6 .56 D6
Benson St DH3 .88 C2
Benson Terr 14 NE10 .71 D8
Bentall Bsns Pk NE37 .83 F7
Bentham Cl SR5 .74 A4
Bentinck Cres
Newcastle-u-T NE4 .54 F4
Pegswood NE61 .4 E3
Bentinck Rd NE4 .54 F5
Bentinck St NE4 .54 F4
Bentinck Villas NE4 .54 F5
Benton Ave SR5 .73 F4
Benton Bank NE2 .39 A1
Benton Cl NE7 .39 B5
Benton Hall Wlk NE7 .39 D2
Benton La NE12 .39 B7
Benton Lodge Ave NE7 .39 B5
Benton Park Prim Sch NE7 .39 B4
Benton Park Rd NE7 .39 A5
Benton Rd
Biddick Hall NE34 .59 C2
Newcastle-u-T NE7 .39 B3
Shiremoor NE27 .30 E1
Benton Square Ind Est NE12 .30 B1
Benton Sta NE12 .39 D6
Benton Terr NE2 .99 C3
Benton Way
Wallsend NE28 .40 B1
Wallsend NE28 .57 B8
Bents Cotts NE33 .42 E2
Bents Cotts App NE33 .42 E2
Bents Park Rd NE33 .42 E3
Bents The SR6 .75 F7
Benwell Dene Terr NE15 .54 C5
Benwell Gr NE4 .54 E5
Benwell Grange 9 NE15 .54 D5
Benwell Grange Ave NE15 .54 D5
Benwell Grange Cl 8 NE15 .54 D5
Benwell Grange Rd NE15 .54 C5
Benwell Grange Terr NE15 .54 C5
Benwell Hall Dr NE15 .54 B6
Benwell Hill Gdns NE5 .54 C7
Benwell Hill Rd NE5 .54 C7
Benwell La
Newcastle-u-T NE15 .54 C5
Newcastle-u-T,Old Benwell NE15 .54 B5
Benwell Roman Temple* NE15 .54 D6
Benwell Vallum Crossing* NE15 .54 D6
Benwell Village NE15 .54 B6
Benwell Village Mews NE15 .54 C6
Berberis Way NE15 .52 E8
Beresford Ave NE31 .57 E3
Beresford Ct NE26 .24 D6
Beresford Gdns 7 NE6 .56 C5
Beresford Pk SR2 .102 C1
Beresford Rd
Seaton Sluice NE26 .24 D5
Tynemouth NE30 .32 A3
Beresford St NE11 .100 A1
Bergen Cl NE29 .41 B4
Bergen Sq SR5 .73 F4
Bergen St SR5 .73 F4
Berkdale Rd NE9 .70 E2
Berkeley Cl
Boldon Colliery NE35 .58 E2
Killingworth NE12 .29 E4
Sunderland SR3 .91 C7
Berkeley Sq NE3 .38 B7
Berkely St NE33 .42 D2
Berkhamstead Ct NE10 .72 C7
Berkley Ave NE21 .53 E2
Berkley Cl NE28 .40 C5
Berkley Rd NE29 .41 D6
Berkley St NE15 .52 F8
Berkley Terr NE15 .52 F8
Berkley Way NE31 .57 F8
Berkshire Cl NE5 .36 F2
Bermondsey St NE2 .99 C2
Bernard Gilpin Prim Sch DH5 .94 E8
Bernard Shaw St 8 DH4 .94 D8
Bernard St
Houghton-le-S DH4 .94 D8
Newcastle-u-T NE6 .57 B4
Berrington Dr NE5 .37 B3
Berrishill Gr NE25 .31 C6
Berry Cl
Newcastle-u-T NE6 .57 A6
Wallsend NE28 .40 C5
Berry Hill NE40 .52 B1
Berryfield Cl SR3 .92 A5
Berryhill Cl NE21 .53 D1
Berrymoor NE63 .6 E4
Bertha Terr DH4 .90 D4
Bertram Cres NE15 .54 C6
Bertram St 3 Birtley DH3 .82 C4
South Shields NE33 .59 C8
Bertram Terr
Ashington NE63 .6 D3
Pegswood NE61 .4 F4
Berwick NE38 .82 F4
Berwick Ave SR5 .73 F4
Berwick Cl NE15 .53 A7
Berwick Ct NE20 .25 F7
Berwick Dr NE28 .40 D5
Berwick Hill Cotts NE20 .19 A4
Berwick Hill Rd NE20 .25 F8
Berwick Sq SR5 .73 F3
Berwick Terr NE29 .41 D4
Besford Gr SR1 .103 B2
Bessemer Rd DH6 .97 F7
Bessie Surtees House Mus* NE1 .101 B4
Bessie Terr NE21 .53 A2
Best View 3 DH4 .90 B6
Bet's La NE61 .13 D8
Bethnell Ave NE6 .56 D7
Betjeman Mews NE8 .101 C1
Betts Ave NE15 .54 B5
Bevan Ave SR2 .92 E6
Bevan Dr NE12 .38 F6
Bevan Gdns NE10 .72 A8
Beverley Cl NE3 .28 B2
Beverley Cres NE9 .71 A6
Beverley Ct
2 Gateshead NE9 .71 A6
1 Jarrow NE32 .58 B7
Washington NE37 .83 D7
Beverley Dr Blaydon NE21 .67 F8
Stakeford NE62 .6 A1
Whickham NE16,NE21 .69 C8
Beverley Gdns
Chester le S DH3 .88 D2
Ryton NE40 .52 A5
Tynemouth NE30 .32 C2
Beverley Pk NE25 .31 E4
Beverley Pl NE28 .40 F3
Beverley Rd
Gateshead NE9 .71 A6
Sunderland SR2 .86 F2
Whitley Bay NE25 .31 F4
Beverley Terr
Newcastle-u-T NE6 .57 A5
Tynemouth NE30 .32 C3
Walbottle NE15 .36 A2
Beverley Villas NE30 .32 C3
Beweshill Cres NE21 .53 A1
Beweshill La NE21 .53 A3
Bewick Cres NE15 .53 D7
Bewick Ct NE1 .99 B2
Bewick Garth NE43 .49 E1
Bewick La NE42 .50 B4
Bewick Pk NE28 .40 F5
Bewick Rd NE8 .101 B1
Bewick St
Newcastle-u-T NE1 .101 A4
South Shields NE33 .59 C8
Bewicke Lodge NE28 .41 A2
Bewicke Main Cvn Site DH2 .81 E5
Bewicke Rd NE28 .41 A1
Bewicke Road Ind Est NE28 .41 A1
Bewicke St NE28 .41 B1
Bewicke View DH3 .82 D5
Bexhill Prim Sch SR5 .73 F3
Bexhill Rd SR5 .73 F3
Bexhill Sq Blyth NE24 .17 E5
Sunderland SR5 .73 F4
Bexley Ave NE15 .54 B6
Bexley Gdns NE28 .40 D5
Bexley Pl NE16 .69 A5
Bexley St SR4 .85 F6
Bickerton Wlk 2 NE5 .36 E1
Bickington Ct DH4 .90 C3
Bicknell Ho NE6 .56 C5
Biddick Hall Dr NE34 .59 B4
Biddick Hall Inf Sch NE34 .59 A3
Biddick Hall Jun Sch NE34 .59 B4
Biddick La NE38 .83 D2
Biddick Prim Sch NE38 .83 D4
Biddick School Sports Coll NE38 .83 E3
Biddick Terr NE38 .83 E3
Biddick View NE38 .83 E3
Biddick Villas NE38 .83 E3
Biddlestone Cres NE29 .41 D5
Biddlestone Rd NE6 .39 C1
Bideford Gdns
Gateshead NE9 .70 F3
Jarrow NE32 .58 E5
South Shields NE34 .43 A1
Whitley Bay NE26 .32 A6
Bideford Gr NE16 .69 A5
Bideford Rd NE3 .37 E4
Bideford St SR2 .86 F2
Big Waters Cl NE13 .28 A6
Big Waters Ctry Pk* NE13 .28 A7
Bigbury Cl DH4 .90 C4
Bigg Mkt NE1 .99 A1
Bigges Gdns NE28 .39 F4
Bilbrough Gdns NE4 .54 D4
Bill Quay Prim Sch NE10 .57 C2
Billy Mill Ave NE29 .41 E6
Billy Mill La NE29 .41 D8
Bilsdale SR6 .75 F7
Bilsdale Pl NE12 .38 F6
Bilsmoor Ave NE7 .39 B2
Bilton Hall NE32 .58 D6
Bilton Hall Rd NE32 .58 D6
Binchester St NE34 .59 A5
Bingfield Gdns NE5 .37 C1
Bingley Cl 8 NE28 .40 E5
Bingley St SR5 .73 F3
Bink Moss NE37 .83 A6
Binsby Gdns NE9 .71 B2
Binswood Ave NE5 .37 C2
Birch Ave Gateshead NE10 .72 A7
Whitburn SR6 .60 F1
Birch Cl NE46 .44 E3
Birch Cres
Burnopfield NE16 .79 A6
Burnside DH4 .90 C2
Birch Ct Prudhoe NE42 .50 A2
Silksworth SR3 .91 E6
Birch Gr Jarrow NE32 .58 A7
Wallsend NE28 .40 C5
Birch Mews NE16 .78 F6
Birch Rd NE21 .53 D3
Birch St NE32 .58 A7
Birch Terr Birtley DH3 .82 B5
Newcastle-u-T NE6 .57 A5
Bircham Dr NE21 .53 D1
Birches Nook Cotts NE43 .64 C7

Birches Nook Rd NE43 .....64 C7
Birches The NE16 ....69 C3
Birchfield NE16 ....69 B5
Birchfield Gdns
  Gateshead NE9 ....71 A2
  Newcastle-u-T NE15 .....53 E7
Birchfield Rd SR2 ....86 B4
Birchfield NE38 ....83 E2
Birchgate Cl NE21 ....53 A1
Birchington Ave NE30 ....59 D7
Birchtree Gdns NE25 .....31 F3
Birchvale Ave NE5 ....37 B2
Birchwood 🖪 NE36 ....74 D7
Birchwood Ave
  Newcastle-u-T NE7 ......39 C3
  Whickham NE16 ....69 A5
  Wideopen NE13 ....28 C5
Birchwood Cl NE23 ....22 F1
Bird St NE30 ....42 C6
Birdhill Pl NE34 ....59 C5
Birds Nest Rd
  Newcastle-u-T NE6 ......56 D4
  Newcastle-u-T NE6 ......56 E4
Birds Terr DH4 ....90 C8
Birkdale
  South Shields NE33 .....42 E1
  Whitley Bay NE25 ....31 D5
Birkdale Ave SR6 ....75 E7
Birkdale Cl
  Newcastle-u-T NE7 ......39 C4
  Wallsend NE28 ....40 C4
  Washington NE37 ....72 B2
Birkdale Dr DH4 ....90 A4
Birkdene NE43 ....64 D6
Birkhead Cotts NE16 .....80 E6
Birkheads La NE11,NE12 ..80 E6
Birkland La DH9,NE11,
  NE16 ....80 E7
Birks Rd NE15 ....35 B5
Birkshaw Wlk 🖪 NE5 ....36 E1
Birling Pl 🖪 NE5 ....37 D2
Birnam Gr NE32 ....58 E2
Birney Edge NE20 ....25 C1
Birnham Pl NE3 ....37 F3
Birnie Cl NE4 ....54 E4
Birrell Sq SR5 ....73 F4
Birrell St SR5 ....73 F4
Birtley Ave Sunderland SR5 .73 F4
  Tynemouth NE30 ....42 D8
Birtley Cl NE3 ....38 A4
Birtley East Com Prim Sch
  DH3 ....82 C6
Birtley Golf Course DH3 .82 D2
Birtley La DH3 ....82 C5
Birtley Villas 🖪 DH3 ....82 C5
Birtwistle Ave NE31 .....57 D3
Biscop Terr NE32 ....58 C4
Biscuit Factory (Art Store)
  The NE2 ....99 C2
Bishop Cres NE32 ....58 E8
Bishop Harland CE Prim Sch
  SR5 ....74 C3
Bishop Ian Ramsey CE Prim
  Sch DH8 ....77 C1
Bishop Morton Gr SR1 ...103 B2
Bishop Ramsay Ct NE34 ..60 A6
Bishop Rock Dr NE12 ....39 A6
Bishop's Ave NE4 ....98 A1
Bishop's Rd NE15 ....54 D5
Bishopbourne Ct 🖪 NE29 .31 F1
Bishopdale Penshaw DH4 ..89 E8
  Wallsend NE28 ....39 F5
Bishopdale Ave NE17 ....16 A6
Bishops Cl NE28 ....40 E2
Bishops Ct NE15 ....53 F8
Bishops Dr NE40 ....52 D4
Bishops Mdw NE22 ....10 F1
Bishops Way SR3 ....91 E5
Bishops Wynd DH5 ....94 E7
Bishopton St Blyth NE24 .17 E6
  Sunderland SR2 ....103 B1
Bishopton Way NE46 .....44 E3
Bisley Cl NE28 ....40 D5
Bisley Dr NE34 ....59 D7
Bittern Cl Dunston NE11 ..54 F2
  Shiremoor NE28 ....41 A6
Biverfield Rd NE42 ......50 E3
Black Boy Rd DH4 ....94 A7
Black Boy Yd NE1 ....99 A1
Black Dr DH3 ....89 B5
Black La Blaydon NE21 ...53 A2
  Gateshead NE9 ....71 C1
Black Rd Hebburn NE31 ..57 F6
  Sunderland SR2 ....92 F7
Blackberries The 🆚 NE6 .71 F1
Blackburn Gn NE10 ......71 C7
Blackcap Cl NE38 ....40 E5
Blackclose Bank NE63 ....6 D1
Blackclose Est NE63 .....6 D1
Blackdene NE63 ....6 B2
Blackett Cotts NE41 ....51 A6
Blackett Ct NE41 ....51 A6
Blackett Pl NE1 ....99 A1
Blackett St
  Hebburn NE31,NE32 .....57 F8
  Newcastle-u-T NE1 .....99 A1
Blackett Terr NE4 ......102 A2
Blackfell Prim Sch NE37 .83 A6
Blackfell Rd NE37 ......82 F6
Blackfriars 🖪 NE1 .....98 C1
Blackfriars Ct 🖪 NE1 ...98 C1
Blackfriars Way NE12 ....39 A6
Blackhams Hill Sta*
  NE9 ....71 E1
Blackheath Ct NE37 .....72 C2

Blackheath Ct NE3 ......37 B5
Blackhill Ave NE28 .....40 F6
Blackhill Cres NE11 ....71 D4
Blackhouse La NE40 .....52 B5
Blackpool Par NE31 .....58 A3
Blackrow La
  Gateshead NE9 ....71 A3
  Heddon-on-t-W NE15 ....35 A4
Blackstone Ct NE21 .....53 A2
Blackthorn Cl NE16 .....69 A2
Blackthorn Dr Blyth NE24 .17 C4
  Wallsend NE28 ....40 C5
Blackthorn Pl NE4 .....100 B3
Blackthorn Way
  Ashington NE63 ....6 B2
  Fence Houses DH4 ......90 A2
Blackthorne NE10 ....71 F5
Blackwater Ho 🖪 SR3 ...92 A6
Blackwell Ave NE6 ......57 A6
Blackwood Rd SR5 ....74 A3
Bladen St NE32 ....58 A7
Bladen Street Ind Est
  NE32 ....58 A7
Blagdon Ave NE34 ......59 E8
Blagdon Cl Morpeth NE61 ..8 E8
  Newcastle-u-T NE1 .....99 C1
Blagdon Cres NE23 .....21 E8
Blagdon Ct NE22 ....11 C2
Blagdon Dr NE24 ....17 C3
Blagdon St NE1 ....99 C1
Blagdon Terr
  Cramlington NE23 ......22 B6
  Seaton Burn NE13 ......28 B8
Blake Ave NE16 ....69 B7
Blake Wlk NE8 ....56 A2
Blakelaw Rd
  🖪 Newcastle-u-T NE5 ..37 B2
  Newcastle-u-T NE5 .....37 C2
Blakemoor Pl NE5 ......37 C1
Blaketown NE23 ....23 A1
Blanche Terr DH9 ....79 B2
Blanchland NE38 ....83 E1
Blanchland Ave
  Newcastle-u-T NE15 ....53 C7
  Wideopen NE13 ....28 B6
Blanchland Cl NE28 .....40 D5
Blanchland Dr
  Holywell NE25 ....23 F2
  Sunderland SR5 ....75 C3
Blanchland Terr NE30 ...42 B7
Blandford Cl NE4 ......100 C4
Blandford Rd NE29 .....41 D8
Blandford Sq NE1 .....100 C4
Blandford St
  Newcastle-u-T NE1 ....100 C4
  Sunderland SR1 ....103 A2
Blandford Way NE28 ....40 D5
Blaxton Pl NE16 ....68 F5
Blaydon Ave SR5 ....74 A4
Blaydon Bank NE21 .....53 C2
Blaydon Bsns Ctr NE21 ..53 E3
Blaydon Bsns Pk NE21 ...53 F4
Blaydon Haughs Ind Est
  NE21 ....53 C3
Blaydon Highway NE21 ..53 D3
Blaydon Ind Pk NE21 ...53 D3
Blaydon Trad Pk NE21 ...53 F3
Blaydon West Prim Sch
  NE21 ....53 C3
Blaykeston Cl NE37 .....92 E1
Blayney Row NE15 ......52 C8
Bleachfield NE10 ....71 E6
Bleasdale Cres DH4 .....90 B7
Blencathra
  Tynemouth NE30 ....32 A2
  Washington NE37 ......83 C6
Blencathra Way NE21 ...68 C8
Blenheim NE12 ....29 D4
Blenheim Ct Blyth NE24 .17 D3
  Gateshead NE10 ....71 C6
Blenheim Dr NE22 ......11 C2
Blenheim Gdns NE61 ....4 E4
Blenheim Ho 🖪 NE11 ...98 C1
Blenheim Pl NE11 ......54 E1
Blenheim Wlk NE33 .....43 D3
Blenkinsop Ct NE34 ....59 B3
Blenkinsop Gr NE32 .....58 B3
Blenkinsop Mews NE32 ..58 A1
Blenkinsop St 🖪 NE28 ..40 B2
Bletchley Ave SR5 ......73 F4
Blezard Bsns Pk NE13 ...21 B1
Blezard Ct NE21 ....53 E4
Blind La Burnside DH4 ...90 B3
  Chester le S DH3 ......88 D6
  New Silksworth SR3 ...92 B7
Blindy La DH5 ....95 C1
Bloomfield Ct SR6 .....75 F2
Bloomfield Dr DH5 ......94 D3
Bloomsbury Ct NE33 ....38 B4
Blossom Gr DH4 ....90 B4
Blossom St NE33 ....95 B5
Blossomfield Way DH6 ...97 F3
Blount St NE6 ....56 D6
Blucher Rd
  Killingworth NE12 ......29 C2
  North Shields NE29 ....41 F3
Blucher Terr NE15 ......36 B1
Blue Anchor Ct NE8 ....101 B4
Blue House Ct NE37 ....83 B8
Blue House La
  Cleadon SR5,SR6 ....75 A6
  Washington NE37 ......83 C8
Blue House Rd NE31 ....57 D3
Blue Quarries Rd NE9 ...71 B6
Blue Reef Aquarium*
  NE30 ....32 D1
Blue Row NE15 ....34 F2
Blue Top Cotts NE23 ...22 D6

Bluebell Cl Gateshead NE9 .71 B5
  Wylam NE41 ....51 B7
Bluebell Dene NE5 ......37 A5
Bluebell Way NE34 .....59 B5
Blueburn Dr NE12 ......29 F3
Blumer St DH4 ....94 A8
Blyth Cl NE23 ....28 F8
Blyth College Com Ed Ctr
  NE24 ....17 D5
Blyth Com Coll NE24 ...16 F7
Blyth Community Hospl
  NE24 ....17 D8
Blyth Ct
  Newcastle-u-T NE15 ....53 C7
  South Shields NE34 ....59 C5
Blyth Dr NE61 ....9 F3
Blyth Rd NE26 ....24 E2
Blyth Sq SR5 ....74 A3
Blyth St Chopwell NE17 ..66 C1
  Seaton Delaval NE25 ...23 C3
  Sunderland SR5 ....74 A4
Blyth Terr Ashington NE63 ..6 A7
  Birtley DH3 ....82 B4
Blythswood NE2 ....99 B4
Blyton Ave Ryhope SR2 ..92 E6
  South Shields NE34 ....58 F5
Bo Elliott Ho The 🖪
  NE24 ....17 E8
Bobby Shafto Cvn Pk
  DH9 ....81 A1
Bodleswell Ho SR1 .....103 B3
Bodlewell La SR1 ......103 B3
Bodley Cl NE37 ....37 D5
Bodmin Cl NE28 ....40 E5
Bodmin Rd NE29 ....41 C8
Bodmin Sq SR5 ....74 A4
Bodmin Way NE3 ....37 F6
Bog Houses NE23 ......16 C2
Bognor St SR5 ....73 F4
Bohemia Terr NE24 .....17 E6
Boker La NE35 ....74 B8
Bolam NE38 ....82 F4
Bolam Ave Blyth NE24 ..17 D7
  Tynemouth NE30 ....32 A1
Bolam Coyne 🆚 NE6 ...56 C5
Bolam Ct NE15 ....35 D1
Bolam Dr NE63 ....6 E2
Bolam Gdns NE28 ....41 B3
Bolam Gr NE30 ....32 A1
Bolam Pl NE22 ....11 C2
Bolam Rd NE12 ....29 C3
Bolam St Gateshead NE8 .70 B8
  Newcastle-u-T NE6 ....56 C5
Bolam Way
  Newcastle-u-T NE6 ....56 C5
  Seaton Delaval NE25 ...23 C3
Boland Rd NE61 ....2 A3
Bolbec Rd NE4 ....54 E7
Bolburn NE10 ....72 A7
Boldon Bsns Pk NE35 ...73 E7
Boldon CE Prim Sch
  NE36 ....73 F7
Boldon Cl NE28 ....40 D5
Boldon Dr NE36 ....74 A7
Boldon Gdns NE9 ....71 C3
Boldon La Cleadon SR6 ..59 F1
  East Boldon NE34,NE36 .59 C1
  South Shields NE34 ....59 B5
Boldon Sch NE35 ....74 B8
Bolingbroke Rd NE29 ...41 D6
Bolingbroke St
  Newcastle-u-T NE6 ....56 A7
  🆚 South Shields NE33 ..42 D2
Bollihope Dr SR3 ......86 B2
Bolsover St NE63 ....6 D3
Bolsover Terr
  Ashington NE63 ....6 D3
  Pegswood NE61 ....4 F4
Bolton's Bglws NE17 ...77 B8
Bomarsund Cvn Site
  NE22 ....11 B6
Bonaventure DH4 ....90 C8
Bonchester Cl NE22 ....10 F2
Bonchester Ct 🆚 NE28 .40 E5
Bonchester Pl NE23 ....22 D8
Bond Cl SR5 ....75 C1
Bond Ct NE4 ....54 E5
Bond St 🆚 NE4 ....54 D5
Bondene Ave NE10 .....71 E8
Bondene Ave W NE10 ...71 E8
Bondene Way NE23 .....16 B2
Bondfield Cl NE28 .....40 F3
Bondfield Gdns NE10 ...72 A8
Bondgate Cl NE46 .....45 B4
Bondgate Ct NE46 .....45 B4
Bondicar Terr NE24 ....17 E7
Bondicarr Pl 🆚 NE5 ...37 D1
Bonemill La
  Chester le S NE38 .....88 F8
  Washington NE38 ......89 C8
Bonington Way NE5 .....37 B2
Bonner's Field SR6 ....103 A4
Bonnivard Gdns NE23 ...23 A1
Bonsall Ct NE34 ....59 D5
Booth St Gateshead NE10 .71 D8
  Sunderland SR4 ....102 A2
Booths Rd NE63 ....6 A4
Bootle St SR5 ....74 A3
Bordeaux Cl SR3 ....91 E6
Border History Mus*
  NE46 ....45 B5
Border Rd NE28 ....40 B1
Boreham Cl NE38 ......40 D5
Borodin Ave SR5 ....73 F4
Borough Rd Jarrow NE32 .58 B6
  North Shields NE29 ....42 A5
  South Shields NE34 ....60 A5

Borough Rd continued
  Sunderland SR1 ....103 B2
Borrowdale Birtley DH3 ..82 D1
  Washington NE37 ......83 C8
  Whickham NE16 ....69 D7
Borrowdale Ave
  Blyth NE24 ....17 A8
  Newcastle-u-T NE6 ....56 F7
  Sunderland SR6 ....75 D5
Borrowdale Cl NE36 ....74 C8
Borrowdale Cres
  Blaydon NE21 ....68 B8
  Penshaw DH4 ....90 A8
Borrowdale Gdns NE9 ...71 B3
Borrowdale St DH5 .....95 A2
Boscombe Dr NE28 .....40 C4
Boston Ave
  Newcastle-u-T NE7 ....39 B5
  Washington NE38 ......83 D6
Boston Cl NE28 ....40 D5
Boston Cres SR5 ....73 E4
Boston Ct NE12 ....39 F8
Boston St SR5 ....73 F4
Bosun's Way NE10 .....57 A2
Boswell Ave NE34 ......59 B3
Bosworth NE12 ....29 D4
Bosworth Gdns NE6 ....39 D2
Bothal Ave NE62 ....10 E7
Bothal Bank NE61 ....5 C2
Bothal Cl Blyth NE24 ...17 C7
  Pegswood NE61 ....4 E3
Bothal Cotts NE63 ......5 F4
Bothal Mid Sch NE63 ...5 F4
Bothal St NE6 ....56 D6
Bothal Terr Ashington NE63 .5 F4
  Stakeford NE62 ....11 B8
Botham Ho NE29 ....41 D3
Bottle Bank NE8 ......101 B4
Bottlehouse St NE6 ....56 C4
Boulby Cl SR3 ....92 C7
Boulevard The NE12 ....39 A6
Boulmer Ave NE23 ......16 B2
Boulmer Cl NE3 ....37 F8
Boulmer Ct DH2 ....88 C2
Boulmer Gdns NE13 ....28 B6
Boulsworth Rd NE29 ...31 E1
Boult Terr DH4 ....90 B6
Boundary Dr NE61 ....9 A7
Boundary Gdns NE7 ....39 A3
Boundary La DH8 ....76 A3
Boundary St SR5 ......75 C2
Boundary Way NE26 ....24 D6
Bourn Lea DH4 ....90 A5
Bourne Ave NE4 ....54 E7
Bournemouth Ct 🆚 NE28 .40 E5
Bournemouth Gdns
  Newcastle-u-T NE5 ....36 F3
  Whitley Bay NE26 .....32 A6
Bournemouth Par NE31 .58 A3
Bournemouth Rd NE29 ..41 C5
Bournmoor Prim Sch
  DH4 ....89 E3
Bourtree Cl NE28 ......40 C4
Bowbank Cl SR3 ....86 B2
Bowburn Ave SR5 ......74 C2
Bowburn Cl NE10 ......72 C7
Bower St SR6 ....75 D4
Bower The NE22 ....73 B8
Bowes Ave DH5 ....95 B1
Bowes Cl NE16 ....54 C8
Bowes Cres NE16 ......79 D8
Bowes Ct Blyth NE24 ...17 E7
  Newcastle-u-T NE3 ....38 E5
Bowes Farm Cotts DH3 .89 D5
Bowes Ho 🖪 SR3 ......91 D7
Bowes Lea DH4 ....89 F4
Bowes Lyon Cl SR3 ....78 D8
Bowes Lyon Ct 🆚 NE9 .70 F8
Bowes Rly* NE9 ....82 E8
Bowes Rly Ctr Mus*
  NE9 ....71 E2
Bowes St Blyth NE24 ...17 E8
  Newcastle-u-T NE3 ....38 E5
Bowes Wlk NE12 ....29 C4
Bowesville NE16 ......79 B5
Bowfell Ave NE5 ......37 D3
Bowfell Cl NE5 ....37 D3
Bowfell Gdns NE12 ....11 A8
Bowfield Ave NE3 .....28 C1
Bowler's Hill NE43 ....64 F7
Bowlynn Cl SR3 ....91 E6
Bowman Dr NE23 ......29 B8
Bowman Pl NE33 ......42 C1
Bowman Sq NE63 ....6 D2
Bowman St SR6 ....60 F1
Bowmont Dr NE23 .....22 D8
Bowmont Wlk DH2 .....88 A1
Bowness Ave NE28 ....40 E6
Bowness Cl NE36 ......74 C7
Bowness Pl NE11 ....71 B4
Bowness Rd
  Newcastle-u-T NE5 ....37 A1
  Whickham NE16 ....69 D7
Bowness St SR5 ....74 A4
Bowood Cl SR3 ....92 D6
Bowsden Ct NE3 ......38 E5
Bowsden Terr NE3 ....38 E5
Bowtrees SR2 ....86 D3
Box Cl NE12 ....29 F8
Boyd Cres NE28 ......40 C2
Boyd Rd NE28 ....40 D2
Boyd St Newburn NE15 ..52 E8
  Newcastle-u-T NE2 ....99 C2
Boyd Terr
  Newcastle-u-T,Walbottle
  NE15 ....36 B1

Boyd Terr continued
  🖪 Newcastle-u-T,Westerhope
  NE5 ....36 F3
Boyne Ct 🖪 NE24 ......17 E8
Boyne Gdns NE27 ......30 E3
Boystones Ct NE37 .....83 F6
Brabourne Gdns 🖥 NE29 .31 F1
Brabourne St NE34 ....59 C6
Brack Terr NE10 ....57 B2
Bracken Ave NE28 ....40 C5
Bracken Cl NE13 ......27 B6
Bracken Dr NE11 ......69 F6
Bracken Pl NE4 ....54 D7
Bracken Ridge NE61 ....3 C3
Bracken Way NE40 ....52 A1
Brackenburn Cl DH4 ...90 C6
Brackenbury Dr NE9 ...70 E3
Brackenfield Rd NE3 ...38 B4
Brackenlaw NE9 ....71 C1
Brackenridge NE16 ....78 E6
Brackenside NE3 ......28 C3
Brackenway NE37 ......83 A6
Brackenwood Gr SR2 ..86 C2
Brackley NE37 ....72 E1
Brackley Gr NE29 .....41 D4
Bracknell Cl SR3 ......92 C6
Bracknell Gdns NE5 ...36 C2
Bradbury Cl NE10 .....72 D2
Bradbury Pl
  New Hartley NE25 .....23 De
  Ponteland NE20 ......25 Fe
Bradbury Pl NE25 .....23 De
Bradford Ave
  Sunderland SR5 ....74 A
  Wallsend NE28 ....40 D
Bradley Ave
  Houghton-le-S DH5 ....94 E
  South Shields NE34 ...60 A
Bradley Cl DH2 ....81 E2
Bradley Fell La NE41 ..51 C5
Bradley Fell Rd NE40,
  NE42 ....66 C
Bradley Rd NE42 ......50 F7
Bradley Terr DH5 .....95 C
Bradley View 🆚 NE40 ..51 F7
Bradman Dr DH3 ....88 E
Bradman Sq SR5 ......74 A
Bradman St SR5 ....74 A
Bradshaw Sq SR5 .....74 A
Bradshaw St SR5 ......74 A
Bradwell Rd NE3 ......37 E
Bradwell Way DH4 ....90 C
Brady & Martin Ct NE1 .99 B
Brady Sq 🖪 NE38 .....83 F
Brady St SR4 ....85 F
Brae The SR2 ....102 B
Braebridge Pl NE3 .....37 F
Braefell Ct NE37 .....83 B
Braemar Ct NE10 ......57 B
Braemar Dr NE34 ......60 A
Braemar Gdns
  Sunderland,East Herrington
  SR3 ....91 C
  Sunderland,Hillview SR3 ..86 B
  Whitley Bay NE25 .....31 C
Braeside Dunston NE11 ..69 F
  Sunderland SR2 ....86 B
Braeside Cl NE30 .....32 A
Brahman Ave NE34 .....41 D
Braintree Gdns NE3 ...37 F
Brama Teams Ind Pk
  NE8 ....70 B
Bramble Cl NE24 ......17 D
Bramble Dykes NE15 ...54 E
Bramblelaw NE9 ......71 C
Brambles The DH3 ....82 D
Brambling Lea NE22 ...11 C
Bramhall Dr NE38 .....89 P
Bramham Ct NE34 .....59 B
Bramhope Gn NE9 .....71 B
Bramley Cl SR4 ....85 A
Bramley Ct
  🆚 Hexham NE46 ......45 B
  Newcastle-u-T NE7 ....39 E
Brampton Ave NE6 ....56 F
Brampton Ct NE23 ....22 C
Brampton Gdns
  Gateshead NE9 ....71 A
  Throckley NE15 ....35 E
  Wallsend NE28 ....41 A
Brampton Pl NE29 .....31 E
Brampton Rd NE34 ....59 A
Bramwell Ct NE3 ......38 E
Bramwell Rd SR2 .....103 B
Brancepeth Ave
  Fence Houses DH4 ....90 A
  Newcastle-u-T NE4 ...54 D
Brancepeth Cl NE15 ...53 C
Brancepeth Rd
  Hebburn NE31 ....57 F
  Washington NE38 .....83 A
Brancepeth Terr NE32 .58 A
Branch End Terr NE43 ..64 C
Branch St NE21 ....53 A
Brancknempeth Mews NE3 .28 E
Brand Ave NE4 ....54 D
Brandling Ct
  🖪 Gateshead NE10 ...56 C
  Newcastle-u-T NE2 ....99 C
  South Shields NE34 ...60 A
Brandling Dr NE3 .....28 C
Brandling La 🆚 NE10 ..56 C
Brandling Mews NE13 ..28 C
Brandling Pk NE2 .....99 B
Brandling Pl NE10 ....56 C
Brandling Pl S NE2 ...99 B
Brandling Prim Sch
  NE10 ....56 C

randling St
Sunderland NE8 . . . . .101 C4
Sunderland SR6 . . . . .75 E2
randling St S SR6 . . . . .75 E1
randling Terr 3 NE30 . . . .42 B6
randon Ave NE27 . . . . .30 E3
randon Cl Blaydon NE21 . . .68 A8
Blyth NE24 . . . . .17 B8
Houghton-le-S DH4 . . . . . . .94 D7
randon Gdns NE9 . . . . . . .71 D3
randon Gr NE2 . . . . .99 C3
randon Rd
Newcastle-u-T NE3 . . . . . . .37 F6
North Shields NE29 . . . . . . .41 D6
randy La NE37 . . . . .83 B7
randywell NE10 . . . . .71 F6
rannen St NE29 . . . . .42 A5
ransdale DH4 . . . . .89 E8
ransdale Ave SR6 . . . . .75 F7
ranston St SR5 . . . . .75 B2
ranton Ave NE31 . . . . .57 D3
rantwood Ave NE25 . . . . . .31 D4
rantwood Terr NE21 . . . . . .53 D2
ranton Cres NE6 . . . . .56 F5
ray Cl NE28 . . . . .40 D5
raydon Dr NE29 . . . . .41 E3
rayside NE32 . . . . .58 D1
reamish NE61 . . . . .1 E5
reamish Dr NE38 . . . . .88 F8
reamish Ho NE1 . . . . .56 A5
reamish St Jarrow NE32 . . .56 A5
Newcastle-u-T NE1 . . . . . . .56 A5
rearley Way NE10 . . . . . . .71 C8
recken Ct NE9 . . . . .70 E4
reckenbeds Rd NE9 . . . . . .70 E4
reckon Cl NE63 . . . . .6 E1
recon Cl NE5 . . . . .37 B4
redon Cl NE38 . . . . .83 B3
rendale Ave NE5 . . . . .36 E3
renkley Ave NE27 . . . . .30 F2
renkley Cl NE13 . . . . .27 B7
renkley Ct NE13 . . . . .28 B8
renkley Way NE13 . . . . . . .21 B1
renlynn Cl SR3 . . . . .91 E6
rennan Cl Ashington NE63 . .7 A3
Newcastle-u-T NE15 . . . . . .54 B6
rentford Ave SR5 . . . . .74 A3
rentford Sq 4 SR5 . . . . . . .74 A3
rentwood Ave
Newbiggin-by-t-S NE64 . . . .7 D5
Newcastle-u-T NE2 . . . . . . .38 E2
rentwood Cl NE25 . . . . . . .23 E2
rentwood Gdns
Newcastle-u-T NE2 . . . . . . .38 D2
Sunderland SR3 . . . . .86 B3
Whickham NE16 . . . . .69 B5
rentwood Gr NE28 . . . . . . .40 D1
rentwood Pl 6 NE3 . . . . . .42 D2
rentwood Rd DH4 . . . . . . .90 A5
rett Cl NE7 . . . . .39 D3
rettanby Gdns NE40 . . . . . .52 C6
rettanby Rd NE10 . . . . .71 A7
retton Gdns NE7 . . . . .39 C2
rettonby Ave NE43 . . . . . . .64 D7
rewer Terr SR2 . . . . .93 A6
rewer's La NE28,NE29 . . . .41 C1
rewery Bank 6 NE16 . . . . .54 A1
rewery Bond NE29 . . . . . . .42 B4
rewery La
Gateshead NE10 . . . . .56 D2
Ponteland NE20 . . . . .25 E6
South Shields NE33 . . . . . . .42 B2
5 Whickham NE16 . . . . . . .54 A1
rewery St 3 NE24 . . . . . . .17 F8
rewery Stables 1 NE1 . .98 C1
rewhouse Bank NE30 . . . . .42 C2
riar Ave
2 Houghton-le-S DH4 . . . .94 D8
Whitley Bay NE26 . . . . .32 A6
riar Cl Blaydon NE21 . . . . .53 A2
Great Lumley DH4 . . . . .89 E1
Shiney Row DH4 . . . . .89 F4
Wallsend NE28 . . . . .40 C5
riar Ct NE26 . . . . .32 A5
riar Edge NE12 . . . . .39 D8
riar La NE15 . . . . .33 E1
riar Lea DH4 . . . . .89 F4
riar Pl NE15 . . . . .54 A5
riar Rd NE39 . . . . .67 D2
riar Terr NE16 . . . . .79 C6
riar Vale NE25 . . . . .31 D3
riardale Bedlington NE22 . .10 E1
Dinnington NE13 . . . . .27 B7
riardale Rd NE24 . . . . .17 A8
riardene Ashington NE63 . . .6 B2
Burnopfield NE16 . . . . .78 E6
riardene Cl SR3 . . . . .91 C6
riardene Cres NE3 . . . . . . .38 A3
riardene Dr NE10 . . . . .72 D8
riarfield NE38 . . . . .83 D1
riarfield Rd NE3 . . . . .38 A5
riarhill DH2 . . . . .88 A4
riarlea NE61 . . . . .9 E4
riars The NE5 . . . . .74 B1
riarside NE5 . . . . .37 A3
riarsyde NE12 . . . . .39 E6
riarsyde Cl NE16 . . . . .68 E5
riarwood NE23 . . . . .29 B8
riarwood Ave NE3 . . . . . . .38 A5
riarwood Cres
3 Dunston NE11 . . . . .69 F8
Newcastle-u-T NE6 . . . . . . .39 F1
riarwood Rd NE24 . . . . . . .17 F6
riarwood St NE4 . . . . .89 E1
riary The NE15 . . . . .35 C2
rick Garth DH5 . . . . .95 C1
rick Row SR2 . . . . .92 E7
rickkirk NE37 . . . . .83 C7

Bridge Cotts NE23 . . . . .29 B8
Bridge Cres SR1 . . . . .103 A3
Bridge End 6 DH3 . . . . . . .88 C4
Bridge End Ind Est NE46 . .45 C6
Bridge Ho SR1 . . . . .103 A3
Bridge Pk NE21 . . . . .38 C8
Bridge Rd NE61 . . . . .2 A2
Bridge Road S NE29 . . . . . .41 E3
Bridge St Blaydon NE21 . . .53 C4
Blyth NE24 . . . . .17 F7
Blyth NE24 . . . . .17 F7
Gateshead NE8 . . . . .101 B4
Morpeth NE61 . . . . .8 F8
Newbiggin-by-t-S NE64 . . . .7 E4
Seaton Burn NE13 . . . . .28 B8
Sunderland SR1 . . . . .103 A3
Bridge Terr
Bedlington NE22 . . . . .11 C3
Shiremoor NE27 . . . . .30 C4
Stakeford NE62 . . . . .11 B8
Bridges The
10 South Shields NE33 . . . .42 D1
Sunderland SR1 . . . . .103 A2
Bridges View NE8 . . . . . . .101 A2
Bridgewater Cl
Newcastle-u-T NE15 . . . . . .53 C7
Wallsend NE28 . . . . .40 C4
Bridgewater Rd NE37 . . . . .83 E7
Bridle Path
East Boldon NE36 . . . . .74 C7
Sunderland SR3 . . . . .91 C8
Bridle The NE27 . . . . .31 B2
Bridlington Ave NE9 . . . . . .70 F3
Bridlington Cl NE28 . . . . . .40 D5
Bridlington Par NE31 . . . . .58 A3
Bridport Rd NE29 . . . . .31 D1
Brier Dene Cres NE26 . . . . .31 F8
Brierdene Cl NE26 . . . . .31 F8
Brierdene Ct NE26 . . . . .31 E8
Brierdene Rd NE26 . . . . . . .24 F1
Brierdene View NE26 . . . . .31 E8
Brierfield Gr SR4 . . . . .85 D4
Brierley Rd NE24 . . . . .17 F7
Brierley Rd NE24 . . . . .17 F7
Briermede Ave NE9 . . . . . . .70 F4
Briermede Pk NE9 . . . . .70 F4
Briery Hill La NE61 . . . . . . .14 C3
Briery Vale Cl SR2 . . . . . .102 C1
Briery Vale Rd SR2 . . . . . . .86 C4
Brieryside NE5 . . . . .37 D2
Brigham Ave NE3 . . . . .37 E3
Brigham Pl NE33 . . . . .42 C3
Bright St
South Shields NE33 . . . . . . .42 E2
Sunderland NE8 . . . . .75 E1
Brightlea DH3 . . . . .82 E5
Brightman Rd NE4 . . . . .42 C3
Brighton Ave Prim Sch
NE8 . . . . .101 A1
Brighton Cl NE28 . . . . .40 E5
Brighton Gdns NE8 . . . . . . .70 E7
Brighton Gr
Newcastle-u-T NE4 . . . . . . .98 A2
Newcastle-u-T NE29 . . . . . .41 F6
Whitley Bay NE26 . . . . .31 F6
Brighton Par NE31 . . . . . . .58 A3
Brighton Rd NE8 . . . . .70 E8
Brighton Terr DH6 . . . . .96 D1
Brignall Gdns NE15 . . . . . .54 A2
Brignall Rise SR3 . . . . .86 B2
Brigside Cotts NE23 . . . . . .28 C8
Brindley Rd NE37 . . . . .83 E6
Brinkburn
Chester le S DH2 . . . . .88 A3
Washington NE38 . . . . .83 E2
Brinkburn Ave Blyth NE24 . .17 F6
Cramlington NE23 . . . . .22 B8
Gateshead NE8 . . . . .70 E8
Newcastle-u-T NE3 . . . . . . .38 B6
Whickham NE16 . . . . .69 B8
Brinkburn Cl
Blaydon NE21 . . . . .68 A8
Newcastle-u-T NE6 . . . . . . .56 B6
Brinkburn Cres
Ashington NE63 . . . . .6 E4
Burnside DH4 . . . . .90 C1
Brinkburn Ct
2 Newcastle-u-T NE6 . . . .56 B6
8 North Shields NE30 . . . .42 B6
Brinkburn Gdns NE62 . . . . .11 A8
Brinkburn La 2 NE6 . . . . .56 B6
Brinkburn Pl 2 NE6 . . . . .56 B6
Brinkburn Sch NE34 . . . . . .59 D6
Brinkburn Sq 7 NE6 . . . . .56 B5
Brinkburn St
7 Newcastle-u-T NE6 . . . .56 B6
Newcastle-u-T,St Lawrence
NE6 . . . . .56 B6
North Shields NE28 . . . . . . .41 C1
South Shields NE34 . . . . . . .59 B6
Sunderland SR4 . . . . .85 C6
Brinkburn St S NE6 . . . . . .56 C4
Brisbane Ave NE34 . . . . . . .58 F3
Brisbane Ct NE23 . . . . . . .101 B3
Brisbane St SR5 . . . . .74 A3
Brislee Ave NE30 . . . . .42 C7
Brislee Gdns NE3 . . . . .37 A6
Bristlecone SR3 . . . . .91 E5
Bristol Ave Sunderland SR5 .73 F4
Washington NE37 . . . . .83 B8
Bristol Dr NE28 . . . . .40 D5
Bristol Terr NE25 . . . . .23 D7
Bristol Terr NE4 . . . . .100 A4
Bristol Wlk NE25 . . . . .23 D7
Britannia Ct NE4 . . . . .100 A4
Britannia Pl NE4 . . . . .98 A1
Britannia Rd SR3 . . . . .92 A7
Britannia Terr DH4 . . . . . . .94 A8

Brittania Ho NE28 . . . . .40 F1
Brixham Ave NE9 . . . . .70 F3
Brixham Cres NE32 . . . . . . .58 D5
Brixham Gdns SR3 . . . . . . .86 B3
Broad Chare NE1 . . . . .101 B4
Broad Garth NE1 . . . . .101 B4
Broad Landing NE33 . . . . . .42 B3
Broad Mdws
Newcastle-u-T NE3 . . . . . . .37 F3
Sunderland SR2 . . . . .102 B1
Broad Oak Terr NE17 . . . . .66 B1
Broadbank NE10 . . . . .72 B8
Broadfield Pl NE34 . . . . . . .59 D5
Broadgates NE46 . . . . .45 B4
Broadlands SR6 . . . . .75 A7
Broadlea NE10 . . . . .72 B8
Broadmayne Ave SR4 . . . . .85 D4
Broadmayne Gdns SR4 . . . .85 D4
Broadmead Way NE15 . . . .54 A5
Broadmeadows
Sunderland NE3 . . . . .91 B6
Washington NE38 . . . . .83 E2
Broadmeadows Cl NE16 . . .54 A1
Broadoak NE10 . . . . .57 B1
Broadpark NE10 . . . . .72 B8
Broadpool Gn NE16 . . . . . . .69 C6
Broadpool Terr NE16 . . . . . .69 C6
Broadsheath Terr SR5 . . . . .74 F2
Broadside NE10 . . . . .72 B8
Broadstairs Ct SR4 . . . . . . .85 D4
Broadstone Gr NE5 . . . . . . .36 C1
Broadstone Way NE28 . . . . .40 A4
Broadview Villas DH6 . . . . .96 A1
Broadwater NE10 . . . . .57 B1
Broadway Blyth NE24 . . . . .17 E6
Chester le S DH3 . . . . .88 D5
Gateshead NE9 . . . . .71 B7
Guide Post NE62 . . . . .10 F7
Newcastle-u-T NE15 . . . . . .53 D7
Ponteland NE20 . . . . .25 C3
Whickham NE16 . . . . .69 A4
Broadway Circ NE24 . . . . . .17 E7
Broadway Cl NE30 . . . . .32 B3
Broadway Cres NE24 . . . . .17 E6
Broadway Ct
Newcastle-u-T NE3 . . . . . . .38 C7
Wallsend NE28 . . . . .40 E6
Broadway E NE3 . . . . .38 D7
Broadway East Fst Sch
NE3 . . . . .38 C7
Broadway Gdns NE46 . . . . .44 F5
Broadway Jun Sch SR4 . . . .85 D7
Broadway The
Houghton-le-S DH4 . . . . . . .94 E8
Sunderland,Castletown SR5 .85 A8
Sunderland,Grindon SR4 . . .85 B3
Sunderland,Springwell SR4 .85 D3
Tynemouth NE30 . . . . .32 B2
Broadway Villas NE15 . . . . .54 B6
Broadway W NE3 . . . . .38 B7
Broadwell Ct NE3 . . . . .37 E2
Broadwood Prim Sch
NE15 . . . . .53 F7
Broadwood Rd NE15 . . . . . .53 F7
Broadwood View NE16 . . . .88 D2
Brock Farm Ct NE30 . . . . . .42 B6
Brock La NE22,NE62 . . . . . .11 C6
Brock Sq 8 NE6 . . . . .56 B5
Brock St NE6 . . . . .56 B5
Brockenhurst Dr SR4 . . . . . .85 A2
Brockhampton Cl NE35 . . . .58 E2
Brockley Ave NE34 . . . . . . .59 B4
Brockley St SR5 . . . . .74 A3
Brockley Terr 4 NE35 . . . . .58 E1
Brockley Whins Sta NE32 . .58 F2
Brockwell Cl NE21 . . . . .53 A1
Brockwell Ct NE24 . . . . . . .17 C5
Brockwell Ctr The NE23 . . .22 B8
Brockwell Dr NE39 . . . . . . .67 E3
Brockwell Ho NE5 . . . . .37 C2
Brockwell Mid Sch NE23 . .22 B8
Brockwell Rd NE38 . . . . . . .82 F5
Brockwell St 1 NE24 . . . . .17 C5
Brockwood Cl NE63 . . . . . . .6 B1
Brodie Cl NE34 . . . . .59 C4
Brodrick Cl NE3 . . . . .37 D5
Brodrick St 15 NE33 . . . . . .42 D3
Brokenheugh NE5 . . . . .36 F1
Bromarsh Ct NE28 . . . . .75 F1
Bromford Rd NE3 . . . . .37 C8
Bromley Ave NE25 . . . . . . .31 E4
Bromley Ct NE3 . . . . .37 D7
Bromley Gdns Blyth NE24 . .17 E5
Wallsend NE28 . . . . .40 D5
Brompton Cl DH2 . . . . .81 E2
Brompton Terr DH4 . . . . . . .90 D4
Brompton Workshops 5
NE11 . . . . .70 A8
Bromsgrove Cl 6 NE28 . . .40 E5
Bronte St NE8 . . . . .56 B1
Brook Ct Bedlington NE22 . .11 A1
Bedlington NE22 . . . . .16 A8
Brook Side Lodge 3
SR2 . . . . .86 C4
Brook St
Newcastle-u-T NE6 . . . . . . .56 D5
Whitley Bay NE26 . . . . .32 B6
Brooke Ave
West Boldon NE35 . . . . .74 B8
Whickham NE16 . . . . .69 A8
Brooke St SR5 . . . . .102 C4
Brooke's Wlk NE34 . . . . . . .59 A2
Brookfield NE3 . . . . .38 B2
Brookfield Cres NE5 . . . . . .36 E2
Brookfield Terr NE10 . . . . . .57 A1
Brookland Dr NE12 . . . . . . .29 E3

Brookland Rd SR4 . . . . .85 F6
Brookland Terr NE29 . . . . . .31 B1
Brooklands NE20 . . . . .25 A3
Brooklands Way NE35 . . . . .73 D8
Brookside Dudley NE23 . . . .29 A7
Houghton-le-S DH5 . . . . . . .94 D6
Brookside Ave Blyth NE24 . .17 B7
Brunswick Village NE13 . . . .28 A6
Brookside Cres NE5 . . . . . . .37 B2
Brookside Gdns 4 SR2 . . . .86 C4
Brookside Terr 2 SR2 . . . . .86 C4
Brookside Wood NE38 . . . . .83 D1
Brooksmead NE28 . . . . .40 A4
Brookvale Ave NE3 . . . . . . .38 A6
Broom Cl Blaydon NE21 . . . .68 B8
Morpeth NE61 . . . . .9 C7
Whickham NE16 . . . . .69 C6
Broom Ct NE9 . . . . .82 F8
Broom Gn NE16 . . . . .69 C6
Broom La NE16 . . . . .69 C6
Broom Terr
Burnopfield NE16 . . . . .79 C6
Whickham NE16 . . . . .69 C6
Broom Wood Ct NE42 . . . . .50 B1
Broome Cl NE3 . . . . .37 F6
Broomfield NE32 . . . . .58 C2
Broomfield Ave
Newcastle-u-T NE6 . . . . . . .39 E1
Wallsend NE28 . . . . .40 C5
Broomfield Cres NE17 . . . . .77 B8
Broomfield Rd NE3 . . . . . . .38 B4
Broomhaugh CE Fst Sch
NE44 . . . . .62 F7
Broomhaugh Cl NE46 . . . . .45 C4
Broomhill Est NE5 . . . . .94 F6
Broomhill Gdns NE5 . . . . . .37 C2
Broomhill Rd NE42 . . . . . . .50 F3
Broomhill Terr DH5 . . . . . . .94 F5
Broomhouse La NE42 . . . . .50 F3
Broomhouse Rd NE42 . . . . .50 F3
Broomlaw NE9 . . . . .71 C4
Broomlea NE29 . . . . .31 B1
Broomlea Ct SR4 . . . . .53 C3
Broomlee NE3 . . . . .6 E2
Broomlee Cl NE7 . . . . .39 D3
Broomlee Rd NE12 . . . . . . .29 D3
Broomley Ct NE3 . . . . .37 F7
Broomley Fst Sch NE43 . . .64 B8
Broomley Wlk NE3 . . . . . . .37 F7
Broomridge Ave NE15 . . . . .53 E5
Brooms The DH2 . . . . .81 F2
Broomsides Ave SR5 . . . . . .75 B3
Broomshields Cl SR5 . . . . . .75 B3
Broomy Hill Rd NE15 . . . . .35 D3
Broomylinn Pl NE23 . . . . . .22 C8
Brotherlee Rd NE3 . . . . .37 F7
Brough Ct 3 NE6 . . . . .56 C7
Brough Pk NE28 . . . . .41 A4
Brough Sq 3 NE6 . . . . .56 C7
Brough St 2 NE6 . . . . .56 C7
Brough Way 20 NE6 . . . . . .56 C7
Brougham St SR1 . . . . .103 A2
Broughton Rd NE33 . . . . . . .42 D2
Brow The NE6 . . . . .56 C7
Brown Cres NE9 . . . . .71 C1
Brown's Bldgs DH3 . . . . . . .82 C5
Browne Rd NE6 . . . . .75 E3
Brownlow Cl NE7 . . . . .39 E3
Brownlow Rd NE34 . . . . . . .59 C6
Brownrigg Dr NE23 . . . . . . .22 C5
Brownriggs Ct NE37 . . . . . .83 B6
Brownsea Pl NE9 . . . . .71 A7
Browntop Pl NE34 . . . . .59 B5
Broxbourne Terr SR4 . . . . .102 A2
Broxburn Cl NE28 . . . . .40 E5
Broxburn Ct NE5 . . . . .36 F1
Broxholm Rd NE6 . . . . .39 B1
Bruce Cl
Newcastle-u-T NE5 . . . . . . .36 F2
Whiteleas NE34 . . . . .59 A2
Bruce Gdns NE5 . . . . .54 C7
Brumell Dr NE61 . . . . .3 D1
Brumwell Cl NE43 . . . . .64 B7
Brundon Ave NE26 . . . . . . .31 F7
Brunel Dr SR6 . . . . .75 E2
Brunel Lodge NE4 . . . . . . .100 A3
Brunel St Gateshead NE8 . .100 D8
Newcastle-u-T NE4 . . . . . . .100 A3
Brunel Terr NE4 . . . . .100 A3
Brunel Wlk NE4 . . . . .100 A3
Brunswick Gr NE13 . . . . . . .28 A6
Brunswick Ind Est NE13 . . .28 B2
Brunswick Park Ind Est
NE13 . . . . .28 B2
Brunswick Pl NE1 . . . . .99 A2
Brunswick Rd
Shiremoor NE27 . . . . .30 F2
Sunderland SR5 . . . . .74 A4
Brunswick Sq NE27 . . . . . . .30 F2
Brunswick St NE33 . . . . . . .42 C1
Brunton Ave
Newcastle-u-T NE3 . . . . . . .37 F6
Wallsend NE28 . . . . .41 B3
Brunton Cl NE27 . . . . .30 D2
Brunton Gr NE3 . . . . .37 E4
Brunton La Hazlerigg NE13 .37 E2
Newcastle-u-T,Brunton Park
NE3 . . . . .37 F2
Brunton Mews NE13 . . . . . .27 F2
5 Bedlington NE22 . . . . . . .11 D3
Brunton Rd NE3 . . . . .37 F6
Brunton St NE29 . . . . .41 D3
Brunton Terr SR4 . . . . .102 A2
Brunton Way
Cramlington NE23 . . . . .16 B2

Brunton Way continued
Gateshead NE10 . . . . .57 B2
Brussels Rd
Sunderland SR4 . . . . .85 D7
Wallsend NE28 . . . . .40 B1
Bryan's Leap NE16 . . . . . . .79 A7
Bryden Ct NE30 . . . . .58 B3
Bryers St SR6 . . . . .60 F1
Buchanan Gn NE11 . . . . . .100 A1
Buchanan St NE31 . . . . . . .57 D5
Buck's Nook La NE40 . . . . .66 C7
Buckingham SR3 . . . . .91 E8
Buckingham Cl 1 SR6 . . . .75 F8
Buckingham St NE4 . . . . . . .98 B1
Buckland Cl Burnside DH4 . .90 C2
Buckingham Rd NE16 . . . . .79 A7
Buckthorne Gr NE7 . . . . . . .39 C3
Buddle Ct NE4 . . . . .54 E4
Buddle Ind Est NE28 . . . . . .57 C8
Buddle Rd NE28 . . . . .54 D4
Buddle St NE28 . . . . .40 C1
Buddle Terr
4 Shiremoor NE27 . . . . . . .30 E1
Sunderland SR2 . . . . .103 B1
Bude Ct NE28 . . . . .40 C4
Bude Gdns NE9 . . . . .70 F3
Bude Gr NE29 . . . . .31 D1
Budle Cl Blyth NE24 . . . . . .17 C7
Newcastle-u-T NE3 . . . . . . .38 A6
Budleigh Rd NE3 . . . . .37 F5
Budworth Ave NE26 . . . . . .24 D6
Bugatti Ind Pk NE29 . . . . . .41 C5
Bugatti's Ent Ho NE1 . . . . . .3 E1
Bullfinch Dr NE16 . . . . .69 A7
Bullion La DH2 . . . . .88 B3
Bullion La Prim Sch DH2 . .88 B3
Bulman's La NE28 . . . . .42 A8
Bulmer Ho NE34 . . . . .60 A7
Bulmer Rd NE34 . . . . .60 A7
Bungalows The
Birtley DH3 . . . . .82 B6
Ebchester DH8 . . . . .76 F4
Gateshead NE10 . . . . .71 E8
Hetton le H DH5 . . . . .94 F6
Kibblesworth NE11 . . . . . . .81 E8
Medomsley NE17 . . . . .77 B4
Wallsend NE28 . . . . .40 F3
Bunyan Ave NE34 . . . . .59 A3
Burdon Ave
Cramlington NE23 . . . . .21 F7
Houghton-le-S DH5 . . . . . . .95 A8
Burdon Cl SR6 . . . . .59 E1
Burdon Cres Cleadon SR6 . .59 E1
Ryhope SR2 . . . . .92 E6
Silksworth SR3 . . . . .92 C5
Burdon La
Ryhope SR2,SR3 . . . . .91 F3
Silksworth SR3 . . . . .91 F3
Burdon Lodge NE16 . . . . . .69 C2
Burdon Main Row NE29 . . .42 A4
Burdon Pk NE16 . . . . .69 C2
Burdon Plain NE16 . . . . . . .80 B2
Burdon Rd Cleadon SR6 . . .59 E1
Silksworth,Doxford Park
SR3 . . . . .92 B5
Sunderland SR1,SR2 . . . . .103 A1
Burdon St NE29 . . . . .41 D3
Burdon Terr
Bedlington NE22 . . . . .10 F1
Newcastle-u-T NE2 . . . . . . .99 B4
Burford Ct NE7 . . . . .39 A4
Burford Gdns NE3 . . . . .86 B3
Burford Way NE35 . . . . .73 F7
Burghley Gdns NE61 . . . . . . .1 E6
Burghley Rd NE10 . . . . .71 C6
Burgoyne Ct NE37 . . . . .83 D8
Burgoyne Terr NE41 . . . . . .51 A6
Burke St 2 SR5 . . . . .74 A3
Burleigh St 9 NE33 . . . . . .42 C3
Burlington Ct SR2 . . . . . . .103 C1
Burlington Ct
Newcastle-u-T NE2 . . . . . . .38 F2
Wallsend NE28 . . . . .40 E7
Burlington Gdns NE6 . . . . . .56 B8
Burlington Rd NE10 . . . . . . .56 D2
Burn Ave
2 Longbenton NE12 . . . . . .39 D8
1 Wallsend NE28 . . . . .40 E2
Burn Crook DH5 . . . . .94 D6
Burn Heads Rd NE31 . . . . .57 D5
Burn La Hetton le H DH5 . . .95 A3
Hexham NE46 . . . . .45 A4
Burn Park Rd
Houghton-le-S DH5 . . . . . . .94 F6
Sunderland SR2 . . . . .102 B1
Burn Prom 5 DH4 . . . . . . .94 B8
Burn Rd NE21 . . . . .53 A1
Burn Terr Hebburn NE31 . . .57 C7
Shiney Row DH4 . . . . .90 B6
Wallsend NE28 . . . . .40 F2
Burn View Dudley NE23 . . . .29 A7
Hedworth NE32 . . . . .73 D8
Burnaby Dr NE21 . . . . .68 A7
Burnaby St SR4 . . . . .102 A1
Burnbank Gateshead NE10 . .72 A6
Seaton Burn NE13 . . . . .28 B8
5 Washington NE38 . . . . . .83 C1
Burnbank Ave NE25 . . . . . .31 B5
Burnbridge NE13 . . . . .28 A4
Burncroft 10 NE46 . . . . . . .45 A4
Burnden Gr DH4 . . . . .90 A5

Burnet Cl NE28 ....40 C5
Burnet Ct NE63 ....6 B1
Burney Villas NE8 ....56 A1
Burneze Pl NE16 ....79 A4
Burnfoot Terr NE26 ....32 C4
Burnfoot Way NE3 ....37 E3
Burnhall Dr SR7 ....93 A1
Burnham Ave NE15 ....53 B7
Burnham Cl Blyth NE24 ...17 E5
■ Penshaw DH4 ....90 B6
Burnham Gr
  East Boldon NE36 ....74 D7
  Newcastle-u-T NE6 ....56 E4
Burnham St NE34 ....59 C6
Burnhills Gdns NE40 ......52 A1
Burnhills La NE40 ....67 B8
Burnhope Dr SR5 ....75 B3
Burnhope Gdns ■ NE9 ....71 D3
Burnhope Rd NE38 ....83 E6
Burnland Terr NE46 ....44 F5
Burnlea ■ DH4 ....94 C8
Burnlea Gdns NE23 ....23 B2
Burnley St NE21 ....53 C2
Burnmoor Gdns NE9 ....71 D3
Burnop Terr NE39 ....67 A2
Burnopfield Gdns NE15 ...54 A6
Burnopfield Prim Sch
  NE16 ....79 A6
Burnopfield Rd NE39 ......67 F1
Burns Ave Blyth NE24 .....17 C5
  West Boldon NE36 ....74 C6
Burns Ave S DH5 ....94 E7
Burns Cl Biddick Hall NE34 .59 B3
  West Rainton NE3 ....94 A2
  Whickham NE16 ....69 A8
Burns Cres NE16 ....69 A8
Burns St NE32 ....58 B7
Burnside Ashington NE63 ..7 A3
  Bedlington NE22 ....11 D3
  East Boldon NE36 ....74 E7
  Gateshead NE10 ....71 E7
  Holywell NE25 ....23 F1
  Jarrow NE32 ....58 C4
  Morpeth NE61 ....4 A1
  Newcastle-u-T NE2 ....98 B3
  Ovington NE42 ....49 D4
  Pontland NE20 ....25 B3
Burnside Ave
  Burnside DH4 ....90 C1
  Dudley NE23 ....29 B8
Burnside Bsns & Ent Coll
  NE28 ....40 D2
Burnside Cl Blyth NE24 ...17 B8
  Ovingham NE42 ....50 A4
  Seghill NE23 ....22 E1
  Whickham NE16 ....69 A4
Burnside Cotts
  Annitsford NE23 ....29 C8
  Mickley Square NE43 .....49 E1
Burnside Fst Sch NE23 ....16 C1
Burnside Prim Sch DH4 ...90 D1
Burnside Rd
  Newcastle-u-T NE3 ....38 C7
  Rowlands Gill NE39 ....92 E3
  Tynemouth NE30 ....32 B3
Burnside The NE5 ....36 E1
Burnside View NE23 ....22 E1
Burnstones NE5 ....36 E1
Burnt House Rd NE25 .....31 E3
Burnt Houses NE40 ....52 B1
Burnthouse Cl NE21 ......68 A8
Burnthouse La
  Whickham NE16 ....69 A5
  Whickham NE16 ....69 A5
  Whickham,Whickham Fell
  NE16 ....69 A4
Burntland Ave SR5 ....74 F2
Burnville NE6 ....56 A7
Burnville Rd S44 ....102 B1
Burnville Rd S SR4 ....102 B1
Burnway Seaham SR7 ......93 A1
  Washington NE37 ....83 B8
Burnwood Cl NE47 ....56 F3
Burradon Farm Cotts
  NE23 ....29 D7
Burradon Prim Sch NE23 .29 C7
Burradon Rd NE23 ....29 C7
Burrow St ■ NE33 ....42 C3
Burscough Cres SR6 ......75 D2
Burstow Ave NE6 ....56 E3
Burswell Ave NE46 ....44 F5
Burswell Villas NE46 ....44 F5
Burt Ave NE29 ....41 E5
Burt Cl DH6 ....97 E3
Burt Cres NE23 ....29 B8
Burt Meml Homes NE10 ..10 E5
Burt Rd NE22 ....11 D3
Burt St NE24 ....17 E8
Burt Terr Morpeth NE61 ..9 A8
  Walbottle NE15 ....36 A2
Burtree NE38 ....83 B3
Burwell Ave NE5 ....53 F8
Burwood Cl NE6 ....57 A4
Burwood Rd
  Newcastle-u-T NE6 ....56 F3
  Tynemouth NE29 ....41 C8
Business & Innovation Ctr
  SR5 ....74 F1
Buston Terr NE2 ....38 F1
Busty Bank
  Burnopfield NE16 ....79 B7
  Burnopfield NE16,NE39 ...79 A8
Butcher's Bridge Rd
  NE32 ....58 B4

Butcher's La NE61 ....4 F5
Bute Ct ■ SR3 ....92 A6
Bute Ct NE33 ....33 A4
Bute Rd N NE39 ....66 F4
Bute Rd S NE39 ....66 F3
Bute St DH9 ....79 A2
Buteland Rd NE15 ....53 F7
Buteland Terr NE64 ....7 D4
Butsfield Gdns SR3 ....86 B2
Butterburn Cl NE7 ....39 E4
Butterfield Cl NE40 .....51 F4
Buttermere Cleadon SR6 ..60 A1
  Gateshead NE10 ....72 A8
Buttermere Ave
  Easington Lane DH5 ......97 C8
  Whickham NE16 ....69 A5
Buttermere Cl
  Chester le S DH2 ....88 C2
  Killingworth NE12 ....29 C3
  ■ Newcastle-u-T NE5 ....37 B1
Buttermere Cres
  Blaydon NE21 ....68 B8
  South Hetton DH6 ....97 E8
Buttermere Gdns
  Gateshead NE9 ....71 A5
  South Shields NE34 ......59 E6
Buttermere Rd NE30 ......32 A2
Buttermere St SR2 ....86 E2
Buttermere Way NE24 ....12 B1
Butterwell Dr NE61 ......4 E3
Buttsfield Terr DH4 .....90 B8
Buxton CI Jarrow NE32 ...58 C5
  Wallsend NE28 ....40 D5
Buxton Gdns
  Newcastle-u-T NE5 ....36 F3
  Sunderland SR3 ....86 B3
Buxton Gn ■ NE5 ....36 F3
Buxton Rd NE32 ....58 C5
Buxton St NE1 ....99 C1
By-Way The NE15 ....35 D1
Byer Sq DH5 ....95 A6
Byer St DH5 ....95 A6
Byermoor Ind Est NE16 ..79 D7
Byers Ct SR3 ....92 B8
Byerside Cvn Site NE17 ..77 C5
Byeways The NE12 ....39 B6
Byewell Terr NE26 ....24 D6
Bygate Cl NE3 ....37 E3
Bygate Rd NE25 ....31 E4
Byker Bank NE6 ....56 B5
Byker Bridge NE1,NE6 ....56 A6
Byker Bsns Development Ctr
  ■ NE6 ....56 B5
Byker Cres ■ NE6 ....56 C6
Byker Prim Sch NE6 ....56 B5
Byker St NE6 ....56 F6
Byker Sta NE6 ....56 F6
Byland Cl DH4 ....90 C2
Byland Ct NE38 ....83 C5
Byland Rd NE12 ....38 B6
Bylands Gdns SR3 ....86 B3
Byony Toft SR3 ....93 A7
Byrne Terr W ■ SR3 .....92 B7
Byrness ■ NE5 ....36 E1
Byrness Cl NE3 ....37 C4
Byrness Ct ■ NE28 ......40 E5
Byrness Row NE23 ....22 C8
Byron Ave Blyth NE24 ....17 C6
  Hebburn NE31 ....57 F6
  ■ Wallsend NE28 ....41 A1
  West Boldon NE35 ....74 A8
Byron Cl
  Newcastle-u-T NE3 ....36 C2
  Whickham NE16 ....69 A8
Byron Ho SR7 ....92 F2
Byron Lodge Est ■ SR7 ..92 E1
Byron Pl NE63 ....6 F2
Byron Rd SR5 ....75 A2
Byron St
  Newcastle-u-T NE2 ....99 B2
  Ouston DH2 ....81 F1
  ■ South Shields NE33 ...59 D8
  Sunderland SR5 ....75 C1
Byron Terr
  Houghton-le-S DH5 ....94 E7
  ■ Seaham SR7 ....92 F1
Byron Wlk NE8 ....56 A2
Byron's Ct SR7 ....93 C2
Bywell Ave Hexham NE46 .45 D4
  Newcastle-u-T,Denton Burn
  NE15 ....53 E7
  Newcastle-u-T,Fawdon NE3 37 F8
  South Shields NE34 ......60 A7
  Sunderland SR5 ....75 C3
Bywell Cl NE40 ....51 E3
Bywell Gdns
  Dunston NE11 ....70 A5
  Gateshead NE9 ....71 B6
Bywell Gr NE27 ....31 A3
Bywell Home Farm NE43 ..48 F3
Bywell Rd Ashington NE63 ..6 D2
  Cleadon SR6 ....74 F8
Bywell St NE6 ....56 D5
Bywell Terr NE32 ....58 B3
Bywell View NE43 ....64 D7

C

Cadehill Rd NE43 ....64 C6
Cadlestone Ct NE23 ......22 D8
Caedmon Com Prim Sch
  NE8 ....101 B1
Caer Urfa Cl NE33 ....42 C4
Caernarvon Cl NE5 ....37 B4

Caernarvon Dr SR3 ....91 C6
Caesar Way NE28 ....40 E4
Caesar's Wlk ■ NE33 ....42 C4
Cairncross SR5 ....74 A1
Cairnglass Gn NE23 ......22 D8
Cairngorm Ave NE38 .....83 A2
Cairnhill Terr DH4 ......90 D4
Cairns Rd SR5 ....75 C4
Cairns Sq SR5 ....75 C4
Cairns Way NE3 ....37 F7
Cairnside SR3 ....91 C7
Cairnside S SR3 ....91 B7
Cairnsmore Cl
  Cramlington NE23 ....22 B4
  Newcastle-u-T NE6 ....57 B8
Cairnsmore Dr NE38 .....83 B3
Cairo St SR2 ....86 F3
Caithness Rd SR5 ....73 F2
Caithness Sq SR5 ....73 F1
Calais Rd SR5 ....73 F1
Calandra Chase NE2 ......98 B4
Caldbeck Ave NE6 ....56 F3
Caldbeck Cl NE6 ....56 F3
Calder Cres NE38 ....83 D1
Calder Ct ■ SR3 ....91 F6
Calder Gn NE32 ....58 C2
Calder Wlk
  Sunnisde NE16 ....69 A2
  Sunnisde NE16 ....69 A3
Calderbourne Ave ■
  SR6 ....75 E4
Calderdale NE28 ....39 F5
Calderdale Ave NE6 .....56 F7
Calderwood Cres NE9 ....71 A3
Caldew Cres NE5 ....54 A8
Caldew Ct DH5 ....95 B2
Caldwell Rd NE3 ....37 F8
Caledonia NE21 ....68 A8
Caledonia St NE6 ....57 A4
Caledonian Rd SR5 .....73 F3
Caledonian St NE31 ....57 D7
Calf Close Dr NE32 .....58 B2
Calf Close Ho NE32 .....58 C2
Calf Close Wlk NE32 ....58 C2
Calfclose La NE32 ......58 C2
California NE21 ....68 A8
California Gdns ■ NE61 ..9 A8
Callaley Ave NE16 ......68 F6
Callaly Ave NE23 ....22 C6
Callaly Cl NE61 ....4 F3
Callaly Way NE6 ....56 D4
Callander DH2 ....82 A2
Callander NE9 ....71 C5
Callerdale Rd NE24 .....17 A7
Callerton Cl NE12 ......29 D5
Callerton Ave NE29 .....41 C6
Callerton Cl
  ■ Ashington NE63 ......6 F2
  Cramlington NE23 ....22 C6
Callerton Ct NE20 ......25 E4
Callerton La NE5,NE15,
  NE20 ....25 E3
Callerton Lane End Cotts
  NE5 ....35 E7
Callerton Parkway Sta
  NE13 ....26 E1
Callerton Pl NE4 ....98 A1
Callerton Rd NE15 ......35 E2
Callerton View NE5 ....36 B4
Callington Cl DH4 ......89 E2
Callington Dr SR2 ......92 F7
Callum Dr NE34 ....60 A8
Calow Way NE16 ....68 F5
Calthwaite Cl SR5 .....74 B2
Calver Ct NE34 ....59 E5
Calvus Dr NE15 ....34 E3
Cam Mead SR3 ....92 A4
Camberley Cl SR3 ......92 C8
Camberley Rd NE28 .....41 A4
Camberwell Cl NE11 ....70 B6
Camberwell Way SR3 ...91 D5
Cambo Ave
  Bedlington NE22 ....11 C1
  Whitley Bay NE25 ......31 D3
Cambo Cl Blyth NE24 ....17 C7
  Newcastle-u-T NE3 ......38 D5
  Wallsend NE28 ....40 D6
Cambo Dr NE23 ....22 C6
Cambo Gn NE5 ....37 C2
Cambo Pl NE30 ....32 A1
Cambois Fst Sch NE24 ..12 C4
Camborne Pl NE8 ....101 C1
Camborne Rd NE8 ......101 C1
Cambourne Ave ■ SR6 ..75 E4
Cambria Gn SR4 ....85 A6
Cambria St SR4 ....85 A6
Cambrian Way NE38 ....83 B3
Cambridge Ave
  Hebburn NE31 ....57 F5
  Longbenton NE12 ......39 D8
  Wallsend NE28 ....40 A3
  Washington NE37 ......83 B8
  Whitley Bay NE26 .....32 A5
Cambridge Cres DH4 ...90 A6
Cambridge Dr DH3 ......82 C1
Cambridge Rd
  New Silksworth SR3 ....92 A7
  Stakeford NE62 ....11 A7
Cambridge St NE4 ......100 B4
Cambridge Terr NE8 ....101 B1
Camden Ct NE1 ....99 B2
Camden Sq NE30 ....42 B5
Camden St
  Newcastle-u-T NE1,NE2 ..99 B2
  North Shields NE30 .....42 B5
  Sunderland SR5 ....75 A1
Camelford Ct NE15 .....53 C8
Cameron Cl NE32 ....58 C3

Cameron Rd NE42 ....50 D3
Camerton Pl NE28 ......40 E7
Camilla Rd NE15 ....34 F2
Camilla St NE8 ....101 C1
Camp Terr NE29 ....42 A6
Campbell Park Rd NE31 ..57 F5
Campbell Pl NE4 ......98 A1
Campbell Rd SR5 ......73 F2
Campbell Sq SR5 ......73 F2
Campbell St NE31 .....57 E7
Campbell Terr DH5 ....95 B1
Camperdown NE5 ......36 F1
Camperdown Ave
  Chester le S DH3 ......88 D5
  Killingworth NE12 ....29 B4
Camperdown Ind Est
  NE12 ....29 B5
Campion Gdns NE10 ...71 D5
Campion Way NE63 ....6 C2
Campsie Cl NE38 ......83 B3
Campsie Cres NE30 ...32 A1
Campus Martius NE15 ..34 E2
Campville NE29 ....42 A6
Camsey Cl NE12 ......38 F7
Camsey Pl NE12 ......38 F7
Canberra Ave NE25 ...31 D3
Canberra Dr NE34 ....58 F4
Canberra Rd SR4 .....85 D4
Candelford Cl NE9 ...71 E3
Candlish St NE33 ....42 D2
Canning St Hebburn NE31 ..57 E5
  Newcastle-u-T NE4 ....54 D4
Canning Street Prim Sch
  NE4 ....54 D5
Cannock Killingworth NE12 ..29 D4
  Ouston DH2 ....82 A2
Cannock Dr NE7 ......39 A4
Cannon St NE8 ....101 B4
Canon Cockin St SR2 ..86 F4
Canon Gr NE32 ....58 C7
Canon Savage Dr NE46 ..44 E4
Canonbie Sq NE23 ....22 D8
Canonsfield Cl
  Newcastle-u-T NE15 ...36 B3
  Silksworth SR3 ....91 F5
Canterbury Ave NE28 ..40 D6
Canterbury Cl
  Ashington NE63 ......6 F2
  Longbenton NE12 .....39 A7
Canterbury Ho SR5 ...73 F4
Canterbury Rd SR5 ...74 A3
Canterbury St
  Newcastle-u-T NE6 ...56 D6
  South Shields NE33 ..59 D8
Canterbury Way
  Hedworth NE32 ....58 A1
  Wideopen NE13 ....28 B5
Capercaillie Lodge NE21 ..22 B1
Capetown Rd SR5 .....73 F2
Capetown Sq SR5 ....73 F2
Caplestone Cl NE38 ..83 B3
Capstan La NE9 ......71 C2
Captains Row The NE33 ..59 B8
Captains Wharf NE33 ..42 C3
Capulet Gr NE34 ....59 A5
Capulet Terr SR2 ....86 E4
Caradoc Cl NE38 ....83 B3
Caragh Rd DH2 ......88 B2
Caraway Wlk NE34 ...59 E2
Carden Ave NE34 ...60 B5
Cardiff Sq SR5 .....73 F1
Cardigan Gr NE30 ...32 A3
Cardigan Rd SR5 ....73 F2
Cardigan Terr NE6 ..56 B7
Cardinal Cl
  Longbenton NE12 ...39 A6
  Newcastle-u-T NE15 ..36 B3
Cardinals Cl ■ SR5 ..91 F5
Cardonnel St NE29 ..42 A4
Cardwell St SR6 ....75 E1
Careen Cres SR3 ....91 B7
Carew Ct NE23 .....22 B5
Carham Ave NE23 ...22 C6
Carham Cl Corbridge NE45 ..47 E5
  Newcastle-u-T NE3 ....38 A1
Caris St NE8,NE9 ....71 A8
Carisbrooke NE23 ...11 A2
Carisbrooke Cl ■ NE37 ..83 D8
Carisbrooke Ct SR1 ..102 B2
Carlcroft ■ SR6 ....75 E1
Carlcroft Pl NE23 ...22 C5
Carley Hill Rd SR5 ..75 B3
Carley Lodge SR5 ...75 B3
Carley Rd SR5 .....75 B2
Carlile Ho NE4 .....98 A1
Carlingford Rd DH2 ..88 B1
Carliol Pl NE1 .....99 B1
Carliol Sq NE1 .....99 B1
Carliol St NE1 .....99 B1
Carlisle Cl NE27 ...30 D1
Carlisle Cres DH4 ..90 B7
Carlisle Ct ■ NE10 ..56 D1
Carlisle Ho ■ SR3 ..91 D7
Carlisle Pl NE10 ...71 B4
Carlisle St NE10 ...56 D1
Carlisle Terr
  ■ Shiremoor NE27 ....30 E1
  ■ Sunderland SR5 ....75 A1
Carlisle Way NE61 ..30 C1
Carlow Dr NE62 ....11 D8
Carlton Ave NE24 ...17 C3
Carlton Cres SR3 ...91 C7
Carlton Ct
  Gateshead NE11 .....70 C5
  North Shields NE29 ..41 F5
Carlton Gdns NE15 ..53 E7

Carlton Gr NE63 ......6 F
Carlton Grange NE3 ...38 A
Carlton Ho NE64 .....7 E
Carlton Rd NE12 .....39 C
Carlton St NE24 ....17 E
Carlton Terr Blyth NE24 ..17 C
  Gateshead NE9 ......70 F
  North Shields NE29 ..41 F
  ■ Springwell NE9 ...71 F
Carlyle Cres NE16 ...69 A
Carlyle Ct ■ NE28 ..41 A
Carlyle St NE28 ....41 A
Carlton Sq SR2 ....103 A
Carmel Gr NE23 ....16 A
Carnaby Cl NE42 ...50 C
Carnaby Rd NE6 ....56 F
Carnation Ave DH4 ..89 E
Carnation Terr ■ NE16 ..69 E
Carnegie Cl SR4 ...59 C
Carnegie St ■ SR2 ..86 E
Carnforth Cl NE28 ..40 E
Carnforth Gdns
  Gateshead NE9 .....71 E
  Rowlands Gill NE39 ..83 E
Carnforth Gn NE3 ...37 E
Carnoustie Ouston DH2 ..82 A
  Washington NE37 ....72 C
Carnoustie Cl NE7 ..39 C
Carnoustie Ct
  Gateshead NE10 .....72 B
  Whitley Bay NE25 ...31 C
Carnoustie Dr NE34 ..59 F
Carol Gdns NE7 .....39 E
Carol St SR4 ....102 B
Caroline Cotts NE5 ..54 E
Caroline Gdns NE28 ..41 A
Caroline St
  Hetton le H DH5 ....95 A
  Jarrow NE32 ....58 A
  Newcastle-u-T NE4 ..54 D
Caroline Terr NE21 ..53 E
Carolyn Cl NE12 ....39 C
Carolyn Cres NE26 ..31 E
Carolyn Way NE26 ..31 E
Carpenter St NE33 ..42 E
Carr Field NE20 ...25 E
Carr Hill Com Prim Sch
  NE9 ....71 E
Carr Hill Rd N10,NE9 ..71 B
Carr St Blyth NE24 ..17 C
  Hebburn NE31 ......57 D
Carrfield Rd NE3 ...37 F
Carrick Dr NE24 ...17 A
Carrigill Dr NE12 ..39 C
Carrington Cl NE23 ..22 B
Carrmere Rd SR2 ...86 E
Carrock Ct SR3 ....91 A1
Carroll Wlk NE34 ..59 A
Carrowmore Rd DH2 ..88 C
Carrs Cl NE42 .....50 E
Carrsfield NE45 ....47 E
Carryside Cl NE10 ..68 B
Carsdale Rd NE3 ...37 E
Carter Ave NE31 ...57 E
Carters Lo ■ NE34 ..59 A
Cartington Ave NE27 ..30 A
Cartington Ct NE3 ..37 E
Cartington Rd NE29 ..41 A
Cartington Terr NE6 ..39 E
Cartmel Ct DH2 ....88 A
Cartmel Gn NE5 ....37 B
Cartmel Gr NE8 ....70 E
Cartmel Pk NE10 ...71 D
Cartwright Rd SR5 ..74 A
Carville Gdns NE28 ..57 E
Carville Prim Sch NE28 ..57 E
Carville Rd NE28 ...40 E
Carville Rise NE6 ..56 E
Carville St NE10 ...55 A
Carville Station Cotts
  NE28 ....40 E
Carvoran ■ NE28 ...40 E
Carwarding Pl NE5 ..37 C
Caseton Cl NE25 ...31 E
Caspian Cl NE32 ...58 C
Caspian Rd SR5 ....73 F
Caspian Sq SR5 ....73 F
Castellian Rd SR5 ..74 A
Casterton Gr NE5 ..36 B
Castle Bank NE61 ..9 B
Castle Cl Chester le S DH3 ..88 B
  Hetton le H DH5 ....95 B
  Morpeth NE61 ....9 B
  ■ Newcastle-u-T NE3 ..37 D
  Prudhoe NE42 ......50 D
  Whickham NE16 ....69 A
Castle Ct NE20 .....25 E
Castle Dene Dr DH4 ..94 A
Castle Farm Mews NE2 ..38 E
Castle Garth NE1 ...101 A
Castle Gn SR3 .....91 F
Castle Gn ■ SR3 ...91 F
Castle Hill Ho NE61 ..9 A
Castle Lea NE61 ...50 A
Castle Leazes (Halls of
  Residence) NE2 .....98 B
Castle Mdws NE61 ...9 A
Castle Mews SR3 ....91 F
Castle Rd Prudhoe NE42 ..50 D
  Washington NE38 ...83 B
Castle Riggs DH2 ...88 B
Castle Sq Backworth NE27 ..30 D
  Morpeth NE61 ....9 B
  Sunderland SR1 .....102 B
Castle St S ■ SR5 ...74 F
Castle Terr NE61 ...9 A

stle View
hester le S DH3 ... 88 C5
orsley NE15 ... 50 C8
vingham NE42 ... 50 B4
enshaw DH4 ... 90 B8
rudhoe NE42 ... 50 C3
underland SR5 ... 74 B1
stle View Sch SR5 ... 74 A1
stle Way NE13 ... 27 B7
stle Wlk NE61 ... 9 A7
stledale Ave NE24 ... 17 A6
stledene Ct
ewcastle-u-T NE3 ... 38 F4
underland SR5 ... 74 A2
stlefields DH4 ... 89 D3
stlefields Dr NE42 ... 50 E3
stleford Rd SR5 ... 73 F2
stlegate Gdns NE8 ... 100 A1
stlemain Cl DH4 ... 89 D3
stlenook Pl NE15 ... 53 F7
stlereagh Homes The
R7 ... 93 D1
stlereagh St SR3 ... 92 A7
stlereigh Cl DH4 ... 89 D3
stles Farm Rd NE2,NE7 ... 38 F4
stles Gn NE12 ... 29 E3
stleside Rd NE15 ... 54 A6
stleton Cl
ramlington NE23 ... 16 A1
ewcastle-u-T NE2 ... 38 F2
stleton Gr NE2 ... 38 F2
stleton Lodge NE4 ... 54 F5
stleton Rd NE32 ... 58 C5
stletown Prim Sch
R5 ... 85 B8
stletown Rd SR5 ... 74 D2
stletown Way SR5 ... 74 D2
stleway NE61 ... 4 F3
stlewood Cl NE5 ... 36 D2
tcheside Cl NE16 ... 69 A5
teran Way NE23 ... 22 C4
tharine St W SR4 ... 102 A2
thedral Ct NE8 ... 56 A3
thedral View DH4 ... 90 D3
therine Cookson Ct
E33 ... 42 E1
therine Rd DH4 ... 90 D6
therine St 3 NE33 ... 42 D3
therine View 9 NE40 ... 51 F3
tholic Row NE22 ... 15 E8
tkin Wlk NE40 ... 52 A3
to Sq SR5 ... 75 A2
o St SR5 ... 75 A2
trail Pl NE23 ... 22 C8
ttle Market NE46 ... 45 B4
tton Gr NE16 ... 69 B3
tton Pl NE28 ... 40 E6
uldwell Ave
uth Shields NE34 ... 59 E7
hitley Bay NE25 ... 31 D3
uldwell Cl NE25 ... 31 E4
uldwell La NE25 ... 31 E4
uldwell Pl NE34 ... 59 E7
uldwell Villas NE34 ... 59 E7
useway Gateshead NE9 ... 71 B6
nderland SR6 ... 103 A4
useway The
teshead NE9 ... 71 A8
rockley NE15 ... 35 D1
usey Arch* DH9 ... 80 A4
usey Arch Sta* NE16 ... 80 A4
usey Bank NE1 ... 99 B1
usey Bldgs NE3 ... 38 C4
usey Brae NE46 ... 44 F3
usey Hill Rd
exham NE46 ... 44 F3
exham NE46 ... 45 B1
usey Hill Way NE46 ... 44 E3
usey Ho NE3 ... 38 C3
usey Pk NE46 ... 44 F4
usey Rd DH9,NE16 ... 80 A3
usey Row NE16 ... 80 B4
usey St NE3 ... 38 C4
usey Way Hexham NE46 ... 44 F3
Hill DH9 ... 80 A1
valier View NE31 ... 57 D7
valier Way SR3 ... 91 F7
vell Rd SR5 ... 74 A2
vendish Gdns NE63 ... 6 D3
vendish Pl
rnopfield NE16 ... 79 A4
w Silksworth SR3 ... 91 F7
wcastle-u-T NE2 ... 38 F1
endish Rd NE2 ... 38 F1
vendish Sq NE61 ... 4 E3
vendish Terr NE63 ... 6 D3
versham Rd NE5 ... 36 B3
vburn Cl NE7 ... 39 E3
vdell Ct NE30 ... 42 B5
vfields Ct NE12 ... 38 F6
vnpore Sq SR4 ... 85 E7
vthorne Terr NE16 ... 79 A4
ton Way DH3 ... 88 D8
ton Wlk NE34 ... 59 A2
nham Cl NE29 ... 41 E8
ton Gr NE5 ... 36 B2
il Ct Ponteland NE20 ... 25 F6
llsend NE28 ... 57 B8
il St NE29 ... 42 A5
il Terr NE46 ... 45 B5
ar Cl Bedlington NE22 ... 10 F2
itley Bay NE25 ... 31 F3
lar Cres
rnopfield NE16 ... 78 F6
nston NE11 ... 69 F7
teshead NE9 ... 70 F4
lar Ct South Hetton DH6 ... 97 F7
nderland SR2 ... 86 D4

Cedar Ct *continued*
Tynemouth NE29 ... 31 E1
Cedar Dr NE32 ... 73 C8
Cedar Gr Blyth NE24 ... 17 C4
Hebburn NE31 ... 57 E3
Ryton NE40 ... 52 C6
South Shields NE34 ... 59 F5
Wallsend NE28 ... 40 D2
Whitburn SR6 ... 60 F2
Cedar Rd Blaydon NE21 ... 53 C2
Newcastle-u-T NE4 ... 54 D7
Cedar Terr Ashington NE63 ... 6 E2
Fence Houses DH4 ... 90 A1
Washington NE38 ... 83 C1
Cedar Way NE12 ... 29 E1
Cedars DH2 ... 88 B5
Cedars Cres SR2 ... 86 E3
Cedars Gn NE9 ... 71 A3
Cedars Pk SR2 ... 86 E3
Cedars Sch The NE9 ... 71 A3
Cedars The
Gateshead NE9 ... 71 C2
Newcastle-u-T NE4 ... 100 B3
Penshaw DH4 ... 90 B8
Sunderland SR2 ... 86 D4
Whickham NE16 ... 69 B4
Cedartree Gdns NE25 ... 31 E3
Cedarway NE10 ... 71 E5
Cedarwood DH4 ... 89 E1
Cedarwood Ave NE6 ... 40 A1
Cedarwood Gr SR2 ... 86 D2
Cedric Cres SR2 ... 86 B4
Celadon Cl NE15 ... 53 C8
Celandine Cl NE3 ... 38 D7
Celandine Ct NE63 ... 6 B1
Celandine Way NE10 ... 71 E5
Cellar Hill Terr DH4 ... 90 D2
Celtic Cl SR6 ... 59 E1
Celtic Cres SR6 ... 59 E1
Cemetery App NE34 ... 59 E8
Cemetery Rd
Gateshead NE8 ... 101 C1
Jarrow NE32 ... 58 C5
Centenary Ave NE34 ... 60 A6
Centenary Cotts NE22 ... 15 F8
Centenary Ct NE4 ... 54 F4
Central Arc NE1 ... 99 A1
Central Ave
Guide Post NE62 ... 10 E7
North Shields NE29 ... 41 E5
South Shields NE34 ... 59 F6
Whitburn SR6 ... 60 E1
Central Bsns & Tech Pk
NE1 ... 99 B1
Central Gdns NE34 ... 59 F6
Central Newcastle High Sch
NE2 ... 99 B4
Central Newcastle High Sch
(Jun Dept) NE3 ... 38 C4
Central Parkway NE1 ... 100 C4
Central Sta (Metro)
NE1 ... 101 A4
Central Way SR4 ... 85 E8
Centralway NE11 ... 70 C4
Centurian Way NE22 ... 10 E2
Centurion Rd NE15 ... 53 F8
Centurion Way
Gateshead NE9 ... 71 B6
Heddon-on-t-W NE15 ... 34 E2
Ceolfrid Terr NE32 ... 58 C4
Cestria Prim Sch DH3 ... 88 D3
Chacombe NE38 ... 83 D3
Chadderton Dr NE5 ... 36 B3
Chadwick St NE28 ... 40 B1
Chadwick Wlk NE8 ... 101 A2
Chaffinch Ct NE63 ... 6 B2
Chaffinch Rd 6 SR5 ... 74 C1
Chaffinch Way NE12 ... 29 C4
Chainbridge Ind Est
NE21 ... 53 F4
Chainbridge Rd
Blaydon NE21 ... 53 D3
Blaydon,Derwenthaugh
NE21 ... 53 F4
Chainbridge Road Ind Est
NE21 ... 53 F4
Chains Dr NE45 ... 46 F6
Chalfont Gr SR4 ... 85 A2
Chalfont Rd NE6 ... 56 F4
Chalford Rd 1 SR5 ... 75 B2
Challoner's Gdns NE61 ... 3 E1
Chaloner Pl NE61 ... 8 F8
Chamberlain St
Blyth NE24 ... 17 F6
Crawcrook NE40 ... 51 F4
Chambers Cres NE9 ... 71 C1
Chancery La NE24 ... 17 D7
Chandler Ct NE2 ... 38 F2
Chandlers Ford DH4 ... 89 F8
Chandlers Quay NE6 ... 56 C4
Chandless St NE8 ... 101 C3
Chandos SR3 ... 92 A4
Chandos St NE8 ... 70 F8
Chandra Pl 3 NE5 ... 37 B2
Chantry Cl SR3 ... 91 E5
Chantry Dr NE13 ... 28 B6
Chantry Est NE45 ... 46 F6
Chantry Ho DH4 ... 94 A2
Chantry Mews 2 NE61 ... 9 A8
Chantry Pl
9 Morpeth NE61 ... 9 A8
West Rainton DH4 ... 94 A2
Chapel Ave NE16 ... 79 B6
Chapel Cl
Kibblesworth NE11 ... 81 D6
Newcastle-u-T NE3 ... 28 D1
Chapel Ct Newburn NE15 ... 52 E8
Seaton Burn NE13 ... 28 B8

Chapel Ct *continued*
Sherburn DH6 ... 96 A1
Chapel Ho NE33 ... 42 E1
Chapel House Dr NE5 ... 36 C1
Chapel House Gr NE5 ... 36 C1
Chapel House Mid Sch
NE5 ... 36 B2
Chapel House Rd NE5 ... 36 C1
Chapel La Haswell DH6 ... 97 F3
Whitley Bay NE25 ... 31 E4
Wylam NE41 ... 51 A6
Chapel Park Mid Sch
NE5 ... 36 C3
Chapel Pl NE13 ... 28 B8
Chapel Rd NE32 ... 58 B7
Chapel Row Birtley DH3 ... 82 E3
Mickley Square NE43 ... 49 E1
Penshaw DH4 ... 90 C5
Chapel St Hetton le H DH5 ... 95 B4
North Shields NE29 ... 41 E5
Tantobie DH9 ... 79 B2
Chapel View
Brunswick Village NE13 ... 28 A6
Rowlands Gill NE39 ... 67 E3
Chapelville NE13 ... 28 B8
Chapman St SR6 ... 75 E4
Chapter Row NE33 ... 42 C3
Chare Bank DH8 ... 76 E3
Chare The NE1 ... 99 A2
Chareway NE46 ... 45 A6
Chareway La NE46 ... 45 A6
Charlbury Cl NE9 ... 71 F1
Charlcote Cres NE36 ... 74 D7
Charles Ave
Longbenton NE12 ... 39 D8
Newcastle-u-T NE3 ... 37 E6
Shiremoor NE27 ... 30 F4
Whitley Bay NE26 ... 32 B5
Charles Baker Wlk NE34 ... 60 B7
Charles Ct 18 NE6 ... 56 C7
Charles Dr NE23 ... 29 B8
Charles Perkins Meml
Cottage Homes DH3 ... 82 C3
Charles St
Boldon Colliery NE35 ... 73 F8
Gateshead NE8 ... 101 C2
Hazlerigg NE13 ... 28 A5
Newbottle DH4 ... 90 D4
Pegswood NE61 ... 4 F3
Ryhope SR2 ... 93 A6
Sunderland SR1 ... 103 B3
Sunderland,Monkwearmouth
SR6 ... 103 A4
Charleswood NE3 ... 38 D8
Charlie St NE40 ... 51 F1
Charlotte Cl NE4 ... 100 B3
Charlotte Mews 7 NE1 ... 98 C1
Charlotte Sq NE1 ... 98 C1
Charlotte St
Crawcrook NE40 ... 51 E3
North Shields NE30 ... 42 B6
South Shields NE33 ... 42 C2
Wallsend NE28 ... 40 C2
Charlotte Terr 12 NE33 ... 42 D2
Charlton Cl NE46 ... 44 F2
Charlton Ct NE25 ... 31 E3
Charlton Gdns NE61 ... 9 B7
Charlton Gr SR6 ... 75 A8
Charlton Mews NE15 ... 53 D6
Charlton Rd SR5 ... 75 C3
Charlton St Ashington NE63 ... 6 C4
Blyth NE24 ... 17 D7
Newcastle-u-T NE15 ... 53 D6
Charlton Villas NE40 ... 52 B1
Charlton Wlk NE8 ... 100 C1
Charman St SR1 ... 103 A3
Charminster Gdns NE6 ... 39 C1
Charnwood Ave NE12 ... 39 A6
Charnwood Ct NE33 ... 42 E2
Charnwood Gdns 1 NE9 ... 71 B5
Charter Dr SR3 ... 91 C7
Charters Cres DH6 ... 97 F6
Chase Ct Sherburn DH6 ... 96 A1
Whickham NE16 ... 69 B7
Chase Farm Dr NE24 ... 16 F7
Chase Mdws NE24 ... 16 F6
Chase Mews NE24 ... 16 F7
Chase Sch NE16 ... 69 B7
Chase The Hexham NE46 ... 44 F3
Longbenton NE12 ... 29 A2
North Shields NE29 ... 41 F6
Washington NE38 ... 82 F1
Chasedale Cres NE24 ... 17 A7
Chatham Cl NE25 ... 23 D1
Chatham Rd SR5 ... 74 A2
Chathill Cl Morpeth NE61 ... 9 B6
Whitley Bay NE25 ... 31 D5
Chathill Terr NE6 ... 56 F5
Chatsworth Cres SR4 ... 86 A4
Chatsworth Ct 8 NE33 ... 42 D3
Chatsworth Dr NE22 ... 11 C3
Chatsworth Gdns
3 Newcastle-u-T NE5 ... 36 F3
Newcastle-u-T,Walker NE6 ... 56 D4
Whitley Bay NE25 ... 31 E3
Chatsworth Pl NE16 ... 69 A5
Chatsworth Rd NE32 ... 58 C5
Chatsworth St SR4 ... 102 A1
Chatsworth St S SR4 ... 86 A4
Chatterton St SR5 ... 75 A2
Chatton Ave
Cramlington NE23 ... 22 C6
South Shields NE34 ... 60 B8
Chatton Cl
Chester le S DH2 ... 88 A1
Morpeth NE61 ... 9 C5
Chatton St NE28 ... 41 C1
Chatton Wynd NE3 ... 38 A7

Chaucer Ave NE34 ... 59 A3
Chaucer Cl NE8 ... 56 A2
Chaucer Rd NE16 ... 69 B8
Chaucer St 9 DH4 ... 94 D8
Chaytor Gr SR1 ... 103 B2
Chaytor St NE32 ... 58 B8
Cheadle Ave
Cramlington NE23 ... 16 A1
Wallsend NE28 ... 40 E6
Cheadle Rd SR5 ... 74 A2
Cheam Cl NE16 ... 69 B5
Cheam Rd SR5 ... 74 A2
Cheddar Gdns NE9 ... 70 F3
Cheldon Cl NE25 ... 31 C6
Chelford Cl NE28 ... 40 E7
Chelmsford Gr NE2 ... 56 A7
Chelmsford Rd SR5 ... 74 A2
Chelmsford Sq SR5 ... 74 A3
Chelmsford St 5 SR3 ... 92 A8
Chelsea Gdns NE8 ... 71 B8
Chelsea Gr NE4 ... 98 A1
Cheltenham Ct NE63 ... 6 C2
Cheltenham Dr NE35 ... 58 E2
Cheltenham Rd SR5 ... 74 A2
Cheltenham Sq SR5 ... 74 A2
Cheltenham Terr NE6 ... 56 B7
Chelton Cl NE13 ... 28 B4
Chepstow Gdns NE8 ... 70 D7
Chepstow Rd NE15 ... 53 F6
Chepstow St SR4 ... 102 B2
Cherribank SR2 ... 92 E6
Cherry Banks DH3 ... 88 D5
Cherry Blossom Way
NE37 ... 73 B1
Cherry Cotts DH9 ... 79 B2
Cherry Dr DH6 ... 97 F3
Cherry Gr
Killingworth NE12 ... 29 C4
Prudhoe NE42 ... 50 B3
Cherry Knowle Hospl
SR2 ... 92 E4
Cherry Tree Dr NE22 ... 10 F1
Cherry Tree Gdns NE15 ... 50 C8
Cherry Tree La NE41 ... 51 A6
Cherry Tree Sq 6 SR2 ... 92 E8
Cherry Tree Wlk NE31 ... 57 E4
Cherry Trees NE24 ... 17 D6
Cherry Way
Fence Houses DH4 ... 90 B1
Killingworth NE12 ... 29 C4
Cherryburn (Mus)*
NE43 ... 49 F2
Cherryburn Cotts NE43 ... 49 E2
Cherryburn Gdns NE4 ... 54 E8
Cherrytree Cl NE12 ... 29 F2
Cherrytree Ct NE22 ... 11 D2
Cherrytree Dr NE16 ... 69 C8
Cherrytree Gdns
Gateshead NE9 ... 71 A4
Whitley Bay NE25 ... 31 F3
Cherrytree Rd DH2 ... 88 A5
Cherrywood NE6 ... 39 E1
Cherrywood Gdns SR3 ... 92 B7
Cherwell NE37 ... 83 F8
Cherwell Sq NE12 ... 29 C1
Chesham Gdns NE5 ... 36 B2
Chesham Gn NE3 ... 37 F5
Cheshire Ave DH3 ... 82 C1
Cheshire Cl NE63 ... 6 A4
Cheshire Ct NE31 ... 57 D5
Cheshire Gdns NE28 ... 40 A3
Cheshire Gr NE34 ... 60 B7
Chesils The NE12 ... 39 A5
Chesmond Dr NE21 ... 53 C3
Chessar Ave NE5 ... 37 B2
Chester Ave NE28 ... 40 F3
Chester Cl NE20 ... 25 B4
Chester Cres
Newcastle-u-T NE2 ... 99 C3
Sunderland SR1 ... 102 B2
Chester Gdns NE34 ... 59 E7
Chester Gr Blyth NE24 ... 17 C6
Seghill NE23 ... 22 E1
Chester Mews SR4 ... 102 B2
Chester Oval SR2 ... 102 B2
Chester Pl NE8 ... 101 B2
Chester Rd
Bournmoor DH3,DH4 ... 89 D3
Chester le S DH3 ... 88 F5
Penshaw DH4 ... 90 B7
Shiney Row DH4 ... 90 B7
Sunderland SR1,SR4 ... 102 B2
Sunderland,Grindon SR4 ... 85 B3
Sunderland,High Barnes
SR1,SR2,SR4 ... 85 F5
Chester Sq NE61 ... 2 A3
Chester St Newbottle DH4 ... 90 D2
Newcastle-u-T NE2 ... 99 C3
Sunderland SR4 ... 102 A2
Chester St E SR4 ... 102 B2
Chester St W SR4 ... 102 A2
Chester Terr SR1 ... 102 B2
Chester Terr N SR4 ... 102 B2
Chester View DH2 ... 81 F1
Chester Way NE32 ... 58 A1
Chester-le-Street CE Jun
Sch DH2 ... 88 B5
Chester-le-Street Com Hospl
DH3 ... 88 C2
Chester-le-Street Sta
DH3 ... 88 C3
Chesterfield Rd NE4 ... 54 F4
Chesterhill NE23 ... 22 B5
Chesters 5 NE28 ... 40 F4
Chesters Ave NE12 ... 39 A5
Chesters Cl NE9 ... 70 F6
Chesters Ct NE12 ... 39 B6
Chesters Dene DH8 ... 76 E3

Chesters Gdns NE40 ... 51 E4
Chesters Pk NE9 ... 70 F6
Chesters The
Ebchester DH8 ... 76 E3
Newcastle-u-T NE5 ... 36 C1
Whitley Bay NE25 ... 31 E6
Chesterton Rd NE34 ... 59 B3
Chesterwood Dr NE28 ... 40 A2
Chesterwood Terr NE10 ... 57 B1
Chestnut Ave Blyth NE24 ... 12 D1
Newcastle-u-T NE5 ... 37 E2
Washington NE38 ... 83 B1
Whickham NE16 ... 69 B5
Whitley Bay NE25 ... 31 F4
Chestnut Cl
Hedworth NE32 ... 58 D1
Killingworth NE12 ... 29 B4
Chestnut Cres SR5 ... 74 F3
Chestnut Gdns NE8 ... 70 C8
Chestnut Gr NE34 ... 59 F4
Chestnut St Ashington NE63 ... 6 D3
Wallsend NE28 ... 40 C1
Chestnut Terr DH4 ... 90 C3
Cheswick Dr NE3 ... 38 D6
Cheswick Rd NE25 ... 23 E2
Chevin Cl NE6 ... 40 B1
Chevington NE10 ... 72 A5
Chevington Cl NE61 ... 4 E3
Chevington Gdns 6 NE5 ... 37 D1
Chevington Gr NE25 ... 31 D7
Cheviot Cl Ellington NE61 ... 1 D4
Tynemouth NE29 ... 31 F2
Washington NE37 ... 83 A6
Cheviot Ct Blaydon NE21 ... 53 C3
Morpeth NE61 ... 9 A6
Newcastle-u-T NE7 ... 39 A4
Whitley Bay NE26 ... 32 C4
Cheviot Gdns NE11 ... 70 A7
Cheviot Gn NE11 ... 70 A8
Cheviot Gr NE61 ... 4 E3
Cheviot Grange NE23 ... 29 C6
Cheviot Ho NE36 ... 74 B7
Cheviot Jun Sch NE34 ... 60 A8
Cheviot La SR2 ... 92 E7
Cheviot Mount NE6 ... 56 C6
Cheviot Prim Sch NE5 ... 37 A4
Cheviot Rd Blaydon NE21 ... 53 C1
Chester le S DH2 ... 88 B1
Hebburn NE32 ... 58 A4
South Shields NE34 ... 60 A7
South Shields NE34 ... 60 A8
Cheviot St SR43 ... 85 F7
Cheviot View
Ashington NE63 ... 6 E5
Brunswick Village NE13 ... 28 A6
Gateshead NE10 ... 71 D6
Longbenton NE12 ... 39 C6
Ponteland NE20 ... 26 A5
Prudhoe NE42 ... 50 E2
Seghill NE23 ... 22 F1
Whitley Bay NE26 ... 32 B5
Cheviot Way
Hexham NE46 ... 45 A4
Stakeford NE62 ... 11 B8
Chevron The 4 NE6 ... 56 B5
Chevychase Ct SR7 ... 92 F2
Cheyne Rd NE42 ... 50 C2
Cheyne The SR3 ... 92 A5
Chichester Ave NE23 ... 21 F8
Chichester Cl
Ashington NE63 ... 7 A2
Gateshead NE8 ... 101 B2
Newcastle-u-T NE3 ... 37 D8
Chichester Gr NE22 ... 10 F2
Chichester Pl NE33 ... 59 C8
Chichester Rd
South Shields NE33 ... 42 D1
Sunderland SR6 ... 75 E4
Chichester Rd E NE33 ... 42 D1
Chichester Sta NE33 ... 59 C8
Chichester Way NE32 ... 58 B1
Chick's La 4 SR6 ... 75 F8
Chicken Rd NE28 ... 40 A4
Chigwell Cl DH4 ... 90 B7
Chilcote NE10 ... 71 D7
Chilcrosse NE10 ... 71 F6
Chilham Ct
Tynemouth NE29 ... 41 B8
Washington NE38 ... 83 B4
Chillingham Cl NE24 ... 17 B5
Chillingham Cres NE63 ... 6 C3
Chillingham Ct 19 NE6 ... 56 C7
Chillingham Dr
Chester le S DH2 ... 88 A1
North Shields NE29 ... 41 D4
Chillingham Ho SR6 ... 103 B4
Chillingham Ind Est NE6 ... 56 C7
Chillingham Rd NE6 ... 56 C8
Chillingham Road Prim Sch
NE6 ... 56 C8
Chillingham Road Sta
NE6 ... 56 D7
Chillingham Terr NE32 ... 58 D4
Chilside Rd NE10 ... 71 D7
Chiltern Ave DH2 ... 88 B2
Chiltern Cl Ashington NE63 ... 6 F1
Washington NE38 ... 83 B3
Chiltern Dr NE12 ... 29 B1
Chiltern Gdns NE11 ... 70 B7
Chiltern Rd NE29 ... 31 F2
Chilton Ave DH4 ... 94 A8
Chilton Gdns 10 DH4 ... 94 A8
Chilton St 1 SR5 ... 75 C1
Chimney Mills NE2 ... 98 C4
China St SR2 ... 86 E4

Chingford Cl DH4 . . . . .90 C7
Chip The NE61 . . . . .8 F5
Chipchase NE38 . . . . .82 F4
Chipchase Ave NE23 . . . . . . .22 B6
Chipchase Cl
  Bedlington NE22 . . . . .10 D1
  Pegswood NE61 . . . . .4 F3
Chipchase Cres NE5 . . . . . .36 E3
Chipchase Ct
  Bournmoor DH4 . . . . .89 D1
  New Hartley NE25 . . . . .23 D6
  Seaham SR7 . . . . .92 F2
Chipchase Mews NE3 . . . . .28 A1
Chipchase Terr NE32 . . . . .58 B3
Chippendale Pl NE17 . . . . . .98 B4
Chirdon Cres NE46 . . . . .45 C4
Chirnside NE23 . . . . .22 B4
Chirton Ave
  North Shields NE29 . . . . .41 F5
  South Shields NE34 . . . . . . .60 C6
Chirton Dene Quays
  NE28 . . . . .41 F2
Chirton Dene Way NE29 . . .42 A3
Chirton Gn Blyth NE24 . . . . .17 B5
  North Shields NE29 . . . . .41 F5
Chirton Gr NE34 . . . . .60 C6
Chirton Hill Dr NE29 . . . . . .41 C7
Chirton La NE29 . . . . .41 E5
Chirton Lodge NE28 . . . . . . .41 A5
Chirton West View NE29 . . .41 F5
Chirton Wynd NE6 . . . . .56 C5
Chisholm Pl ⬛ NE46 . . . . . .45 B5
Chislehurst Rd DH4 . . . . . . .90 B7
Chiswick Gdns NE8 . . . . . . .71 A8
Chiswick Rd SR5 . . . . .74 A2
Chiswick St SR5 . . . . .74 A2
Chollerford Ave
  North Shields NE29 . . . . .41 D6
  Whitley Bay NE25 . . . . .32 B4
Chollerford Cl NE3 . . . . . . .38 A4
Chollerford Mews NE25 . . .23 F2
Chollerton Dr
  Bedlington NE22 . . . . .11 A1
  Longbenton NE12 . . . . .40 A8
Choppington Fst Sch
  NE62 . . . . .10 E5
Choppington Rd
  Bedlington NE22,NE62 . . . . . .10 F2
  Morpeth NE61 . . . . .9 B6
Chopwell Gdns NE9 . . . . . .71 D2
Chopwell Prim Sch NE17 .66 B1
Chopwell Rd NE17 . . . . .77 C6
Chopwell Wood Wlks*
  NE39 . . . . .66 F2
Christ Church CE Prim Sch
  Newcastle-u-T NE1 . . . . .99 C2
  North Shields NE30 . . . . .42 A6
Christal Terr SR6 . . . . .75 D3
Christie Terr NE6 . . . . .56 E6
Christmas Pl NE8 . . . . .100 B2
Christon Cl NE3 . . . . .38 E5
Christon Rd NE3 . . . . .38 D5
Christon Way NE10 . . . . . . .57 B2
Christopher Rd NE6 . . . . . . .56 E7
Chudleigh Gdns NE5 . . . . .36 B2
Church Ave
  Choppington NE62 . . . . .10 E5
  Newcastle-u-T NE3 . . . . .38 D5
  West Sleekburn NE62 . . . . . .11 D7
Church Bank Jarrow NE32 .58 D7
  Newburn NE15 . . . . .52 F7
  Sunderland SR5 . . . . .75 A1
  Wallsend NE28 . . . . .40 D2
Church Chare
  Chester le S DH3 . . . . .88 D3
  Ponteland NE20 . . . . .25 F7
  Whickham NE16 . . . . .69 B7
Church Cl Bedlington NE22 .15 F8
  Bournmoor DH4 . . . . .89 E4
  Dinnington NE13 . . . . .27 B7
  Ebchester DH8 . . . . .76 E3
  Seaton Burn NE13 . . . . .28 A6
  Whitley Bay NE25 . . . . .31 C4
Church Ct Bedlington NE22 .15 F8
  ⬛ Gateshead NE10 . . . . . . .56 D1
Church Dr NE9 . . . . .71 A6
Church Flatt NE20 . . . . .25 F7
Church Gn 🔳 NE16 . . . . . . .69 B7
Church High Sch NE2 . . . . .99 B4
Church La
  Bedlington NE22 . . . . .16 A7
  Gateshead NE9 . . . . .71 B6
  Newcastle-u-T NE3 . . . . .38 D5
  Riding Mill NE44 . . . . .62 E7
  Sunderland SR1 . . . . .102 C2
  Whitburn SR6 . . . . .75 F8
Church Mews
  Ashington NE63 . . . . .6 B4
  Backworth NE27 . . . . .30 C5
Church Pl NE10 . . . . .56 D1
Church Rd
  Backworth NE27 . . . . .30 C5
  Gateshead NE9 . . . . .71 A5
  Hetton le H DH5 . . . . .95 A5
  Newburn NE15 . . . . .52 F7
  Newcastle-u-T NE3 . . . . .38 D5
  Stannington NE61 . . . . .14 C3
  Wylam NE41 . . . . .51 A6
Church Rise Ryton NE40 . . .52 E5

Church Rise continued
  Whickham NE16 . . . . .69 B7
Church Row ⬛ NE46 . . . . .45 B5
Church Sq NE61 . . . . .8 B3
Church St Birtley DH3 . . . . .82 C4
  Blaydon NE21 . . . . .53 B1
  Blyth NE24 . . . . .17 E8
  Cramlington NE23 . . . . .22 B6
  Dunston NE11 . . . . .100 A1
  Gateshead NE8 . . . . .101 B4
  Gateshead,Felling NE10 . . . .71 D8
  Haswell DH6 . . . . .97 E3
  Hebburn NE31 . . . . .57 D7
  🔳 Houghton-le-S DH4,DH5 .94 E8
  Newcastle-u-T NE6 . . . . .57 A4
  North Shields NE30 . . . . .42 A6
  Penshaw DH4 . . . . .90 B6
  🔳 Sunderland SR5 . . . . . . .75 A1
  Sunderland,South Hylton
  SR4 .85 A6
  Sunniside NE16 . . . . .69 A1
  West Rainton DH4 . . . . .94 A2
Church St E SR1 . . . . .103 C3
Church St N SR6 . . . . .103 B4
Church Terr NE21 . . . . .53 C3
Church Vale DH6 . . . . .96 C4
Church View
  Boldon Colliery NE35 . . . . . . .58 E1
  Earsdon NE25 . . . . .31 A5
  Haswell DH6 . . . . .97 F3
  New Silksworth SR3 . . . . . . .92 A7
  Newbiggin-by-t-S NE64 . . . . .7 C5
  Wallsend NE28 . . . . .40 D2
  Washington NE37 . . . . .83 D7
Church Way Earsdon NE25 .31 A5
  North Shields NE29,NE30 . . .42 A6
  South Shields NE33 . . . . . . .42 C3
Church Wlk Morpeth NE61 . .8 E8
  Newcastle-u-T NE5 . . . . .36 F3
  Sunderland SR1 . . . . .103 C3
Churchburn Dr NE61 . . . . . .8 F6
Churchdown Cl NE35 . . . . .58 E2
Churchdown Cl NE28 . . . . .40 A4
Churchill Ave
  Sunderland SR5 . . . . .75 A2
  Whitley Bay NE25 . . . . .31 F3
Churchill Com Coll NE28 . .40 F4
Churchill Gdns NE2 . . . . . .39 A1
Churchill Mews NE6 . . . . . .56 C4
Churchill Sq DH4 . . . . .94 B8
Churchill St
  Newcastle-u-T NE1 . . . . . . .100 C4
  Sunderland SR1 . . . . .103 B2
  Wallsend NE28 . . . . .40 F4
Churchlands NE46 . . . . .45 D4
Churchwalk Ho NE6 . . . . . .57 A5
Churston Cl NE6 . . . . .90 C4
Cicero Terr 🔳 SR5 . . . . . . .75 A2
Cinderford Cl NE35 . . . . . . .58 E2
Circle Pl NE46 . . . . .45 A5
Circle The NE32 . . . . .58 C4
Cirencester St SR4 . . . . . .102 B3
Cirrus Ho 🔳 SR3 . . . . .92 A6
Citadel E NE12 . . . . .29 D3
Citadel W NE12 . . . . .29 D3
City Hall NE1 . . . . .99 B2
City of Sunderland Coll
  (Hylton Ctr) SR5 . . . . .74 E2
City of Sunderland Coll Bede
  Ctr SR3 . . . . .85 F3
City of Sunderland Coll
  Shiney Row Ctr DH4 . . . . . . .90 B5
City Rd NE1 . . . . .99 C1
City Way SR3 . . . . .91 C6
Citygate NE4 . . . . .98 C1
Civic Ct NE31 . . . . .57 F5
Clacton Rd SR5 . . . . .73 F1
Clanfield Ct NE3 . . . . .38 F4
Clanny Ho SR4 . . . . .85 F6
Clanny St Sunderland SR1 .102 B2
  Sunderland SR1 . . . . .102 C2
Clapham Ave NE6 . . . . .56 D5
Clara Ave NE27 . . . . .30 F4
Clara St Blaydon NE21 . . . . .53 A4
  Newcastle-u-T NE4 . . . . .54 D4
Clarabad Terr NE12 . . . . . . .30 A1
Clarance Pl NE3 . . . . .38 E6
Clare Lea NE43 . . . . .65 A3
Claremont Ave
  Newcastle-u-T NE15 . . . . . . .53 D7
  Sunderland SR6 . . . . .75 E3
Claremont Cres NE26 . . . . .31 E7
Claremont Ct NE26 . . . . . . .31 E8
Claremont Dr DH4 . . . . .90 A6
Claremont Gdns
  East Boldon NE36 . . . . .74 D7
  Whitley Bay NE26 . . . . .31 F6
Claremont North Ave
  NE8 . . . . .101 B2
Claremont Pl
  Gateshead NE8 . . . . .101 B2
  Newcastle-u-T NE2 . . . . .98 C3
Claremont Rd
  Newcastle-u-T NE2 . . . . .98 B4
  Sunderland SR6 . . . . .75 E3
  Whitley Bay NE26 . . . . .31 F7
Claremont South Ave
  NE8 . . . . .101 B1
Claremont St
  Gateshead NE8 . . . . .101 B1
  Newcastle-u-T NE2 . . . . .98 C3
Claremont Terr
  Blyth NE24 . . . . .17 D7
  Gateshead NE10 . . . . .57 B1
  Newcastle-u-T NE2 . . . . .98 C3
  🔳 Springwell NE9 . . . . .71 F1
  Sunderland SR2 . . . . .102 C1
Claremont Wlk NE8 . . . . . .101 A1

Claremont Ct NE36 . . . . . . .74 B7
Clarence Cres 🔳 NE26 . . .32 B4
Clarence Ho NE2 . . . . .99 C2
Clarence St
  Newcastle-u-T NE1,NE2 . . . .99 C2
  Seaton Sluice NE26 . . . . . . .24 D5
  🔳 Sunderland SR5 . . . . . . .75 A2
  Tantobie DH9 . . . . .79 B2
Clarence Terr DH3 . . . . .88 C3
Clarendon Mews NE3 . . . . .28 C2
Clarendon Rd NE6 . . . . .39 C1
Clarendon Sq SR5 . . . . .75 B3
Clarewood Ave NE34 . . . . . .60 A8
Clarewood Ct NE4 . . . . .98 B2
Clarewood Gn NE4 . . . . . . .98 A2
Clarewood Pl NE5 . . . . .54 C8
Clark's Terr 🔳 SR7 . . . . . . .92 E1
Clarke Terr NE10 . . . . .71 C8
Clarke's Terr NE23 . . . . .29 A6
Clarks Field NE61 . . . . .8 E8
Clarks Hill Wlk NE15 . . . . . .52 F7
Clasper Ct 🔳 NE33 . . . . . . .42 C4
Clasper St NE4 . . . . .100 B3
Clasper Way NE16 . . . . .54 A3
Claude St
  🔳 Crawcrook NE40 . . . . . . .51 F3
  Hetton le H DH5 . . . . .95 A3
Claudius Ct NE33 . . . . .42 C4
Claverdon St NE5 . . . . .36 B4
Clavering Pl ⬛ NE1 . . . . . .101 A4
Clavering Rd
  Blaydon NE21 . . . . .53 C1
  Whickham NE16 . . . . .54 B1
Clavering Sq NE11 . . . . .69 F8
Clavering St NE28 . . . . .41 B1
Clavering Way NE21 . . . . . .53 E2
Claverley Dr NE27 . . . . .30 C5
Claxheugh Cotts SR4 . . . . .85 B7
Claxheugh Rd SR4 . . . . . . .85 B7
Claymere Rd SR2 . . . . .86 E1
Claypath NE10 . . . . .71 F4
Claypath La NE33 . . . . .42 D2
Claypath Rd DH5 . . . . .95 B2
Claypath St ⬛ NE6 . . . . . . .56 A6
Claypool Ct NE34 . . . . .59 C5
Clayside Ho NE4 . . . . .54 F4
Clayton Park Sq NE2 . . . . .99 B4
Clayton Rd NE2 . . . . .99 B4
Clayton St
  Bedlington NE22 . . . . .11 D3
  Dudley NE23 . . . . .28 F8
  Jarrow NE32 . . . . .58 B7
  Newcastle-u-T NE1 . . . . .99 A1
Clayton St W NE1 . . . . . . .100 C4
Clayton Terr
  Gateshead NE8 . . . . .56 C1
  Heddon-on-t-W NE15 . . . . . .34 F2
Clayton Terrace Rd
  Chopwell NE17 . . . . .66 C2
  High Spen NE13,NE39 . . . . .66 D4
Clayworth Rd NE2 . . . . .28 B1
Cleadon Gdns
  Gateshead NE9 . . . . .71 D3
  Wallsend NE28 . . . . .41 A5
Cleadon Hill Dr NE34 . . . . .60 A4
Cleadon Hill Rd NE34 . . . . .60 A4
Cleadon La Cleadon SR6 . . .60 C1
  East Boldon NE36,SR6 . . . . .60 C1
Cleadon Lane Ind Est
  NE36 . . . . .74 E8
Cleadon Lea SR6 . . . . .59 F1
Cleadon Mdws SR6 . . . . . . .60 A2
Cleadon Old Hall SR6 . . . . .60 A1
Cleadon St NE6 . . . . .56 E6
Cleadon Twrs NE34 . . . . . . .60 A4
Cleadon Village CE Prim Sch
  SR6 .59 F1
Cleasby Gdns NE9 . . . . .70 F3
Cleasewell Terr NE62 . . . . .11 A7
Cleaside Ave NE34 . . . . .60 A4
Cleaswell Hill NE62 . . . . . . .10 F7
Cleaswell Hill Special Sch
  NE62 . . . . .10 F7
Cleehill Dr NE29 . . . . .31 F1
Cleeve Ct NE38 . . . . .83 C5
Cleghorn St 🔳 NE6 . . . . . . .56 C8
Clegwell Terr NE31 . . . . . . .57 F6
Clematis Cres NE9 . . . . .71 D2
Clement Ave NE22 . . . . .11 C1
Clement St NE9 . . . . .70 F5
Clementina Ct NE23 . . . . . .103 B1
Clennel Ave NE31 . . . . .57 D5
Clennell Ho 🔳 NE4 . . . . . . .54 E5
Clent Way NE12 . . . . .39 A6
Clephan St NE11 . . . . .54 F1
Clervaux Terr NE32 . . . . . . .58 C5
Cleveland Ave
  Chester le S DH2 . . . . .88 B2
  Newbiggin-by-t-S NE64 . . . . .7 D4
  North Shields NE29 . . . . .41 F6
Cleveland Cres NE29 . . . . .42 A6
  🔳 South Shields NE33 . . . . .42 C4
Cleveland Dr NE38 . . . . .83 B3
Cleveland Gdns
  Newcastle-u-T NE7 . . . . .39 A3
  Wallsend NE28 . . . . .40 A3
Cleveland Mews NE11 . . . .100 A1
Cleveland Rd
  North Shields NE29 . . . . .42 A6
  Sunderland SR4 . . . . .85 F5
Cleveland St 🔳 NE33 . . . . .42 D4
Cleveland Terr
  Newbiggin-by-t-S NE64 . . . . .7 D4
  North Shields NE29 . . . . .42 A6
  Sunderland SR4 . . . . .85 F5
Clickemin NE20 . . . . .26 A6
Cliff Rd SR2 . . . . .93 A6

Cliff Row NE26 . . . . .32 C4
Cliff Terr SR2 . . . . .93 A6
Cliff View SR2 . . . . .93 A6
Cliffe Ct NE6 . . . . .75 F4
Cliffe Pk SR6 . . . . .75 F8
Clifford Gdns 🔳 NE4 . . . . . .51 F3
Clifford Rd NE6 . . . . .56 D5
Clifford St Blaydon NE21 . . .53 C3
  Chester le S DH3 . . . . .88 C1
  Newcastle-u-T NE6 . . . . .56 B6
  North Shields NE30 . . . . .42 C6
  Sunderland SR4 . . . . .102 A2
Clifton Ave
  South Shields NE34 . . . . . . .59 E7
  🔳 Wallsend NE28 . . . . .40 B2
Clifton Cl Ryton NE40 . . . . . .52 E4
  Stakeford NE62 . . . . .11 A8
Clifton Ct
  🔳 Gateshead NE9 . . . . .71 E1
  Newcastle-u-T NE3 . . . . .37 D7
  Whitley Bay NE26 . . . . .31 E7
Clifton Gdns Blyth NE24 . . .17 D7
  Gateshead NE9 . . . . .70 F7
  Newcastle-u-T NE3 . . . . .37 E3
Clifton Gr NE25 . . . . .23 D3
Clifton La NE61 . . . . .9 B2
Clifton Rd
  Cramlington NE23 . . . . .22 C5
  Newcastle-u-T NE4 . . . . .54 F5
  Sunderland SR6 . . . . .75 E4
Clifton Terr
  Longbenton NE12 . . . . .39 D7
  South Shields NE33 . . . . . . .59 C8
  Whitley Bay NE26 . . . . .32 B5
Clifton Wlk NE5 . . . . .36 B2
Cliftonbourne Ave 🔳
  SR6 .75 E4
Cliftonville Ave NE4 . . . . . .54 F5
Cliftonville Gdns NE26 . . . .32 A6
Climbing Tree Wlk NE61 . . .4 E3
Clintburn Ct NE23 . . . . .22 C3
Clinton Pl
  Newcastle-u-T NE3 . . . . .28 B2
  Sunderland SR3 . . . . .91 C6
Clipsham Cl NE12 . . . . .39 B6
Clipstone Ave NE6 . . . . .56 E3
Clipstone Cl NE15 . . . . .35 C2
Clithroe Gdns NE12 . . . . . .10 D2
Clive Pl NE6 . . . . .56 B5
Clive St North Shields NE29 .42 B5
  🔳 South Shields NE34 . . . . .59 A4
Clockburn Lonnen NE16 . . .68 C5
Clockburnsyde Cl NE16 . . .68 C5
Clockmill Rd NE11,NE8 . . .100 A1
Cloggs The NE20 . . . . .25 F7
Cloister Ave NE34 . . . . .59 A5
Cloister Ct NE8 . . . . .101 C3
Cloister Garth NE7 . . . . .38 F5
Cloister Wlk NE32 . . . . .58 C7
Cloisters The
  Newcastle-u-T NE7 . . . . .38 F5
  South Shields NE34 . . . . . . .59 F7
  Sunderland SR2 . . . . .103 A1
Close NE1 . . . . .101 A4
Close E The DH2 . . . . .88 C5
Close St
  🔳 Sunderland SR5 . . . . . . .75 B1
  Sunderland,Millfield SR4 . . .102 A3
Close The Blaydon NE21 . . .68 C5
  Blyth NE24 . . . . .12 E1
  Burnopfield NE16 . . . . .79 C7
  Chester le S DH2 . . . . .88 C5
  Cleadon SR6 . . . . .59 F1
  Houghton-le-S DH5 . . . . .94 F8
  Newcastle-u-T NE5 . . . . .53 E8
  Ponteland NE20 . . . . .25 E5
  Seghill NE23 . . . . .22 F2
  Stannington NE61 . . . . .14 C3
Closeburn Sq SR3 . . . . .92 B6
Closefield Gr NE25 . . . . . . .31 E4
Cloth Mkt NE1 . . . . .99 A1
Clough Dene
  Tantobie DH9 . . . . .79 B2
  Tantobie,Pickering Nook
  NE16 . . . . .79 A2
Clough La NE1 . . . . .99 A1
Clousden Dr NE12 . . . . .29 E1
Clousden Grange NE12 . . .29 E1
Clovelly Ave NE4 . . . . .54 E5
Clovelly Gdns
  Bedlington NE22 . . . . .15 F8
  Whitley Bay NE26 . . . . .32 A6
Clovelly Pl Jarrow NE32 . . .58 E5
  Ponteland NE20 . . . . .25 C2
Clovelly Sq 🔳 SR5 . . . . . . .74 A3
Clover Ave
  Gateshead NE10 . . . . .56 B2
  Shiney Row DH4 . . . . .90 B4
  Winlaton Mill NE21 . . . . .67 E2
Clover Hill NE16 . . . . .69 B2
Clover Hill Com Prim Sch
  NE16 . . . . .68 F4
Clover Ho SR3 . . . . .92 A4
Cloverdale NE22 . . . . .10 E1
Cloverdale Gdns
  Newcastle-u-T NE7 . . . . .39 B3
  Whickham NE16 . . . . .69 B5
Cloverfield Ave NE3 . . . . . .37 F6
Cloverhill NE32 . . . . .58 C1
Cloverhill Ave NE31 . . . . . .57 D3

Cloverhill Cl NE23 22
Cloverhill Dr NE40 52
Clumber St NE4 100
Clumber St N NE4 100
Clyde Ave NE31 57
Clyde Ct 🔳 SR3 91
Clyde St Chopwell NE17 66
  Gateshead NE8 71
Clydedale Ave NE12 39
Clydesdale Ave DH4 90
Clydesdale Mount 🔳
  NE6 .56
Clydesdale Rd NE6 56
Clydesdale St DH5 95
Clyvedon Rise NE34 60
Co-operative Bldgs
  NE23 23
Co-operative Cres 🔳
  NE10 71
Co-operative St DH3 88
Co-Operative Terr
  Backworth NE27 30
  Brunswick Village NE13 28
  Burnopfield NE16 79
  Gateshead NE10 71
  High Spen NE39 66
  Longbenton NE12 30
  Medomsley DH8 77
  Pegswood NE61 4
  🔳 Shiremoor NE27 30
  Sunderland SR4 102
  🔳 Washington NE37 83
Co-operative Villas DH6 . .96
Coach La
  Brunswick Village NE13 27
  Hazlerigg NE13 28
  Newcastle-u-T NE7 39
  North Shields NE29 42
Coach Open NE28 41
Coach Rd
  Kibblesworth NE11 70
  Throckley NE15 35
  Wallsend NE28 40
  Washington NE37 72
Coach Rd Est NE37 72
Coach Road Gn NE10 56
Coal La NE42 49
Coalbank Rd DH5 94
Coalbank Sq DH5 94
Coalburn Terr NE61 9
Coaley La DH4 90
Coalford La DH6 96
Coalway La
  Greenside NE40,NE41 51
  Whickham NE16 69
Coalway La N NE16 54
Coanwood Dr NE23 22
Coanwood Gdns NE11 70
Coanwood Rd NE15 54
Coanwood Way NE16 54
Coast Rd
  Newcastle-u-T NE6,NE7,
  NE28 39
  North Shields NE28,NE29 . . .41
  South Shields NE34,SR6 . . .60
  Wallsend NE28,NE29 41
Coatsworth Ct NE8 101
Coatsworth Rd NE8 101
Cobalt Cl NE15 53
Cobbett Cres NE34 59
Cobbler's La NE43 49
Cobblestone Ct NE6 56
Cobden Rd NE23 22
Cobden St Gateshead NE8 .56
  🔳 Wallsend NE28 40
Cobden Terr NE8 56
Cobham Pl NE6 56
Cobham Sq SR5 75
Coble Dene NE29 41
Coble Landing NE33 42
Coburg St Blyth NE24 17
  Gateshead NE8 101
  North Shields NE30 42
Coburn Cl NE23 22
Cochran St NE21 53
Cochrane Ct NE4 54
Cochrane Park Ave NE7 . . .39
Cochrane St NE4 54
Cochrane Terr NE13 27
Cockburn Terr NE29 41
Cockermouth Gn NE5 54
Cockermouth Rd SR5 73
Cockshaw NE46 45
Cockshaw Ct 🔳 NE46 45
Cockshaw Terr 🔳 NE46 . . .45
Cockshott Dean NE42 49
Cohen Ct NE8 70
Cohort Cl DH8 77
Colbeck Ave NE16 69
Colbeck Terr 🔳 NE30 42
Colbourne Ave NE23 15
Colbourne Cres NE23 15
Colbury Cl NE23 15
Colby Ct NE4 100
Colchester St NE34 59
Colchester Terr SR4 85
Coldbeck Ct NE23 21
Coldingham Gdns NE5 36
Coldstream DH2 88
Coldstream Ave SR5 75
Coldstream Cl DH4 90
Coldstream Dr NE21 67
Coldstream Gdns NE28 41
Coldstream Rd NE15 53
Coldstream Way NE29 41
Coldwell Cl DH6 96

Coldwell La NE10 ....71 C7
Coldwell Park Ave NE10 ..71 D7
Coldwell Park Dr NE10 ..71 D7
Coldwell Rd NE42 ....50 F3
Coldwell St NE10 ....71 D8
Coldwell Terr 2 NE10 ..71 C7
Cole Gdns NE10 ....72 A8
Coledge Cl NE5 ....37 C3
Colebrooke DH3 ....82 D2
Colegate NE10 ....71 F7
Colegate Com Prim Sch
  NE10 ....71 F7
Colegate W NE10 ....71 F7
Colepeth NE10 ....71 F7
Coleridge Ave
  Gateshead NE47 ....70 E4
  South Shields NE33 ....42 E1
Coleridge Rd NE5 ....74 B2
Coleridge Sq NE31 ....57 E6
Coley Gn NE5 ....36 B4
Coley Hill Cl NE5 ....36 C4
Coley Terr SR6 ....75 F2
Colgrove Pl NE3 ....37 E5
Colgrove Way NE3 ....37 F5
Colima Ave SR5 ....85 C8
Colin Pl NE6 ....57 A8
Colin Terr 7 SR2 ....92 F6
College Burn Rd SR3 ....91 E5
College Dr NE33 ....59 E8
College La
  Longbenton NE12 ....39 C6
  Newcastle-u-T NE1 ....99 B2
College Pl NE63 ....6 E2
College Rd Ashington NE63 ..6 E2
  Hebburn NE31 ....57 D2
College St NE1 ....99 B2
College View 4 SR5 ....75 C1
Collier Cl NE15 ....35 D1
Colliery La DH9 ....78 D1
Colliery La
  Hetton le H DH5 ....95 B2
  Newcastle-u-T NE4 ....98 B1
Colliery Rd NE11 ....54 F2
Collin Ave NE34 ....60 B5
Collingdon Gn NE39 ....67 A4
Collingdon Rd NE39 ....67 A4
Collingwood Ave NE28 ..30 B4
Collingwood Cl NE23 ....21 F8
Collingwood Cotts NE20 ..25 D7
Collingwood Cres NE20 ..25 D6
Collingwood Ct 1 NE37 ..83 F8
Collingwood Cnr NE29 ..31 F1
Collingwood Dr
  Hexham NE46 ....44 F2
  Shiney Row DH4 ....90 A6
Collingwood Gdns NE10 ..56 D2
Collingwood Ho
  North Shields NE29 ....41 F5
  South Shields NE33 ....42 D5
Collingwood Mans NE2 ..42 B4
Collingwood Mews NE3 ..38 C5
Collingwood Pl NE62 ....11 A7
Collingwood Prim Sch
  NE29 ....41 D5
Collingwood Rd
  Earsdon NE25 ....31 A5
  Newbiggin-by-t-S NE64 ....7 D5
Collingwood St
  16 Gateshead NE10 ....56 D1
  Hebburn NE31 ....58 A6
  Hetton le H DH5 ....95 B6
  Newcastle-u-T NE1 ....101 A4
  South Shields NE33 ....59 C8
  3 Sunderland SR5 ....75 B2
Collingwood Terr
  Blyth NE24 ....17 E7
  Dunston NE11 ....100 A1
  1 Newcastle-u-T NE2 ....38 F1
  Tynemouth NE30 ....42 D7
  Whitley Bay NE26 ....32 C4
Collingwood View NE3 ..41 F5
Collywell Bay Rd NE26 ..24 D5
Collywell Ct NE24 ....24 D6
Colman Ave NE34 ....59 A5
Colmet Ct NE11 ....70 D4
Colnbrook Cl NE3 ....37 D7
Colombo Rd SR5 ....73 F1
Colston St NE4 ....54 D6
Colston Way NE25 ....31 D7
Colt Pk NE17 ....77 B5
Coltere Ave NE36 ....74 E7
Colton Gdns NE9 ....71 A3
Coltpark NE5 ....36 F1
Coltpark Pl NE5 ....22 B5
Coltsfoot Gdns NE10 ....71 C5
Coltspool NE11 ....81 D6
Columba St SR5 ....75 B2
Columbia Wlk NE3 ....38 E5
Columbia Grange NE3 ..37 E5
Columbia Terr NE24 ....17 E6
Colwell Pl NE5 ....54 B7
Colwell Rd Ashington NE63 ..6 F1
  Shiremoor NE27 ....30 F2
  3 Tynemouth NE29 ....31 F1
Colwyn Par NE31 ....58 A2
Colwyne Pl NE5 ....37 B2
Combe Dr NE15 ....53 B7
Comet Row NE29 ....29 C2
Comet Sq SR3 ....92 A7
Comical Cnr NE33 ....42 B4
Comma Ct NE11 ....70 B7
Commercial Pl 4 NE46 ..45 B4
Commercial Rd
  8 Blyth NE24 ....17 E8
  Jarrow NE32 ....58 C8
  Newcastle-u-T NE6 ....56 C5
  Newcastle-u-T,South Gosforth
  NE3 ....38 E5

Commercial Rd continued
  South Shields NE33 ....42 B1
  Sunderland SR2 ....86 F4
Commercial St 9 NE21 ..53 B1
Commissioners' Wharf
  NE29 ....42 A2
Common Ave NE34 ....59 D7
Compton Cl NE38 ....83 B5
Compton Rd NE29 ....41 F5
Concorde Ho NE25 ....23 E1
Concorde Sq 5 SR3 ....92 A7
Concorde Way NE32 ....58 B6
Condercum Ct NE15 ....54 C5
Condercum Ind Est NE4 ..54 D5
Condercum Rd NE4 ....54 D5
Cone St NE33 ....42 B2
Cone Terr DH3 ....88 D4
Conewood Ho NE4 ....37 F6
Conhope La NE15,NE4 ....54 D5
Conifer Cl NE21 ....68 B8
Conifer Ct NE12 ....39 F8
Coniscliffe Ave NE3 ....37 F4
Coniscliffe Pl 1 SR6 ....75 E1
Conishead Terr DH6 ....97 F8
Coniston Birtley DH3 ....82 D2
  Gateshead NE10 ....72 A8
Coniston Ave
  Easington Lane DH5 ....97 C8
  Hebburn NE31 ....57 F6
  Newbiggin-by-t-S NE64 ....7 C3
  Sunderland SR5 ....74 C4
  Whickham NE16 ....69 D7
Coniston Cl
  Chester le S DH2 ....88 C2
  Killingworth NE12 ....29 C3
  Newburn NE15 ....52 E7
Coniston Cres NE21 ....68 B8
Coniston Ct
  Newcastle-u-T NE5 ....54 B8
  Wallsend NE28 ....28 A3
Coniston Dr NE32 ....58 D3
Coniston Gdns NE9 ....71 B5
Coniston Grange NE36 ..74 B7
Coniston Ho NE38 ....83 C6
Coniston Pl NE9 ....71 B5
Coniston Rd Blyth NE24 ..12 A1
  Tynemouth NE30 ....32 A2
  Wallsend NE28 ....40 A4
Connaught Cl DH4 ....90 C5
Connaught Gdns NE12 ..39 D7
Connaught Terr NE32 ....58 B6
Conningsby Cl NE3 ....38 D8
Conniscliffe Rd NE46 ....44 F3
Conniscliffe Rd NE46 ....44 F3
Connolly Terr NE17 ....77 C6
Consett Rd NE11 ....70 A5
Constable Cl NE40 ....52 C4
Constable Gdns NE34 ..59 C4
Constables Garth 7 DH3 ..82 C4
Content St NE21 ....53 C1
Convent Rd NE4 ....54 D7
Conway Cl
  Bedlington NE22 ....10 D1
  Ryton NE40 ....52 D4
Conway Dr NE7 ....39 A4
Conway Gdns
  Sunderland SR3 ....91 C7
  Wallsend NE28 ....40 A4
Conway Gr NE26 ....24 B7
Conway Rd SR5 ....73 F2
Conway Sq Gateshead NE9 ..71 A8
  Sunderland SR5 ....73 F2
Conyers Ave DH2 ....88 B5
Conyers Pl DH2 ....88 B5
Conyers Rd
  Chester le S DH2 ....88 C5
  Newcastle-u-T NE3 ....37 F7
Cook Cl NE33 ....59 B8
Cook Gdns NE10 ....72 B8
Cook Sq SR5 ....74 A2
Cooks Wood NE38 ....83 D3
Cookshold La DH6 ....96 B2
Cookson Cl
  Corbridge NE45 ....46 F6
  Newcastle-u-T NE4 ....98 B1
Cookson Ho NE33 ....42 C3
Cookson St NE4 ....98 A1
Cookson Terr DH2 ....88 B3
Cookson's La NE1 ....101 A4
Coomassie Rd NE24 ....17 E7
Coomside NE23 ....22 C4
Coop Bldgs 10 DH3 ....82 C4
Cooperage 5 SR6 ....75 E1
Cooperative Terr
  Great Lumley DH4 ....89 F1
  Hetton le H DH5 ....95 A5
Coopie's La NE61 ....9 B7
Coopies Field NE61 ....9 B8
Coopies Haugh NE61 ....9 C7
Coopies Lane Ind Est
  NE61 ....9 C7
Coopies Way NE61 ....9 C7
Copland Terr NE2 ....99 C2
Copley Ave NE34 ....59 C2
Copley Dr SR3 ....86 B2
Copper Chare NE61 ....3 F1
Copperas La NE15 ....53 F7
Coppergate Ct NE31 ....57 F7
Coppice Cl NE11 ....70 B7
Coppice The NE6 ....24 C6
Coppice Way NE2 ....99 C2
Coppy La DH9,NE16 ....80 C4
Copse The Blaydon NE21 ..53 F2
  Burnopfield NE16 ....78 F6
  Longbenton NE12 ....29 E1
  Newcastle-u-T NE3 ....38 D8

Copse The continued
  Prudhoe NE42 ....50 E2
  Washington NE37 ....72 B2
Coptleigh DH5 ....95 A7
Coquet NE38 ....82 F1
Coquet Ave Blyth NE24 ..17 E5
  Newcastle-u-T NE3 ....38 B6
  South Shields NE34 ....60 B8
  Whitley Bay NE26 ....32 A5
Coquet Bldgs NE15 ....36 B1
Coquet Dr NE61 ....1 E5
Coquet Gr NE15 ....35 C2
Coquet Ho 16 SR3 ....91 F6
Coquet Park Fst Sch
  NE26 ....31 F7
Coquet St Ashington NE63 ..6 E4
  Chopwell NE17 ....66 C1
  Hebburn NE31 ....57 D6
  Jarrow NE32 ....58 A5
  Newcastle-u-T NE1 ....56 A6
Coquet Terr Dudley NE23 ..28 B6
  Newcastle-u-T NE6 ....56 F6
Coquetdale Ave NE6 ....57 A6
Coquetdale Cl NE61 ....4 E3
Coquetdale Pl NE22 ....11 C1
Coquetdale Villas 5 SR6 ..75 E2
Corbiere Cl SR3 ....91 E6
Corbitt St NC8 ....100 C1
Corbridge Ave NE3 ....28 B6
Corbridge CE Fst Sch
  NE45 ....47 A6
Corbridge Cl NE28 ....40 E6
Corbridge Cl NE12 ....38 F6
Corbridge Mid Sch NE45 ..46 F7
Corbridge Rd
  Hexham NE46 ....45 D4
  Newcastle-u-T NE6 ....56 C6
Corbridge Roman Site*
  NE45 ....46 E6
Corbridge St NE6 ....56 B6
Corbridge Sta NE45 ....46 F6
Corby Gate SR2 ....86 D4
Corby Gdns NE6 ....56 F6
Corby Hall Dr SR2 ....86 D4
Corchester Ave NE45 ....46 F6
Corchester La NE46,NE45 ..46 F7
Corchester Rd NE22 ....10 F2
Corchester Terr NE45 ....46 F6
Corchester Twrs NE45 ....46 F7
Corchester Wlk NE7 ....39 C4
Corfu Rd SR5 ....74 A2
Corinthian Sq SR5 ....74 A2
Cork St SR1 ....103 B3
Cormorant Cl
  Ashington NE63 ....6 E1
  Blyth NE24 ....17 F4
  4 Washington NE38 ....82 F3
Cormorant Dr NE11 ....100 A4
Corn Mill Dr DH5 ....94 D6
Cornbank Cl SR3 ....92 A5
Corndean NE38 ....84 A4
Cornel Mews NE7 ....39 C3
Cornel Rd NE7 ....39 C3
Cornelia Ct 7 SR3 ....92 A7
Corney St NE33 ....59 B7
Cornfields The NE31 ....57 E6
Cornforth Cl
  Ashington NE63 ....6 E1
  Gateshead NE10 ....72 C6
Cornhill Herdworth NE32 ..58 C1
  Newcastle-u-T NE5 ....36 F1
Cornhill Ave NE3 ....37 F7
Cornhill Cres NE29 ....41 D7
Cornhill Rd
  Cramlington NE23 ....22 C6
  6 Sunderland SR5 ....75 B2
Cornmoor Gdns NE16 ....69 B5
Cornmoor Rd NE16 ....69 B6
Cornthwaite Dr SR6 ....75 E8
Cornwall Rd NE31 ....57 F3
Cornwallis NE37 ....72 E1
Cornwallis Sq NE33 ....42 C3
Cornwallis St 18 NE33 ..42 C3
Cornwell Cres NE22 ....16 B8
Cornwell Ct NE3 ....38 F4
Coronation Ave
  6 Ryhope SR2 ....92 F6
  Sunniside NE16 ....69 B2
Coronation Bglws NE3 ..38 D5
Coronation Cl SR1 ....103 B3
Coronation Cotts NE61 ....2 A3
Coronation Cres
  Burnside DH4 ....90 C2
  High Pittington DH6 ....96 B6
  Whitley Bay NE25 ....31 F4
Coronation Gn DH5 ....97 D8
Coronation Rd
  Newcastle-u-T NE5 ....36 F1
  Seaton Delaval NE25 ....23 C3
  Sunniside NE16 ....69 A2
Coronation St
  Annitsford NE23 ....22 B1
  Blyth NE24 ....17 F8
  Chester le S DH3 ....88 D1
  Newbiggin-by-t-S NE64 ....7 E5
  North Shields NE29 ....42 A4
  Ryton NE40 ....52 E4
  South Shields NE33 ....42 C2
  Sunderland SR1 ....103 B3
  Wallsend NE28 ....40 C2
Coronation Terr
  8 Boldon Colliery NE35 ..58 E1
  Chester le S DH3 ....88 C2
  7 Gateshead NE10 ....56 C1
  Hetton le H DH5 ....95 A2
  Kibblesworth NE11 ....81 C6
  21 Springwell NE9 ....71 F1
  Sunderland SR4 ....85 B6

Coronation Terr continued
  Tynemouth NE29 ....31 B1
Corporation Rd SR2 ....86 F4
Corporation St 9 NE4 ....98 C1
Corporation Yd 9 NE61 ....3 F1
Corpus Christi RC Prim Sch
  NE8 ....70 E8
Correction House Bank
  NE30 ....42 C6
Corrighan Terr DH5 ....94 C4
Corrofell Gdns NE10 ....56 F1
Corry Ct SR4 ....85 E4
Corsair NE16 ....68 F6
Corsenside NE5 ....36 F1
Corstopitum 3 NE28 ....40 F4
Corstorphine Town NE33 ..42 B1
Cortina Ave SR4 ....85 D4
Corvan Terr DH9 ....79 A2
Cosford Ct NE3 ....37 C7
Cossack Terr SR4 ....85 E7
Cosser St NE24 ....17 E8
Cosserat Pl NE31 ....57 D7
Cosyn St NE6 ....56 A5
Cotehill Dr NE20 ....25 B4
Cotehill Rd 2 NE5 ....37 B1
Cotemede NE10 ....72 A5
Cotemede Ct NE10 ....72 A6
Cotfield Wlk NE8 ....101 A1
Cotgarth The NE10 ....71 E7
Cotherstone Ct SR3 ....86 B2
Cotman Gdns NE34 ....59 D2
Cotswold Ave
  Chester le S DH2 ....88 B1
  Longbenton NE12 ....29 B1
Cotswold Cl NE38 ....83 B4
Cotswold Dr
  Ashington NE63 ....6 F1
  Whitley Bay NE25 ....31 F3
Cotswold Gdns
  Dunston NE11 ....70 A7
  Newcastle-u-T NE7 ....39 A3
Cotswold La NE35 ....58 F2
Cotswold Rd
  Sunderland SR5 ....74 A2
  Tynemouth NE29 ....31 E2
Cotswold Sq SR5 ....74 A3
Cottage Farm NE7 ....39 D3
Cottage La NE5 ....37 D1
Cottenham Chare NE4 ..98 B1
Cottenham St NE4 ....98 B1
Cotter Riggs Pl NE5 ....36 B2
Cotter Riggs Wlk NE5 ....36 B2
Cotterdale NE10 ....72 A5
Cotterdale Ave NE6 ....39 F5
Cotterdale Cl 6 NE8 ....70 F8
Cottersdale Gdns NE5 ....36 B3
Cottingley NE10 ....72 A5
Cottingvale NE61 ....3 F2
Cottingwood Ct NE4 ....98 B2
Cottingwood Gdns
  Morpeth NE61 ....3 F1
  Newcastle-u-T NE4 ....98 B2
Cottingwood Gn NE24 ..17 C3
Cottingwood La NE61 ....3 F2
Cottonwood
  Shiney Row DH4 ....89 F6
  Silksworth SR3 ....91 E5
Coulson Cl NE46 ....44 E6
Coulson Park Fst Sch
  NE63 ....6 F2
Coulthards La NE8 ....101 C3
Coulthards Pl NE8 ....56 A4
Coulton Dr NE36 ....74 D7
Council Ave NE9 ....71 B8
Council Rd NE63 ....6 C2
Council Terr NE37 ....83 D7
Counden Rd 4 NE6 ....36 E3
Countess Ave NE26 ....32 A5
Countess Dr NE15 ....54 A7
Coupland Gr NE32 ....58 B3
Coupland Rd NE63 ....6 C3
Court Rd NE22 ....10 F1
Court The NE16 ....69 C6
Courtfield Rd NE6 ....56 F8
Courtney Ct NE3 ....37 B8
Courtney Dr SR3 ....91 F8
Cousin St SR1 ....103 C3
Coutts Rd NE6 ....56 E8
Cove The DH4 ....90 B6
Coventry Gdns
  Newcastle-u-T NE4 ....54 E4
  North Shields NE29 ....41 E4
Coventry Way SR3 ....92 A5
Coverdale Gateshead NE10 ..72 A6
  Wallsend NE28 ....39 F5
Coverdale Ave Blyth NE24 ..17 A7
  Washington NE37 ....83 C8
Coverdale Wlk SR3 ....59 C7
Coverley Rd SR5 ....74 B2
Covers The
  Longbenton NE12 ....39 E6
  Morpeth NE61 ....9 A7
  Wallsend NE28 ....40 B3
  Whickham NE16 ....53 F1
Cow La NE45 ....46 F7
Cowan Cl NE21 ....53 A4
Cowan Terr SR2 ....103 A2
Cowans Ave NE12 ....29 C4
Cowans Ho NE15 ....53 C7
Cowdray Ct NE3 ....37 C7
Cowdray Rd SR5 ....74 B2
Cowdrey Ho NE29 ....41 D3
Cowell Gr NE39 ....67 C2
Cowen Gdns NE9 ....71 A1
Cowen Rd NE21 ....53 D3
Cowen St Blaydon NE21 ..68 B8
  Newcastle-u-T NE6 ....56 F6
Cowen Terr NE39 ....67 F3

Cowgarth NE46 ....45 A5
Cowgate NE1 ....99 B1
Cowley Cres DH5 ....94 C4
Cowley Pl NE24 ....17 B8
Cowley Rd NE24 ....12 B1
Cowpath Gdns NE10 ....57 A1
Cowpen Hall Rd NE24 ..17 A8
Cowpen Rd NE24 ....17 C8
Coxfoot Cl NE34 ....59 C5
Coxgreen Rd DH4,SR4 ..84 B2
Coxlodge Rd NE3 ....38 A5
Coxlodge Terr NE3 ....38 A5
Coxon St Gateshead NE10 ..57 B2
  Sunderland SR2 ....103 B1
Coxon Terr NE8 ....56 C1
Crabtree Rd NE43 ....64 C7
Cradock Ave NE31 ....57 D4
Craggyknowe NE37 ....82 E6
Craghall Dene NE2 ....38 E4
Craghall Dene Ave NE2 ..38 E4
Cragleas NE16 ....79 A4
Cragside
  Brunswick Village NE13 ..28 B6
  Chester le S DH2 ....88 A4
  Corbridge NE45 ....47 B7
  Cramlington NE23 ....22 B4
  Newcastle-u-T NE7 ....39 B3
  South Shields NE34 ....60 B5
  Whitley Bay NE26 ....31 E7
Cragside Ave NE29 ....41 D8
Cragside CE Fst Sch
  NE23 ....22 B4
Cragside Ct Dunston NE11 ..70 A6
  4 Houghton-le-S DH5 ....94 F8
Cragside Gdns
  Bedlington NE22 ....11 C3
  Dunston NE11 ....70 A5
  Killingworth NE12 ....29 F4
  Wallsend NE28 ....40 F3
Cragside Ho NE3 ....91 D7
Cragside Prim Sch NE7 ..39 A3
Cragside Rd NE37 ....83 A7
Cragston Ave NE5 ....37 C3
Cragston Cl NE5 ....37 C2
Cragton Gdns NE24 ....17 B7
Craig Cres NE23 ....29 A8
Craig St 2 DH3 ....82 C4
Craigavon Rd SR5 ....74 B2
Craigend NE23 ....22 B5
Craighill DH4 ....90 A6
Craiglands The SR3 ....86 C3
Craigmill Pk NE24 ....17 A8
Craigmillar Ave NE5 ....37 C3
Craigmillar Cl NE5 ....37 C3
Craigmont Ct NE12 ....39 D6
Craigshaw Rd SR5 ....73 F3
Craigshaw Sq SR5 ....73 F3
Craigwell Dr SR3 ....92 A4
Craik Park (Morpeth Town
  AFC) NE61 ....8 D6
Crake Way NE38 ....82 F2
Cramer St NE8 ....101 C1
Cramlington Beaconhill Fst
  Sch NE23 ....21 E6
Cramlington Com High Sch
  NE23 ....22 A4
Cramlington Eastlea Fst Sch
  NE23 ....22 C8
Cramlington Hareside Fst
  Sch NE23 ....22 A5
Cramlington Hillcrest Sch
  NE23 ....22 B6
Cramlington Kramel Fst Sch
  NE23 ....22 B5
Cramlington Parkside Mid
  Sch NE23 ....22 B7
Cramlington Rd SR5 ....73 F2
Cramlington Shanklea Fst
  Sch NE23 ....21 F7
Cramlington Sq SR5 ....73 F2
Cramlington Sta NE23 ....21 F7
Cramlington Terr
  2 Blyth NE24 ....17 C4
  16 Shiremoor NE27 ....30 E1
Cramond Ct NE9 ....70 E3
Cramond Way NE23 ....22 B4
Cranberry Dr NE38 ....83 E3
Cranberry Rd SR5 ....74 B2
Cranberry Sq SR5 ....74 A2
Cranborne SR3 ....91 C6
Cranbourne Gr NE30 ....32 B3
Cranbrook SR3 ....86 A3
Cranbrook Ave NE3 ....38 C7
Cranbrook Ct NE3 ....37 E7
Cranbrook Dr NE42 ....50 B2
Cranbrook Rd NE15 ....54 B4
Cranemarsh Cl NE40 ....6 C1
Craneshaugh Cl NE46 ..45 B4
Cranesville NE9 ....71 C5
Craneswater Ave NE26 ..24 F1
Cranfield Pl NE15 ....53 C7
Cranford Gdns NE15 ....53 E7
Cranford St NE34 ....59 C6
Cranford Terr SR4 ....102 A1
Cranham Cl NE12 ....29 F4
Cranlea NE3 ....37 C2
Cranleigh Av NE3 ....37 C7
Cranleigh Gr NE42 ....50 D3
Cranleigh Pl NE25 ....31 D6
Cranleigh Rd SR5 ....74 A2
Cranleigh SR5 ....22 C5
Cranston Pl SR2 ....93 A6
Crantock Rd NE3 ....37 F5
Crantock Rd NE3 ....37 F5
Cranwell Ct NE3 ....37 C7
Cranwell Dr NE13 ....28 B6

Craster Ave
Longbenton NE12 . . . . .29 F1
Shiremoor NE27 . . . . .30 F3
South Shields NE34 . . . . .60 B8
Craster Cl Blyth NE24 . . . . . .17 C7
Whitley Bay NE25 . . . . .31 D7
Craster Ct NE11 . . . . .70 C6
Craster Gdns NE28 . . . . .40 F3
Craster Rd NE29 . . . . .41 D5
Craster Sq NE3 . . . . .38 A6
Craster Terr NE7 . . . . .39 B2
Crathie DH3 . . . . .82 C7
Crathorne Ct NE16 . . . . .78 F6
Craven Ct SR6 . . . . .75 F1
Crawcrook La NE40,NE41 . .51 D5
Crawcrook Terr NE41 . . . . . .51 E3
Crawford Cotts NE61 . . . . . .4 A1
Crawford Ct SR3 . . . . .91 F6
Crawford Pl NE25 . . . . .31 E4
Crawford St NE24 . . . . .12 D1
Crawford Terr
Morpeth NE61 . . . . .4 A1
Newcastle-u-T NE6 . . . . .56 F5
Crawhall Cres NE61 . . . . . . .8 F2
Crawhall Rd NE1 . . . . .99 C1
Crawley Ave NE31 . . . . .57 D3
Crawley Gdns NE16 . . . . . . .69 C7
Crawley Rd NE28 . . . . .40 B1
Crawley Sq NE31 . . . . .57 D3
Craythorne Gdns NE6 . . . . .39 D2
Creevelea NE38 . . . . .83 C3
Creighton Ave NE3 . . . . .37 E4
Creland Way NE5 . . . . .37 C3
Crescent Ave NE46 . . . . .44 F5
Crescent The
Chester le S DH2 . . . . .88 B3
Cleadon SR6 . . . . .74 F8
5 Dunston NE11 . . . . .69 F8
Hetton le H DH5 . . . . .95 A3
High Spen NE39 . . . . .66 F3
Jarrow NE32 . . . . .58 A4
Kibblesworth NE11 . . . . .81 C6
Morpeth NE61 . . . . .8 F6
New Silksworth SR3 . . . . . . .86 A1
Newbottle DH4 . . . . .90 D4
Newcastle-u-T NE7 . . . . .39 B5
Newcastle-u-T,Kenton Bankfoot
NE13 . . . . .37 B6
Ponteland NE20 . . . . .25 A3
Rowlands Gill NE39 . . . . . . .67 F2
Ryton NE40 . . . . .52 D5
Seghill NE23 . . . . .22 F1
Shiney Row DH4 . . . . .90 A5
South Shields NE34 . . . . . . .59 F5
Sunniside NE16 . . . . .69 B2
9 Throckley NE15 . . . . . . .35 D2
Tynemouth NE30 . . . . .42 C8
Wallsend NE28 . . . . .40 B3
Whickham NE16 . . . . .69 C6
Whitley Bay NE26 . . . . .32 B4
Wylam NE41 . . . . .51 B5
Crescent Vale NE26 . . . . . . .32 A4
Crescent Way NE12 . . . . . . .39 E8
Crescent Way N NE12 . . . . .39 E8
Crescent Way S NE12 . . . . .39 E8
Cressbourne Ave **5** SR6 . .75 E1
Cresswell Ave
Longbenton NE12 . . . . .29 F1
Seaton Sluice NE26 . . . . . . .24 C6
Tynemouth NE29 . . . . .41 F7
Cresswell Cl Blaydon NE21 .68 A8
Whitley Bay NE25 . . . . .31 E3
Cresswell Dr Blyth NE24 . . .17 B7
Newcastle-u-T NE3 . . . . .37 E7
Cresswell Home Farm Cotts
NE61 . . . . .2 B4
Cresswell Rd Ellington NE61 .1 E6
Wallsend NE28 . . . . .40 A1
Cresswell St NE6 . . . . .56 D6
Cresswell Terr
Ashington NE63 . . . . .6 C4
Sunderland SR2 . . . . .102 C1
Crest The Bedlington NE22 .10 E1
Dinnington NE13 . . . . .27 B7
Seaton Sluice NE26 . . . . . . .24 E4
Cresthaven NE10 . . . . .71 E6
Crichton Ave DH3 . . . . .88 D1
Cricket Terr NE16 . . . . .79 A6
Cricklewood Dr DH4 . . . . . .90 B6
Cricklewood Rd SR5 . . . . . .74 A1
Criddle St NE8 . . . . .56 A4
Crieff Gr NE32 . . . . .58 D3
Crieff Sq SR5 . . . . .73 F2
Crigdon Hill NE5 . . . . .36 F1
Crighton NE38 . . . . .83 A5
Crimdon Dr DH4 . . . . .94 C7
Crimea Rd SR5 . . . . .73 F2
Crindledykes NE38 . . . . .83 E2
Cripps Ave NE10 . . . . .72 B8
Crocus Cl NE21 . . . . .53 A2
Croft Ave Longbenton NE12 .39 E7
Sunderland SR4 . . . . .102 A2
Wallsend NE28 . . . . .40 C4
Croft Cl NE40 . . . . .52 D4
Croft Cotts NE43 . . . . .64 D7
Croft Ho NE42 . . . . .50 A4
Croft Rd NE24 . . . . .17 E7
Croft St NE1 . . . . .99 B1
Croft Terr
18 Hexham NE46 . . . . . . .45 A4
Horsley NE15 . . . . .50 C8
Jarrow NE32 . . . . .58 B6
Croft The Hexham NE46 . . .44 F5
Killingworth NE12 . . . . .29 E4

Croft The continued
Nedderton NE22 . . . . .15 A8
Newcastle-u-T NE3 . . . . .38 A4
Ryton NE40 . . . . .52 D4
Sherburn Hill DH6 . . . . .96 D1
Croft View
Crawcrook NE40 . . . . .51 E3
Ovingham NE42 . . . . .50 B4
Croft Villas **2** NE40 . . . . . .51 E3
Croft's La NE15 . . . . .50 C8
Croftdale Rd NE21 . . . . .53 B2
Crofter Cl NE23 . . . . .22 A1
Crofthead Dr NE23 . . . . .22 B4
Crofton Mill Ho **2** NE24 . .17 F7
Crofton Mill Ind Est NE24 .17 F7
Crofton St Blyth NE24 . . . . . .17 E7
South Shields NE34 . . . . . . .59 C6
Crofton Way NE15 . . . . .53 B7
Crofts Ave NE45 . . . . .47 B5
Crofts Cl NE45 . . . . .47 B5
Crofts Pk NE61 . . . . .9 E5
Crofts The NE20 . . . . .25 F6
Crofts Way NE45 . . . . .47 A6
Croftside DH3 . . . . .82 C5
Croftside Ave **2** SR6 . . . . .75 F8
Croftside Ho
4 Silksworth SR3 . . . . . . .91 F5
Whitburn SR6 . . . . .60 F1
Croftsway NE4 . . . . .54 F4
Croftway Fst Sch NE24 . . . .17 E6
Croftwell Cl NE21 . . . . .53 D1
Cromarty DH2 . . . . .81 F2
Cromarty St SR6 . . . . .75 D2
Cromdale Pl NE5 . . . . .36 F3
Cromer Ave NE9 . . . . .70 F3
Cromer Ct NE9 . . . . .71 A3
Cromer Gdns
Newcastle-u-T NE2 . . . . .38 E3
Whitley Bay NE26 . . . . .32 A6
Crompton Rd NE6 . . . . .56 B8
Cromwell Ave NE21 . . . . . . .53 B2
Cromwell Ct
Newcastle-u-T NE10 . . . . . . .57 C2
Ryton NE21 . . . . .53 A4
Cromwell Pl NE21 . . . . .53 A4
Cromwell Rd
Gateshead NE10 . . . . .57 B2
Whickham NE16 . . . . .69 C8
Cromwell St
Gateshead NE8 . . . . .56 A4
Ryton NE21 . . . . .53 A4
Sunderland SR4 . . . . .102 A3
Cromwell Terr
Gateshead NE8 . . . . .101 A1
Newcastle-u-T NE10 . . . . . . .57 B2
North Shields NE29 . . . . .41 F6
Crondall St NE33 . . . . .59 D7
Cronin Ave NE34 . . . . .59 B4
Cronniewell NE17 . . . . .77 B5
Crookham Gr NE61 . . . . .9 B5
Crookham Rd NE23 . . . . . . .22 C4
Crookhill Com Prim Sch
NE40 . . . . .52 E5
Crookhill Terr NE40 . . . . . . .52 E4
Croome Gdns NE61 . . . . . . .4 F4
Cropthorne NE10 . . . . .72 B6
Crosby Gdns NE9 . . . . .71 B3
Crosland Pk NE23 . . . . .15 F2
Cross Ave NE28 . . . . .39 F4
Cross Carliol St NE1 . . . . . .99 B1
Cross Dr NE40 . . . . .52 C6
Cross Keys La NE9 . . . . .70 F5
Cross La Dunston NE11 . . . .54 D2
Kibblesworth NE11 . . . . .70 B4
Cross Morpeth St NE2 . . . . .98 B4
Cross Par NE4 . . . . .100 B4
Cross Pl **1** SR1 . . . . .103 B3
Cross Rigg Cl
Penshaw DH4 . . . . .90 A7
Shiney Row DH4 . . . . .89 F7
Cross Row Gateshead NE8 .56 B1
Ryton NE40 . . . . .52 E4
Cross Sheraton St NE2 . . . .98 B4
Cross St
8 Fence Houses DH4 . . . .94 A8
Gateshead NE8 . . . . .101 C1
High Pittington DH6 . . . . . . .96 D3
Houghton-le-S DH4 . . . . . . .90 D1
Newcastle-u-T NE1 . . . . .99 A1
Newcastle-u-T,St Ann's NE6 .56 A5
Prudhoe NE42 . . . . .50 D3
Cross Terr NE39 . . . . .67 D1
Cross Vale Rd SR2 . . . . .86 C4
Cross Villa Place No 1
NE4 .98 C1
Cross Villa Place No 2
NE4 .98 C1
Cross Villa Place No 3
NE4 .98 C1
Cross Villa Place No 4
NE4 .98 B1
Cross Villa Place No 5
NE4 .98 B1
Cross Way The NE61 . . . . . .8 F6
Crossbank Rd NE5 . . . . .37 D3
Crossbrook Rd **2** NE5 . . . .37 D2
Crossby Ct SR2 . . . . .103 C1
Crossfell NE20 . . . . .25 C4
Crossfell Gdns NE62 . . . . . .11 A8
Crossfield Pk NE10 . . . . .71 C6
Crossfield Terr NE6 . . . . .57 A4
Crossgate NE33 . . . . .42 C2
Crossgate Rd DH5 . . . . .95 A2
Crossgill NE37 . . . . .83 B7
Crosshill Rd NE15 . . . . .54 B4
Crosslaw NE5 . . . . .36 F1
Crosslea Ave SR3 . . . . .86 B3

Crossley Terr
Longbenton NE12 . . . . .29 F1
Newcastle-u-T NE4 . . . . .98 A2
Crossway Gateshead NE9 . .71 B6
Guide Post NE62 . . . . .10 F7
Newcastle-u-T NE2 . . . . .38 E3
South Shields NE34 . . . . . . .60 A5
Tynemouth NE30 . . . . .42 C8
Crossway Ct NE5 . . . . .37 F3
Crossway The
Newcastle-u-T,Kenton NE3 . .37 F4
Newcastle-u-T,Lemington
NE15 . . . . .53 D7
Crossway Villas **1** NE9 . . .71 A6
Crossways
East Boldon NE36 . . . . .74 E7
Hedworth NE32 . . . . .58 C1
New Silksworth SR3 . . . . . . .91 F7
Crossways The NE13 . . . . . .28 A4
Crosthwaite Gr SR5 . . . . . . .74 A1
Croudace Rd **2** NE10 . . . .71 D8
Crow Bank NE28 . . . . .40 C2
Crow Hall La NE23 . . . . .21 F7
Crow Hall Rd NE23 . . . . .15 F1
Crow La SR3 . . . . .91 B7
Crowhall La NE10 . . . . .71 D8
Crowhall Twrs **7** NE10 . . .71 D8
Crowley Ave NE16 . . . . .69 C8
Crowley Gdns NE21 . . . . . . .53 C2
Crowley Rd NE21 . . . . .54 A1
Crowley Villas **2** NE21 . . .54 A1
Crown & Anchor Cotts
NE15 . . . . .50 C8
Crown Rd SR5 . . . . .75 A1
Crown St Blyth NE24 . . . . . . .17 F7
12 Morpeth NE61 . . . . . . .9 A8
Crown Terr NE40 . . . . .52 B1
Crowther Ind Est
Birtley NE37 . . . . .82 F4
Washington NE38 . . . . .82 F5
Crowther Rd NE38 . . . . .82 F5
Crowtree L Ctr SR1 . . . . . . .102 C2
Crowtree Rd SR1 . . . . .102 C3
Croxdale Ct **3** NE34 . . . . .59 A5
Croxdale Gdns NE10 . . . . . .57 A2
Croxdale Terr
Gateshead NE10 . . . . .57 A1
Greenside NE40 . . . . .52 C1
Croydon Rd NE4 . . . . .98 A2
Crozier St SR5 . . . . .75 C1
Cruddas Pk NE4 . . . . .100 A4
Cruddas Pk Sh Ctr NE4 . . .100 A4
Crudwell Cl NE35 . . . . .58 E2
Crummock Ave SR6 . . . . . . .75 F6
Crummock Ct NE28 . . . . . . .41 A4
Crummock Rd NE5 . . . . .54 B8
Crumstone Ct NE12 . . . . . . .29 E4
Crusade Wlk NE32 . . . . .58 A5
Cty Cricket Gd NE2 . . . . . . .99 C4
Cuba St NE32 . . . . .58 A4
Cuillin Cl NE38 . . . . .83 B3
Culford Pl NE28 . . . . .40 E6
Cullercoats Prim Sch
NE30 . . . . .32 C3
Cullercoats Rd SR5 . . . . . . .73 F1
Cullercoats Sq SR5 . . . . . . .73 F1
Cullercoats St NE6 . . . . .56 F6
Cullercoats Sta NE30 . . . . . .32 C3
Culloden Wlk NE12 . . . . .29 D4
Culzean Rd **6** SR3 . . . . . . .91 D7
Cumberland Ave
Bedlington NE22 . . . . .10 E1
Newbiggin-by-t-S NE64 . . . .7 D4
Cumberland Pl
Birtley DH3 . . . . .82 D1
South Shields NE34 . . . . . . .60 B7
Cumberland Rd
New Silksworth SR3 . . . . . . .92 A8
Shiremoor NE27 . . . . .41 B7
Cumberland St
Sunderland SR1 . . . . .103 A3
Wallsend NE28 . . . . .40 C2
Wallsend,Willington Quay
NE28 . . . . .41 B1
Cumberland Way NE37 . . . .72 D2
Cumberland Wlk NE7 . . . . .39 B4
Cumbria Wlk NE4 . . . . .98 A1
Cumbrian Ave
Chester le S DH2 . . . . .88 C2
Sunderland SR5 . . . . .75 C5
Cumbrian Gdns NE11 . . . . .70 A6
Cummings St NE24 . . . . . . .17 E8
Curlew Cl Ashington NE63 . .11 E8
Longbenton NE12 . . . . .39 A7
Ryton NE40 . . . . .52 A5
Washington NE38 . . . . .83 A2
Curlew Hill NE61 . . . . .3 D2
Curlew Ho NE33 . . . . .42 D3
Curlew Rd Jarrow NE32 . . . .58 C8
Jarrow NE32 . . . . .58 D8
Curlew Way NE24 . . . . .17 E4
Curly Kews NE61 . . . . .4 A5
Curran Ho NE32 . . . . .58 C8
Curren Gdns NE10 . . . . .56 C2
Curtis Rd NE4 . . . . .54 F7
Curzon Pl **6** NE5 . . . . .37 B2
Curzon Rd W NE28 . . . . . . .40 B1
Curzon St NE8 . . . . .70 E8
Curzon Terr NE10 . . . . .56 C5
Cut Bank NE1 . . . . .56 A5
Cut Throat La NE17,NE39 . .77 C4
Cuthbert Ct NE32 . . . . .58 C3
Cuthbert St
Gateshead NE8 . . . . .101 A2
Hebburn NE31 . . . . .57 D7
Sunniside NE16 . . . . .69 A1
Cuthbert Wlk NE3 . . . . .38 E5

Cuthbertson Ct SR6 . . . . . .75 E5
Cutting St **3** SR7 . . . . .92 F1
Cygnet Cl Ashington NE63 . .11 D8
Newcastle-u-T NE5 . . . . .36 D4
Cyncopa Way NE5 . . . . .37 D2
Cypress Ave NE4 . . . . .54 D8
Cypress Cres Blyth NE24 . .17 F7
Dunston NE11 . . . . .70 A7
Cypress Dr NE24 . . . . .17 E7
Cypress Gdns Blyth NE24 . .17 E7
Killingworth NE12 . . . . .29 C4
Cypress Gr NE40 . . . . .52 C6
Cypress Rd Blaydon NE21 . .53 C2
Gateshead NE9 . . . . .71 D2
Cypress Sq **12** SR3 . . . . . .92 A8
Cyprus Gdns NE9 . . . . .71 A6

D

D'arcy Ct SR1 . . . . .103 B2
Dacre Ct NE25 . . . . .31 D7
Dacre St NE61 . . . . .4 A1
Dacre Rd SR6 . . . . .75 D4
Dacre St Morpeth NE61 . . . .3 F1
South Shields NE33 . . . . . . .59 C8
Daffodil Cl NE21 . . . . .53 B2
Dahlia Ct SR4 . . . . .102 B3
Dahlia Pl NE4 . . . . .54 D7
Dahlia Way NE31 . . . . .57 E4
Dainton Cl DH4 . . . . .90 C6
Dairnbrook **7** NE37 . . . . . .83 A6
Dairy La DH4 . . . . .94 C8
Daisy Cotts **10** DH3 . . . . .82 C4
Dalamere Cl NE38 . . . . .89 B7
Dale Rd NE25 . . . . .31 D4
Dale St Cambois NE24 . . . . .12 E1
Newcastle-u-T NE4 . . . . .54 F8
South Shields NE33 . . . . . . .61 D3
Dale Terr SR6 . . . . .75 E3
Dale Top NE25 . . . . .23 F1
Dale View Gdns NE40 . . . . .51 F3
Dalegarth Gr SR6 . . . . .75 C5
Dales The NE5 . . . . .37 E2
Dalla St SR4 . . . . .85 A7
Dally Mews NE3 . . . . .28 B1
Dalmahoy NE37 . . . . .72 D3
Dalmatia Terr NE24 . . . . . . .17 E6
Dalston Pl NE24 . . . . .17 E4
Dalton Ave NE61 . . . . .2 A3
Dalton Ct NE23 . . . . .22 B6
Dalton Cres **28** NE6 . . . . .56 B6
Dalton Ct NE28 . . . . .39 F5
Dalton Pl
Newcastle-u-T NE5 . . . . .36 C3
Sunderland SR4 . . . . .102 B2
Dalton St
Newcastle-u-T NE6 . . . . .56 B5
Newcastle-u-T NE6 . . . . .56 B6
Dalton Terr NE17 . . . . .77 B8
Dalton Way NE40 . . . . .90 A7
Daltons La NE33 . . . . .42 B2
Dame Allan's Boys Sch
NE4 .54 E7
Dame Allan's Girls Sch
NE4 .54 E7
Dame Dorothy Cres **5**
SR6 .75 E1
Dame Dorothy Prim Sch
SR6 .103 B4
Dame Dorothy St SR6 . . . . .103 A4
Dame Flora Robson Ave
NE34 . . . . .58 F4
Dame Margaret Hall
NE38 . . . . .83 E5
Damside **8** NE61 . . . . .9 A8
Danby Cl Silksworth SR3 . . .92 B6
Washington NE38 . . . . .88 F8
Danby Gdns NE6 . . . . .39 C3
Danville Rd SR6 . . . . .75 E4
Darden Cl NE12 . . . . .29 F4
Darden Lough NE5 . . . . .36 F1
Darenth St NE34 . . . . .59 C6
Darien Ave SR6 . . . . .75 D4
Dark La NE61 . . . . .4 A1
Darley Cl **15** SR3 . . . . .91 F6
Darley Pl NE15 . . . . .54 A5
Darnell Pl NE4 . . . . .98 B2
Darnley Rd NE63 . . . . .6 C3
Darras Ct NE33 . . . . .42 D1
Darras Dr NE29 . . . . .41 C7
Darras Hall Fst Sch NE20 .25 C3
Darras Mews NE20 . . . . .25 C4
Darras Rd NE20 . . . . .25 D4
Darrell St NE13 . . . . .28 A6
Dartford Cl NE25 . . . . .23 E3
Dartford Rd
South Shields NE33 . . . . . . .42 F2
Sunderland SR6 . . . . .75 D4
Dartmouth Ave NE9 . . . . . . .70 F2
Darvall Cl NE25 . . . . .31 D7
Darwin Cres NE3 . . . . .38 A4
Darwin St SR5 . . . . .74 F2
Daryl Cl NE21 . . . . .53 A1
Daryl Way NE10 . . . . .72 D8
Davenport Dr NE3 . . . . .28 B1
Davenport Sch DH5 . . . . . . .94 D7
David Adams Ho **7** NE5 .54 D5
David Gdns SR6 . . . . .75 F3
David St NE28 . . . . .40 B2
David Terr **3** NE40 . . . . . . .51 F3
Davidson Cotts NE2 . . . . . . .38 E1
Davidson Rd NE10 . . . . .57 B2
Davidson St NE10 . . . . .71 D8
Davison Ave
New Silksworth SR3 . . . . . . .92 B7
Whitley Bay NE26 . . . . .31 F6
Davison St Blyth NE24 . . . . .17 E8

Davison St continued
Boldon Colliery NE35 . . . . . .58 A1
Newburn NE15 . . . . .52 E8
Davison Terr **3** SR5 . . . . . .75 A2
Davy Bank NE28 . . . . .40 D1
Dawlish Cl NE29 . . . . .41 D8
Dawlish Gdns NE9 . . . . .70 F3
Dawlish Pl NE5 . . . . .36 C3
Dawson Pl NE61 . . . . .3 F1
Dawson Sq **4** NE30 . . . . . .42 D7
Dawson St **5** NE6 . . . . . . .57 A6
Dawson Terr SR4 . . . . .85 A7
Daylesford Dr NE3 . . . . .38 F4
Daylesford Rd NE23 . . . . . . .16 A2
Dayshield NE5 . . . . .36 F1
De Merley Rd NE61 . . . . .3 F1
De Mowbray Way NE61 . . . .3 D2
De Walden Sq NE61 . . . . . . .4 E3
De Walden Terr NE61 . . . . . .4 F3
Deacon Cl NE15 . . . . .36 B2
Deacon Ct NE12 . . . . .39 A7
Deaconsfield Cl SR3 . . . . . . .91 F5
Deadridge La NE45 . . . . .47 B7
Deal Cl NE24 . . . . .17 E4
Dean Cl **8** NE24 . . . . .17 D8
Dean Ho NE6 . . . . .57 A8
Dean Rd
South Shields NE33 . . . . . . .59 B7
South Shields,Dean NE33 . .59 C8
Dean St Gateshead NE9 . . . .71 F1
Hexham NE46 . . . . .45 C5
Newcastle-u-T NE1 . . . . .99 B1
Dean Terr Ryton NE40 . . . . .52 C5
South Shields NE33 . . . . . . .59 B7
Sunderland SR5 . . . . .75 A1
Dean View Dr NE24 . . . . . . .17 B8
Deanery St NE22 . . . . .10 F1
Deanham Gdns NE5 . . . . . . .54 D8
Deans Ave NE64 . . . . .7 C5
Deans Cl **1** NE16 . . . . .69 B7
Deansfield Gr NE15 . . . . . . .36 B3
Deansfield St SR3 . . . . .91 F5
Dearham Gr NE23 . . . . .16 A2
Debden Ho **7** NE11 . . . . . .70 A8
Debdon Gdns NE6 . . . . .39 D1
Debdon Pl NE23 . . . . .22 A6
Debdon Rd NE63 . . . . .6 F2
Debussy Ct NE32 . . . . .58 C6
December Ctyd NE8 . . . . . .100 B2
Deckham St **11** NE8 . . . . .71 A8
Deckham Terr NE8,NE9 . . . .71 A8
Dee Rd NE31 . . . . .57 F3
Dee St NE32 . . . . .58 C7
Deel Ho **2** NE9 . . . . .71 F2
Deepbrook Rd **5** NE5 . . . .37 C1
Deepdale Wallsend NE28 . .39 F5
Washington NE38 . . . . .83 A1
Deepdale Cl NE16 . . . . .68 F4
Deepdale Cres NE5 . . . . . . .37 E2
Deepdale Gdns NE12 . . . . . .29 C3
Deepdale Gn NE5 . . . . .37 E2
Deepdale Rd NE30 . . . . .32 E2
Deepdale St DH5 . . . . .95 A2
Deepdene Gr SR6 . . . . .75 E5
Deepdene Rd SR6 . . . . .75 D5
Deer Bush NE5 . . . . .36 F1
Deer Park Way NE21 . . . . . .53 E1
Deerbolt Pl NE12 . . . . .39 C7
Deerfell Cl NE63 . . . . .6 B2
Deerness Rd SR2 . . . . .103 B1
Dees Ave NE28 . . . . .40 B3
Defender Ct SR5 . . . . .85 C8
Defoe Ave NE34 . . . . .59 C3
Deighton Wlk NE5 . . . . .36 F1
Delacour Rd NE21 . . . . .53 C3
Delamere Cres NE23 . . . . . .16 A2
Delamere Ct **8** SR3 . . . . . .92 A6
Delamere Rd NE3 . . . . .37 F5
Delaval DH2 . . . . .88 B7
Delaval Ave
North Shields NE29 . . . . .41 E6
Seaton Delaval NE25 . . . . . .23 C3
Delaval Com Mid Sch
NE24 . . . . .17 D5
Delaval Com Prim Sch
NE24 . . . . .17 B5
Delaval Cres NE24 . . . . .17 B4
Delaval Ct
Bedlington NE22 . . . . .11 C2
Longbenton NE12 . . . . .29 E1
15 Sunderland SR3 . . . . .92 A6
Delaval Gdns Blyth NE24 . .17 B4
Newcastle-u-T NE15 . . . . . . .54 B4
Delaval Rd
Newcastle-u-T,Delaval NE15 .54 B4
Newcastle-u-T,Old Benwell
NE15 . . . . .54 B5
Whitley Bay NE26 . . . . .32 C4
Longbenton NE12 . . . . .29 D1
Delaval St NE24 . . . . .17 B4
Delaval Terr Blyth NE24 . . . .17 E8
Newcastle-u-T NE3 . . . . .38 A3
Delaval Trad Est NE25 . . . . .23 C5
Delhi Cres NE40 . . . . .52 A3
Delhi Gdns NE40 . . . . .52 A3
Delhi View NE40 . . . . .52 A3
Dell The Morpeth NE61 . . . .3 F2
Newbottle DH4 . . . . .90 D3
Dellfield Dr SR4 . . . . .85 A4
Della Bank Rd NE11 . . . . . . .54 C3
Delton Cl NE38 . . . . .83 C1
Demesne Dr NE22 . . . . .15 F8
Demesne The NE63 . . . . .7 B2
Dempsey Rd NE13 . . . . .28 B4
Denbigh Pl NE12 . . . . .39 C7
Denbigh Ave
Sunderland SR6 . . . . .75 D4
Wallsend NE28 . . . . .41 A3

Denbigh Com Prim Sch
NE28 . . . . .41 A3
Denby Cl NE23 . . . . .16 A2
Dene Ave
Brunswick Village NE13 . . . .28 A6
Hexham NE46 . . . . .45 C4
Houghton-le-S DH5 . . . . . .95 A7
Killingworth NE12 . . . . .29 A2
Newcastle-u-T,Denton Burn
NE15 . . . . .53 D7
Newcastle-u-T,South Gosforth
NE3 . . . . .38 E4
Rowlands Gill NE39 . . . . . .67 D1
Dene Bank View NE3 . . . .37 E3
Dene Cl Newcastle-u-T NE7 .39 A1
Ovingham NE42 . . . . .50 B5
Riding Mill NE44 . . . . .62 F8
Ryton NE40 . . . . .52 D5
Dene Cres
Newcastle-u-T NE3 . . . . . . .38 E4
Rowlands Gill NE39 . . . . . .67 D1
Ryton NE40 . . . . .52 D5
Wallsend NE28 . . . . .40 D2
Whitley Bay NE26 . . . . .31 F6
Dene Ct Birtley DH3 . . . . .82 C7
Hamsterley NE17 . . . . .77 B6
Newcastle-u-T NE7 . . . . . . .39 B1
Washington NE38 . . . . .83 C6
Dene Farm Cotts NE15 . . .35 E2
Dene Garth NE42 . . . . . . .50 A5
Dene Gdns
Gateshead NE10 . . . . .57 B1
Houghton-le-S DH5 . . . . . .94 F7
Newcastle-u-T NE15 . . . . . .53 D6
Whitley Bay NE25 . . . . .31 E5
Dene Gr
Newcastle-u-T NE3 . . . . . . .38 E4
Prudhoe NE42 . . . . .50 B3
Seghill NE23 . . . . .23 B2
Dene La Cleadon SR6 . . . .75 C7
Sunderland SR6 . . . . .75 D4
Dene Mews SR5 . . . . .74 C1
Dene Pk Hexham NE46 . . .45 C4
Ponteland NE20 . . . . .25 B3
Sunderland SR5 . . . . .74 C1
Dene Rd Blaydon NE21 . . . .53 D3
Guide Post NE62 . . . . .10 E7
Rowlands Gill NE39 . . . . . .67 D1
Sunderland SR5 . . . . .74 C1
Tynemouth NE30 . . . . .42 C8
Wylam NE41 . . . . .51 B7
Dene Side NE21 . . . . .53 D2
Dene St Hetton le H DH5 . .95 B6
Holywell NE25 . . . . .23 F2
New Silksworth SR3 . . . . . .86 A1
Prudhoe NE42 . . . . .50 E3
Sunderland SR4 . . . . .85 F7
Dene Terr Blaydon NE21 . . .53 B2
Jarrow NE32 . . . . .58 A4
Newburn NE15 . . . . .52 F8
Newcastle-u-T NE3 . . . . . . .38 E4
Ovington NE42 . . . . .49 D4
Riding Mill NE44 . . . . .62 F8
Dene Terr E NE41 . . . . . . .51 A7
Dene Terr W NE41 . . . . . . .51 A7
Dene The Medomsley DH8 .77 A2
West Rainton DH4 . . . . .94 A2
Whitley Bay NE25 . . . . .31 E5
Wylam NE41 . . . . .51 B6
Dene View Ashington NE63 . .6 B7
Bedlington NE22 . . . . .11 C1
Burnopfield NE16 . . . . .79 A6
Ellington NE61 . . . . .1 E4
High Spen NE39 . . . . .67 A3
Newcastle-u-T NE3 . . . . . . .38 E4
Rowlands Gill NE39 . . . . . .67 C2
Dene View Cres SR4 . . . . .85 B6
Dene View Ct NE24 . . . . . . .17 B7
Dene View Dr NE24 . . . . . .17 B8
Dene View E NE22 . . . . . . .11 C1
Dene View W NE22 . . . . . .16 B8
Dene Villas DH3 . . . . .88 B8
Denebank NE25 . . . . .31 E5
Deneburn NE10 . . . . .72 A7
Denecrest DH8 . . . . .77 A2
Denecroft NE41 . . . . .51 A6
Denefold NE9 . . . . .71 A1
Deneholm Wallsend NE28 .40 D3
Whitley Bay NE25 . . . . .31 E5
Denelands NE46 . . . . .45 C5
Deneside Dunston NE11 . . .69 F7
Hedworth NE32 . . . . .58 C1
Newcastle-u-T NE5 . . . . . . .36 F4
Newcastle-u-T,Denton Burn
NE15 . . . . .54 A7
Seghill NE23 . . . . .23 A2
South Shields NE34 . . . . . .60 C6
Deneside Ave NE9 . . . . . . .70 F4
Deneside Cl NE15 . . . . . . .35 D2
Deneside Ct
Newcastle-u-T NE4 . . . . . . .56 A8
Whitley Bay NE26 . . . . .31 E8
Denesyde DH8 . . . . .77 A2
Deneway NE39 . . . . .68 A4
Denewell Ave
Gateshead NE9 . . . . .70 F5
Newcastle-u-T NE7 . . . . . . .39 A3
Denewood NE12 . . . . .29 E2
Denewood Ct NE28 . . . . . .41 A2
Denham Ave SR6 . . . . .75 D4
Denham Dr NE25 . . . . .23 D2
Denham Gr NE21 . . . . .67 F8
Denham Wlk NE5 . . . . .36 C3
Denhill Pk NE15 . . . . .54 B6
Denholm Ave NE23 . . . . . .16 A2
Denholme Lodge NE11 . . .100 A1
Denmark Ctr 10 NE6 . . . . . .56 C7
Denmark Ctr 14 NE33 . . . .42 C3

Denmark St
Gateshead NE8 . . . . .101 C2
2 Newcastle-u-T NE6 . . . .56 C6
Dennison Cres DH3 . . . . . .82 C6
Denshaw Cl NE23 . . . . .16 B2
Dent Cl DH6 . . . . .97 E3
Dent St Blyth NE24 . . . . . . .17 F6
Sunderland SR4 . . . . .75 D4
Dentdale DH4 . . . . .89 E8
Denton Ave
Newcastle-u-T NE15 . . . . . .53 D6
North Shields NE29 . . . . . . .41 C6
Denton Chare NE1 . . . . . .101 A4
Denton Ct NE5 . . . . .54 A7
Denton Gate NE5 . . . . .37 A3
Denton Gdns NE15 . . . . . .54 C5
Denton Gr NE5 . . . . .37 A3
Denton Park Ho NE5 . . . . . .36 E2
Denton Park Sch Ctr NE5 . .36 E2
Denton Rd NE15 . . . . .53 F6
Denton View NE21 . . . . . . .53 B2
Denver Gdns NE6 . . . . .56 E5
Denway Gr NE26 . . . . .24 B7
Denwick Ave NE15 . . . . . . .53 C6
Denwick Terr NE30 . . . . . .42 C7
Depot Rd NE6 . . . . .56 D7
Deptford Rd
Gateshead NE8 . . . . .56 A4
Sunderland SR4 . . . . .102 B3
Deptford Terr SR4 . . . . . . .102 A4
Derby Cres NE31 . . . . .57 D5
Derby Ct NE4 . . . . .98 B2
Derby Gdns NE28 . . . . .40 A3
Derby St Jarrow NE32 . . . . .58 C7
Newcastle-u-T NE4 . . . . . . .98 B2
South Shields NE33 . . . . . .42 D5
Sunderland SR2 . . . . .102 C2
Derby Terr NE33 . . . . .42 D5
Dereham Cl NE26 . . . . .24 D5
Dereham Ct NE5 . . . . .37 B4
Dereham Rd NE26 . . . . . . .24 D5
Dereham Terr NE62 . . . . . .11 C8
Dereham Way NE29 . . . . . .41 B8
Derry Ave SR6 . . . . .75 E4
Derwent Ave
Gateshead NE11 . . . . .70 D5
Hebburn NE31 . . . . .57 E3
Newburn NE15 . . . . .52 E7
Rowlands Gill NE39 . . . . . .67 E1
Derwent Cote NE17 . . . . . .77 B5
Derwent Cres
Hamsterley NE17 . . . . .77 A7
Wickham NE16 . . . . .69 B8
Derwent Crook Dr NE9 . . . .70 E5
Derwent Ct
Gateshead NE11 . . . . .70 D5
Newcastle-u-T NE7 . . . . . . .39 A4
Derwent Gdns
Gateshead NE9 . . . . .71 A5
Wallsend NE28 . . . . .41 A4
Derwent Haven NE17 . . . . .77 B5
Derwent Rd Hexham NE46 .45 C4
Seaton Sluice NE26 . . . . . .24 C6
Tynemouth NE30 . . . . .32 B2
Derwent St
Blackhall Mill NE17 . . . . . . .77 C6
Chopwell NE17 . . . . .66 B1
Hetton le H DH5 . . . . .95 B2
Newcastle-u-T NE15 . . . . . .54 B5
Penshaw DH4 . . . . .90 B6
Sunderland SR1 . . . . .102 C2
Derwent Terr
Burnopfield NE16 . . . . .79 B7
South Hetton DH6 . . . . .97 E8
Washington NE38 . . . . .83 E4
Derwent Twr NE11 . . . . . .100 A1
Derwent Valley Cotts
NE39 . . . . .67 F1
Derwent Valley Villas
NE17 . . . . .77 A6
Derwent View
Blaydon NE21 . . . . .53 B1
Burnopfield NE16 . . . . .79 B6
Chopwell NE17 . . . . .66 C2
Derwent View Terr DH9 . . . .78 D1
Derwent Walk Cty Pk* NE16,NE21,NE39 . . . . .68 C5
Derwent Way
Blaydon NE21 . . . . .53 E1
Killingworth NE12 . . . . .29 C3
Derwentcote Steel Furnace*
NE17 . . . . .77 E6
Derwentdale Gdns NE7 . . .39 B3
Derwenthaugh Ind Est
NE16 . . . . .53 F3
Derwenthaugh Marina
NE21 . . . . .54 A3
Derwenthaugh Rd NE21 . . .54 A3
Derwentwater Ave 1
DH2 . . . . .88 B1
Derwentwater Ct NE8 . . . .101 A1
Derwentwater Gdns
NE16 . . . . .69 D7
Derwentwater Rd
Gateshead NE8 . . . . .100 C1
Newbiggin-by-t-S NE64 . . . . .7 C3
Gateshead NE8 . . . . .70 B8
Deuchar Ho NE2 . . . . .99 C3
Deuchar St NE2 . . . . .99 C4
Devon Ave NE16 . . . . .69 C7
Devon Cl NE63 . . . . .5 F4
Devon Cres DH3 . . . . .82 B6
Devon Dr SR3 . . . . .92 A8
Devon Gdns
Gateshead NE9 . . . . .70 F7
South Shields NE34 . . . . . .60 B7
Devon Rd Hebburn NE31 . . .57 F3

Devon Rd *continued*
Tynemouth NE29 . . . . .31 D1
Devon St Hetton le H DH5 . .94 F4
Penshaw DH4 . . . . .90 C6
Devon Wlk NE37 . . . . .72 D1
Devonport DH4 . . . . .90 C3
Devonshire Dr NE27 . . . . . .30 C1
Devonshire Gdns NE28 . . .40 A3
Devonshire Pl NE2 . . . . . . .38 F1
Devonshire St
South Shields NE33 . . . . . .59 B7
Sunderland SR5 . . . . .75 C1
Devonshire Terr
Newcastle-u-T NE2 . . . . . . .99 A3
7 Whitley Bay NE26 . . . . . .32 B4
Devonshire Twr 1 SR5 . . .75 D1
Dewberry Cl NE24 . . . . . . .17 C4
Dewhurst Terr 5 NE16 . . . .69 B2
Dewley NE23 . . . . .22 B5
Dewley Ct NE23 . . . . .22 B5
Dewley Pl NE5 . . . . .36 E4
Dewley Rd NE5 . . . . .37 B1
Dewsgreen NE23 . . . . .22 B6
Dexter Ho NE29 . . . . .41 D3
Dexter Way NE10 . . . . .71 C8
Deyncourt NE20 . . . . .25 D1
Deyncourt Cl NE20 . . . . . . .25 D1
Dial Cottage Mus* NE12 . . .29 C1
Diamond Ct NE3 . . . . .37 D5
Diamond Hall Jun & Inf Sch
SR4 . . . . .85 F7
Diamond Sq NE46 . . . . . . .45 B4
Diamond St NE28 . . . . .40 B2
Diana St NE4 . . . . .98 B1
Dibley Sq 5 NE6 . . . . .56 B5
Dibley St 6 NE6 . . . . .56 B5
Dick St 12 NE40 . . . . .51 F3
Dickens Ave
Biddick Hall NE34 . . . . .59 B3
Whickham NE16 . . . . .69 A8
Dickens St
Houghton-le-S DH4 . . . . . . .94 D8
Sunderland SR5 . . . . .75 A1
Dickens Wlk NE5 . . . . .36 C3
Dickson Dr NE46 . . . . .44 E3
Didcot Ave NE29 . . . . .41 E4
Didcot Way NE36 . . . . .73 E7
Dillon St NE32 . . . . .58 A5
Dilston Ave Hexham NE46 . .45 D4
Whitley Bay NE25 . . . . .32 B4
Dilston Cl Pegswood NE61 . . .5 A3
Shiremoor NE27 . . . . .30 D7
Washington NE38 . . . . .83 A4
Dilston Dr Ashington NE63 . .6 D2
Newcastle-u-T NE5 . . . . . . .36 E3
Dilston Gdns SR4 . . . . .85 F5
Dilston Haugh Cotts
NE45 . . . . .46 A4
Dilston Rd NE4 . . . . .98 A2
Dilston Terr Jarrow NE32 . . .58 C3
Newcastle-u-T NE3 . . . . . . .38 E4
Dilston West Cotts NE45 . . .46 C2
Dimbula Gdns NE7 . . . . . . .39 B2
Dimmont Pl NE23 . . . . .22 B5
Dimmington Fst Sch NE13 .27 C7
Dinsdale Ave NE28 . . . . . . .40 C4
Dinsdale Cotts 3 SR2 . . . . .92 F6
Dinsdale Pl NE2 . . . . .99 C3
Dinsdale Rd
Newcastle-u-T NE2 . . . . . . .99 C3
2 Newcastle-u-T NE2 . . . .75 E2
Dinsdale St SR2 . . . . .92 F6
Dinsdale St S SR2 . . . . . . .92 F6
Dipe La NE36 . . . . .73 F6
Dipton Ave NE4 . . . . .54 E4
Dipton Cl NE46 . . . . .45 E4
Dipton Gdns SR3 . . . . .86 B2
Dipton Gr NE23 . . . . .22 B6
Dipton Rd NE25 . . . . .31 D7
Dipwood Rd NE39 . . . . . . .67 E1
Dipwood Way NE39 . . . . . .78 D8
Discovery Ct SR3 . . . . .91 F7
Dishforth Gn NE9 . . . . .71 B1
Dispensary La 3 NE1 . . . . .99 A1
Disraeli St Blyth NE24 . . . . .17 D8
Blyth NE24 . . . . .17 E8
Fence Houses DH4 . . . . . . .94 B8
Disraeli Terr NE17 . . . . .66 B1
Dissington Pl
Newcastle-u-T NE5 . . . . . . .54 C8
Whickham NE16 . . . . .69 A5
Ditchburn Terr SR4 . . . . . . .85 F8
Dixon Ave DH8 . . . . .76 F4
Dixon Pl NE11 . . . . .69 F8
Dixon Rd DH5 . . . . .94 D6
Dixon St Gateshead NE8 . .100 C1
South Shields NE33 . . . . . .42 C1
Dixon's Sq SR6 . . . . .103 A4
Dobson Cl NE4 . . . . .100 B3
Dobson Cres NE6 . . . . .56 C4
Dock Rd NE29 . . . . .42 A4
Dock Rd S NE29 . . . . .42 A3
Dock St South Shields NE33 .59 B7
Sunderland SR1 . . . . .75 E1
Dockendale La NE16 . . . . . .69 C7
Dockendale Mews NE16 . . .69 C7
Dockray Cl NE30 . . . . .42 C6
Dockray Sq NE30 . . . . .42 B5
Doddfell Cl NE37 . . . . .90 D7
Doddington Cl NE15 . . . . . .53 B7
Doddington Dr NE23 . . . . . .22 B6
Doddington Villas NE10 . . .71 C7
Dodds Cl 3 SR5 . . . . .74 A3
Dodds Farm NE3 . . . . .38 A5
Dodds Terr DH3 . . . . .82 C6
Dodsworth N NE40 . . . . . . .52 B1
Dodsworth Terr NE40 . . . . .52 B1

Dodsworth Villas NE40 . . . .52 B1
Dog Bank NE1 . . . . .101 B4
Dogger Bank NE61 . . . . .3 E1
Dolphin Ct 1 NE4 . . . . .54 D5
Dolphin Quay NE29 . . . . . .42 B5
Dolphin St NE4 . . . . .54 D5
Dolphin Villas NE13 . . . . . .28 A4
Dominies Cl NE39 . . . . .67 F3
Don Dixon Dr NE32 . . . . . . .58 B1
Don Gdns
Washington NE37 . . . . .72 D1
West Boldon NE36 . . . . . . .73 F7
Don Rd NE32 . . . . .58 D7
Don St NE11 . . . . .70 C4
Don View NE36 . . . . .74 A7
Donald Ave DH6 . . . . .97 F8
Donald St NE3 . . . . .38 E5
Doncaster Rd NE2 . . . . .99 C3
Doncrest Rd NE37 . . . . .72 B1
Donkin Rd NE37 . . . . .82 F7
Donkin Terr
Crawcrook NE40 . . . . .51 E3
North Shields NE30 . . . . . . .42 C7
Donkins St NE35 . . . . .58 E1
Donnington Ho 2 SR3 . . . .91 D7
Donnington Cl SR5 . . . . . . .74 A1
Donnington Ct NE3 . . . . . . .38 F4
Donnison Gdns SR1 . . . . .103 B3
Donridge NE37 . . . . .72 B1
Donside NE10 . . . . .71 F4
Donvale Rd NE37 . . . . .72 A1
Dorcas Ave NE15 . . . . .54 C5
Dorcas Terr 8 NE37 . . . . . .83 D8
Dorchester Cl NE5 . . . . .36 B3
Dorchester Ct NE25 . . . . . .23 C6
Dorchester Gdns NE9 . . . . .70 F2
Doris Wilkes Ho NE6 . . . . . .56 B6
Dorking Ave NE29 . . . . .41 E4
Dorking Cl NE24 . . . . .17 C4
Dorking Rd NE6 . . . . .75 E4
Dornoch Cres NE10 . . . . . .71 C6
Dorrington Rd NE3 . . . . .37 E7
Dorset Ave Birtley DH3 . . . .82 D1
Hebburn NE31 . . . . .57 F5
South Shields NE34 . . . . . .60 B7
Sunderland SR6 . . . . .75 E4
Wallsend NE28 . . . . .40 A3
Dorset Cl NE63 . . . . .5 F4
Dorset Gr NE29 . . . . .31 D1
Dorset Rd Gateshead NE8 . .56 B1
Newcastle-u-T NE15 . . . . . .53 F6
Dorset St DH5 . . . . .97 C8
Dotland Cl NE46 . . . . .45 E4
Double Row NE25 . . . . .23 B5
Douglas Ave NE3 . . . . .38 A4
Douglas Bader Ho NE24 . . .17 F6
Douglas Cl NE34 . . . . .59 C4
Douglas Ct
Gateshead NE11 . . . . .70 E2
Sunderland SR3 . . . . .103 B3
Douglas Gdns NE11 . . . . . .70 A7
Douglas Par NE31 . . . . .58 A2
Douglas Rd SR6 . . . . .75 E4
Douglas St NE28 . . . . .41 A1
Douglas Terr
Newcastle-u-T NE4 . . . . . . .98 B1
Penshaw DH4 . . . . .90 C8
Washington NE37 . . . . .72 D1
Douglass St 7 NE28 . . . . . .40 B2
Dove Ave NE32 . . . . .58 C3
Dove Cl NE12 . . . . .29 C4
Dove Ct Birtley DH3 . . . . . .82 D5
Tynemouth NE30 . . . . .32 C3
Dove Ho NE30 . . . . .32 C3
Dove Row NE30 . . . . .32 C3
Dovecote Cl NE25 . . . . .31 C6
Dovecote Rd NE12 . . . . . . .39 E7
Dovecrest Ct 7 NE28 . . . . .40 F4
Dovedale Ave NE24 . . . . . . .17 A8
Dovedale Ct NE34 . . . . .59 A5
Dovedale Gdns
Gateshead NE9 . . . . .71 A4
Newcastle-u-T NE7 . . . . . . .39 B3
Dovedale Rd SR6 . . . . .75 C5
Dover Cl Bedlington NE22 . .10 D1
Newcastle-u-T NE5 . . . . . . .36 C3
Dovercourt Rd NE6 . . . . . . .57 A4
Dowdale Cl NE34 . . . . .59 A5
Downe Cl NE24 . . . . .17 E4
Downend Rd NE5 . . . . .36 B3
Downfield NE37 . . . . .72 D3
Downham NE5 . . . . .36 F3
Downham Ct NE33 . . . . .42 C1
Downhill Inf Sch NE34 . . . . .60 B7
Downhill La
Sunderland SR5,NE36 . . . . .73 F5
West Boldon NE36 . . . . . . .73 D4
Downing Dr NE61 . . . . .8 F7
Downs La DH5 . . . . .95 B5
Downs Pit La DH5 . . . . .95 C5
Downswood NE12 . . . . .29 F3
Doxford Ave DH5 . . . . .94 F6
Doxford Gdns 4 NE5 . . . . .37 D1
Doxford Park Way SR3 . . . .91 E5
Doxford Pl NE23 . . . . .22 B5
Doxford Terr DH5 . . . . .94 F6
Dr Pit Cotts NE22 . . . . .10 F1
Dr Ryman Ho NE6 . . . . .56 B4
Drake Cl NE33 . . . . .59 B8
Drawback NE42 . . . . .50 E2
Drawback Cl NE42 . . . . . . .50 D2
Drayton Rd
Newcastle-u-T NE3 . . . . . . .37 E4
Sunderland SR6 . . . . .75 D4
Drey The NE20 . . . . .25 B3
Drive Com Prim Sch The
NE10 . . . . .71 E8

Drive The Birtley DH3 . . . . .82 D1
Gateshead,Felling NE10 . . . .71 E8
Gateshead,Saltwell NE9 . . . .70 F6
Newcastle-u-T NE7 . . . . . . .39 B4
Newcastle-u-T,East Denton
NE5 . . . . .54 A8
Newcastle-u-T,Gosforth
NE3 . . . . .38 C3
Stannington NE61 . . . . .14 D6
Tranwell NE61 . . . . .8 D1
Tynemouth NE30 . . . . .42 D8
Wallsend NE28 . . . . .40 B2
Washington NE37 . . . . .72 C1
Whickham NE16 . . . . .69 C6
Drivecote NE10 . . . . .71 E8
Dronfield Cl 2 DH2 . . . . . . .88 A1
Drove Rd NE15 . . . . .35 B3
Drum Ind Est DH2 . . . . .88 B7
Drum Rd DH2,DH3 . . . . . . .88 B8
Drumaldrace 5 NE37 . . . . .83 A6
Drummond Cres NE34 . . . . .58 F5
Drummond Rd NE3 . . . . . . .37 F4
Drummond Terr NE30 . . . . .42 B6
Drumoyne Cl SR3 . . . . .91 B6
Drumoyne Gdns NE25 . . . .31 D3
Drumsheugh Pl NE5 . . . . . .37 B2
Druridge Ave SR6 . . . . .75 E5
Druridge Cres Blyth NE24 . .17 B5
South Shields NE34 . . . . . .60 B8
Druridge Dr Blyth NE24 . . . .17 B5
Newcastle-u-T NE5 . . . . . . .37 D1
Drury La
Newcastle-u-T NE1 . . . . . . .99 A1
Sunderland SR1 . . . . .103 B3
Tynemouth NE30 . . . . .41 C7
Drybeck Ct
Cramlington NE23 . . . . .22 A4
Newcastle-u-T NE4 . . . . . . .98 B1
Drybeck Sq SR3 . . . . .92 B6
Drybeck Wlk NE23 . . . . . . .22 D8
Dryborough St SR4 . . . . . .102 B3
Dryburgh NE38 . . . . .83 D5
Dryburgh Cl NE29 . . . . .41 E8
Dryden Cl NE34 . . . . .59 B2
Dryden Ct 3 NE9 . . . . .70 F7
Dryden Rd NE9 . . . . .70 F7
Dryden Road Hospl NE9 . . .70 F7
Dryden Sch NE9 . . . . .71 A7
Dryden St SR5 . . . . .75 A2
Drysdale Cres NE13 . . . . . .28 A6
Drysdale Ct NE13 . . . . .28 B6
Dubmire Cotts DH4 . . . . . . .94 A8
Dubmire Ct DH4 . . . . .94 A8
Dubmire Ind Est DH4 . . . . .90 B1
Dubmire Prim Sch DH4 . . . .94 A8
Duchess Cres NE32 . . . . . .58 B3
Duchess Cres E NE32 . . . . .58 B3
Duchess Dr NE15 . . . . .54 A7
Duchess St NE26 . . . . .32 A5
Duckets Dean NE42 . . . . . . .50 D3
Duckpool La NE16 . . . . .69 C7
Duckpool La N NE16 . . . . . .69 C7
Duddon Pl NE9 . . . . .71 B4
Dudley Ave SR6 . . . . .75 D4
Dudley Bsns Ctr NE22 . . . .22 A2
Dudley Dr NE23 . . . . .29 A8
Dudley Gdns SR3 . . . . .91 C7
Dudley Ho NE4 . . . . .98 B2
Dudley La Annitsford NE23 . .22 A4
Cramlington,Collingwood
NE23 . . . . .22 A4
Cramlington,Hall Close
NE23 . . . . .22 A6
Seaton Burn NE13,NE23 . . .28 D8
Dudley Lane Cotts NE13 . . .28 C8
Dugdale Ct 6 NE6 . . . . .57 A5
Dugdale Rd NE3 . . . . .37 D5
Duke of Northumberland Ct
9 NE37 . . . . .40 E5
Duke St Ashington NE63 . . . .6 C1
Gateshead NE8 . . . . .57 A1
Newcastle-u-T NE1 . . . . . .100 C1
North Shields NE29 . . . . . . .42 B4
Sunderland SR4 . . . . .102 A2
Whitley Bay NE26 . . . . .32 A5
**Duke St N SR6 . . . . .75 D2
Duke Wlk NE8 . . . . .100 C1
Duke's Ave NE31 . . . . .57 D4
Duke's Gdns NE24 . . . . .17 C8
Dukes Cott NE15 . . . . .35 A1
Dukes Ct NE42 . . . . .50 E4
Dukes Dr NE3 . . . . .28 B1
Dukes Mdw NE13 . . . . .28 A5
Dukes Rd NE46 . . . . .44 E5
Dukes Way NE42 . . . . .50 E4
Dukesfield NE23 . . . . .22 B6
Dukesway NE11 . . . . .70 C3
Dukesway Ct NE11 . . . . . . .70 C2
Dukesway W NE11 . . . . . . .70 C2
Dulverton Ct NE25 . . . . .36 C3
Dulverton Ave NE33 . . . . . .59 D7
Dulverton Ct NE22 . . . . .38 F2
Dumas Wlk NE5 . . . . .36 C3
Dumbarton Cl SR4 . . . . . . .85 D3
Dumbarton Cres NE32 . . . .58 E3
Dun Cow St NE1 . . . . .102 C3
Dunbar Cl NE5 . . . . .36 C3
Dunbar St SR4 . . . . .85 F5
Dunblane Cres NE5 . . . . . . .36 F1
Dunblane Dr NE24 . . . . .17 E4
Dunblane Rd SR6 . . . . .75 E4
Dunbreck Gr SR4 . . . . .86 A4
Duncan St Gateshead NE8 . .56 B1
Newcastle-u-T NE6 . . . . . . .57 A5

Duncan St continued
Sunderland SR4 .... 85 F7
Dunces Hos NE61 .... 9 D7
Dundas St SR6 .... 103 A4
Dundas Way NE10 .... 71 C8
Dundee Cl NE5 .... 36 C3
Dundee Ct NE32 .... 58 E3
Dundrennan NE38 .... 83 C3
Dunelm SR2 .... 86 B4
Dunelm Cl 6 DH3 .... 82 C4
Dunelm Dr
  Houghton-le-S DH4 .... 94 D7
  West Boldon NE36 .... 74 B8
Dunelm Rd DH5 .... 94 F4
Dunelm S SR4 .... 86 B4
Dunelm St NE33 .... 42 D2
Dunford Gdns NE5 .... 36 D4
Dunholme Cl DH5 .... 94 E7
Dunholme Rd NE4 .... 54 F5
Dunira Cl NE2 .... 38 F2
Dunira Ho NE2 .... 38 F2
Dunkeld Cl Blyth NE24 .... 17 E4
  Gateshead NE10 .... 72 B8
  Shiney Row DH4 .... 89 F5
Dunkirk Ave DH5 .... 94 F7
Dunlin Cl NE40 .... 52 E4
Dunlin Ct NE61 .... 2 A3
Dunlin Dr Blyth NE24 .... 17 E4
  Washington NE38 .... 82 F3
Dunlop Cl NE7 .... 39 C4
Dunlop Cres NE34 .... 60 A6
Dunmoor Cl NE3 .... 38 A4
Dunmoor Ct DH2 .... 88 A1
Dunmore Ave SR6 .... 75 E4
Dunmorlie St NE6 .... 56 D6
Dunn Ave SR3 .... 86 A1
Dunn St NE4 .... 100 B3
Dunn Street Prim Sch
  NE32 .... 58 C7
Dunn Terr NE6 .... 56 B6
Dunne Rd NE21 .... 53 E4
Dunning St SR1 .... 102 C3
Dunnington Ct SR3 .... 91 E6
Dunnock Dr
  Sunniside NE16 .... 69 A3
  Washington NE38 .... 82 F2
Dunnock Lodge NE15 .... 53 D6
Dunnykirk Ave 2 NE3 .... 37 D5
Dunscar DH4 .... 90 B1
Dunsdale Dr NE23 .... 22 D8
Dunsdale Rd NE25 .... 23 E2
Dunsgreen NE20 .... 25 E5
Dunsgreen Ct NE20 .... 25 E5
Dunsley Gdns NE13 .... 27 B7
Dunslow Croft NE15 .... 33 C1
Dunsmuir Gr NE8 .... 70 D8
Dunstable Pl NE5 .... 36 B3
Dunstan Cl DH2 .... 88 A1
Dunstan Wlk NE5 .... 36 F1
Dunstanburgh Cl
  Bedlington NE22 .... 10 D1
  Newcastle-u-T NE6 .... 56 D5
  Washington NE38 .... 83 B4
Dunstanburgh Ct
  Bournmoor DH4 .... 89 D1
  Gateshead NE10 .... 72 B7
  Jarrow NE32 .... 58 F5
Dunstanburgh Rd NE6 .... 56 D5
Dunster Ho 3 SR3 .... 91 D7
Dunston Bank NE11 .... 69 F7
Dunston Ent Pk NE11 .... 54 E2
Dunston Hill Com Prim Sch
  NE11 .... 69 F8
Dunston Hill Hospl NE11 .... 69 D7
Dunston Pl NE24 .... 17 B8
Dunston Rd NE11 .... 54 F1
Dunston Riverside Prim Sch
  NE11 .... 54 F2
Dunston Sta NE11 .... 70 A8
Dunston Workshops
  NE11 .... 54 F2
Dunvegan DH3 .... 82 E2
Dunvegan Ave DH2 .... 88 B1
Dunwoodie Terr 2 NE46 .... 45 A5
Duoro Terr SR2 .... 103 A1
Durant Rd NE1 .... 99 B2
Durban St NE24 .... 17 D8
Durham Ave NE37 .... 83 B8
Durham Cl NE22 .... 10 D2
Durham Ct NE31 .... 57 D5
Durham City Cricket Gd (The
  Riverside) DH3 .... 88 E2
Durham Dr NE32 .... 58 B2
Durham Gr NE32 .... 58 B2
Durham Ho SR5 .... 73 F4
Durham La Haswell DH6 .... 97 C1
  Sherburn Hill DH6 .... 96 D1
3 Gateshead NE10 .... 56 F1
Newcastle-u-T NE4 .... 54 F5
Wallsend NE28 .... 40 C2

Durham Street W NE28 .... 40 C2
Durham Terr SR3 .... 86 A1
Durken Bsns Pk NE23 .... 22 F2
Dutton Ct NE21 .... 53 E4
Duxbury Pk NE38 .... 89 D8
Duxfield Rd NE7 .... 39 B3
Dwyer Cres SR2 .... 92 F6
Dyer Sq SR5 .... 75 B2
Dyke Heads La NE40 .... 52 B1
Dykefield Ave NE3 .... 37 E7
Dykelands Rd NE33 .... 75 E5
Dykelands Way NE34 .... 58 F3
Dykenook Cl NE16 .... 69 A4
Dykes Way NE10 .... 71 D5
Dymock Ct NE3 .... 37 B5

E

E D Morel Terr NE17 .... 77 C8
Eaglescliffe Dr NE7 .... 39 D2
Eaglesdene DH5 .... 95 A4
Ealing Ct NE3 .... 37 B6
Ealing Dr NE30 .... 32 C1
Ealing Sq NE23 .... 21 D6
Eardulph Ave DH3 .... 88 D3
Earl Grey Way NE29 .... 41 F3
Earl St SR4 .... 102 B2
Earl's Dr NE15 .... 54 A7
Earl's Gdns NE24 .... 17 C8
Earlington Ct NE12 .... 29 E1
Earls Ct Gateshead DH98 .... 70 D5
  Prudhoe NE42 .... 50 E4
  Sunderland SR5 .... 75 A4
Earls Dene 5 NE9 .... 70 F4
Earls Dr NE9 .... 70 F4
Earls Gn DH5 .... 94 D3
Earls Pk N Trad Est NE11 .... 70 C7
Earls Ct NE23 .... 75 A4
Earlston Way NE23 .... 16 C2
Earlsway DH98,NE11,NE82 .... 70 D5
Earlswood Ave NE9 .... 70 F4
Earlswood Gr NE24 .... 17 D3
Earlswood Pk NE9 .... 70 F4
Earnshaw Way NE25 .... 31 D7
Earsdon Cl NE5 .... 37 A1
Earsdon Ct NE25 .... 31 D4
Earsdon Rd
  Houghton-le-S DH5 .... 94 F8
  Newcastle-u-T NE3 .... 37 E4
  Shiremoor NE27 .... 30 E4
  Whitley Bay NE25 .... 31 C4
Earsdon Terr
2 Ryhope SR2 .... 92 F6
3 Shiremoor NE27 .... 30 E4
Earsdon View NE27 .... 30 E1
Earth Balance * NE22 .... 11 C5
Easby Cl NE3 .... 38 D8
Easby Rd NE38 .... 83 D4
Easdale Ave NE3 .... 28 C1
Easedale NE26 .... 24 C6
Easedale Gdns NE9 .... 71 B3
Easington Ave
  Cramlington NE23 .... 16 C2
  Gateshead NE9 .... 71 C3
Easington Lane Inf Sch
  DH5 .... 97 D8
Easington St SR5 .... 102 C4
Easington St N SR5 .... 102 C4
East Acres Blaydon NE21 .... 53 D1
  Dinnington NE13 .... 27 C8
East Ave Longbenton NE12 .... 39 D6
  South Shields NE34 .... 60 A6
  Washington NE38 .... 83 B1
  Whitley Bay NE25 .... 31 E5
East Back Par SR2 .... 103 C1
East Bailey NE12 .... 29 F3
East Benton Cotts NE12 .... 39 E5
East Boldon Inf Sch
  NE36 .... 74 D7
East Boldon Jun Sch
  NE36 .... 74 D7
East Boldon Rd SR6 .... 59 F1
East Boldon Sta NE36 .... 74 E8
East Bridge St DH4 .... 83 E1
East Cl NE34 .... 60 A6
East Cleft Rd SR2 .... 102 B2
East Cres NE22 .... 11 D2
East Cross St SR1 .... 103 A3
East Dr Blyth NE24 .... 17 C4
  Cleadon SR6 .... 75 E8
East End NE26 .... 24 E4
East Farm Ct NE16 .... 69 C3
East Farm Terr NE23 .... 22 B6
East Fields SR6 .... 75 H8
East Ford Rd NE62 .... 11 C8
East Forest Hall Rd NE12 .... 39 E8
East Front NE2 .... 98 A4
East Gate Gateshead NE8 .... 101 D3
  Morpeth NE61 .... 9 A6
East George Potts St 8
  NE33 .... 42 D1
East George St NE30 .... 42 C6
East Gr SR4 .... 85 B5
East Grange
  Holywell NE25 .... 23 F2
  Sunderland SR5 .... 75 C3
East Hartford Sch NE23 .... 16 B3
East Herrington Prim Sch
  SR3 .... 91 C7
East Hill Rd NE8 .... 56 B1
East Holburn NE33 .... 42 E4
East Law DH8 .... 76 D1
East Lea Blaydon NE21 .... 68 C8
  Newbiggin-by-t-S NE64 .... 7 E5
East Loan NE61 .... 1 A6
East Moffett St 11 NE33 .... 42 D1
East Moor Rd SR4 .... 85 F7

East Oakwood NE46 .... 45 E8
East Par NE26 .... 32 B5
East Park Gdns NE21 .... 53 C1
East Park Rd NE9 .... 70 F6
East Park View NE24 .... 18 A7
East Pastures NE63 .... 6 B2
East Percy St NE30 .... 42 C6
East Rainton Prim Sch
  DH5 .... 94 C4
East Riggs NE22 .... 15 F8
East Sea View NE64 .... 7 F5
East St Chopwell NE17 .... 66 D1
  Gateshead NE8 .... 101 C3
  Hebburn NE31 .... 57 F7
  High Spen NE39 .... 66 F4
  Mickley Square NE43 .... 49 F1
  South Shields NE33 .... 42 C3
  Tynemouth NE30 .... 42 E7
  Whitburn SR6 .... 75 F8
East Stainton St 10 NE33 .... 42 D1
East Stevenson St 12
  NE33 .... 42 D1
East Tanfield Sta* DH9 .... 79 E2
East Terr Chopwell NE17 .... 77 C7
  Stakeford NE62 .... 11 C7
East Thorp NE5 .... 36 F5
East View
8 Bedlington NE22 .... 11 D3
  Blaydon NE21 .... 53 D3
  Boldon Colliery NE35 .... 73 F8
  Burnopfield NE16 .... 79 A6
  Crawcrook NE40 .... 51 E6
  Hebburn NE31 .... 57 F6
  Morpeth NE61 .... 9 A8
  New Hartley NE25 .... 23 C5
  Rowlands Gill NE39 .... 67 C2
  Ryhope SR2 .... 92 E6
1 Seaham SR7 .... 92 F1
  Seghill NE23 .... 22 F1
  Sherburn Hill DH6 .... 96 D1
  Stakeford NE62 .... 11 C7
  Sunderland,Castletown SR5 .... 74 C3
  Sunderland,Monkwearmouth
  SR6 .... 75 E3
  Wideopen NE13 .... 28 B7
East View Ave NE23 .... 22 B6
East View S 5 SR5 .... 74 C1
East View Terr
  Dudley NE23 .... 29 A8
  Gateshead NE10 .... 71 F6
  Wickham NE16 .... 69 B8
East Villas DH6 .... 97 F4
East Vines SR1 .... 103 C3
East Wing The NE38 .... 83 E5
East Woodlands NE46 .... 45 D4
Eastbourne Ave
  Gateshead NE8 .... 70 E8
  Newcastle-u-T NE6 .... 57 A6
Eastbourne Ct 1
  Cramlington NE23 .... 21 D6
  Newcastle-u-T NE6 .... 57 A6
  Whitley Bay NE26 .... 32 A6
Eastbourne Gdns
  Cramlington NE23 .... 21 D6
  Newcastle-u-T NE6 .... 57 A6
  Whitley Bay NE26 .... 32 A6
Eastbourne Gr 12 NE6 .... 42 D3
Eastbourne Par NE31 .... 58 A2
Eastbourne Sq NE6 .... 75 A4
Eastburn Gdns NE10 .... 57 B2
Eastcheap NE6 .... 39 C1
Eastcliffe Ave NE3 .... 38 A3
Eastcombe Cl NE35 .... 58 E2
Eastcote Terr NE6 .... 56 F4
Easten Terr NE28 .... 41 C1
Easterfield Ct NE61 .... 4 A1
Eastern Ave NE11,NE9 .... 70 D4
Eastern Gdns 4 NE10 .... 56 D1
Eastern Way
  Newcastle-u-T NE5 .... 37 D2
  Ponteland NE20 .... 25 D3
Eastfield Ave
  Newcastle-u-T NE28,NE6 .... 57 A8
  Whitley Bay NE25 .... 31 D4
Eastfield Ho NE6 .... 57 A8
Eastfield Rd
  Longbenton NE12 .... 39 D6
  South Shields NE34 .... 59 F8
Eastfield St SR4 .... 85 F5
Eastfield Terr NE12 .... 39 D6
Eastfields NE46 .... 45 A5
Eastgarth NE5 .... 37 A5
Eastgate Choppington NE62 .... 10 F5
  Hexham NE46 .... 45 B4
Eastgate Bank NE43 .... 64 F8
Eastgate Gdns NE4 .... 54 E4
Eastgreen NE62 .... 10 F5
Eastlands Blaydon NE21 .... 53 B1
  Chester le S NE38 .... 88 E7
  Newcastle-u-T NE7 .... 39 A3
Eastleigh Ct NE35 .... 73 E8
Easton Holmes NE11 .... 11 C2
Eastward Gn NE25 .... 31 D4
Eastway SR4 .... 60 B5
Eastwood Ave NE24 .... 17 D3
Eastwood Cl NE23 .... 29 C5
Eastwood Ct NE3 .... 37 D2
Eastwood Gdns
  Gateshead,Low Fell NE9 .... 71 A6
  Gateshead,Old Fold NE10 .... 56 D2
  Newcastle-u-T NE3 .... 37 F4
Eastwood Grange Ct
  NE46 .... 45 E4
Eastwood Grange Rd
  NE46 .... 45 E4
Eastwood Mid Sch NE42 .... 50 F3
Eastwood Pl NE23 .... 16 C2
Eastwood Villas NE42 .... 50 F3
Eastwoods Rd NE62 .... 11 B8
Eaton Cl NE38 .... 89 B8
Eaton Pl NE4 .... 54 F5

Eavers Ct NE34 .... 59 C5
Ebba Wlk NE3 .... 38 D5
Ebchester Ave NE9 .... 71 D3
Ebchester CE Prim Sch
  DH8 .... 76 E3
Ebchester Ct NE3 .... 37 C5
Ebchester Hill DH8 .... 76 F2
Ebchester St NE34 .... 59 A5
Ebdon La SR6 .... 75 H4
Ebor St Newcastle-u-T NE6 .... 56 C8
  South Shields NE34 .... 59 A4
Eccles Cl NE27 .... 30 C5
Eccles Terr 2 NE27 .... 30 E1
Eccleston Cl NE27 .... 30 C4
Eccleston Rd NE33 .... 42 E2
Ecgfrid Terr NE32 .... 58 C4
Eddison Rd NE38 .... 83 F4
Eddiston Rd NE38 .... 83 A1
Eddleston Ave NE3 .... 38 A3
Eddrington Gr NE5 .... 36 C2
Ede Ave Dunston NE11 .... 69 F8
  South Shields NE34 .... 60 B7
Eden Ave NE16 .... 79 A6
Eden Cl NE5 .... 36 C2
Eden Ct Bedlington NE22 .... 16 A8
8 Wallsend NE28 .... 59 E8
Eden Dale NE40 .... 51 F4
Eden Gr NE61 .... 9 A6
Eden House Rd SR2,SR4 .... 102 B1
Eden Pl NE30 .... 32 A1
Eden St NE28 .... 40 B1
Eden St W SR1 .... 102 C3
Eden Terr Lynemouth NE61 .... 2 A3
  Penshaw DH4 .... 90 B6
  Sunderland SR2 .... 102 B1
Eden Vale SR2 .... 102 B1
Eden Villas NE38 .... 83 E4
Eden Wlk NE32 .... 58 C3
Edenbridge Cres NE12 .... 39 B7
Edendale Ave Blyth NE24 .... 17 B8
  Newcastle-u-T NE6 .... 56 A8
Edendale Ct Blyth NE24 .... 17 B8
1 South Shields NE34 .... 59 A4
Edendale Ho NE24 .... 17 B7
Edendale Terr NE8 .... 70 F8
Edengarth NE30 .... 32 A2
Edgar St NE3 .... 38 F5
Edge Hill NE20 .... 25 C1
Edge Mount NE12 .... 29 F4
Edgecote NE37 .... 83 F8
Edgefield Ave NE3 .... 28 D3
Edgefield Dr NE23 .... 16 C2
Edgehill Cl NE20 .... 25 C1
Edgeware Ct SR5 .... 75 A3
Edgeware Wlk NE4 .... 54 E3
Edgewell Ave NE42 .... 50 B1
Edgewell Grange NE42 .... 50 C2
Edgewell House Rd NE42,
  NE43 .... 65 B8
Edgewell Rd NE42 .... 50 B1
Edgewood Hexham NE46 .... 45 D4
  Ponteland NE20 .... 25 D2
Edgeworth Cl NE38 .... 83 D6
Edgeworth Cres SR6 .... 75 D2
Edgmond Ct SR2 .... 92 E8
Edgware Rd NE8 .... 71 A8
Edhill Ave NE34 .... 59 A4
Edhill Gdns NE34 .... 58 F4
Edinburgh Ct NE3 .... 37 D8
Edinburgh Dr NE22 .... 10 E2
Edinburgh Rd NE32 .... 58 E4
Edinburgh Sq SR5 .... 75 A3
Edington Gdns NE40 .... 51 E6
Edington Gr NE30 .... 32 A1
Edington Rd NE30 .... 32 A1
Edison Gdns NE8 .... 70 E7
Edison St SR4 .... 53 C2
Edith Moffat Ho 7 NE29 .... 42 A5
Edith St Jarrow NE32 .... 58 A7
  Sunderland,Hendon SR2 .... 86 E4
  Sunderland,Monkwearmouth
  SR5 .... 75 C2
  Tynemouth NE30 .... 42 C8
Edith Terr Newbottle DH4 .... 90 D3
8 Whickham NE16 .... 69 A7
Edlingham Cl NE3 .... 38 A4
Edlingham Ct 1 DH5 .... 94 F8
Edmonton Sq 1 SR5 .... 75 A3
Edmund Pl NE9 .... 70 F5
Edmund Rd NE27 .... 30 D1
Edna Terr NE5 .... 37 A3
Edrich Ho NE29 .... 41 D3
Edward Burdis St SR5 .... 75 B2
Edward Graveling Ho
  NE30 .... 42 C6
Edward Ho 2 NE2 .... 102 C2
Edward Pl NE4 .... 98 B1
Edward Rd
  Bedlington NE22 .... 11 D3
  Birtley DH3 .... 82 B5
  Newcastle-u-T NE28 .... 40 F3
Edward St Blyth NE24 .... 17 D7
  Burnopfield NE16 .... 79 A4
  Chester le S DH3 .... 88 C3
  Crawcrook NE40 .... 51 E3
  Hebburn NE31 .... 57 C6
  Hetton le H DH5 .... 95 A4
  Morpeth NE61 .... 9 A8
  New Silksworth SR3 .... 92 A7
  Newcastle-u-T NE3 .... 38 C5
  Pegswood NE61 .... 4 C3
Edward's Wlk NE1 .... 99 A2
Edwards Rd NE26 .... 32 C4
Edwin Gr NE28 .... 41 A3

Edwin St
  Brunswick Village NE13 .... 28 A6
  Houghton-le-S DH5 .... 90 E1
14 Newcastle-u-T NE6 .... 56 B6
  Sunderland SR4 .... 85 E7
Edwin Terr NE40 .... 52 C2
Edwin's Ave S NE12 .... 39 E8
Edwina Gdns NE29 .... 41 E7
Edwins Ave NE12 .... 39 E8
Egerton Rd NE34 .... 59 C6
Egerton St
  Newcastle-u-T NE4 .... 54 D4
  Sunderland SR2 .... 103 B1
Eggleston Dr SR3 .... 86 A2
Egham Rd NE5 .... 36 C2
Eglesfield Rd NE33 .... 59 C8
Eglingham Ave NE30 .... 32 C1
Eglingham Way NE61 .... 9 B6
Eglinton St SR5 .... 75 C1
Eglinton St N SR5 .... 75 C1
Eglinton Twr 2 SR5 .... 75 D1
Egremont Dr 4 NE9 .... 71 A6
Egremont Gdns NE9 .... 71 A6
Egremont Pl NE26 .... 32 B4
Egremont Way NE23 .... 16 C2
Egton Terr DH3 .... 82 C5
Eider Cl NE24 .... 17 E3
Eider Wlk NE12 .... 29 C4
Eighteenth Ave NE24 .... 17 D5
Eighth Ave Ashington NE63 .... 6 E2
  Blyth NE24 .... 17 D6
  Chester le S DH2 .... 88 B3
  Gateshead NE11 .... 69 C7
  Morpeth NE61 .... 9 B7
  Newcastle-u-T NE6 .... 56 C8
Eighth Row NE63 .... 6 B4
Eighton Terr NE9 .... 71 E3
Eilansgate NE46 .... 45 A5
Eilansgate Ho NE46 .... 44 F5
Eilansgate Terr NE46 .... 45 A5
Eilanville NE46 .... 45 A5
Eishort Way NE12 .... 39 B6
Eland Cl NE3 .... 37 D5
Eland Edge NE20 .... 25 F6
Eland La NE20 .... 25 F7
Eland View NE20 .... 25 F6
Elberfeld Ct NE32 .... 58 B6
Elder Gdns NE9 .... 71 C1
Elder Gr 3 Gateshead NE9 .... 70 F5
  South Shields NE34 .... 59 F3
Elder Sq NE23 .... 6 E2
Elderwood Gdns NE11 .... 70 B5
Eldon Cl 1 NE40 .... 41 B1
Eldon Gn NE1 .... 99 A2
Eldon La NE1 .... 99 A1
Eldon Pl
  Newcastle-u-T NE1 .... 99 A3
  Newcastle-u-T,Lemington
  NE15 .... 53 D7
Eldon Rd Hexham NE46 .... 45 D4
  Newcastle-u-T NE15 .... 53 D7
Eldon Sq NE1 .... 99 A2
Eldon Square Sh Ctr NE1 .... 99 A2
Eldon St Gateshead NE8 .... 56 A2
  South Shields NE33 .... 42 B1
  Sunderland SR4 .... 102 A2
  Wallsend NE28 .... 41 B2
Eleanor St
  South Shields NE33 .... 42 D3
  Tynemouth NE30 .... 32 C3
Eleanor Terr
  Crawcrook NE40 .... 52 A4
8 Whickham NE16 .... 69 A7
Electric Cres DH4 .... 90 D4
Elemore Hall Sch DH6 .... 97 A5
Elemore La
  Easington Lane DH5 .... 97 A7
  High Pittington DH6 .... 96 E6
Elemore St DH6 .... 96 B5
Elenbel Ave NE22 .... 11 C1
Eleventh Ave Blyth NE24 .... 17 E6
  Chester le S DH2 .... 88 B3
  Gateshead NE11 .... 70 E2
  Morpeth NE61 .... 9 B7
Eleventh Ave N NE11 .... 70 E3
Eleventh Row NE63 .... 6 B4
Elford Cl NE25 .... 31 D5
Elfordleigh DH4 .... 90 C4
Elgar Ave 3 NE5 .... 36 C2
Elgin Ave NE28 .... 40 F4
Elgin Cl Bedlington NE22 .... 11 D2
  Cramlington NE23 .... 21 D6
  Tynemouth NE29 .... 41 C8
Elgin Ct NE10 .... 57 B2
Elgin Gdns NE6 .... 56 F6
Elgin Pl DH3 .... 82 D2
Elgin Rd NE9 .... 71 B8
Elgin St NE32 .... 58 B4
Elgy Rd NE3 .... 38 B3
Elisabeth Ave DH3 .... 82 B6
Elizabeth Cres NE23 .... 29 A8
Elizabeth Ct
  High Pittington DH6 .... 96 C5
  Longbenton NE12 .... 30 A1
Elizabeth Diamond Gdns
  NE33 .... 59 B8
Elizabeth Dr NE12 .... 40 A8
Elizabeth Rd NE28 .... 41 A2
Elizabeth St
  Chopwell NE17 .... 66 B1
  East Cramlington NE23 .... 22 F5
  Houghton-le-S DH5 .... 90 E1
7 South Shields NE33 .... 42 D2
  Sunderland,Castletown SR5 .... 74 B1

lizabeth St *continued*
Sunderland,Monkwearmouth
SR5 ....75 C3
izabeth Woodcock
Maritime Inst The SR2 .103 A1
I-Dene Cres NE10 ....71 E7
len Ct **3** NE32 ....58 B7
len Terr NE37 ....83 F8
llerbeck Cl **3** NE10 ....71 C8
llersmere Gdns NE30 ...32 B2
llerton Way
Cramlington NE23 ....16 C2
Gateshead NE10 ....71 C8
llesmere DH4 ....89 D3
llesmere Ave
Newcastle-u-T,South Gosforth
NE3 ....38 E4
Newcastle-u-I,Walkergate
NE6 ....56 E8
Newcastle-u-T,Westerhope
NE5 ....37 A2
llesmere St SR2 ....86 E1
llesmere Gdns NE62 ....11 C8
llesmere Rd NE4 ....54 E5
llesmere Terr SR6 ....75 E3
lington Cl
Newcastle-u-T NE15 .....53 B7
1 Ryhope SR2 ....92 F5
lrpeth DH2? 81 E2
lington Cvn Pk NE61 ....1 D7
lington Fst Sch NE61 ...1 E5
lington Terr NE63 ....5 F4
lington Way NE61 ....1 C4
liot Cl DH4 ....90 B7
liot Gdns NE34 ....59 D2
liot Rd NE10 ....56 B1
liot St NE31 ....71 D8
liott Gdns NE28 ....40 A4
liott St NE24 ....17 C4
liott Terr
Newcastle-u-T NE4 ......98 A1
1 Washington NE37 ...83 E8
lis Rd SR5 ....75 A3
lis Sq Pegswood NE61 ...4 F3
Sunderland SR5 ....75 B3
lison Pl
1 Gateshead NE9 ......70 F4
arrow NE32 ....58 B8
Newcastle-u-T NE1 ......99 B2
ison Rd NE11,NE8 ......69 F8
ison St Gateshead NE8 .101 C3
lebburn NE13 ....57 C7
lebburn NE31 ....57 D6
Jarrow NE32 ....58 B7
ison Terr NE46 ....51 F1
ison Villas **8** NE8 ....71 A8
wood Gdns **3** NE9 ...70 F8
n Ave Dinnington NE13 ..17 C1
lington NE11 ....69 F7
outh Shields NE34 ....59 F4
Whickham NE16 ....69 C8
n Bank Rd NE41 ....51 B5
n Cl Cramlington NE23 ...16 C2
exham NE46 ....44 E3
n Ct NE10 ....69 B5
n Dr Bedlington NE22 ...15 F8
hitburn SR6 ....61 A2
n St Burnopfield NE16 ..78 F6
llingworth NE12 ....29 D1
ewcastle-u-T NE3 ....37 F7
hiney Row DH4 ....90 C5
outh Shields NE34 ....59 F4
n Pl DH4 ....90 D3
n Rd Blaydon NE21 .....53 D2
onteland NE20 ....26 A5
ynemouth NE29 ....41 B8
n St Chester le S DH3 ..88 C3
arrow NE32 ....58 A7
hickley Square NE43 ....64 E8
eaton Burn NE13 ....28 C8
nniside NE16 ....69 A6
n St W NE10 ....69 B2
n Terr Birtley DH3 ....82 B5
antobie DH9 ....79 B2
n Trees NE10 ....17 D6
ncroft Rd NE12 ....39 E7
nfield DH5 ....95 A6
nfield Cl SR3 ....91 C6
nfield Terr
ewcastle-u-T NE3 ....38 B4
Vallsend NE28 ....39 F4
Vhitley Bay NE25 ....31 D3
nfield Gr NE3 ....38 B4
nfield Pk NE3 ....38 B4
nfield Rd Hebburn NE31 .57 F3
ewcastle-u-T NE3 ....38 C3
arockley NE15 ....35 E2
nfield Terr
ateshead NE10 ....57 A1
lebburn NE31 ....57 F4
ns The
asington Lane DH5 ......97 D8
llington NE61 ....1 D4
ewcastle-u-T NE23 ....38 B3
underland SR2 ....103 A1
ns W SR2 ....103 A1
nsford Gr NE12 ....39 B6
nsleigh Gdns SR6 ......60 A2
ntree Dr NE40 ....52 B1
ntree Gdns NE25 ....31 E3
ntree Gr NE3 ....38 B3
nway DH2 ....88 A5
nwood NE15 ....53 C8
nwood Ave
underland SR5 ....74 F3
allsend NE28 ....40 F2
ideopen NE13 ....28 C5

Elmwood Cres NE6 ......39 F1
Elmwood Dr NE20 ....25 E7
Elmwood Gdns NE11 ....70 B6
Elmwood Gr NE26 ....32 A6
Elmwood Ho NE7 ....39 A4
Elmwood Mews NE13 ...28 B4
Elmwood Rd NE25 ......31 E4
Elmwood Sq **5** SR5 ...74 F2
Elmwood St
Great Lumley DH4 ....89 E1
Sunderland SR2 ....102 B1
Elrick Cl NE5 ....36 C2
Elrington Gdns NE5 .....54 B8
Elsdon Ave NE25 ....23 D3
Elsdon Ct NE24 ....17 C7
Elsdon Ct NE16 ....69 A5
Elsdon Dr Ashington NE63 ..6 C3
Longbenton NE12 ....39 F8
Elsdon Gdns NE11 ......70 A8
Elsdon Pl **7** NE29 .....42 A4
Elsdon Rd
Newcastle-u-T NE3 ......38 C5
Whickham NE16 ....69 A6
Elsdon St NE29 ....42 A4
Elsdon Terr
North Shields NE29 ......41 D4
Wallsend NE28 ....40 B1
Elsdonburn Rd SR3 .....91 E5
Elsham Gn NE3 ....37 E6
Elsing Cl NE5 ....37 B4
Elstob Farm Cvns SR3 ..86 B2
Elstob Pl
Newcastle-u-T NE6 ......56 E4
Sunderland SR3 ....36 C2
Elstree Cl NE5 ....36 C2
Elstree Ct NE3 ....37 B7
Elstree Gdns NE24 .....17 D3
Elstree Sq SR5 ....75 A3
Elswick East Terr NE4 .100 B4
Elswick Rd
Newcastle-u-T NE4 .....100 A4
Washington NE37 ....83 A7
Elswick Row NE4 ....98 B1
Elswick St NE4 ....98 B1
Elswick Way Ind Est
NE34 ....59 A6
Elsworth Gn NE5 ....37 C3
Elterwater Rd DH2 ......88 B1
Elton St E NE28 ....40 B1
Elton St W NE28 ....40 B1
Eltringham NE42 ....40 A2
Eltringham Cotts NE43 ..49 F1
Eltringham Rd NE42 ....50 A2
Elvaston Dr NE46 ....45 B3
Elvaston Gr NE46 ....45 B3
Elvaston Park Rd NE46 .45 A3
Elvaston Rd Hexham NE46 ..45 B4
Ryton NE40 ....52 C6
Elvet Cl
Brunswick Village NE13 ..28 B6
6 Newcastle-u-T NE6 .56 C7
Elvet Ct NE6 ....56 C7
Elvet Gn Chester le S DH2 .88 C2
Hetton le H DH5 ....95 A1
Elvet Way **5** NE6 ....56 C7
Elvington St SR6 ....75 E3
Elwin Cl NE26 ....24 D5
Elwin Pl NE26 ....24 D5
Elwin Terr SR2 ....102 B2
Ely Cl NE12 ....39 D4
Ely St NE8 ....101 B1
Ely Way NE32 ....58 B1
Elysium La NE8 ....101 A1
Embankment Rd SR7 ...93 B1
Embassy Gdns NE15 ...54 B6
Emblehope NE37 ....83 A6
Emblehope Ho SR3 .....91 E8
Embleton Ave
Newcastle-u-T NE3 ......38 A6
South Shields NE34 ......60 B8
Wallsend NE28 ....40 C5
Embleton Cres NE29 ...41 C8
Embleton Dr Blyth NE24 .17 C3
Chester le S DH3 ....88 A1
Embleton Gdns
Gateshead NE10 ....56 D1
5 Newcastle-u-T NE5 .37 D1
Embleton Rd
Gateshead NE10 ....57 B2
Tynemouth NE29 ....41 C8
Emden Rd NE3 ....37 F6
Emily Davison Ave NE61 .8 E3
Emily St Gateshead NE8 .56 B1
Newbottle DH4 ....90 D4
Newcastle-u-T NE6 ......56 E6
Emlyn Rd NE34 ....59 A6
Emma Ct SR2 ....103 B1
Emma View **7** NE40 ..51 F3
Emmanuel Coll NE11 ...70 A5
Emmaville NE40 ....52 A4
Emmaville Prim Sch
NE40 ....51 F4
Emmbrook Cl DH5 ......94 D4
Emmerson Ct NE27 ....30 E3
Emmerson Pl NE27 .....30 E3
Emmerson Rd NE64 ....7 D5
Emmerson Terr NE38 ..83 E5
Emmerson Terr W **1**
SR3 ....92 B7
Emperor Way SR3 .....91 C5
Empress Rd NE6 ....57 B4
Empress St **3** SR6 ...75 C1
Emsworth Rd SR5 ......75 A3
Enderby Dr NE46 ....44 E3
Enderby Rd SR4 ....102 B3
Enfield Ave NE16 ......54 B1

Enfield Gdns NE16 .....69 B5
Enfield Rd NE9 ....70 F8
Enfield St SR4 ....85 F7
Engel St NE19 ....67 B2
Engine Inn Rd NE28 .....40 F4
Engine La NE9 ....70 F8
Engine Rd
Hedley on t H NE17 ......65 E4
Prudhoe NE42 ....65 F5
Englefield NE10 ....71 F4
Englefield Cl NE3 ......37 D7
Englemann Way SR3 ...91 E5
English Martyrs RC Prim Sch
SR5 ....74 F2
English Martyrs' RC Prim Sch
NE5 ....54 C8
Enid Ave SR6 ....75 D3
End St NE13 ....28 A4
Ennerdale Birtley DH3 ...82 D2
Gateshead NE10 ....72 A8
Sunderland SR2 ....86 C4
Washington SR7 ....83 C7
Ennerdale Cres
Blaydon NE21 ....68 B8
Penshaw DH4 ....90 A8
Ennerdale Gdns
Gateshead NE9 ....71 A5
Wallsend NE28 ....41 A4
Ennerdale Pl DH2 ....88 B1
Ennerdale Rd Blyth NE24 .16 F8
Newcastle-u-T NE6 ......56 F6
Tynemouth NE30 ....32 A2
Ennerdale St DH5 ......94 F2
Ennerdale Terr NE17 ...77 A5
Ennerdale Wlk NE16 ...68 F5
Ennis Cl NE62 ....11 D8
Ennismore Ct NE12 ....39 D6
Ensign Ho **21** NE30 ...42 D7
Enslin St NE6 ....56 F3
Enterprise Ct
Cramlington NE23 ....15 F1
Seaham SR7 ....92 F2
Enterprise Ho NE11 ....70 D4
Epinay Sch NE32 ....58 C6
Epping Ct NE23 ....21 D6
Epping Sq **4** SR5 ....75 A3
Eppleton Ave DH5 ......95 B5
Eppleton Row DH5 .....95 A4
Eppleton Terr DH5 .....95 B4
Eppleton Terr W DH5 ..95 B5
Epsom Ct NE29 ....41 F4
Epsom Ct NE33 ....37 C2
Epsom Dr NE63 ....6 C2
Epsom Sq **5** SR5 ....75 A3
Epsom Way NE24 ......17 D3
Epwell Gr NE23 ....16 C2
Epworth Gr NE8 ....101 B1
Equitable St NE28 ......40 B1
Eric Tolhurst Ctr **12** NE24 .17 F8
Erick St NE1 ....99 B1
Erin Sq SR5 ....75 A3
Erith Terr SR4 ....85 F6
Ermine Cres NE4 ....85 A4
Ernest Mackley Ho NE34 .59 A5
Ernest St
8 Gateshead NE8 .....86 C4
West Boldon NE35 ......74 A8
Ernest Terr
Chester le S DH3 ....88 C2
Ryhope SR2 ....93 A6
Ernwill Ave SR5 ....75 B4
Errington Pl NE20 ......25 C2
Errington Rd NE20 .....25 C2
Errington Rd NE20 .....25 B2
Errington St NE24 .....29 E1
Errol Pl DH3 ....38 F2
Erskine Ct NE2 ....38 F2
Erskine Rd NE33 ....42 D2
Esdale SR2 ....92 E6
Esher Ct NE3 ....37 D3
Esher Gdns NE24 ......17 D3
Esher Pl NE23 ....16 C2
Eshmere Cres NE5 .....36 C3
Eshott Cl
Newcastle-u-T,East Denton
NE5 ....37 A1
Newcastle-u-T,Fawdon NE3 .38 A6
Eshott Cl NE5 ....37 A1
Esk Ave DH5 ....95 A1
Esk Ct **12** SR3 ....91 F6
Esk Rd N10,NE9 ....17 B7
Esk Terr **2** SR3 ......91 F6
Eskdale Birtley DH3 .....82 E1
Penshaw DH4 ....90 A8
Eskdale Ave Blyth NE24 .17 A8
Wallsend NE28 ....40 C5
Eskdale Cres NE37 ....72 B1
Eskdale Ct NE34 ....59 C2
Eskdale Dr NE32 ....58 D3
Eskdale Gdns NE9 .....71 A3
Eskdale Mans NE2 .....99 B4
Eskdale Rd SR6 ....75 F6
Eskdale St Hetton le H DH5 .94 F2
South Shields NE34 .....59 C5
Eskdale Terr
Newcastle-u-T NE2 .....99 B4
Whitley Bay NE26 ......32 C4
Eslington Ct NE3 ....70 B8
Eslington Ho NE2 ......99 B4
Eslington Mews NE63 ..6 A4
Eslington Rd NE2 ......99 B3
Eslington Sch NE8 ....100 C1
Eslington Terr NE2 .....99 B4
Esmeralda Gdns NE23 .22 F1
Esplanade NE26 ....32 B5
Esplanade Ave NE26 ..32 B5

Esplanade Mews SR2 .103 A1
Esplanade Pl NE26 .....32 B5
Esplanade The SR2 ....103 A1
Esplanade W SR2 .....103 A1
Espley Ct NE12 ....40 A8
Espley Ho NE3 ....37 E7
Essen Way SR3 ....86 B3
Essex Cl Ashington NE63 .6 A4
Newcastle-u-T NE4 .....100 B3
Essex Ct NE37 ....72 D1
Essex Gdns Gateshead NE9 .70 F7
South Shields NE34 .....60 C7
Wallsend NE28 ....40 E3
Essex Gr SR3 ....92 A8
Essex St DH5 ....94 F4
Estate Houses DH4 ....89 F4
Esther Campbell Ct NE2 .98 C3
Eston Ct Blyth NE24 ....17 B8
Wallsend NE28 ....39 F5
Eston Gr SR5 ....75 C3
Estuary Way SR4 ......85 B7
Etal Ave
North Shields NE29 .....41 D4
Whitley Bay NE25 ......32 B4
Etal Cl NE2? 30 F3
Etal Cres Jarrow NE32 ..58 E4
Shiremoor NE27 ....30 F3
Etal Ct NE29 ....42 A6
Etal Ho NE63 ....6 F4
Etal La NE5 ....37 A3
Etal Pl NE3 ....38 A7
Etal Rd NE24 ....17 B3
Etal Way NE5 ....37 A3
Ethel Ave Blaydon NE21 .53 C2
Ryhope SR2 ....93 A6
Ethel St Dudley NE23 ...29 A6
Newcastle-u-T NE4 .....54 D4
Ethel Terr
2 Hexham NE46 ......45 A4
High Spen NE39 ....66 F3
South Shields NE34 .....59 B5
Sunderland SR5 ....74 B1
Etherley Rd NE6 ....56 D7
Etherstone Ave NE7 ...39 C3
Eton Cl NE23 ....16 C2
Eton Sq NE31 ....57 F6
Ettrick Cl NE12 ....29 C4
Ettrick Gdns
Gateshead NE8 ....71 B8
Sunderland SR4 ....85 F4
Ettrick Gr SR3 ....85 F4
Ettrick Lodge NE3 .....38 D4
Ettrick Rd NE32 ....58 A5
European Way SR4 ....85 E8
Euryalus Ct NE31 ......42 F1
Eustace Ave NE29 .....41 E5
Euston Ct SR5 ....75 A4
Eva St NE15 ....53 C6
Evanlade NE10 ....72 B6
Evelyn St SR2 ....102 B1
Evelyn Terr NE21 ......53 C3
Evenwood Gdns NE9 ..71 B5
Ever Ready Ind Est DH9 .79 D2
Everard St NE23 ....16 B3
Everest Gr NE36 ....74 A7
Everest Sq SR5 ....75 A4
Eversleigh Pl NE15 ....35 E2
Eversley Cres SR5 .....75 B3
Eversley Pl
1 Newcastle-u-T NE6 .56 B7
2 Wallsend NE28 .....40 F3
Everton La SR5 ....75 A4
Evesham SR4 ....85 A6
Evesham Ave NE26 ....31 F6
Evesham Cl NE35 ......58 F1
Evesham Garth NE3 ...37 E3
Evesham Pl NE23 .....21 D7
Evistones Gdns NE6 ...56 E3
Evistones Rd NE9 .....71 A7
Ewart Cres NE34 ......58 E4
Ewart St NE33 ....59 D3
Ewbank Ave NE4 ......54 E7
Ewe Hill Cotts DH4 ....89 F1
Ewe Hill Terr DH4 ......89 F1
Ewe Hill Terr W DH4 ..89 F1
Ewehurst Cres DH9 ...78 E1
Ewehurst Gdns DH9 ...78 E1
Ewehurst Par DH9 .....78 E1
Ewehurst Rd DH9 ......78 E1
Ewehurst Terr DH9 ....78 E1
Ewen Ct NE28 ....41 B8
Ewesley SR4 ....85 A6
Ewesley Cl NE5 ....37 A1
Ewesley Rd SR4 ....85 A6
Ewesley Rd SR4 ....85 F5
Ewing Rd SR4 ....102 A1
Exchange Bldgs NE26 .32 B5
Exelby Cl NE3 ....38 D8
Exeter Cl Ashington NE63 .6 A4
Cramlington NE23 ....21 E6
Exeter Ct NE31 ....57 F6
Exeter Rd Tynemouth NE29 .31 C1
Wallsend NE28 ....40 A5
Exeter St Gateshead NE8 .101 C1
Newcastle-u-T NE6 .....56 C6
Sunderland SR4 ....102 A2
Exeter Way NE32 ......58 B2
Exmouth Rd NE29 .....41 C5
Exmouth Sq SR5 ......75 A3
Exmouth St SR5 ....75 A3
Extension Rd SR1 ....103 C2
Eyemouth Ct **2** NE34 .59 A5
Eyemouth La SR5 ......75 A4
Eyemouth Rd NE29 ....41 C5

F

Faber Rd SR5 ....75 A3
Factory Rd NE21 ....53 D4
Fair Gn NE25 ....31 C4
Fair View Burnopfield NE16 .78 E6
Prudhoe NE42 ....50 C2
West Rainton DH4 ......94 A2
Fairburn Ave
Houghton-le-S DH5 .....94 E6
Newcastle-u-T NE7 .....39 C4
Fairdale Ave NE7 ....39 C4
Fairfield
Fence Houses DH4 ......90 B1
Hexham NE46 ....44 F4
Longbenton NE12 ....38 F6
3 Longbenton NE12 ..17 D4
Whickham NE16 ....69 A5
Fairfield Cl NE11 ....54 E1
Fairfield Cres NE46 ....4 C2
Fairfield Dr Ashington NE63 .7 A2
Tynemouth NE30 ....32 B2
Whitley Bay SR26 ......60 F2
Whitley Bay NE25 ......31 D4
Fairfield Gn NE25 ......31 C4
Fairfield Ind Est NE10 ..1 B2
Fairfield Rd NE2 ....38 D1
Fairfield Terr NE10 .....57 A1
Fairfields NE40 ....52 B5
Fairgreen Cl SR3 ....91 F5
Fairhaven Ave NE6 ....57 A6
Fairhaven Ave NE34 ...57 C4
Fairhill Cl NE7 ....39 C4
Fairholm Rd NE4 ....54 E5
Fairholme Ave NE34 ..59 F6
Fairholme Rd SR3 .....86 C3
Fairisle DH2 ....82 A1
Fairlands E SR6 ....75 D2
Fairlands W SR6 ....75 D2
Fairles St NE33 ....42 D4
Fairmead Way SR4 ....85 A6
Fairmile Dr SR3 ....91 E6
Fairmont Way NE7 ....39 C4
Fairney Cl NE20 ....25 E6
Fairney Edge NE20 ....25 E6
Fairney Wlk NE20 .....25 F6
Fairspring NE5 ....37 A2
Fairview Ave NE34 ....59 F7
Fairville Cres NE7 .....39 C4
Fairville Cl NE23 ....21 E6
Fairville Cres NE7 .....39 C4
Fairway Morpeth NE61 .11 A8
Stakeford NE62 ....11 A8
Fairway **1** NE32 .....38 B8
Fairway The
Newcastle-u-T NE3 .....38 B8
Ryton NE21 ....53 A4
Washington NE37 ......72 D3
Fairways
New Silksworth SR3 ....92 B7
Whitley Bay NE25 ......31 D5
Fairways Ave NE7 .....39 C4
Fairways The NE36 ....74 A7
Fairwood Rd NE46 ....45 D4
Fairy St NE35 ....95 A4
Falcon Cl NE63 ....6 B2
Falcon Hill NE61 ....8 D7
Falcon Pl NE12 ....39 D4
Falcon Terr NE41 ......51 B6
Falconar St NE2 ....99 B2
Falconar's Ct NE1 .....99 A1
Faldonside NE6 ....39 D2
Falkirk NE12 ....29 D4
Falkland Ave
Hebburn NE31 ....57 E6
Newcastle-u-T NE3 .....37 F3
Falkland Rd SR4 ....85 E6
Fallin Park Com Prim Sch
NE10 ....71 C8
Falla Park Cres NE10 ..71 C8
Falla Park Rd NE10 ....71 C8
Fallodon Ave NE3 .....37 F8
Fallodon Gdns NE5 ....37 D2
Fallow Park Ave NE24 .17 C6
Fallow Rd NE34 ....60 D6
Fallowfeld NE10 ....72 A7
Fallowfield NE10 ....37 F6
Fallowfield Way
Ashington NE63 ....6 B2
Washington NE38 ......83 E2
Falmouth Rd
Newcastle-u-T NE29 ....56 B7
South Shields NE34 ....41 C5
Sunderland SR4 ....85 E7
Falmouth Sq SR4 .....85 E6
Falmouth Sq SR4 .....22 A8
Falsgrave Pl NE16 .....68 F5
Falstaff Rd NE29 ......41 C5
Falston Rd NE24 ......17 C5
Falstone Gateshead NE10 .72 A8
Washington NE38 ......83 F2
Falstone Ave
Newcastle-u-T NE15 ...53 E8
South Shields NE34 ....60 A6
Falstone Cl NE12 .....40 A8
Falstone Cres NE63 ...6 B1
Falstone Sq NE3 ......38 A6

Falstone Way NE46 . . . . . .44 F3
Faraday Cl NE38 . . . . . . .84 B5
Faraday Gr Gateshead NE8 .70 E7
  Sunderland SR4 . . . . . . .85 F6
Faraday Terr DH6 . . . . . . .97 E3
Farbridge Cres DH8 . . . . .76 F3
Farding Lake Ct NE34 . . . .60 C6
Farding Sq NE34 . . . . . . .60 C6
Fareham Gr NE35 . . . . . . .73 D8
Fareham Way NE23 . . . . . .22 B7
Farlam Ave NE30 . . . . . . .32 A1
Farlam Rd NE5 . . . . .54 B8
Farleigh Ct NE29 . . . . . . .41 B8
Farm Cl Sunnisde NE16 . . .69 B2
  Washington NE37 . . . . . .72 B1
Farm Cotts NE25 . . . . . . .23 F2
Farm Hill Rd SR6 . . . . . . .60 A2
Farm St SR5 . . . . .75 B1
Farm View Ho NE23 . . . . .22 C5
Farm Well Pl NE42 . . . . . .50 D3
Farn Ct NE3 . . . . .37 D8
Farnborough Cl NE23 . . . .22 B8
Farnborough Dr SR3 . . . . .92 B8
Farndale NE28 . . . . .39 F5
Farndale Ave
  Stakeford NE62 . . . . . . .11 A8
  Sunderland SR6 . . . . . . .75 F6
Farndale Cl Blaydon NE21 ..67 F8
  Dinnington NE13 . . . . . .27 B7
Farndale Ct NE24 . . . . . . .17 D4
Farndale Rd NE4 . . . . . . .54 E5
Farne Ave Ashington NE63 ..6 D2
  Newcastle-u-T NE3 . . . . .38 A7
  South Shields NE34 . . . .60 B8
Farne Prim Sch NE5 . . . . .37 A3
Farne Rd NE27 . . . . .30 F3
Farne Sq SR4 . . . . .85 D7
Farne Terr NE6 . . . . .56 E6
Farnham Cl NE15 . . . . . . .53 D6
Farnham Gr NE24 . . . . . . .17 D4
Farnham Rd NE34 . . . . . . .59 C6
Farnham St NE15 . . . . . . .53 D6
Farnham Terr SR4 . . . . . . .85 F4
Farnley Rd NE6 . . . . .39 C1
Farnon Rd NE3 . . . . .38 A5
Farnsworth Ct NE2 . . . . . .38 D7
Farquhar St ◆ NE2 . . . . . .38 F1
Farrfield NE37 . . . . .71 F4
Farrier Cl NE38 . . . . .83 E2
Farriers Ct NE22 . . . . . . .11 C5
Farrington Com Sports Coll SR3 . . . . .91 D7
Farringdon Prim Sch SR3 . . . . .91 D8
Farringdon Rd NE10 . . . . .32 A2
Farringdon Row SR4 . . . . .102 C3
Farrington Ave SR3 . . . . . .91 C8
Farrow Dr SR6 . . . . .60 E1
Farthings The NE37 . . . . .72 B2
Fatfield Pk NE38 . . . . . . .83 D1
Fatfield Prim Sch NE38 . . .83 D1
Fatfield Rd NE38 . . . . . . .83 E4
Fatherly Terr DH4 . . . . . . .94 B8
Faversham Ct NE3 . . . . . .37 D7
Faversham Pl NE23 . . . . . .22 B8
Fawcett St SR1 . . . . .103 A2
Fawcett Terr SR2 . . . . . . .93 A6
Fawcett Way NE33 . . . . . .42 C3
Fawdon Cl NE3 . . . . .37 F8
Fawdon Gr NE61 . . . . .4 D5
Fawdon House Farm NE3 . .4 D5
Fawdon La NE3 . . . . .37 F7
Fawdon Park Ho NE3 . . . .37 F6
Fawdon Park Rd NE3 . . . .37 F6
Fawdon Pl NE29 . . . . .41 C6
Fawdon Sta NE3 . . . . . . .37 D7
Fawdon Wlk NE3 . . . . . . .37 D7
Fawlee Gn NE5 . . . . .37 C4
Fawley Cl NE35 . . . . .58 E1
Fawn Rd SR4 . . . . .85 C6
Feather Bed La SR7 . . . . .93 A6
Featherstone NE38 . . . . . .82 F5
Featherstone Gr
  Bedlington NE22 . . . . . . .10 E2
  Jarrow NE32 . . . . .58 A3
  Newcastle-u-T NE3 . . . . .28 A8
Featherstone St SR6 . . . . .75 F2
Federation Terr DH9 . . . . .79 B2
Federation Way NE11 . . . .54 E1
Fee Terr SR2 . . . . .92 E6
Feetham Ave NE12 . . . . . .40 A8
Feetham Ct NE12 . . . . . . .30 A1
Felixstowe Dr NE7 . . . . . .39 D3
Fell Bank DH3 . . . . .82 D4
Fell Cl Birtley DH3 . . . . . .82 E3
  Sunniside NE16 . . . . . . .69 B2
  Washington NE37 . . . . . .83 B7
Fell Ct ◆ NE9 . . . . .71 B5
Fell Dyke Com Prim Sch NE9 . . . . .71 D3
Fell Pl ◆ NE9 . . . . .71 F1
Fell Rd Springwell NE9 . . .71 F1
  Sunderland SR4 . . . . . . .85 D7
Fell Sq SR4 . . . . .85 D7
Fell Terr NE16 . . . . .79 B6
Fell The NE16 . . . . .79 B6
Fell View
  ◆ Crawcrook NE40 . . . . .51 F3
  High Spen NE39 . . . . . . .67 A3
Fell View ◆ NE40 . . . . . . .53 F1
Fell Way The NE5 . . . . . . .36 D1
Fellcross DH3 . . . . .82 C5
Felldyke NE10 . . . . .71 F5
Fellgate Ave NE32 . . . . . .58 C1
Fellgate Gdns NE10 . . . . .72 C8

Fellgate Prim Sch NE32 . . .58 B1
Fellgate Sta NE32 . . . . . . .58 C2
Felling Bsns Ctr NE10 . . . .56 D2
Felling Dene Gdns NE10 . .56 E1
Felling Gate NE10 . . . . . . .56 C1
Felling House Gdns
  NE10 . . . . .56 D2
Felling Sta NE10 . . . . .56 D3
Felling View NE6 . . . . .56 F3
Fellmere Ave NE10 . . . . . .72 A8
Fells Rd NE11 . . . . .70 D7
Fells The ◆ NE9 . . . . .71 A6
Fellsdyke Ct NE9 . . . . . . .71 C6
Fellside Birtley DH3 . . . . . .82 D3
  Ponteland NE20 . . . . . . .25 B1
  Sunniside NE34 . . . . . . .60 B5
Fellside Ave NE16 . . . . . . .69 B3
Fellside Cl NE20 . . . . .25 B1
Fellside Com Prim Sch
  NE16 . . . . .69 A6
Fellside Ct
  Washington NE37 . . . . . .83 B6
  Whickham NE16 . . . . . . .69 A7
Fellside Rd
  Byermoor NE16 . . . . . . .79 C8
  Sunniside NE16 . . . . . . .68 F3
Fellside The NE3 . . . . .37 E6
Felsham Sq SR4 . . . . .85 E7
Felstead Cres SR4 . . . . . .85 D7
Felstead Pl NE24 . . . . . . .17 D4
Felstead Sch SR4 . . . . . . .85 D6
Felstead Sq SR4 . . . . . . .85 D6
Felthorpe Ct NE5 . . . . . . .37 B4
Felton Ave
  Newcastle-u-T NE3 . . . . .38 A6
  South Shields NE34 . . . .60 A7
  Whitley Bay NE25 . . . . . .32 B4
Felton Cl Morpeth NE61 . . .9 B6
  Shiremoor NE27 . . . . . . .30 F3
Felton Cres NE8 . . . . .70 E7
Felton Dr NE12 . . . . .29 F1
Felton Gn ⑱ NE6 . . . . . . .56 C6
Felton Ho NE4 . . . . .56 C6
Felton Terr NE63 . . . . . . .6 D2
Felton Wlk ⑱ NE6 . . . . . .56 C6
Fence Rd DH3 . . . . .89 E5
Fencer Ct NE3 . . . . .38 A5
Fenham Chase NE4 . . . . . .54 E8
Fenham Ct NE4 . . . . .54 E8
Fenham Hall Dr NE4 . . . . .54 E8
Fenham Rd Lynemouth NE61 .1 F3
  Newcastle-u-T NE4 . . . . .98 A2
Fenkle St NE1 . . . . .99 A1
Fennel NE9 . . . . .71 C4
Fennel Gr NE34 . . . . .59 E3
Fenning Pl ⑱ NE6 . . . . . .56 C4
Fenside Rd SR2 . . . . .92 F8
Fenton Cl DH2 . . . . .88 A2
Fenton Sq SR4 . . . . .85 D6
Fenton Terr DH4 . . . . .90 D6
Fenton Wlk NE5 . . . . .37 A2
Fenwick Ave Blyth NE24 . .17 D5
  South Shields NE34 . . . .59 A5
Fenwick Cl
  ⑧ Newcastle-u-T NE2 . . . .38 F1
  Penshaw DH4 . . . . .90 B8
Fenwick Gr
  ④ Hexham NE46 . . . . . .45 A5
  Morpeth NE61 . . . . .4 A1
Fenwick St Penshaw DH4 ..90 B8
  Boldon Colliery NE35 . . .73 E8
Fenwick Terr
  ⑧ Newcastle-u-T NE2 . . . .38 F1
  North Shields NE29 . . . .42 A6
Fenwicks St NE35 . . . . . . .58 E1
Ferguson Cres NE13 . . . . .28 A4
Ferguson St SR2 . . . . . . .103 C2
Ferguson's La NE15 . . . . .54 B6
Fern Ave Cramlington NE23 .16 B2
  Newcastle-u-T,Fawdon NE3 .38 A7
  Newcastle-u-T,Jesmond
  NE2 . . . . .38 F1
  North Shields NE29 . . . .41 F6
  Sunderland SR5 . . . . . . .75 A2
  Whitburn SR6 . . . . .60 F2
Fern Cl NE62 . . . . .10 E7
Fern Dene Rd NE8 . . . . . .70 E8
Fern Dr Cleadon SR6 . . . . .59 F1
  Dudley NE23 . . . . .29 B8
Fern Gdns NE9 . . . . .70 F6
Fern St SR4 . . . . .102 B3
Fern Terr DH9 . . . . .78 F1
Fernbank NE26 . . . . .24 C6
Fernclough NE9 . . . . .71 C5
Ferndale Ave
  ④ East Boldon NE36 . . . .74 D7
  Newcastle-u-T NE3 . . . . .28 D1
  Wallsend NE28 . . . . . . .40 C2
Ferndale Cl NE24 . . . . . . .17 A8
Ferndale Gr NE36 . . . . . . .74 D7
Ferndale La NE36 . . . . . . .74 D7
Ferndale Rd DH4 . . . . .90 A8
Ferndale Terr
  ◆ Springwell NE9 . . . . . .71 F1
  Sunderland SR4 . . . . . . .85 E8
Ferndene
  Longbenton NE12 . . . . . .29 B3
  Wallsend NE28 . . . . . . .40 E4
Ferndene Cres NE3 . . . . . .85 F6
Ferndene Ct NE3 . . . . . . .38 D4
Ferndene Gr
  Newcastle-u-T NE7 . . . . .39 C3
  Ryton NE40 . . . . .52 D4
Ferndown Ct
  Gateshead NE10 . . . . . .72 B7
  Ryton NE40 . . . . .52 D4

Ferngrove NE32 . . . . .73 C8
Fernhill Ave NE16 . . . . . . .69 A7
Fernlea NE23 . . . . .29 B8
Fernlea Cl NE38 . . . . .83 E2
Fernlea Gdns NE40 . . . . . .52 A4
Fernlea Gn NE3 . . . . .37 F5
Fernley Villas NE23 . . . . . .22 D6
Fernsway SR3 . . . . .86 B3
Fernville Ave NE16 . . . . . .69 B2
Fernville Rd NE3 . . . . .38 B3
Fernville St SR4 . . . . .102 B1
Fernway NE61 . . . . .9 B8
Fernwood NE2 . . . . .99 B4
Fernwood Ave NE3 . . . . . .38 D6
Fernwood Cl SR3 . . . . . . .92 A5
Fernwood Gr NE39 . . . . . .77 F5
Fernwood Rd
  Newcastle-u-T,Jesmond
  NE2 . . . . .99 B4
  Newcastle-u-T,Lemington
  NE15 . . . . .53 D6
Fernyhough Hall NE31 . . . .57 F5
Ferrand Dr DH4 . . . . .94 D8
Ferriby Cl NE3 . . . . .38 D8
Ferrisdale Way NE3 . . . . . .37 F7
Ferry App NE33 . . . . .42 C3
Ferry Landing NE42 . . . . . .49 F3
Ferry Mews
  North Shields NE29 . . . .42 B4
  South Shields NE33 . . . .42 B3
Ferry Rd NE46 . . . . .45 C6
Ferry St Jarrow NE32 . . . . .58 B8
  South Shields NE33 . . . .42 B3
Ferryboat La
  Sunderland,Castletown SR5 .85 A7
  Sunderland,Hylton Castle
  SR5 . . . . .73 F2
Ferrydene Ave NE3 . . . . . .37 F4
Festival Cotts NE12 . . . . . .29 B5
Festival Park Dr NE11 . . . .70 B7
Festival Way NE11,NE8 . . .100 A1
Fetcham Ct NE3 . . . . .37 C7
Fewster Sq NE10 . . . . . . .72 A8
Field Cl NE2 . . . . .99 C2
Field Ho
  ⑨ North Shields NE30 . . .42 B6
  Silksworth SR3 . . . . . . .92 A3
Field House Farm SR7 . . . .92 F1
Field House Rd NE6 . . . . . .57 A8
Field House Terr DH6 . . . . .97 F3
Field La NE10 . . . . .72 A8
Field Sq SR4 . . . . .85 D6
Field St
  ⑧ Gateshead NE10 . . . . .56 D1
  Newcastle-u-T NE3 . . . . .38 E5
Field Terr Jarrow NE32 . . . .58 B5
  ② Throckley NE15 . . . . . .35 D2
Fieldfare Cl NE38 . . . . . . .82 F3
Fieldfare Cl NE16 . . . . . . .79 C5
Fieldfare Ho ⑨ NE9 . . . . . .17 F8
Fieldhouse La NE61 . . . . . .9 F5
Fielding Ct NE34 . . . . .59 A3
Fielding Pl NE9 . . . . .71 B8
Fieldside East Rainton DH5 .94 C3
  Whitburn SR6 . . . . .60 E1
Fieldway NE32 . . . . .73 D8
Fife Ave
  Brockley Whins NE32 . . .58 E3
  Chester le S DH2 . . . . . .88 C3
Fife St NE8 . . . . .56 A1
Fife Terr NE17 . . . . .77 B6
Fifteenth Ave NE24 . . . . . .17 D6
Fifth Ave Ashington NE63 . .6 E3
  Blyth NE24 . . . . .17 D6
  Chester le S DH2 . . . . . .88 B3
  Gateshead DH98,NE11 . .70 D5
  Morpeth NE61 . . . . .9 B7
  Newcastle-u-T NE6 . . . . .56 C7
Fifth Row NE63 . . . . .1 A3
Filey Cl NE23 . . . . .22 B8
Filton Cl NE23 . . . . .22 B8
Finchale NE38 . . . . .83 C3
Finchale Cl Dunston NE11 ..69 F6
  Houghton-le-S DH4 . . . . .94 D8
  Sunderland SR2 . . . . . . .103 B1
Finchale Gdns
  Gateshead NE9 . . . . . . .71 C2
  Throckley NE15 . . . . . . .35 D2
Finchale Rd NE31 . . . . . . .57 E3
Finchale Terr
  Great Lumley DH4 . . . . .89 E1
  Jarrow NE32 . . . . .58 D4
  ② Newcastle-u-T NE6 . . . .56 C4
Finchdale Cl NE29 . . . . . . .41 C5
Finchdale Terr ② DH3 . . . .88 C3
Finchley Cres NE6 . . . . . .57 A8
Finchley Ct NE6 . . . . .57 A8
Findon Gr NE29 . . . . .41 E4
Fine La DH8 . . . . .76 B3
Fines Rd DH8 . . . . .77 B1
Finsbury Ave NE6 . . . . . . .56 E4
Finsbury St ② SR5 . . . . . .75 C1
Finsmere Pl ① NE5 . . . . . .37 B1
Finstock Ct NE7 . . . . .38 F4
Fir Gr ⑤ South Shields NE34 .59 F5
Fir St NE32 . . . . .58 A7
Fir Terr NE16 . . . . .79 B6
Firbank Ave NE30 . . . . . . .32 B2
Firbanks NE32 . . . . .58 E3
Fire Station Cotts SR6 . . . .75 D4
Firfield Rd NE5 . . . . .37 D2
Firs The NE3 . . . . .38 B6
First Ave Ashington NE63 . .6 E4
  Blyth NE24 . . . . .17 E7
  Chester le S DH2 . . . . . .88 B8
  Gateshead NE11 . . . . . .70 C6

First Ave continued
  Morpeth NE61 . . . . .9 B7
  Newcastle-u-T NE6 . . . . .56 C7
  North Shields NE29 . . . .41 C4
First Row Ashington NE63 . .6 A4
  Ellington NE61 . . . . .1 E4
  Linton NE61 . . . . .1 A3
First St NE8 . . . . .101 A1
Firth Sq SR4 . . . . .85 D7
Firtree Ave
  Longbenton NE12 . . . . . .29 D1
  Wallsend NE6 . . . . .40 A1
  Washington NE38 . . . . . .83 C1
Firtree Cres NE12 . . . . . . .29 C1
Firtree Gdns NE25 . . . . . .31 F3
Firtree Rd NE16 . . . . .69 A6
Firtrees Chester le S DH2 ..88 B5
  Gateshead NE12 . . . . . .41 B3
Firtrees Ave NE28 . . . . . . .41 B3
Firwood Cres NE39 . . . . . .67 A3
Firwood Gdns NE11 . . . . . .70 B5
Fish Quay NE30 . . . . .42 C6
Fisher Ind Est NE6 . . . . . .57 B7
Fisher La NE13,NE23 . . . . .21 B5
Fisher Rd NE27 . . . . .30 B6
Fisher St NE6 . . . . .57 B7
Fisherwell Rd NE10 . . . . . .57 A1
Fitzpatrick Pl NE33 . . . . . .42 E2
Fitzroy Terr ⑦ SR5 . . . . . .74 F2
Fitzsimmons Ave NE28 . . . .40 B3
Flag Ho NE33 . . . . .42 E1
Flag Lo NE33 . . . . .42 E1
Flagg Ct NE33 . . . . .42 D3
Flaunden Cl NE34 . . . . . . .60 B5
Flax Sq SR4 . . . . .85 C7
Flaxby Cl NE3 . . . . .38 D8
Fleet Ct SR1 . . . . .103 C2
Fleming Bsns Ctr NE2 . . . .99 B4
Fleming Ct NE8 . . . . .100 C2
Fleming Gdns NE10 . . . . . .71 D7
Fletcher Cres DH4 . . . . . . .90 E6
Fletcher Rd NE29 . . . . . . .41 E3
Fletcher Terr DH4 . . . . . . .90 D4
Flexbury Gdns
  Gateshead,Linghurst NE9 .71 A2
  Gateshead,Mount Pleasant
  NE10 . . . . .71 C8
  Newcastle-u-T NE15 . . . .53 E7
Flint Hill Bank DH9 . . . . . .78 E1
Flixton DH4 . . . . .90 B1
Flock Sq SR4 . . . . .85 C7
Flodden NE12 . . . . .29 D4
Flodden Rd SR4 . . . . .85 D6
Flodden St NE6 . . . . .56 D5
Flora St ⑫ NE6 . . . . .56 B6
Floral Dene SR4 . . . . .85 A6
Floralia Ave SR2 . . . . .93 A6
Florence Ave NE9 . . . . . . .71 A6
Florence Cres ④ SR5 . . . .74 F2
Florence St NE21 . . . . . . .53 B2
Florence Terr DH5 . . . . . . .95 A2
Florida St SR4 . . . . .85 F8
Flotterton Gdns NE5 . . . . .54 C7
Flour Mill Rd NE11 . . . . . .54 F2
Fold The Burnopfield NE16 .79 A7
  Newcastle-u-T NE6 . . . . .57 A8
  Silksworth SR3 . . . . . . .92 B5
  Whitley Bay NE25 . . . . . .31 E5
Folds The
  East Rainton DH5 . . . . . .94 D4
  Fence Houses DH4 . . . . .94 B8
Folldon Ave SR6 . . . . .75 D3
Follingsby Ave NE10 . . . . .72 C6
Follingsby Dr NE10 . . . . . .72 C7
Follingsby La NE10 . . . . . .72 E5
Follingsby Pk NE10 . . . . . .72 E5
Follingsby Terr NE10 . . . . .72 E7
Folly La NE40 . . . . .52 B2
Folly The NE36 . . . . .74 A7
Folly Yd NE40 . . . . .52 C2
Font Side NE61 . . . . .3 A1
Fontburn NE61 . . . . .1 E6
Fontburn Ct
  North Shields NE29 . . . .41 D4
  Sunderland SR5 . . . . . . .74 F4
Fontburn Gdns NE61 . . . . .8 E7
Fontburn Pl NE7 . . . . .39 A5
Fontburn Rd
  Bedlington NE22 . . . . . . .11 C1
  Seaton Delaval NE25 . . . .23 D3
Fontburn Terr NE30 . . . . . .42 B6
Fonteyn Pl NE23 . . . . .16 B2
Fontwell Dr NE10 . . . . . . .70 D7
Forbeck Rd SR4 . . . . .85 D6
Forber Ave NE34 . . . . .60 B6
Forbes Terr SR2 . . . . .92 E6
Ford Ave Ashington NE63 . .6 D2
  North Shields NE29 . . . .41 D4
  Sunderland SR4 . . . . . . .85 A6
Ford Cres Jarrow NE32 . . . .58 B3
  Shiremoor NE27 . . . . . . .30 E3
Ford Dr NE24 . . . . .17 C7
Ford Hall Dr SR4 . . . . . . .85 E6
Ford Oval SR4 . . . . .85 B7
Ford Pk NE62 . . . . .11 C8
Ford Rise NE43 . . . . .64 C7
Ford St Gateshead NE8 . . .56 B1
  Newcastle-u-T NE6 . . . . .56 A5
Ford Terr Guide Post NE62 .10 F7
  Riding Mill NE44 . . . . . .63 A8
  Wallsend NE28 . . . . . . .40 F2
Ford The NE42 . . . . .50 C3
Ford View NE23 . . . . .22 A1

Fordenbridge Cres SR4 . . .85
Fordenbridge Rd SR4 85
Fordenbridge Sq SR4 85
Fordham Rd SR4 85
Fordham Sq SR4 85
Fordland Pl SR4 85
Fordley Com Prim Sch
  NE23 29
Fordmoss Wlk NE5 37
Fore St Hexham NE46 45
  Newcastle-u-T NE2 56
Forest Ave NE12 39
Forest Dr NE38 88
Forest Gate NE12 30
Forest Hall Prim Sch
  NE12 29
Forest Hall Rd NE12 29
Forest Rd
  Newcastle-u-T NE15 54
  South Shields NE15 54
  Sunderland SR4 85
Forest Rd Ind Est ⑤ NE33 .42
Forest Villa NE12 29
Forfar St SR6 75
Forge Cl NE17 77
Forge La Bournmoor DH3 ..89
  Hamsterley Mill NE17 . . .77
Forge Rd NE1,NE8 70
Forge The SR4 85
Forge Wlk NE15 35
Forres Pl NE23 22
Forrest Rd NE28 40
Forster Ave
  Bedlington NE22 10
  Sherburn DH6 96
  South Shields NE34 59
Forster Ct ⑥ NE9 71
Forster St Blyth NE24 17
  Newcastle-u-T NE1 99
  Sunderland SR6 75
Forsyth Rd NE2 38
Forsyth St NE29 31
Fort Sq ② NE33 42
Fort St NE33 42
Forth Banks NE1 101
Forth Ct ① Silksworth SR3 .91
  South Shields NE34 59
Forth La NE1 101
Forth Pl NE1 100
Forth St Chopwell NE17 . . .66
  Newcastle-u-T NE1 101
Fortrose Ave SR3 86
Forum Ct NE22 10
Forum The
  Newcastle-u-T NE15 53
  ② Wallsend NE28 40
Forum Way NE23 22
Foss Way Ebchester DH8 ..76
  South Shields NE34 59
Fossdyke NE10 71
Fosse Law NE15 35
Fosse Terr NE9 71
Fossefeld NE10 71
Fossway NE6 56
Foster Ct NE11 70
Foster Dr NE8 56
Foster St
  Newcastle-u-T,Low Walker
  NE6 57
  Newcastle-u-T,Wincomblee
  NE6 57
Foundary Ct NE6 57
Foundry Ct NE6 56
Foundry La NE6 56
Fountain Cl NE22 10
Fountain Gr NE34 59
Fountain Head Bank
  NE26 24
Fountain La NE21 53
Fountain Row NE2 98
Fountains Cl
  Dunston NE11 69
  Washington NE38 83
Fountains Cres
  Burnside DH4 90
  Hebburn NE31 57
Four Lane Ends
  Hetton le H DH5 95
  Houghton-le-S DH5 94
Four Lane Ends Sta NE7 . .39
Fouracres Rd NE5 37
Fourstones NE5 37
Fourstones Cl NE3 37
Fourstones Rd SR4 85
Fourteenth Ave NE24 17
Fourth Ave Ashington NE63 .6
  Blyth NE24 17
  Chester le S DH2 88
  Gateshead NE11 70
  Morpeth NE61 9
  ① Newcastle-u-T NE6 56
Fourth Row NE61 1
Fourth St NE8 101
Fowberry Cres NE4 54
Fowberry Rd NE15 53
Fowler Cl DH4 90
Fowler Gdns ② NE11 54
Fowler St NE33 42
Fox & Hounds La NE15 . . .54
Fox & Hounds Rd NE5 36
Fox Ave NE34 59
Fox Covert La NE20 25
Fox Ho SR3 92
Fox Lea Wlk NE23 22

Fox St Gateshead NE10 .....56 C1
Sunderland SR2 ....102 B1
Foxcover NE63 ....6 F1
Foxcover La SR3 ....91 B7
Foxcover Rd
Sunderland,Middle Herrington
SR3 ....91 A8
Sunderland,Offerton SR4 ..84 F2
Foxglove NE44 ....89 F5
Foxglove Cl NE24 ....17 C4
Foxglove Ct NE34 ....59 B4
Foxhill Cl NE63 ....6 B1
Foxhills Cl NE38 ....83 E2
Foxhills Covert NE16 .....68 E5
Foxhills The NE16 ....68 E6
Foxhomes NE32 ....73 D8
Foxhunters Light Ind Site
NE25 ....31 F3
Foxhunters Rd NE25 ......31 F3
Foxlair Cl SR3 ....92 A4
Foxley NE37 ....83 E8
Foxley Cl NE12 ....29 F4
Foxton Ave
Newcastle-u-T NE3 ......37 F7
Tynemouth NE30 ....32 B3
Foxton Cl NE29 ....41 E3
Foxton Ct SR6 ....60 A1
Foxton Gn NE13 ....37 E5
Foxton Hall NE37 ....72 D3
Foxton Way NE10 ....57 B2
Foyle St SR1 ....103 A2
Framlington Ho NE2 ......98 C3
Framlington Pl NE2 ......98 C3
Frances St Blaydon NE21 ..53 A2
New Silksworth SR3 ......92 B7
Frances Ville NE62 ....10 E4
Francis St Beamish DH9 ...80 D1
Sunderland SR6 ....75 D2
Francis Way NE27 ....30 D1
Frank Bushell Ho NE34 ...59 C5
Frank Pl NE29 ....42 A6
Frank St Greenside NE40 ..51 F1
Sunderland SR5 ....92 B6
Wallsend NE28 ....40 B1
Frankham St NE5 ....36 F2
Frankland Dr NE25 ....31 E3
Franklin Ct NE37 ....83 D8
Franklin Pk SR3 ....53 E4
Franklin St
South Shields NE33 ......42 C2
Sunderland SR4 ....102 A3
Franklyn Ave NE26 ....24 B7
Fraser Cl NE33 ....59 B8
Frazer Terr NE10 ....57 A1
Freda St SR5 ....74 F1
Frederick Gdns DH4 ......90 A3
Frederick Rd SR1 ....103 A3
Frederick St
Chopwell NE17 ....77 B8
South Shields NE33 ......42 C1
Sunderland SR1 ....103 A2
Sunderland,South Hylton
SR4 ....85 A6
Frederick Terr
Hetton le H DH5 ....95 B1
South Hetton DH6 ....97 F6
Freehold Ave NE62 ....10 F7
Freehold St NE24 ....17 F8
Freeman Hospl NE7 ......39 A4
Freeman Rd NE3,NE7 .....38 F4
Freeman Way
Ashington NE63 ....6 F1
Whitley Bay NE26 ....31 E7
Freesia Grange NE38 .....83 E3
Freezemoor Rd DH4 ......90 D6
Fremantle Rd NE34 ......60 B5
French St NE24 ....17 E8
Frenchman's Row NE15 ...35 B2
Frenchman's Way NE34 ...60 B8
Frensham NE38 ....84 A4
Frenton Cl NE5 ....36 C2
Friar Gdns NE10 ....56 D6
Friar Sq NE4 ....85 D6
Friar Way NE32 ....58 C7
Friar's Row NE11 ....78 F5
Friarage Ave SR6 ....75 D3
Friars NE1 ....98 C1
Friars Dene Rd NE10 .....56 C2
Friars Gate NE61 ....8 D7
Friars St NE1 ....98 B1
Friars Way NE5 ....54 C8
Friarsfield Cl SR3 ....91 E5
Friarside Cres NE39 .....78 D8
Friarside Gdns
Burnopfield NE16 ....78 F6
Whickham NE16 ....69 A6
Friarside Rd NE4 ....54 E8
Friary Gdns NE10 ....56 C1
Frinton Pk SR3 ....86 A3
Frobisher Ct SR3 ....91 F6
Frobisher St NE31 ....58 A6
Frome Gdns NE9 ....70 F2
Frome Pl NE23 ....22 B8
Frome Sq SR4 ....85 C6
Front Rd SR4 ....85 C6
Front St Annitsford NE23 ..22 B1
Blaydon NE21 ....53 B1
Blyth NE24 ....16 E7
Boldon Colliery NE35 .....58 E1
Burnopfield NE16 ....79 B6
Burnopfield,Hobson NE16 ..79 A4
Chester le S DH3 ....88 C3
Cleadon SR6 ....60 A1
Corbridge NE45 ....46 F5
Cramlington NE23 ....22 B6
Dinnington NE13 ....27 B7

Front St continued
Dipton DH9 ....78 E1
Earsdon NE25 ....31 A5
East Boldon NE36 ....74 C7
Ebchester DH8 ....76 E3
Ellington NE61 ....1 C5
Fence Houses DH4 ....94 A8
Guide Post NE62 ....10 E7
Haswell DH6 ....97 E1
Hetton le H DH5 ....95 A3
Hetton le Hole,Low Moorsley
DH5 ....94 E1
High Pittington DH6 ......96 B6
High Spen NE39 ....67 A5
Killingworth NE12,NE23 ...29 B5
Longbenton NE7,NE12 ....39 C5
Newbiggin-by-t-S NE64 ....7 E4
Newbottle DH4 ....90 D3
Newbottle DH4 ....90 D4
North Shields NE29 ......41 E5
Prudhoe NE42 ....50 D2
Prudhoe,Hagg Bank NE41 ..50 F5
Seghill NE23 ....22 F2
Sherburn DH6 ....96 A1
Sherburn Hill DH6 ....96 D1
South Hetton DH6 ....97 D3
Tanfield DH9 ....79 B2
Tantobie DH9 ....79 B2
Tynemouth NE30 ....42 D7
Tynemouth,Cullercoats
NE30 ....31 A5
Tynemouth,Preston NE29 ..42 A8
Washington NE37 ....83 D8
Whickham NE16 ....69 B7
Whickham,Swalwell NE16 ..54 A1
Whitburn SR6 ....75 F8
Whitley Bay NE25,NE26 ...31 E4
Front St E Bedlington NE22 ..16 A8
Haswell DH6 ....97 F3
Penshaw DH4 ....90 B8
Front St W
Bedlington NE22 ....15 F8
Penshaw DH4 ....90 B8
Front Street Com Prim Sch
NE16 ....69 A7
Frosterley Cl DH5 ....97 D8
Frosterley Gdns SR3 .....86 B2
Frosterley Pl NE4 ....98 A2
Frosterley Wlk NE16 .....69 B3
Froude Ave NE34 ....59 C3
Fuchsia Gdns NE31 ......57 E3
Fuchsia Pl NE5 ....37 D2
Fulbrook Cl NE23 ....16 B2
Fulbrook Rd NE3 ....37 F5
Fuller Rd SR2 ....86 E4
Fullerton Pl NE9 ....71 A8
Fulmar Dr Blyth NE24 ....17 E3
Washington NE38 ....42 F2
Fulmar Lodge NE33 ......42 F2
Fulmar Wlk SR6 ....60 F7
Fulwell Ave NE34 ....60 B7
Fulwell Gn NE5 ....37 B1
Fulwell Inf Sch SR6 .....75 E4
Fulwell Jun Sch SR6 .....75 E4
Fulwell Mill* SR5 ....75 C3
Fulwell Rd SR6 ....75 D2
Furnace Bank NE22 .....11 D1
Furness Ct SR3 ....91 F6
Furrowfield NE10 ....71 C6
Furrowfield Jun Sch
DH3 ....82 D3
Furrowfield Sch NE10 ....71 C6
Furzefield Rd NE3 ....38 B4
Fyling Ho SR3 ....91 F5
Fylingdale Dr SR3 ....92 C7

G

Gables Ct SR4 ....85 C3
Gables The Blyth NE24 ...17 D8
Newcastle-u-T NE13 .....37 C4
Wallsend NE28 ....83 E4
Gadwall Rd NE4 ....94 B6
Gainers Terr NE28 ....57 C8
Gainford Chester le S DH2 ..88 A3
Gateshead NE9 ....70 F2
Gainsborough Ave
Washington NE38 ....83 E4
Whiteleas NE34 ....59 C2
Gainsborough Cl NE25 ...31 C7
Gainsborough Cres
Gateshead NE9 ....71 B7
Shiney Row DH4 ....90 A5
Gainsborough Pl NE23 ...22 B3
Gainsborough Rd SR4 ....85 C2
Gainsborough Sq SR4 ....85 C2
Gainsford Ave NE9 ......70 E4
Gairloch Cl NE23 ....16 B1
Gairloch Dr NE38 ....83 A3
Gairloch Rd SR4 ....85 C3
Gairsay Cl SR2 ....92 E8
Galashiels Gr DH4 ....90 B5
Galashiels Rd SR4 ....85 C3
Galen Ho NE1 ....99 A1
Gallalaw Terr NE3 ....38 F5
Gallant Terr NE28 ....41 C1
Galleries The NE38 ......83 C5
Galley's Gill Rd SR1 ....102 C3
Galloping Green Cotts
NE9 ....71 D2
Galloping Green Farm Cl
NE9 ....71 D2
Galloping Green Rd NE9 ..71 D2
Gallowgate NE1 ....98 C1
Gallowhill La NE15,NE42 ..50 B7

Gallows Bank NE46 ......45 B3
Galsworthy Ctr The NE34 ..59 B2
Galsworthy Rd
Biddick Hall NE34 ....59 B3
Sunderland SR4 ....85 C3
Whiteleas NE34 ....59 C3
Galway Rd SR4 ....85 B3
Galway Sq SR4 ....85 B3
Gambia Rd SR4 ....85 B2
Gambia Sq SR4 ....85 B2
Ganton Ave NE23 ....22 B4
Ganton Cl NE37 ....72 C2
Ganton Ct NE34 ....59 F3
Gaprigg Ct NE46 ....45 B4
Gaprigg La NE46 ....45 A4
Garasdale Cl NE24 ....17 C4
Garcia Terr SR6 ....75 D4
Garden City Villas NE63 ...6 D3
Garden Cl NE13 ....28 B8
Garden Cres DH8 ....76 F4
Garden Croft NE12 ......39 E8
Garden Dr NE31 ....57 D4
Garden Est NE35 ....95 B4
Garden House Cres NE16 ..68 B4
Garden House Est NE40 ...51 F4
Garden House Farm DH2 ..88 B1
Garden La Cleadon SR6 ...74 F8
South Shields NE33 ......42 C2
Garden Pk NE28 ....40 F4
Garden Pl Penshaw DH4 ..90 B7
Sunderland SR1 ....102 C3
Garden St Blaydon NE21 ...53 C3
Newbottle DH4 ....90 D3
Newcastle-u-T NE3 ......38 C4
Garden Terr
Boldon NE21 ....53 B1
Crawcrook NE40 ....51 F4
Crawcrook,Ryton Woodside
NE40 ....52 A3
Earsdon NE25 ....31 A5
Hexham NE46 ....45 A5
Newbottle DH4 ....90 D3
Gardener St NE4 ....100 A3
Gardens The
Chester le S DH2 ....88 B3
Washington NE38 ....83 E4
Whitley Bay NE25 ....31 F4
Gardiner Rd SR4 ....85 B3
Gardiner Sq
Kibblesworth NE11 ......81 C6
Sunderland SR4 ....85 B3
Gardner Pk NE29 ....41 F5
Gardner Pl NE29 ....42 B5
Garesfield Gdns
Burnopfield NE16 ....78 F6
Rowlands Gill NE39 ......67 E3
Garesfield La NE21,NE39 ..67 E2
Gareston Cl NE24 ....17 B7
Garfield St SR4 ....85 F7
Garforth Cl NE23 ....22 A4
Garland Terr DH4 ....94 A8
Garleigh Cl NE12 ....29 F3
Garmondsway NE6 ......56 C5
Garner Cl NE5 ....36 D3
Garnet St SR4 ....85 F7
Garrett Cl NE28 ....39 F6
Garrick Cl NE29 ....41 C7
Garrick St NE33 ....59 C8
Garrigill NE38 ....83 F1
Garsdale DH3 ....82 E1
Garsdale Ave NE37 ......83 C8
Garsdale Rd NE26 ....24 E1
Garside Ave DH3 ....82 E2
Garstin Cl NE7 ....39 E3
Garth Cres Blaydon NE21 ..53 B1
South Shields NE33 ......43 A1
Garth Farm Rd NE21 ....53 B1
Garth Heads NE1 ....99 C1
Garth Sixteen NE12 .....29 D4
Garth The
Blaydon NE21 ....53 B1
Medomsley DH8 ....77 C2
Newcastle-u-T NE5 ......36 E1
Newcastle-u-T,Kenton NE3 ..37 F4
Garth Thirty Three NE12 ..29 D3
Garth Thirty Two NE12 ...29 E3
Garth Twenty NE12 ......29 E3
Garth Twenty Five NE12 ..29 F3
Garth Twenty Four NE12 ..29 E3
Garth Twenty One NE12 ..29 E4
Garth Twenty Seven
NE12 ....29 E3
Garth Twenty Two NE12 ..29 E3
Garthfield Cl NE5 ....37 A3
Garthfield Cnr NE5 ......37 A3
Garthfield Cres NE5 .....37 A3
Gartland Rd SR4 ....85 B3
Garvey Villas N10,NE9 ...71 C6
Garwood St NE33 ....59 B8
Gas House La NE61 ......4 A1
Gas La NE21 ....53 C4
Gaskell Ave NE34 ....59 B3
Gatacre St NE24 ....17 E8
Gate The NE1 ....98 B2
Gateley Ave NE24 ....17 D4
Gatesgarth NE9 ....71 A5
Gatesgarth Gr SR6 .....75 D5
Gateshead Coll NE10 ....70 F7
Gateshead Coll (Annexe)
NE9 ....71 A7
Gateshead Highway
NE8 ....101 C2
Gateshead International Stad
(Athletics Gd) NE10 .....56 C3
Gateshead Jewish Boarding
Sch NE8 ....101 B1

Gateshead Jewish Prim Sch
NE8 ....101 B1
Gateshead Jewish Teachers
Training Coll NE8 ......101 B1
Gateshead Rd NE16 ......69 C3
Gateshead Sta NE8 .....101 B3
Gateshead Stadium Sta
NE8 ....56 A2
Gateshead Talmudical Coll
NE8 ....101 B1
Gatwick Ct NE3 ....37 C7
Gatwick Rd SR4 ....85 B3
Gaughan Cl NE4 ....56 F3
Gaweswell Terr DH4 .....90 D4
Gayhurst Cres SR3 .....92 B6
Gayton Rd NE37 ....72 E1
Geddes Rd SR4 ....85 B3
Gellesfield Chare NE16 ...69 B4
Gelt Cres DH5 ....95 B2
General Graham St SR4 ..102 A1
General Havelock Rd
SR4 ....85 E6
General's Wood The
NE38 ....89 B8
Geneva Rd 6 SR4 ......85 B3
Genister Pl NE4 ....54 D8
Geoffrey St Whitburn SR6 ..60 F1
Whiteleas NE34 ....59 C3
George Rd
Bedlington NE22 ....11 D2
Wallsend NE28 ....57 B8
George Scott St NE33 ...42 D4
George Smith Gdns
NE10 ....56 C2
George Sq NE30 ....42 B6
George St Ashington NE63 ..6 E4
Birtley DH3 ....82 B4
Blaydon NE21 ....53 D3
Blyth NE24 ....17 E6
Brunswick Village NE13 ..28 A6
Chester le S DH3 ....88 B2
6 Crawcrook NE40 ......51 F3
6 Gateshead NE8 ....56 F1
Haswell DH6 ....97 F3
Hetton le H DH5 ....95 A5
Newcastle-u-T NE1,NE4 ..100 C4
Newcastle-u-T,Coxlodge
NE3 ....38 A5
North Shields NE30 .....42 B6
Ryhope SR2 ....93 A6
Sherburn DH6 ....96 A1
Walbottle NE15 ....35 F2
Wallsend NE28 ....41 B1
Whickham NE16 ....69 A7
George St E SR3 ....92 A8
George St N SR6 ....103 A4
George St W 8 SR3 .....92 A8
George Stephenson Com
High Sch NE12 ....29 D3
George Stephenson Way
NE29 ....42 A3
George Stephenson's
Cottage* NE41 ....51 D7
George Washington Prim Sch
NE37 ....72 C1
George's View NE23 .....29 A7
Georges Rd
Newcastle-u-T NE4 ......54 F4
Newcastle-u-T,Elswick NE4 ..54 F3
Georgian Ct
Longbenton NE12 ....29 B1
Sunderland SR4 ....86 A4
Gerald St
Newcastle-u-T NE4 ......54 D4
Whiteleas NE34 ....59 C3
Gerrard Cl
Cramlington NE23 ....22 B4
Whitley Bay NE26 ....24 E1
Gerrard Rd
6 Sunderland SR4 ......85 B3
Whitley Bay NE26 ....24 F1
Gertrude St DH4 ....90 D2
Ghyll Edge NE61 ....3 C1
Gibbon's Wlk NE34 .....59 A2
Gibbs Ct 3 DH2 ....88 C2
Gibside Chester le S DH2 ..88 A3
* Rowlands Gill NE16 ....68 B2
Gibside Chapel* NE16 ...68 A1
Gibside Cres NE16 ......79 D8
Gibside Ct
Burnopfield NE16 ....79 B6
Dunston NE11 ....69 F6
Gibside Gdns NE15 .....85 A6
Gibside Sch NE16 ......68 A5
Gibside Terr NE16 ......79 B6
Gibside View NE21 .....68 B8
Gibson Cl NE35 ....73 F8
Gibson Fields NE46 .....45 B4
Gibson Ho 8 NE46 .....45 B4
Gibson Pl 8 NE46 ......45 A5
Gibson St
Newbiggin-by-t-S NE64 ...7 D4
Newcastle-u-T NE1 .....99 C1
Wallsend NE28 ....40 F5
Gipton Terr NE40 ....52 A4
Gifford Sq SR4 ....85 C4
Gilberdyke NE10 ....72 A5
Gilbert Rd SR4 ....85 B3
Gilbert Sq SR4 ....85 B2
Gilbert St NE35 ....73 F8
Gilderdale DH4 ....89 E8
Gilderdale Way NE23 ...22 A4
Giles Pl 11 NE46 ....45 A5
Gilesgate NE46 ....45 A5
Gilesgate Ct 18 NE46 ...45 A5
Gilesgate Rd DH5 ....95 B1

Gilhespy Green Cvn Pk
NE24 ....17 F4
Gilhurst Grange SR1 ...102 B2
Gill Burn NE39 ....67 E3
Gill Crescent N DH4 .....89 E1
Gill Crescent S DH4 .....89 E1
Gill Ct NE13 ....28 A6
Gill Side Gr SR6 ....75 E2
Gill St NE4 ....54 E5
Gillas La DH5 ....95 A7
Gillas La E DH5 ....94 F7
Gillas La W DH5 ....94 E6
Gillas Lane Prim Sch
DH5 ....94 F7
Gillhurst Ho SR1 ......102 B3
Gillies St NE6 ....58 D6
Gilliland Cres DH3 ......82 C6
Gillingham Rd SR4 ......85 C3
Gillside Ct 4 NE34 .....59 A5
Gillwood Ct NE4 ....90 A6
Gilmore Cl NE5 ....36 D3
Gilmore Ho NE8 ....70 E8
Gilpin St DH4 ....90 D8
Gilsland Ave NE28 ......40 F3
Gilsland Gr NF73 ....16 B1
Gilsland St SR4 ....102 A2
Gilwell Way NE3 ....28 B1
Gingler La NE40 ....52 A2
Girtin Rd NE34 ....59 D7
Girven Terr DH5 ....95 B1
Girven Terr W DH5 .....95 B1
Gisburn Ct NE23 ....16 B1
Gishford Way NE5 ......37 B2
Givens St SR6 ....75 E2
Glade The Hedworth NE32 ..73 B8
Walbottle NE15 ....36 A2
Gladeley Way NE16 .....68 C2
Gladewell Ct NE62 ......10 E7
Gladstonbury Pl NE12 ...39 C7
Gladstone Ave NE26 ....31 F6
Gladstone Pl NE2 ......99 B3
Gladstone St Blyth NE24 ..17 D8
Fence Houses DH4 ....94 B8
Hebburn NE31,NE32 ....58 A6
Morpeth NE61 ....9 B8
Newcastle-u-T NE15 ....53 C6
Sunderland SR6 ....75 D1
3 Wallsend NE28 ......40 F2
Gladstone Terr
Bedlington NE22 ....11 A1
Birtley DH3 ....82 B4
2 Boldon Colliery NE35 ..58 E1
Gateshead NE8 ....101 C1
Newcastle-u-T NE2 .....99 B3
Penshaw DH4 ....89 F8
Washington NE37 ....83 F8
8 Whitley Bay NE26 ....32 B4
Gladstone Terr W NE8 ..101 B1
Gladwyn Rd 2 SR4 .....85 B2
Gladwyn Sq SR4 ....85 B2
Glaholm Rd SR2 ....103 C2
Glaisdale Cl NE34 ......59 A4
Glaisdale Dr SR6 ....75 E6
Glaisdale Rd NE7 ......39 A5
Glamis Ave
Newcastle-u-T NE3 ......28 C1
Sunderland SR4 ....85 C4
Glamis Cres NE39 ......68 B4
Glamis Ct Bournmoor DH4 ..89 D1
Glamis Terr NE16 ......69 A1
Glamis Villas DH3 ......82 C6
Glanmore Rd 3 SR4 ....85 B3
Glantlees NE5 ....37 A2
Glanton Ave NE25 ......23 C3
Glanton Cl
Chester le S DH2 ....88 A2
Newcastle-u-T NE2 .....72 C7
Morpeth NE61 ....9 B5
3 Newcastle-u-T NE6 ...56 C4
Wallsend NE28 ....40 E3
Glanton Ct NE11 ......100 A1
Glanton Ho NE24 ....17 B8
Glanton Rd Hexham NE46 ..45 D4
Tynemouth NE29 ....42 A7
Glanton Sq SR4 ....85 C3
Glanton Wynd NE3 .....38 B7
Glanville Cl NE11 ....70 B7
Glanville Rd SR3 ....91 D5
Glasbury Ave SR4 ......85 C4
Glasgow Rd NE32 ......58 E3
Glassey Terr NE22 .....11 D1
Glasshouse St NE6 .....56 C4
Glastonbury NE38 ......83 D3
Glastonbury Gr NE2 ....38 F2
Glazebury Way NE23 ...16 B1
Glebe Ave
Longbenton NE12 ......39 D7
Whickham NE16 ....69 B7
Glebe Cl
Newcastle-u-T NE5 ......36 D3
Ponteland NE20 ....25 E7
Glebe Cres
Longbenton NE12 ......29 D1
Washington NE38 ......83 E6
Glebe Ct NE22 ....11 F1
Glebe Dr SR7 ....92 F2
Glebe Est SR7 ....92 F2
Glebe Farm NE62 ......10 F1
Glebe Mews NE22 .....10 F1
Glebe Rd Bedlington NE22 ..10 F1
Longbenton NE12 ......29 D1
Glebe Rise NE16 ....69 B7
Glebe Sq NE4 ....54 E6

Glebe Terr
Choppington NE62 . . . .**10** E4
1 Dunston NE11 . . . .**69** F8
2 Houghton-le-S DH4 . . . . . .**90** D1
Longbenton NE12 . . . .**29** D1
Glebe The
6 South Shields NE33 . . . . . .**42** D1
Stannington NE61 . . . .**14** C4
Glebe Village Prim Sch
NE38 . . . .**83** D5
Glebe Villas NE12 . . . .**29** C1
Glebe Wlk NE16 . . . .**69** B7
Glebelands NE45 . . . .**47** A6
Glen Ave NE43 . . . .**64** C2
Glen Barr DH2 . . . .**88** B4
Glen Cl NE39 . . . .**67** E3
Glen Ct NE31 . . . .**57** D5
Glen Luce Dr SR2 . . . .**86** F2
Glen Path SR2 . . . .**86** D3
Glen St NE31 . . . .**57** D5
Glen Terr Chester le S DH2 .**88** A4
Hexham NE46 . . . .**45** C4
Washington NE38 . . . .**83** E4
Glen The SR2 . . . .**86** D3
Glen Thorpe Ave SR6 . . . . . .**75** E2
Glen's Flats DH6 . . . .**96** B5
Glenallen Gdns NE30 . . . . . .**32** C1
Glenavon Ave DH2 . . . .**88** B4
Glenbrooke Terr NE9 . . . . . .**70** F4
Glenburn Cl NE38 . . . .**82** F3
Glencarron Cl NE38 . . . .**83** A3
Glencoe NE12 . . . .**29** D4
Glencoe Ave
Chester le S DH2 . . . .**88** B4
Cramlington NE23 . . . .**22** B3
Glencoe Rd SR4 . . . .**85** B2
Glencoe Rise NE39 . . . .**67** C1
Glencoe Sq SR4 . . . .**85** B3
Glencoe Terr NE39 . . . .**67** C1
Glencourse NE36 . . . .**74** E7
Glendale Ave Blyth NE24 . . .**16** E8
Newcastle-u-T NE3 . . . .**38** A4
North Shields NE29 . . . .**41** F6
Stakeford NE62 . . . .**11** A8
Wallsend NE28 . . . .**40** C2
Washington NE37 . . . .**83** C8
Whickham NE16 . . . .**69** A6
Whitley Bay NE26 . . . .**32** A7
Glendale Cl Blaydon NE21 . . .**67** F8
Newcastle-u-T NE5 . . . .**36** D3
Sunderland SR3 . . . .**91** C6
Glendale Gdns
Gateshead NE9 . . . .**71** B5
Stakeford NE62 . . . .**11** A8
Glendale Gr NE29 . . . .**41** F6
Glendale Rd
Ashington NE63 . . . .**7** A2
Shiremoor NE27 . . . .**31** A3
Glendale Terr 6 NE6 . . . .**56** C6
Glendford Rd NE24 . . . .**17** D4
Glendower Ave NE29 . . . .**41** D6
Glendyn Cl NE7 . . . .**39** A1
Gleneagle Cl NE5 . . . .**36** D3
Gleneagles
South Shields NE33 . . . .**42** F1
Whitley Bay NE25 . . . .**31** D6
Gleneagles Cl NE7 . . . .**39** C5
Gleneagles Ct NE25 . . . .**31** D6
Gleneagles Dr NE37 . . . .**72** C2
Gleneagles Rd
Gateshead NE9 . . . .**70** E3
Sunderland SR4 . . . .**85** B2
Gleneagles Sq 1 SR4 . . . . . .**85** B2
Glenesk Gdns SR2 . . . .**86** C2
Glenesk Rd SR2 . . . .**86** C3
Glenfield Ave NE23 . . . .**16** B1
Glenfield Rd
Longbenton NE12 . . . .**39** B7
Longbenton NE12 . . . .**39** C7
Glengarvan Cl NE38 . . . .**83** A3
Glenholme 7 NE38 . . . .**82** F3
Glenhurst Dr
Newcastle-u-T NE5 . . . .**36** D3
Whickham NE16 . . . .**68** F4
Glenhurst Gr NE34 . . . .**59** F6
Glenkerry Cl NE38 . . . .**83** A3
Glenleigh Dr SR4 . . . .**85** C4
Glenluce Ct NE23 . . . .**22** B4
Glenluce Dr NE23 . . . .**22** B3
Glenmoor NE31 . . . .**57** D7
Glenmore Ave DH2 . . . .**88** C4
Glenmuir Ave NE23 . . . .**22** A3
Glenorrin Cl NE38 . . . .**83** A3
Glenridge Ave 8 NE6 . . . .**39** B1
Glenroy Gdns DH2 . . . .**88** B4
Glenshiel Cl NE38 . . . .**83** A3
Glenside Ellington NE61 . . . . . .**1** E5
Hedworth NE32 . . . .**58** C2
Glenside Ct NE9 . . . .**70** E4
Glenthorn Rd NE2 . . . .**38** E2
Glenthorne Rd 1 SR6 . . . . . .**75** E2
Glenthorpe NE10 . . . .**72** B8
Glenuce DH3 . . . .**82** E3
Glenwood NE63 . . . .**6** C2
Glenwood Wlk NE5 . . . .**36** D3
Gloria Ave NE25 . . . .**23** D6
Glossop St NE39 . . . .**66** F4
Gloucester Ave NE6 . . . .**75** E4
Gloucester Ct NE3 . . . .**37** C8
Gloucester Pl NE34 . . . .**60** A5
Gloucester Rd
Newcastle-u-T NE4 . . . .**98** A1
Shiremoor NE27 . . . .**41** B7
Gloucester St NE25 . . . .**23** D6

Gloucester Terr
Haswell DH6 . . . .**97** E1
Newcastle-u-T NE4 . . . .**100** A4
Gloucester Way
Hedworth NE32 . . . .**58** B2
Newcastle-u-T NE4 . . . .**100** B4
Glover Ind Est NE37 . . . .**83** E7
Glover Network Ctr NE37 . . .**83** F7
Glover Rd Sunderland SR4 . . .**85** B2
Washington NE37 . . . .**83** F8
Glover Sq SR4 . . . .**85** B2
Glovers Pl 14 NE46 . . . .**45** A5
Glynfellis NE10 . . . .**71** F4
Glynfellis Ct NE10 . . . .**71** F5
Glynwood Cl NE23 . . . .**16** B1
Glynwood Com Prim Sch
NE9 . . . .**71** A5
Glynwood Gdns NE9 . . . .**71** A5
Goalmouth Cl 6 SR6 . . . .**75** E2
Goathland Ave NE12 . . . .**39** C6
Goathland Cl SR3 . . . .**92** C7
Goathland Dr SR3 . . . .**92** B6
Goathland Prim Sch
NE12 . . . .**39** C6
Godfrey Rd SR4 . . . .**85** B3
Gofton Wlk NE5 . . . .**37** A2
Goldcrest Rd NE38 . . . .**82** F3
Goldfinch Cl NE4 . . . .**54** F4
Goldlynn Dr SR3 . . . .**91** E6
Goldsbrough Ct NE2 . . . .**98** C3
Goldsmith Rd SR4 . . . .**85** B2
Goldspink La NE2 . . . .**56** A7
Goldstone Ct NE12 . . . .**29** E4
Goldthorpe Cl NE23 . . . .**16** B1
Golf Course Rd DH4 . . . .**90** A4
Gompertz Gdns NE33 . . . .**59** B8
Gooch Ave NE22 . . . .**11** A4
Goodrich Cl DH4 . . . .**90** C5
Goodwood NE12 . . . .**29** E3
Goodwood Ave NE8 . . . .**70** C8
Goodwood Cl NE5 . . . .**36** D3
Goodwood Ct NE63 . . . .**6** D2
Goodwood Rd SR4 . . . .**85** A3
Goodwood Sq SR4 . . . .**85** A3
Goole Rd SR4 . . . .**85** C3
Goose Hill NE61 . . . .**9** A8
Gordon Ave
Newcastle-u-T NE3 . . . .**38** C4
Sunderland SR5 . . . .**85** A8
Gordon Ct 8 NE10 . . . .**56** D1
Gordon Dr NE36 . . . .**74** D7
Gordon Ho
Newcastle-u-T NE6 . . . .**56** B5
Whitley Bay NE26 . . . .**32** C4
Gordon Rd Blyth NE24 . . . . . .**17** F6
Newcastle-u-T NE6 . . . .**56** B5
South Shields NE34 . . . .**59** C6
Sunderland SR4 . . . .**85** B2
Gordon Sq
Newcastle-u-T NE6 . . . .**56** B5
Whitley Bay NE26 . . . .**32** C4
Gordon St NE33 . . . .**59** D8
Gordon Terr
Bedlington NE22 . . . .**16** A8
Prudhoe NE42 . . . .**50** D2
Ryhope SR2 . . . .**93** A6
Stakeford NE62 . . . .**11** C7
Sunderland SR5 . . . .**75** A2
Whitley Bay NE26 . . . .**32** C5
Gordon Terrace W NE12 . . . .**11** C7
Gorleston Way SR3 . . . .**92** A4
Gorse Ave NE34 . . . .**60** A5
Gorse Hill Way NE5 . . . .**37** C2
Gorse Rd SR2 . . . .**103** A1
Gorsedene Ave NE26 . . . .**24** F1
Gorsedene Rd NE26 . . . .**24** F1
Gorsehill NE7 . . . .**71** C5
Gorseway NE61 . . . .**8** D7
Goschen St Blyth NE24 . . . . . .**17** D8
Gateshead NE8 . . . .**70** D8
Gosforth Ave NE34 . . . .**59** C3
Gosforth Bsns Pk NE12 . . . .**38** F7
Gosforth Central Mid Sch
NE3 . . . .**38** D6
Gosforth Ctr NE3 . . . .**38** C4
Gosforth East Mid Sch
NE3 . . . .**38** D7
Gosforth High Sch NE3 . . . . .**38** C6
Gosforth Park Fst Sch
NE3 . . . .**38** D7
Gosforth Park Villas
NE13 . . . .**28** C4
Gosforth Park Way NE3 . . . . .**39** A8
Gosforth St
20 Gateshead NE10 . . . .**56** D1
Newcastle-u-T NE2 . . . .**99** C2
Gosforth Terr
Gateshead NE10 . . . .**56** F1
Newcastle-u-T NE3 . . . .**38** E5
Gosforth West Mid Sch
NE3 . . . .**38** B5
Gosport Way NE24 . . . .**17** D4
Gossington NE38 . . . .**84** A5
Goswick Ave NE7 . . . .**39** B3
Goswick Dr NE3 . . . .**37** F8
Goundry Ave SR2 . . . .**93** A6
Gourock Sq SR4 . . . .**85** A3
Govt Bldgs (DSS) NE98 . . . . .**39** A5
Gowan Terr NE2 . . . .**38** F1
Gowanburn
Cramlington NE23 . . . .**22** A3
Washington NE38 . . . .**83** F2
Gower Rd SR5 . . . .**75** A2
Gower St NE6 . . . .**57** A4
Gower Wlk NE10 . . . .**71** C8
Gowland Ave NE4 . . . .**54** E6
Grace Gdns NE28 . . . .**40** A4

Grace Ho NE29 . . . .**41** E3
Grace St Dunston NE11 . . . . . .**69** F8
Newcastle-u-T,Byker NE6 . . . . .**56** C6
Newcastle-u-T,Walker NE6 . . . .**56** D6
Gracefield Cl NE5 . . . .**36** D3
Gradys Yd NE15 . . . .**35** D3
Grafton Cl 6 NE6 . . . .**56** B6
Grafton Ho 7 NE6 . . . .**56** B6
Grafton Rd NE26 . . . .**32** C4
Grafton St
11 Newcastle-u-T NE6 . . . . . .**56** B6
Sunderland SR4 . . . .**102** B3
Gragareth Way NE37 . . . .**83** A6
Graham Ave NE16 . . . .**69** B8
Graham Park Rd NE3 . . . .**38** C3
Graham Rd NE31 . . . .**57** D5
Graham St NE33 . . . .**42** D2
Graham Terr DH6 . . . .**96** B8
Grahamsley St 6 NE8 . . . . . .**101** C2
Grainger Ct NE4 . . . .**54** F5
Grainger Mkt NE1 . . . .**99** A1
Grainger Park Rd NE4 . . . . . .**54** F5
Grainger St NE1 . . . .**99** A1
Graingerville N NE4 . . . .**98** A1
Graingerville S NE4 . . . .**98** A1
Grampian Ave DH2 . . . .**88** B2
Grampian Cl 8 NE29 . . . .**31** F1
Grampian Gdns NE11 . . . .**70** B6
Grampian Gr NE36 . . . .**74** F7
Grampian Pl NE12 . . . .**29** B1
Granaries The
Fence Houses DH4 . . . .**94** B8
High Spen NE39 . . . .**66** F4
Sunderland SR4 . . . .**84** F3
Granby Cl Sunderland SR3 . . .**86** B3
Sunnside NE16 . . . .**69** B3
Granby Terr 4 NE16 . . . .**69** B2
Grand Par NE30 . . . .**32** D1
Grandstand Rd NE2 . . . .**38** B2
Grandstand The NE61 . . . .**8** B6
Grange Ave
Bedlington NE22 . . . .**11** E3
Fence Houses DH4 . . . .**90** A1
Longbenton NE12 . . . .**39** E6
Shiremoor NE27 . . . .**30** F4
Grange Cl Blyth NE24 . . . .**17** D4
Tynemouth NE30 . . . .**32** D3
Wallsend NE28 . . . .**40** C2
Whitley Bay NE25 . . . .**31** D4
Grange Cres
Gateshead NE10 . . . .**72** A7
Ryton NE40 . . . .**52** C4
Sunderland SR2 . . . .**103** A1
Grange Ct Gateshead NE10 . . .**72** A7
6 Jarrow NE32 . . . .**58** B7
Morpeth NE61 . . . .**9** A7
Prudhoe NE42 . . . .**50** D2
Ryton NE40 . . . .**52** C4
Grange Dr NE40 . . . .**52** C4
Grange Est NE11 . . . .**81** C6
Grange Farm Dr NE16 . . . . . .**69** A5
Grange Fst Sch NE3 . . . .**38** B6
Grange La NE16 . . . .**69** B5
Grange Lonnen NE40 . . . .**52** B5
Grange Nook NE16 . . . .**69** A5
Grange Park Ave
Bedlington NE22 . . . .**11** E3
Sunderland SR5 . . . .**75** C3
Grange Park Prim Sch
SR5 . . . .**75** C2
Grange Pk NE25 . . . .**31** D4
Grange Pl NE32 . . . .**58** B7
Grange Rd
Gateshead NE10 . . . .**72** A7
Jarrow NE32 . . . .**58** B7
Morpeth NE61 . . . .**9** A6
Newburn NE15 . . . .**52** E8
Newcastle-u-T,Fenham NE4 . . .**54** D7
Newcastle-u-T,Gosforth
NE3 . . . .**38** C7
Ponteland NE20 . . . .**25** F7
Ryton NE40 . . . .**52** C5
Sunderland SR5 . . . .**85** A8
Grange Rd W NE32 . . . .**58** B7
Grange St S SR2 . . . .**86** F2
Grange Terr
1 East Boldon NE36 . . . .**74** D7
6 Gateshead NE9 . . . .**71** A8
Kibblesworth NE11 . . . .**81** C6
Medomsley DH8 . . . .**77** B1
Prudhoe NE42 . . . .**50** D2
2 Sunderland,High Southwick
SR5 . . . .**75** D3
Grange The
Prudhoe NE42 . . . .**50** A1
East Boldon NE36 . . . .**74** D7
Grange View
East Rainton DH5 . . . .**94** D5
Newbottle DH4 . . . .**90** B3
Ryton NE40 . . . .**52** C4
Sunderland SR5 . . . .**75** C3
Grange Villas NE38 . . . . .69** A5
Grange Wlk 3 NE16 . . . .**69** A5
Grangemere Cl SR2 . . . .**86** F1
Grangeside Ct 8 SR2 . . . .**31** F1
Grangetown Prim Sch
SR2 . . . .**86** F3
Grangewood Cl DH4 . . . .**90** A5
Grangewood Ct 3 DH4 . . . . .**90** A6
Grant St NE32 . . . .**58** A7
Grantham Dr NE9 . . . .**71** A4
Grantham Pl NE23 . . . .**22** A4
Grantham Rd
Newcastle-u-T NE2 . . . .**99** C3
Sunderland SR6 . . . .**75** E2
Grantham St NE24 . . . .**17** F6

Granville Ave
Longbenton NE12 . . . .**29** E1
Seaton Sluice NE26 . . . .**24** D5
Granville Cres NE22 . . . .**39** E7
Granville Ct NE2 . . . .**99** C4
Granville Dr
Longbenton NE12 . . . .**39** E7
Newcastle-u-T NE5 . . . .**36** D3
Shiney Row DH4 . . . .**90** C5
Granville Gdns
Newcastle-u-T NE12 . . . .**56** A8
Stakeford NE62 . . . .**11** A8
Granville Lodge NE12 . . . . . .**39** E8
Granville Rd
Newcastle-u-T,Gosforth
NE3 . . . .**38** D7
Newcastle-u-T,Jesmond
NE2 . . . .**99** C4
Granville St
Gateshead NE8 . . . .**101** C1
Sunderland SR4 . . . .**102** B3
Grasmere Birtley DH3 . . . .**82** E2
Cleadon SR6 . . . .**60** A1
Grasmere Ave
Easington Lane DH5 . . . .**97** C8
Hebburn NE31 . . . .**71** F8
Hedworth NE32 . . . .**58** D2
Newburn NE15 . . . .**52** E7
Newcastle-u-T NE6 . . . .**56** F5
Grasmere Cres
Blaydon NE21 . . . .**68** B8
5 Penshaw DH4 . . . .**90** B6
Sunderland SR5 . . . .**75** C3
Whitley Bay NE26 . . . .**31** F7
Grasmere Ct
Killingworth NE12 . . . .**29** C4
Newburn NE15 . . . .**52** E7
Grasmere Gdns
South Shields NE34 . . . .**59** E6
Washington NE38 . . . .**83** E4
Grasmere Ho NE6 . . . .**56** E5
Grasmere Pl NE3 . . . .**38** C7
Grasmere Rd
Chester le S DH2 . . . .**88** B1
Hebburn NE31 . . . .**57** F4
Wallsend NE28 . . . .**40** A1
Whickham NE16 . . . .**69** C7
Grasmere St NE8 . . . .**101** B1
Grasmere St W NE8 . . . .**101** B1
Grasmere Terr
Newbiggin-by-t-S NE64 . . . .**7** D8
Washington NE38 . . . .**83** E5
Grasmere Way NE24 . . . .**17** A8
Grasmoor Pl NE15 . . . .**53** B7
Grassbanks NE10 . . . .**72** A6
Grassholm Pl NE12 . . . .**39** A7
Grassholme Mdws SR3 . . . . .**86** B2
Grassington Dr NE23 . . . .**22** A4
Grasslees NE38 . . . .**83** A4
Grasswell Cvn Site DH4 . . . . .**90** D3
Grasswell Dr NE5 . . . .**37** D3
Grasswell Terr DH4 . . . .**90** D2
Gravel Wlks DH5 . . . .**90** F1
Gravesend Rd SR4 . . . .**85** B2
Gravesend Sq SR4 . . . .**85** C2
Gray Ave Chester le S DH2 . . .**88** B7
Widopen NE13 . . . .**28** C2
Gray Ct SR2 . . . .**103** A2
Gray Rd Sunderland SR2 . . . .**103** A2
Sunderland SR2 . . . .**103** C2
Gray St NE24 . . . .**12** E1
Gray's Wlk NE34 . . . .**59** A2
Graylands NE38 . . . .**88** E8
Grayling Ct SR3 . . . .**91** C5
Grayling Rd NE11 . . . .**70** B7
Grays Cross SR1 . . . .**103** B3
Grays Terr 8 NE35 . . . .**58** C1
Graystones NE10 . . . .**72** B6
Great Lime Rd
Dudley NE12,NE13,NE23 . . . . .**29** A5
Longbenton NE12 . . . .**29** D1
Great North Rd
Newcastle-u-T,Gosforth
NE3 . . . .**38** C7
Newcastle-u-T,West Jesmond
NE2 . . . .**38** D2
Stannington NE61 . . . .**9** A4
Great Park Way
Hazlerigg NE13 . . . .**27** F2
Newcastle-u-T NE13 . . . .**28** A3
Greathead St NE33 . . . .**59** B7
Grebe Cl Ashington NE63 . . . . .**6** E1
Blyth NE24 . . . .**17** E5
Dunston NE11 . . . .**100** A2
Grebe Ct NE2 . . . .**38** F1
Greely Rd NE5 . . . .**36** F2
Green Acres Morpeth NE61 . . .**8** F7
Ponteland NE20 . . . .**25** C1
Green Ave DH4 . . . .**90** C4
Green Bank Cl Stannington NE61 . .**14** C4
Tynemouth NE30 . . . .**32** B1
Whitley Bay NE25 . . . .**31** D4
Green Cres NE23 . . . .**22** B6
Green Gr NE40 . . . .**52** B3
Green Hill Wlk NE34 . . . .**60** C6
Green La Ashington NE63 . . . . . .**6** C3
Dudley NE23 . . . .**28** F8
East Boldon NE36 . . . .**74** C7
Gateshead,Felling NE10 . . . . . .**56** D2
Gateshead,Pelaw NE10 . . . . . .**71** E8
Haswell DH6 . . . .**97** B3
Killingworth NE12 . . . .**29** E2
Pontefract NE20 . . . .**4** B1
Seaham SR7 . . . .**95** F6
South Shields NE34 . . . .**59** B4
Stannington NE61 . . . .**13** D2

Green La continued
Stannington,Duddo Hill
NE61 . . . .**13** D5
Woolsington NE13 . . . .**36** F8
Morpeth,Stobhillgate NE61 . . . .**9** B7
Green Lane Gdns NE10 . . . . . .**56** C2
Green Pk NE28 . . . .**39** E3
Green Sq NE25 . . . .**31** D4
Green St SR1 . . . .**103** A3
Green Terr SR1 . . . .**102** C2
Green The
Chester le S DH2 . . . .**88** B3
Chopwell NE17 . . . .**77** B8
Gateshead NE10 . . . .**71** E8
Houghton-le-S DH5 . . . .**90** F1
New Silksworth SR3 . . . .**92** C7
Newcastle-u-T NE3 . . . .**37** F3
Ovington NE42 . . . .**49** C4
Ponteland NE20 . . . .**25** F7
Rowlands Gill NE39 . . . .**67** C2
Sunderland,Bishopwearmouth
SR1 . . . .**102** C2
Sunderland,Southwick SR5 . . .**75** A1
Walbottle NE15 . . . .**35** F1
Whitley Bay NE25 . . . .**31** E6
Green's Pl NE33 . . . .**42** C4
Green-Fields NE40 . . . .**52** B3
Greenacre Pk NE9 . . . .**70** E3
Greenacres Cl NE40 . . . .**52** A3
Greenbank Blaydon NE21 . . . .**53** C2
Jarrow NE32 . . . .**58** B7
Greenbank Dr SR4 . . . .**85** A5
Greenbank St 4 DH3 . . . .**88** C3
Greenbank Villas NE32 . . . . .**58** B7
Greenbourne Gdns NE10 . . .**71** C7
Greencroft NE63 . . . .**6** C2
Greencroft Ave
Corbridge NE45 . . . .**47** A6
Newcastle-u-T NE6 . . . .**57** A8
Greendale Cl NE24 . . . .**17** A8
Greendale Gdns DH5 . . . .**94** F2
Greendyke Ct NE5 . . . .**37** A5
Greener Ct NE42 . . . .**50** B1
Greenesfield Bsns Ctr
NE8 . . . .**101** B3
Greenfield Ave NE5 . . . .**37** A2
Greenfield Dr NE62 . . . .**10** E6
Greenfield Pl
Newcastle-u-T NE4 . . . .**98** C1
Ryton NE40 . . . .**52** D5
Greenfield Rd NE3 . . . .**28** B1
Greenfield Terr 2 NE10 . . . . .**56** F1
Greenfields DH2 . . . .**82** A2
Greenfields Com Prim Sch
NE13 . . . .**28** C6
Greenfields Sch NE31 . . . .**58** A6
Greenfinch Cl NE38 . . . .**82** F3
Greenford NE11 . . . .**81** D6
Greenford La DH2,NE11 . . . . .**81** A6
Greenford Rd NE6 . . . .**57** A4
Greenhead NE38 . . . .**82** F4
Greenhaugh Rd NE25 . . . .**31** B5
Greenhead NE38 . . . .**82** F4
Greenhead Rd NE17 . . . .**66** B3
Greenhead Terr NE17 . . . .**66** B2
Greenhill View NE5 . . . .**37** E2
Greenhills NE12 . . . .**29** D5
Greenholme Cl NE23 . . . .**16** B1
Greenhow Cl 2 SR2 . . . .**92** F5
Greenlands NE32 . . . .**58** C2
Greenlands Ct NE25 . . . .**23** D4
Greenlaw NE5 . . . .**53** E8
Greenlaw Rd NE23 . . . .**22** A3
Greenlea NE29 . . . .**31** B1
Greenlea Cl
High Spen NE39 . . . .**67** A3
Sunderland SR4 . . . .**85** C3
Greenlee Dr NE63 . . . .**6** E2
Greenlee Dr NE7 . . . .**39** D3
Greenmount DH4 . . . .**90** B1
Greenock Rd SR4 . . . .**85** B2
Greenrigg Gdns 4 SR3 . . . . .**86** B3
Greenriggs Ave NE3 . . . .**28** D1
Greenrising NE42 . . . .**49** D4
Greenshields Rd SR4 . . . .**85** B2
Greenside Sq 6 SR4 . . . .**85** B2
Greenside Ashington NE63 . . . .**6** C4
South Shields NE34 . . . .**60** B6
Greenside Ave
Brunswick Village NE13 . . . . . .**28** A6
Wallsend NE28 . . . .**40** F3
Greenside Cres NE15 . . . .**54** A7
Greenside Ct SR3 . . . .**86** C3
Greenside Drift NE33 . . . .**42** F2
Greenside Prim Sch
NE40 . . . .**51** F1
Greenside Rd
Crawcrook NE40 . . . .**51** F3
Greenside NE40 . . . .**51** F2
Greentree Sq NE5 . . . .**37** B2
Greenway
Newcastle-u-T NE5 . . . .**36** D4
Newcastle-u-T,Fenham NE4 . . .**54** D8
Whitley Bay NE25 . . . .**31** D4
Greenway The NE34 . . . .**85** C4
Greenwell Cl NE21 . . . .**53** A1
Greenwell Dr NE42 . . . .**50** D3
Greenwell Terr NE40 . . . .**51** F4
Greenwich Pl NE8 . . . .**56** A4
Greenwood NE12 . . . .**29** F3
Greenwood Ave
Bedlington NE22 . . . .**11** D3
Houghton-le-S DH4 . . . .**94** C8
Wallsend NE28 . . . .**40** A1
Greenwood Cl NE38 . . . .**83** F3

enwood Gdns
ston NE11 ....70 B5
eshead NE10 ....56 D2
enwood Rd SR4 ....85 B3
enwood Sq **3** SR4 ....85 B2
gory Rd **6** SR4 ....85 B2
gory Rd SR4 ....86 C2
gory Terr DH4 ....90 A1
gson Terr SR7 ....92 F1
nada Cl NE26 ....31 F8
nada Dr NE26 ....31 F8
nada Pl NE26 ....31 F8
nfell Sq **7** SR4 ....85 B2
nville Ct
　amlington NE23 ....22 A5
　tland NE20 ....25 A4
nville Dr NE3 ....28 B1
nville Terr NE3 ....99 C1
nville Way NE26 ....31 F7
sford St NE13 ....59 C6
sham Cl NE23 ....22 B4
ta Ave DH4 ....90 A6
ta Gdns NE33 ....59 D8
ta Terr SR4 ....102 A1
tna Dr NE32 ....58 F2
tna Rd NE15 ....54 B6
ttn Pl NE7 ....39 A3
y Ave NE23 ....22 A3
y Pl **15** NE61 ....9 A8
y St
　nswick Village NE13 ....28 A6
　ighton-le-S DH4 ....90 D1
　ncastle-u-T NE1 ....99 A1
　th Shields NE30 ....42 B6
　lsend NE28 ....40 C2
y Terr **10** SR2 ....92 F6
y's Cl NE1 ....99 A1
ybourne Gdns SR2 ....86 C2
yfriars La NE12 ....39 A6
ystead Cl NE5 ....36 D3
ystead Rd NE25 ....31 B5
ystoke Ave
　ncastle-u-T NE4 ....56 A7
　nderland SR2 ....86 B2
　ickham NE16 ....69 B5
ystoke Gdns
　eshead NE9 ....71 B2
　Morpeth NE61 ....3 F1
　ncastle-u-T NE1 ....56 A8
　dand Terr SR2 ....86 C3
ystoke Rd NE28 ....69 B5
ystoke Pl NE3 ....38 C8
ystoke Pl NE23 ....22 A3
ystoke Wlk **2** NE16 ....69 A5
ystone Pl SR5 ....75 A2
ywood Ave NE4 ....54 E7
yes' Row NE23 ....22 A1
rith Terr **8** NE27 ....30 C1
nsby St NE24 ....17 E6
ndleford St NE34 ....59 E5
don Ave SR4 ....85 B5
don Cl
　amlington NE23 ....22 A3
　tley Bay NE25 ....31 E2
don Cotts SR4 ....85 C3
don Gdns SR4 ....85 B5
don Hall Christian Sch
......................................85 C4
don Inf Sch SR4 ....85 B5
don La
　nderland,South Hylton 85 B5
don Pk SR4 ....85 D3
don Terr SR4 ....102 A1
stead Ct NE34 ....59 F7
edale Gdns NE9 ....71 A3
edale St NE34 ....59 E5
edale Ct SR6 ....75 C5
dat Mkt NE1 ....99 A1
venor Ave
　ncastle-u-T NE2 ....38 F1
　ckham NE16 ....69 B8
venor Cl NE23 ....57 F4
venor Ct NE5 ....36 D3
venor Dr Cleadon SR6 ......74 E8
　tley Bay NE26 ....31 E1
venor Gdns
　ncastle-u-T NE2 ....56 A8
　th Shields NE34 ....59 F6
　lsend NE28 ....41 A3
venor Mews
　North Shields NE29 ....42 A6
　th Shields NE33 ....59 E8
venor Pl Blyth NE24 ....16 F6
　ncastle-u-T NE2 ....38 F1
　th Shields NE29 ....42 A6
venor Rd
　ncastle-u-T NE2 ....38 F1
　th Shields NE33 ....59 E8
venor St SR5 ....75 A2
venor Villas NE2 ....38 F1
venor Way NE5 ....36 D3
to Gdns NE34 ....60 D6
to Rd NE34 ....60 D6
semoor **7** NE37 ....83 A7
semoor Dr NE63 ....6 C1
e Ave NE3 ....38 D6
e Cotts **9** DH3 ....84 B7
e Ho NE3 ....38 D4
e St Gateshead NE9 ....71 A6
ndle NE15 ....35 F2

Grove Terr
　Burnopfield NE16 ....79 B6
　Sunniside NE16 ....69 B1
Grove The Hedworth NE32 ..73 B8
　Houghton-le-S DH5 ....94 D6
　Longbenton NE12 ....39 D6
　Newcastle-u-T NE5 ....36 D1
　NE3 ....38 D4
　Newcastle-u-T,Gosforth
　NE3 ....38 D4
　Newcastle-u-T,Jesmond
　NE2 ....38 F2
　Ponteland NE20 ....25 D5
　Rowlands Gill NE39 ....67 F1
　Ryhope SR2 ....92 F6
　Stocksfield NE43 ....64 C3
　6 Sunderland SR5 ....74 B1
　Sunderland,Ashbrooke SR2 ..86 D4
　Whickham NE16 ....69 C6
　Whitley Bay NE25 ....31 F4
Guardian Ct NE26 ....32 C4
Guardians Ct NE20 ....25 F7
Gubeon Wood NE61 ....8 C2
Guelder Rd NE7 ....39 C3
Guernsey Rd SR4 ....85 B2
Guernsey Sq SR4 ....85 B2
Guessburn NE43 ....64 B6
Guide Post Mid Sch
　NE62 ....10 F7
Guide Post Ringway Fst Sch
　NE62 ....10 F8
Guildford Pl NE6 ....56 B7
Guildford Sq NE61 ....2 A3
Guildford St **2** SR4 ....86 C4
Guillemot Cl NE24 ....17 E5
Guillemot Row NE12 ....29 C4
Guillmot Ho NE33 ....42 D5
Guisborough Dr NE29 ....41 B8
Guisborough St SR4 ....85 F5
Gullane NE37 ....72 D3
Gullane Cl NE10 ....57 C2
Gunn St NE11 ....69 F8
Gunnerston Gr **1** NE2 .....58 D8
Gunnerton Cl NE23 ....22 B4
Gunnerton Pl NE29 ....41 D6
Gurney Ho NE2 ....99 B3
Gurteen Yd DH4 ....90 D3
Gut Rd NE28 ....40 F1
Guyzance Ave NE3 ....38 B6

H

Hackwood Pk NE46 ....45 B3
Hackwood Gdns NE41 ....51 B6
Hackworth Way NE29 ....41 F3
Haddington Rd NE25 ....31 D7
Haddon Cl NE25 ....31 B5
Haddon Gn NE25 ....31 B5
Haddon Rd NE25 ....31 B5
Haddricks Mill Rd NE3 ....38 E4
Haddricksmill Ct NE3 ....38 E4
Hadleigh Ct **9** DH4 ....90 B6
Hadleigh Rd SR4 ....88 D5
Hadrian Ave DH3 ....88 D5
Hadrian Ct
　Killingworth NE12 ....29 E3
　Ponteland NE20 ....25 B1
Hadrian Gdns NE21 ....53 D1
Hadrian Ho **2** NE15 ....35 D2
Hadrian Lodge NE34 ....58 F5
Hadrian Park Prim Sch
　NE28 ....40 E7
Hadrian Pl Gateshead NE9 ..71 B7
　Throckley NE15 ....35 E2
Hadrian Prim Sch NE33 ......42 C4
Hadrian Rd Blyth NE24 ....17 C3
　Jarrow NE32 ....58 D4
　Newcastle-u-T NE4 ....54 E6
　Wallsend NE28 ....40 D1
Hadrian Road Sta NE28 ......40 E2
Hadrian Sch NE15 ....54 C6
Hadrian St NE34 ....102 A3
Hadrian's Wall* NE15 ....34 D3
Hadrians Ct NE11 ....54 E4
Hadrians Way DH8 ....76 E3
Hadstone Pl **3** NE5 ....37 C1
Hagan Hall NE32 ....58 C1
Hagg Bank Cotts NE41 ....50 F5
Haggerston Cl NE5 ....37 B4
Haggerston Cres NE5 ....37 B4
Haggerston Ct NE5 ....37 B4
Haggerston Terr NE32 ....58 E4
Haggerstone Dr SR5 ....85 A8
Haggie Ave NE28 ....40 D3
Hahnemann Ct SR5 ....75 B2
Haig Ave NE25 ....31 F3
Haig Cres NE15 ....54 B5
Haig Rd NE22 ....16 B8
Haig St NE11 ....69 F8
Haigh Terr NE9 ....71 C1
Hailsham Ave NE12 ....39 C7
Hainingwood Terr NE10 ......57 B2
Haldane Ct NE2 ....99 B4
Haldane St NE63 ....6 C2
Haldane Terr NE2 ....99 B4
Halewood Ave NE3 ....37 F4
Half Fields Rd NE21 ....53 B1
Half Moon La
　Gateshead NE8 ....101 B4
　Tynemouth NE30 ....42 D7
Half Moon St NE62 ....11 B8
Halidon Rd NE25 ....31 C4
Halidon Sq SR2 ....86 D1
Halifax Pl Dunston NE11 .....54 E1
　9 Ryhope SR2 ....92 F6
Halifax Rd NE11 ....54 E1
Halkirk Way NE23 ....16 A1

Hall Ave NE4 ....54 E6
Hall Cl Seaham SR7 ....92 D1
　West Rainton DH4 ....94 A2
Hall Dene Way SR7 ....92 F2
Hall Dr NE12 ....29 C5
Hall Farm NE43 ....64 B8
Hall Farm Rd SR3 ....92 A5
Hall Garth NE33 ....38 C8
Hall Gdns Gateshead NE10 ..71 C8
　Seaton Sluice NE26 ....24 A6
　Shiremoor DH6 ....96 A1
　West Boldon NE36 ....74 A7
Hall La Haswell DH6 ....97 F3
　Houghton-le-S DH5 ....94 F7
　West Rainton DH4 ....94 A2
Hall Pk NE21 ....53 A4
Hall Rd Chopwell NE17 ....66 B2
　Hebburn NE31 ....57 E5
　Washington NE37 ....83 E8
Hall Road Bglws NE17 ....66 B2
Hall Terr NE24 ....17 E8
Hall View SR6 ....75 F8
Hallview Ave NE6 ....39 C4
Halleypike Cl NE7 ....39 C3
Hallfield Cl SR3 ....92 A5
Hallgarth NE10 ....72 A7
Hallgarth Ct SR6 ....75 F1
Hallgarth Rd NE13 ....59 C8
Hallgarth La NE65 ....96 B5
Hallgarth Rd NE21 ....53 B2
Hallgarth View NE6 ....96 C5
Hallgarth Villas DH6 ....96 A1
Hallgate NE46 ....45 A5
Halling Cl NE6 ....57 A4
Hallington Dr NE25 ....23 D3
Hallington Mews NE23 ....29 C3
Halliwell St DH4 ....90 D1
Hallorchard Rd NE46 ....45 B5
Hallow Dr NE15 ....35 D1
Hallside Rd NE24 ....17 B6
Hallstile Bank NE46 ....45 B5
Hallwood Cl NE22 ....15 A8
Halstead Pl **2** NE33 ....42 D1
Halstead Sq SR4 ....85 D5
Halterburn Cl NE3 ....38 A4
Halton Dr Backworth NE27 ..30 D3
　Wideopen NE13 ....28 A6
Halton Way NE3 ....28 A1
Hamar Cl NE29 ....41 C4
Hambard Way NE34 ....83 D4
Hambledon Ave
　Chester le S DH2 ....88 B2
　Tynemouth NE30 ....32 A3
Hambledon Cl NE35 ....73 E8
Hambledon Gdns NE7 ....39 A3
Hambledon St NE24 ....17 D8
Hambleton Ct NE63 ....6 F1
Hambleton Gn NE9 ....71 B1
Hambleton Rd NE38 ....83 B3
Hamilton Cres
　Newcastle-u-T NE29 ....98 B2
　Tynemouth NE29 ....41 C8
Hamilton Ct
　7 Gateshead NE8 ....71 A8
　Sunderland SR5 ....75 F2
Hamilton Dr NE26 ....31 F8
Hamilton Pl NE4 ....98 B2
Hamilton Terr
　14 Morpeth NE61 ....9 A8
　West Boldon NE36 ....74 A7
Hamilton Way **2** NE26 .....31 F8
Hammer Square Bank
　DH9 ....78 A4
Hammerton Ct NE28 ....40 A1
Hampden Rd SR6 ....75 E2
Hampden St NE33 ....59 C8
Hampshire Ct NE4 ....100 A2
Hampshire Gdns NE28 ....40 E4
Hampshire Pl NE37 ....72 D1
Hampshire Way NE34 ....60 C7
Hampstead Cl NE24 ....17 C4
Hampstead Gdns NE32 ....58 D2
Hampstead Rd
　Newcastle-u-T NE4 ....54 E5
　Sunderland SR4 ....85 C4
Hampstead Sq SR4 ....85 C4
Hampton Cl NE23 ....22 D7
Hampton Dr
　Gateshead NE10 ....71 C8
　Whitley Bay NE25 ....31 C4
Hampton Rd NE30 ....32 A2
Hamsterley Cres
　Gateshead NE9 ....71 C3
　Newcastle-u-T NE15 ....53 B7
Hamsterley Ct **6** SR3 ......92 A6
Hamsterley Dr NE12 ....29 C4
Hanby Gdns SR3 ....86 A3
Hancock Mus* NE2 ....99 B4
Hancock St NE1,NE2 ....99 A3
Handel St NE33 ....42 C3
Handley Cres DH5 ....94 C4
Handley Cross DH8 ....77 C2
Handy Dr NE11 ....54 E2
Hangmans La SR3,SR7 ....91 E4
Hanlon Ct Hebburn NE32 ....57 F7
　Jarrow NE32 ....58 A8
Hann Terr NE37 ....83 F8
Hannington Pl **3** NE6 ....56 A6
Hannington St **2** NE6 ......56 A6
Hanover Cl **2** NE5 ....36 C2
Hanover Ct
　Annitsford NE23 ....22 B1
　5 Gateshead NE9 ....71 A2

Hanover Dr NE21 ....53 A1
Hanover Gdns **8** NE28 .....41 A1
Hanover Ho NE2 ....58 B4
Hanover Pl
　Cramlington NE23 ....16 A2
　Sunderland SR4 ....102 B4
Hanover Sq NE1 ....101 A4
Hanover St NE1 ....101 A4
Hanover Wlk
　Blaydon NE21 ....68 A8
　1 Newcastle-u-T NE3 .....36 C2
Harbord Terr NE26 ....23 F5
Harbottle Ave
　Newcastle-u-T NE3 ....38 A6
　Shiremoor NE27 ....31 A2
Harbottle Cres NE32 ....58 C4
Harbottle St NE6 ....56 C4
Harbottle St **4** NE6 ....56 C4
Harbour Dr NE33 ....42 E4
Harbour The NE10 ....90 B6
Harbour View
　Cambois NE22 ....12 B3
　South Shields NE33 ....42 D5
　Sunderland SR6 ....75 H4
Harcourt Pk **1** NE9 ....71 A5
Harcourt Rd NE2 ....86 D1
Harcourt St **2** NE9 ....71 A5
Hardgate Rd SR2 ....86 D1
Hardie Ave NE16 ....69 A8
Hardie Dr NE36 ....74 B7
Hardman Gdns NE40 ....52 D5
Hardwick Ct NE8 ....56 A1
Hardwick Pl NE3 ....38 A3
Hardwick Rise SR6 ....103 B4
Hardy Ave NE34 ....59 B3
Hardy Ct **5** NE30 ....42 B6
Hardy Gr NE28 ....40 A5
Hardy Sq SR5 ....75 A2
Hardyards Ct NE34 ....59 C5
Harebell Rd NE5 ....37 D3
Harehills Ave NE5 ....37 D3
Harehills Terr NE5 ....37 D3
Harelaw Dr Ashington NE63 ..6 A7
　Sunderland SR5 ....75 E1
Harelaw Gr NE5 ....36 D1
Hareshaw Pk NE25 ....31 B5
Hareside NE23 ....22 A5
Hareside Cl NE15 ....52 F8
Hareside Ct NE15 ....52 F8
Hareside Wlk NE15 ....52 F8
Harewood Cl
　Whickham NE16 ....69 A4
　Whitley Bay NE25 ....31 B4
Harewood Cres NE25 ....31 B4
Harewood Dr NE22 ....11 C2
Harewood Gdns
　Pegswood NE61 ....4 E4
　Sunderland SR3 ....86 A3
Harewood Gn NE9 ....71 B2
Harewood Rd NE3 ....38 C6
Hareydene NE5 ....36 F5
Hargill Dr NE38 ....83 A1
Hargrave Ct NE24 ....17 D8
Harle Cl SR3 ....83 D5
Harle Ct NE5 ....36 E1
Harle Rd NE27 ....30 D3
Harle St NE28 ....40 B2
Harlebury NE27 ....30 C1
Harlequin Lodge **9**
　NE10 ....71 D8
Harleston Way NE10 ....71 E6
Harley Terr NE3 ....38 D5
Harlow Ave
　Backworth NE27 ....30 D3
　Newcastle-u-T NE3 ....37 F7
Harlow Cl NE23 ....16 A1
Harlow Green Com Inf Sch
　NE9 ....71 A2
Harlow Green Jun Sch
　NE9 ....71 A2
Harlow Green La NE9 ....71 A2
Harlow Pl NE7 ....39 B3
Harlow St SR4 ....102 B2
Harnham Ave NE29 ....41 D5
Harnham Gdns NE5 ....37 C1
Harold Sq SR2 ....22 A5
Harold St NE32 ....58 C7
Harper St NE24 ....17 D7
Harperley Dr SR3 ....86 B2
Harperley La DH9 ....79 B1
Harraby Gdns NE9 ....71 B3
Harras Bank DH3 ....82 C3
Harraton Ct
　15 Birtley DH3 ....82 C4
　Bournmoor DH3 ....89 C7
Harriet Pl **16** NE6 ....56 C6
Harriet St Blaydon NE21 .....53 C2
　6 Newcastle-u-T NE6 .....56 C6
Harrington Gdns NE62 ....11 C8
Harrington St **6** NE28 ......40 B2
Harriot Dr NE12 ....29 B2
Harrison Ct
　Annitsford NE23 ....29 B8
　Birtley DH3 ....82 C3
Harrison Gdns NE8 ....70 D7
Harrison Pl NE2 ....99 B3
Harrison Rd NE28 ....41 A3
Harrogate St SR2 ....103 B1
Harrow Cres DH4 ....90 A6
Harrow Gdns NE13 ....28 B5
Harrow Sq SR4 ....85 D5
Hart Ct SR1 ....103 A3
Hart Sq SR4 ....85 D5
Hart Terr SR6 ....75 F5
Hartburn NE10 ....72 A6

Hartburn Dr SR3 ....36 D3
Hartburn Pl NE4 ....54 F7
Hartburn Rd NE30 ....32 A1
Hartburn Terr NE25 ....23 D3
Hartburn Wlk NE3 ....37 C5
Hartford Cl NE12 ....29 C5
Hartford Bank NE23 ....15 C4
Hartford Bridge Farm
　NE22 ....15 C5
Hartford Cres
　Ashington NE63 ....6 D2
　Bedlington NE22 ....15 E8
Hartford Ct NE22 ....15 E8
Hartford Cvn Pk NE22 ....15 E5
Hartford Dr NE22 ....15 E5
Hartford Ho NE4 ....98 B2
Hartford Rd
　Bedlington NE22 ....15 D6
　Newcastle-u-T NE3 ....38 D7
　South Shields NE34 ....59 A5
Hartford Rd E NE22 ....15 F8
Hartford Rd W NE22 ....15 F8
Hartford St **1** NE6 ....56 C8
Harthope Cl NE61 ....1 F5
Harthope Ave SR5 ....74 C3
Harthope Cl NE38 ....88 F8
Harthope Dr NE29 ....41 E3
Hartington Rd NE30 ....32 B2
Hartington St
　Gateshead NE8 ....101 C1
　Newcastle-u-T NE4 ....98 A1
　Sunderland SR6 ....75 E1
Hartington Terr NE33 ....59 D8
Hartland Dr DH3 ....82 D3
Hartlands NE22 ....15 E8
Hartleigh Pl NE24 ....17 F7
Hartley Ave NE26 ....31 E5
Hartley Ct
　Brunswick Village NE13 ....27 F5
　New Hartley NE25 ....23 D6
Hartley Gdns NE25 ....23 C3
Hartley Ho NE26 ....31 F5
Hartley La Holywell NE25 ....31 B7
　Whitley Bay NE25,NE26 ....24 C2
Hartley Sq NE26 ....24 D4
Hartley St
　Seaton Delaval NE25 ....23 C3
　Sunderland SR1 ....103 C3
Hartley St N NE25 ....23 C3
Hartley Terr NE4 ....17 C4
Hartleyburn Ave NE31 ....57 D3
Harton Ct NE34 ....59 F7
Harton Gr NE34 ....59 F6
Harton House Rd NE34 ....59 F7
Harton House Rd E NE34 ....60 A7
Harton Inf Sch NE34 ....60 B6
Harton Jun Sch NE34 ....60 A6
Harton La NE34 ....59 D6
Harton Lea NE34 ....59 F6
Harton Quay NE33 ....42 D2
Harton Rise NE34 ....60 A7
Harton Sch NE34 ....60 A6
Harton View NE36 ....74 A7
Hartside Birtley DH3 ....82 D1
　Newcastle-u-T NE15 ....53 C7
Hartside Cres
　Backworth NE27 ....30 D3
　Cramlington NE23 ....16 A2
Hartside Gdns
　Easington Lane DH5 ....95 C1
　Newcastle-u-T NE2 ....38 F1
Hartside Pl NE3 ....28 C1
Hartside Rd SR4 ....85 D4
Hartside Sq SR4 ....85 D4
Harvard Rd NE3 ....37 E6
Harvest Cl SR3 ....91 F5
Harvey Cl Washington NE63 ..7 A3
　Washington NE38 ....82 F5
Harvey Cres NE10 ....72 B8
Harwood Cl
　Cramlington NE23 ....22 A5
　Washington NE38 ....83 A1
Harwood Ct **10** SR6 ....75 E1
Harwood Dr NE12 ....30 A4
Hascombe Cl NE26 ....31 D6
Haslemere Dr SR3 ....86 A3
Hassop Way NE22 ....10 F2
Hasting Hill Prim Sch
　SR3 ....85 C1
Hastings Ave
　Cramlington NE23 ....39 D7
　Newcastle-u-T NE7 ....37 D7
　Seaton Sluice NE26 ....24 B7
　Whitley Bay NE26 ....31 E5
Hastings Ct
　Bedlington NE22 ....11 C2
　New Hartley NE25 ....23 D6
Hastings Dr NE30 ....42 C8
Hastings Gdns NE25 ....23 D6
Hastings Par NE31 ....58 A3
Hastings St
　Cramlington NE23 ....22 C5
　Sunderland SR2 ....86 E3
Hastings Terr
　Cramlington NE23 ....16 D1
　Newcastle-u-T NE7 ....23 D7
　Sunderland SR2 ....86 F3
Haswell Cl NE10 ....72 C7
Haswell Gdns NE30 ....42 A6
Hatfield Ave NE31 ....57 F6
Hatfield Dr NE23 ....23 A2

Hatfield Gdns
Sunderland SR3 . . . . .86 A3
Whitley Bay NE25 . . . . . . .31 B5
Hatfield Ho 10 NE2 . . . . . .42 A4
Hatfield Sq 8 NE33 . . . . . .42 D3
Hathaway Gdns SR3 . . . . .86 A3
Hathersage Gdns NE5 . . . .59 D5
Hatherton Ave NE30 . . . . .32 B3
Hathery La NE24 . . . . . . .16 D5
Haugh La Hexham NE46 . . .45 B5
Ryton NE15,NE40 . . . . . . .52 E6
Ryton,Ryton Haugh NE21 . . .52 D5
Haugh Lane Ind Est NE46 .45 A4
Haughs The NE42 . . . . . . .50 D3
Haughton Cres
Hedworth NE32 . . . . .58 B2
Newcastle-u-T NE5 . . . . . .36 E1
Haughton Ct NE4 . . . . . .100 A3
Haughton Terr NE24 . . . . .17 E7
Hautmont Rd NE31 . . . . . .57 F4
Hauxley NE12 . . . . .29 D5
Hauxley Dr
Cramlington NE23 . . . . . . .16 A1
Newcastle-u-T NE3 . . . . . .37 F7
Hauxley Gdns NE5 . . . . . .37 D2
Havanna NE12 . . . . .29 D5
Havannah Cres NE13 . . . . .27 B6
Havannah Rd NE37 . . . . . .83 B7
Havant Gdns NE13 . . . . . .28 B7
Havelock Cl NE8 . . . . . . .101 B2
Havelock Cres NE22 . . . . .11 F3
Havelock Ct SR4 . . . . . . .85 D6
Havelock Ho SR4 . . . . . . .85 D6
Havelock Mews NE22 . . . .11 F3
Havelock Pl NE4 . . . . .98 B1
Havelock Prim Sch SR4 . . .85 D6
Havelock Rd NE27 . . . . . .30 D3
Havelock St Blyth NE24 . . .17 E8
South Shields NE33 . . . . . .42 B1
South Shields NE33 . . . . . .42 C1
Sunderland SR1 . . . . .103 C3
Havelock Terr
Chopwell NE17 . . . . .66 B1
Gateshead NE8 . . . . .101 B2
Jarrow NE32 . . . . .58 B5
Sunderland SR2 . . . . .102 B1
Tantobie DH9 . . . . .79 B2
Havelock Villas NE22 . . . .11 F3
Haven Ct Blyth NE24 . . . . .17 C6
Sunderland SR6 . . . . .75 F1
Haven The
North Shields NE29 . . . . . .42 A3
Penshaw DH4 . . . . .90 B6
Prudhoe NE42 . . . . .50 D2
Haven View NE64 . . . . . . .7 E4
Havercroft NE10 . . . . .72 B7
Haverley Dr 1 SR7 . . . . . .92 E1
Haversham CL NE7 . . . . . .39 A5
Haversham Pk SR5 . . . . . .75 C5
Hawarden Cres SR4 . . . . .102 A1
Hawes Ave DH2 . . . . .88 C1
Hawes Ct SR6 . . . . .75 C5
Hawesdale Cres NE21 . . . .68 B8
Haweswater Cl NE34 . . . . .59 D6
Haweswater Cres NE64 . . .7 C4
Hawick Cres NE6 . . . . . . .56 B4
Hawk Terr DH3 . . . . .82 E2
Hawkesley Rd SR4 . . . . . .85 D5
Hawkey's La NE29 . . . . . .41 F6
Hawkhills Terr 8 DH3 . . . .82 C5
Hawkhurst NE38 . . . . . . .83 E2
Hawkins Ct SR3 . . . . .91 F6
Hawks St NE8 . . . . .56 A4
Hawksbury NE16 . . . . . . .69 A7
Hawksfeld NE10 . . . . .71 E4
Hawkshead Ct NE3 . . . . . .37 D7
Hawkshead Pl NE9 . . . . . .71 B4
Hawksley NE5 . . . . .36 F2
Hawksmoor Cl NE63 . . . . .6 C1
Hawkwell Rise NE15 . . . . .35 D1
Hawsker Cl SR3 . . . . .92 C7
Hawthorn Ave
Brunswick Village NE13 . . . .28 A6
New Silksworth SR3 . . . . . .92 B8
Hawthorn CE Fst Sch
NE63 . . . . .6 D1
Hawthorn Cl NE16 . . . . . .69 B5
Hawthorn Cres NE38 . . . . .83 C1
Hawthorn Ct Morpeth NE61 .8 F7
Newcastle-u-T NE3 . . . . . .38 C4
Hawthorn Dr
Dunston NE11 . . . . .69 F8
Hedworth NE32 . . . . .58 D2
Hawthorn Gdns
8 Gateshead NE10 . . . . . .56 D1
Newcastle-u-T NE3 . . . . . .37 F4
Ryton NE40 . . . . .52 E4
Tynemouth NE29 . . . . . . .41 F7
Whitley Bay NE26 . . . . . . .31 F5
Hawthorn Gr NE28 . . . . . .40 B2
Hawthorn Mews NE3 . . . . .38 C4
Hawthorn Pl
Killingworth NE12 . . . . . . .29 C4
Newcastle-u-T NE4 . . . . . .100 B4
Hawthorn Prim Sch
NE4 . . . . .100 A4
Hawthorn Rd
Ashington NE63 . . . . .6 E3
Blaydon NE21 . . . . .53 C1
Newcastle-u-T NE3 . . . . . .38 C4
Hawthorn Rd W NE3 . . . . .38 C4
Hawthorn St
Burnside DH4 . . . . .90 C2
Jarrow NE32 . . . . .58 A7
Sunderland SR4 . . . . .102 A2

Hawthorn St continued
Walbottle NE15 . . . . .35 F2
Hawthorn Terr
Chester le S DH3 . . . . . . .88 D2
Crawcrook NE40 . . . . .51 E3
8 Dunston NE11 . . . . . . .69 F8
Gateshead NE9 . . . . .71 D1
Newcastle-u-T NE4 . . . . .100 A4
12 Springwell NE9 . . . . . .71 F1
Sunderland SR6 . . . . .75 E6
Hawthorn Villas NE23 . . . .22 D6
Hawthorn Way NE20 . . . . .25 D3
Hawthorn Wlk NE4 . . . . .100 B4
Hawthorne Ave
Hebburn NE31 . . . . .57 F6
South Shields NE34 . . . . . .59 F4
Hawthorne Gdns NE9 . . . .70 F6
Hawthorne Rd NE24 . . . . .17 F7
Hawthorne Terr DH9 . . . . .79 D3
Hawthorns The
East Boldon NE36 . . . . . . .74 D7
Gateshead NE9 . . . . .71 D1
Newcastle-u-T NE4 . . . . .100 A3
Hay St NE5 . . . . .102 C4
Haydock Dr NE10 . . . . . . .72 C7
Haydon NE38 . . . . .83 E1
Haydon Cl NE3 . . . . .37 F8
Haydon Dr NE25 . . . . . . .31 F3
Haydon Gdns NE27 . . . . . .30 D4
Haydon Rd NE63 . . . . . . .6 D2
Haydon Sq SR4 . . . . .85 D5
Hayes Wlk NE13 . . . . .28 B6
Hayfield La NE16 . . . . . . .69 B6
Hayhole Rd NE29 . . . . . . .41 E2
Haylands Sq NE34 . . . . . .59 D5
Hayleazes Rd NE15 . . . . . .53 F7
Haymarket NE1 . . . . .99 A2
Haymarket Sta NE1 . . . . . .99 A2
Haynyng The DH9 . . . . . . .71 E7
Hayricks The DH9 . . . . . . .79 D4
Hayton Ave NE34 . . . . . . .60 A5
Hayton Cl NE23 . . . . .22 C7
Hayton Rd NE30 . . . . .32 A2
Hayward Ave NE25 . . . . . .23 D3
Hazard La DH5 . . . . .94 E3

Hazel Ave
3 Houghton-le-S DH4 . . . .94 C8
New Silksworth SR3 . . . . . .92 B8
Tynemouth NE29 . . . . . . .41 F7
Hazel Cl NE12 . . . . .39 D7
Hazel Gr Burnopfield NE16 .79 C6
Chester le S DH2 . . . . . . .88 A5
Ellington NE61 . . . . .1 E5
Gateshead NE10 . . . . .72 B7
Killingworth NE12 . . . . . . .29 B2
South Shields NE34 . . . . . .59 F4
Hazel Rd Blaydon NE21 . . .53 D2
Gateshead NE8 . . . . .70 C8
Hazel St NE32 . . . . .58 A7
Hazel Terr DH4 . . . . .90 C2
Hazeldene Hedworth NE32 .73 C8
Whitley Bay NE25 . . . . . . .31 E5
Hazeldene Ave NE3 . . . . .37 C5
Hazeldene Ct NE30 . . . . . .42 C7
Hazeley Gr 4 NE3 . . . . . .37 D5
Hazeley Way NE3 . . . . . . .37 D5
Hazelmere Ave
Bedlington NE22 . . . . .10 E1
Newcastle-u-T NE3 . . . . . .28 D1
Hazelmere Cres NE23 . . . .22 C8
Hazelmere Dene NE23 . . . .22 E1
Hazelmoor NE31 . . . . .57 D7
Hazelwood Jarrow NE32 . . .58 D6
Killingworth NE12 . . . . . . .29 F3
Hazelwood Ave
Newbiggin-by-t-S NE64 . . . .7 D5
Newcastle-u-T NE2 . . . . . .38 E2
Sunderland SR5 . . . . .74 F2
Hazelwood Cl NE10 . . . . . .71 D2
Hazelwood Com Prim Sch
NE13 . . . . .28 B5
Hazelwood Gdns NE38 . . . .83 C1
Hazelwood Terr NE28 . . . .41 A3
Hazlitt Ave NE34 . . . . . . .59 B3
Hazlitt Pl NE23 . . . . .23 A1
Headlam Gn 2 NE6 . . . . . .56 C5
Headlam Ho 11 NE6 . . . . . .56 C6
Headlam St 4 NE6 . . . . . .56 C6
Headlam View NE28 . . . . .41 A2
Healey Dr SR3 . . . . .86 B2
Heartsbourne Dr NE34 . . . .59 F3
Heath Cl NE11 . . . . .70 B7
Heath Cres NE15 . . . . . . .54 A4
Heath Grange DH5 . . . . . .94 F3
Heath Sq SR4 . . . . .85 E5
Heathcote Gn NE5 . . . . . .37 B3
Heathdale Gdns NE7 . . . . .39 B3
Heather Cl SR6 . . . . .60 A2
Heather Dr DH5 . . . . .95 A5
Heather Hill 4 NE9 . . . . . .71 F1
Heather Lea DH9 . . . . . . .78 E2
Heather Lea La NE42 . . . . .50 D3
Heather Pl
Crawcrook NE40 . . . . .52 A4
Newcastle-u-T NE3 . . . . . .54 E8
Heather Terr NE16 . . . . . .79 B6
Heatherdale Terr NE9 . . . .71 B3
Heatherlaw
Gateshead NE9 . . . . .71 C5
Washington NE37 . . . . . . .82 F6
Heatherlea Gdns 1 SR2 . . .86 B3
Heatherlea Pl NE37 . . . . . .72 D1
Heatherlee Gdns NE62 . . . .11 A8
Heatherslaw Rd NE5 . . . . .54 C8
Heatherwell Gn NE10 . . . . .71 E7
Heathery La NE13 . . . . . . .38 E7
Heatheryhill NE46 . . . . . . .44 A4

Heathfield Morpeth NE61 . . .9 86
Sunderland SR2 . . . . .86 C2
Heathfield Cres NE5 . . . . .37 D3
Heathfield Farm NE40 . . . .52 A1
Heathfield Gdns NE40 . . . .52 A1
Heathfield Ho NE9 . . . . . .70 F6
Heathfield Pl
Gateshead NE9 . . . . .70 F6
Newcastle-u-T NE3 . . . . . .28 D1
Heathfield Rd NE9 . . . . . .70 F6
Heathway NE32 . . . . .58 C2
Heathwell Gdns NE16 . . . .69 B8
Heathwell Rd NE15 . . . . . .53 F7
Heathwood Ave 1 NE46 . . .69 A7
Heaton Cl NE6 . . . . .56 B7
Heaton Gr NE6 . . . . .56 B7
Heaton Hall Rd NE6 . . . . .56 B7
Heaton Manor Sch NE7 . . .39 A2
Heaton Park Ct 9 NE6 . . . .56 B7
Heaton Park Rd NE6 . . . . .56 B7
Heaton Park View NE6 . . . .56 B7
Heaton Pl NE6 . . . . .56 B6
Heaton Rd NE6 . . . . .56 B7
Heaton Terr
Newcastle-u-T NE3 . . . . . .56 A6
North Shields NE29 . . . . . .41 E6
Heaton Wlk 4 NE6 . . . . . .56 B6
Hebburn Comp Sch NE31 . .57 E4
Hebburn Hospl NE31 . . . . .57 D4
Hebburn Sta NE31 . . . . . .57 D6
Heber St NE1 . . . . .98 C1
Hebron Ave NE61 . . . . . . .4 F4
Hebron Pl NE63 . . . . .6 F3
Hebron Way NE23 . . . . . . .22 A5
Hector St NE27 . . . . .30 F4
Heddon Ave NE13 . . . . . . .28 A4
Heddon Banks NE15 . . . . .34 E1
Heddon Cl
Newcastle-u-T NE3 . . . . . .38 A6
Ryton NE40 . . . . .52 D5
Heddon View
Blaydon NE21 . . . . .53 B2
Ryton NE40 . . . . .52 D5
Heddon Way NE34 . . . . . .59 B6
Hedge Cl NE11 . . . . .70 B7
Hedgefield Ave NE21 . . . . .52 F5
Hedgefield Cotts NE21 . . . .52 F5
Hedgefield Ct NE21 . . . . . .52 F5
Hedgefield Gr NE24 . . . . . .17 C3
Hedgefield View NE23 . . . .22 A1
Hedgehope 8 NE37 . . . . . .83 A6
Hedgehope Rd NE5 . . . . . .37 A4
Hedgelea NE40 . . . . .52 A5
Hedgelea Rd DH5 . . . . . . .94 C3
Hedgeley Rd
Hebburn NE31 . . . . .57 E6
Newcastle-u-T NE5 . . . . . .53 E8
Tynemouth NE29 . . . . . . .41 D7
Hedgeley Terr NE6 . . . . . .56 C6
Hedgerow Mews NE63 . . . .6 B2
Hedley Ave NE24 . . . . . . .17 F6
Hedley Cl 7 NE33 . . . . . . .42 C4
Hedley Ct NE24 . . . . .17 F6
Hedley La NE11,NE16 . . . .80 C6
Hedley Pl NE28 . . . . .40 B1
Hedley Rd
North Shields NE29 . . . . . .41 F3
Seaton Delaval NE25 . . . . .23 E2
Wylam NE41 . . . . .51 B6
Hedley St Gateshead NE8 . .70 D8
Newcastle-u-T NE3 . . . . . .38 C5
8 South Shields NE33 . . . .42 C4
Hedley Terr
Newcastle-u-T NE3 . . . . . .38 C5
Ryhope SR2 . . . . .93 A6
South Hetton DH6 . . . . . . .97 F7
Hedworth Ave NE34 . . . . .59 A4
Hedworth Ct SR1 . . . . . . .103 B2
Hedworth La
Boldon Colliery NE35 . . . . .58 E1
Hedworth NE32 . . . . .58 D2
Hedworth Lane Prim Sch
NE35 . . . . .58 D1
Hedworth Pl NE9 . . . . . . .71 C3
Hedworth St DH3 . . . . . . .88 C2
Hedworth Terr DH4 . . . . . .90 B6
Hedworth View NE32 . . . . .58 D1
Hedworthfield Prim Sch
NE32 . . . . .58 D1
Heighley St NE15 . . . . . . .53 F5
Helen St Blaydon NE21 . . .53 C3
East Cramlington NE23 . . . .22 F2
Sunderland SR6 . . . . .75 E4
Helena Ave NE36 . . . . . . .32 B5
Helena Ho SR2 . . . . .102 B1
Hellpool La NE46 . . . . . . .44 C3
Helmdon NE37 . . . . .83 E8
Helmsdale Ave 10 NE10 . . .56 D1
Helmsdale Rd SR4 . . . . . .85 B5
Helmsley Cl DH4 . . . . .90 A6
Helmsley Ct SR5 . . . . .74 B3
Helmsley Dr NE28 . . . . . .40 F2
Helmsley Gn NE2 . . . . . . .39 A1
Helmsley Rd NE2 . . . . . . .99 C3
Helston Ct NE15 . . . . .53 B7
Helvellyn Ave NE38 . . . . . .83 A3
Helvellyn Cl NE21 . . . . . . .68 C8
Helvellyn Rd SR2 . . . . . . .86 D3
Hemel St 8 DH3 . . . . .88 C2
Hemlington Cl 2 SR2 . . . . .92 F6
Hemming St 9 SR2 . . . . . .86 F2
Hemsley Rd NE34 . . . . . . .43 A1
Hencotes NE46 . . . . .45 A4
Hencotes Ct 7 NE46 . . . . .45 A4
Hencotes Mews 4 NE46 . . .45 A4
Henderson Ave NE16 . . . . .69 A8
Henderson Cl NE46 . . . . . .44 F3

Henderson Ct NE29 . . . . . .41 F3
Henderson Gdns NE10 . . . .72 B8
Henderson Rd
South Shields NE34 . . . . . .58 F4
Sunderland SR4 . . . . .85 F6
Wallsend NE28 . . . . .40 B3
Wallsend NE28 . . . . .40 B4
Henderson's Bldgs NE64 . . .7 E5
Hendersyde Cl NE5 . . . . . .37 B3
Hendon Burn Ave SR2 . . .103 B1
Hendon Burn Ave W 2
SR2 . . . . .86 C4
Hendon Cl
North Shields NE29 . . . . . .42 A3
Sunderland SR1 . . . . .103 B2
Hendon Gdns NE32 . . . . . .58 D2
Hendon Ho NE6 . . . . .6 A4
Hendon Rd
Gateshead NE8,NE9 . . . . . .71 B8
Sunderland SR1 . . . . .103 B3
Sunderland,Hendon SR1,
SR2 . . . . .103 C2
Hendon Rd E SR1 . . . . . .103 C2
Hendon St SR1 . . . . .103 C2
Hendon Valley Ct 7 SR2 . .86 E4
Hendon Valley Rd SR2 . . .103 B1
Henley Cl NE23 . . . . .22 D7
Henley Gdns NE28 . . . . . .41 B4
Henley Ho NE35 . . . . .73 E8
Henley Rd Sunderland SR4 .85 D5
Tynemouth NE30 . . . . . . .32 C1
Henley Sq NE61 . . . . .2 A3
Henley Way NE35 . . . . . . .73 E8
Henlow Rd NE15 . . . . .53 C7
Henry Nelson St NE33 . . . .42 D4
Henry Robson Way NE33 . .42 C2
Henry Sq NE2 . . . . .99 C2
Henry St Hetton le H DH5 . .95 A5
Houghton-le-S DH5 . . . . . .90 E1
Newcastle-u-T NE3 . . . . . .38 C5
North Shields NE29 . . . . . .42 A4
Shiney Row DH4 . . . . .90 A6
South Shields NE33 . . . . . .42 D4
Henry St E SR2 . . . . .103 C2
Henry Terr DH4 . . . . .89 F2
Hensby St NE5 . . . . .37 B4
Henshaw Ct NE3 . . . . .38 A6
Henshaw Gr NE25 . . . . . . .23 F2
Henshaw Pl NE5 . . . . .54 B7
Henshelwood Terr 2
NE2 . . . . .38 E1
Henson Cl NE38 . . . . .83 D4
Hepburn Gdns NE10 . . . . .56 C1
Hepburn Gr SR5 . . . . .73 F1
Hepple Ct NE24 . . . . .17 C6
Hepple Rd NE64 . . . . .7 C3
Hepple Way NE3 . . . . .38 A6
Hepscott Dr NE25 . . . . . . .31 D6
Hepscott Manor Cotts
NE61 . . . . .2 A2
Hepscott Terr NE33 . . . . . .59 D8
Hepscott Wlk NE61 . . . . . .4 E3
Herbert St NE8 . . . . .56 A1
Herbert Terr SR5 . . . . . . .75 B5
Herd Ct NE21 . . . . .53 A1
Herd House La NE21 . . . . .52 F2
Herdinghill NE37 . . . . .82 F6
Herdlaw NE23 . . . . .22 A6
Hereford Ct
Newcastle-u-T NE3 . . . . . .37 D8
Sunderland SR2 . . . . .86 D1
Hereford Rd SR2 . . . . .86 D1
Hereford Sq SR2 . . . . .86 D1
Hereford Way NE32 . . . . . .58 B2
Heritage Cl NE8 . . . . .100 C1
Hermiston NE25 . . . . .31 E5
Hermitage Gdns DH2 . . . . .88 B1
Hermitage Pk DH3 . . . . . .88 C1
Hermitage Sch The DH2 . . .88 A2
Heron Cl Ashington NE63 . . .6 A4
Blyth NE24 . . . . .17 E4
Washington NE38 . . . . . . .83 A2
Heron Dr NE33 . . . . .42 C4
Heron Pl NE12 . . . . .39 A7
Heron Villas NE34 . . . . . . .59 B4
Herrick St NE5 . . . . .37 A3
Herring Gull Cl NE24 . . . . .17 E3
Herrington Mews DH4 . . . .90 E6
Herrington Rd SR3,DH4 . . .91 B6
Herriott St NE24 . . . . .17 D7
Hersham Cl NE3 . . . . .37 D7
Hertburn Gdns NE37 . . . . .83 E7
Hertburn Ind Est NE37 . . . .83 E7
Hertford NE9 . . . . .70 F2
Hertford Ave NE34 . . . . . .60 C7
Hertford Cl NE25 . . . . .31 D6
Hertford Cres DH5 . . . . . . .94 F4
Hertford Gr NE23 . . . . .22 C7
Hesket Ct NE3 . . . . .37 E7
Hesleyside 4 NE63 . . . . . .6 F2
Hesleyside Dr NE5 . . . . . .54 C8
Hesleyside Rd NE25 . . . . .31 B5
Hessewelle Cres DH6 . . . . .97 F1
Hester Ave NE25 . . . . .23 D6
Hester Bglws NE25 . . . . . .23 D6
Hester Gdns NE25 . . . . . . .23 E6
Heswall Rd NE23 . . . . .16 A2
Hetton Lyons Ctry Pk*
DH5 . . . . .95 C4
Hetton Lyons Ind Est
DH5 . . . . .95 B3
Hetton Lyons Prim Sch
DH5 . . . . .95 A2
Hetton Moor Terr DH5 . . . .95 B2
Hetton Prim Sch DH5 . . . . .94 F3
Hetton Rd DH5 . . . . .94 F4
Hetton Sch DH5 . . . . .94 F3
Heugh Hill NE9 . . . . .72 A2
Hewison Terr NE10 . . . . . .71 C8

Hewitt Ave SR2 9
Hewley Cres NE15 35
Heworth Burn Cres NE10 . .7
Heworth Cres 1 NE37 83
Heworth Ct 6 NE34 5
Heworth Dene Gdns
NE10 5
Heworth Gr NE37 83
Heworth Grange Comp Sch
NE10 7
Heworth Rd NE37 72
Heworth Sta (BR & Metro)
NE10 7
Heworth Way NE10 7
Hewson Pl NE9 7
Hexham NE38 8
Hexham Abbey* NE46 4
Hexham Ave
Cramlington NE23 2
Hebburn NE31 5
Newcastle-u-T NE6 5
Hexham Bsns Pk NE46 4
Hexham East Fst Sch
NE46 4
Hexham General Hospl
NE46 4
Hexham Ho 8 NE6 5
Hexham Mid Sch NE46 4
Hexham Old Rd NE21,
NE40 6
Hexham Priory Sch NE46 . .4
Hexham Race Course
NE46 4
Hexham Rd
Heddon-on-t-W NE15 3
Sunderland SR4 8
Throckley NE15 3
Whickham NE16 5
Hexham Sta NE46 4
Hextol Cres NE46 4
Hextol Ct NE46 4
Hextol Gdns NE15 5
Hextol Terr NE46 4
Heybrook Ave NE29 4
Heyburn Gdns NE15 5
Hi-Tec Village NE35 7
Hibernia Rd NE6 5
Hibernian Rd NE32 5
Hickling Ct NE5 3
Hickstead Cl NE28 4
Hickstead Gr NE23 2
Hiddleston Ave NE7 3
High Axwell NE21 5
High Back Cl NE32 5
High Barnes Terr SR4 10
High Bridge NE1,NE99 9
High Burswell NE46 4
High Chare DH3 8
High Cl NE42 5
High Croft NE37 8
High Croft Cl NE31 5
High Dene NE7 3
High Dewley Burn NE15 . . .3
High Downs Sq DH5 9
High Flatworth NE29 4
High Friar La NE1 9
High Friarside NE16 7
High Gables 9 NE46 4
High Gate The NE3 3
High Gosforth Park
(Newcastle Race Course)
. 2
High Gr NE40 5
High Grindon Ho SR4 8
High Hamsterley Rd
NE39 7
High Hedgefield Terr
NE21 5
High Heworth La NE10 7
High Horse Cl NE39 7
High Horse Close Wood
NE39 7
High House Ct NE61 4
High House Gdns NE10 5
High La DH4 9
High Lane Row NE31 5
High Lanes NE10 5
High Laws NE3 3
High Level Rd NE8 10
High Market NE63 6
High Mdw
South Shields NE34 6
South Shields NE34 6
High Mdws NE3 3
High Mill Rd NE39 7
High Moor Ct NE5 3
High Moor Pl NE34 6
High Pasture NE38 8
High Pk NE61 4
High Primrose Hill DH4 8
High Quay Blyth NE24 1
Newcastle-u-T NE1 9
High Rd The NE34 6
High Reach NE10 7
High Reins NE46 4
High Ridge
Bedlington NE22 1
Hazlerigg NE13 2
High Row
Great Lumley DH4 9
Newcastle-u-T NE15 3
Ryton NE40 5
Washington NE37 8
High Sandgrove SR6 6
High Shaw NE42 5
High Spen Ct NE39 7

h Spen Ind Est NE39 ......66 F5
h Spen Prim Sch
39 ....66 F3
h St Blyth NE24 ....17 D7
h NE24 ....17 E7
oppington NE62 ....10 E6
ington Lane DH5 ....95 C1
eshead NE3 ....101 C3
eshead,Felling NE10 ....71 D8
eshead,Wrekenton NE9 ..71 C1
de Post NE22 ....10 E7
sh Pittington DH6 ....96 B6
row NE32 ....58 C7
row NE32 ....58 D7
row NE23 ....7 F5
wburn NE15 ....3 C2
wcastle-u-T NE3 ....38 C4
nderland SR4 ....85 A6
h St Bk NE3 ....38 C5
h St E Sunderland SR1 .103 B3
llsend NE28 ....40 C1
View
nderland SR1 ....103 A3
nshead NE28 ....40 A1
h Stanners NE61 ....3 F1
h Stobhill NE61 ....9 A6
h Swinburne Pl NE4 ......98 B1
View
teland NE20 ....23 D2
teland NE28 ....40 B3
h View N NE28 ....40 B4
h Weetslade Farm Cotts
23 ....29 A6
h Well Gdns NE10 ....56 E1
h West St NE8 ....101 C2
nam Pl NE1 ....99 B2
bridge NE3 ....38 C7
wburn NE23 ....22 A5
bury Gateshead NE10 ..71 E8
wcastle-u-T NE2 ....38 D2
tley Bay NE25 ....31 E5
bury Ave NE9 ....72 A2
bury Cl NE9 ....72 A2
bury Gr NE29 ....41 F6
clere DH4 ....89 F5
clere Dr SR2 ....92 D6
cliffe Gdns NE8 ....71 A8
croft Dr SR6 ....60 E1
croft Pk SR6 ....60 F1
crofts NE15 ....50 C8
cross Rd NE30 ....32 A3
field Birtley DH3 ....82 C6
h NE24 ....14 F7
thoe NE42 ....50 D2
nside NE16 ....69 B3
field Ave NE12 ....39 D8
field Cl NE5 ....36 F3
field Com Prim Sch
9 ....67 C2
field Cres DH3 ....88 C5
field Ct NE10 ....71 E7
field Day Hospl DH3 ....88 C5
field Dr
ington NE63 ....7 A2
ce Houses DH4 ....94 B7
th Shields NE34 ....59 F8
field Gdns DH4 ....94 B7
field Grange DH4 ....94 B7
field Inf Sch NE34 ......43 A1
field Jun Sch NE34 ......50 C1
field Pl
nswick Village NE13 ....28 A5
Sunderland SR4 ....85 F6
field Rd
shead NE8 ....56 A1
castle-u-T NE5 ....36 F3
lands Gill NE39 ....90 A6
g Row DH4 ....90 A6
th Shields NE33,NE34 ..59 F8
field Rise 88 C5
field Terr
castle-u-T NE6 ....57 A4
thoe NE42 ....50 D2
fields Mid Sch NE42 ....50 C2
field Gdns NE61 ....8 E7
ford La NE46 ....44 E4
gate Gdns NE32 ....58 D2
gate Rd NE4 ....85 D5
green Chase NE16 ......69 A4
grove NE5 ....36 D2
heath **1** NE37 ....83 A6
land Rd NE5 ....37 D3
laws Gdns NE9 ....71 B2
moor NE61 ....8 D7
ridge DH3 ....82 C5
side Dr SR3 ....86 A3
stead Ave NE23 ....16 A1
steads DH8 ....77 B1
tree Cl SR3 ....91 F5
well La **4** NE5 ....36 E1
wood Rd NE15 ....53 F7
worth Dr
castle-u-T NE7 ....39 D3
springwell NE9 ....71 F1
a Pk DH2 ....88 B5
a St Gateshead NE8 ..101 A1
derland SR6 ....75 D3
Terr
castle-u-T NE6 ....57 A4
thoe NE42 ....50 D2
brockley NE15 ....38 C4
bington NE62 ....39 C2
en Gdns NE7 ....39 C2
Ave NE23 ....23 A2
Brow SR3 ....92 B6
Crest Burnopfield NE16 79 B6
eshead NE10 ....71 E6
Crest Gdns 38 E4

Hill Croft NE15 ....33 C1
Hill Dyke NE9 ....71 C2
Hill Gate NE61 ....9 A8
Hill Head Dr NE5 ....36 D1
Hill House Rd NE15 ....35 C2
Hill La DH4 ....84 C1
Hill Park Rd NE32 ......55 C5
Hill Pk NE20 ....25 D2
Hill Rise Crawcrook NE40 ..51 F3
Washington NE38 ....83 E6
Hill St Corbridge NE45 ..46 F5
Jarrow NE32 ....58 A7
New Silksworth SR3 ....92 A7
South Shields NE33 ......42 B1
Hill Terr DH4 ....90 E6
Hill The NE42 ....50 B4
Hill Top Birtley DH3 ....82 D4
Blaydon NE21 ....53 B1
Hill Top Ave NE9 ....71 B5
Hill Top Cl NE10 ....10 F8
Hill Top Gdns NE9 ......71 A5
Hill Top Sch NE10 ......18 C1
Hill View Gdns SR3 ....86 B3
Hill View Inf Sch SR2 ..86 D2
Hill View Jun Sch SR2 ..86 D2
Hill View Rd SR2 ....86 D2
Hill View Sq SR2 ....86 D2
Hillary Ave NE12 ....39 E8
Hillcrest Ashington NE63 ..7 A2
Hedworth NE32 ....58 D2
Prudhoe NE42 ....50 D7
South Shields NE34 ....60 B5
Sunderland SR3 ....91 B8
Whitley Bay NE25 ......31 E5
Hillcrest Ave NE62 ......10 F8
Hillcrest Ct NE42 ....50 D2
Hillcrest Dr Dunston NE11 ..69 E7
Hexham NE46 ....45 C4
Hillcroft **3** Birtley DH3 ..82 C5
Gateshead NE9 ....71 A6
Rowlands Gill NE39 ....67 C2
Hillfield NE23 ....31 D5
Hillfields Gdns SR3 ....86 B3
Hillfield St NE8 ....101 B2
Hillford Terr NE17 ......66 B1
Hillgate NE8 ....101 B4
Hillhead Gdns NE11 ....70 A6
Hillhead La NE16 ....68 D2
Hillhead Parkway NE5 ..36 C2
Hillhead Rd NE5 ....36 D2
Hillhead Way NE5 ......36 E3
Hillheads Ct NE25 ......32 A4
Hillheads Rd NE25,NE26 ..32 A4
Hillingdon Gr SR4 ......85 A2
Hillrise Cres SR7 ....92 D1
Hills St NE21 ....53 E4
Hills St NE8 ....101 B3
Hillsden Rd NE25 ....31 D7
Hillside Ashington NE63 ..6 C4
Birtley DH3 ....82 C4
Blaydon NE21 ....53 B2
Chester le S DH3 ....88 C4
Dunston NE11 ....69 F7
Killingworth NE12 ......29 E2
Morpeth NE61 ....8 F7
Ponteland NE20 ....25 C1
South Shields NE34 ....60 B4
Sunderland SR3 ....86 C3
West Boldon NE36 ......36 F8
Hillside Ave NE15 ......53 F8
Hillside Cl NE30 ....67 E3
Hillside Cres NE15 ......54 A4
Hillside Dr SR6 ....60 E1
Hillside Gdns SR3 ......86 C3
Hillside Gr DH6 ....96 B5
Hillside Pl NE9 ....71 A6
Hillside Rd NE46 ....45 D4
Hillside Way DH4 ......90 E1
Hillsleigh Rd NE5 ......37 D2
Hillsview Ave NE3 ......37 E5
Hillthorne Cl NE38 ......83 E4
Hilltop Gdns SR3 ....92 C7
Hilltop Ho NE5 ....37 A2
Hilltop View SR6 ....60 E2
Hillview NE3 ....91 B7
Hillview Cres DH4 ......90 D3
Hillview Gr DH4 ....90 D3
Hillview Rd DH4 ....90 D3
Hilton Ave NE5 ....37 B2
Hilton Cl NE23 ....16 A2
Hilton Prim Sch NE5 ....37 B2
Hind St SR1 ....102 C2
Hindley Cl NE40 ....51 E3
Hindley Gdns NE4 ......54 C7
Hindmarch Dr NE35,NE36 ..74 B7
Hindson's Cres N DH4 ..90 A5
Hindson's Cres S DH4 ..90 A5
Hinkley Cl SR3 ....91 B5
Hippingstones La NE45 ..46 F6
Hipsburn Dr SR3 ....86 A3
Hiram Dr NE36 ....74 D7
Hirst Head N NE62 ......11 A2
Hirst High Sch NE63 ....6 F2
Hirst Terr N NE22 ....11 A1
Hirst Villas NE22 ....11 B1
Histon Ct NE5 ....37 B3
Histon Way NE5 ....37 B3
Hither Gn NE32 ....58 D2
Hobart DH2 ....88 A7
Hobart Ave NE5 ....54 B8
Hobart Gdns NE7 ....39 A5
Hobson Ind Est NE16 ..80 A5
Hodgkin Ho NE2 ....99 A3
Hodgkin Park Cres NE15 ..54 C5
Hodgkin Park Rd NE15 ..54 C5
Hodgson Terr **6** NE37 ..83 F8
Hodgson's Rd NE24 ....12 D1
Hodkin Gdns NE9 ....71 B6

Hogarth Cotts NE22 ....16 A8
Hogarth Dr NE38 ....83 E3
Hogarth Rd NE34 ....59 C2
Holbein Rd NE34 ....59 C3
Holborn Ho NE33 ....42 B2
Holborn Pl NE5 ....36 E1
Holborn Rd SR4 ....85 D5
Holborn Sq SR4 ....85 D4
Holburn Cl NE40 ....52 D5
Holburn Cres NE40 ....52 E5
Holburn Gdns NE40 ....52 E5
Holburn La NE40 ....52 D6
Holburn Lane Ct NE40 ..52 D5
Holburn Terr NE40 ......52 E5
Holburn Way NE40 ....52 D5
Holburn Wlk NE40 ......52 E5
Holden Pl NE6 ....37 D2
Holder House La NE34 ..59 E4
Holder House Way NE34 ..59 E2
Holderness Rd
Newcastle-u-T NE6 ....39 B1
Wallsend NE28 ....41 B3
Hole La Sunnside NE16 ..69 B3
Whickham NE16 ....68 F4
Holeyn Hall Rd NE41 ..51 A7
Holeyn Rd NE15 ....35 C1
Holland Dr NE2 ....98 B3
Holland Park Dr NE32 ..58 D2
Holland Pk NE28 ....39 E3
Holley Park Prim Sch
NE38 ....83 A3
Hollinghill Rd NE25 ....23 E2
Hollings Cres NE28 ....40 B4
Hollings Terr NE17 ......66 A1
Hollingside Way NE34 ..59 D5
Hollinhill NE39 ....40 A5
Hollinhill La NE39 ......67 F4
Hollinhill Rd NE37 ......83 E7
Hollinhill Terr NE44 ....62 F8
Hollinside NE16 ....69 A5
Hollinside Gdns NE15 ..54 B6
Hollinside Rd
Sunderland SR4 ....85 D4
Whickham NE11 ....54 B2
Hollinside Sq SR4 ......85 C5
Hollinside Terr NE39 ..67 D2
Hollon St 3 E1
Hollow The Ashington NE63 ..7 B2
Hedworth NE32 ....58 B2
Hollowdene DH5 ....95 A3
Holly Ave Dunston NE11 ..69 B8
Earsdon NE25 ....31 B5
Houghton-le-S DH5 ......94 F8
Longbenton NE12 ....29 D1
Morpeth NE61 ....8 F7
New Silksworth SR3 ....92 B8
Newcastle-u-T,Jesmond
NE2 ....38 F1
Ryton NE40 ....52 C6
South Shields NE34 ....60 A5
Wallsend NE28 ....40 C1
Whitburn SR6 ....75 F8
Whitley Bay NE26 ......31 F5
Winlaton Mill NE21 ....68 C6
Holly Ave W NE2 ....98 C3
Holly Bush Gdns NE40 ..52 E3
Holly Cl Hexham NE46 ..44 F3
Killingworth NE12 ......29 C4
Holly Cres NE38 ....83 C1
Holly Ct Newcastle-u-T NE5 ..37 B2
Sunderland SR4 ....102 A2
Holly Gdns NE9 ....71 A6
Holly Gr NE42 ....50 B3
Holly Haven DH5 ....94 D4
Holly Hill NE10 ....71 D8
Holly Ho SR1 ....103 C3
Holly Mews NE26 ....32 A5
Holly Park View NE10 ..71 D8
Holly Rd NE29 ....41 F7
Holly St Ashington NE63 ..6 F3
Jarrow NE32 ....58 A7
Holly Terr NE10 ....71 D8
Holly Terr W NE10 ......71 C8
Hollybush Rd **4** NE10 ..71 C8
Hollycarrside Rd SR2 ..92 E8
Hollycrest DH2 ....88 B5
Hollydene
Kibblesworth NE11 ......81 D6
Rowlands Gill NE39 ....67 F2
Hollyhock Hebburn NE31 ..57 D5
Washington NE38 ....83 E2
Hollymount Ave NE22 ..16 A8
Hollymount Sq NE22 ..16 A8
Hollymount Terr NE22 ..16 A8
Hollyoak Ho NE24 ......17 B5
Hollys The DH2 ....82 B7
Hollywell Gr NE13 ......36 F8
Hollywell Rd NE29 ......41 D6
Hollywood Ave
Newcastle-u-T,Gosforth
NE3 ....38 D6
Sunderland SR5 ....74 F2
Wallsend NE28 ....40 A1
Hollywood Cres NE3 ..38 D6
Hollywood Gdns NE11 ..70 B5
Holm Gn NE25 ....31 B7
Holman Ct NE33 ....42 C2
Holmcroft NE34 ....7 C5
Holmdale Ashington NE63 ..7 A1
Hexham NE46 ....44 E5
Holme Ave
Newcastle-u-T NE6 ......39 D1
Whickham NE16 ....69 B7

Holme Gdns
Sunderland SR3 ....86 B3
Wallsend NE28 ....41 A2
Holme Rise NE16 ....69 B7
Holmesdale Rd NE5 ....37 D1
Holmeside SR1 ....103 A2
Holmewood Dr NE30 ..78 D8
Holmfield Ave NE34 ....59 E7
Holmland NE15 ....54 C4
Holmlands NE25 ....31 E5
Holmlands Cl NE25 ....31 E5
Holmlands Pk DH3 ......88 D2
Holmlands Pk N NE25 ..31 E5
Holmlands Pk S SR3 ..86 C4
Holmside Ave NE11 ....70 A8
Holmside Terr NE11 ....69 C2
Holmwood Ave
Newbiggin-by-t-S NE64 ..7 D5
Whitley Bay NE25 ......31 D4
Holmwood Gr NE2 ......38 D2
Holwick Cl NE38 ....83 A2
Holy Cross RC Prim Sch
NE28 ....40 F4
Holy Island **11** NE46 ..45 A5
Holy Jesus Bglws NE2 ..98 B4
Holyfields NE27 ....30 E2
Holylake Sq SR4 ....85 B5
Holyoake Gdns
Birtley DH3 ....82 C4
Gateshead NE9 ....70 F8
Holyoake St NE42 ......50 D3
Holyoake Terr
Sunderland SR6 ....75 E3
8 Washington NE37 ....83 D8
Holyrood Rd **2** SR2 ....86 F2
Holystone Ave Blyth NE24 ..17 C5
Newcastle-u-T NE3 ......38 B6
Whitley Bay NE25 ......32 B4
Holystone Cl Blyth NE24 ..17 B5
Burnside DH4 ....90 B2
Holystone Cres NE7 ....39 B4
Holystone Dr NE27 ....30 C2
Holystone Gdns NE29 ..41 D8
Holystone Grange NE27 ..30 C1
Holystone Prim Sch
NE27 ....30 C2
Holystone St **11** NE31 ..57 D6
Holystone Way NE12,
NE27 ....40 C8
Holywell Ave
Holywell NE25 ....23 F2
Newcastle-u-T NE6 ......56 E3
Whitley Bay NE26 ......31 F6
Holywell Cl Blaydon NE21 ..53 D1
Newcastle-u-T NE4 ......98 B2
Holywell Dene Rd NE25 ..23 F2
Holywell La NE25 ....69 B3
Holywell Mews NE26 ..31 F6
Holywell Terr NE27 ....30 D1
Holywell Village Fst Sch
NE25 ....23 F2
Home Ave **2** NE9 ....70 F4
Home Farm Cl NE63 ....5 F4
Home Pk NE28 ....39 E3
Homedale NE42 ....50 E2
Homedale Pl NE42 ......50 E2
Homedale Terr NE42 ..50 D2
Homedowne Ho NE3 ..38 C5
Homeforth Ho NE3 ......38 C5
Homeprior Ho NE25 ....31 E4
Homeside Pl **6** NE6 ....56 B7
Homestall Cl NE34 ......59 D5
Honeycomb Cl **7** SR3 ..91 F5
Honeycrook Dr NE7 ....39 E3
Honeysuckle Ave NE34 ..59 B5
Honeysuckle Cl SR3 ..92 A5
Honister Ave NE2 ....38 E3
Honister Cl NE15 ....53 D7
Honister Dr SR5 ....75 C3
Honister Pl NE15 ....53 D7
Honister Rd NE30 ......32 B2
Honister Way NE24 ....17 C8
Honiton Ct NE3 ....37 B6
Honiton Way NE29 ....41 B8
Hood Cl SR5 ....75 C1
Hood Sq NE21 ....53 A1
Hood St Morpeth NE61 ..3 F1
Newcastle-u-T NE1 ......99 A1
4 Whickham NE16 ......54 A1
Hookergate La NE39 ..67 A2
Hookergate Sch NE39 ..67 B3
Hope Shield NE38 ......82 F1
Hope St Jarrow NE32 ..58 C7
Sunderland SR1 ....102 C2
Hope View SR2 ....92 F7
Hopedene NE10 ....72 A5
Hopgarth Ct DH3 ....88 D4
Hopgarth Gdns DH3 ..88 D4
Hopkins Ct SR4 ....85 F7
Hopkins Wlk NE34 ......59 A2
Hopper Pl **8** NE8 ....101 C3
Hopper Rd NE10 ....71 C7
Hopper St
Gateshead NE8 ....101 C3
5 North Shields NE29 ..41 F5
8 Wallsend NE28 ....40 B2
Horatio St
Newcastle-u-T NE1 ......56 A5
Sunderland SR1 ....75 E1
Hornbeam DH4 ....89 F5
Hornbeam Pl NE4 ......100 B3
Horncliffe Gdns NE16 ..69 C8
Horncliffe Pl NE15 ......35 B2
Horncliffe Wlk NE15 ..53 A7
Horning Ct NE5 ....37 B4

Hornsea Cl NE13 ....28 B5
Hornsey Cres DH5 ......95 B1
Hornsey Terr DH5 ......95 B1
Horse Crofts NE21 ......53 C3
Horsegate Bank NE17,
NE40 ....86 D5
Horsham Gdns SR3 ....86 A3
Horsham Gr NE29 ......41 E4
Horsley Ave
Crawcrook NE40 ....51 E3
Shiremoor NE27 ....30 F2
Horsley Cl NE62 ....10 F8
Horsley Ct NE3 ....37 E6
Horsley Gdns
Dunston NE11 ....70 A8
Holywell NE25 ....23 F2
Horsley Hill Rd NE33 ..42 E1
Horsley Hill Sq NE34 ..60 B7
Horsley Rd
Newcastle-u-T NE7 ......39 B2
Ovingham NE42 ....50 A5
Washington NE38 ....84 A5
Horsley Terr
Newcastle-u-T NE6 ......56 F5
Newcastle-u-T NE30 ..42 D7
Horsley Vale NE34 ......60 A8
Horsley View NE42 ....50 F3
Horsley Wood Cotts
NE15 ....50 D7
Horsleys Bldgs **3** NE61 ..9 A8
Horton Ave
Bedlington NE22 ....15 F8
Shiremoor NE27 ....30 F2
Whiteleas NE34 ....59 D3
Horton Cres NE13 ......27 B7
Horton Dr NE23 ....16 B2
Horton Grange Fst Sch
NE24 ....16 F8
Horton Manor NE24 ....16 F8
Horton Pl NE24 ....17 B4
Horton Rd NE22,NE24 ..16 C5
Horton St **3** NE24 ......17 F7
Hortondale Gr NE24 ..17 B7
Horwood Ave NE5 ......37 B2
Hospital Dr NE31 ....57 D4
Hospital La NE15 ....53 B8
Hospital Of King James The
..................................56 B1
Hospl of St Mary the Virgin
The NE4 ....100 B4
Hotch Pudding Pl NE5 ..36 F1
Hotspur Ave
Bedlington NE22 ....15 F8
South Shields NE34 ....59 F7
Whitley Bay NE25 ......32 A4
Hotspur Prim Sch NE2 ..56 A6
Hotspur Rd NE28 ......40 A5
Hotspur St
Newcastle-u-T NE6 ......56 A7
Tynemouth NE30 ....42 D8
Houghton Ave
Newcastle-u-T NE5 ......37 E3
Tynemouth NE30 ....32 B3
Houghton Cut DH5 ......90 E1
Houghton Ent Ctr DH5 ..94 E8
Houghton Gate DH3 ....89 B3
Houghton Kepier Sch
DH4 ....94 D8
Houghton Rd
Hetton le H DH5 ....95 A4
Newbottle DH4 ....90 D3
Houghton Rd W DH5 ..95 A4
Houghton St SR4 ......102 A2
Houghtonside DH4 ......90 E1
Houlet Garth **11** NE6 ..56 C5
Houlsyke Cl SR3 ....92 C7
Houndelee Pl NE5 ......36 E2
Houndslow Dr NE63 ....6 B2
Hounslow Gdns NE32 ..58 D2
House Terr NE37 ....83 E6
Housesteads Gdns NE12 ..38 F6
Housing La DH8 ....77 D1
Housteads **6** NE30 ......42 A7
Houston St NE4 ....100 B4
Houston St NE4 ....100 B4
Houxty Rd NE25 ....31 B5
Hovingham Gdns SR3 ..86 A3
Howard Cl NE27 ....30 C1
Howard Ct NE30 ....42 B5
Howard Gr NE61 ....4 E3
Howard Pl NE3 ....38 C4
Howard Rd NE61 ....4 A1
Howard St
Gateshead,Mount Pleasant
NE8 ....56 B1
Gateshead,Windy Nook
NE10 ....71 C6
Jarrow NE32 ....58 C7
Newcastle-u-T NE1 ......99 C1
North Shields NE30 ....42 B5
3 Sunderland SR5 ......75 D1
Howarth St
High Spen NE39 ....66 F4
Sunderland SR4 ....3 F1
Howardian Cl NE38 ....83 B3
Howarth St SR4 ....102 A2
Howarth Terr DH6 ......97 F3
Howat Ave NE5 ....37 E1
Howburn Cres NE61 ....4 E3
Howdene Rd NE15 ......53 F6
Howdon Green Ind Est
NE28 ....41 B2
Howdon La NE28 ....41 A2

Howdon Rd
North Shields,Howdon Pans
NE28 ....41 C2
North Shields,Redburn Dene
NE28,NE29 ....41 E3
Howdon Sta NE28 ....41 A2
Howe Sq SR4 ....85 C5
Howe St Gateshead NE8 ...56 A1
Hebburn NE31 ....58 A6
Howick Ave NE3 ....38 A7
Howick Pk SR6 ....103 A4
Howlett Hall Rd NE15 ....53 F6
Howley Ave SR5 ....74 C2
Hownam Cl NE3 ....38 A4
Hoy Cres SR7 ....92 F1
Hoylake Ave NE7 ....39 C5
Hoyle Ave NE4 ....54 E6
Hoyle Fold SR3 ....92 A4
Hubert St NE35 ....73 F8
Hucklow Gdns NE34 ....59 D5
Huddart Terr **2** DH3 ....82 C5
Huddleston Rd NE6 ....56 D7
Huddlestone Rise SR6 ....103 B4
Hudleston NE26 ....32 C4
Hudshaw Gdns NE46 ....45 D4
Hudson Ave
Bedlington NE22 ....11 B1
Dudley NE23 ....29 B8
Hudson Rd SR1 ....103 B2
Hudson Road Prim Sch
SR1 ....103 B2
Hudson St
Gateshead NE8 ....101 B3
North Shields NE30 ....42 C6
South Shields NE33 ....59 B6
Hugar Rd NE39 ....67 A3
Hugh Ave NE27 ....30 F4
Hugh Gdns NE4 ....54 E4
Hugh St Sunderland SR6 ....75 E4
Wallsend NE28 ....40 B1
1 Washington NE38 ....83 F4
Hull St NE4 ....54 F5
Hulne Ave NE30 ....42 D7
Hulne Terr NE15 ....53 C6
Humber Ct **11** SR3 ....91 F6
Humber Gdns NE8 ....56 B1
Humber St NE17 ....66 C1
Humbert St NE32 ....58 B6
Humbledon Pk SR3 ....86 A3
Humbledon View **3** SR2 ..86 C4
Hume St
Newcastle-u-T NE6 ....56 A5
Sunderland SR4 ....102 A2
Humford Gn NE24 ....16 F7
Humford Ho NE24 ....17 B6
Humford Way NE22 ....16 A7
Humsford Gr NE23 ....22 C8
Humshaugh Cl NE12 ....40 A8
Humshaugh Rd NE29 ....41 C6
Hunn's Bldgs NE62 ....10 E5
Hunstanton Ct NE9 ....70 E3
Hunt Lea NE16 ....68 E5
Huntcliffe Ave NE6 ....75 E6
Huntcliffe Gdns NE6 ....39 D1
Huntcliffe Ho NE34 ....59 C3
Hunter Ave NE4 ....17 F6
Hunter Cl NE36 ....74 D6
Hunter Ho NE6 ....57 A4
Hunter St Shiney Row SR4 ..90 A5
South Shields NE33 ....42 D1
Hunter Terr SR2 ....86 E3
Hunter's Moor Cl NE2 ....98 B4
Hunter's Moor Hospl
NE2 ....98 B4
Hunter's Pl NE2 ....98 B4
Hunter's Rd
Newcastle-u-T,South Gosforth
NE3 ....38 C7
Newcastle-u-T,Spital Tongues
NE2 ....98 B3
Hunters Ct DH8 ....77 C1
Hunters Ct
Newcastle-u-T NE3 ....38 E5
Wallsend NE28 ....40 C2
Hunters Hall Rd SR4 ....102 B1
Hunters Lodge NE4 ....40 C2
Huntingdon Cl NE3 ....37 D8
Huntingdon Gdns SR3 ....86 A3
Huntington Pl NE30 ....42 D7
Huntington Dr NE23 ....29 D7
Huntley Cres NE21 ....68 A8
Huntley Sq SR4 ....85 D5
Huntley Terr **4** SR2 ....92 F6
Huntly Rd NE25 ....31 D7
Huntsmoor Ho NE2 ....98 B3
Hurst Terr NE6 ....56 E6
Hurstwood Rd SR4 ....86 A4
Hurworth Ave NE34 ....60 B7
Hurworth Pl NE32 ....58 B6
Hutton Cl Chester le S DH3 ..88 E1
Houghton-le-S DH4 ....94 C8
Washington NE38 ....82 F5
Hutton Ho NE29 ....41 E3
Hutton Row NE33 ....42 E2
Hutton St
Boldon Colliery NE35 ....58 F1
Newcastle-u-T NE3 ....38 A5
Sunderland SR4 ....102 B1
Hutton Terr
Gateshead NE9 ....70 F4
Newcastle-u-T NE2 ....99 C3
Huxley Cl NE34 ....59 B2
Huxley Cres NE8 ....70 D7
Hyacinth Ct SR4 ....102 B3
Hybrid Cl DH4 ....89 F5

Hyde Park St NE8 ....70 D8
Hyde Pk NE28 ....39 F3
Hyde St
South Shields NE33 ....42 D2
Sunderland SR2 ....86 F4
Hyde Terr NE3 ....38 D5
Hylton Ave NE34 ....60 B7
Hylton Bank SR4 ....85 B6
Hylton Castle* SR5 ....74 B2
Hylton Castle Prim Sch
SR5 ....74 A2
Hylton Castle Rd SR5 ....74 B2
Hylton Cl NE12 ....10 D1
Hylton Ct NE38 ....83 B5
Hylton Grange SR5 ....84 F8
Hylton La NE36,SR5 ....74 A5
Hylton Park Rd SR5 ....74 E1
Hylton Pk SR5 ....74 E1
Hylton Rd Jarrow NE32 .....58 C3
Sunderland SR4 ....85 D5
Hylton Red House Prim Sch
SR5 ....74 D2
Hylton Red House Sch
SR5 ....74 E4
Hylton St Gateshead NE8 ...56 B1
Newbottle DH4 ....90 D2
17 North Shields NE29 ....42 A5
Sunderland SR4 ....102 A2
Hylton Terr
Newcastle-u-T NE10 ....57 C2
6 North Shields NE29 ....42 A5
Ryhope SR2 ....92 E6
Hylton Wlk SR4 ....85 A5
Hymers Ave NE34 ....58 F4
Hyperion Ave NE34 ....59 A5

I

Ilderton Pl NE5 ....53 E8
Ilford Ave NE23 ....16 A1
Ilford Pl NE8,NE9 ....71 A8
Ilford Rd
Newcastle-u-T NE2 ....38 D3
Wallsend NE28 ....40 F3
Ilford Road Sta NE2 ....38 D3
Ilfracombe Ave NE4 ....54 E5
Ilfracombe Gdns
Gateshead NE9 ....70 F3
Whitley Bay NE26 ....31 F6
Illingworth Ho NE29 ....41 E3
Ilminster Ct NE3 ....37 C6
Imeary Gr **2** NE33 ....42 D1
Imeary St NE33 ....42 D1
Imperial Bldgs **9** DH4 ......94 E8
Inchberry Cl NE4 ....54 E4
Inchcliffe Cres NE5 ....37 C2
Industrial Rd NE37 ....83 E7
Industry Rd NE6 ....39 D2
Ingham Gr NE23 ....16 A1
Ingham Grange NE33 ....42 C1
Ingham Pl NE2 ....99 C2
Ingham Terr NE41 ....51 B6
Ingleborough Cl **3** NE37 ..83 A6
Ingleby Terr
Lynemouth NE61 ....2 A3
Sunderland SR4 ....102 A1
Ingleby Way NE24 ....17 D3
Inglemere Pl NE15 ....54 A6
Ingleside
South Shields NE34 ....60 B6
Whickham NE16 ....68 F6
Ingleton Ct SR4 ....102 B1
Ingleton Dr NE15 ....35 B2
Ingleton Gdns NE24 ....17 C3
Inglewood Cl NE24 ....16 F7
Inglewood Pl NE3 ....28 C1
Ingoe Ave NE3 ....37 F7
Ingoe Cl NE24 ....17 C7
Ingoe St
Newcastle-u-T NE15 ....53 C6
North Shields NE30 ....41 C2
Ingoldsby Ct SR4 ....85 E4
Ingram Ave NE3 ....37 F8
Ingram Cl
Chester le S DH2 ....88 A1
Wallsend NE28 ....40 F5
Ingram Dr Blyth NE24 ....17 B7
Newcastle-u-T NE5 ....36 D4
Ingram Terr NE6 ....57 A6
Inkerman Rd NE37 ....72 D1
Inkerman St SR5 ....75 A1
Inleborough Dr NE40 ....52 D4
Innesmoor NE31 ....57 D7
Inskip Ho NE34 ....59 C5
Inskip Terr NE8 ....70 F8
Inst for Higher Rabbinical
Studies NE8 ....101 B1
Institute Rd NE63 ....6 B4
Intake Way NE46 ....45 F2
International Ctr for Life
The* NE1 ....100 C4
Inverness Rd NE32 ....58 C2
Inverness St SR5 ....75 D2
Invertay NE3 ....38 B4
Invincible Dr NE4 ....100 A3
Iolanthe Cres NE6 ....56 E7
Iolanthe Terr NE33 ....42 E1
Iona Ct **10** NE28 ....40 F4
Iona Pl NE6 ....57 A6
Iona Rd
Brockley Whins NE32 ....58 E3
Gateshead N10,NE9 ....71 B7
Irene Ave SR2 ....86 F1
Iris Cl NE21 ....53 A2
Iris Cres DH2 ....81 F2
Iris Pl NE4 ....54 D7
Iris Steedman Ho NE4 ....98 A2

Iris Terr Bournmoor DH4 ...89 E3
Crawcrook NE40 ....51 F2
Ironside St DH5 ....90 E1
Irthing NE61 ....1 E5
Irthing Ave NE6 ....56 E6
Irton St NE33 ....38 C5
Irvine Ho **7** NE12 ....39 D8
Irwin Ave NE28 ....40 C3
Isabella Cl NE4 ....54 E3
Isabella Rd NE24 ....17 C6
Isabella Wlk NE15 ....35 D1
Islay Ho **9** SR3 ....92 A6
Ivanhoe NE25 ....31 E5
Ivanhoe Cres SR2 ....86 B4
Ivanhoe Terr
11 Chester le S DH3 ....88 C2
Dipton DH9 ....78 E1
Ivanhoe View NE9 ....71 B2
Iveagh Cl NE4 ....54 D4
Iveson Rd NE46 ....44 E3
Ivor St SR2 ....87 A2
Ivy Ave
Newbiggin-by-t-S NE64 ....7 C5
Ryton NE40 ....52 C6
Ivy Cl Newcastle-u-T NE4 ..100 B3
Ryton NE40 ....52 C6
Ivy La NE9 ....71 A3
Ivy Pl DH9 ....79 C3
Ivy Rd Longbenton NE12 ....39 E8
Newcastle-u-T,Gosforth
NE3 ....38 C4
Newcastle-u-T,Walkergate
NE6 ....56 F8
Ivy Road Prim Sch NE12 ...39 E8
Ivy St NE13 ....28 C8
Ivy Terr Crawcrook NE40 ....51 F2
Penshaw DH4 ....90 B6
Ivymount Rd NE6 ....39 B1

J

Jack Common Ho **3** NE6 ..56 B7
Jack's Terr NE34 ....59 C5
Jackson Ave NE20 ....25 F7
Jackson Rd NE41 ....51 B6
Jackson St
Gateshead NE8 ....101 C3
Newcastle-u-T NE6 ....56 F6
North Shields NE30 ....42 B6
Sunderland SR4 ....102 A1
Jackson St W NE30 ....42 B6
Jacksons Terr **11** NE61 ......9 A8
Jacksons Pl DH3 ....82 C5
Jacobins Chare **9** NE1 ....98 C1
Jacques St SR4 ....85 F8
Jacques Terr DH2 ....88 A4
Jade Cl NE15 ....53 C8
James Armitage St SR5 .....75 B2
James Ave NE27 ....30 F4
James Mather St NE33 ....42 C3
James Pl St NE6 ....56 A6
James St Kip Hill DH9 ....79 F1
Newcastle-u-T NE5 ....36 F2
Newcastle-u-T,Elswick NE4 ..54 F4
Sunderland SR5 ....75 A2
10 Whickham NE16 ....69 A7
James Steel Pk The*
NE8 ....84 A2
James Terr
Easington Lane DH5 ....97 B8
Fence Houses DH4 ....94 A8
Wallsend NE28 ....40 B1
James Williams St SR1 ....103 B3
Jameson Dr NE45 ....47 B7
Jane Eyre Terr NE6 ....56 B1
Jane St Hetton le H DH5 .....95 A6
22 Newcastle-u-T NE6 ....56 C6
Jane Terr NE6 ....57 A4
Janet Sq NE6 ....56 C5
Janet St
17 Newcastle-u-T,St Lawrence
NE6 ....56 C5
Newcastle-u-T,St Peters
NE6 ....56 C4
Janus Cl NE5 ....36 C4
Jarrow Cross CE Prim Sch
NE32 ....58 B6
Jarrow Rd NE32,NE34 ....58 F6
Jarrow Sch (Cornhill)
NE32 ....58 B6
Jarrow Sch (Field Terrace)
NE32 ....58 B5
Jarrow Sta NE32 ....58 B7
Jasmin Ave NE6 ....36 C4
Jasmine Cl NE6 ....39 E1
Jasmine Ct Ashington NE63 ..6 C1
Sunderland SR4 ....102 B3
Jasmine Terr DH3 ....82 D4
Jasmine Villas **7** NE16 .....69 A7
Jasper Ave NE40 ....52 B1
Jaycroft Ct NE32 ....58 C3
Jedburgh Cl
Gateshead NE8 ....101 C1
Newcastle-u-T NE5 ....36 C4
Tynemouth NE29 ....41 E8
Jedburgh Ct NE11 ....70 E2
Jedburgh Gdns NE15 ....54 A8
Jedburgh Rd DH4 ....90 B6
Jedmoor NE31 ....57 D7
Jefferson Cl SR5 ....75 C4
Jefferson Pl NE4 ....98 B2
Jellicoe Rd NE6 ....56 E3
Jenifer Gr NE7 ....39 A4
Jenison Ave NE15 ....54 A5
Jennifer Ave **9** SR5 ....74 B1
Jersey Sq NE61 ....2 A3
Jervis St NE31 ....57 F6

Jesmond Dene Rd
Newcastle-u-T,Jesmond
NE2 ....38 F2
Newcastle-u-T,West Jesmond
NE2 ....38 D3
Jesmond Gdns
Newcastle-u-T NE2 ....38 F1
Whiteleas NE34 ....59 C3
Jesmond Park Ct **1** NE7 ...39 B1
Jesmond Pk E NE7 ....39 B1
Jesmond Pk W NE7 ....39 B1
Jesmond Pl **1** NE2 ....38 E1
Jesmond Rd NE2 ....99 C4
Jesmond Rd W NE2 ....99 B3
Jesmond Sta NE2 ....99 B3
Jesmond Terr NE26 ....32 B4
Jesmond Vale NE2 ....56 A7
Jesmond Vale La NE6 ....56 B8
Jesmond Vale Terr NE6 ......56 B8
Jessel St NE7 ....70 F4
Jetty The NE10 ....57 A2
Joan Ave SR2 ....86 F1
Joan St NE4 ....54 D4
Joannah St SR5 ....75 C3
Jobling Ave NE21 ....53 B2
Jobling Cres NE61 ....9 B6
Jobling Ho SR4 ....85 F7
Joel Terr NE10 ....57 B2
John & Margaret Common
Homes for Aged Miners 8
NE24 ....16 B8
John Ave NE40 ....52 B1
John Brown Ct NE22 ....10 F1
John Candlish Rd SR4 ......102 A3
John Clay St
3 South Shields NE33 ....42 D1
5 South Shields,Dean
NE33 ....59 D8
John Dobson St NE1,
NE99 ....99 B2
John F Kennedy Est
NE38 ....83 E5
John F Kennedy Prim Sch
NE38 ....83 E5
John Reid Rd NE34 ....59 C4
John Spence Community
High Sch NE29 ....42 A8
John St Ashington NE63 ....6 C4
Blyth NE24 ....17 B8
Boldon Colliery NE35 ....73 F8
Earsdon NE25 ....31 A5
Fence Houses DH4 ....94 A8
Gateshead,Old Fold NE8 .....71 C8
1 Gateshead,Pelaw NE10 ..56 F1
Hetton le H DH5 ....95 A3
Houghton-le-S DH5 ....94 F8
Newcastle-u-T NE5 ....38 A5
Pegswood NE61 ....4 F3
Prudhoe NE42 ....50 E3
Ryhope SR2 ....93 A6
Sunderland SR1 ....103 A3
Sunderland,South Hylton
SR4 ....85 A7
Tynemouth NE30 ....32 C3
Wallsend NE28 ....40 B2
John Taylor Ct SR5 ....75 A3
John Wesley Ct NE42 ....50 D2
John Williamson St
SR5 ....59 C7
Johnson St
6 Dunston NE11 ....54 F1
Gateshead NE8 ....100 B1
Newcastle-u-T NE15 ....53 C6
South Shields NE33 ....59 C7
Sunderland SR1 ....102 C3
Johnson Terr
High Spen NE39 ....66 F4
8 Washington NE37 ....83 F8
Johnson's Villas NE62 ....10 B7
Johnston Ave NE31 ....57 D3
Joicey Aged Miners Homes
7 DH4 ....90 B6
Joicey Rd NE9 ....70 F6
Joicey Road Sch NE9 ....70 F6
Joicey St NE10 ....57 A1
Joliffe St DH3 ....88 D1
Jonadab Rd NE10 ....57 A2
Jonadab St NE10 ....57 A1
Jones St **4** DH3 ....82 C4
Jonquil Cl NE5 ....36 C4
Joseph Cl NE4 ....54 E4
Joseph Hopper Aged
Miners' Homes DH3 ....82 C7
Joseph Hopper Meml Homes
NE9 ....71 C6
Joseph Swan Sch NE9 ....70 E3
Joseph Terr NE17 ....66 B1
Jowett Sq SR5 ....75 A2
Joyce Cl NE10 ....72 D8
Joyce Terr **5** SR5 ....74 B1
Jubilee Ave NE9 ....71 C1
Jubilee Bldgs **3** NE46 ......45 B4
Jubilee Cotts
Greenside NE40 ....66 D7
Houghton-le-S DH4 ....94 D8
Lynemouth NE61 ....2 A3
Jubilee Cres
Newcastle-u-T NE3 ....38 A5
Sherburn Hill DH6 ....96 D1
Jubilee Ct Annitsford NE23 ..22 B1
Blyth NE24 ....17 D6
Gateshead NE9 ....70 C8
Hebburn NE31 ....58 A6
Jubilee Est NE63 ....6 D3
Jubilee Ho DH5 ....95 C1
Jubilee Ind Est NE63 ....6 D1
Jubilee Lodge 22 B4
Jubilee Mews NE3 ....38 B5

Jubilee Rd Blyth NE24 ....1 .
Newcastle-u-T NE1 ....9 .
Newcastle-u-T,Coxlodge
NE3 ....3 .
Ovington NE42 ....4 .
Jubilee Sq
Easington Lane DH5 ....9 .
South Hetton DH6 ....9 .
Jubilee St **3** NE28 ....4 .
Jubilee Terr
Bedlington NE22 ....1 .
Crawcrook NE40 ....5 .
Newbiggin-by-t-S NE64 ....2 .
Seaton Burn NE13 ....2 .
Tantobe DH9 ....2 .
Washington NE38 ....5 .
7 Whickham NE16 ....5 .
Jubilee Terrs Newcastle-u-T
Julian Ave
Newcastle-u-T NE6 ....5 .
South Shields NE33 ....5 .
Julian Rd NE10 ....7 .
Julian St NE33 ....4 .
Juliet Ave NE29 ....4 .
Juliet St NE63 ....4 .
Julius Caesar St **5** SR5 ....7 .
Julius Ct NE33 ....4 .
June Ave NE21 ....6 .
Juniper Cl Blyth NE24 ....1 .
Newcastle-u-T NE3 ....2 .
Juniper Ct NE21 ....5 .
Juniper Wlk NE5 ....3 .
Jutland Ave NE31 ....5 .

K

Kane Gdns NE10 ....7 .
Kateregina DH3 ....8 .
Katherine St NE63 ....8 .
Katrine Cl DH2 ....8 .
Katrine Ct SR3 ....9 .
Kay's Cotts **5** NE10 ....7 .
Kayll Rd SR4 ....8 .
Kearsley Cl NE25 ....2 .
Kearton Ave NE5 ....5 .
Keats Ave Blyth NE24 ....1 .
Sunderland SR5 ....7 .
West Boldon NE35 ....7 .
Keats Gr NE63 ....6 .
Keats Rd NE15 ....5 .
Keats Wlk
Biddick Hall NE34 ....5 .
Gateshead NE8 ....5 .
Keeble Ct NE63 ....6 .
Keebledale Ave NE6 ....5 .
Keebledale Ho NE6 ....5 .
Keel Row **11** Blyth NE24 ....1 .
Whickham NE16 ....5 .
Keele Dr NE23 ....2 .
Keelman's La SR4 ....8 .
Keelman's Rd SR4 ....8 .
Keelmans Ho **8** NE34 ....5 .
Keelmans Terr NE24 ....1 .
Keelmans Flats NE1 ....5 .
Keighley Ave SR5 ....7 .
Keighley Sq SR5 ....7 .
Keir Hardie Ave NE10 ....7 .
Keir Hardie Ct NE64 ....7 .
Keir Hardie St
Fence Houses DH4 ....9 .
Rowlands Gill NE39 ....6 .
Keir Hardie Way SR5 ....7 .
Keith Cl NE4 ....5 .
Keith Sq SR5 ....7 .
Kelburn Ho NE1 ....5 .
Keldane Gdns NE4 ....5 .
Kelfield Gr NE23 ....2 .
Kelham Sq SR5 ....7 .
Kell Cres DH6 ....5 .
Kell's Way NE39 ....6 .
Kellfield Ave NE9 ....7 .
Kellfield Rd NE9 ....7 .
Kells Gdns NE9 ....7 .
Kells La NE9 ....7 .
Kells Lane Prim Sch NE9 ....7 .
Kellsway NE10 ....7 .
Kellsway Ct NE10 ....7 .
Kelly Rd NE31 ....5 .
Kelpie Gdns **3** SR6 ....7 .
Kelsey Way NE23 ....2 .
Kelso Dr NE29 ....4 .
Kelso Gdns
Bedlington NE22 ....1 .
Newcastle-u-T NE15 ....5 .
Wallsend NE28 ....4 .
Kelso Gr DH4 ....9 .
Kelso Pl NE8 ....10 .
Kelson Way NE5 ....3 .
Kelston Way NE5 ....3 .
Kelvin Gdns **3** NE11 ....7 .
Kelvin Gro **1** Gateshead NE8 .5 .
Newcastle-u-T NE2 ....5 .
South Shields NE33 ....5 .
Sunderland SR6 ....7 .
Tynemouth NE29 ....5 .
Kelvin Grove Com Prim Sch
NE8 ....5 .
Kelvin Pl NE12 ....5 .
Kemble Cl NE23 ....5 .
Kemble Sq SR5 ....7 .
Kempton Gdns NE8 ....5 .
Kendal Ave Blyth NE24 ....1 .
Tynemouth NE30 ....4 .

Kendal Cres NE9 . . . . .71 B5
Kendal Dr
　Cramlington NE23 . . . . .22 C8
　East Boldon NE36 . . . . .74 C8
Kendal Gdns NE28 . . . . .41 A4
Kendal Gn 6 NE6 . . . . .56 B6
Kendal Ho 7 NE6 . . . . .56 B6
Kendal Pl 20 NE6 . . . . .56 B6
Kendal Rise NE22 . . . . .10 D2
Kendale Wlk NE5 . . . . .36 E3
Kendor Gr NE61 . . . . .8 F6
Kenilworth Ct
　Newcastle-u-T NE4 . . . . . .100 A4
　4 Washington NE37 . . . . .83 F8
Kenilworth Rd
　Ashington NE63 . . . . .6 C3
　Newcastle-u-T NE4 . . . . . .100 A4
　Whitley Bay NE25 . . . . .31 F4
Kenilworth Sq SR5 . . . . .74 C4
Kenilworth View 7 NE9 . .71 A2
Kenley Rd
　Newcastle-u-T NE5 . . . . .54 A8
　Sunderland SR5 . . . . .74 C4
Kenmoor Way NE5 . . . . .36 C3
Kenmore Cl NE10 . . . . .72 B8
Kenmore Cres NE40 . . . . . . .52 B2
Kennersdene NE30 . . . . .42 C8
Kennet Ave NE32 . . . . .58 C3
Kennet Sq SR5 . . . . .74 B4
Kennford NE9 . . . . .71 A1
Kennington Gr NE6 . . . . .56 E5
Kensington Ave NE3 . . . . . . .38 C7
Kensington Cl NE25 . . . . . . .31 F5
Kensington Cotts NE61 . . . . .9 B8
Kensington Ct
　6 Gateshead NE10 . . . . . . .71 C8
　Hebburn NE31 . . . . .57 D5
　South Shields NE33 . . . . . . .59 C5
Kensington Gdns
　1 North Shields NE30 . . . . .42 B6
　Wallsend NE28 . . . . .39 E3
　Whitley Bay NE25 . . . . .31 F5
Kensington Gr NE30 . . . . . . .42 B7
Kensington Terr
　2 Dunston NE11 . . . . .69 F8
　Newcastle-u-T NE2 . . . . .99 A3
Kensington Villas 5 NE5 . .36 E3
Kent Ave 3 Dunston NE11 .70 A8
　Hebburn NE31 . . . . .57 D5
　Wallsend NE28 . . . . .40 F2
Kent Ct NE63 . . . . .6 A4
Kent Ct NE3 . . . . .37 D8
Kent Gdns DH5 . . . . .94 F4
Kent Pl NE34 . . . . .60 A6
Kent St NE32 . . . . .58 A6
Kent Terr DH6 . . . . .97 E1
Kentchester Rd SR5 . . . . . . .74 C4
Kentmere DH3 . . . . .82 E1
Kentmere Ave
　Newcastle-u-T NE6 . . . . .56 F7
　Sunderland SR5 . . . . .75 C5
Kentmere Cl NE23 . . . . .23 A2
Kenton Ave NE3 . . . . .38 A3
Kenton Bank NE5 . . . . .37 E4
Kenton Bar Prim Sch
　NE3 . . . . .37 D4
Kenton Cres NE3 . . . . .37 F4
Kenton Ct NE33 . . . . .42 D1
Kenton Gr NE6 . . . . .75 D1
Kenton La NE3 . . . . .37 E4
Kenton Park Sch Ctr NE3 . .38 A4
Kenton Rd
　Newcastle-u-T NE3 . . . . .38 A3
　Tynemouth NE29 . . . . .41 C7
Kenton Sch NE3 . . . . .37 E4
Kentucky Rd SR5 . . . . .74 A4
Kenwood Gdns NE9 . . . . . . .71 A2
Kenya Rd SR5 . . . . .74 C4
Kepier Chare Com Prim Sch
　NE40 . . . . .51 F3
Kepier Gdns 6 SR4 . . . . . . .85 A6
Keppel St Dunston NE11 . . . .54 F1
　6 South Shields NE33 . . . . .42 C3
Kepwell Bank Top NE42 . . . .50 C2
Kepwell Ct NE42 . . . . .50 C3
Kepwell Rd NE42 . . . . .50 C2
Kerry Cl NE24 . . . . .17 E8
Kerry Sq SR5 . . . . .74 B4
Kesteven Sq SR5 . . . . .74 B4
Keston Dr NE23 . . . . .16 B2
Kestrel Cl NE38 . . . . .83 A2
Kestrel Ct 11 DH3 . . . . .82 C4
Kestrel Dr NE63 . . . . .6 B1
Kestrel Lodge Flats 6
　NE33 . . . . .42 D3
Kestrel Mews NE16 . . . . .69 A7
Kestrel Pl NE12 . . . . .39 A7
Kestrel Sq SR5 . . . . .74 B4
Kestrel Way
　North Shields NE29 . . . . . . .42 A3
　South Shields NE34 . . . . . . .59 B4
Keswick Ave SR6 . . . . .75 D4
Keswick Dr NE30 . . . . .32 B2
Keswick Gdns NE28 . . . . . . .41 A3
Keswick Gr NE5 . . . . .54 A8
Keswick St NE8 . . . . .101 B1
Keswick Terr DH6 . . . . .97 E8
Kettering Pl NE23 . . . . .22 C8
Kettering Sq SR5 . . . . .74 B4
Kettlewell Terr 7 NE30 . . . .42 B6
Ketton Cl NE12 . . . . .39 B6
Kew Gdns NE26 . . . . .32 A6
Keyes Gdns NE2 . . . . .38 E3
Kibblesworth Bank NE11 . .81 B6
Kibblesworth Prim Sch
　NE11 . . . . .81 D6

Kidd Sq SR5 . . . . .74 B4
Kidderminster Dr NE5 . . . . . .36 C3
Kidderminster Rd SR5 . . . . .74 B3
Kidderminster Sq SR5 . . . . .74 B3
Kidland Cl NE63 . . . . .6 F4
Kidlandlee Gn NE5 . . . . .37 A4
Kidlandlee Pl NE5 . . . . .37 A4
Kidsgrove Sq SR5 . . . . .74 B3
Kielder NE38 . . . . .82 F4
Kielder Ave NE23 . . . . .21 D6
Kielder Cl Blyth NE24 . . . . . .17 B5
　Killingworth NE12 . . . . .29 C4
Kielder Ct NE15 . . . . .37 A4
Kielder Dr NE63 . . . . .6 C3
Kielder Gdns Jarrow NE32 .58 B3
　Stakeford NE62 . . . . .6 A1
Kielder Ho 15 SR3 . . . . .92 A6
Kielder Pl NE25 . . . . .31 B5
Kielder Rd Earsdon NE15 . . .31 B5
　Newcastle-u-T NE15 . . . . . . .53 C7
Kielder Terr NE30 . . . . .42 B6
Kielder Way NE3 . . . . .38 B7
Kilburn Cl SR2 . . . . .93 A6
Kilburn Gdns NE29 . . . . .41 D3
Kilburn Gn NE9 . . . . .71 B1
Kilburn Cl NE7 . . . . .39 E3
Kildale DH4 . . . . .89 E8
Kildale Sq SR5 . . . . .74 B4
Kilkenny Ave SR5 . . . . .74 B4
Killarney Sq SR5 . . . . .74 B4
Killebrigs NE15 . . . . .34 E2
Killin Cl NE23 . . . . .16 E1
Killingworth Ave NE27 . . . . .30 B4
Killingworth Ctr The
　NE12 . . . . .29 D3
Killingworth Dr
　Killingworth NE12 . . . . .29 B2
　Sunderland SR3,SR4 . . . . . . .85 E4
Killingworth Hall NE12 . . . . .29 E2
Killingworth La NE27 . . . . . . .30 A5
Killingworth Pl NE1 . . . . .99 A2
Killingworth Rd
　Killingworth NE12 . . . . .29 E3
　Newcastle-u-T NE3 . . . . .38 F5
Killingworth Way NE12,
　NE27 . . . . .29 D2
Killowen St NE9 . . . . .70 E4
Kiln Rise NE16 . . . . .69 A4
Kilnshaw Pl NE3 . . . . .28 D1
Kilsyth Ave NE29 . . . . .31 E2
Kilsyth Sq SR5 . . . . .74 B4
Kimberley NE38 . . . . .84 A5
Kimberley Ave NE29 . . . . . . .41 E6
Kimberley Gdns
　Newcastle-u-T NE2 . . . . .56 A8
　Stocksfield NE43 . . . . .64 C7
Kimberley St Blyth NE24 . . .17 D8
　Sunderland SR4 . . . . .85 F6
Kimberley Terr 4 NE24 . . . .17 E8
Kinfauns Terr 5 NE9 . . . . . .71 A5
King Charles Ct SR5 . . . . . . .74 A4
King Charles Twr NE1 . . . . . .99 C2
King Edward Pl NE8 . . . . . . .56 B1
King Edward Prim Sch
　NE30 . . . . .42 B7
King Edward St
　Gateshead NE8 . . . . .56 B1
　Tanfield Lea DH9 . . . . .79 C1
King Edward VI Sch The
　NE61 . . . . .3 F2
King George Ave NE11 . . . . .69 F8
King George Rd
　Newcastle-u-T NE3 . . . . .37 E6
　South Shields NE34 . . . . . . .59 E5
King George V Sch NE34 . . .59 E3
King George's Rd NE64 . . . . .7 D5
King Henry Ct SR5 . . . . .74 A4
King James Ct SR5 . . . . .74 A4
King James St NE8 . . . . .101 C1
King John St NE6 . . . . .56 B8
King John Terr NE6 . . . . .56 B8
King John's Ct NE20 . . . . . . .25 A4
King St Birtley DH3 . . . . .82 B4
　Blyth NE24 . . . . .17 E8
　Gateshead,Bensham NE8 . . .70 C8
　Gateshead,Pelaw NE10 . . . . .57 A1
　Newbiggin-by-t-S NE64 . . . . .7 F5
　Newcastle-u-T NE1 . . . . . . .101 B4
　North Shields NE30 . . . . . . .42 B6
　South Shields NE33 . . . . . . .42 C3
　Sunderland SR1 . . . . .103 A4
　Sunderland,Fulwell SR6 . . . .75 D4
King's Ave NE16 . . . . .3 F1
King's Dr Greenside NE40 . . .52 A3
　Whitley Bay NE26 . . . . .32 A4
King's Gdns NE24 . . . . .17 C8
King's Pl SR4 . . . . .102 A3
King's Rd Bedlington NE22 . .11 C6
　Newcastle-u-T NE1,NE2 . . . . .99 A2
　Whitley Bay NE26 . . . . .31 F6
King's Rd The SR5 . . . . .75 A2
King's School Tynemouth
　NE30 . . . . .42 B6
King's Terr SR4 . . . . .102 A3
King's Wlk NE1 . . . . .99 A2
Kingarth Ave SR6 . . . . .75 E5
Kingdom Pl NE12 . . . . .29 C4
Kingfisher Bvd NE15 . . . . . . .53 D5
Kingfisher Cl NE63 . . . . .11 E8
Kingfisher Ct NE11 . . . . . . .100 A1
Kingfisher Lodge NE32 . . . .58 A6
Kingfisher Rd NE12 . . . . .39 A7

Kingfisher Way
　Blyth NE24 . . . . .17 F4
　Shiremoor NE28 . . . . .41 A6
Kingham Ct NE3 . . . . .38 F4
Kinghorn Sq SR5 . . . . .74 B4
Kings Ave Hebburn NE31 . . . .57 F5
　Sunderland SR5 . . . . .75 E5
Kings Cl NE8 . . . . .56 B1
Kings Ct NE2 . . . . .99 C2
Kings Lodge NE30 . . . . .42 B6
Kings Mdw NE32 . . . . .58 C1
Kings Mdws NE4 . . . . .54 C5
Kings Pk NE62 . . . . .10 F5
Kings Rd Cl NE29 . . . . .29 C1
Kings Road N NE28 . . . . . . .40 B4
Kings Road S NE28 . . . . . . .40 B3
Kings Terr 28 NE9 . . . . .71 F1
Kings Vale NE28 . . . . .40 C4
Kings Wlk NE5 . . . . .36 C4
Kingsbridge NE12 . . . . .38 F7
Kingsbridge Cl NE29 . . . . . .41 E4
Kingsclere Ave SR5 . . . . .74 B3
Kingsclere Sq SR5 . . . . .74 B3
Kingsdale Ave Blyth NE24 . . .17 A7
　Washington NE37 . . . . .83 C8
Kingsdale Rd NE12 . . . . .38 F7
Kingsgate 6 NE46 . . . . .45 A5
Kingsgate Terr NE46 . . . . . . .45 A5
Kingsley Ave
　Biddick Hall NE34 . . . . .59 A3
　Newcastle-u-T NE3 . . . . .28 D1
　Whitley Bay NE25 . . . . .32 A4
Kingsley Cl 4 SR5 . . . . .75 A1
Kingsley Pl
　6 Dunston NE11 . . . . .54 F1
　2 Newcastle-u-T NE6 . . . . .56 B7
　Wallsend NE28 . . . . .40 F3
　Whickham NE16 . . . . .69 B8
Kingsley Rd NE61 . . . . .2 A2
Kingsley Terr
　Crawcrook NE40 . . . . .51 E4
　Newcastle-u-T NE4 . . . . .98 A1
Kingsmeadow Com Comp
　Sch NE11 . . . . .68 C2
Kingsmere DH3 . . . . .88 C7
Kingsmere Gdns NE6 . . . . . .57 A4
Kingston Ave NE6 . . . . .56 D4
Kingston Cl NE26 . . . . .31 F8
Kingston Cres DH6 . . . . .97 E3
Kingston Ct 6 NE26 . . . . . . .31 F8
Kingston Dr NE26 . . . . .31 F8
Kingston Gn NE6 . . . . .56 D5
Kingston Mews DH4 . . . . . . .90 C5
Kingston Park Ave NE3 . . . . .37 C6
Kingston Park Rd NE3 . . . . . .37 C6
Kingston Park Prim Sch
　NE3 . . . . .37 C7
Kingston Park Rd NE3 . . . . . .37 F7
Kingston Park S NE3 . . . . . . .37 C6
Kingston Rd NE8 . . . . .71 B8
Kingston Terr SR6 . . . . .75 D2
Kingston Way NE26 . . . . .31 F8
Kingsway Blyth NE24 . . . . . . .17 E6
　Houghton-le-S DH5 . . . . . . .94 F8
　Newcastle-u-T NE4 . . . . .54 E8
　Ponteland NE20 . . . . .25 C6
　South Shields NE33 . . . . . . .42 C2
　Sunnisid NE16 . . . . .69 A2
　Tynemouth NE30 . . . . .42 C8
Kingsway Ave NE3 . . . . .38 C7
Kingsway Ho NE11 . . . . .70 D4
Kingsway Intc NE11 . . . . . . .70 E3
Kingsway N NE11 . . . . .70 C5
Kingsway S NE11 . . . . .70 D3
Kingsway Sq SR5 . . . . .74 B4
Kingsway Sq SR5 . . . . .74 B4
Kingswell NE61 . . . . .9 B7
Kingswood Ave NE2 . . . . . . .38 D3
Kingswood Cl NE35 . . . . .58 E1
Kingswood Ct 18 NE30 . . . .42 D7
Kingswood Dr NE20 . . . . . . .25 C4
Kingswood Gr SR4 . . . . .85 A2
Kingswood Rd NE12 . . . . . . .29 B3
Kingswood Sq SR5 . . . . .74 B3
Kinlett NE38 . . . . .84 A5
Kinloch Ct DH2 . . . . .88 B1
Kinloss Sq NE23 . . . . .22 C8
Kinnaird Ave NE15 . . . . .54 A6
Kinnock Cl DH6 . . . . .96 A1
Kinross Cl DH3 . . . . .82 D2
Kinross Ct NE10 . . . . .72 B8
Kinross Dr NE3 . . . . .37 F5
Kinsale Sq SR5 . . . . .74 B4
Kinver Dr NE5 . . . . .36 D3
Kipling Ave Hebburn NE31 . . .57 F6
　West Boldon NE36 . . . . .74 A7
　Whickham NE16 . . . . .69 B8
Kipling Cl NE16 . . . . .69 B8
Kipling St SR5 . . . . .75 A1
Kipling Wlk NE8 . . . . .56 A2
Kirby Cl NE7 . . . . .39 A3
Kirk St NE6 . . . . .56 C5
Kirk View DH4 . . . . .90 D3
Kirkbride Pl NE23 . . . . .22 C8
Kirkdale Ct 2 NE34 . . . . . . .59 A4
Kirkdale Gn NE4 . . . . .100 B4
Kirkdale Sq SR5 . . . . .74 B4
Kirkdale St DH5 . . . . .94 F2
Kirkham NE38 . . . . .83 D4
Kirkham Rd NE3 . . . . .37 C7
Kirkharle Dr NE61 . . . . .4 E1
Kirkheaton Pl NE5 . . . . .54 C8
Kirkland Wlk NE27 . . . . .30 E3
Kirklands NE21 . . . . .29 C5
Kirklea Rd DH5 . . . . .94 F8
Kirkleatham Gdns NE6 . . . . .39 D2

Kirkley Ave NE34 . . . . .60 A6
Kirkley Cl NE3 . . . . .38 B6
Kirkley Dr Ashington NE63 . . .6 E2
　Ponteland NE20 . . . . .25 E7
Kirkley Lodge NE3 . . . . .38 B6
Kirkley Rd NE27 . . . . .30 F2
Kirklinton Rd NE30 . . . . .32 A2
Kirknewton Cl 7 DH5 . . . . . .94 F8
Kirkside DH4 . . . . .90 E6
Kirkston Ave NE15 . . . . .53 D7
Kirkstone DH3 . . . . .82 D2
Kirkstone Ave
　Hedworth NE32 . . . . .58 D3
　Sunderland SR5 . . . . .75 C3
　Tynemouth NE30 . . . . .32 A2
Kirkstone Cl Blaydon NE21 . .68 C8
　8 Houghton-le-S DH5 . . . . .94 F8
Kirkstone Gdns NE7 . . . . . . .39 A3
Kirkstone Rd NE10 . . . . .71 F8
Kirkwall Cl SR5 . . . . .74 A3
Kirkwood NE23 . . . . .29 C5
Kirkwood Ave SR4 . . . . .85 A2
Kirkwood Dr NE3 . . . . .37 F5
Kirkwood Gdns NE10 . . . . . .72 B8
Kirkwood Pl NE3 . . . . .28 B1
Kirton Ave NE4 . . . . .54 E6
Kirton Park Terr NE29,
　NE30 . . . . .42 A7
Kirton Way NE23 . . . . .22 C8
Kismet St SR5 . . . . .75 A2
Kitchener Rd SR6 . . . . .60 F4
Kitchener St
　Gateshead NE9 . . . . .71 B8
　Sunderland SR4 . . . . .85 F4
Kitchener Terr
　Jarrow NE32 . . . . .58 B5
　New Herrington DH4 . . . . . .90 D6
　North Shields NE30 . . . . . . .42 C7
　Sunderland SR2 . . . . .86 F2
Kittiwake Cl Blyth NE24 . . . .17 E3
　Shiremoor NE38 . . . . .41 A7
Kittiwake Dr NE38 . . . . .82 F3
Kittiwake Ho NE26 . . . . .32 B5
Kitty Brewster Ind Est
　NE24 . . . . .12 B1
Kitty Brewster Rd NE24 . . . .16 F8
Knaresborough Cl NE12 . . . .10 D2
Knaresborough Sq SR5 . . . .74 C4
Knaresdale DH3 . . . . .82 D1
Knarsdale Ave NE23 . . . . . . .41 D6
Knarsdale Pl 8 NE5 . . . . . .36 E1
Knightsbridge
　Newcastle-u-T NE3 . . . . .38 C6
　Sunderland SR3 . . . . .91 E8
Knightsbodge Cl NE3 . . . . . .38 C6
Knightside Gdns NE11 . . . . .70 A7
Knightside Wlk NE5 . . . . . . .36 C3
Knivestone Ct NE12 . . . . . . .29 E4
Knobbyends La NE21 . . . . . .67 F8
Knoll Rise NE11 . . . . .69 F7
Knoll The Ellington NE61 . . . .1 C5
　Sunderland SR2 . . . . .102 B1
Knollside Cl SR3 . . . . .91 F5
Knop Law Fst Sch NE5 . . . . .36 C3
Knott Meml Flats 13
　NE30 . . . . .42 D7
Knott Pl NE15 . . . . .54 B5
Knoulberry NE37 . . . . .83 A6
Knoulberry Rd NE37 . . . . . . .83 A6
Knowle Pl NE12 . . . . .39 B5
Knowledge Hill NE21 . . . . . .53 B1
Knowsley Ct NE3 . . . . .37 B5
Knox Cl NE22 . . . . .11 D2
Knox Rd NE22 . . . . .16 B8
Knox Sq SR5 . . . . .75 A2
Knutsford Wlk NE23 . . . . . . .22 C8
Kristin Ave NE32 . . . . .58 C4
Kyffin View NE34 . . . . .60 B5
Kyle Cl NE4 . . . . .100 B4
Kyle Rd NE8 . . . . .70 C8
Kylins The NE61 . . . . .9 A6
Kyloe Ave NE25 . . . . .23 D2
Kyloe Cl NE3 . . . . .37 E7
Kyloe Pl Bedlington NE22 . . .10 F5
　Newcastle-u-T NE3 . . . . .37 A3
Kyloe Villas NE5 . . . . .37 A3
Kyo Bog La NE41,NE42 . . . .51 B1
Kyo La NE40 . . . . .66 D7

L

L'Arbre Cres NE16 . . . . .68 F7
La Sagesse Sch NE2 . . . . . .38 E3
Laburnum Ave Blyth NE24 . .17 D8
　Gateshead NE9 . . . . .72 A7
　Newcastle-u-T NE6 . . . . .56 F8
　Wallsend NE28 . . . . .40 B2
　Washington NE38 . . . . .83 B1
Laburnum Cres NE11 . . . . . .81 C6
Laburnum Ct NE29 . . . . .29 C4
Laburnum Gdns
　6 Gateshead,Felling NE10 . .56 D1
　Gateshead,Low Fell NE9 . . .70 F6
　Jarrow NE32 . . . . .58 B4
Laburnum Gr Cleadon SR6 . .60 C4
　Hebburn NE31 . . . . .57 E3
　South Shields NE34 . . . . . . .59 F5
　Sunderland SR5 . . . . .85 A8
　Sunniside NE16 . . . . .69 A7
　Whickham NE16 . . . . .69 A7
Laburnum Rd
　Blaydon NE21 . . . . .53 C2
　Sunderland SR6 . . . . .75 D3

Laburnum Terr
　Ashington NE63 . . . . .6 D3
　Wylam NE41 . . . . .51 A6
Laburnum Ct NE62 . . . . .10 E7
Lacebark Shiney Row DH4 . .89 F6
　Silksworth SR3 . . . . .91 E4
Ladock Cl SR2 . . . . .93 A8
Lady Beatrice Terr DH4 . . . . .90 E7
Lady St DH5 . . . . .95 A5
Lady's Piece La DH6 . . . . . . .96 A5
Lady's Wlk Morpeth NE61 . . . .3 E1
　South Shields NE33 . . . . . . .42 C4
Ladybank NE5 . . . . .36 B4
Ladycutters La NE45 . . . . . . .46 F3
Ladyhaugh Dr NE16 . . . . . . .69 A4
Ladykirk Rd NE4 . . . . .54 E5
Ladyridge SR2 . . . . .20 D4
Ladysmith St NE33 . . . . .42 D2
Ladywell NE43 . . . . .64 D6
Ladywell Rd NE21 . . . . .53 C2
Ladywell Way NE20 . . . . .25 D7
Ladywood Pk DH4 . . . . .89 F8
Laet St NE29 . . . . .42 B5
Laindon Ave SR6 . . . . .75 D4
Laing Art Gallery & Mus*
　NE1 . . . . .99 C2
Laing Gr NE28 . . . . .41 B3
Laith Rd NE3 . . . . .37 F5
Lake App NE21 . . . . .53 F1
Lake Ave NE34 . . . . .60 C6
Lake Ct SR3 . . . . .92 A6
Lake View NE61 . . . . .3 C7
Lakeside Blaydon NE21 . . . . .53 F1
　South Shields NE34 . . . . . . .60 D6
Laleham Ct NE3 . . . . .30 D7
Lamara Dr SR5 . . . . .75 C3
Lamb St
　East Cramlington NE23 . . . . .22 F5
　Newcastle-u-T NE6 . . . . .57 A5
Lamb Terr 8 NE27 . . . . .30 E1
Lambden Cl NE29 . . . . .41 E3
Lambert Rd NE37 . . . . .82 F7
Lambert Sq NE3 . . . . .38 A5
Lambeth Pl NE8 . . . . .71 A8
Lambley Ave NE30 . . . . .32 B2
Lambley Cl NE16 . . . . .69 A2
Lambley Cres NE31 . . . . .57 D2
Lambourn Ave
　Longbenton NE12 . . . . .39 C7
　North Shields NE29 . . . . . . .41 E3
Lambourne Cl DH4 . . . . .89 E3
Lambourne Rd SR2 . . . . .86 C3
Lambrook Ho NE7 . . . . .17 A7
Lambton Ave NE16 . . . . .69 C8
Lambton Cl NE40 . . . . .51 F4
Lambton Ct
　Sunderland SR3 . . . . .91 C7
　Washington NE38 . . . . .88 E8
Lambton Dr DH5 . . . . .95 A1
Lambton Gdns NE16 . . . . . . .78 E5
Lambton Lea DH4 . . . . .90 A4
Lambton Prim Sch NE38 . . .83 B3
Lambton Rd Hebburn NE31 . .57 F7
　Newcastle-u-T NE2 . . . . .99 B4
Lambton St
　Chester le St DH3 . . . . .88 D2
　Gateshead NE8 . . . . .101 B3
　Sunderland SR1 . . . . .103 A3
Lambton Terr
　Jarrow NE32 . . . . .58 B4
　Penshaw DH4 . . . . .90 B8
Lambton Twr SR1 . . . . .103 B3
Lamonby Way NE23 . . . . . . .22 A4
Lampeter Cl NE5 . . . . .37 B4
Lamport St NE31 . . . . .57 C5
Lampton Ct NE22 . . . . .11 C2
Lanark Cl NE29 . . . . .41 E6
Lanark Dr NE32 . . . . .58 E2
Lancaster Cl NE63 . . . . .7 C2
Lancaster Dr NE28 . . . . .40 D7
Lancaster Ho NE22 . . . . .22 D5
Lancaster Rd NE11 . . . . .54 F1
Lancaster St NE4 . . . . .98 B1
Lancaster Terr
　Chester le S DH3 . . . . .88 D2
　Morpeth NE61 . . . . .4 A1
Lancaster Way NE32 . . . . . . .58 E2
Lancastrian Rd NE23 . . . . . . .22 A5
Lancefield Ave NE6 . . . . .56 F4
Lancet Ct NE8 . . . . .101 C4
Lanchester Ave NE9 . . . . . . .71 E3
Lanchester Cl NE10 . . . . .72 C2
Lanchester Gn NE22 . . . . . . .10 F2
Lanchester Pk NE38 . . . . . . .83 C7
Lanchester Ct 3 . . . . .37 C7
Landscape Terr NE40 . . . . . .52 B1
Landsdowne Gdns NE62 . . .11 A8
Landseer Gdns
　Gateshead NE9 . . . . .71 B7
　Whiteleas NE34 . . . . .59 D2
Landswood Terr NE21 . . . . . .68 C2
Lane Cnr NE34 . . . . .59 C5
Lane Head NE40 . . . . .52 C8
Lanercost NE38 . . . . .83 D5
Lanercost Ave NE21 . . . . . . .53 B2
Lanercost Dr NE5 . . . . .54 C8
Lanercost Gdns
　Gateshead NE10 . . . . .71 C6
　Throckley NE15 . . . . .35 D2
Lanercost Pk NE23 . . . . .16 D1
Lanercost Rd NE23 . . . . .22 A5
Lanesborough Ct NE3 . . . . . .38 A5
Langdale Birtley DH3 . . . . . . .82 C1

Langdale *continued*
Washington NE37 .83 C7
Whitley Bay NE25 .31 E5
Langdale Cl NE12 .39 A6
Langdale Cres NE21 .68 B8
Langdale Dr NE23 .21 E6
Langdale Gdns
Newcastle-u-T NE6 .57 A6
Wallsend NE28 .41 A5
Langdale Rd
Gateshead NE9 .71 A5
Penshaw DH4 .90 A8
Langdale St DH5 .95 A2
Langdale Terr NE17 .77 A5
Langdale Way NE36 .74 C7
Langdon Cl NE29 .31 F1
Langdon Rd NE5 .36 E2
Langeeford Pl 4 SR6 .75 E1
Langford Dr NE35 .58 F2
Langham Rd NE15 .54 A5
Langholm Ave NE29 .41 C8
Langholm Rd
East Boldon NE36 .74 D8
Newcastle-u-T NE3 .38 C7
Langhorn Cl NE6 .56 B7
Langhurst SR2 .92 E8
Langleeford Rd NE5 .37 A4
Langley Ave Blyth NE24 .17 B8
Gateshead NE10 .72 B6
Hexham NE46 .45 D4
Shiremoor NE27 .31 A3
Whitley Bay NE25 .31 D3
Langley Cl NE38 .83 B4
Langley Fst Sch NE25 .31 D3
Langley Mere 8 NE12 .39 D8
Langley Rd Ashington NE63 .6 C3
Newcastle-u-T,Walker NE6 .56 F6
Newcastle-u-T,West Denton NE5 .53 F8
North Shields NE29 .41 D6
Sunderland SR3 .86 B2
Langley St DH4 .90 D6
Langley Tarn 1 NE29 .42 A4
Langley Terr NE32 .58 B3
Langport Rd SR2 .86 D3
Langton Cl SR4 .102 B2
Langton Ct NE20 .25 B4
Langton Dr NE23 .16 C2
Langton St NE8 .101 C1
Langton Terr
Bournmoor DH4 .89 E2
Newcastle-u-T NE7 .39 B2
Langwell Cres NE63 .6 C4
Langwell Terr NE61 .4 F4
Lanivet Cl 4 SR2 .92 F8
Lannerwood 5 NE29 .42 A4
Lansbury Cl DH3 .82 B6
Lansbury Dr DH3 .82 B5
Lansbury Gdns NE10 .72 A8
Lansbury Rd NE16 .69 C6
Lansbury Way SR5 .74 B1
Lansdowne SR2 .92 E7
Lansdowne Cres NE3 .38 C5
Lansdowne Ct NE46 .44 F3
Lansdowne Gdns NE2 .56 A8
Lansdowne Pl NE3 .38 C5
Lansdowne Rd NE12 .39 D8
Lansdowne St SR4 .102 B3
Lansdowne Terr
Newcastle-u-T NE3 .38 C5
North Shields NE29 .41 F6
Lansdowne Terr E NE3 .38 C5
Lansdowne Terrace W NE29 .41 F6
Lanthwaite Rd NE9 .71 A4
Lanton St DH4 .90 D6
Lapford Dr NE23 .16 C1
Lapwing Cl Blyth NE24 .17 E4
Washington NE38 .82 F3
Lapwing Ct
Burnopfield NE16 .79 C5
Haswell DH6 .97 F3
South Shields NE34 .59 E5
Larch Ave
Houghton-le-S DH4 .90 D1
South Shields NE34 .60 A5
Whitburn SR6 .61 A2
Larch Cl NE9 .71 D2
Larch Gr NE24 .17 C4
Larch Rd NE21 .53 D3
Larch St 2 NE16 .69 B2
Larch Terr DH9 .79 A1
Larches The
Burnopfield NE16 .79 B7
Newcastle-u-T NE4 .100 A3
Larchlea NE20 .25 C2
Larchlea S NE20 .25 C2
Larchwood NE38 .83 B1
Larchwood Ave
Newcastle-u-T,Fawdon NE3 .37 F7
Newcastle-u-T,Walkergate NE6 .56 E8
Wideopen NE13 .28 C5
Larchwood Dr NE63 .6 C1
Larchwood Gdns NE11 .70 B5
Larchwood Gr SR2 .86 C2
Larkfield Cres DH4 .90 A5
Larkfield Rd SR2 .86 C3
Larkhill SR2 .92 F7
Larkrise Cl NE7 .39 D3
Larkspur NE9 .71 C4
Larkspur Com Prim Sch NE9 .71 C4
Larkspur Rd NE16 .69 B6
Larkspur Terr NE2 .38 E1
Larkswood NE34 .60 B7
Larne Cres NE9 .71 A5
Larriston NE42 .50 B1
Larriston Pl NE23 .21 F6
Lartington Gdns NE3 .38 F5
Larwood Ct DH3 .88 E1
Lascelles Ave NE34 .59 E5
Laski Gdns NE10 .72 B8
Lassells Rigg NE42 .50 D4
Latimer St NE30 .42 D8
Latrigg Ct 25 SR3 .91 F6
Latton Cl NE23 .22 A4
Lauderdale Ave NE28 .40 C4
Launceston Cl NE3 .37 D8
Launceston Dr SR3 .91 C7
Laura St SR1 .103 B2
Laurel Ave
Longbenton NE12 .30 A1
Newcastle-u-T NE3 .38 A7
Laurel Cres Burnside DH4 .90 C3
Newcastle-u-T NE6 .39 F1
Laurel Ct Chester le S DH2 .88 B5
North Shields NE30 .42 B5
Laurel Dr NE63 .6 C1
Laurel End NE12 .30 A1
Laurel Gr SR2 .86 D2
Laurel Rd NE21 .53 D2
Laurel St Throckley NE15 .35 D3
Wallsend NE28 .40 C1
Laurel Terr
Burnopfield NE16 .78 F6
Seaton Delaval NE25 .23 E2
Laurel Way NE40 .52 A3
Laurel Wlk NE3 .38 C5
Laurelwood Gdns NE11 .70 B5
Laurens Ct NE37 .83 D8
Lavender Ct NE63 .6 C1
Lavender Gdns
Gateshead NE9 .70 F6
Newcastle-u-T NE2 .38 D1
Lavender Gr
Hedworth NE32 .73 C8
Sunderland SR5 .74 A1
Lavender La NE34 .59 B5
Lavender Rd NE16 .69 A6
Lavender Row 2 NE9 .71 B5
Lavender St 4 SR4 .85 A6
Lavender Wlk NE31 .57 E3
Lavendon Cl NE23 .22 A4
Laverick NE10 .71 F6
Laverock Ct 12 NE6 .56 C5
Laverock Hall Rd NE24 .17 B3
Laverock Pl Blyth NE24 .17 B3
3 Newcastle-u-T NE3 .37 D5
Lavers Rd DH3 .82 C5
Lavington Rd NE34 .59 E8
Lawe Rd NE33 .42 D4
Lawn Cotts SR3 .91 F6
Lawn Ct NE63 .6 B3
Lawn Dr NE36 .73 F6
Lawn The NE40 .52 C6
Lawnhead Sq SR3 .92 B6
Lawns The
Easington Lane DH5 .95 C1
Newcastle-u-T NE2 .38 F2
Silksworth SR3 .91 F6
Whitburn SR6 .75 F8
Lawnsway NE32 .58 C1
Lawnswood DH5 .94 F7
Lawrence Ave
Blaydon NE21 .53 C3
Whiteleas NE34 .59 D3
Lawrence Ct NE21 .53 C3
Lawrence Hill Ct NE10 .72 C8
Lawrence St SR1 .103 C2
Laws St SR6 .75 D4
Lawson Ave NE32 .58 D3
Lawson Cres SR6 .75 D4
Lawson Ct
Boldon Colliery NE35 .73 F7
6 Chester le S DH2 .88 C2
Lawson St
North Shields NE29 .42 A4
Wallsend NE28 .40 C1
Lawson St W 8 NE29 .42 A4
Lawson Terr
Hetton le H DH5 .95 B1
Newcastle-u-T NE4 .54 E4
Laxford DH3 .82 D2
Laxford Ct SR3 .92 A5
Laybourn Gdns 5 NE34 .59 A4
Layburn Gdns NE15 .53 E8
Laycock Gdns NE23 .22 F1
Layfield Rd NE3 .28 C1
Laygate NE33 .42 C1
Laygate Pl NE33 .42 C1
Laygate Sch NE33 .42 C1
Laygate St NE33 .42 B1
Lea Ave NE32 .58 C2
Lea Gn DH3 .82 E1
Lea Riggs DH4 .94 A2
Leabank NE15 .53 D8
Leaburn Terr NE42 .50 B2
Lead La Horsley NE15 .33 C1
Newlands DH8 .76 C6
Lead Rd Greenside NE40 .52 B1
High Spen NE17,NE40 .66 D6
Stocksfield NE43 .64 B2
Leadgate Cotts NE17 .66 A4
Leafield Cl DH3 .82 D6
Leafield Cres NE34 .60 A8
Leagreen Ct NE3 .38 A5
Leaholme Cres NE24 .17 C6
Lealholm Rd NE7 .39 A5
Leam Gdns NE10 .72 C8
Leam La Gateshead NE10 .72 B6
Jarrow NE32 .58 C3
Leam La/Newcastle Rd NE32,NE34 .58 F5
Leamington St SR4 .102 B1
Leamside Gateshead NE10 .71 F6
Jarrow NE32 .58 C4
Leander Ave
Chester le S DH3 .88 D7
Stakeford NE62 .11 B8
Leander Ct NE62 .11 B8
Leander Dr NE35 .73 E8
Leaplish NE38 .83 F2
Leas The Newbottle DH4 .90 D3
Whitley Bay NE25 .31 D4
Leasyde Wlk NE16 .68 F5
Leatham SR2 .92 E8
Leaway NE42 .50 B2
Leazes Arc NE1 .99 A2
Leazes Cres Hexham NE46 .44 F5
Newcastle-u-T NE1 .98 C2
Leazes Ct NE4 .98 B2
Leazes La Corbridge NE45 .47 A8
Hexham NE46 .44 E5
Newcastle-u-T NE1 .99 A2
Leazes Par NE2 .98 B2
Leazes Park Rd NE1 .99 A2
Leazes Parkway NE15 .35 D1
Leazes Pk NE46 .44 E5
Leazes Terr
Corbridge NE45 .46 F6
Hexham NE46 .44 F5
Newcastle-u-T NE1 .98 C2
Leazes The
Burnopfield NE16 .78 F6
South Shields NE34 .59 F6
Sunderland SR1 .102 B2
Throckley NE15 .35 C1
Leazes View
Ovington NE42 .49 D4
Rowlands Gill NE39 .67 D2
Leazes Villas NE16 .79 A6
Lecondale NE10 .71 F5
Lecondale Ct NE10 .71 F5
Ledbury Rd SR2 .86 D3
Lee Cl NE38 .84 B6
Lee St
Sunderland,Fulwell SR6 .75 D4
6 Sunderland,Southwick SR5 .75 B1
Lee Terr DH5 .95 B2
Leechmere Cres SR7 .92 F1
Leechmere Ind Est SR2 .86 E1
Leechmere Rd SR2 .86 D1
Leechmere View 5 SR2 .92 F8
Leechmere Way SR2 .92 F8
Leeds St SR6 .75 E2
Leeholme DH5 .94 F7
Leeming Gdns NE9 .71 B6
Legg Ave NE22 .11 E3
Legges Dr NE13 .20 D6
Legion Gr NE15 .53 F7
Legion Rd NE15 .53 F7
Leicester Cl NE28 .40 A5
Leicester St NE6 .56 E5
Leicester Way NE32 .58 A1
Leighton Rd SR2 .86 D2
Leighton St
7 Newcastle-u-T NE6 .56 A6
South Shields NE33 .42 E2
Leighton Terr DH3 .82 B5
Leith Ct NE34 .59 C5
Leith Gdns DH9 .79 D1
Leland Pl NE61 .8 D7
Lemington Gdns NE5 .54 C7
Lemington Rd NE15 .53 B6
Lemington Riverside Prim Sch NE15 .53 D6
Lemon St NE33 .59 B6
Lena Ave NE25 .31 E4
Lenin Terr NE17 .77 C8
Lenore Terr NE40 .52 B2
Lenthorn Mews 2 SR6 .75 E1
Leominster Rd SR2 .86 D2
Leopold Ho SR2 .102 C1
Leopold St NE32 .58 B6
Lesbury Ave
Ashington NE63 .6 D2
Shiremoor NE27 .30 E3
Stakeford NE62 .6 A1
Wallsend NE28 .40 F3
Lesbury Chase NE3 .38 B7
Lesbury Gdns NE13 .28 C6
Lesbury Rd NE6 .56 B8
Lesbury St
Newcastle-u-T NE15 .53 C6
North Shields NE28 .41 C1
Lesbury Terr NE17 .77 B8
Lesley Ct NE3 .38 C5
Leslie Ave NE31 .57 E5
Leslie Cl NE40 .52 E4
Leslie Cres NE3 .38 C3
Leslies View NE61 .3 E2
Letch Way NE15 .53 C7
Letchwell Villas NE12 .29 E1
Leuchars Ct DH3 .82 C3
Leven Ave DH2 .88 B1
Leven Ho 10 SR3 .92 A6
Levens Wlk NE23 .21 E7
Levisham Cl SR3 .92 C7
Lewis Cres SR2 .103 C1
Lewis Dr NE4 .54 F6
Lewis Gdns NE34 .59 C3
Leybourne Ave NE12 .29 D1
Leybourne Dene NE12 .29 D2
Leybourne Hold DH3 .82 C6
Leyburn Cl
Houghton-le-S DH4 .90 D1
Urpeth DH2 .81 D1
Leyburn Ct NE23 .22 A4
Leyburn Dr NE7 .39 A3
Leyburn Gr DH4 .90 D1
Leyburn Pl DH3 .82 B6
Leyfield Cl SR3 .92 B5
Leyton Pl NE8 .71 B8
Liberty Ho NE2 .38 E1
Liberty Terr DH9 .79 B2
Liburn Cl NE36 .74 C8
Lichfield Ave NE6 .56 E4
Lichfield Cl Ashington NE63 .6 F2
Newcastle-u-T NE3 .37 E7
Lichfield Rd SR5 .75 A3
Lichfield Way NE32 .58 A1
Lidcombe Cl SR3 .92 C7
Liddell Ct SR6 .75 F2
Liddell St
North Shields NE29,NE30 .42 B5
Sunderland SR6 .103 A4
Liddell Terr
Gateshead NE8 .70 D8
Kibblesworth NE11 .81 C6
Liddle Ct NE4 .98 A1
Liddle Rd NE4 .98 A1
Liddles St 1 NE22 .11 D3
Lieven St NE13 .28 A4
Liffey Rd NE31 .57 F3
Lightbourne Rd NE6 .57 A6
Lightfoot Sports Ctr The NE6 .56 F4
Lightwood Ave NE15 .54 A4
Lilac Ave Blyth NE24 .17 D8
11 Houghton-le-S DH5 .94 E8
Longbenton NE12 .39 F8
New Silksworth SR3 .92 B8
South Shields NE34 .60 A5
Whitburn SR6 .60 F3
Lilac Cl NE5 .36 B4
Lilac Cres NE16 .79 A6
Lilac Ct Ashington NE63 .6 C1
Ellington NE61 .1 E6
Lilac Gdns Cleadon SR6 .60 A2
Gateshead NE9 .70 F6
Washington NE38 .83 C1
Whickham NE16 .69 A6
Lilac Gr Chester le S DH2 .88 A5
Sunderland SR6 .75 D3
Lilac Rd NE6 .40 A1
Lilac Sq DH4 .89 E3
Lilac St SR4 .85 A6
Lilac Wlk NE31 .57 E3
Lilburn Cl 5 NE6 .56 C4
Lilburn Gdns NE3 .38 F4
Lilburn Pl SR5 .75 A1
Lilburn Rd NE27 .30 E2
Lilburn St NE29 .41 F5
Lilburne Cl SR1 .103 B3
Lilian Ave Sunderland SR2 .92 E8
Wallsend NE28 .40 A1
Lilley Gr SR5 .74 B1
Lilley Terr NE39 .67 F3
Lilleycroft NE39 .67 F2
Lillico Ho NE2 .99 C3
Lily Ave Bedlington NE22 .16 B8
Newcastle-u-T NE2 .38 E1
Lily Bank NE28 .40 C2
Lily Cl NE21 .53 A2
Lily Cres
Newcastle-u-T NE2 .38 E1
Whitburn SR6 .60 F3
Lily Est NE15 .35 D3
Lily Gdns DH9 .78 E1
Lily St SR4 .102 B3
Lily Terr Newbottle DH4 .90 D4
Newcastle-u-T NE5 .37 A3
Lilywhite Terr DH5 .95 B1
Lime Ave DH4 .90 C1
Lime Gr Prudhoe NE42 .50 B3
Ryton NE40 .52 C5
Lime St Blaydon NE21 .53 D1
Newcastle-u-T NE1,NE6 .56 A5
Sunderland SR4 .102 B3
Throckley NE15 .35 D3
Limecroft NE32 .58 C1
Limekiln Ct NE28 .40 D2
Limekiln Rd NE28 .40 D2
Limes Ave NE24 .12 D1
Limes The Penshaw DH4 .90 B8
Stannington NE61 .14 C3
Sunderland SR2 .86 D4
Limestone La NE20 .25 B7
Limetree NE38 .83 E2
Limetrees Gdns NE9 .70 F7
Limewood Ct NE2 .98 B4
Limewood Gr NE13 .28 B5
Linacre Cl NE3 .37 B6
Linbridge Dr NE5 .36 E1
Linburn NE38 .89 B8
Lincoln Ave
New Silksworth SR3 .92 A8
Wallsend NE28 .40 A3
Lincoln Cres DH5 .94 F4
Lincoln Ct NE31 .57 D5
Lincoln Gn NE3 .28 C1
Lincoln Rd
Cramlington NE23 .16 C1
South Shields NE34 .60 B7
Lincoln St
Gateshead NE8 .101 B1
Sunderland SR4 .85 F7
Lincoln Way NE32 .58 B1
Lincrest Ct NE5 .36 F2
Lindale Ave NE16 .69 A5
Lindale Rd NE4 .54 E8
Lindean Pl NE23 .21 F6
Linden NE9 .71 D4
Linden Ave
Newcastle-u-T,Fenham NE4 .54 D7
Linden Ave *continued*
Newcastle-u-T,Gosforth NE3 .38 C4
Linden Cl NE62 .11 A8
Linden Gdns SR2 .86 C3
Linden Gr
1 Dunston NE11 .70 A8
Houghton-le-S DH4 .94 D8
Linden Rd Blaydon NE21 .53 D2
Longbenton NE12 .39 D6
Newcastle-u-T NE3 .38 C4
Seaton Delaval NE25 .23 B3
Sunderland SR2 .86 C3
Linden Sch NE12 .39 D8
Linden Terr
Longbenton NE12 .39 D6
25 Springwell NE9 .71 F1
Whitley Bay NE26 .32 B5
Linden Way Ellington NE61 .1 D5
Gateshead NE9 .71 D2
Ponteland NE20 .25 C3
Lindfield Ave NE5 .37 C1
Lindisfarne Ryhope SR2 .92 E6
Washington NE38 .83 C4
Lindisfarne Ave DH3 .88 D3
Lindisfarne Cl
Burnside DH4 .90 C2
Chester le S DH2 .88 A1
Morpeth NE61 .9 A6
Newcastle-u-T NE5 .36 F1
Newcastle-u-T,Jesmond NE2 .38 F2
Pegswood NE61 .5 A4
Lindisfarne Com Prim Sch NE8 .56 A2
Lindisfarne Ct NE32 .58 F6
Lindisfarne Dr NE8 .101 C2
Lindisfarne La NE61 .9 A6
Lindisfarne Pl NE28 .40 D3
Lindisfarne Rd
Hebburn NE31 .57 E3
Jarrow NE32 .58 D4
Newcastle-u-T NE2 .38 F2
Lindisfarne Recess NE32 .58 D4
Lindisfarne Terr NE30 .42 A7
Lindisfarne Wlk NE62 .10 E7
Lindom Ave DH3 .88 D3
Lindrick Ct NE10 .72 C7
Lindsay Ave NE24 .17 C8
Lindsay Cl SR2 .103 B1
Lindsay Ct SR6 .60 F2
Lindsay Rd SR2 .103 B1
Lindsay St DH5 .95 B5
Lindsey Cl NE23 .21 E6
Lindum Rd NE9 .70 F8
Linfield SR2 .92 E7
Lingcrest NE9 .71 C5
Lingdale Ave SR6 .75 E6
Lingey Gdns NE10 .72 C8
Lingey House Prim Sch NE10 .72 B7
Lingey La NE10 .72 B7
Lingfield DH5 .94 F7
Lingholme DH2 .88 A4
Lingmell NE37 .83 B6
Lingshaw NE10 .72 B7
Lingside NE32 .58 C1
Linhope Ave NE3 .37 F7
Linhope PRU NE5 .36 F2
Linhope Rd NE5 .36 F2
Link Ave NE22 .10 D1
Link Rd Hazlerigg NE13 .28 A4
Newcastle-u-T NE5 .37 E2
Link The NE46 .44 F5
Links Ave Tynemouth NE30 .32 C2
Whitley Bay NE26 .31 F7
Links Ct NE26 .32 A7
Links Gn NE3 .38 D6
Links Green Wlk NE3 .38 D6
Links Rd Blyth NE24 .17 F4
Seaton Sluice NE24 .18 A2
Tynemouth NE30 .32 C2
Links The NE26 .32 A7
Links View
Ashington NE63 .12 A8
Blyth NE24 .17 C4
Links Wlk NE5 .36 F2
Linkway NE32 .58 D1
Linley Hill NE16 .68 E4
Linnel Dr NE15 .53 E7
Linnet Cl NE38 .83 A3
Linnet Ct NE63 .6 B2
Linnet Gr SR5 .74 C1
Linnetsfield NE6 .56 F8
Linney Gdns NE34 .59 A4
Linnheads NE42 .50 B1
Linshiels Gdns 1 NE63 .6 F2
Linskell SR2 .92 E8
Linskill Ctr PRU NE30 .42 B7
Linskill Pl
Newcastle-u-T NE3 .37 F3
North Shields NE30 .42 B7
Linskill St NE30 .42 B5
Linskill Terr
North Shields NE30 .42 B7
Tynemouth NE30 .42 B7
Linslade Wlk NE23 .21 F6
Lintfort NE38 .88 E7
Linthorpe Ct 1 NE34 .59 A5
Linthorpe Rd
Newcastle-u-T NE3 .38 C7
Tynemouth NE30 .32 B1
Linton NE12 .29 D5
Linton Fst Sch NE61 .1 A3
Linton Rd Gateshead NE9 .70 F3
Whitley Bay NE26 .24 E1
Lintonville Ent Pk NE63 .6 D5
Lintonville Parkway NE63 .6 D5

Lintonville Rd NE63 . . . . .6 C4
Lintz Green La NE16,NE39 .78 F4
Lintz La NE16 . . . . .78 E4
Lintz Terr NE15 . . . . .78 F6
Lintzford Gdns
Newcastle-u-T NE15 . . . . .53 E7
Rowlands Gill NE39 . . . . .78 D8
Lintzford La NE39 . . . . .67 B1
Lintzford Rd NE39 . . . . .78 C7
Linum Pl NE4 . . . . .54 E8
Linwood Pl NE3 . . . . .28 C1
Lion Wlk NE29 . . . . .42 A3
Lisa Ave SR4 . . . . .85 A5
Lisburn Terr SR4 . . . . .102 A3
Lish Ave NE26 . . . . .32 C4
Lishman Terr NE40 . . . . .52 A4
Lisle Ct **11** NE28 . . . . .40 B2
Lisle Gr NE28 . . . . .41 A3
Lisle Rd NE34 . . . . .60 A6
Lisle St Newcastle-u-T NE1 . .99 A2
Wallsend NE28 . . . . .40 C1
Lismor Terr **10** NE9 . . . . .71 F1
Lismore Ave NE33 . . . . .59 D7
Lismore Pl NE15 . . . . .54 D6
Lister Ave Dunston NE11 . . . .54 F1
Greenside NE40 . . . . .66 F8
Lister Cl DH5 . . . . .94 D6
Lister St NE15 . . . . .53 F5
Listers La NE9 . . . . .71 A8
Litchfield Cres **2** NE21 . .53 B1
Litchfield La NE21 . . . . .53 B1
Litchfield St **1** NE21 . . . . .53 B1
Litchfield Terr **3** NE21 . .53 B1
Little Bedford St NE29,
NE30 . . . . .42 B5
Little Bldgs NE42 . . . . .49 D4
Little Dene NE2 . . . . .38 D3
Little Villiers St SR1 . . . . . . .103 B3
Little Way NE15 . . . . .54 B4
Littleburn Cl DH4 . . . . .90 C2
Littledene NE9 . . . . .70 F7
Littletown La DH6 . . . . .96 D3
Litton Ct **14** SR3 . . . . .91 F1
Littondale NE28 . . . . .39 F4
Livingstone Pl **2** NE33 . . .42 C4
Livingstone Rd SR1 . . . . . . .102 C3
Livingstone St **2** NE33 . . .42 D4
Livingstone View NE30 . . . . .42 C7
Lizard La NE34,SR6 . . . . .60 E4
Lizard View SR6 . . . . .60 E2
Lloyd Ave DH5 . . . . .94 C4
Lloyd Cl NE11 . . . . .54 E2
Lloyd St **18** NE40 . . . . .51 F3
Lobban Ave NE31 . . . . .57 D3
Lobelia Ave NE10 . . . . .56 B2
Lobelia Cl NE5 . . . . .36 B3
Lobley Gdns NE11 . . . . .70 A6
Lobley Hill Prim Sch
NE11 . . . . .70 A6
Lobley Hill Rd NE11,NE8 . . .70 C7
Lobleyhill Rd
Byermoor NE16 . . . . .79 D8
Sunniside NE16 . . . . .79 D8
Local Ave DH6 . . . . .96 C1
Locarno Pl NE64 . . . . .7 E4
Lochcraig Pl NE23 . . . . .16 B1
Lochfield Gdns NE11 . . . . . . .81 C6
Lochnaben Terr SR5 . . . . .75 D2
Lockerbie Gdns NE15 . . . . . .53 E7
Lockerbie Rd NE23 . . . . .21 F6
Lockhaugh Rd NE39 . . . . .68 A4
Locksley Cl NE29 . . . . .31 B1
Locomotion Way
Killingworth NE12 . . . . .29 B5
North Shields NE29 . . . . .42 A4
Locomotive Ct NE42 . . . . .50 C2
Lodge Cl NE39 . . . . .78 A5
Lodges Rd The NE9 . . . . .70 F2
Lodgeside Mdw SR3 . . . . .92 B5
Lodore Ct **5** SR3 . . . . .91 F6
Lodore Gr NE32 . . . . .58 D3
Lodore Rd NE2 . . . . .38 D3
Lodsworth Dr NE23 . . . . .22 A4
Loft Hill **1** SR3 . . . . .91 F1
Logan Rd NE6 . . . . .39 F1
Logan St DH5 . . . . .95 A3
Logan Terr DH6 . . . . .97 E8
Lola St NE13 . . . . .27 F4
Lombard Dr DH3 . . . . .88 D7
Lombard St
Newcastle-u-T NE1 . . . . .101 B4
Sunderland SR1 . . . . .103 B3
Lomond Cl NE38 . . . . .83 B3
Lomond Ct **11** SR3 . . . . .92 A6
Lomond Pl DH2 . . . . .88 B1
London Ave NE37 . . . . .72 C2
Londonderry Mews 5
SR3 . . . . .92 B7
Londonderry St SR3 . . . . .92 A7
Londonderry Terr SR3 . . . . . .92 B7
Londonderry Twr SR1 . . . . . .103 B3
Londonderry Way DH4 . . . . .90 A7
Long Bank Birtley DH3 . . . .82 C7
Gateshead NE9 . . . . .71 C1
Long Close Rd NE39 . . . . .77 F5
Long Crag NE37 . . . . .83 A5
Long Gr NE61 . . . . .8 F5
Long Gair NE21 . . . . .53 A2
Long Headlam 11 NE6 . . .56 C6
Long Mdw Cl NE40 . . . . . . .52 A4
Long Pk NE64 . . . . .7 A4
Long Ridge Rd NE21,
NE40 . . . . .52 D2
Long Rigg NE16 . . . . .54 A2
Long Row NE33 . . . . .42 B4
Long Row NE40 . . . . .66 F8
Longacre
Houghton-le-S DH4 . . . . .94 C8

Longacre continued
Washington NE38 . . . . .83 E1
Longbenton Com Coll
NE12 . . . . .39 C7
Longbenton Sta NE12 . . . . . .39 A5
Longclose Bank DH8,
NE39 . . . . .77 E3
Longdean Cl NE31 . . . . .57 C5
Longdean Pk DH3 . . . . .88 D6
Longfellow St DH5 . . . . .94 E7
Longfield Cl NE34 . . . . .59 D4
Longfield Rd SR6 . . . . .75 D3
Longfield Terr NE6 . . . . .56 B3
Longhirst Gateshead NE10 .72 A7
Killingworth NE12 . . . . .29 D5
Newcastle-u-T NE5 . . . . .36 F7
Longhirst Rd NE61 . . . . .4 F4
Longhirst Dr
Cramlington NE23 . . . . .22 A4
Wideopen NE13 . . . . .28 B5
Longhirst Rd NE61 . . . . .4 F4
Longhirst Village NE61 . . . .4 F7
Longlands **11** NE46 . . . . .45 A4
Longlands Dr DH5 . . . . .94 E7
Longleat Gdns
Pegswood NE61 . . . . .4 E4
11 South Shields NE33 . . . .42 D3
Longley St NE4 . . . . .98 A2
Longmeadows
Ponteland NE20 . . . . .25 B3
Sunderland SR3 . . . . .91 C6
Longniddry NE37 . . . . .72 C3
Longniddry Ct NE9 . . . . .70 E3
Longridge NE21 . . . . .53 A2
Longridge Ave
Newcastle-u-T NE7 . . . . .39 D2
Washington NE38 . . . . .83 B3
Longridge Ct NE22 . . . . .11 A4
Longridge Dr NE26 . . . . .31 E7
Longridge Sq SR2 . . . . .86 D2
Longridge Way
Bedlington NE22 . . . . .11 A4
Cramlington NE23 . . . . .21 F6
Longriggs The NE44 . . . . .62 E7
Longshank La NE23 . . . . .82 A6
Longstaff Gdns NE34 . . . . . . .58 F4
Longstone Ct NE12 . . . . .29 E4
Longstone Sq NE5 . . . . .36 D1
Longwood Cl NE16 . . . . .69 B2
Lonnen Ave NE4 . . . . .54 D7
Lonnen Dr NE16 . . . . .69 A8
Lonnen The Ryton NE40 . . . . .52 E5
South Shields NE34 . . . . .60 B4
Lonsdale 82 E1
Lonsdale Ave Blyth NE24 . .16 E8
Sunderland SR6 . . . . .75 E7
Lonsdale Ct
Medomsley NE17 . . . . .77 B4
South Shields NE34 . . . . .59 A4
Lonsdale Gdns NE28 . . . . .41 A4
Lonsdale Rd SR6 . . . . .75 E7
Lonsdale Terr NE2 . . . . .38 E2
Lonsdale Terr NE15 . . . . . . .53 C6
Lord Blyton Prim Sch
NE34 . . . . .58 F5
Lord Byrons Wlk SR7 . . . . . . .93 B1
Lord Gort Cl **1** SR5 . . . . . . .75 A1
**Lord Lawson of Beamish Com
Sch** DH3 . . . . .82 D3
Lord Nelson St NE33 . . . . .42 D3
Lord St New Silksworth SR3 .92 B7
Newcastle-u-T NE1 . . . . .100 C4
South Shields NE33 . . . . .42 E1
Lordenshaw NE5 . . . . .36 F1
Lorne St DH5 . . . . .97 B8
Lorne Terr SR2 . . . . .103 A4
Lorrain Rd NE34 . . . . .59 D2
Lort Ho NE2 . . . . .99 C2
Lorton Ave NE30 . . . . .32 A2
Lorton Rd NE9 . . . . .71 A4
Losh Terr NE6 . . . . .56 F6
Lossiemouth Rd NE29 . . . . . .41 C5
Lothian Cl Birtley DH3 . . . . . .82 D1
Sunderland SR4 . . . . .85 D3
Lothian Ct NE5 . . . . .37 C3
Lotus Cl NE5 . . . . .36 B3
Lotus Pl NE4 . . . . .54 D7
Loudon St NE34 . . . . .59 C5
Lough Ct NE9 . . . . .71 B5
Loughborough Ave
Sunderland SR2 . . . . .86 C3
Tynemouth NE30 . . . . .32 C1
Loughbrow Pk NE46 . . . . .45 B2
Loughrigg Ave NE23 . . . . .21 F6
Louie Terr NE9 . . . . .71 A5
Louis Ave SR6 . . . . .75 D3
Louise Ho SR2 . . . . .102 C1
Louise Terr DH3 . . . . .88 C3
Louisville NE20 . . . . .25 F7
Loup St NE21 . . . . .53 C3
Louvain Terr
Guide Post NE62 . . . . .10 F7
Hetton le H DH5 . . . . .95 A5
Louvain Terr W DH5 . . . . . .95 A5
Lovaine Ave
6 North Shields NE29 . . . . .42 A5
Whitley Bay NE25 . . . . .31 F3
Lovaine Flats NE1 . . . . .99 B2
Lovaine Pl NE29 . . . . .42 A5
Lovaine Place W 6 NE29 .41 F5
Lovaine Row NE30 . . . . .42 D6
Lovaine Terr NE29 . . . . .42 A5
Love Ave NE23 . . . . .22 B7
Love Avenue Cotts NE23 . . . .23 B8

Love La NE1 . . . . .99 C1
Loveless Gdns NE10 . . . . .72 A8
Lovett Wlk NE8 . . . . .100 C2
Low Burswell NE46 . . . . .44 F5
Low Chare DH3 . . . . .88 D3
Low Cl NE42 . . . . .50 E3
Low Downs Rd DH5 . . . . .95 A6
Low Downs Sq DH5 . . . . .95 B6
Low Farm NE61 . . . . .1 D4
Low Flatts Rd DH3 . . . . .88 B6
Low Fold NE6 . . . . .56 B5
Low Friar La **4** NE1 . . . . . . .99 A1
Low Friar St NE1 . . . . .99 A1
Low Gate Fst Sch NE46 . . . . .44 A4
Low Gosforth Ct NE3 . . . . . . .28 D1
Low Haugh NE20 . . . . .25 F7
Low Heworth La NE10 . . . . . .56 F1
Low La NE34 . . . . .59 C5
Low Main Pl NE23 . . . . .22 B6
Low Mdw SR6 . . . . .75 E8
Low Prudhoe Ind Est
NE42 . . . . .50 D4
Low Quay NE24 . . . . .17 F8
Low Reach NE10 . . . . .57 A2
Low Row Ryton NE40 . . . . . . .52 E3
Sunderland SR1 . . . . .102 C2
Low St SR1 . . . . .103 C3
Low Stobhill NE61 . . . . .9 A7
Low Well Gdns NE10 . . . . . . .56 E1
Low West Ave NE39 . . . . .67 D1
Lowbiggin NE5 . . . . .36 E5
Lowdham Ave NE29 . . . . .41 E4
Lowdon Ct NE2 . . . . .98 C3
Lower Crone St NE27 . . . . . . .30 F4
Lower Dundas St SR6 . . . . . .103 A4
Lower Rudyerd St NE29 . . . . .42 B5
Lowerson Ave DH4 . . . . .90 A5
Lowery Pl NE2 . . . . .99 C2
Loweswater Ave
Chester le S DH2 . . . . .88 B1
Easington Lane DH5 . . . . .97 C8
Loweswater Cl NE24 . . . . .11 F1
Loweswater Rd
Gateshead NE9 . . . . .71 A4
Newcastle-u-T NE5 . . . . .54 B8
Loweswood Cl NE7 . . . . .39 A1
Lowfield Terr NE6 . . . . .56 F4
Lowfield Wlk NE16 . . . . .69 A6
Lowgate NE15 . . . . .35 D1
Lowick Cl DH3 . . . . .82 D1
Lowick Ct NE3 . . . . .38 E4
Lowland Cl SR3 . . . . .92 A5
Lowlean Ct NE5 . . . . .36 F1
Lownds Terr NE6 . . . . .56 E6
Lowrey's La NE9 . . . . .70 F5
Lowry Gdns NE34 . . . . .59 D2
Lowry Rd NE34 . . . . .75 E5
Lowther Ave DH2 . . . . .88 B2
Lowther Cl NE63 . . . . .6 D2
Lowther Sq NE23 . . . . .21 E6
Lowthian Cres NE6 . . . . .56 E5
Lowthian Terr NE38 . . . . .83 F4
Loxton Sq NE23 . . . . .22 A3
Lucknow St SR1 . . . . .103 C3
Lucock St NE34 . . . . .59 B5
Lucombe Cl DH4 . . . . .89 F5
Lucy St Blaydon NE21 . . . . . . .53 D3
4 Chester le S DH3 . . . . . . .88 C4
Ludlow Ave NE29 . . . . .41 E8
Ludlow Ct NE3 . . . . .37 E7
Ludlow Dr NE25 . . . . .31 B5
Ludlow Rd SR2 . . . . .86 D3
Luffness Dr NE34 . . . . .59 F3
Luke's La NE10,NE31 . . . . . . .57 F1
Lukes Lane Com Sch
NE31 . . . . .58 A3
Lulsgate SR5 . . . . .74 A1
Lulworth Ave NE32 . . . . .58 D5
Lulworth Ct SR3 . . . . .91 C7
Lulworth Gdns SR2 . . . . .86 C3
Lumley Ave
South Shields NE34 . . . . .60 B6
Whickham NE16 . . . . .54 B1
Lumley Cl
Chester le S DH2 . . . . .88 B3
Washington NE38 . . . . .83 B5
Lumley Cres NE34 . . . . .90 C4
Lumley Ct Bedlington NE22 .11 C2
Hebburn NE31 . . . . .57 F8
Sunderland SR3 . . . . .91 C7
Lumley Gdns
Burnopfield NE16 . . . . .78 E5
Gateshead NE8 . . . . .56 B1
Lumley New Rd DH3,DH4 .89 C1
Lumley St Newbottle DH4 . . .90 D2
Sunderland SR4 . . . . .102 B2
Lumley Terr
Chester le S DH3 . . . . .88 D2
Jarrow NE32 . . . . .58 C4
1 Ryhope SR2 . . . . .92 F6
Lumley Thicks DH3 . . . . .89 C1
Lumley Twr SR1 . . . . .103 B3
Lumley Wlk NE11 . . . . .100 A1
Lumley's La NE43 . . . . .65 B6
Lumsden's La NE61 . . . . .3 F1
Lune Gn NE32 . . . . .58 C2
Lunedale Ave SR6 . . . . .75 D3
Lunedale Rd DH1 . . . . .95 A2
Lupin Cl NE5 . . . . .36 C4
Luss Ave NE32 . . . . .58 E3
Lutterworth Cl NE12 . . . . .39 B6
Lutterworth Pl NE12 . . . . .39 B5
Lutterworth Rd
Longbenton NE12 . . . . .39 B5
Sunderland SR2 . . . . .86 C3
Luxembourg Rd SR4 . . . . .85 D7
Lychgate Ct NE8 . . . . .101 C3
Lydbury Cl NE23 . . . . .16 C1

Lydcott NE38 . . . . .84 B5
Lyden Gate NE9 . . . . .71 A3
Lydford Ct Newbottle DH4 . .90 C3
Newcastle-u-T NE3 . . . . .37 C6
Lydford Way DH3 . . . . .82 D3
Lydney Cl NE15 . . . . .35 C1
Lyncroft NE63 . . . . .6 C2
Lyncroft Rd NE29 . . . . .41 E6
Lyndale NE23 . . . . .16 C1
Lynden Gdns NE5 . . . . .37 A3
Lynden Rd SR2 . . . . .92 F8
Lyndhurst Ave
Chester le S DH3 . . . . .88 C6
Gateshead NE9 . . . . .71 A4
Newcastle-u-T NE2 . . . . .38 E2
Lyndhurst Cl NE21 . . . . .68 A8
Lyndhurst Cres NE9 . . . . .71 A4
Lyndhurst Dr NE9 . . . . .71 A3
Lyndhurst Gdns NE2 . . . . .38 D2
Lyndhurst Gn NE9 . . . . .70 F4
Lyndhurst Gr NE9 . . . . .70 F4
Lyndhurst Lodge NE25 . . . . .31 E5
Lyndhurst Rd
Ashington NE63 . . . . .6 F1
Longbenton NE12 . . . . .39 D7
Whitley Bay NE25 . . . . .31 E5
Lyndhurst St **3** NE33 . . . . .42 D2
Lyndhurst Terr
Sunderland SR4 . . . . .85 E8
1 Whickham NE16 . . . . . . .54 A1
Lyndon Cl NE36 . . . . .74 B7
Lyndon Dr NE36 . . . . .74 B7
Lyndon Gr NE36 . . . . .74 B7
Lyndon Wlk NE24 . . . . .16 C3
Lyne Terr NE61 . . . . .1 F3
Lyneburn Grange NE61 . . . . .1 D5
Lynemouth Fst Sch NE61 . .2 B3
Lynemouth Rd NE61 . . . . .1 D4
Lynfield NE26 . . . . .31 E7
Lynfield Pl NE5 . . . . .37 A2
Lynford Gdns SR2 . . . . .86 C3
Lyngrove SR2 . . . . .92 F8
Lynholm Gr NE12 . . . . .39 D8
Lynholme Ct **9** NE8 . . . . . .71 A8
Lynmouth Pl NE7 . . . . .39 B3
Lynmouth Rd
Gateshead NE9 . . . . .70 F3
North Shields NE29 . . . . .41 C5
Lynn Rd Tynemouth NE29 . . .41 D7
18 Chester le S DH3 . . . . . .88 C2
Wallsend NE28 . . . . .40 A1
Lynn St Blyth NE24 . . . . .17 D7
18 Chester le S DH3 . . . . . .88 C2
Lynndale Ave NE24 . . . . .16 A7
Lynnholm Cl NE7 . . . . .39 B2
Lynnholme Gdns
4 Gateshead NE9 . . . . .70 F8
Gateshead,Deckham NE9 . . .71 A8
Lynnwood Ave NE4 . . . . .54 F5
Lynnwood Terr NE4 . . . . .54 F5
Lynthorpe SR2 . . . . .92 F8
Lynton Ave NE32 . . . . .58 E3
Lynton Ct Newbottle DH4 . . .90 C3
Newcastle-u-T NE5 . . . . .37 B3
Lynton Pl NE5 . . . . .37 B3
Lynton Way NE5 . . . . .37 B3
Lynwood Ave
Blaydon NE21 . . . . .53 C3
Newbiggin-by-t-S NE64 . . . . .7 D5
Sunderland SR4 . . . . .85 A2
Lynwood Bsns Dev Ctr
NE4 . . . . .54 F5
Lynwood Cl NE20 . . . . .25 C2
Lyon St **3** NE31 . . . . .57 D7
Lyons Ave DH5 . . . . .95 B2
Lyons Cotts DH5 . . . . .95 B2
Lyons La DH5 . . . . .95 C1
Lyons The DH5 . . . . .95 B2
Lyric Cl NE27 . . . . .31 A2
Lysdon Ave NE25 . . . . .23 D6
Lyster Cl SR7 . . . . .92 E1
Litchfield NE10 . . . . .72 B7
Lytham Cl
Cramlington NE23 . . . . .21 E6
Wallsend NE28 . . . . .40 A2
Washington NE37 . . . . .72 C2
Lytham Dr NE25 . . . . .31 D5
Lytham Gn NE10 . . . . .57 B2
Lytham Grange DH4 . . . . .90 A4
Lytham Pl NE6 . . . . .56 B5
Lythe Way NE12 . . . . .39 C6

Magdelene Pl SR4 . . . . .85 F7
Magenta Cres NE5 . . . . .36 C4
Magnet Ct **1** NE1 . . . . .99 A1
Magnolia Cl NE4 . . . . .54 D7
Magnolia Dr NE63 . . . . .6 C1
Magnolia Gr NE16 . . . . .79 B6
Magpie Ct NE63 . . . . .6 B2
Mahogany Row NE9 . . . . .80 D1
Maiden La NE40 . . . . .52 A2
Maiden Law DH4 . . . . .94 A7
Maiden St NE4 . . . . .100 B3
Maiden's Wlk NE46 . . . . .45 C4
Maidenhair DH4 . . . . .89 F5
Maidens Croft NE46 . . . . .44 F4
Maidstone Cl SR3 . . . . .91 D6
Maidstone Terr NE38 . . . . . . .90 D4
Main Cres NE28 . . . . .39 F4
Main Rd Dinnington NE13 . .27 B6
Newcastle-u-T NE3 . . . . .37 B6
Ryton NE40 . . . . .52 B5
Wylam NE41 . . . . .51 B6
Main St Corbridge NE45 . . .47 A5
Crawcrook NE40 . . . . .51 F4
Ponteland NE20 . . . . .25 C6
Main St N NE23 . . . . .22 F1
Main St S NE23 . . . . .22 F1
Mains Park Rd DH3 . . . . .88 D3
Mains Pl NE21 . . . . .53 C3
Mainsforth Terr SR2 . . . . . . .103 C1
Mainsforth Terr W SR2 . . . . .86 E4
Mainstone Cl NE23 . . . . .22 A6
Maitland Terr NE64 . . . . .7 D4
Makendon St NE31 . . . . .57 E7
Makepeace Terr **8** NE1 . . .1 C5
Malaburn Way **2** SR5 . . . . .75 A1
Malaga Cl NE5 . . . . .36 B4
Malaya Dr NE6 . . . . .57 B5
Malcolm Cl NE25 . . . . .31 D4
Malcolm St NE6 . . . . .56 A6
Malden Cl NE23 . . . . .21 F6
Maling Cl NE6 . . . . .56 A4
Maling Pk SR4 . . . . .85 B7
Maling St NE6 . . . . .56 A5
Malings Cl SR1 . . . . .103 C2
Mallard Cl Ashington NE63 .11 D8
Washington NE38 . . . . .82 F4
Mallard Ct NE12 . . . . .29 C4
Mallard Lodge **1** NE10 . . .71 D8
Mallard Way Blyth NE24 . . . .17 D3
Fence Houses DH4 . . . . .94 B7
Shiremoor NE28 . . . . .41 A6
Mallowburn Cres NE3 . . . . . .37 E4
Malmo Cl NE29 . . . . .41 B5
Malone Gdns DH3 . . . . .82 D6
Malory Pl NE8 . . . . .101 C2
Maltby Cl
2 Silksworth SR3 . . . . .91 E5
Washington NE38 . . . . .83 D4
Maltings The SR3 . . . . .92 C7
Maltkiln NE46 . . . . .45 A4
Malton Cl Blyth NE24 . . . . . . .17 B8
Newcastle-u-T NE15 . . . . .53 E6
Malton Cres NE29 . . . . .41 F4
Malton Ct NE32 . . . . .58 B2
Malton Gdns NE28 . . . . .40 B4
Malton Gn NE9 . . . . .71 B1
Malvern Ave DH2 . . . . .88 B2
Malvern Cl NE63 . . . . .6 A4
Malvern Ct Cleadon SR6 . . . .59 F1
Dunston NE11 . . . . .70 A6
Newcastle-u-T NE15 . . . . .53 B7
Malvern Gdns
Dunston NE11 . . . . .70 A7
Sunderland SR6 . . . . .75 E3
Malvern Rd
Seaton Sluice NE26 . . . . .24 D5
Tynemouth NE29 . . . . .41 E8
Wallsend NE28 . . . . .83 B3
Malvern St
Newcastle-u-T NE4 . . . . .100 A4
South Shields SR3 . . . . .59 C7
Malvin's Close Fst Sch
NE24 . . . . .17 C7
Malvins Close Rd NE24 . . . . .17 C7
Malvins Rd NE24 . . . . .17 B8
Manchester St NE61 . . . . .3 F1
Mandale Cres NE30 . . . . .32 A3
Mandarin Cl NE5 . . . . .36 A3
Mandarin Lodge **8** NE10 .71 D8
Mandarin Way NE38 . . . . .84 C6
Mandela Cl SR1 . . . . .103 C3
Mandela Way NE11 . . . . .54 F2
Mandeville NE37 . . . . .83 F8
Manet Gdns NE34 . . . . .59 D2
Mangrove Cl NE5 . . . . .36 A3
Manila St SR2 . . . . .86 E4
Manisty Ho NE4 . . . . .100 A3
Manley View NE63 . . . . .7 A3
Manners Gdns NE25 . . . . .22 A5
Manningford Cl NE23 . . . . . . .22 A5
Manningford Dr SR3 . . . . .91 E5
Manor Ave
Longbenton NE7 . . . . .39 C5
Newburn NE15 . . . . .52 F8
Manor Chare NE1 . . . . .99 B1
Manor Cl
Newcastle-u-T NE3 . . . . .38 D5
Riding Mill NE44 . . . . .62 F7
Manor Cotts NE45 . . . . .46 F6
Manor Ct NE32 . . . . .58 C4
Manor Dr Longbenton NE7 . .39 C5
Newbiggin-by-t-S NE64 . . . . .7 A5
Manor Gdns
Gateshead NE10 . . . . .72 C8

Manor Gdns continued
Longbenton NE7 . . . . .39 C5
Manor Gr Longbenton NE7 . .39 C5
New Herrington DH4 . . . . . .90 F7
Newburn NE15 . . . . .52 F7
Manor House Cl 1 NE6 . .56 C5
Manor House Farm Cotts
NE5 . . . . .37 D4
Manor House Rd NE2 . . . .38 C1
Manor Pk Corbridge NE45 . .46 F6
Washington NE37 . . . . .83 D8
Manor Pl NE7 . . . . .39 C5
Manor Rd Longbenton NE7 . .39 C5
Medomsley DH8 . . . . .77 C1
Washington NE37 . . . . .42 D7
Tynemouth NE30 . . . . .83 D8
Manor Terr Blaydon NE21 . .53 A1
Winlaton Mill NE21 . . . . . . .68 C7
Manor The NE37 . . . . .72 E2
Manor View
High Pittington DH6 . . . . . .96 B4
Newbiggin-by-t-S NE64 . . . .7 E5
Washington NE37 . . . . .83 E8
Manor View E 2 NE37 . . . .83 E8
Manor Walks Sh Ctr
NE23 . . . . .22 A6
Manor Wlk NE7 . . . . .39 C5
Manorfields NE12 . . . . . . .39 D6
Manors Sta NE1 . . . . .99 B1
Manors Sta (Metro) NE1 . .99 B1
Manors The NE42 . . . . . . .50 E3
Manorway Hedworth NE32 .58 C1
Tynemouth NE30 . . . . .42 D8
Mansel Terr NE24 . . . . . . .16 F7
Mansell Pl NE3 . . . . .37 E3
Mansfield Cres SR6 . . . . .75 E2
Mansfield Ct NE36 . . . . . .74 A7
Mansfield Pl NE4 . . . . . . .98 B1
Mansfield St NE4 . . . . . . .98 B1
Mansion Ho NE36 . . . . . . .74 A7
Mansion Hts NE11 . . . . . .69 E7
Manston Cl SR3 . . . . .91 D6
Manx Sq SR5 . . . . .75 B3
Maple Ave Dunston NE11 . .70 A7
New Silksworth SR3 . . . . . .92 B8
Whitley Bay NE25 . . . . .31 F4
Maple Cl Bedlington NE22 . .10 F1
Newcastle-u-T NE5 . . . . . . .36 D1
Maple Cres NE24 . . . . . . .16 F8
Maple Ct Killingworth NE12 . .29 C4
New Hartley NE25 . . . . .23 D6
Maple Gr
Gateshead,Felling NE10 . . .71 E8
Gateshead,Saltwell NE8 . . .70 F2
Prudhoe NE42 . . . . .50 B2
South Shields NE34 . . . . . .59 F5
Whitburn SR6 . . . . .60 F1
Maple Rd NE21 . . . . .53 C2
Maple Row NE11 . . . . . . .54 B2
Maple St Ashington NE63 . .6 D3
Jarrow NE32 . . . . .58 A7
Newcastle-u-T NE4 . . . . . .100 B4
Maple Terr
Burnopfield NE16 . . . . .78 F6
Newcastle-u-T NE4 . . . . . .100 B4
Shiney Row DH4 . . . . .90 A5
Maplebeck Cl SR3 . . . . . .91 D5
Mapledene NE38 . . . . . . .83 E2
Mapledene Rd NE3 . . . . . .37 F6
Maplewood
Chester le S DH2 . . . . .88 A4
Newcastle-u-T NE6 . . . . . . .56 E8
Maplewood Ave SR5 . . . . .74 F3
Maplewood Cres NE38 . . .83 B1
Maplewood Dr DH6 . . . . . .97 E1
Maplewood Sch SR5 . . . .74 E3
Maplewood St DH4 . . . . . .89 E1
Mapperley Dr NE15 . . . . .53 E7
Marblet Ct NE11 . . . . .70 B7
Marbury Cl SR3 . . . . .91 D6
March Rd NE23 . . . . .29 B7
March Terr NE13 . . . . .27 A7
Marchburn La NE44 . . . . . .62 E7
Marcia Ave SR6 . . . . .75 D3
Marconi Way NE11 . . . . . .54 B2
Marcross Cl NE15 . . . . . . .36 B2
Marcross Dr SR3 . . . . .83 B7
Mardale NE37 . . . . .83 B7
Mardale Ave NE9 . . . . . . .71 A3
Mardale Rd NE5 . . . . .37 B1
Mardale St DH5 . . . . .95 A2
Marden Ave NE30 . . . . . . .32 C3
Marden Bridge Mid Sch
NE25 . . . . .32 A4
Marden Cl NE16 . . . . .8 D7
Marden Cres NE26 . . . . . .32 C4
Marden Ct NE26 . . . . .24 B7
Marden Farm Dr NE30 . . . .32 B3
Marden High Sch NE30 . . .32 B1
Marden Rd NE26 . . . . .32 B4
Marden Rd S NE25 . . . . . .32 B4
Marden Terr NE30 . . . . . . .32 C2
Mare Cl NE23 . . . . .23 A3
Mareburn Cres NE10 . . . . .71 E8
Maree Cl SR3 . . . . .91 E5
Margaret Alice St SR4 . . . .85 E7
Margaret Collins Ho NE6 .56 D6
Margaret Cotts NE25 . . . . .31 F2
Margaret Dr NE12 . . . . . . .40 A8
Margaret Gr NE34 . . . . . . .59 A5
Margaret Rd NE26 . . . . . . .32 C4
Margaret St SR2 . . . . .87 A2
Margaret Sutton Sch
NE34 . . . . .59 D6

Margaret Terr
Penshaw DH4 . . . . .90 C6
Rowlands Gill NE39 . . . . . . .67 C1
Tanfield Lea DH9 . . . . .79 C1
Margate St SR3 . . . . .92 A8
Marguerite Ct SR4 . . . . . .102 B3
Maria St
New Silksworth SR3 . . . . . .92 A7
Newcastle-u-T NE4 . . . . . . .54 E4
Marian Ct NE8 . . . . .101 A1
Marian Dr NE10 . . . . .57 C3
Marian Way
Ponteland NE20 . . . . .25 B2
South Shields NE34 . . . . . .59 F3
Marie Curie Dr NE4 . . . . . .54 F4
Marigold Ave NE10 . . . . . .56 B2
Marigold Cres DH4 . . . . . .89 E3
Marigold Ct NE3 . . . . . . .102 B3
Marigold Wlk NE34 . . . . . .59 B5
Marina Ave SR6 . . . . .75 D3
Marina Ct SR6 . . . . .75 D3
Marina Dr
South Shields NE33 . . . . . .42 E3
Whitley Bay NE25 . . . . .31 C4
Marina Gr SR6 . . . . .75 D3
Marina Terr
1 Ryhope SR2 . . . . .92 F6
Whitburn SR6 . . . . .60 F1
Marina View
Hebburn NE31 . . . . .57 D6
Wallsend NE28 . . . . .40 F2
Marine App NE33 . . . . . . .42 E2
Marine Ave NE26 . . . . . . .31 F5
Marine Ct E NE26 . . . . . . .32 A6
Marine Ct W NE26 . . . . . . .32 A6
Marine Dr Jarrow NE31 . . .58 A3
Ryhope SR2 . . . . .93 A8
Marine Gdns NE26 . . . . . .32 A6
Marine Park Fst Sch
NE26 . . . . .32 A6
Marine Park Prim Sch
NE33 . . . . .42 D3
Marine St NE64 . . . . .7 E5
Marine Terr NE24 . . . . . . .17 E7
Marine View NE26 . . . . . . .24 C7
Marine Wlk SR6 . . . . .75 F2
Mariners Point 8 NE30 . . .42 D7
Mariners Wharf NE1 . . . . .56 A5
Mariners' Cotts NE33 . . . .42 E3
Mariners' La NE30 . . . . . . .42 C7
Mariners' St SR2 . . . . .86 E4
Maritime Pl 4 NE61 . . . . . . .3 F1
Maritime St SR1 . . . . .103 A2
Maritime Terr SR1 . . . . . .102 C2
Marius Ave NE15 . . . . . . .34 F7
Mariville E SR2 . . . . .93 A5
Mariville W SR2 . . . . .93 A5
Marjorie St NE23 . . . . .22 C5
Mark Rise DH5 . . . . .95 A5
Mark's La DH4 . . . . .94 A3
Markby Cl SR3 . . . . .91 E5
Market Cres DH4 . . . . .90 C6
Market La
Dunston NE11,NE16 . . . . . .69 D8
Newcastle-u-T NE1 . . . . . . .99 B1
Market Pl Bedlington NE22 .15 F8
Blyth NE24 . . . . .17 E8
Corbridge NE45 . . . . .46 F5
2 Hexham NE46 . . . . .45 B5
Houghton-le-S DH5 . . . . . .94 F8
Morpeth NE61 . . . . .8 F8
South Shields NE33 . . . . . .42 C3
Market Place Ind Est
DH5 . . . . .90 F1
Market Sq Jarrow NE32 . . .58 B7
Lynemouth NE61 . . . . .2 B2
Sunderland SR1 . . . . .103 A2
Market St Blyth NE24 . . . . .17 E8
Dudley NE23 . . . . .29 A8
Hetton le H DH5 . . . . .95 B4
Newcastle-u-T NE1 . . . . . . .99 B1
Market Way NE11 . . . . . . .70 D6
Markham Ave SR6 . . . . . . .61 A1
Markham St SR2 . . . . .86 F2
Markington Dr SR2 . . . . . .92 F5
Markle Gr DH5 . . . . .94 D5
Marlboro Ave NE16 . . . . . .69 B8
Marlborough App NE3 . . . .38 C7
Marlborough Ave NE3 . . . .38 C7
Marlborough Cres
Gateshead NE9 . . . . .71 C3
Newcastle-u-T NE1 . . . . . .100 C4
Marlborough Ct
Houghton-le-S DH5 . . . . . .94 E6
Jarrow NE32 . . . . .58 B5
Newcastle-u-T NE3 . . . . . . .37 D7
Marlborough Ho NE26 . . . .31 F6
Marlborough Rd
Sunderland SR4 . . . . .85 A3
Washington NE37 . . . . .83 F8
Marlborough St N NE33 . . .59 D8
Marlborough St S NE33 . . .59 D8
Marlborough Terr NE62 . . .10 F4
Marleen Ave NE6 . . . . .56 C8
Marleen Ct 1 NE6 . . . . . . .56 C8
Marlesford Cl SR3 . . . . . . .91 D6
Marley Cres SR5 . . . . .74 F3
Marley Hill Com Prim Sch
NE16 . . . . .80 A8
Marlfield Ct NE5 . . . . .37 B3
Marlow Dr SR3 . . . . .91 D5
Marlow St NE24 . . . . .17 E8
Marlow Way NE16 . . . . . . .68 F5
Marlowe Gdns NE8 . . . . .101 C1
Marlowe Pl DH5 . . . . .94 F7

Marlowe Wlk NE34 . . . . . .59 A3
Marmion Rd NE26 . . . . . . .57 A8
Marmion Terr NE25 . . . . . .31 F4
Marne St DH4 . . . . .90 C6
Marondale Ave NE6 . . . . . .56 F7
Marquis Ave NE5 . . . . .36 C4
Marquis Cl NE12 . . . . .39 D5
Marquis Ct
Gateshead NE11 . . . . .70 D3
4 New Silksworth SR3 . . . .92 B7
Prudhoe NE42 . . . . .50 A3
Marquisway NE11 . . . . . . .70 D2
Marr Ho SR4 . . . . .85 F7
Marr Rd NE31 . . . . .57 F5
Marris Ho NE2 . . . . .98 C3
Marsden Ave SR6 . . . . . . .60 F3
Marsden Cl DH4 . . . . .94 C8
Marsden Cliffs Nature
Reserve* NE34 . . . . .60 E6
Marsden Gr
Gateshead NE9 . . . . .71 D3
Whitburn SR6 . . . . .60 F1
Marsden La
Newcastle-u-T NE5 . . . . . . .37 A3
South Shields NE34 . . . . . .60 C7
Marsden Prim Sch SR6 . .60 F3
Marsden Rd Cleadon SR6 . .60 E4
South Shields NE34 . . . . . .60 A7
Marsden St 6 NE33 . . . . . .59 D8
Marsden View SR6 . . . . . .60 F3
Marsh Ct NE11 . . . . .70 B7
Marshall St SR6 . . . . .75 D3
Marshall Wallis Rd NE33 .59 C8
Marsham Cl Cleadon SR6 . .60 F3
Newcastle-u-T NE15 . . . . . .53 E7
Marsham Rd 3 NE5 . . . . . .36 E3
Marshes' Houses NE62 . . .11 D7
Marshmont Ave NE30 . . . .32 C1
Marske Terr NE6 . . . . .56 E6
Marston NE12 . . . . .29 D4
Marston Wlk NE16 . . . . . . .68 F5
Martello Gdns NE7 . . . . . .39 D3
Martha St DH9 . . . . .79 B2
Martin Ct NE38 . . . . .82 F2
Martin Hall NE38 . . . . .58 C6
Martin Terr 7 SR4 . . . . . . .85 F7
Martin Way NE13 . . . . .28 A6
Martindale Ave SR6 . . . . . .75 C5
Martindale Pk DH5 . . . . . .94 E8
Martindale Rd NE38 . . . . . .83 A5
Martindale Wlk NE12 . . . . .29 C3
Marwell Dr NE37 . . . . .72 E2
Marwood Ct NE25 . . . . . . .31 D6
Marx Terr NE17 . . . . .77 C8
Mary Agnes St NE3 . . . . . .38 A5
Mary Ave DH3 . . . . .82 B6
Mary Magdalene Bglws
NE2 . . . . .98 B4
Mary St Blaydon NE21 . . . .53 C3
Blaydon,Winlaton NE21 . . . .53 A2
New Silksworth SR3 . . . . . .92 A8
Sunderland SR1 . . . . .102 C2
Mary Terr NE5 . . . . .37 A3
Mary's Pl NE6 . . . . .57 B6
Maryhill Cl NE4 . . . . .54 E4
Maryside Pl NE40 . . . . . . .51 F7
Mascot Ho 3 NE1 . . . . . . .98 C1
Masefield Ave NE16 . . . . . .54 B1
Masefield Dr NE34 . . . . . . .59 A2
Masefield Pl NE8 . . . . . . .101 C2
Mason Ave NE26 . . . . .32 B5
Mason Rd NE28 . . . . .40 A4
Mason St
Brunswick Village NE13 . . .28 A6
4 Newcastle-u-T NE6 . . . .56 C5
Mason View NE13 . . . . . . .28 B8
Massingham Way NE34 . . .59 B5
Mast La NE30 . . . . .32 B3
Master Mariners' Homes
NE30 . . . . .42 C7
Master's Cres NE42 . . . . . .50 B2
Matamba Terr SR4 . . . . . .102 B2
Matanzas St SR2 . . . . . . .86 E3
Matfen Ave
Hazlerigg NE13 . . . . .28 A4
Shiremoor NE27 . . . . .31 A2
Matfen Cl Blyth NE24 . . . . .17 C7
Newcastle-u-T NE15 . . . . . .53 E6
Matfen Ct DH2 . . . . .88 A3
Matfen Dr SR3 . . . . .91 D6
Matfen Gdns NE28 . . . . . . .40 F5
Matfen Pl
Newcastle-u-T,Fawdon NE3 .38 A4
Newcastle-u-T,Fenham NE4 .54 F7
Matfen Terr NE64 . . . . .7 D3
Mathematical NE4 . . . . . .100 B4
Mathesons Gdns NE61 . . . .8 F8
Matlock Gdns NE15 . . . . . .36 F3
Matlock Rd NE32 . . . . .58 C5
Matlock Sq NE61 . . . . .2 A2
Matlock St SR1 . . . . .103 A3
Matthew Bank NE2 . . . . . .38 E3
Matthew Cl NE6 . . . . .56 B6
Matthew Rd NE24 . . . . . . .17 F5
Matthew St 13 NE6 . . . . . .56 B6
Maud St
Newcastle-u-T NE15 . . . . . .53 C6
Sunderland SR2 . . . . .55 E4
Maud Terr
5 Shiremoor NE27 . . . . . .30 E1
Tanfield DH9 . . . . .79 D3
Maud's Terr NE64 . . . . .7 F5
Maudlin Pl 8 NE5 . . . . . . .37 D1
Maudlin St NE5 . . . . .36 F1
Mauds La SR1 . . . . .103 B3
Maughan St SR6 . . . . .17 F7

Maurice Rd NE28 . . . . . . .57 B8
Maurice Road Ind Est
NE28 . . . . .57 B8
Mautland St DH4 . . . . .90 E1
Maxton Cl SR3 . . . . .91 D5
Maxwell NE33 . . . . .42 C2
Maxwell St Gateshead NE8 .70 D7
South Shields NE33 . . . . . .42 C2
2 Sunderland SR4 . . . . . .85 F7
Maxwell St Ind Est 6
NE33 . . . . .42 C2
May Ave Ryton NE40 . . . . .52 C6
Winlaton Mill NE21 . . . . . . .68 C7
May Gr SR6 . . . . .60 F3
May St Birtley DH3 . . . . . . .82 C4
Blaydon NE21 . . . . .53 C3
South Shields NE33 . . . . . .42 D1
Sunderland SR4 . . . . .85 A7
Maybury Villas NE12 . . . . .39 A5
Maydown Cl SR5 . . . . .74 A8
Mayfair Cl NE31 . . . . .57 D5
Mayfair Gdns
Gateshead NE8 . . . . .71 A8
Ponteland NE20 . . . . .25 F6
South Shields NE34 . . . . . .59 F7
Mayfair Rd NE2 . . . . .38 D2
Mayfield Morpeth NE61 . . . .8 E7
Whickham NE16 . . . . .69 B5
Mayfield Ave
Cramlington NE23 . . . . .22 C6
Throckley NE15 . . . . .35 E1
Mayfield Ct SR6 . . . . .75 D3
Mayfield Dr SR6 . . . . .75 B8
Mayfield Gdns
Newcastle-u-T NE3 . . . . . . .58 A6
Throckley NE15 . . . . .35 E1
Wallsend NE28 . . . . .40 A3
Mayfield Gr SR4 . . . . .85 A2
Mayfield Pl NE13 . . . . .28 A5
Mayfield Rd
Newcastle-u-T NE3 . . . . . . .38 C4
Sunderland SR4 . . . . .85 A2
Mayo Dr 1 SR3 . . . . .91 E5
Mayoral Way NE11 . . . . . . .70 D3
Maypole Cl 8 SR5 . . . . . . .75 B2
Mayswood Rd SR6 . . . . . . .75 B8
Maytree Ho NE4 . . . . .100 A4
Maywood Cl NE3 . . . . .37 E4
Mazine Terr DH6 . . . . .97 E2
McAnany Ave NE34 . . . . . .59 D5
McAteer Ct DH6 . . . . .97 E1
McClaren Way DH4 . . . . . .90 F7
McCracken Cl NE3 . . . . . . .38 C8
McCracken Dr NE13 . . . . . .28 C7
McCutcheon Ct NE6 . . . . .56 E3
McCutcheon St 7 SR7 . . . .92 E1
McErlane Sq NE10 . . . . . . .57 A1
McEwan Gdns NE4 . . . . . .54 E5
McGowen Ct 8 NE6 . . . . . .56 C5
McIlvenna Gdns NE28 . . . .40 B4
Mcintyre Hall NE31 . . . . . .57 F7
Mcintyre Rd NE31 . . . . . . .57 F7
McKendrick Villas NE5 . . . .37 D1
McLennan Ct NE38 . . . . . . .83 D6
McNamara Rd NE28 . . . . . .40 F3
Mcnulty Ct NE23 . . . . .28 F8
Meacham Way NE16 . . . . .69 A5
Mead Ave NE12 . . . . .39 E8
Mead Cres NE12 . . . . .39 E8
Mead Way NE12 . . . . .39 E8
Mead Wlk NE6 . . . . .56 F6
Meadow Bank Dr NE12 . . .11 F2
Meadow Brook Dr NE17 . . .66 C2
Meadow Cl Blaydon NE21 . .52 F1
Dunston NE11 . . . . .54 E1
Houghton-le-S DH5 . . . . . . .94 F7
Longbenton NE12 . . . . .39 B7
Ryton NE40 . . . . .52 D5
Seghill NE23 . . . . .22 F2
Meadow Ct
Bedlington NE22 . . . . .10 E1
Ponteland NE20 . . . . .25 E5
Meadow Dr
Seaton Burn NE13 . . . . . . .28 C8
Sunderland,East Herrington
SR3 . . . . .91 B6
Sunderland,South Hylton
SR4 . . . . .85 A3
Meadow Gdns SR3 . . . . . .86 B3
Meadow Gr SR3 . . . . .85 B5
Meadow Grange DH4 . . . . .89 E2
Meadow Ho NE12 . . . . . . .39 A5
Meadow La
Crawcrook NE40 . . . . .52 A4
Dunston NE11 . . . . .54 F1
Sunderland SR3 . . . . .91 B6
Meadow Laws NE34 . . . . . .60 A4
Meadow Pk NE44 . . . . .62 F7
Meadow Rd
Newcastle-u-T NE15 . . . . . .53 D8
Seaton Sluice NE26 . . . . . .24 C6
Wallsend NE28 . . . . .40 F4
Whitley Bay NE25 . . . . .31 D4
Meadow Rise
Gateshead NE9 . . . . .71 C5
Newcastle-u-T NE5 . . . . . . .37 B4
Meadow St DH5 . . . . .94 C3
Meadow Terr DH4 . . . . .90 C6
Meadow Vale SR2 . . . . . . .86 E2
Meadow View Dipton DH9 . .78 E1
Hedworth NE32 . . . . .58 D2
New Hartley NE25 . . . . .23 D6
North Shields NE29 . . . . . . .41 E4
Sunderland SR3 . . . . .91 B5
Meadow Well Sta NE29 . . .41 D5
Meadow Well Way NE29 . . .41 E4
Meadow Wlk NE40 . . . . . . .52 D5

Meadowbank NE23 . . . . . .29 A8
Meadowbrook Dr NE10 . . .72 C7
Meadowcroft Mews
NE8 . . . . .101 A1
Meadowdale Cres
Bedlington NE22 . . . . .10 D1
Newcastle-u-T NE5 . . . . . . .37 D3
Meadowdale Mid Sch
NE22 . . . . .10 D1
Meadowfield
Ashington NE63 . . . . .7 A2
Ponteland NE20 . . . . .25 E7
Whitley Bay NE25 . . . . .31 D5
Meadowfield Ave NE3 . . . .38 A6
Meadowfield Cres NE40 . . .52 A4
Meadowfield Ct NE20 . . . . .25 E7
Meadowfield Dr SR6 . . . . . .60 B1
Meadowfield Est NE61 . . . .7 B6
Meadowfield Gdns NE6 . . .40 A1
Meadowfield Ind Est
NE20 . . . . .25 E6
Meadowfield Pk NE20 . . . .25 E6
Meadowfield Pk S NE43 . . .64 C5
Meadowfield Rd
Newcastle-u-T NE3 . . . . . . .38 A4
Stocksfield NE43 . . . . .64 C5
Meadowfield Terr
Longbenton NE12 . . . . .29 F1
Stocksfield NE43 . . . . .64 D7
Meadows Crest NE43 . . . . .65 A5
Meadows La DH4,DH5 . . . .94 B3
Meadows The
Bournmoor DH4 . . . . .89 D3
Burnopfield NE16 . . . . .79 A4
Newcastle-u-T NE3 . . . . . . .37 F6
Ryton NE40 . . . . .52 D5
West Rainton DH4 . . . . .94 A3
Meadowside SR2 . . . . .86 B4
Meadowsweet Cl 3
NE24 . . . . .17 C4
Meadowvale
Backworth NE27 . . . . .30 D3
Ponteland NE20 . . . . .25 A2
Meadway Dr NE12 . . . . . . .39 F8
Meal Mkt NE46 . . . . .45 B5
Means Ct NE23 . . . . .29 B6
Means Dr NE23 . . . . .29 B5
Medburn Ave NE30 . . . . . .32 C2
Medburn Rd
Newcastle-u-T NE15 . . . . . .53 C7
Seaton Delaval NE25 . . . . . .23 E2
Medina Cl SR3 . . . . .91 E5
Medlar NE9 . . . . .71 D4
Medlar Cl DH4 . . . . .89 F6
Medomsley Gdns NE9 . . . .71 E4
Medomsly St SR4 . . . . . . .102 A3
Medway NE32 . . . . .58 C2
Medway Ave NE31 . . . . . . .57 E3
Medway Cres NE8 . . . . . . .71 A8
Medway Gdns
Sunderland SR4 . . . . .85 D4
Tynemouth NE30 . . . . .42 A7
Medway Pl NE23 . . . . .16 D1
Medwood Cl NE13 . . . . . . .37 E3
Medwyn Cl Blyth NE24 . . . .17 D5
Bournmoor DH4 . . . . .89 E3
Megstone Ave NE23 . . . . . .22 A2
Megstone Ct NE23 . . . . . . .22 A2
Melbeck Dr DH2 . . . . .81 E2
Melbourne Cres NE25 . . . .31 E3
Melbourne Ct
Gateshead NE8 . . . . .101 B3
Newcastle-u-T NE1 . . . . . . .99 C1
Melbourne Gdns NE34 . . . .59 C5
Melbourne Pl SR4 . . . . . . .85 E4
Melbourne St NE1 . . . . . . .99 B1
Melbury NE25 . . . . .31 D6
Melbury Ct SR6 . . . . .75 D2
Melbury Rd NE7 . . . . .39 A1
Meldon Ave
Newcastle-u-T NE3 . . . . . . .37 F7
Sherburn DH6 . . . . .96 A1
South Shields NE34 . . . . . .59 E6
Meldon Ct NE20 . . . . .40 E1
Meldon Ct NE40 . . . . .51 E3
Meldon Gdns
Dunston NE11 . . . . .70 A5
Stakeford NE62 . . . . .10 F8
Meldon Ho NE24 . . . . .17 B8
Meldon Rd SR4 . . . . .85 F7
Meldon St NE28 . . . . .41 C2
Meldon Terr
Greenside NE40 . . . . .51 F1
Newbiggin-by-t-S NE64 . . . .7 D3
Newcastle-u-T NE6 . . . . . . .56 A6
Melgarve Dr SR3 . . . . .91 E5
Melkington Ct NE5 . . . . . . .36 C2
Melkridge Gdns NE7 . . . . .39 D2
Melkridge Pl NE23 . . . . . . .22 A1
Mellendean Cl NE5 . . . . . .37 B3
Melling Rd NE23 . . . . .22 A1
Melmerby Cl NE3 . . . . .38 D2
Melness Rd NE13 . . . . .28 A1
Melock Ct NE13 . . . . .28 A4
Melrose NE38 . . . . .83 D2
Melrose Ave
Backworth NE27 . . . . .30 C2
Bedside NE22 . . . . .11 D3
Gateshead NE9 . . . . .71 E1
Hebburn NE31 . . . . .57 E2
Seaton Delaval NE25 . . . . . .23 A3
Tynemouth NE30 . . . . .32 A4
Whitley Bay NE25 . . . . .31 F4
Melrose Cl
Newcastle-u-T NE3 . . . . . . .28 B7
Newcastle-u-T,Bell's Close
NE15 . . . . .53 E6

Melrose Ct NE22 11 D2
Melrose Gdns
Newbottle DH4 90 C3
Sunderland SR6 75 E3
Wallsend NE28 41 A4
Melrose Gr NE32 58 E4
Melrose Terr
Bedlington NE22 11 D2
Newbiggin-by-t-S NE64 7 D3
Melrose Villas NE22 11 D2
Melsonby Cl SR3 91 D6
Meltham Ct NE15 36 B2
Meltham Dr SR3 91 E5
Melton Ave NE6 56 F5
Melton Cres NE26 24 D5
Melton Dr NE25 23 D6
Melvaig Cl SR3 91 E5
Melville Ave NE24 17 D5
Melville Gdns NE25 31 C4
Melville Gr NE7 39 A4
Melville St DH3 88 C2
Melvin Pl [5] NE5 37 B2
Melvyn Gdns SR6 75 E3
Membury Cl [4] SR3 91 E5
Memorial Sq NE64 7 D5
Menai Ct [9] SR3 91 F6
Menceforth Cotts DH2 88 B4
Mendham Cl NE10 71 E6
Mendip Ave DH2 88 C2
Mendip Cl Ashington NE63 6 E1
Tynemouth NE29 31 F1
Mendip Dr NE38 83 B3
Mendip Gdns NE11 70 B6
Mendip Way NE12 38 F6
Mentieth Cl NE38 83 B3
Menvill Pl SR1 103 B2
Mercantile Rd DH4 94 C7
Merchants Wharf [10] NE6 56 C4
Mercia Way NE15 53 E5
Mere Knolls Rd SR6 75 E4
Meredith Gdns NE8 101 C1
Meresyde NE10 72 A7
Meresyde Ct NE10 72 A7
Merevale Cl NE37 72 E2
Merganser Lodge [10]
NE10 71 D8
Meridan Way NE7 39 D3
Meridian Ho [8] NE33 59 E8
Merlay Dr NE13 27 B6
Merlay Hall NE6 57 A4
Merle Gdns Morpeth NE61 3 D2
[16] Newcastle-u-T NE6 56 C5
Merle Terr SR4 85 F7
Merley Gate NE61 9 A6
Merlin Cres NE28 40 F3
Merlin Ct [17] NE10 56 D1
Merlin Dr DH3 88 D7
Merlin Pl NE12 39 A7
Merlin Way Earsdon NE27 31 A1
Shiremoor NE27 41 A8
Merrick Ho [21] SR3 91 F6
Merrington Cl
New Hartley NE25 23 D7
Silksworth SR3 91 D6
Merrion Cl SR3 91 D6
Merryfield Gdns SR6 75 E3
Merryshields Terr NE43 64 C8
Mersey Ct [17] SR3 91 F6
Mersey Pl NE8 71 B8
Mersey Rd Gateshead NE8 71 B8
Hebburn NE31 57 F3
Mersey St NE17 66 C1
Merton Ct NE4 54 D4
Merton Rd NE20 25 E6
Merton Sq [3] NE24 17 E8
Merton Way NE20 25 E6
Methuen St NE9 71 A8
Methven Way NE23 16 C2
Metro Ctr Sta NE11 54 D2
Metro Ret Pk NE11 54 B2
MetroCentre The NE11 54 C2
Metroland Indoor Theme
Pk* NE11 54 C2
Mews Ct DH5 94 E8
Mews Gdns NE1 99 B1
Mews The Blaydon NE21 53 E2
Fence Houses DH4 94 A7
Gateshead NE10 72 B8
Newcastle-u-T NE1 99 A2
North Shields NE30 42 A6
Sunderland SR3 91 B7
Tynemouth NE30 42 E8
Michaelgate [24] NE6 56 C6
Mickle Cl NE37 83 A6
Mickleton Gdns SR3 86 B2
Micklewood Cl NE61 4 E6
Mickley Fst Sch NE43 49 E1
Middle Chare DH3 88 D3
Middle Cl NE38 83 B1
Middle Dr Ponteland NE20 25 C3
Woolsington NE13 26 F1
Middle Engine La
Shiremoor NE27,NE28,NE29 41 A7
Wallsend NE27,NE28,NE29 40 F5
Middle Farm Ct NE23 22 B7
Middle Garth [1] NE5 37 D2
Middle Gate Morpeth NE61 8 F6
Newcastle-u-T NE5 36 D1
Middle Gn NE25 31 C4
Middle Row
Great Lumley DH4 89 E1
Ryton NE40 52 E3
Middle St Blyth NE24 17 B4
Corbridge NE45 46 F5
Newcastle-u-T NE6 56 F6
Sunderland SR1 102 C3
Sunderland SR1 103 A3
Tynemouth NE30 42 E7
Middle St E NE6 57 A6
Middlebrook NE20 25 B3
Middlefields Ind Est
NE33 59 B6
Middleham Cl DH2 81 E1
Middleham Ct SR5 74 E3
Middleton Ave
Newcastle-u-T NE4 54 E6
Rowlands Gill NE39 67 F1
Middleton Cl SR7 92 E1
Middleton Ct NE2 99 C3
Middleton St NE24 17 E7
Middlewood Pk NE4 54 F7
Midfield Dr [11] SR6 75 E2
Midgley Dr SR3 91 E5
Midhurst Ave NE34 60 A8
Midhurst Cl SR3 91 D6
Midhurst Rd NE12 39 D7
Midlothian Cl SR4 85 D3
Midmoor Rd SR4 85 E7
Midsomer Cl SR3 91 D5
Midway NE6 57 A6
Milbanke Cl DH2 81 F1
Milbanke St DH2 81 F1
Milburn Cl
Chester le S DH3 88 E2
Hexham NE46 44 F2
Milburn Dr NE15 54 B6
Milburn Rd NE63 6 D2
Milburn Terr
Shiney Row DH4 90 B6
Stakeford NE62 11 C6
Milcombe Cl SR3 91 D6
Mildmay Rd NE2 38 D2
Mildred St DH5 90 E1
Mile End Rd NE33 42 C4
Milecastle Ct NE5 36 D2
Milecastle Fst Sch NE5 36 C2
Milfield Ave
Shiremoor NE27 31 A3
Wallsend NE28 40 C4
Milford Gdns NE3 28 B1
Milford Rd NE15 54 C5
Military Rd
Heddon-on-t-W NE15 34 C3
North Shields NE30 42 B6
Military Vehicle Mus*
NE2 99 A4
Milk Mkt NE1 99 C1
Milkhope Ctr NE13 20 D5
Milkwell NE45 47 A6
Milkwell La NE45 47 A7
Mill Bank SR5 75 C4
Mill Cl North Shields NE29 41 E5
Riding Mill NE44 62 F7
Mill Cres Hebburn NE31 57 C2
Penshaw DH4 90 B6
Mill Ct Bournmoor DH4 89 E2
Ellington NE61 1 C4
Hamsterley NE17 77 B6
Mill Dam NE33 42 B2
Mill Dene View NE32 58 C5
Mill Dyke Cl NE25 31 C6
Mill Farm NE61 1 C4
Mill Farm Cl NE4 98 B1
Mill Farm Rd NE39 78 A5
Mill Gr South Shields NE34 60 B4
Tynemouth NE30 42 C8
Mill Grange NE44 63 A8
Mill Hill DH5 94 D6
Mill Hill Prim Sch SR3 92 A6
Mill Hill Rd
Newcastle-u-T NE5 53 F8
Silksworth SR3 92 A6
Mill Ho NE2 98 B4
Mill La Ebchester DH8 76 E4
Hebburn NE10,NE31 57 E2
Heddon-on-t-W NE15 34 F3
Newcastle-u-T NE4 100 A4
North Shields NE29 42 B4
Seghill NE23 22 D1
Sherburn DH6 96 A1
Slaley NE44 62 A1
Urpeth DH2 81 D1
Whitburn SR6 60 F2
Winlaton Mill NE21 68 B7
Mill Pit DH4 90 B6
Mill Race Cl NE17 77 B6
Mill Rd Chopwell NE17 77 B8
Gateshead NE8 101 C4
Mill Rise NE3 38 E4
Mill St SR4 102 B3
Mill Terr
Houghton-le-S DH5 94 D6
Shiney Row DH4 90 B6
Mill View Gateshead NE10 71 C7
West Boldon NE36 74 A7
Mill View Ave SR6 75 D3
Mill View Rise NE42 50 D4
Mill Way NE15,NE42 50 D7
Millais Gdns NE34 59 C2
Millbank Cres NE22 11 A1
Millbank Ind Est [3] NE33 42 C2
Millbank Pl NE22 16 B8
Millbank Rd
Bedlington NE22 11 B1
Newcastle-u-T NE6 57 A4
Millbank Terr NE22 11 A1
Millbeck Gdns NE9 71 B2
Millbeck Gr DH5 94 D6
Millbrook Gateshead NE10 71 E7
North Shields NE29 41 E5
Millbrook Rd NE23 16 D1
Millburn St SR4 102 B3
Milldale Ave NE24 17 A7
Milldene Ave NE30 42 C8
Millennium Way SR5 102 C4
Miller St NE8 70 D8
Miller Terr SR3 92 A8
Miller's La NE16 54 B1
Millers Hill DH4 90 C6
Millers Rd NE6 56 C7
Millfield Bedlington NE22 16 A7
Seaton Sluice NE26 24 D5
Millfield Ave NE3 37 E3
Millfield Cl
Chester le S DH2 88 A1
Newburn NE15 52 F7
Millfield Ct
Bedlington NE22 16 A8
Hexham NE46 44 F5
Seaton Sluice NE26 24 D5
Whickham NE16 69 C7
Millfield E NE22 16 A7
Millfield Gdns Blyth NE24 12 D1
Gateshead NE10 71 C8
Hexham NE46 44 F5
Tynemouth NE30 42 C8
Millfield Gr NE30 42 C8
Millfield La NE15 52 F8
Millfield N NE22 16 A8
Millfield Rd
Riding Mill NE44 62 F7
Whickham NE16 69 B6
Millfield S NE22 16 A7
Millfield Sta SR4 102 B3
Millfield Terr
Hexham NE46 44 F5
Whitburn SR6 60 F2
Millfield W NE22 16 A8
Millford NE10 72 B6
Millford Ct NE10 72 B6
Millgrove View NE3 37 F3
Milling Ct NE8 100 C2
Millne Ct NE22 10 F1
Millom Pl NE9 71 B4
Mills Gdns NE28 40 B3
Millside NE61 8 F8
Millthorp Cl SR2 87 A1
Millview Dr NE30 42 C8
Millway Gateshead NE9 71 A7
Seaton Sluice NE26 24 D5
Millway Gr NE26 24 D5
Milne Way NE3 37 F6
Milner Cres NE21 53 A1
Milner St NE33 42 E2
Milrig Cl SR3 91 E5
Milsted Cl SR3 91 D5
Milsted Ct NE15 36 B2
Milton Ave Hebburn NE31 57 E6
Houghton-le-S DH5 94 F7
Milton Cl NE2 99 C3
Milton Gn NE2 99 C3
Milton Gr Ashington NE63 6 F3
North Shields NE29 41 F6
Prudhoe NE42 50 B2
Milton Pl
Newcastle-u-T NE2 99 C3
North Shields NE29 41 F6
[22] Springwell NE9 71 F1
Milton Rd NE16 69 B8
Milton Sq NE8 56 A2
Milton St Greenside NE40 51 E1
Jarrow NE32 58 B8
[1] South Shields NE33 59 D8
Sunderland SR4 102 A3
Milton Terr NE29 41 F6
Milvain Ave NE4 54 E6
Milvain Cl NE8 101 C1
Milvain St NE8 101 C1
Milverton Ct NE3 37 C6
Mimosa Dr NE31 57 E3
Mimosa Pl NE4 54 D8
Minden St NE1 99 B1
Mindrum Terr
Newcastle-u-T NE6 56 F5
North Shields NE29 41 D4
Mindrum Way NE25 23 D3
Minehead Gdns [9] SR3 92 A8
Miner's Cotts NE16 69 C6
Miners Cotts NE15 54 A7
Minerva Cl NE5 36 C4
Mingarry DH3 82 E2
Mingary Cl DH5 94 C4
Minorca Cl SR1 103 C2
Minorca Pl NE3 37 F3
Minskip Cl SR3 91 E5
Minster Ct NE8 101 C3
Minster Gr NE15 36 B3
Minster Par NE32 58 C7
Minting Pl NE23 22 A5
Minton Ct NE29 41 F4
Minton La NE29 41 F4
Minton Sq [4] SR4 85 E7
Mirk La NE8 101 B4
Mirlaw Rd NE23 21 F5
Mistletoe Rd NE2 38 E1
Mitcham Cres NE7 39 B4
Mitchell Ave
Newcastle-u-T NE2 38 E2
Whitley Bay NE25 31 D4
Mitchell Dr NE63 7 B3
Mitchell Gdns NE34 59 F7
Mitchell St Birtley DH3 82 C4
Crawcrook NE40 51 E3
Newcastle-u-T NE6 57 B5
Mitchell Terr DH9 79 B2
Mitchell's Bldgs NE9 72 A1
Mitford Ave Blyth NE24 17 C6
Pegswood NE61 4 E4
Seaton Delaval NE25 23 C3
Mitford Cl
Chester le S DH3 88 D8
Washington NE38 83 B4
Mitford Dr Ashington NE63 6 D2
Newcastle-u-T NE5 36 E3
Mitford Dr *continued*
Sherburn DH6 96 A2
Mitford Gdns
Dunston NE11 70 A5
Stakeford NE62 10 F8
Wallsend NE28 40 F5
Wideopen NE13 28 C6
Mitford Pl NE3 38 A6
Mitford Rd Morpeth NE61 3 E1
South Shields NE34 59 E6
Mitford St
North Shields NE28 41 C2
Sunderland SR6 75 E4
Mitford Terr NE32 58 B2
Mitford Way NE13 27 B7
Mithras Gdns NE15 34 E2
Mitre Ind Est NE33 59 B7
Mitre Pl NE33 59 B7
Moat Gdns NE10 72 C8
Mobray First Sch NE62 10 F7
Modder St NE6 56 F3
Model Dwellings [1]
NE38 83 E4
Model Terr DH4 90 A8
Modigars La NE43 64 F4
Moffat Ave NE32 58 E4
Moffat Cl NE29 41 C8
Moine Gdns SR6 75 E3
Moir Terr SR2 93 A6
Molesdon Cl NE30 32 A1
Molineux Cl [6] NE6 56 B6
Molineux Ct [8] NE6 56 B6
Molineux St NE6 56 B6
Mollyfair Cl NE40 52 A4
Monarch Rd NE4 100 A2
Monarch Terr NE21 53 C2
Monarch Way SR3 91 C5
Monastery Ct [11] NE32 58 B7
Monday Cres NE4 98 B2
Monday Pl NE4 98 B2
Monk Ct NE8 101 C2
Monk St
Newcastle-u-T NE1 98 C1
Sunderland SR6 75 D1
Monk's Terr NE46 45 D4
Monkchester Gn NE6 56 E5
Monkchester Rd NE6 56 E4
Monkdale Ave NE24 17 A6
Monkhouse Ave NE30 32 A1
Monkhouse Prim Sch
NE30 32 B1
Monkridge
Newcastle-u-T NE15 36 B2
Whitley Bay NE26 31 E7
Monkridge Ct NE3 38 E4
Monkridge Gdns NE11 70 A7
Monks Ave NE25 31 D3
Monks Mdws NE46 45 D4
Monks Park Way NE12 39 A6
Monks Rd NE25 31 C3
Monks Ridge NE61 8 D7
Monks Way NE30 32 C1
Monks Wood NE29 41 F8
Monkseaton Com High Sch
NE25 31 E2
Monkseaton Dr NE25,
NE26 31 E6
Monkseaton Mid Sch
NE25 31 E4
Monkseaton Rd NE25 31 B5
Monkseaton Sta NE25 31 F5
Monkseaton Terr NE63 6 E1
Monksfeld NE10 71 E7
Monksfield Cl [6] SR3 91 F5
Monkside
Cramlington NE23 21 F5
Newcastle-u-T NE6 56 D8
Monkside Cl NE38 83 A2
Monkstone Ave NE30 42 C8
Monkstone Cl NE30 42 C8
Monkstone Cres NE30 32 C1
Monkstone Grange NE30 32 B1
Monksway NE32 58 E6
Monkswood Sq SR3 92 B6
Monkton NE10 71 F6
Monkton Ave NE34 59 A4
Monkton Bsns Pk NE31 57 F2
Monkton Bsns Pk S NE10 57 F1
Monkton Hall NE32 57 F4
Monkton Hall Hospl
NE31 57 F4
Monkton Inf Sch NE34 59 A3
Monkton Jun Sch NE34 58 F4
Monkton La Hebburn NE32 57 F4
Jarrow NE31,NE32 57 F2
Monkton Rd NE32 58 B7
Monkton Terr NE32 58 C6
Monkwearmouth Hospl
SR5 75 C2
Monkwearmouth Sch
SR6 75 C5
Monkwearmouth Station
Mus* SR5 103 A4
Monmouth Gdns NE28 41 A4
Monroe Pl NE5 37 D2
Mons Ave NE31 57 E6
Mons Cres DH4 90 C6
Montagu Ave NE3 38 A2
Montagu Ct NE3 38 A2
Montagu Prim Sch NE5 37 E2
Montague Ct NE9 70 F8
Montague St
Newcastle-u-T NE15 53 D6
Sunderland SR6 75 D3
Monterey Silksworth SR3 91 E5
Washington NE37 72 D1
Montford Cl SR3 91 D5
Montpellier Pl NE3 37 F3
Montpellier Terr SR2 86 E3
Montrose Cl NE25 23 D6
Montrose Cres NE9 71 B7
Montrose Dr NE10 72 C7
Montrose Gdns
Morpeth NE61 8 F7
Sunderland SR3 86 A3
Monument Mall Sh Ctr
NE1 99 A1
Monument Sta NE1 99 A1
Monument Terr
[11] Birtley DH3 82 C4
Penshaw DH4 90 A8
Monument View DH4 90 B8
Moonfield NE46 45 B4
Moor Cl Sunderland SR1 103 C3
Tynemouth NE29 41 C8
Moor Cres NE3 38 C3
Moor Crest Terr [2] NE29 41 F8
Moor Croft NE64 7 E5
Moor Ct Bournmoor DH4 89 E3
Newcastle-u-T NE3 38 B2
Whitburn SR6 75 E8
Moor Edge Prim Sch
NE12 29 C3
Moor Edge Rd NE27 30 E4
Moor Gdns NE29 41 C8
Moor Grange NE42 50 D1
Moor Ho NE4 98 B2
Moor La Cleadon SR6 75 A7
Newcastle-u-T NE5 37 D4
Ponteland NE20 25 C4
South Shields NE34 59 E6
Stannington NE61 14 C6
Whitburn SR6 75 D8
Moor La E NE34 59 F7
Moor Park Ct NE29 41 C7
Moor Park Rd NE29 41 C7
Moor Pl NE3 38 C3
Moor Rd NE42 65 E7
Moor Rd N NE3 38 D4
Moor Rd S NE2,NE3 38 D3
Moor St SR1 103 B3
Moor Terr SR1 103 C3
Moor View
Crawcrook NE40 52 A4
High Pittington DH6 96 D4
Killingworth NE12 29 C4
Newbiggin-by-t-S NE64 7 E5
Whitburn SR6 75 E8
Moor View Cl NE61 4 E3
Moor View Wlk NE12 29 C4
Moorcroft Cl NE15 53 D7
Moorcroft Rd NE15 53 E6
Moordale Ave NE24 17 A6
Moore Ave Dunston NE11 69 F8
South Shields NE34 59 F6
Moore Cres DH3 82 C6
Moore Cres N DH5 94 E7
Moore Cres S DH5 94 E7
Moore Ct NE15 52 B7
Moore St NE8 56 A1
Moorfield NE2 38 D3
Moorfield Gdns SR6 75 A8
Moorfields NE61 9 A6
Moorfoot Ave DH2 88 C2
Moorfoot Gdns NE11 70 A7
Moorhead NE5 37 E1
Moorhead Mews NE5 37 E1
Moorhouse Cl NE34 59 D5
Moorhouse Est NE63 6 F3
Moorhouse Gdns DH5 95 B2
Moorhouse La NE63 6 F3
Moorhouses Rd NE29 41 C7
Moorings The [8] NE6 56 C4
Moorland Ave NE22 11 E3
Moorland Cotts [6] NE22 11 D3
Moorland Cres
Bedlington NE22 11 E3
Newcastle-u-T NE6 56 E7
Moorland Ct NE22 11 E3
Moorland Dr NE22 11 E3
Moorland Ho NE5 37 C2
Moorland View NE17 77 B8
Moorland Villas NE22 11 E3
Moorland Way NE23 15 E1
Moorlands Dipton DH9 78 E1
Hedworth NE32 58 D1
Prudhoe NE42 50 E1
Moormill NE11 81 D6
Moormill La NE11 81 E6
Moors Cl DH4 94 B8
Moorsburn Dr DH4 90 C1
Moorsfield DH4 94 B8
Moorside Hedworth NE32 58 C1
Longbenton NE12 29 B2
Washington NE37 83 B7
Moorside Com Prim Sch
NE4 98 A2
Moorside Ct NE5 37 E1
Moorside N NE4 54 F8
Moorside Pl NE4 54 F8
Moorside Rd SR3 91 D5
Moorside S NE4 54 F7
Moorsley Rd DH5 94 F2
Moorvale La NE5 37 E2
Moorview Cres NE5 37 E2
Moorway NE37 83 B6
Moorway Dr NE15 53 E7
Moraine Cres NE17 77 B6
Moralee Cl NE7 39 D3
Moran St SR6 75 D4
Moray Cl DH3 82 D1
Moray St SR6 75 D3
Morcott Gdns NE29 41 F4

Morden St NE1 ....99 A2
Mordey Cl SR2 ....103 B1
Morecambe Par NE31 ....58 A2
Moreland Rd NE14 ....59 D3
Moreland St SR6 ....75 D2
Moresby Rd NE23 ....16 C2
Morgan Bsns Ctr NE12 ...29 B5
Morgan St SR5 ....75 B2
Morgans Way NE21 ......53 A2
Morgy Hill E **3** NE40 ...51 F3
Morgy Hill W **2** NE40 ..51 F3
Morinda Cl DH4 ....89 F5
Morland Ave NE38 ....83 E4
Morland Gdns NE9 ......71 B7
Morley Ave NE10 ....57 B2
Morley Ct **10** NE6 ....56 C7
Morley Hill NE5 ....53 F8
Morley Pl NE27 ....30 F4
Morley Terr
  Fence Houses DH4 ......90 A1
  6 Gateshead NE10 ....71 D8
Morningside NE38 ....88 E8
Morningside Ct **5** DH3 ..88 C4
Mornington Ave NE3 .....37 F3
Morpeth All Saints CE Fst
  Sch NE61 ....3 E2
Morpeth Ave Jarrow NE32 .58 B3
  Pegswood NE61 ....4 E4
  South Shields NE34 ....59 E7
  Wideopen NE13 ....28 C7
Morpeth Chantry Bagpipe
  Mus* NE61 ....9 A8
Morpeth Chantry Mid Sch
  NE61 ....3 E1
Morpeth Cl
  Guide Post NE62 ....10 E7
  Washington NE38 ......83 A4
Morpeth Clock Twr*
  NE61 ....8 F8
Morpeth Collingwood Sch
  NE61 ....9 B7
Morpeth Cottage Hospl
  NE61 ....8 F6
Morpeth Ct NE61 ....9 A8
Morpeth Dr SR3 ....91 D6
Morpeth Fst Sch NE61 ...9 A8
Morpeth Newminster Mid
  Sch NE61 ....3 E1
Morpeth Rd Ashington NE63 .5 F4
  Guide Post NE62 ....10 E7
Morpeth Road Fst Sch
  NE24 ....17 D8
Morpeth St NE2 ....98 B4
Morpeth Sta NE61 ....9 A7
Morpeth Stobhillgate Fst Sch
  NE61 ....9 B7
Morpeth Terr NE29 ......41 D4
Morris Ave NE34 ....59 B3
Morris Cres NE35 ....74 A8
Morris Gdns NE9 ....29 B8
Morris Rd NE10 ....72 B8
Morris Rd NE16 ....69 B8
Morris St Birtley DH3 ....82 C4
  Gateshead NE8 ....70 C8
  Washington NE37 ......83 C8
Morrison Rd NE61 ....4 A1
Morrison St NE8 ....100 C2
Morriss Terr DH5 ....94 F7
Morrit Ct NE7 ....39 C5
Morston Dr NE15 ....53 E6
Mortimer Ave
  Newcastle-u-T NE6 .....36 F3
  North Shields NE29 ....41 D6
Mortimer Chase NE23 ...16 C3
Mortimer Comp Sch
  NE33 ....59 D7
Mortimer Prim Sch NE34 .59 D7
Mortimer Rd NE33,NE34 .59 D7
Mortimer St SR4 ....85 F7
Mortimer Terr
  Pegswood NE61 ....4 F4
  Seaton Delaval NE25 ...23 E2
Morton Cl NE38 ....83 D4
Morton Cres
  Great Lumley DH4 ......89 F1
  Woolsington NE5 ......54 B6
Morton Grange Terr DH4 .89 E1
Morton St
  Newcastle-u-T NE6 .....56 D6
  1 South Shields NE33 .42 D4
Morton Wlk **6** NE33 ...42 D4
Morval Cl SR3 ....91 D5
Morven Dr NE10 ....57 B1
Morven Lea NE21 ....53 B2
Morven Pl NE63 ....6 B4
Morven Terr NE63 ....6 B4
Morwick Cl NE23 ....22 A5
Morwick Pl **3** NE5 ....37 D1
Morwick Rd NE29 ....41 D8
Moss Bank NE9 ....71 B3
Moss Cl NE15 ....53 C8
Moss Cres NE40 ....52 A4
Moss Side NE9 ....71 C3
Mosspool NE21 ....53 A2
Mostyn Gn NE3 ....37 F5
Motcombe Way NE26 ...16 C2
Moulton Ct NE5 ....37 C2
Moulton Pl NE5 ....37 C2
Mount Cl
  Killingworth NE12 ......29 D4
  Sunderland SR4 ....85 B6
  Whitley Bay NE25 .....31 D3
Mount Ct DH3 ....82 D5
Mount Gr Dunston NE11 ..69 F7

Mount Gr continued
  Sunderland SR4 ....86 A4
Mount La NE9 ....82 E8
Mount Lonnen NE9 ......82 E8
Mount Pleasant
  Birtley DH3 ....82 C5
  6 Blaydon NE21 ......53 B1
  Dipton DH9 ....78 E1
  Houghton-le-S DH5 ....94 F8
  10 Newcastle-u-T NE6 .56 C6
  3 Sunderland SR5 ....75 A1
Mount Pleasant Bglws **4**
  DH3 ....79 B2
Mount Pleasant Ct NE15 .35 D2
Mount Pleasant Gdns
  NE8 ....56 A1
Mount Rd Birtley DH3 ...82 D5
  Gateshead NE9 ....82 E8
  Sunderland SR4 ....85 F4
Mount Terr NE33 ....42 C2
Mount The Ryton NE40 ...52 C5
  Sunderland SR4 ....85 C2
Mount View
  7 Crawcrook NE40 ...51 F3
  Whickham NE16 ....69 B8
Mount View Terr NE43 ...64 A7
Mountbatten Ave NE31 ..57 E4
Mountfield Gdns NE3 ....37 F5
Mountfield Prim Sch
  NE3 ....37 E5
Mountford Rd NE25 .....23 D7
Mountside Gdns NE11 ...69 F7
Mourne Gdns NE11 .....70 A6
Mowbray Cl SR2 ....103 A1
Mowbray Mews NE33 ...42 E2
Mowbray Rd
  Longbenton NE12 ......39 E8
  North Shields NE29 ....41 D6
  South Shields NE33 ....42 E1
  Sunderland SR2 ......103 B1
Mowbray St NE6 ....56 A7
Mowbray Terr NE62 ....10 F7
Mowden Hall (Prep Sch)
  NE43 ....48 E7
Moyle Terr NE16 ....79 A4
Mozart St NE33 ....42 D2
Muirfield
  South Shields NE33 ....42 F1
  Whitley Bay NE25 .....31 D5
Muirfield Dr
  Gateshead NE10 ....71 E6
  Washington NE37 ......72 C2
Muirfield Rd NE7 ....39 C5
Mulben Cl NE4 ....54 E4
Mulberry Cl NE24 ......17 D4
Mulberry Gdns NE10 ...56 C2
Mulberry Gr NE11 ......79 A4
Mulberry Pk NE9 ....70 F5
Mulberry Pl NE4 ....100 B3
Mulberry St NE10 ......56 C1
Mulcaster Gdns NE28 ...40 A3
Mulgrave Dr SR6 ....75 E1
Mulgrave Terr NE8 .....101 B3
Mulgrave Villas NE8 ....101 B2
Mull Gr NE32 ....58 E3
Mullen Dr NE40 ....52 D4
Mullen Gdns NE28 .....40 A4
Mullen Rd NE28 ....40 B4
Mundella Terr NE6 .....56 B7
Mundle Ave NE21 ......68 C6
Mundles La NE36 ....74 D6
Municipal Terr NE38 ...83 D6
Munslow Rd SR3 ....91 D8
Murphy Gr SR2 ....92 E7
Murray Ave DH4 ....90 A1
Murray Ct DH2 ....88 B3
Murray Gdns **1** NE11 ..70 A7
Murray Pl DH2 ....88 C3
Murray St NE21 ....53 C3
Murrayfield NE23 ......22 F2
Murrayfield Rd NE5 ....37 D3
Murston Ave NE23 .....16 C2
Murton La
  Easington Lane DH5 ...95 D1
  Tynemouth NE27,NE29 ..31 B2
Murton St SR1 ....103 B2
Muscott Gr NE15 ....54 A6
Musgrave Prim Sch NE9 .70 F6
Musgrave Rd
  Gateshead NE10 ....57 A1
  Newcastle-u-T NE6 ....56 B6
  Washington NE38 ......83 D6
Muswell Hill NE15 .....54 A5
Mutual St NE28 ....40 B1
Mylord Cres NE12 .....29 B5
Myre Hall **8** DH5 ....94 E8
Myrella Cres SR2 ......86 C2
Myreside Pl NE12 ......39 E7
Myrtle Ave Dunston NE11 .69 F8
  Whitburn SR6 ....62 E1
Myrtle Cres NE12 ....29 D1
Myrtle Gr Burnopfield NE16 .78 F6
  Gateshead NE11 ......70 F5
  Newcastle-u-T NE2 ....38 E2
  South Shields NE34 ...59 F4
  Wallsend NE28 ....40 D1
Myrtle Rd NE21 ....53 C1
Myrtle St NE63 ....6 D4
Myrtles DH2 ....88 B5

National Glass Ctr (Mus)*
  SR6 ....103 B4
Natley Ave NE36 ....74 E7
Navan Cl NE62 ....11 D8
Navenby Cl
  Cramlington NE23 .....38 D8
  Seaham SR7 ....93 A1
Naworth Ave NE30 .....32 A1
Naworth Dr NE5 ....36 E3
Naworth Terr NE34 ....58 D4
Nawton Ave NE5 ....75 C2
Nayland Rd NE23 ......22 A7
Naylor Ave NE21 ......53 A3
Naylor Bldgs NE21 ....68 C6
Naylor Ct NE21 ....53 E4
Naylor Pl NE26 ....24 B7
Neale St Prudhoe NE42 ..50 D3
  Sunderland SR6 ....75 E3
  Tantobie DH9 ....79 B2
Neale Terr **1** DH3 ....82 C4
Nearlane Cl NE13 ......28 C8
Neasdon Cres NE30 ....32 B1
Neasham Rd NE7 ....93 A1
Nedderton Cl NE5 ......36 B4
Needham Pl NE23 ......22 B7
Neil St DH5 ....95 C1
Neill Dr NE16 ....69 B2
Neilson Rd NE10 ....56 B3
Nellie Gormley Ho NE12 .29 B2
Nelson Ave
  Cramlington NE23 .....21 F8
  Newcastle-u-T NE3 ....38 A5
  South Shields NE33 ...42 E3
Nelson Cl NE63 ....6 C2
Nelson Cres NE29 .....41 D2
Nelson Dr NE23 ....15 F1
Nelson Ho **4** NE30 ...42 D7
Nelson Ind Est NE23 ...15 E2
Nelson Park Ind Est
  NE23 ....15 E1
Nelson Park Networkctr
  NE23 ....15 D1
Nelson Rd
  Cramlington NE23 .....15 D1
  Earsdon NE25 ....31 B5
  Newcastle-u-T NE7 ....57 B4
  Stakeford NE62 ....11 A7
Nelson St Chester le S DH3 .88 C2
  Dunston NE11 ....54 F2
  Gateshead NE8 ....101 C3
  Greenside NE40 ....51 F1
  Hetton le H DH5 ....95 A3
  Newcastle-u-T NE1 ....99 A1
  11 South Shields NE33 .42 C3
  Sunderland SR2 ....92 F7
  Washington NE38 .....83 E4
Nelson Terr
  Chopwell NE17 ....66 B1
  North Shields NE29 ...41 D3
  Sherburn DH6 ....96 A1
Nelson Way NE23 ......15 E2
Nene Ct **11** NE37 ....83 E8
Nent Gr NE46 ....45 C4
Neptune Rd
  Newcastle-u-T,Denton Burn
  NE15 ....53 E7
  Newcastle-u-T,Lemington
  NE15 ....53 D6
  Wallsend NE28 ....57 B8
Nesburn Rd SR4 ....102 A1
Nesham Pl DH5 ....94 F8
Nesham Terr SR1 ......103 C3
Ness Ct NE21 ....53 A2
Nest Rd NE10 ....56 D8
Nether Farm Rd NE10 ..56 F1
Nether Riggs NE22 ....15 F8
Netherburn Rd SR5 ....75 C2
Netherby Dr NE5 ......54 C8
Netherdale NE22 ......10 D1
Netherton NE12 ....29 C4
Netherton Ave NE29 ...41 D7
Netherton Gdns NE13 ..28 B6
Netherton Gr NE29 ....41 D7
Netherton La NE22 ....10 C1
Netherwitton Way NE3 ..28 B1
Nettleham Rd SR5 .....75 C2
Nettles La SR3 ....92 B6
Nevill Rd NE43 ....64 D7
Neville Cres DH3 ......82 C6
Neville Ct NE37 ....83 F8
Neville Rd
  Newcastle-u-T NE15 ...53 E7
  Sunderland SR4 ....85 F7
Neville Sq NE61 ....2 A2
Neville St NE1 ....101 A4
Neville's Cross Rd NE31 .57 F5
Nevinson Ave NE34 ....59 E3

Nevis Cl NE26 ....31 E8
Nevis Ct NE26 ....31 E8
Nevis Gr NE36 ....74 B7
Nevis Way NE26 ....31 E8
New Bridge St NE1 .....99 C1
New Bridge St W NE1,
  NE99 ....99 B2
New Cotts NE61 ....3 A1
New Delaval Fst Sch
  NE24 ....17 B4
New Durham Rd SR2 ..102 C2
New Front St DH9 ......79 D1
New George St NE33 ...42 C1
New Green St NE33 ....42 C1
New Hartley Fst Sch
  NE25 ....23 D6
New Herrington Ind Est
  DH4 ....90 D6
New Horton Grange Cotts
  NE13 ....19 F4
New King St NE64 ......7 F5
New Mills NE4 ....98 B2
New Mills Ho NE4 .....98 B2
New Moor Cl NE63 .....5 F4
New Penshaw Prim Sch
  DH4 ....90 B8
New Phoenix Yd **1** NE61 .9 A8
New Quay NE29 ....42 B4
New Queen St NE64 ....7 E8
New Rainton St DH4 ...90 E8
New Rd Burnopfield NE16 .79 B7
  Dunston NE11 ....68 D8
  Gateshead NE10 ......72 C5
  Washington NE38 .....89 C8
  West Boldon NE35 ....74 B8
New Ridley Rd NE43 ...64 D5
New Sandridge NE64 ...7 F5
New Seaham Prim Sch
  SR7 ....92 F1
New Silksworth Inf Sch
  SR3 ....92 B7
New Silksworth Jun Sch
  SR3 ....92 B7
New South Terr DH3 ...82 D4
New St Sherburn DH6 ..96 A6
  5 Sunderland SR4 ....85 A6
New York Ind Pk NE27 ..41 A8
New York Prim Sch
  NE29 ....41 C8
New York Rd
  Shiremoor NE27 ....30 E2
  Tynemouth NE29 .....31 B1
New York Way NE27 ...41 A8
Newark Cl NE22 ....10 D1
Newark Cres SR7 ......93 A1
Newark Dr SR7 ....75 F8
Newark Sq NE29 ......41 F4
Newarth Cl NE15 ......53 E7
Newbank Wlk NE21 ....53 A1
Newbiggin Hall Ctr NE5 .37 A5
Newbiggin La NE5 .....36 F4
Newbiggin Mid Sch NE64 .7 C4
Newbiggin Rd NE23 ....6 E1
Newbiggin-by-the-Sea
  Moorside Fst Sch NE64 .7 D5
Newbold Ave SR5 .....75 C2
Newbold St NE6 ....56 A2
Newbottle Prim Sch DH4 .90 D3
Newbottle St DH4 .....90 E1
Newbridge Ave SR5 ...75 C2
Newbridge Bank DH3 ..88 F5
Newbrough Cres NE2 ..38 E2
Newburgh Ave NE25 ...23 D2
Newburn Ave SR5 .....75 C2
Newburn Bridge Rd
  NE15,NE21 ....52 E6
Newburn Cres DH4 ....90 D1
Newburn Hall Motor Mus*
  NE15 ....53 C6
Newburn Ind Est NE21 ..52 F5
Newburn Lane End NE15 .35 D2
Newburn Manor Fst Sch
  NE15 ....52 F8
Newburn Rd
  Newburn NE15 ....53 C6
  Throckley NE15 ....35 E1
Newbury Cl NE12 ......29 D4
Newbury Ave NE8 .....70 D8
Newbury Cl NE15 .....53 C6
Newbury St
  South Shields NE33 ...59 D7
  Sunderland SR5 ....75 D3
Newby Cl NE22 ....11 C3
Newby La DH6 ....96 C5
Newby Pl NE9 ....71 B4
Newcastle Arena NE4 ..100 C3
Newcastle Bank NE9 ...82 A7
Newcastle Bsns Pk NE4 .100 A3
Newcastle Coll Trevelyan
  Bldg NE4 ....100 B4
Newcastle Discovery Mus*
  NE1 ....100 C4
Newcastle General Hospl
  NE4 ....54 F6
Newcastle International
  Airport NE13 ....26 D3
Newcastle Nuffield Hospl The
  NE2 ....99 B4
Newcastle Rd Birtley DH3 .82 C6
  Blyth NE24 ....17 C4
  Chester le S DH3 .....88 C5
  Corbridge NE45 ......47 B5
  Sunderland SR5 ....75 C3
  West Boldon NE10,NE36 .73 C2

Newcastle Rd/Leam La
  NE34 ....58 F5
Newcastle St NE29 ....42 A5
Newcastle Terr **6** NE30 .42 D7
Newcastle Trade Ctr
  NE4 ....100 B3
Newcastle Upon Tyne Central
  Sta NE1 ....101 A4
Newdene Wlk NE15 ....53 D7
Newfield Wlk NE16 ....69 A6
Newgate Sh Ctr NE1 ...99 A1
Newgate St Morpeth NE61 .3 F1
  Newcastle-u-T NE1 ....99 A1
Newham Ave NE13 ....28 A4
Newhaven Ave SR5 ....75 C2
Newington Cr
  Sunderland SR5 ....75 C1
  Washington NE37 .....83 C8
Newington Dr NE29 ...31 F1
Newington Rd NE6 .....56 A8
Newker Prim Sch DH2 ..88 B2
Newland Ct NE34 .....59 C5
Newlands NE30 ....32 A2
Newlands Ave Blyth NE24 .17 D5
  Newcastle-u-T NE3 ....38 D3
  Sunderland SR3 ....86 B3
  Whitley Bay NE25 ....31 D3
Newlands Pl NE24 .....17 D5
Newlands Rd Blyth NE24 .17 D5
  Newcastle-u-T NE2 ....38 D3
Newlands Rd W SR7 ...93 A1
Newlands St NE3 ......38 D4
Newlyn Cres NE29 ....41 E5
Newlyn Dr
  Cramlington NE23 ....22 B8
  Jarrow NE32 ....58 D6
Newlyn Rd NE3 ....37 E5
Newman St **10** NE8 ..71 A8
Newman Terr NE8 .....71 A8
Newman's Way **2** NE46 .44 E4
Newmarch St NE32 ....58 D1
Newmarket Wlk **1** NE33 .42 D1
Newmin Way NE16 ....68 F5
Newminster Cl DH4 ....90 B2
Newminster Rd NE4 ...54 D7
Newport Gr **6** SR3 ...92 A8
Newquay Gdns **4** NE9 .71 A2
Newriggs NE38 ....83 E2
Newsham Cl NE15 .....36 B4
Newsham Fst Sch NE24 .17 C5
Newstead Ct NE38 ....83 C5
Newstead Rd DH4 .....90 C2
Newstead Sq SR3 .....92 A6
Newsteads Cl NE25 ...31 D5
Newsteads Dr NE25 ...31 D5
Newton Ave
  Tynemouth NE30 ......32 B3
  Wallsend NE28 ....40 F3
Newton Cl NE15 ......53 E7
Newton Gr NE34 ......59 A5
Newton Ho NE4 ....98 B2
Newton Pl NE7 ....39 B2
Newton St Dunston NE11 .54 F2
  Gateshead NE8 ....70 D8
Newton Terr NE43 ....49 E1
Nichol Ct NE4 ....54 D5
Nichol St NE4 ....54 D5
Nicholas Ave SR6 .....75 F8
Nicholas St DH5 ....95 B5
Nicholson Cl SR1 .....103 B2
Nicholson Terr NE12 ..29 E1
Nidderdale Ave DH5 ..94 F2
Nidderdale Cl NE24 ...17 A8
Nidsdale Ave NE6 .....57 A7
Nightingale Cl SR4 ...85 B4
Nile Cl NE15 ....53 C8
Nile Ct SR1 ....56 A1
Nile St North Shields NE29 .42 B5
  South Shields NE33 ...42 B3
  Sunderland SR1 ......103 B3
Nilverton Ave SR2 ....86 D3
Nimbus Ct **15** SR3 ..92 A6
Nine Lands DH4 ....94 C8
Ninth Ave NE11 ....17 D6
  Chester le S DH2 .....88 B3
  Gateshead NE11 ......70 D3
  Morpeth NE61 ....3 A3
  Newcastle-u-T NE6 ....56 C8
Ninth Ave E NE11 .....70 D3
Ninth Row NE63 ......6 B4
Nissan Way SR5 ......84 B2
Nithdale Cl NE16 .....57 B8
Nixon St NE8 ....70 C8
Nixon Terr NE24 ......17 F6
Noble Gdns NE34 .....58 F4
Noble St
  8 Gateshead NE10 ..56 D2
  Newcastle-u-T NE4 ...54 F3
  Sunderland SR2 ......103 C2
Noble Terr
  18 Morpeth NE61 ....9 A8
  Sunderland SR2 ......103 C2
Noble's Bank Rd SR2 ..103 C2
Noel Ave NE21 ....68 C6
Noel Terr NE21 ....68 D6
Noirmont Way SR3 ...91 E6
Nolan Hall NE32 ......58 B6
Nook The
  North Shields NE29 ...41 F5
  Whitley Bay NE25 ....31 F3
Nookside SR4 ....85 C6
Nookside Ct SR4 ......85 C6
Nora St South Shields NE34 .59 C5
  Sunderland SR4 ......85 F6
Norbury Gr NE6 ......56 D7
Nordale Ho NE34 .....17 A8

Nafferton Pl NE5 ....54 C8

Nordale Way NE24 ... 17 A8
Norfolk Ave Birtley DH3 ... 82 D1
New Silksworth SR3 ... 91 F8
Norfolk Cl Ashington NE63 ... 6 A4
Seaham SR7 ... 93 A1
Norfolk Ct 10 NE30 ... 42 B6
Norfolk Dr NE37 ... 72 D2
Norfolk Gdns NE28 ... 40 E4
Norfolk Mews 11 NE30 ... 42 A6
Norfolk Pl DH3 ... 82 D1
Norfolk Rd Gateshead NE8 ... 56 A4
South Shields NE34 ... 60 C7
Norfolk Sq 19 NE6 ... 56 B6
Norfolk St Hetton le H DH5 ... 94 F4
North Shields NE30 ... 42 B5
Sunderland SR1 ... 103 A3
Norfolk Way NE15 ... 53 E7
Norham Ave N NE34 ... 60 A8
Norham Ave S NE34 ... 60 A8
Norham Cl Blyth NE24 ... 17 C7
Brunswick Village NE13 ... 28 A5
Norham Com Tech Coll
NE29 ... 41 D5
Norham Ct
Bournmoor DH4 ... 89 D1
Washington NE38 ... 83 B4
Norham Dr Morpeth NE61 ... 9 B5
Newcastle-u-T NE5 ... 36 E3
Norham Gdns NE62 ... 6 A1
Norham Pl NE2 ... 38 E1
Norham Rd Ashington NE63 ... 6 D2
Newcastle-u-T NE3 ... 38 B6
North Shields NE29 ... 41 C5
Whitley Bay NE25,NE26 ... 31 F5
Norham Road N NE29 ... 41 B7
Norham Terr NE32 ... 58 B3
Norhurst NE16 ... 68 E5
Norland Rd NE15 ... 53 F6
Norley Ave SR5 ... 75 C2
Norma Cres NE26 ... 32 C4
Norman Ave SR3 ... 92 B7
Norman Rd NE39 ... 67 F1
Norman Terr
High Pittington DH6 ... 96 C5
Morpeth NE61 ... 9 A8
Wallsend NE28 ... 41 B2
Normanby Cl SR7 ... 93 A1
Normanby Ct SR6 ... 75 F1
Normandy Cres DH5 ... 94 F8
Normanton Terr NE4 ... 98 A1
Normount Ave 2 NE4 ... 54 E5
Normount Gdns NE4 ... 54 E6
Normount Rd NE4 ... 54 E5
North App DH2 ... 88 B4
North Ave Guide Post NE62 ... 10 E7
Longbenton NE12 ... 39 D6
Newcastle-u-T NE5 ... 36 F2
Newcastle-u-T,Gosforth
NE3 ... 38 C4
South Shields NE34 ... 59 F6
Washington NE37 ... 72 C1
North Balkwell Farm Ind Est
NE29 ... 41 B7
North Bank Ct 7 SR5 ... 75 B2
North Bridge St SR5 ... 103 A4
North Burns DH3 ... 88 C4
North Church St 2 NE30 ... 42 B6
North Cl
4 Newcastle-u-T NE6 ... 56 C7
Ryton NE40 ... 52 C5
South Shields NE34 ... 59 F6
North Cres NE38 ... 83 B1
North Croft NE12 ... 39 E7
North Cross St NE3 ... 38 C5
North Ct 5 NE32 ... 58 B7
North Dene DH3 ... 82 C7
North Dr Chester le S NE38 ... 88 E7
Cleadon SR6 ... 59 F1
Hebburn NE31 ... 57 C4
North Durham St SR1 ... 103 B3
North East Aircraft Mus*
SR5 ... 73 E3
North East Bus Mus*
NE10 ... 72 B6
North Eastern Ct NE16 ... 69 E8
North Farm NE22 ... 15 A8
North Farm Ave SR4 ... 85 B2
North Farm Rd NE31 ... 57 D5
North Fawdon Prim Sch
NE3 ... 37 F7
North Gr Ryton NE40 ... 52 D5
Sunderland SR6 ... 75 E3
North Grange NE20 ... 25 E8
North Guards SR6 ... 75 F8
North Hall Rd SR4 ... 85 D4
North Hylton Rd SR5 ... 74 E2
North Hylton Road Ind Est
SR5 ... 74 D2
North Jesmond Ave NE2 ... 38 E2
North King St NE30 ... 42 B6
North La East Boldon NE36 ... 74 C7
Hetton le H DH5 ... 95 E5
North Leech NE61 ... 3 D2
North Leigh DH9 ... 79 D1
North Lodge DH3 ... 88 D7
North Lodge Apartments 11
NE21 ... 53 B1
North Magdalene DH8 ... 77 B1
North Mason Lodge
NE13 ... 27 B8
North Mdws NE42 ... 50 B5
North Milburn St SR4 ... 102 B3
North Moor Ct SR3 ... 85 E1
North Moor La SR3 ... 91 E8
North Moor Rd SR3 ... 85 E1
North Par
Choppington NE62 ... 10 E6
Whitley Bay NE26 ... 32 B5
North Pl NE61 ... 3 E1
North Ravensworth St
SR4 ... 102 B3
North Rd
Boldon Colliery NE35 ... 58 E1
Boldon Colliery,New Town
NE35,NE36 ... 73 F7
Chester le S DH3 ... 88 C7
Dipton DH9 ... 78 E1
East Boldon NE36 ... 74 C7
Hetton le H DH5 ... 94 E4
Houghton-le-S DH5 ... 94 E4
Ponteland NE20 ... 25 E8
Seaham SR7 ... 93 D1
Slaley NE47 ... 62 A4
Tynemouth NE29 ... 42 A8
Wallsend NE28 ... 40 B2
North Ridge
Bedlington NE22 ... 10 D1
Bedlington NE22 ... 10 E1
Whitley Bay NE25 ... 31 C6
North Row NE42 ... 50 A2
North Sands Bsns Ctr
SR6 ... 103 B4
North Seaton Ind Est NE63 ... 6 F1
North Seaton Rd
Ashington NE63 ... 6 D2
Newbiggin-by-t-S NE64 ... 7 D3
North Shields Sta NE29 ... 42 A5
North Side NE8 ... 100 B2
North St Birtley DH3 ... 82 E3
Blaydon NE21 ... 53 A2
Cleadon SR6 ... 60 A1
East Rainton DH5 ... 94 D4
Jarrow NE32 ... 58 B7
New Silksworth SR3 ... 92 A8
Newbottle DH4 ... 90 D4
Newcastle-u-T NE1 ... 99 A2
South Shields NE33 ... 42 C3
5 Sunderland SR5 ... 75 C1
West Rainton DH4 ... 94 A2
North St E NE1 ... 99 B2
North Terr Chopwell NE17 ... 66 B2
Hexham NE46 ... 45 B4
11 New Silksworth SR3 ... 92 A8
Newcastle-u-T NE2 ... 98 C3
1 Shiremoor NE27 ... 30 E1
Wallsend NE28 ... 40 E2
North Tyne Ind Est NE12 ... 40 A8
North Tyneside Coll
NE28 ... 40 E5
North Tyneside General
Hospl NE29 ... 31 E1
North Tyneside Steam Rly*
NE28,NE29 ... 41 C5
North View Ashington NE63 ... 6 C4
7 Bedlington NE22 ... 11 D3
Bournmoor DH4 ... 89 E2
Cambois NE24 ... 12 C6
Crawcrook NE40 ... 51 E7
Dinnington NE13 ... 27 B7
Easington Lane DH5 ... 95 C1
Gateshead NE9 ... 71 B3
Haswell DH6 ... 97 E1
Hazlerigg NE13 ... 28 A4
High Spen NE39 ... 66 F3
Jarrow NE32 ... 58 A6
4 Longbenton NE12 ... 39 D8
Medomsley DH8 ... 77 B1
Mickley Square NE43 ... 49 E1
Newbiggin-by-t-S NE64 ... 7 D3
Newcastle-u-T NE6 ... 56 B7
Newcastle-u-T NE6 ... 56 C7
Ouston DH2 ... 81 F1
Rowlands Gill NE39 ... 67 C2
Ryton NE40 ... 52 A5
Sherburn Hill DH6 ... 96 D1
South Shields NE34 ... 59 F8
Stakeford NE62 ... 11 C8
Sunderland,Castletown SR5 ... 74 C1
Sunderland,Monkwearmouth
SR6 ... 75 D3
Sunderland,South Hylton
SR4 ... 85 B5
Tynemouth NE29 ... 41 F8
Wallsend NE28 ... 40 C2
Washington NE37 ... 83 D8
Whickham NE11 ... 69 A7
Whitley Bay NE30 ... 32 C4
North View Terr
Fence Houses DH4 ... 94 B8
Gateshead NE8 ... 56 C1
Prudhoe NE42 ... 50 B2
Stocksfield NE43 ... 64 C7
North View W NE39 ... 67 C2
North Villas NE23 ... 22 A1
North Walbottle Rd
Newcastle-u-T NE5 ... 36 B4
Walbottle NE15 ... 36 A2
North West Side NE8 ... 100 B2
North Wylam View NE42 ... 50 E4
Northbourne Ave NE61 ... 3 F2
Northbourne Ho NE9 ... 70 F5
Northbourne Rd NE31,
NE32 ... 58 A6
Northbourne St
Gateshead NE8 ... 70 F8
Newcastle-u-T NE4 ... 54 F4
Northburn Fst Sch NE23 ... 16 A1
Northcote NE16 ... 69 A5
Northcote Ave
Newcastle-u-T NE5 ... 36 C1
Sunderland SR1 ... 103 B2
Whitley Bay NE25 ... 31 D4
Northcote St
Newcastle-u-T NE4 ... 98 A1
8 South Shields NE33 ... 59 D8
Northcott Gdns NE23 ... 22 E1
Northern Counties Sch
NE2 ... 38 D1
Northern Terr NE23 ... 22 A1
Northern Way SR5 ... 75 A2
Northfield NE22 ... 12 B4
Northfield Cl NE16 ... 68 F5
Northfield Dr
Killingworth NE12 ... 29 B2
Sunderland SR4 ... 85 B2
Northfield Gdns NE34 ... 59 F8
Northfield Rd
Newcastle-u-T NE3 ... 38 B4
South Shields NE33 ... 42 F1
Northfields 23 NE6 ... 56 C7
Northfields Ho 22 NE6 ... 56 C7
Northgate NE12 ... 29 D4
Northgate & Prudhoe NHS
Trust Northgate Hospl
NE61 ... 3 D4
Northland Cl SR4 ... 85 B2
Northlands Blaydon NE21 ... 53 B1
Chester le S DH3 ... 88 C5
Tynemouth NE30 ... 32 B1
Northlands Rd NE61 ... 3 F2
Northlea NE15 ... 53 E8
Northmoor Rd NE6 ... 56 E8
Northolt Ave NE23 ... 22 B7
Northside DH3 ... 82 D6
Northside Pl NE25 ... 23 E2
Northumberland Aged
Mineworkers Homes
NE23 ... 22 D5
Northumberland Ave
Bedlington NE22 ... 10 E1
Longbenton NE12 ... 39 D7
Newbiggin-by-t-S NE64 ... 7 D4
Newcastle-u-T NE3 ... 38 A3
Wallsend NE28 ... 40 F2
Northumberland Cl NE63 ... 6 A4
Northumberland Coll
NE63 ... 6 E2
Northumberland Ct
Hebburn NE31 ... 57 D5
Prudhoe NE42 ... 50 E4
Northumberland Dock Rd
NE28 ... 41 C1
Northumberland Gdns
Newcastle-u-T NE5 ... 36 B3
Newcastle-u-T,Jesmond Vale
NE2 ... 56 A8
Northumberland Pl
Birtley DH3 ... 82 D1
Newcastle-u-T NE1 ... 99 A2
9 North Shields NE30 ... 42 A6
Northumberland Rd
Newcastle-u-T NE1,NE99 ... 99 B2
Newcastle-u-T,Lemington
NE15 ... 53 C6
Ryton NE40 ... 52 C6
Northumberland Sq
4 North Shields NE30 ... 42 B6
Whitley Bay NE26 ... 32 A5
Northumberland St
Gateshead NE8 ... 100 C1
Newcastle-u-T NE1 ... 99 A2
North Shields NE30 ... 42 C6
Wallsend NE28 ... 40 C2
Northumberland Terr
29 Newcastle-u-T NE6 ... 56 B6
Tynemouth NE30 ... 42 D7
Wallsend NE28 ... 40 F2
Northumberland Villas
NE28 ... 40 E2
Northumberland Way
Washington,Columbia NE37,
NE38 ... 83 F4
Washington,Usworth NE10,
NE37 ... 72 D3
Northumbria Ctr For Ent
NE63 ... 6 D5
Northumbria Lodge NE5 ... 37 E1
Northumbria Police
Headquarters NE20 ... 25 D8
Northumbria Univ, Coach
Lane Campus NE7 ... 39 C4
Northumbria Wlk
Newcastle-u-T NE5 ... 36 F1
Newcastle-u-T,East Denton
NE5 ... 37 A2
Northumbrian Rd NE23 ... 22 B6
Northumbrian Way
Killingworth NE12 ... 29 C2
North Shields NE29 ... 42 A3
Northway Gateshead NE9 ... 71 B7
Guide Post NE62 ... 10 F7
Throckley NE15 ... 35 D3
Northwood Ct SR5 ... 75 C2
Norton Ave SR7 ... 93 A1
Norton Cl 1 DH2 ... 88 A1
Norton Rd SR5 ... 75 A3
Norton Way NE15 ... 53 E6
Norway Ave SR4 ... 85 E4
Norwich Ave NE13 ... 28 B5
Norwich Cl NE63 ... 7 A2
Norwich Way
Cramlington NE23 ... 22 A7
Hedworth NE32 ... 58 B1
Norwood Ave
Newcastle-u-T,Brunton Park
NE3 ... 28 C1
Newcastle-u-T,Heaton NE6 ... 39 B1
Norwood Cres NE39 ... 67 F2
Norwood Ct
Gateshead NE9 ... 71 C2
Longbenton NE12 ... 39 D6
Norwood Gdns 4 NE9 ... 71 A8
Norwood Rd
Gateshead NE11 ... 70 B7
Norwood Rd *continued*
Newcastle-u-T NE15 ... 53 D8
Nottingham Ct NE22 ... 10 D2
November Ctyd NE8 ... 100 B2
Numbers Garth SR1 ... 103 B3
Nun St NE1 ... 99 A1
Nuneaton Way NE5 ... 36 B4
Nunn Gdns 12 NE16 ... 69 A7
Nunn St DH4 ... 90 A5
Nunnykirk Cl NE42 ... 50 A4
Nuns La Gateshead NE8 ... 101 C3
Newcastle-u-T NE1 ... 99 A1
Nuns Moor Cres NE4 ... 54 E7
Nuns Moor Rd NE4 ... 54 E7
Nunthorpe Ave SR2 ... 86 F1
Nunwick Gdns NE29 ... 41 C6
Nunwick Way NE7 ... 39 D4
Nursery Cl SR3 ... 86 A2
Nursery Ct NE17 ... 77 B6
Nursery Gdns NE5 ... 54 B8
Nursery Grange NE46 ... 44 F3
Nursery La Cleadon SR6 ... 60 A1
Gateshead NE10 ... 71 C7
Nursery Pk NE63 ... 6 E1
Nursery Rd SR3 ... 86 A2
Nutley Pl NE15 ... 54 A5
Nye Bevan Ho NE24 ... 17 F6
Nye Dene SR5 ... 74 B1

O

O'Hanlon Cres NE28 ... 40 A4
Oak Ave Dinnington NE13 ... 27 C7
Dunston NE11 ... 69 F7
5 Houghton-le-S DH4 ... 94 D8
South Shields NE34 ... 60 A5
Oak Cl NE46 ... 44 E3
Oak Cres SR6 ... 61 A2
Oak Gr Longbenton NE12 ... 39 D8
Wallsend NE28 ... 40 D1
Oak Rd NE29 ... 41 B7
Oak Sq NE8 ... 100 C1
Oak St Great Lumley DH4 ... 89 E1
Jarrow NE32 ... 58 A7
Mickley Square NE43 ... 64 E8
Seaton Burn NE13 ... 28 C8
Sunderland SR1 ... 103 C2
1 Throckley NE15 ... 35 D2
Washington NE38 ... 83 F4
Oak Terr Blaydon NE21 ... 53 C1
Burnopfield NE16 ... 79 C6
Tantobie DH9 ... 79 B2
Oakapple Cl NE22 ... 10 F1
Oakdale NE22 ... 15 B8
Oakdale Cl NE15 ... 53 D6
Oakdale Terr DH3 ... 88 C2
Oakenshaw NE15 ... 53 E6
Oakey's Rd DH9 ... 79 F1
Oakfield Ave NE16 ... 69 B6
Oakfield Cl
Sunderland SR3 ... 91 C6
Whickham NE16 ... 69 B6
Oakfield Ct SR3 ... 91 C6
Oakfield Dr
Killingworth NE12 ... 29 F3
Whickham NE16 ... 69 B6
Oakfield Gdns
Newcastle-u-T NE15 ... 54 D5
Wallsend NE28 ... 39 F3
Oakfield Grange NE13 ... 27 B7
Oakfield Inf & Jun Schs
NE9 ... 70 F3
Oakfield N NE40 ... 52 B5
Oakfield Pk NE42 ... 50 D2
Oakfield Rd Dunston NE11 ... 70 A6
Newcastle-u-T NE3 ... 38 B3
Whickham NE16 ... 69 A5
Oakfield Terr
Gateshead NE10 ... 57 A1
Killingworth NE12 ... 29 E1
Newcastle-u-T NE3 ... 38 B4
Oakfield Way NE23 ... 22 F1
Oakfields NE16 ... 79 B7
Oakham Ave NE16 ... 68 F6
Oakham Gdns NE29 ... 41 E5
Oakhurst Dr NE3 ... 38 A3
Oakhurst Terr NE12 ... 39 D7
Oakland Rd
Newcastle-u-T NE2 ... 38 D2
Whitley Bay NE25 ... 31 D4
Oakland Terr
Ashington NE63 ... 6 C3
Lynemouth NE61 ... 2 A2
Oaklands
Newcastle-u-T NE3 ... 38 C3
Ponteland NE20 ... 25 D4
Riding Mill NE44 ... 62 F7
Whickham NE16 ... 69 C8
Oaklands Ave NE3 ... 38 C3
Oaklands Cres SR5 ... 75 A2
Oaklands Ct NE20 ... 25 D4
Oaklands Pl NE42 ... 50 E2
Oaklands Rise NE44 ... 62 F7
Oaklands Terr SR4 ... 102 A1
Oaklea Chester le S DH2 ... 88 A5
Shiney Row DH4 ... 89 F4
Oakleigh Gdns SR6 ... 60 A2
Oakley Cl NE23 ... 29 B8
Oakley Dr NE23 ... 22 D7
Oakley Gardens Sch SR6 ... 60 B2
Oakmere Cl 2 DH4 ... 90 B6
Oakridge NE16 ... 68 F6
Oaks The Greenside NE40 ... 52 B1
Hexham NE46 ... 44 F3
Penshaw DH4 ... 90 B8
Sunderland SR2 ... 103 B1
Oaks W The SR2 ... 103 B1
Oaktree Ave NE6 ... 40 A1
Oaktree Gdns NE25 ... 31 E3
Oaktree Terr NE42 ... 50 D2
Oakville NE63 ... 7 A2
Oakwell Ct NE17 ... 77 C5
Oakwell Terr NE42 ... 50 D2
Oakwellgate NE8 ... 101 C4
Oakwood Gateshead NE10 ... 57 E5
Hebburn NE31 ... 57 C7
Oakwood Ave
Gateshead NE9 ... 71 A3
Newbiggin-by-t-S NE64 ... 7 D5
Wideopen NE13 ... 28 C5
Oakwood Bank NE46 ... 45 C7
Oakwood Cl NE9 ... 71 F1
Oakwood Gdns NE11 ... 70 B5
Oakwood Pl 2 NE5 ... 37 C1
Oakwood St SR2 ... 102 B1
Oatens Bank NE15 ... 33 A2
Oates St SR4 ... 102 A2
Oatfield Cl NE63 ... 6 B2
Oatlands Rd SR4 ... 85 E4
Oban Ave NE28 ... 40 F4
Oban Ct NE6 ... 56 C5
Oban Gdns 9 NE6 ... 56 C5
Oban St
Brockley Whins NE32 ... 58 E3
Gateshead NE10 ... 56 C1
Ocean Rd
South Shields NE33 ... 42 D3
Sunderland SR2 ... 86 F2
Ocean Rd N 6 SR2 ... 86 F2
Ocean Rd S 7 SR2 ... 86 F2
Ocean View
Newbiggin-by-t-S NE64 ... 7 E4
Sunderland SR2 ... 92 F8
Whitley Bay NE26 ... 32 B5
Ochiltree Ct NE26 ... 24 D6
Octavia Cl NE22 ... 10 E2
Octavia Ct NE28 ... 40 F4
Octavian Way NE11 ... 70 C3
October Ctyd NE8 ... 100 B2
Odinel Ct NE42 ... 50 D3
Off Quay Bldg The NE6 ... 56 B5
Offerton Cl 7 SR4 ... 85 A6
Offerton La
Sunderland,Offerton SR4 ... 84 F4
Sunderland,South Hylton
SR4 ... 85 A5
Offerton St SR4 ... 102 B2
Office Pl DH5 ... 95 A3
Office Row
New Herrington DH4 ... 90 E7
Washington NE38 ... 83 A1
Ogden St SR4 ... 102 B2
Ogle Ave Hazlerigg NE13 ... 28 A4
Morpeth NE61 ... 8 E8
Ogle Dr NE24 ... 17 C7
Ogle Gr NE32 ... 58 A3
Oil Mill Rd NE6 ... 57 B7
Okehampton Ct 2 NE9 ... 71 A2
Okehampton Dr DH4 ... 90 C4
Okehampton Sq SR5 ... 75 A3
Old Bakehouse Yd 11
NE61 ... 3 F1
Old Brewery Sq NE42 ... 49 C4
Old Brewery The 10 DH4 ... 94 E8
Old Coastguard Cotts
NE30 ... 42 E7
Old Coronation St NE33 ... 42 C2
Old Course Rd SR6 ... 75 A8
Old Custom Ho NE29 ... 42 B4
Old Durham Rd NE8,NE9 ... 71 B6
Old Farm Ct NE16 ... 69 B2
Old Fold Rd NE10,NE8 ... 56 B2
Old Forge The NE43 ... 48 C5
Old George Yd 7 NE1 ... 99 A1
Old Main St NE40 ... 51 E3
Old Mill Rd
Sunderland SR5 ... 75 A3
Sunderland,Hendon SR2 ... 103 C1
Old Orchard The NE44 ... 63 A7
Old Rectory Cl DH9 ... 79 D4
Old Sawmill NE61 ... 8 A8
Old Station Ct NE20 ... 25 C3
Old Vicarage Wlk 21 NE6 ... 56 C6
Old Well Ave 4 NE21 ... 53 B1
Old Well La NE21 ... 53 B1
Oldfield Rd NE6 ... 56 F3
Oldgate NE61 ... 8 F8
Oldgate Ct NE61 ... 8 F8
Oldstead Gdns SR4 ... 85 E4
Olga Terr NE39 ... 67 C1
Olive Gdns NE9 ... 71 A6
Olive Pl NE4 ... 54 D7
Olive St South Shields NE33 ... 59 B6
Sunderland SR1 ... 102 C2
Oliver Ave NE4 ... 54 E6
Oliver Cres DH3 ... 82 C6
Oliver St 2 NE38 ... 83 E4
Olivers Mill NE61 ... 8 F8
Ollerton Dr NE15 ... 35 B2
Ollerton Gdns NE10 ... 71 C6
Olney Cl NE23 ... 22 D7
Olympia Ave NE62 ... 10 F7
Olympia Gdns NE61 ... 4 A1
Olympia Hill NE61 ... 3 F2
Ongar Way NE12 ... 39 B7
Onslow Gdns NE9 ... 70 F5
Onslow St SR4 ... 85 E7
Open The NE1 ... 99 A2
Oram Cl NE61 ... 9 B8
Orange Gr Annitsford NE23 ... 22 B1
Whickham NE16 ... 69 C8
Orchard Ave NE39 ... 67 D1

Orchard Cl
Killingworth NE12 ....29 F2
Morpeth NE61 ....9 B8
Prudhoe NE42 ....50 D1
Rowlands Gill NE39 ....78 D8
Sunniside NE16 ....69 B3
Orchard Cres NE45 ......47 A5
Orchard Ct
Greenside NE40 ....51 F1
Ryton NE40 ....52 C5
Tynemouth NE29 ....42 A8
Orchard Dene NE39 ......67 D1
Orchard Gdns
Chester le S DH3 ....88 C1
Gateshead NE28 ....71 A4
Wallsend NE28 ....40 A4
Whitburn SR6 ....75 E8
Orchard Gn NE5 ....37 D4
Orchard Hill NE45 ....50 D3
Orchard Mews NE61 ......3 F1
Orchard Pk B DH3 ......82 C4
Orchard Pl NE2 ....38 F1
Orchard Rd
Rowlands Gill NE39 ....67 D1
Whickham NE16 ....69 C7
Orchard Rise NE15 ....53 B7
Orchard St Birtley DH3 ..82 A2
Newcastle-u-T NE1 ....101 A4
Sunderland SR4 ....85 F7
Orchard Terr
Chester le S DH3 ....88 C1
4 Hexham NE46 ....45 B5
Newcastle-u-T NE15 ....53 C6
Rowlands Gill NE39 ....78 D8
8 Throckley NE15 ....35 D2
Orchard The
Chester le S DH3 ....88 D4
East Boldon NE36 ....74 C7
Hepscott NE61 ....9 E5
Newcastle-u-T NE15 ....53 D6
4 North Shields NE29 ..42 A6
Whickham NE16 ....69 C7
Wylam NE41 ....51 A6
Orchard View NE45 ......46 F6
Orchard-Leigh NE15 .....53 E6
Orchards The NE24 ....17 C8
Orchid Cl Ashington NE63 ..6 C2
South Shields NE34 ....59 B5
Ord Ct NE4 ....54 D7
Ord St NE4 ....100 C3
Ord Terr NE62 ....11 B8
Orde Ave NE28 ....40 E3
Ordley Cl NE15 ....53 B6
Oriole Ho NE12 ....39 D7
Orkney Dr SR2 ....92 D8
Orlando Rd NE29 ....41 E6
Ormesby Rd SR6 ....75 D3
Ormiscraig NE15 ....53 E6
Ormiston NE15 ....53 E6
Ormonde Ave NE15 ......54 A6
Ormonde St Jarrow NE32 ..58 B7
Sunderland SR4 ....102 A1
Ormsby Gn NE5 ....54 A8
Ormskirk Cl NE15 ....53 D6
Ormskirk Gr NE23 ....22 C7
Ormston St NE23 ....16 B3
Orpen Ave NE34 ....59 C3
Orpine Cl NE63 ....6 C2
Orpington Ave NE6 ......56 E6
Orpington Rd NE23 ......22 C7
Orr Ave SR3 ....92 B6
Orton Cl NE4 ....54 E4
Orwell Cl NE34 ....59 B2
Orwell Gn NE3 ....37 E3
Osbaldeston Gdns NE3 ..38 B3
Osborne Ave
Hexham NE46 ....44 F5
Newcastle-u-T NE2 ....99 C4
South Shields NE33 ....42 E1
Osborne Cl NE22 ....11 C2
Osborne Ct NE2 ....99 C4
Osborne Gdns
Tynemouth NE29 ....42 A7
Whitley Bay NE26 ....31 F5
Osborne Ho NE28 ....40 E2
Osborne Pl NE12 ....29 F1
Osborne Rd
Chester le S DH3 ....88 C3
Newcastle-u-T NE2 ....38 E2
Sunderland SR5 ....85 A7
Osborne St
South Shields NE33 ....42 E2
Sunderland SR2 ....75 D2
Osborne Terr
Cramlington NE23 ....22 A7
Gateshead NE8 ....101 A1
Newcastle-u-T NE2 ....99 B3
Osborne Villas NE2 .....99 B4
Osier Ct NE11 ....11 C7
Oslo Cl NE29 ....41 B4
Osman Cl SR2 ....103 B1
Osmund Terr 2 DH4 .....90 B6
Osprey Dr Blyth NE24 ...17 F5
Shiremoor NE28 ....41 A6
Osprey Ho 4 NE2 ....38 E1
Osprey Way NE34 ....59 B4
Oswald Rd
Hetton le H DH5 ....95 A5
Morpeth NE61 ....4 A2
Newbiggin-by-t-S NE64 ....7 D5
Oswald St
Sunderland SR4 ....102 A3
Whiteleas NE34 ....59 C3
Oswald Terr
Gateshead NE8 ....101 A1

Oswald Terr continued
Sunderland SR5 ....74 C1
11 Sunderland,Grangetown
SR2 ....86 F2
Oswald Terr S SR5 ......74 C1
Oswald Wlk NE3 ....38 E5
Oswestry Pl NE23 ....22 C7
Oswin Ave NE12 ....39 D8
Oswin Ct NE12 ....29 E3
Oswin Rd NE12 ....29 E1
Oswin Terr NE29 ....41 D5
Otley Cl NE23 ....22 D7
Otter Burn Way NE42 ...50 B1
Otterburn Ave
Earsdon NE25 ....31 B4
Newcastle-u-T NE3 ....38 A4
Otterburn Cl NE12 ....39 F8
Otterburn Cres DH4 .....90 C1
Otterburn Ct
Gateshead NE8 ....101 A1
Whitley Bay NE25 ....31 B4
Otterburn Dr NE63 ....6 B1
Otterburn Gdns
Dunston NE11 ....70 A7
Gateshead NE9 ....70 E5
South Shields NE34 ....59 E6
Whickham NE16 ....69 B7
Otterburn Gr NE24 ....17 B5
Otterburn Rd NE29 ......41 F7
Otterburn Terr NE2 ......38 E1
Otterburn Villas S NE2 ..99 B4
Ottercap Cl NE15 ....53 D6
Ottercops NE42 ....50 B1
Otterington NE38 ....84 B4
Ottershaw NE15 ....53 E6
Otto Terr SR2 ....102 B1
Ottovale Cres NE21 ......53 A1
Ottringham Cl NE15 .....53 D6
Oulton Cl
Cramlington NE23 ....22 C7
Newcastle-u-T NE5 ....37 B4
Our Lady & St Anne's RC
Prim Sch NE4 ....100 C4
Our Lady Queen of Peace RC
Prim Sch DH4 ....90 A7
Ousby Ct NE3 ....37 D7
Ouse St NE1 ....56 A5
Ouseburn Cl NE22 ....92 F8
Ouseburn Rd
Newcastle-u-T,Jesmond Vale
NE2,NE6 ....56 B3
Newcastle-u-T,St Ann's NE1 ..56 A4
Ouselaw NE11 ....81 D6
Ouslaw La NE11 ....81 B6
Ouston Cl NE10 ....72 C7
Ouston Inf Sch DH2 .....81 A8
Ouston Jun Sch DH2 ....81 F1
Ouston St NE15 ....53 F5
Outram St DH5 ....90 E1
Oval Park View NE10 ....71 D7
Oval The Bedlington NE22 ..11 C1
Blyth NE24 ....17 B3
Houghton-le-S DH4 ....94 D8
Longbenton NE12 ....39 E6
Newcastle-u-T NE6 ....56 D4
Ouston DH2 ....81 F2
4 Sunderland SR7 ....75 B2
Washington NE37 ....83 D8
Woolsington SL13 ....36 F8
Overdale Ct NE62 ....10 B7
Overdene NE15 ....53 F7
Overfield Rd NE3 ....37 C3
Overhill NE15 ....34 E2
Overhill Terr NE8 ......101 A1
Overstone Ave NE40 ....51 F2
Overstone Gdns NE46 ...45 A3
Overton Cl NE15 ....53 D6
Overton Rd NE29 ....41 E8
Ovett Gdns NE8 ....56 B2
Ovingham CE Fst Sch
NE42 ....50 A3
Ovingham Cl NE38 ....83 F5
Ovingham Gdns NE13 ...28 B6
Ovingham Mid Sch NE42 ..50 A2
Ovingham Rd NE41 ......51 A6
Ovington Gr NE5 ....54 D8
Ovington View NE42 .....50 B1
Owen Brannigan Dr
NE23 ....29 B7
Owen Ct NE2 ....98 C3
Owen Dr NE35,NE36 .....74 B8
Owen Terr Chopwell NE17 ..77 C8
Tantobie DH9 ....79 B2
Owlet Cl NE21 ....53 A1
Owlet Grange NE39 ......77 E5
Oxberry Gdns NE10 ......71 C7
Oxbridge St SR2 ....86 F2
Oxclose Com Sch NE38 ..83 A4
Oxclose Rd NE38 ....83 E4
Oxclose Village Prim Sch
NE38 ....83 A5
Oxford Ave
Cramlington NE23 ....22 C7
10 South Shields NE33 ..59 D8
Wallsend NE28 ....40 A3
Washington NE37 ....83 B8
Oxford Cl SR3 ....91 F8
Oxford Cres Hebburn NE31 ..57 F6
Hetton le H DH5 ....94 F4
Oxford Pl DH3 ....82 C1
Oxford Rd NE62 ....11 A7
Oxford St Blyth NE24 ....17 E8
Newcastle-u-T NE1 ....99 B2
South Shields NE33 ....59 D8
Sunderland SR4 ....85 E7
Tynemouth NE30 ....42 D7
Whitley Bay NE26 ....32 B5

Oxford Terr
Gateshead NE8 ....101 B1
Shiney Row DH4 ....90 A6
Oxford Way NE32 ....58 B1
Oxley Mews 7 NE35 .....58 E1
Oxnam Cres NE2 ....98 B3
Oxted Cl NE23 ....22 D7
Oxted Pl NE6 ....56 E3
Oystershell La NE4 ....98 C1
Oyston St NE33 ....42 C2
Ozanan Cl NE23 ....29 B7

P

Packham Rd SR4 ....85 C5
Paddock Cl Cleadon SR6 ..59 E1
Prudhoe NE42 ....50 E2
Shiney Row DH4 ....89 F5
Paddock Hill NE20 ....25 F7
Paddock La SR3 ....92 C7
Paddock Rise NE63 ....6 B2
Paddock The
Ashington NE63 ....7 B2
Blyth NE24 ....17 C7
East Cramlington NE23 ....22 D5
Gateshead NE10 ....71 F6
New Herrington DH4 ......90 F7
Seaton Delaval NE25 ......23 E3
Stocksfield NE43 ....64 C5
Walbottle NE15 ....35 F1
Woolsington SL13 ....36 F8
Paddock Wood NE42 .....50 E2
Paddocks The NE12 .....12 C7
Pader Cl NE13 ....28 B5
Padgate Rd SR4 ....85 C6
Padonhill 5 SR3 ....91 E5
Padstow Cl 3 SR2 ....92 F8
Padstow Gdns NE9 ....70 F2
Padstow Rd NE29 ....41 E4
Page Ave NE34 ....59 E7
Page St NE31 ....57 F7
Page's Bldgs NE35 ......73 E8
Paignton Ave
Newcastle-u-T NE4 ....54 F5
Whitley Bay NE25 ....31 E4
Paignton Sq SR3 ....85 E2
Painshawfield Rd NE43 ..64 C6
Paisley Sq SR3 ....85 E2
Palace Rd NE22 ....11 D2
Palace St NE4 ....100 B4
Palatine View DH6 ....96 C1
Paley St SR1 ....102 C3
Palgrave Rd SR4 ....85 C5
Palgrave Sq SR4 ....85 C5
Pallinsburn Ct NE5 ......37 B3
Pallion Ind Est SR4 ......85 D7
Pallion New Rd SR4 ......85 E7
Pallion Prim Sch SR4 ....85 F7
Pallion Ret Pk SR4 ....85 E6
Pallion Sta SR4 ....85 E8
Pallion Subway SR4 .....85 F8
Pallion Way SR4 ....85 E7
Pallion West Ind Est SR4 ..85 D7
Palm Ave
Newcastle-u-T NE4 ....54 D7
South Shields NE34 ....60 A5
Palm Ct NE12 ....29 F1
Palm Terr DH9 ....79 C3
Palmer Community Hospl
NE32 ....58 B7
Palmer Cres NE31 ....57 F6
Palmer Gdns NE10 ......72 C8
Palmer Rd DH9 ....78 E1
Palmer St NE32 ....58 A7
Palmer's Hill Rd SR6 ...103 A4
Palmers Gn NE12 ....29 F1
Palmerston Ave NE6 .....56 E7
Palmerston Rd NE10 .....85 B3
Palmerston Sq SR4 ......85 C4
Palmerston St NE33 .....59 C8
Palmerston Wlk NE8 ...101 A2
Palmersville NE12 ....29 F1
Palmersville Sta NE12 ...30 A1
Palmstead Rd SR4 ....85 C5
Palmstead Sq SR4 ....85 C5
Pancras Rd SR3 ....85 E2
Pandon NE1 ....99 B1
Pandon Bank NE1 ....99 B1
Pandon Ct NE2 ....99 C2
Pandon Quays NE1 ....99 C1
Panfield Terr DH4 ....89 E2
Pangbourne Cl NE15 ....53 C8
Pankhurst Gdns NE10 ...72 A8
Pann La SR1 ....103 A3
Panns Bank SR1 ....103 A3
Pantiles The NE37 ....72 D2
Parade Cl NE6 ....57 A5
Parade The
Chester le S DH3 ....88 D1
Hebburn NE31 ....57 A5
Newcastle-u-T NE6 ....57 A6
Sunderland SR2 ....103 C1
Wallsend NE28 ....40 D5
Washington NE38 ....83 E4
Paradise Row NE23 ......22 B6
Park Ave Bedlington NE22 ..11 E3
Blaydon NE21 ....53 C2
Blaydon,Bleach Green NE21 ..53 B2
Hexham NE46 ....44 F6
New Silksworth SR3 ....92 B7
Newcastle-u-T,Fawdon NE3 ..37 F7
Newcastle-u-T,Gosforth
NE3 ....38 B6
North Shields NE30 ....42 C7

Park Ave continued
Prudhoe NE42 ....50 E1
Shiremoor NE27 ....31 A3
South Shields NE34 ....59 F4
Sunderland SR6 ....75 E7
Wallsend NE28 ....40 B2
Washington NE37 ....83 D8
Whitley Bay NE26 ....32 A5
Park Chare NE38 ....83 D5
Park Cl NE4 ....100 A4
Park Cotts NE17 ....77 B6
Park Cres
North Shields NE30 ....42 B7
Shiremoor NE27 ....30 F3
Park Cres E NE30 ....42 C7
Park Ct Gateshead NE8 ..101 C3
Gateshead,Chowdene NE11 ..70 D3
Wallsend NE6 ....40 A1
Park Dr Blyth NE24 ......17 B4
Longbenton NE12 ....39 E8
Morpeth NE61 ....8 F7
Newcastle-u-T NE3 ....28 C1
Stannington NE61 ....22 F8
Whickham NE16 ....69 C8
Park Farm Villas NE24 ..17 C7
Park Field NE61 ....52 C5
Park Field Terr NE26 ....24 C6
Park Gate SR6 ....75 E3
Park Gdns NE26 ....32 A5
Park Gr Shiremoor NE27 ..30 F3
Washington NE37 ....72 D1
Park Hall SR2 ....103 A1
Park Head Rd NE7 ....39 A1
Park House Gdns DH6 ..96 A2
Park La Blaydon NE21 ...68 B8
Gateshead NE8 ....56 A3
Prudhoe NE42 ....50 D1
Shiremoor NE27 ....30 F2
Sunderland SR1 ....103 A2
Park Lane Intc SR1 .....103 A2
Park Lane Sta SR1 .....103 A2
Park Lea SR3 ....91 B6
Park Lea Rd SR6 ....75 E3
Park Par Sunderland SR6 ..75 E2
Whitley Bay NE26 ....32 A5
Park Pl DH3 ....88 D5
Park Pl E SR2 ....103 A1
Park Pl W SR2 ....103 A1
Park Rd Ashington NE63 ..6 B3
Bedlington NE22 ....16 A8
Blyth NE24 ....17 F7
Gateshead NE10,NE8 ......56 B2
Hebburn NE31 ....57 C5
Jarrow NE32 ....58 A5
Lynemouth NE61,NE63 .....2 A2
Newburn NE15 ....52 F8
Newcastle-u-T NE4 ......100 A3
Rowlands Gill NE39 ....67 D2
Seaton Delaval NE25 ......23 C3
Shiremoor NE27 ....30 F3
Sunderland SR2 ....103 A1
Wallsend NE28 ....40 C1
Whitley Bay NE26 ....32 A6
Park Rd N DH3 ....88 D4
Park Rd S DH3 ....88 D3
Park Rise NE15 ....53 C7
Park Road Central DH3
DH3 ....88 D3
Park Road E NE6 ....6 C4
Park Row
3 Gateshead NE10 ......71 D8
Sunderland SR5 ....75 A1
Park Side NE61 ....9 F5
Park St S SR5 ....74 C1
Park Terr Bedlington NE22 ..11 D3
Blaydon NE21 ....53 D2
Burnopfield NE16 ....79 A6
Dunston NE11 ....69 F8
Killingworth NE12 ....29 B2
Newcastle-u-T NE1,NE2 ...99 A3
North Shields NE30 ....42 C7
Sunderland SR5 ....74 C1
Wallsend NE28 ....40 B2
Washington NE37 ....72 D1
Whickham NE16 ....54 A1
Whitley Bay NE26 ....32 A6
Park View Ashington NE63 ..6 B4
Blaydon NE21 ....68 C8
Blyth NE24 ....17 F7
Bournmoor DH4 ....89 D4
Burnopfield NE16 ....79 B6
Chester le S DH2 ....88 B5
Hetton le H DH5 ....95 A3
Jarrow NE32 ....58 B4
Longbenton NE12 ....29 B2
Longbenton,Forest Hall
NE12 ....39 B2
Lynemouth NE61 ....2 A2
Newcastle-u-T NE6 ....57 A5
Seaton Delaval NE25 ......23 D3
Shiney Row DH4 ....90 B6
Wallsend NE28 ....40 B2
Whitley Bay NE26 ....32 A6
Widopen NE13 ....28 C6
Park View Cl NE40 ....52 C5
Park View Com Sch DH3 ..88 D3
Park View Com Sch (Lower)
DH3 ....88 D7
Park View Ct NE26 ......32 A5
Park View Gdns NE40 ...52 D5
Park View Sh Ctr NE26 ..32 A5
Park Villas Ashington NE63 ..6 B4
Wallsend NE28 ....40 B2
Park Wall Cnr SR3 ....91 A6
Parkdale Rise NE16 .....69 A7
Parker Ave NE3 ....38 B3
Parker Ct NE11 ....54 E2
Parkfield NE32 ....58 C1
Parkgate DH5 ....95 C3

Parkgate La NE21 ....68 B8
Parkham Cl NE23 ....16 B1
Parkhead Com Prim Sch
NE21 ....68 C8
Parkhead Gdns NE21 ....68 B8
Parkhead Sq NE21 ....53 C1
Parkhouse Ave SR5 .....85 B8
Parkhurst Rd SR4 ....85 B4
Parkin Gdns NE10 ....71 E7
Parkinson's Cotts NE40 ..52 E4
Parkland Longbenton NE12 ..39 D6
Ryton NE21 ....53 A4
Parkland Ave NE21 ......68 B8
Parklands
Gateshead,Eighton Banks NE10 ..72 C8
Hamsterley Mill NE39 .....77 F5
Ponteland NE20 ....25 B2
Parklands Ct NE10 ....57 C1
Parklands Way NE10 ....72 C8
Parklea NE26 ....24 C6
Parkmore Rd SR4 ....85 A3
Parks The DH3 ....88 E1
Parkshiel NE34 ....60 A4
Parkside Bedlington NE22 ..11 E3
Dunston NE11 ....69 F8
Hebburn NE31 ....57 D4
Sunderland SR3 ....90 B4
Throckley NE15 ....79 C1
Tynemouth NE30 ....32 D1
Wallsend NE28 ....40 D3
Parkside Ave
Blaydon NE21 ....53 C1
Newcastle-u-T NE7 ....39 B5
Parkside Cotts DH9 ......79 C1
Parkside Cres NE30 .....42 D8
Parkside Ct Ashington NE63 ..6 E2
Whitley Bay NE26 ....31 F5
Widopen NE13 ....28 C6
Parkside S SR3 ....91 B6
Parkside Sch NE28 ......40 A5
Parkside Terr NE28 ......40 A4
Parkstone Cl SR4 ....85 A3
Parkville NE6 ....56 A7
Parkway Guide Post NE62 ..10 F8
Washington,Biddick NE38 ..83 C4
Washington,Washington Village
NE38 ....83 D5
Whickham NE16 ....68 E6
Parkwood Ave NE42 .....50 F3
Parliament St NE31 ......57 C7
Parmontley St NE15 .....53 F5
Parnell St DH4 ....94 B8
Parrish View NE1 ....99 A1
Parry Dr SR6 ....60 E1
Parson Rd NE41 ....51 B6
Parson's Ave NE6 ....56 F5
Parsons Ind Est NE37 ...83 B8
Parsons Rd NE37 ....83 B7
Parsons St 10 NE26 .....17 E8
Parsons' Gdns 5 NE11 ..54 F1
Partick Rd SR4 ....85 A4
Partick Sq SR4 ....85 C4
Partnership Ct SR7 ......92 E2
Partridge Cl NE38 ....82 F4
Pasteur Rd DH6 ....97 F7
Pastures The Blyth NE24 ..17 D4
Morpeth NE61 ....8 D7
Stocksfield NE43 ....64 B8
Path The 8 NE9 ....70 F4
Pathside NE32 ....58 C2
Patience Ave NE13 ......28 C8
Patina Cl NE15 ....53 C8
Patina Ct NE3 ....85 F2
Paton Rd SR3 ....85 F2
Patrick Cain Ho NE33 ...59 B8
Patrick Cres DH6 ....97 E8
Patrick Terr NE23 ....29 B7
Patterdale Cl NE36 ......74 C7
Patterdale Gdns NE7 ....39 B4
Patterdale Gr SR5 ....75 C4
Patterdale Ho NE24 .....17 A8
Patterdale Rd NE24 .....17 A8
Patterdale St DH5 ....95 A2
Patterdale Terr NE8 .....70 F8
Patterson Cl NE46 ....44 E3
Patterson St NE21 ....53 C4
Pattinson Gdns
Gateshead,Carr Hill NE9 ..71 B7
Gateshead,Old Fold NE10 ..56 C2
Pattinson Ind Est
Washington NE38 ....84 B6
Washington,Swan NE38 ...83 B3
Pattinson Rd NE38 ....84 B3
Patton Way NE61 ....4 E3
Pauline Ave SR6 ....75 D3
Pauline Gdns NE15 ......54 A2
Pauls Gn DH5 ....95 A6
Pauls Rd SR1 ....103 B2
Paulsway NE32 ....58 E6
Pavilion Mews NE2 ......99 C4
Pavilion Terr DH5 ....95 A3
Pavilion The NE16 ....53 F1
Pavillion Cl SR1 ....103 A2
Pawston Rd NE21,NE39 ..67 B5
Paxford Cl NE7 ....39 A4
Paxton Terr SR4 ....102 A3
Peacehaven Ct NE37 ....72 C2
Peacock Cl NE11 ....70 B7
Peacock St W SR4 ....85 F6
Pear Tree Terr
Chopwell NE17 ....77 B8
Great Lumley DH4 ....89 B2
Peareth Edge 2 NE9 .....71 F3
Peareth Ct NE8 ....101 C2
Peareth Gr SR2 ....75 F3
Peareth Hall Rd NE37,
NE9 ....72 A2

eareth Rd SR6 .... .75 F4
eareth Terr DH3 .... .82 C3
earey Ho NE29 .... .42 A7
earl Rd SR3 .... .85 F2
earson Pl Jarrow NE32 .. .58 C8
North Shields NE30 ...... .42 B6
earson St NE33 .... .42 D4
earson's Terr ◼ NE46 .. .45 A5
eart Cl DH6 .... .96 A1
eartree Bglws NE17 .... .77 C6
eartree Ct NE17 .... .77 C6
eartree Gdns NE4 ..... .40 A1
eartree Mews ◻ SR2 .. .86 C4
eary Cl NE15 .... .36 F2
ease Ave NE15 .... .54 C6
easemoor Rd SR4 ..... .85 B5
ebble Beach SR6 ...... .75 F7
ecket Cl NE24 .... .17 A5
eddars Way NE44 ..... .59 B5
eebles Cl NE29 .... .41 C8
eebles Rd SR3 .... .85 E2
eel Ct NE13 .... .28 B8
eel Ctr The NE37 ..... .83 F7
eel Gdns NE34 .... .58 E4
eel La NE1 .... .100 C4
eel St
Newcastle-u-T NE1 .... .100 C4
Sunderland SR2 ...... .103 B1
eepy Cotts NE43 ..... .48 D2
egswood Fst Sch NE61 .. .4 F4
egswood Ho NE4 ..... .98 B2
egswood Ind Est NE61 .. .4 F3
egswood Prec NE61 ... .4 F3
egswood Sta NE61 .... .4 F3
egswood Village NE61 .. .4 A4
egswood Rd SR4 ..... .85 C5
elaw Ave
Chester le S DH2 ..... .88 C5
Newbiggin-by-t-S NE64 ... .7 D5
elaw Bank DH3 .... .88 C4
elaw Cres DH2 .... .88 B5
elaw Grange Ct DH3 ... .88 C8
elaw Ind Est NE10 .... .72 A8
elaw Pl DH2 .... .88 C5
elaw Rd DH2 .... .88 C5
elaw Sq Chester le S DH2 .88 B5
Sunderland SR4 ...... .85 C7
elaw Sta NE10 ...... .57 A1
elaw Way NE10 ...... .57 A1
eldon Cl NE7 .... .38 F5
elham Ct NE3 .... .37 D7
eldon Fell Rd DH2 .... .88 B4
elton La DH2 .... .88 B5
elton Rd SR4 .... .85 C4
eltondale Ave NE17 ... .16 A6
emberton Bank DH5 ... .95 C1
emberton Ct ◼ SR5 .. .75 B1
emberton Gdns ◼ SR3 .86 B3
emberton St NE38 .... .95 A4
embridge NE38 ...... .83 A5
embroke Ave
Birtley DH3 .... .82 D1
Newcastle-u-T NE6 ... .56 E7
Silksworth SR3 ..... .92 A6
embroke Ct
◼ Blyth NE24 ...... .17 F7
Newbiggin-by-t-S NE64 ... .7 E5
embroke Dr NE37 .... .37 D7
embroke Dr NE20 ... .25 B4
embroke Gdns
Ashington NE63 ..... .7 A1
Wallsend NE28 ...... .41 A4
embroke Terr NE33 ... .59 C7
embrooke Ave NE6 ... .56 E7
enandor Ct NE61 .... .5 D8
endeford NE38 ..... .84 A4
endle Cl NE38 ...... .83 B3
endle Gn SR4 ..... .102 A1
endleton Dr NE23 .... .16 B1
endower Way NE15 ... .54 C5
enfold Cl NE7 ...... .39 D4
enhale Dr SR2 ..... .92 F7
enhill Cl DH2 ...... .81 F1
enistone Rd SR4 .... .85 A4
enman Pl NE29 ..... .42 A4
enman Sq SR4 ..... .85 C4
enman St NE29 ..... .42 A4
enn Sq SR4 .... .85 C6
enn St NE4 .... .100 A4
ennant Sq SR4 ..... .85 C6
ennine Ave DH2 .... .88 B2
ennine Ct ◼ SR3 ... .91 F6
ennine Dr NE23 ..... .6 E1
ennine Gdns NE11 ... .70 A6
ennine Gr NE36 ..... .74 B7
ennine View NE17 ... .77 B8
ennine Way NE12 ... .39 A6
ennycross Rd SR4 ... .85 A4
ennycross Sq SR4 ... .85 A5
ennyfine Cl NE29 ... .42 A8
ennyfine Rd NE12 ... .69 C2
ennygate Sq SR4 ... .85 A5
ennymore Sq SR4 ... .85 A5
ennymore Bsns Ctr SR4 .85 C5
ennywell Fst Sch SR4 .85 A3
ennywell Ind Est SR4 .85 A4
ennywell Rd SR4 ... .85 C4
ennywell Sh Prec SR4 .85 C4
enrith Ave NE30 .... .32 A2
enrith Cl NE22 ..... .10 D2
enrith Gdns NE9 ... .71 B4
enrith Gr NE9 .... .71 B4
enrith Rd Hebburn NE31 .57 F4
Sunderland SR5 .... .75 C4
enrose Gn NE3 .... .37 F5
enrose Rd SR4 ..... .85 B4
nsford Ct NE3 .... .37 C6

Penshaw Gn NE5 ..... .37 D3
Penshaw La DH4 ..... .90 B8
Penshaw Monument* ▪
SR4 .... .84 C1
Penshaw View
Birtley DH3 .... .82 E3
Gateshead NE10 .... .72 C8
Hebburn NE31 ..... .57 E4
Jarrow NE32 ...... .58 B4
Penshaw Way DH3 ... .82 E4
Pensher St
Gateshead NE10 .... .56 C1
Sunderland SR4 ... .102 B2
Pensher St E NE10 ... .56 C1
Pensher View NE37 ... .72 E1
Pent Ct NE40 ..... .52 A1
Pentland Cl Ashington NE63 .6 E1
Cramlington NE23 ... .16 B1
Tynemouth NE29 ... .31 F1
Washington NE38 ... .83 B3
Pentland Ct ◼ DH2 ... .88 C2
Pentland Gdns NE11 .. .70 A7
Pentland Gr NE12 ... .29 B1
Pentridge Cl NE23 ... .22 C7
Penwood Rd SR4 ... .85 C5
Penyghent Way NE37 .. .83 A6
Penzance Par NE31 .. .58 A2
Penzance Rd SR4 ... .85 B4
Peplow Sq SR4 ..... .85 C/
Peppercorn Ct NE1 .. .101 B4
Percival St SR4 .... .85 F7
Percy Ave
Tynemouth NE30 .... .32 C3
Whitley Bay NE26 ... .32 A5
Percy Cl NE46 ..... .44 F3
Percy Cotts NE25 ... .23 E2
Percy Cres NE29 ... .41 D3
Percy Ct NE29 ..... .41 D3
Percy Gardens Cotts
NE30 .... .42 D8
Percy Gdns Dunston NE11 .70 A7
Longbenton NE12 ... .39 D8
Stakeford NE62 .... .11 A8
Tynemouth NE30 .... .42 D8
Whitley Bay NE25 ... .32 A4
Percy Hedley Sch The
NE12 .... .29 D2
Percy Lonnen NE42 .. .50 D3
Percy Main Prim Sch
NE29 .... .41 D2
Percy Main Sta NE29 .. .41 D3
Percy Main Village Sta
NE29 .... .41 C3
Percy Park Rd NE30 ... .42 D8
Percy Pk NE30 ..... .42 D8
Percy Rd NE26 .... .32 B5
Percy Scott St NE34 .. .59 C3
Percy St Ashington NE63 .6 E4
Blyth NE24 .... .17 F8
Cramlington NE23 ... .22 C5
Hetton le H DH5 .... .95 B4
Jarrow NE32 ...... .58 C7
Longbenton NE12 ... .29 C7
Newcastle-u-T,Lemington
NE15 .... .53 C6
◼ South Shields NE33 .42 D2
Tynemouth NE30 ... .42 C2
Wallsend NE28 .... .40 C2
Percy St S SR4 .... .17 F7
Percy Terr Newburn NE15 .52 F7
Newcastle-u-T NE3 ... .38 E5
Penshaw DH4 ..... .90 A8
Sunderland SR2 ... .86 E4
◻ Whitburn SR6 ... .60 F1
Whitley Bay NE25 ... .31 E5
Percy Terr S SR2 ... .86 F4
Percy Way NE15 ... .36 A1
Peregrine Cl NE38 ... .41 F6
Peregrine Pl NE12 ... .39 A7
Perivale Rd SR4 .... .85 B4
Perry St NE8 ...... .70 F8
Perry Stone Mews NE22 .16 A8
Perrycrofts SR3 .... .92 A4
Perth Ave NE32,NE34 .58 E3
Perth Cl Tynemouth NE29 .31 F1
Wallsend NE28 .... .40 F4
Perth Ct Gateshead NE11 .70 F3
Sunderland SR3 ... .85 E1
Perth Gdns NE28 ... .40 F4
Perth Rd SR3 ..... .85 F2
Perth Sq SR3 ..... .85 F2
Pescott Ct ◼ NE46 ... .45 B4
Pesspool Ave DH6 ... .97 F3
Pesspool Bglws DH6 .. .97 F3
Pesspool La DH6 .... .97 F3
Pesspool Terr DH6 ... .97 F3
Peter Stracey Ho SR6 .75 F2
Peterborough Cl NE8 .101 B2
Peterborough Way NE32 .58 B1
Petersfield Rd SR4 .. .85 B4
Petersham Rd SR4 ... .85 B4
Peth Gn DH5 ...... .95 B1
Peth Head NE46 ... .45 C5
Peth La NE40 ..... .52 D6
Petherton Ct NE3 ... .37 C6
Pethgate Ct ◼ NE61 ... .9 A8
Petrel Cl ◼ NE61 ... .42 C4
Petrel Way SR4 .... .17 F4
Petteril NE38 ..... .83 A1
Petworth Cl NE33 ... .42 D3
Petworth Gdns NE61 ... .4 E4
Pevensey Cl NE29 ... .31 F1
Pexton Way NE5 ... .54 A8
Pheasantmoor ◼ NE37 .83 A7
Philadelphia Aged Miners
Homes ◻ DH4 ...... .90 B6

Philadelphia Complex
DH4 .... .90 D6
Philadelphia La DH4 ... .90 C4
Philip Pl NE4 ..... .98 A2
Philip Sq SR3 .... .85 E2
Philip St NE4 .... .98 A2
Philip's Ct ◼ NE9 ... .71 B5
Philiphaugh NE28 ... .57 B8
Philipson St NE6 ... .56 F6
Phillips Ave NE16 ... .69 A8
Phillips Cl DH6 .... .97 E3
Phobe Grange Cotts
NE42 .... .50 D2
Phoenix Chase NE29 .41 C8
Phoenix Ct Morpeth NE61 .8 F8
Tynemouth NE29 ... .41 C8
Phoenix Rd
Sunderland SR4 ... .85 C5
Washington NE38 ... .82 E6
Phoenix St NE24 ... .17 B4
Phoenix Way NE24 .. .94 C7
Piccadilly SR3 ..... .91 E8
Picherwell NE10 ... .71 D7
Pickard St SR4 ... .102 A3
Pickering Cl NE32 ... .58 B7
Pickering Gn NE9 ... .71 B2
Pickering Rd SR4 ... .85 B3
Pickering Sq SR4 ... .85 B3
Pickersgill Ho SR5 ... .74 C3
Pickhurst Rd SR4 ... .85 B3
Pickhurst Sq SR4 ... .85 B3
Picktree Cotts ◻ DH3 .88 D4
Picktree Cotts ◼ DH3 .88 D4
Picktree Farm Cotts
NE38 .... .88 C2
Picktree La
Chester le S DH3 ... .88 D4
Chester le S,Picktree DH3,
NE38 .... .88 D7
Picktree Lodge
Birtley NE38 ..... .82 E1
Chester le S DH3 ... .88 D8
Picktree Mews ◻ DH3 .88 D4
Picktree Terr ◼ DH3 .88 D4
Pier Par NE33 .... .42 E4
Pier Rd NE30 .... .42 E7
Pier View SR6 ... .75 F2
Pikestone Cl NE38 ... .83 A3
Pilgrim Cl SR5 .... .75 C1
Pilgrim St
Newcastle-u-T NE1 .101 B4
Newcastle-u-T NE1 ... .99 B1
Pilgrims Ct NE2 ... .98 B1
Pilgrims Way NE61 ... .8 D7
Pilgrimsway
Gateshead NE9 .... .71 B7
Jarrow NE32 ...... .58 E6
Pilton Rd NE5 .... .36 F3
Pilton Wlk ◼ NE5 .. .36 F3
Pimlico Ct NE9 .... .70 F4
Pimlico Rd
Hetton le H DH5 ... .95 B1
Sunderland SR4 ... .85 B4
Pinders Way DH6 ... .96 D1
Pine Ave Burnopfield NE16 .78 F6
Dinnington NE13 ... .27 C7
Guide Post NE62 ... .11 A8
◼ Houghton-le-S DH4 .94 D8
Newcastle-u-T NE7 .. .37 F7
South Shields NE34 .. .60 A5
Pine Rd NE21 .... .53 C2
Pine St Birtley DH3 ... .82 C5
◻ Chester le S DH3 .88 C3
Greenside NE40 ... .52 A5
Jarrow NE32 ..... .58 A6
Seaton Burn NE13 .. .28 C8
Sunderland SR4 ... .85 F7
Throckley NE15 .... .35 D1
Pinedale Dr DH6 ... .97 F7
Pinegarth NE20 ... .25 C2
Pines The Greenside NE40 .52 B1
Newcastle-u-T NE4 .100 A3
Pinesway SR3 .... .86 B3
Pinetree Gdns NE25 .. .31 E3
Pinetree Way NE11 .. .54 B2
Pinewood NE31 ... .57 C7
Pinewood Ave
Cramlington NE23 ... .16 B1
Washington NE38 ... .83 F3
Widopen NE13 .... .28 C5
Pinewood Cl
Newcastle-u-T,Kingston Park
NE3 .... .37 B7
Newcastle-u-T,Walkerville
NE6 .... .39 F1
Washington NE38 ... .83 F3
Pinewood Dr NE61 ... .3 D2
Pinewood Gdns NE11 .70 A5
Pinewood Rd SR5 ... .74 F2
Pinewood Sq ◼ SR5 .74 F2
Pinewood St DH4 ... .90 A8
Pinewood Villas NE34 .60 A6
Pink La NE1 .... .100 C4
Pinner Pl NE6 .... .56 E4
Pinner Rd SR4 ... .85 B3
Pintail Cl ◼ NE34 ... .59 A4
Pioneer Terr NE22 .. .11 C3
Pipe Track La NE4 .. .64 B4
Piper Rd NE42 .... .50 B5
Pipershaw NE37 ... .82 F6
Pipewellgate NE8 ... .101 B3
Pit Row SR3 ..... .91 F8
Pitcairn Rd SR4 ... .85 B3
Pitt St NE4 ..... .98 C2
Pittington La DH6 ... .96 A4
Pittington Prim Sch DH6 .96 B5
Pittington Rd DH5,DH6 .96 A7

Plains Farm Prim Sch
SR3 .... .85 F2
Plains Rd SR3 .... .85 F2
Plaistow Sq SR4 ... .85 C6
Plaistow Way NE23 ... .16 B1
Plane Tree Ct SR3 ... .91 E6
Planesway NE10 ... .71 E5
Planet Ho SR1 ... .103 A3
Planet Pl NE12 ... .29 C2
Plantree Ave NE4 ... .54 D8
Plantagenet Ave DH3 .88 D2
Plantation Ave
High Pittington DH6 ... .96 E3
Whickham NE16 .... .69 A8
Plantation Ct NE40 ... .66 E8
Plantation Gr NE10 ... .57 C2
Plantation Rd SR4 ... .85 E7
Plantation Sq ◼ SR4 .85 E7
Plantation St NE28 .. .57 B8
Plantation The NE9 ... .71 A4
Plantation Wlk DH6 .. .97 F7
Plawsworth Gdns NE9 .71 C3
Pleasant Pl ◼ DH3 ... .82 C5
Plenmeller Pl NE16 .. .69 A3
Plessey Ave NE24 ... .17 F6
Plessey Cres NE25 .. .32 B4
Plessey Ct NE24 ... .17 B4
Plessey Gdns NE29 .. .41 D5
Plessey Rd NE24 ... .17 D5
Plessey Road Fst Sch
NE24 .... .17 F7
Plessey Road Workshops
NE24 .... .17 B4
Plessey St NE23 ... .16 B3
Plessey Terr NE7 ... .39 B2
Plessey Woods Ctry Pk*
NE22 .... .15 B4
Plough Rd SR3 .... .91 F5
Plover Cl Blyth NE24 .. .17 E4
◻ Washington NE38 .. .82 F3
Plover Dr NE24 .... .17 E5
Plover Lodge DH3 ... .82 C6
Ploverfield Cl NE63 .. .6 C2
Plummer St NE4 ... .100 C3
Plumtree Ave SR5 ... .74 C2
Plunkett Rd DH9 ... .78 E1
Plymouth Sq SR3 ... .85 E2
Point Pleasant Ind Est
NE28 .... .40 F1
Point Pleasant Terr NE28 .40 F1
Polden Cres NE29 ... .31 F1
Polebrook Rd SR4 ... .85 C6
Pollard St NE33 ... .42 D3
Polmaise St NE21 ... .53 C2
Polmuir Rd SR3 ... .85 F2
Polmuir Sq SR3 ... .85 F2
Polperro Cl DH3 .... .82 D3
Polperro Cl ◻ SR2 ... .92 F8
Polton Sq SR4 .... .85 C6
Polwarth Cres NE3 ... .38 C8
Polwarth Dr NE3 ... .28 C1
Polwarth Pl NE3 ... .28 C1
Polwarth Rd NE3 ... .28 C1
Pont Haugh NE20 ... .25 C2
Pont Pk NE20 .... .19 A2
Pont St NE63 ..... .6 D3
Pont View NE20 ... .25 F7
Pontdyke NE10 ... .71 D6
Pontefract Rd ◼ SR3 .85 B3
Ponteland Cl
Tynemouth NE29 ... .41 C7
Washington NE38 ... .82 F4
Ponteland Com High Sch
NE20 .... .25 F5
Ponteland Fst Sch NE20 .25 F5
Ponteland Mid Sch NE20 .25 F5
Ponteland Rd
Newcastle-u-T,Blakelaw
NE5 .... .37 D3
Newcastle-u-T,Kenton Bankfoot
NE3 .... .37 B6
Newcastle-u-T,Spital Tongues
NE2 .... .98 A3
Ponteland NE20 .... .26 A5
Throckley NE15 .... .35 D5
Woolsington NE13 .. .37 A7
Ponthaugh NE39 ... .67 F3
Pontop Sq NE39 ... .67 D3
Pontop St DH5 .... .94 C4
Pontop View NE39 .. .67 D2
Pontville Ct NE23 .. .22 C7
Poole Rd SR4 .... .85 C6
Pooley Cl SR4 .... .85 B3
Pooley Rd NE5 ... .37 B1
Poplar Ave Blyth NE24 .12 D1
Burnopfield NE16 ... .78 F6
Dinnington NE13 ... .27 C7
◼ Houghton-le-S DH4 .94 D8
Newcastle-u-T NE6 .. .39 F1
Poplar Cl NE11 ... .70 A6
Poplar Cres Birtley DH3 .82 B5
Dunston NE11 ... .70 A6
Gateshead NE8 ... .101 B2
Poplar Dr SR6 .... .60 F1
Poplar Gr Bedlington NE22 .11 C1
South Shields NE34 .. .59 F5
◼ Sunderland SR2 .. .92 F8
Poplar Pl NE3 .... .38 C5
Poplar St Ashington NE63 .6 D4
◻ Chester le S DH3 .88 C3
Throckley NE15 .... .35 D3
Poplar Terr DH3 ... .88 C7
Poplars The
Easington Lane DH5 .95 C1
Newcastle-u-T,Elswick
NE4 .... .100 A3

Poplars The continued
Newcastle-u-T,Gosforth
NE3 .... .38 C3
Penshaw DH4 ..... .90 B8
◼ Sunderland SR5 .. .74 F2
◼ Sunderland,South Hylton
NE38 .... .83 A4
Washington NE38 .. .83 D4
Popplewell Gdns NE9 .71 A4
Popplewell Terr NE29 .42 A8
Popular Cr ◼ DH3 .. .88 C3
Porchester Dr NE23 .. .22 C7
Porlock Ct NE23 ... .16 A1
Porlock Ho NE12 ... .58 D5
Porlock Rd NE12 ... .58 D5
Portadown Rd ◼ SR4 .85 B3
Portberry St NE33 ... .42 B1
Portberry Street Ind Est
NE33 .... .59 B8
Portberry Way NE33 .42 B1
Portchester Gr NE35 .73 E8
Portchester Rd SR4 .. .85 C5
Portchester Sq SR4 .. .85 C4
Porthcawl Dr NE37 .. .72 C2
Portia St NE63 ..... .6 E4
Portland Cl DH2 ... .88 A1
Portland Gdns
Cramlington NE23 ... .22 C7
◼ Gateshead NE9 ... .70 F2
Tynemouth NE30 ... .42 A7
Portland Ind Pk NE63 .5 F5
Portland Mews NE2 .. .99 C3
Portland Rd
Newcastle-u-T NE2 ... .99 C2
Sunderland SR3 ... .85 F3
Throckley NE15 ... .35 E2
Portland Sch
Silksworth SR3 .... .91 E5
Sunderland SR3 ... .85 F3
Portland Sq ◼ SR3 .. .85 F3
Portland St ◻ Blyth NE24 .17 D8
Gateshead NE10 ... .57 A1
Newcastle-u-T NE4 .. .54 F4
Portland Terr
Ashington NE63 .... .5 F5
Hexham NE46 ..... .44 F5
Newcastle-u-T NE2 .. .99 C3
Portman Mews NE6 .. .99 C2
Portman Pl NE6 .... .56 E3
Portman Sq SR4 ... .85 C5
Portmarnock NE37 .. .72 B2
Portmeads Rd DH3 .. .82 D4
Portmeads Rise DH3 .82 D4
Portobello Ind Est DH3 .82 E4
Portobello La SR5,SR6 .75 D1
Portobello Prim Sch
DH3 .... .82 D2
Portobello Terr DH3 .82 E2
Portobello Way DH3 .82 D4
Portree Cl DH3 .... .82 D1
Portree Sq SR3 .... .85 E2
Portrush Cl NE37 ... .72 C2
Portrush Rd SR4 ... .85 C6
Portrush Way NE7 .. .39 C5
Portslade Rd SR4 ... .85 B4
Portsmouth Rd
North Shields NE29 ... .41 C5
Sunderland SR4 ... .85 B5
Portsmouth Sq SR4 .. .85 B5
Portugal Pl NE28 ... .40 B1
Post Office La NE42 .. .42 A8
Post Office St ◼ NE24 .17 F8
Postern Cres NE61 .. .8 F7
Potland View NE61 .. .1 A3
Potter Sq SR3 .... .85 F2
Potter St Jarrow NE32 .58 A7
Potteries The NE33 .. .42 E1
Potterway NE9 ... .71 B7
Pottery Bank Morpeth NE61 .3 E2
Newcastle-u-T NE6 .. .56 F3
Pottery Bank Ct NE61 ..3 E2
Pottery La
Newcastle-u-T NE1 .100 C3
Sunderland SR4 ... .85 A7
Pottery Rd SR5 .... .75 A1
Pottery Yd ◼ DH4 .. .94 E8
Potts St SR6 .... .56 C6
Poulton Cl NE38 ... .89 B8
Powburn Cl DH2 ... .88 A1
Powburn Gdns NE4 .. .54 E8
Powis Rd SR3 .... .85 F2
Powys Pl NE4 .... .98 B2
Powys Pl NE4 .... .37 C5
Poynings Cl NE5 ... .37 C5
Praetorian Dr NE28 .. .40 B1
Precinct The
Blaydon NE21 .... .53 D3
Sunderland SR2 ... .102 B2
Sunderland,Hillview SR2 ..86 C2
Prefect Pl NE7 .... .71 A7
Premier Rd SR3 ... .85 F2
Prendwick Ct NE31 .. .57 D3
Prendwick Rd NE31 .. .57 D3
Prengarth Way NE34 .58 F3
Prescot Rd SR4 .... .85 C5
Press La SR1 .... .103 A3
Prestbury Ave NE23 .16 A1
Prestbury Rd NE31 .. .85 A3
Prestdale Ave NE24 .. .17 A7
Prestmede NE10 ... .71 E7
Preston Ave NE30 ... .42 B7
Preston Ct NE29 ... .42 A8

Preston Gate NE29 ....31 F1
Preston Grange Prim Sch NE29 ....31 E1
Preston North Rd NE29 ....31 F1
Preston Pk NE29 ....42 A7
Preston Rd Sunderland SR2 ....86 F4
Tynemouth NE29,NE30 ....42 A7
Preston Terr
12 Shiremoor NE27 ....30 E1
1 Tynemouth NE29 ....41 F8
Preston Twrs NE29 ....42 A7
Preston Wood NE30 ....32 A1
Prestonhill 8 SR3 ....91 E5
Prestwick NE10 ....71 E5
Prestwick Ave NE12 ....41 C6
Prestwick Carr Rd NE13 ....27 A8
Prestwick Cl NE37 ....72 C2
Prestwick Dr NE10 ....72 C7
Prestwick Gdns NE3 ....37 F4
Prestwick Ho NE4 ....98 B2
Prestwick Rd SR4 ....85 C6
Prestwick Terr NE20 ....26 C3
Pretoria Ave NE61 ....8 F8
Pretoria Sq SR3 ....85 E2
Pretoria St NE15 ....54 A5
Price St Hebburn NE31 ....57 C7
Morpeth NE61 ....3 E1
Priestclose Cotts NE42 ....50 F2
Priestclose Rd NE42 ....50 D2
Priestfield Cl SR3 ....91 F5
Priestfield Gdns NE16 ....78 F6
Priestlands Ave 12 NE46 ....45 A4
Priestlands Cl NE46 ....45 A3
Priestlands Cres NE46 ....45 A4
Priestlands Dr NE46 ....45 A4
Priestlands Gr NE46 ....45 A4
Priestlands La NE46 ....45 A4
Priestlands Rd NE46 ....45 A4
Priestley Ct NE34 ....59 A3
Priestley Gdns NE10 ....72 B7
Priestly Cres SR4 ....102 B4
Priestman Ct SR4 ....85 D6
Priestpopple NE46 ....45 B4
Primary Gdns SR2 ....103 C1
Primate Rd SR3 ....85 E2
Primrose Ave NE9 ....59 B5
Primrose Cl NE23 ....29 A8
Primrose Cres
Bournmoor DH4 ....89 E3
Sunderland SR6 ....75 D3
Primrose Gdns
Ouston DH2 ....81 D2
Wallsend NE28 ....40 A4
Primrose Hill NE9 ....71 A5
Primrose Hill Hospl NE32 ....58 C4
Primrose Hill Terr NE32 ....58 C3
Primrose Prec SR6 ....75 D3
Primrose St 3 SR5 ....85 A6
Primrose Terr Birtley DH3 ....82 D4
Jarrow NE32 ....58 C4
Prince Albert Terr NE2 ....99 C2
Prince Consort Ind Est NE31 ....57 C7
Prince Consort La NE31 ....57 D6
Prince Consort Rd
Gateshead NE8 ....101 C1
Hebburn NE31 ....57 C6
Jarrow NE32 ....58 C6
Prince Consort Way NE29 ....42 A3
Prince Edward Ct NE34 ....60 A5
Prince Edward Gr NE34 ....60 C6
Prince Edward Rd NE34 ....60 A5
Prince Edward Rd E NE34 ....60 C6
Prince George Ave SR6 ....75 D3
Prince George Sq 13 NE33 ....42 D3
Prince Of Wales Cl NE34 ....59 E5
Prince Philip Cl NE15 ....54 C5
Prince Rd NE28 ....40 B3
Prince St Chopwell NE17 ....66 B1
Sunderland SR1 ....103 A3
Prince's Gdns NE24 ....17 C8
Prince's Mdw NE3 ....38 A5
Princes Ave
Newcastle-u-T NE3 ....38 B7
Sunderland SR3 ....75 E5
Princes Cl NE3 ....38 B8
Princes Gdns
Sunderland SR6 ....75 E5
Whitley Bay NE25 ....31 E5
Princes Pk Dunston NE11 ....70 B6
Gateshead NE8 ....70 C5
Princes Rd NE3 ....38 C7
Shiney Row DH4 ....90 A5
Tynemouth NE30 ....42 B7
Princess Ct NE42 ....50 D4
Princess Dr NE8 ....100 A1
Princess Gdns DH5 ....95 A5
Princess Louise Fst Sch NE24 ....17 D7
Princess Louise Rd NE24 ....17 E7
Princess Mary Ct NE2 ....99 A4
Princess Sq NE1 ....99 B2
Princess St
Gateshead NE10 ....57 A1
Sunderland SR2 ....102 C1
Sunniside NE16 ....69 B2
Princess Way NE42 ....50 C4
Princesway NE11 ....70 C5

Princesway Central NE11 ....70 C4
Princesway S NE11 ....70 C3
Princetown Terr SR3 ....85 E2
Princeway NE30 ....42 D8
Prinn Pl NE16 ....69 B2
Prior Terr Corbridge NE45 ....46 F6
Hexham NE46 ....45 A6
Prior's Ho NE30 ....42 E7
Prior's Terr NE30 ....42 D7
Priors Grange DH6 ....96 B5
Priors Way NE28 ....40 E2
Priors Wlk NE61 ....8 E7
Priory Ave NE25 ....31 F4
Priory Ct Gateshead NE8 ....101 C3
Gateshead,Wardley NE10 ....72 B8
South Shields NE33 ....42 D5
Tynemouth NE30 ....42 E8
Priory Gdns NE45 ....46 F7
Priory Gn 20 NE6 ....56 B6
Priory Gr SR4 ....85 F5
Priory Grange NE24 ....17 C8
Priory Mews 7 NE30 ....42 D7
Priory Pl
Brunswick Village NE13 ....28 A5
Newcastle-u-T NE6 ....56 C5
Stakeford NE62 ....11 A8
Priory Prim Sch NE30 ....42 D8
Priory Rd NE32 ....58 C8
Priory Way NE5 ....36 C8
Proctor Ct NE6 ....57 A5
Proctor Sq SR3 ....85 F2
Proctor St NE6 ....57 A5
Promenade
Newbiggin-by-t-S NE64 ....7 E4
Seaham SR7 ....93 D1
South Shields NE33 ....42 F3
Sunderland SR2 ....87 A3
Whitley Bay NE26 ....32 B5
Promontory Terr NE26 ....32 C4
Promotion Cl 9 SR6 ....75 E2
Prospect Ave
Seaton Delaval NE25 ....23 C3
Wallsend NE28 ....40 B3
Prospect Avenue N NE28 ....40 B4
Prospect Cotts NE22 ....11 C5
Prospect Cres SR7 ....97 C8
Prospect Ct NE4 ....98 A1
Prospect Gdns NE36 ....74 A7
Prospect Pl
Newbiggin-by-t-S NE64 ....7 F5
Newcastle-u-T NE4 ....98 A1
Prospect Row SR1 ....103 C3
Prospect St 2 DH3 ....88 C1
Prospect Terr
Burnopfield NE16 ....79 A4
1 Chester le S DH3 ....88 C4
East Boldon NE36 ....74 C7
Ebchester DH8 ....76 F4
Gateshead NE9 ....71 D1
Kibblesworth NE11 ....81 C6
North Shields NE30 ....42 C6
Prudhoe NE42 ....50 B2
Prospect Terr Ind Est NE10 ....42 C6
Providence Pl 10 NE10 ....56 D1
Provident Terr NE28 ....40 A2
Provost Gdns NE4 ....54 D4
Prudhoe Castle* NE42 ....50 C3
Prudhoe Castle Fst Sch NE42 ....50 B2
Prudhoe Chare NE1 ....99 A2
Prudhoe Com High Sch NE42 ....50 D1
Prudhoe Ct NE32 ....37 E2
Prudhoe Gr NE32 ....58 B3
Prudhoe Hospl NE42 ....50 F1
Prudhoe Pl NE1 ....99 A2
Prudhoe St
Newcastle-u-T NE1 ....99 A2
North Shields NE29 ....42 A5
6 Sunderland SR4 ....85 F7
Prudhoe Sta NE42 ....50 B4
Prudhoe Street Back 19 NE29 ....42 A5
Prudhoe Terr
10 North Shields NE29 ....42 A5
Tynemouth NE30 ....42 D8
Prudhoe West Fst Sch NE42 ....50 B2
Pudding Chare NE1 ....99 A1
Pudding Mews 3 NE46 ....45 B5
Puffin Cl NE12 ....17 F3
Pullman Ct NE9 ....70 E5
Purbeck Cl NE29 ....31 F2
Purbeck Gdns NE23 ....22 C7
Purbeck Rd NE12 ....39 B6
Purdy's Ho NE61 ....3 E1
Purley NE38 ....84 A4
Purley Cl NE28 ....40 F4
Purley Gdns NE3 ....37 F4
Purley Rd SR3 ....85 E2
Purley Sq SR3 ....85 E2
Putney Sq SR4 ....85 B4
Pykerley Mews NE25 ....31 E4
Pykerley Rd NE25 ....31 E5

Q

Quadrant The
North Shields NE29 ....41 E5
Sunderland SR1 ....103 C3
Quality Row NE6 ....56 A5
Quality Row Rd NE16 ....54 A1
Quantock Ave DH2 ....88 A2
Quantock Cl NE29 ....31 F2
Quarry Bank Ct NE4 ....98 B1
Quarry Cotts NE63 ....7 B6

Quarry Edge NE46 ....45 C3
Quarry Hos NE23 ....29 C6
Quarry House Gdns DH5 ....94 C4
Quarry House La DH5 ....94 C4
Quarry La
South Shields NE34 ....60 B5
South Shields NE34 ....60 B6
Quarry Rd Hebburn NE31 ....57 E5
New Silksworth SR3 ....92 B7
Newcastle-u-T NE15 ....53 C6
Quarry Row 18 NE10 ....56 D1
Quarry Sq DH9 ....79 B2
Quarry St SR3 ....92 A7
Quarry View Prim Sch SR4 ....85 C6
Quarryfield Rd NE8 ....101 C4
Quatre Bras NE46 ....44 F5
Quay Corner Ave NE32 ....58 D8
Quay Rd NE24 ....18 A7
Quay The DH5 ....95 A3
Quay View NE28 ....41 A2
Quayside Blyth NE24 ....17 F8
Newcastle-u-T NE1 ....101 A4
Newcastle-u-T,St Lawrence NE1,NE6 ....56 A5
Quayside Ct 8 Blyth NE24 ....17 F8
North Shields NE30 ....42 B5
Quayside Ho SR1 ....103 B3
Queen Alexandra Mews SR2 ....86 D3
Queen Alexandra Rd
Sunderland SR2 ....86 D3
Tynemouth NE29 ....42 A7
Queen Alexandra Road W NE29 ....42 A7
Queen Ann Ct 21 NE6 ....56 C7
Queen Elizabeth Ave NE9 ....71 B6
Queen Elizabeth Ct NE34 ....58 F3
Queen Elizabeth Dr DH5 ....97 D8
Queen Elizabeth High Sch NE46 ....44 E4
Queen Elizabeth Hospl NE9 ....71 A6
Queen Elizabeth II Ctry Pk* NE63 ....6 F4
Queen St Ashington NE63 ....6 E4
Birtley DH3 ....82 B4
Gateshead NE8 ....70 C8
Hetton le H DH5 ....95 A5
Lynemouth NE61 ....1 A2
Morpeth NE61 ....9 A8
Newbiggin-by-t-S NE64 ....7 E1
Newcastle-u-T NE1 ....101 B4
North Shields NE30 ....42 B6
South Shields NE33 ....42 C3
Sunderland SR1 ....103 A3
Sunderland,Grangetown SR2 ....92 F8
Queen St E SR1 ....103 B3
Queen Victoria Rd NE1,NE2 ....99 A3
Queen Victoria St NE10 ....57 A1
Queen's Cres
Hebburn NE31 ....57 D4
Sunderland SR4 ....102 A1
Wallsend NE28 ....40 B3
Queen's Dr NE26 ....32 A5
Queen's Gdns Blyth NE24 ....17 C8
Morpeth NE61 ....8 E7
Queen's Par NE26 ....75 F5
Queen's Pk DH3 ....88 D2
Queen's Rd
Bedlington NE22 ....11 D2
Newcastle-u-T NE2 ....38 F1
Sunderland SR5 ....75 B1
Whitley Bay NE26 ....31 F6
Queen's Terr NE2 ....38 F1
Queens Ave SR6 ....75 E5
Queens Ct
Gateshead NE8 ....100 C1
Newcastle-u-T NE4 ....98 B2
Newcastle-u-T,Brunton Park NE3 ....28 C2
Walbottle NE15 ....35 D2
Queens Dr Sunniside NE16 ....69 B2
Whickham NE16 ....69 C5
Queens Gdns
Annitsford NE23 ....22 B1
Longbenton NE12 ....39 D6
Queens La NE1 ....101 A4
Queens Pl NE64 ....7 E5
Queens Rd
Annitsford NE23 ....22 B1
Newcastle-u-T NE5 ....37 A3
Seaton Sluice NE26 ....24 D6
Walbottle NE15 ....36 A1
Queens Terr NE28 ....40 C3
Queens Way NE46 ....44 F4
Queensberry St SR4 ....102 B3
Queensbridge NE12 ....38 F7
Queensbury Dr NE15 ....36 B2
Queensbury Gate NE12 ....39 A6
Queensland Ave NE34 ....58 F4
Queensmere DH3 ....88 C7
Queensway
Houghton-le-S DH5 ....94 F8
Morpeth NE61 ....9 A6
Newcastle-u-T,Fenham NE4 ....54 D8
Ponteland NE20 ....25 D2
Tynemouth NE30 ....42 D8
3 Washington NE38 ....83 E4
Queensway Cl NE11 ....70 C6
Queensway N NE11 ....70 C5
Queensway S NE11 ....70 C5
Quentin Ave NE3 ....37 D5

Quick Silver Way NE27 ....30 E1
Quigley Terr DH3 ....82 B6

R

Rabbit Banks Rd NE8 ....101 A3
Raby Cl Bedlington NE22 ....10 D1
Fence Houses DH4 ....90 A1
Raby Cres 8 NE6 ....56 C6
Raby Cross 10 NE6 ....56 C5
Raby Dr SR3 ....91 C7
Raby Gdns
Burnopfield NE16 ....78 E6
Jarrow NE32 ....58 B4
Raby Rd NE38 ....83 A5
Raby St Gateshead NE8 ....70 F8
10 Newcastle-u-T,Byker NE6 ....56 B6
Newcastle-u-T,St Lawrence NE6 ....56 C5
Sunderland SR4 ....102 B2
Raby Way NE6 ....56 C5
Rabygate 7 NE6 ....56 C6
Rachel Cl SR2 ....92 C7
Rackly Way SR5 ....75 F8
Radcliffe Cotts 5 NE15 ....35 C5
Radcliffe Pl 3 NE5 ....37 D2
Radcliffe Rd
Hexham NE46 ....45 C4
Sunderland SR5 ....74 C2
Radcliffe St DH3 ....82 C3
Radlett Rd SR5 ....74 D2
Radnor Gdns NE28 ....41 A3
Radnor St NE1 ....99 B2
Radstock Pl NE12 ....39 C7
Rae Ave NE28 ....40 B4
Raeburn Ave NE38 ....83 E4
Raeburn Gdns NE9 ....71 B7
Raeburn Rd
Sunderland SR5 ....74 C3
Whiteleas NE34 ....59 D2
Raglan NE38 ....83 A5
Raglan Ave SR2 ....86 E3
Raglan Pl NE16 ....79 B6
Raglan Row DH4 ....90 C5
Raglan St NE32 ....58 C7
Railton Gdns NE9 ....71 B6
Railway Arches NE1 ....99 B1
Railway Cotts Birtley DH3 ....82 B4
Blyth,Bebside NE24 ....16 E8
Blyth,South Newsham NE24 ....17 C2
Cleadon NE36 ....59 D1
Penshaw NE38 ....90 A4
Riding Mill NE44 ....63 A8
Wylam NE41 ....53 C5
Railway Mus* NE41 ....51 B6
Railway Row SR1 ....102 B3
Railway St Dunston NE11 ....100 A1
Dunston NE11 ....54 F2
Hebburn NE31 ....57 F7
Hetton le H DH5 ....95 A4
Jarrow NE32 ....58 A7
Newbottle DH4 ....90 C2
Newcastle-u-T NE4 ....100 B3
Sunderland SR1 ....103 C2
Railway Terr Blyth NE24 ....17 D7
New Herrington DH4 ....90 D6
Newcastle-u-T NE4 ....100 B3
North Shields NE29 ....42 A5
Penshaw DH4 ....90 A4
2 Sunderland SR4 ....85 A6
Washington NE38 ....40 D1
Railway Terr N DH4 ....90 D7
Raine Gr SR1 ....103 B2
Rainford Ave SR2 ....86 E3
Rainhill Cl NE37 ....72 F1
Rainhill Rd NE37 ....72 F1
Rainton Bridge Ind Est DH4 ....94 C7
Rainton Cl NE10 ....72 C6
Rainton Gr DH5 ....94 E6
Rainton Meadows (Nature Reserve)* DH4 ....94 B6
Rainton St Penshaw DH4 ....90 B8
Sunderland SR4 ....102 A2
Rainton View DH4 ....94 A2
Rake La NE29 ....31 E1
Raleigh Cl NE33 ....59 B8
Raleigh Rd SR5 ....74 E2
Raleigh Sq SR5 ....74 D2
Ralph Ave SR2 ....92 E8
Ralph St NE31 ....57 F7
Ramilies SR2 ....92 D6
Ramillies Rd SR5 ....74 C3
Ramillies Sq SR5 ....74 C3
Ramparts The NE15 ....53 F8
Ramsay Rd NE17 ....66 B2
Ramsay Sq SR5 ....74 D2
Ramsay St Blaydon NE21 ....53 B1
High Spen NE39 ....67 A5
Ramsey St DH3 ....88 C2
Ramsgate Rd SR5 ....74 C3
Ramshaw Cl NE7 ....39 E3
Randolph St NE32 ....58 C7
Rangoon Rd SR5 ....74 C3
Ranmere Rd NE15 ....54 A5
Ranmore Cl NE23 ....22 B7
Rannoch Ave DH2 ....88 B1
Rannoch Cl NE10 ....72 C8
Rannoch Ho NE2 ....38 F2
Rannoch Rd SR5 ....74 C3
Ranson Cres NE34 ....58 F5
Ranson St SR4,SR2 ....86 B4
Raphael Ave NE34 ....59 B5
Rapperton Ct 7 NE5 ....36 F3

Rathmore Gdns NE30 ....42 A8
Ratho Ct NE10 ....71 E...
Ravel Ct NE32 ....58 C...
Raven Terr 7 DH3 ....82 C...
Ravensbourne Ave NE36 ....74 D...
Ravensburn Gdns NE15 ....53 F...
Ravenna Rd SR5 ....74 B...
Ravens Hill Dr NE63 ....6 A...
Ravensbourne Ave NE36 ....74 D...
Ravensburn Wlk 8 NE15 ....35 D...
Ravenscar Cl NE16 ....68 F...
Ravenscourt Pl NE8 ....101 A...
Ravenscourt Rd SR5 ....74 D...
Ravensdale Cres 3 NE9 ....71 A...
Ravensdale Gr NE24 ....17 A...
Ravenshill Rd NE5 ....36 E...
Ravenside Rd NE4 ....54 E...
Ravenside Terr NE17 ....66 A...
Ravenstone NE37 ....83 B...
Ravenswood 5 NE9 ....71 A...
Ravenswood Cl NE12 ....39 E...
Ravenswood Gdns NE9 ....71 A...
Ravenswood Prim Sch NE6 ....39 C...
Ravenswood Rd
Newcastle-u-T NE6 ....39 C...
Sunderland SR5 ....74 E...
Ravenswood Sq SR5 ....74 E...
Ravensworth 7 NE2 ....92 C...
Ravensworth Apartments 6 NE11 ....70 A...
Ravensworth Ave
Fence Houses DH4 ....90 A...
Gateshead NE9 ....71 C...
Ravensworth Cl NE28 ....40 F...
Ravensworth Cres NE16 ....79 D...
Ravensworth Ct
Bedlington NE22 ....11 D...
Dunston NE11 ....100 A...
Newcastle-u-T NE3 ....37 C...
South Hetton DH6 ....97 F...
Ravensworth Gdns NE11 ....1 ...
Ravensworth Rd
Birtley DH3 ....82 B...
Dunston NE11 ....100 A...
Fence Houses DH4 ....89 F...
Ravensworth St
2 Bedlington NE22 ....11 D...
Sunderland SR4 ....102 B...
Wallsend NE28 ....40...
Ravensworth Terr
3 Bedlington NE22 ....11 D...
Birtley DH3 ....82 B...
Jarrow NE32 ....58...
Newcastle-u-T NE4 ....98...
South Shields NE33 ....59 D...
Sunniside NE16 ....69...
Ravensworth Terrace Prim Sch DH3 ....82 C...
Ravine Ct SR6 ....75...
Ravine Terr SR6 ....75...
Rawdon Rd SR5 ....74...
Rawling Rd NE8 ....70...
Rawlston Way NE5 ....37...
Rawmarsh Rd NE63 ....74...
Raydale SR5 ....74...
Raydale Ave NE37 ....83...
Raylees Gdns NE11 ....70...
Rayleigh Dr NE13 ....28...
Rayleigh Gr NE8 ....70...
Raynes Cl NE61 ....8...
Raynham Cl NE23 ....21...
Raynham Ct 8 NE32 ....42...
Readhead Ave NE33 ....42...
Readhead Bldgs 2 NE33 ....42 ...
Readhead Dr NE6 ....56...
Readhead Rd NE34 ....59...
Reading Rd
South Shields NE33 ....59...
Sunderland SR5 ....74...
Reasby Gdns NE40 ....52...
Reasby Villas NE40 ....52...
Reavley Ave NE22 ....11...
Reay Cres NE35 ....74...
Reay Ct 4 DH2 ....88...
Reay Gdns NE5 ....37...
Reay Pl Newcastle-u-T NE3 ....38...
South Shields SR4 ....59...
Reay St NE10 ....
Rectory Ave NE3 ....38...
Rectory Bank NE36 ....74...
Rectory Ct 6 NE16 ....69...
Rectory Dene NE61 ....8...
Rectory Gn NE36 ....73...
Rectory Gr NE3 ....38...
Rectory La Blaydon NE21 ....68...
Ebchester DH8 ....76...
Whickham NE16 ....69...
Rectory Pk NE61 ....8...
Rectory Pl NE8 ....101...
Rectory Rd
Gateshead,Carr Hill NE10 ....71...
Gateshead,Shipcote NE8, NE9 ....70...
Hetton le H DH5 ....95...
Newcastle-u-T NE3 ....38...
Rectory Rd E NE10 ....71...
Rectory Terr NE3 ....38...
Red Admiral Ct NE11 ....70...
Red Barns NE1 ....99...
Red Bglws NE9 ....71...
Red Hall Dr NE7 ....39...
Red House Dr NE25 ....23...
Red House Farm NE22 ....15...
Red House Rd NE31 ....57...
Red Lion Bldgs NE37 ....72...
Red Lion La NE37 ....72...

Red Rose Prim Sch DH3 ..88 D1
Red Rose Terr DH3 ....88 D2
Red Row CE NE22 ....11 C4
Red Row Dr NE22 ....11 C3
Red Wlk NE7 ....39 A1
Redberry Way NE34 ....59 B4
Redburn CI DH4 ....94 C8
Redburn Rd NE5 ....36 F4
Redby CI SR6 ....75 D2
Redby Prim Sch SR6 .....75 E2
Redcar Rd
  Newcastle-u-T NE6 ....39 D1
  Sunderland SR5 ....74 E2
  Wallsend NE28 ....41 A3
Redcar Sq SR5 ....74 E2
Redcliffe Way NE5 ....37 B3
Redcroft Gn NE5 ....37 B3
Redditch Sq SR5 ....74 D2
Rede Ave Hebburn NE31 ...57 E6
  Hexham NE46 ....45 C4
Rede Ct NE61 ....1 E5
Rede St Gateshead NE11 ..70 C5
  Jarrow NE32 ....58 A5
Rede Terr NE46 ....45 C4
Redemarsh NE10 ....71 F6
Redesdale Ave
  Blaydon NE21 ....67 F8
  Newcastle-u-T NE3 ....38 A6
Redesdale Cl
  Longbenton NE12 ....39 C8
  Newcastle-u-T NE15 .....53 E7
Redesdale Gdns NE11 ....69 F7
Redesdale Gr NE29 ....41 D6
Redesdale PI NE24 ....17 B7
Redesdale Prim Sch
  NE28 ....39 F4
Redesdale Rd
  Chester le S DH3 ....88 A1
  North Shields NE29 ......41 D6
  Sunderland SR5 ....74 C3
Redewater Gdns NE16 ....69 A6
Redewater Rd NE4 ....64 A8
Redewood CI NE5 ....37 A1
Redford PI NE23 ....29 C5
Redheugh Bridge Rd
  NE1,NE4 ....100 C3
Redheugh Ct NE8 ....70 B8
Redheugh Rd NE8 ....31 B5
Redhill NE38 ....75 E8
Redhill Rd SR5 ....68 E4
Redhill Wlk NE23 ....22 B7
Redhills Way DH5 ....95 A2
Redland Ave NE3 ....37 E6
Redmayne Ct 1 NE10 ....71 D8
Redmires CI DH2 ....81 E1
Redmond Rd SR5 ....74 E3
Redmond Sq SR5 ....74 E3
Rednam PI NE5 ....37 B2
Redruth Gdns NE9 ....70 F2
Redruth Sq SR5 ....74 D3
Redshank CI NE38 ....82 F2
Redshank Dr NE24 ....17 E4
Redstart Ct NE39 ....67 D2
Redwell Ct Prudhoe NE42 .50 C7
  South Shields NE34 ......60 C7
Redwell La NE34 ....60 D7
Redwell Rd NE42 ....50 E2
Redwing Ct NE38 ....82 F3
Redwing Ct NE6 ....56 E7
Redwood Cl
  Hetton le H DH5 ....94 F4
  Killingworth NE12 ....29 C4
Redwood Ct NE3 ....6 E2
Redwood Gdns NE11 .....70 B5
Redwood Gr SR3 ....92 B7
Reed Ave NE12 ....29 C4
Reed St North Shields NE30 .42 B6
  South Shields NE33 ......59 C8
Reedham Ct NE5 ....37 B4
Reedling Cl SR5 ....74 C4
Reedside NE40 ....52 D5
Reedsmouth PI NE5 ......54 D3
Reedswood Cres NE23 ...22 E5
Reestones PI NE3 ....37 D5
Reeth Rd SR5 ....74 D2
Reeth Sq SR5 ....74 D2
Reeth Way NE15 ....35 C1
Regal Rd SR4 ....102 A3
Regency Ct NE2 ....99 C4
Regency Dr
  New Silksworth SR3 ......92 B8
  Whickham NE16 ....68 F6
Regency Gdns NE29 .....41 E7
Regent Ave NE3 ....38 B5
Regent Centre Sta NE3 ..37 E6
Regent Ct Blyth NE24 ....17 D7
  Gateshead NE8 ....101 C2
  Hebburn NE31 ....57 D5
  Longbenton NE12 ....29 B2
  South Shields NE33 ......42 C1
Regent Ctr The NE3 ......38 C6
Regent Dr NE16 ....68 F4
Regent Farm Ct NE3 .....38 A6
Regent Farm Fst Sch
  NE3 ....38 A6
Regent Farm Rd NE3 ....38 A6
Regent Rd Jarrow NE32 ..58 C6
  Newcastle-u-T NE3 ......38 A6
  Ryhope SR2 ....93 A5
  Wallsend NE28 ....40 A3
Regent Rd N NE3 ....38 C5
Regent St Blyth NE24 ....17 D8
  Hetton le H DH5 ....95 A5
Regent Terr
  Gateshead NE8 ....101 B2

Regent Terr continued
  North Shields NE29 ......41 E6
  Sunderland SR2 ....86 F2
Regents Cl SR6 ....75 F8
Regents Ct NE28 ....39 E4
Regents Dr Prudhoe NE42 .50 E4
  Tynemouth NE30 ....32 C1
Regents Pk NE28 ....39 E3
Regina Sq SR5 ....74 D3
Reginald St
  Boldon Colliery NE35 .....73 F8
  Gateshead NE8 ....56 B1
  4 Sunderland SR4 ......85 F7
Regrave Ct NE8 ....56 B2
Reid Ave NE28 ....40 B3
Reid Park Cl NE2 ....38 F2
Reid Park Ct NE2 ....38 F2
Reid Park Rd NE2 ....38 F2
Reid St NE61 ....9 A8
Reid's La SR5 ....22 E1
Reigate Sq NE23 ....22 B7
Reins Ct NE46 ....44 E5
Reiverdale Rd NE63 ....6 D4
Rekendyke Ind Est NE33 .42 B1
Rekendyke La NE33 ......42 B1
Relton Ave NE6 ....56 D4
Relton Cl DH4 ....94 A7
Relton Ct NE25 ....31 E5
Relton PL NE25 ....31 E5
Relton Terr
  Chester le S DH3 ....88 C2
  Whitley Bay NE25 ....31 E5
Rembrandt Ave NE34 ....59 C2
Remscheid Way NE63 .....6 C1
Remus Ave NE15 ....34 D2
Remus Cl NE13 ....28 B5
Renaissance Point NE30 .42 C6
Rendel St NE11 ....54 F1
Rendle Rd NE6 ....57 B4
Renforth Cl NE8 ....56 B2
Renforth St NE11 ....56 B2
Renfrew Cl NE29 ....41 C8
Renfrew Gn NE5 ....37 B3
Renfrew PI DH3 ....82 D2
Renfrew Rd SR5 ....74 D3
Rennie Rd SR5 ....74 B3
Rennie Sq SR5 ....74 B3
Rennington NE10 ....72 A5
Rennington Ave NE30 ...32 C1
Rennington Cl
  Morpeth NE61 ....9 B5
  Tynemouth NE30 ....32 C1
Renoir Gdns NE34 ....59 D2
Renwick Ave NE3 ....37 E6
Renwick Ct NE8 ....70 C8
Renwick Ho NE61 ....8 E7
Renwick Rd NE24 ....17 D7
Renwick St NE6 ....56 D6
Renwick Wlk NE61 ....8 E8
Rescue Station Cotts
  DH5 ....94 F6
Resida Cl NE15 ....53 C8
Retford Rd SR5 ....74 D3
Retford Sq SR5 ....74 D3
Retreat The
  Newburn NE15 ....52 F7
  Sunderland SR2 ....102 B2
Revell Terr NE5 ....37 E1
Revelstoke Rd SR5 ......74 C3
Revesby St NE33 ....59 C6
Reynolds Ave
  Killingworth NE12 ....29 B2
  Washington NE34 ....83 E4
  Whiteleas NE34 ....59 D3
Reyrolle Ct NE31 ....57 D5
Rheims Ct SR4 ....85 D7
Rheydt Ave NE28 ....39 F2
Rhoda Terr NE2 ....86 F1
Rhodes St NE6 ....57 A5
Rhodesia Rd SR5 ....74 D3
Rhondda Rd SR5 ....74 B3
Rhuddlan Ct NE5 ....37 B4
Rhyl Par NE5 ....58 A2
Rhyl Sq SR5 ....74 E3
Ribble Rd SR5 ....74 C2
Ribble Wlk NE32 ....58 C2
Ribbledale Gdns NE7 ....39 B3
Ribblesdale Penshaw DH4 .90 B8
  Washington NE28 ....39 F4
Ribblesdale Ave NE24 ...17 A8
Richard Ave SR4 ....84 A4
Richard Avenue Prim Sch
  SR4 ....84 B4
Richard Browell Rd NE15 .35 E1
Richard Coates CE Mid Sch
  NE20 ....25 E7
Richard St Blyth NE24 ...17 E7
  Hetton le H DH5 ....95 A3
Richard Stannard Ho 11
  NE24 ....17 F8
Richardson Ave 2 NE34 .58 F4
Richardson Dees Prim Sch
  NE28 ....40 D2
Richardson Rd NE1,NE2 .98 C3
Richardson St
  Ashington NE63 ....6 E1
  3 Newcastle-u-T NE6 ...56 C8
  Wallsend NE28 ....40 C2
Richardson Terr
  Chopwell NE17 ....66 B1
  Ryhope SR2 ....93 A6
  5 Washington NE37 .....83 D6
Richmond's Bldgs NE62 ..10 E5
Richmond Ave
  Gateshead NE10 ....57 C2
  Washington NE38 ....83 D6

Richmond Ave continued
  Whickham NE16 ....54 B1
Richmond Cl NE22 ....10 E2
Richmond Ct
  Gateshead NE8 ....101 C1
  1 Gateshead,Low Fell NE9 .70 F4
  Jarrow NE32 ....58 A7
Richmond Dr DH4 ....89 D1
Richmond Fields NE20 ...25 A5
Richmond Gdns NE28 ....40 E3
Richmond Gr NE29 ......41 E5
Richmond Lodge NE3 ....38 D4
Richmond Mews NE3 ....38 B3
Richmond Pk NE28 ......39 E3
Richmond Rd NE34 ......59 C6
Richmond St SR5 ....102 C4
Richmond Terr
  Gateshead NE8 ....101 B1
  18 Gateshead,Felling NE10 .71 D8
  Haswell DH6 ....97 F3
  Walbottle NE15 ....35 F1
  Whitley Bay NE26 ....31 F7
Richmond Way
  Cramlington NE23 ....22 A3
  Ponteland NE20 ....25 A3
Rickaby St SR1 ....103 C4
Rickgarth NE10 ....71 F5
Rickleton Ave DH3 ....88 D5
Rickleton Prim Sch NE38 .88 F8
Rickleton Village Ctr
  NE38 ....88 F8
Rickleton Way NE38 ....83 A1
Riddel Ave NE15 ....54 C5
Riddell Ct 7 DH2 ....88 C2
Riddings Sq SR5 ....74 D3
Riddings Sq SR5 ....74 D3
Ridge Ct NE13 ....28 B3
Ridge Terr NE40 ....52 C4
Ridge Villas NE22 ....10 E1
Ridge Way The NE3 ......37 F4
Ridgely Cl NE20 ....26 A6
Ridgely Dr NE20 ....26 A6
Ridgeway Ashington NE63 .7 A2
  Birtley DH3 ....82 C6
  Gateshead NE10 ....72 B6
  Newcastle-u-T NE4 ......54 E8
  Ryhope SR2 ....93 A5
  Seaton Delaval NE25 ....23 E1
  Stakeford NE62 ....11 A8
Ridgeway Cres SR3 .....86 B3
Ridgeway Prim Sch NE34 .59 F4
Ridgeway The NE7 ....59 F3
Ridgewood Cres NE3 ....38 F5
Ridgewood Gdns NE3 ...38 E5
Ridgewood Villas NE3 ...38 E5
Riding Barns Way NE16 ..69 A2
Riding Cl NE40 ....51 E3
Riding Cotts NE46 ....45 A8
Riding Dene NE43 ....49 F1
Riding Grange NE44 .....62 E8
Riding La DH2,NE11 .....81 B4
Riding Lea NE21 ....53 A1
Riding Mill Sta NE44 ....62 F8
Riding Terr NE43 ....49 F1
Riding The NE3 ....37 E3
Ridings Ct NE40 ....51 E3
Ridings The NE25 ....31 C6
Ridley Ave Blyth NE24 ...17 F7
  Chester le S DH2 ....88 B2
  Sunderland SR2 ....92 F7
  Wallsend NE28 ....41 B4
Ridley Cl 11 Hexham NE46 .44 F3
  Morpeth NE61 ....9 E8
  Newcastle-u-T NE3 ......38 C6
Ridley Gdns NE16 ....54 A1
Ridley Gr NE34 ....60 A7
Ridley Mill Cotts NE43 ...64 B6
Ridley Mill Rd NE43 .....64 B5
Ridley PI NE1,NE99 .....99 B2
Ridley St Blyth NE24 ....17 F8
  Cramlington NE23 ....22 C5
  Gateshead NE8 ....70 E8
  Sunderland SR5 ....75 B2
Ridley Terr Cambois NE24 .12 D4
  Gateshead NE10 ....57 B1
  Hexham NE46 ....45 A6
  Sunderland SR2 ....103 C1
Ridsdale NE42 ....50 B1
Ridsdale Ave NE34 ......59 E5
Ridsdale Cl
  Seaton Delaval NE25 ....23 C3
  Wallsend NE28 ....40 A1
Ridsdale Sq NE63 ....6 C3
Rievaulx NE38 ....83 C6
Riga Sq SR5 ....74 C3
Riggs The Corbridge NE45 .46 F7
  Houghton-le-S DH4 ......94 F8
Rignall NE38 ....84 A5
Riley St NE32 ....58 A7
Riley Street Ind Est NE32 .58 A7
Ringlet Ct NE11 ....70 B7
Ringmore Ct SR2 ....86 E4
Rington Cl 8 NE30 ......42 D7
Ringway Stakeford NE62 ..6 A1
  Sunderland SR5 ....85 A8
Ringwood Dr NE23 ......22 B7
Ringwood Gn NE12 ......39 C7
Ringwood Rd SR5 ....74 D3
Ringwood Sq SR5 ....74 D3
Rink St NE24 ....17 F8
Ripley Ave NE29 ....41 F6
Ripley Cl NE22 ....10 D2
Ripley Ct NE9 ....71 B1
Ripley Terr NE6 ....56 E6
Ripon Cl NE23 ....21 F3

Ripon Gdns
  Newcastle-u-T NE2 ......56 A8
  Wallsend NE28 ....40 E3
Ripon Sq NE32 ....73 B8
Ripon St Chester le S DH3 .88 C1
  Gateshead NE8 ....101 B1
  Sunderland SR6 ....75 E1
Rise The
  Newcastle-u-T NE3 ......37 E4
  Ponteland NE20 ....25 B2
  Ryton NE21 ....53 A4
  Seaton Sluice NE26 .....24 E4
Rishton Sq SR5 ....74 C3
Rising Sun Cotts NE28 ..40 B5
Rising Sun Cntry Pk*
  NE28 ....41 E7
Ritson Cl NE29 ....41 D6
Ritson St SR6 ....75 E4
River Bank NE62 ....11 C8
River Bank E NE62 ......11 C8
River Dr NE33 ....42 C4
River Garth SR1 ....103 C4
River Lawn NE62 ....11 D1
River Terr 5 DH3 ....88 D4
River View Bedside NE22 .11 D1
River View Cl NE22 ......11 D1
Riverbank Rd SR5 ....74 D2
Riverdale SR5 ....85 B8
Rivermead NE38 ....83 E1
Rivermede NE20 ....25 F7
Riversdale NE17 ....77 B6
Riversdale Ave NE62 ....11 A8
Riversdale Ct
  Newcastle-u-T NE15 .....53 C6
  Stakeford NE62 ....11 A7
Riversdale Ho NE62 .....11 A7
Riversdale Terr SR2 .....102 B1
Riversdale Way NE15 ...53 C6
Riverside Morpeth NE61 ..8 F8
  Ponteland NE20 ....25 E6
Riverside Ave NE10 ......10 D7
Riverside Bsns Pk NE28 ..41 A1
Riverside Ct
  Dunston NE11 ....100 A1
  South Shields NE33 .....42 B2
Riverside Lodge NE15 ...52 A8
Riverside Pk SR4 ....85 B7
Riverside Prim Sch NE29 .41 D4
Riverside Rd SR5 ....74 E2
Riverside The NE31 ......57 C7
Riverside Way
  Rowlands Gill NE39 .....78 D8
  Whickham NE11,NE16 ...69 B4
Riverslea NE34 ....60 A6
Riverview Lodge NE4 ....54 B3
Roachburn Rd NE5 ......36 E2
Robert Allan Ct NE13 ...28 A7
Robert Owen Gdns NE10 .71 C7
Robert St Blyth NE24 ....17 F7
  New Silksworth SR3 .....92 B7
  South Shields NE33 .....42 D1
  Sunderland SR4 ....102 A3
Robert Terr NE39 ....66 F4
Robert Terr Cotts NE39 ..66 F4
Robert Westall Way
  NE29 ....42 A3
Robert Wheatman Ct
  SR2 ....86 E2
Roberts St NE15 ....54 A8
Roberts Terr NE35 ......58 B5
Robertson Ct 14 DH3 ...88 C2
Robertson Rd SR5 ....74 B2
Robertson Sq SR5 ......74 B2
Robin Ct DH5 ....94 C3
Robin Gr SR5 ....74 C1
Robin La
  East Rainton DH4,DH5 ..94 C2
  West Rainton DH4,DH5 ..94 C2
Robinson Gdns
  Wallsend NE28 ....41 A3
  2 Whitburn SR6 ....60 F1
Robinson St
  5 Newcastle-u-T NE6 ...56 C6
  8 South Shields NE33 ...42 D2
Robinson Terr
  Burnopfield NE16 ....79 A6
  Sunderland SR2 ....103 C1
  2 Washington NE37 ....83 A6
Robinswood 8 NE9 ......70 F5
Robsheugh PI NE5 ......54 D8
Robson Dr NE46 ....44 F6
Robson PI SR2 ....93 A6
Robson St
  7 Gateshead NE9 ......70 F5
  Newcastle-u-T NE6 .....56 E6
Robson Terr
  Hexham NE46 ....45 A6
  High Spen NE39 ....67 B3
  Tantobel DH9 ....79 D1
Rochdale Rd SR5 ....74 D3
Rochdale St
  Hetton le H DH5 ....95 A2
  Wallsend NE28 ....40 C1
Rochdale Way SR5 ......74 D3
Roche Ct NE38 ....83 C4
Rochester Gdns NE11 ...70 A8
Rochester Sq NE25 .....31 E5
Rochester St NE6 ....57 A4
Rochester Terr 1 NE10 .71 C8
Rochford Gr NE23 ....22 A3
Rochford Rd SR5 ....74 C3

Rock Gr 4 NE9 ....70 F5
Rock Lodge Gdns SR6 ...75 F3
Rock Lodge Rd SR6 .....75 F3
Rock Terr
  Newcastle-u-T NE2 ......99 C2
  7 Washington NE37 ....83 E8
Rockcliffe
  South Shields NE33 ......42 F1
  Whitley Bay NE26 ....32 C5
Rockcliffe Ave NE26 ....32 C4
Rockcliffe Fst Sch NE26 .32 C4
Rockcliffe Gdns
  Newcastle-u-T NE15 .....53 F7
  Whickham NE16 ....32 C4
Rockcliffe St NE26 ......32 C4
Rockcliffe Way NE9 .....71 D1
Rockhope NE38 ....88 F8
Rockingham Cl SR7 .....93 C1
Rockingham Rd SR5 ....74 C3
Rockingham Sq SR5 ....74 C3
Rockmore Rd NE21 .....53 C1
Rockville SR6 ....75 E4
Rockwood Gdns NE40 ...51 F1
Rockwood Hill Est NE40 .66 E8
Rockwood Hill Rd NE40 .51 F1
Rockwood Terr NE40 ....51 F1
Rodin Ave NE34 ....59 D2
Rodney Cl Ryhope SR2 ..92 C6
  Tynemouth NE30 ....42 D7
Rodney Ct NE6 ....56 B5
Rodney St NE6 ....56 B5
Rodney Way NE26 ......31 D7
Rodsley Ave NE8,NE9 ...70 F8
Roeburn Way NE3 ....37 F3
Roedean Rd SR5 ....74 E3
Roehedge NE10 ....72 B6
Rogan Ave 8 NE37 .....83 A6
Roger St NE6 ....56 B6
Rogerson Terr NE5 .....36 E3
Rogues La NE39 ....67 A5
Rokeby Ave NE15 ....53 D6
Rokeby Dr NE3 ....37 F4
Rokeby St
  Newcastle-u-T NE15 .....53 D6
  Sunderland SR4 ....102 B2
Rokeby Terr NE6 ....39 C1
Rokeby View NE9 ....71 A1
Roker Ave Sunderland SR6 .75 E1
  Whitley Bay NE25 ....31 F1
Roker Baths Rd SR6 .....75 E2
Roker Park Cl 10 SR6 ...75 E2
Roker Park Rd SR6 ......75 E2
Roker Park Terr SR6 ....75 F3
Roker Terr SR6 ....75 F3
Rokerby Ave NE16 ......69 B7
Roland Rd NE28 ....40 E2
Roland St NE38 ....83 E4
Rollesby Ct NE5 ....37 B4
Rolley Way NE42 ....50 E3
Rolling Mill Rd NE32 ...58 A8
Romaldskirk Cl SR4 ....85 B5
Roman Ave
  Chester le S DH3 ....88 D3
  Newcastle-u-T NE6 ......56 E6
Roman Rd Hedworth NE10 .72 D8
  South Shields NE33 .....42 D4
Roman Road Prim Sch
  NE10 ....72 A5
Roman Way NE45 ....46 F6
Roman Way The NE5 ...53 D8
Romford PI NE23 ....22 A3
Romford St 4 SR4 ......85 F6
Romilly Gr NE10 ....72 D7
Romilly St SR3 ....92 A3
Romney Ave
  Sunderland SR2 ....86 E3
  Washington NE34 ....83 E4
  Whiteleas NE34 ....59 D3
Romney Cl
  Shiney Row DH4 ....90 C5
  Sunderland NE26 ....32 C4
Romney Gdns NE9 ......71 B7
Romney Villas 5 NE8 ...83 E4
Romsey Cl NE23 ....22 A3
Romsey Dr NE35 ....73 E8
Romsey Gr NE15 ....54 A6
Ronald Dr NE15 ....54 A6
Ronald Gdns NE31 .....57 D4
Ronald Sq NE5 ....36 D3
Ronaldsay Cl 4 SR2 ....92 E8
Ronan Mews DH4 ......94 A2
Ronsdorf Ct NE32 ......58 B6
Rookery Cl NE16 ....68 E4
Rookery La NE16 ....68 E4
Rookery The NE6 ....78 F6
Rooksleigh 6 NE21 ....53 B1
Rookwood NE26 ....32 C4
Rookwood Dr NE13 .....28 C8
Rookwood Gdns NE62 ..27 E3
Rookwood Rd NE15 .....54 A7
Ropery La Bournmoor DH3 .88 F3
  Chester le S DH3 ....88 D7
  Hebburn NE31 ....57 D6
  Wallsend NE28 ....40 E2
Ropery Rd Gateshead NE8 .70 B8
  Sunderland SR4 ....102 A4
Ropery The NE6 ....57 B5
Rosa St NE33 ....42 D2
Rosalie Terr SR2 ....86 F4
Rosalind Ave NE22 .....11 B1
Rosalind St Ashington NE63 .6 E4

Rosalind St *continued*
Ashington,Hirst NE63 . . . .**6** E3
Rosamond Pl NE24 . . . .**17** F7
Rose Ave
Cramlington NE23 . . . .**21** F8
Fence Houses DH4 . . . .**89** F1
Whickham NE16 . . . .**69** B7
Rose Bery Cres NE2 . . . .**56** A8
Rose Cotts NE41 . . . .**51** A6
Rose Cres Bournmoor DH4 . .**89** D3
Whitburn SR6 . . . .**60** F2
Rose Ct NE31 . . . .**57** D5
Rose Gdns
Kibblesworth NE11 . . . .**81** C6
Wallsend NE28 . . . .**40** B4
Rose St Gateshead NE8 . . .**100** C2
Hebburn NE31 . . . .**57** D5
7 Houghton-le-S DH4 . . . . .**94** D8
Sunderland SR4 . . . .**102** B3
Rose St E DH4 . . . .**90** B8
Rose St W DH4 . . . .**90** B8
Rose Terr Greenside NE40 . . .**52** C2
Newcastle-u-T NE3 . . . .**37** E1
Rose Villa La NE16 . . . .**69** B7
Roseberry Ct 13 NE37 . . . . . .**83** E8
Roseberry Grange NE12 . . . .**30** A1
Roseberry Pl NE2 . . . .**99** C4
Roseberry Terr 1 NE35 . . . . .**58** E1
Roseberry Ave Blyth NE24 . .**17** D7
Gateshead NE8 . . . .**71** A8
South Shields NE33 . . . .**42** E1
Tynemouth NE29 . . . .**42** A8
Rosebery Pl NE2 . . . .**56** A8
Rosebery St 4 SR5 . . . .**75** D1
Rosebud Cl 8 NE15 . . . .**54** A1
Rosedale Bedlington NE22 . . .**10** E1
Wallsend NE28 . . . .**39** F4
Rosedale Ave SR6 . . . .**75** E6
Rosedale Cres DH4 . . . .**90** C2
Rosedale Ct NE15 . . . .**36** D2
Rosedale Rd NE40 . . . .**51** F3
Rosedale St
Hetton le H DH5 . . . .**94** E1
Sunderland SR1 . . . .**102** B1
Rosedale Terr
Newcastle-u-T NE2 . . . .**99** C3
North Shields NE30 . . . .**42** A7
Sunderland SR6 . . . .**75** E4
Roseden Ct NE12 . . . .**39** C7
Rosedene Villas NE23 . . . .**22** B7
Rosefinch Lodge NE9 . . . .**70** F5
Rosegill NE37 . . . .**83** B6
Rosehill NE28 . . . .**40** E2
Rosehill Rd NE28 . . . .**40** F2
Rosehill Way NE5 . . . .**37** C1
Roselea NE32 . . . .**58** A3
Roselea Ave SR2 . . . .**92** F7
Rosemary Gdns NE9 . . . .**71** D2
Rosemary Rd SR5 . . . .**74** D3
Rosemary Terr NE24 . . . .**17** F6
Rosemount Haswell DH6 . . . . .**97** F4
Morpeth NE61 . . . .**9** A7
Newcastle-u-T NE5 . . . .**36** F2
Sunderland SR4 . . . .**85** A5
Rosemount Ave NE10 . . . .**72** B7
Rosemount Cl NE37 . . . .**72** C2
Rosemount Ct NE36 . . . .**74** B7
Rosemount Way
Newcastle-u-T NE7 . . . .**39** C5
Whitley Bay NE25 . . . .**31** C5
Roseneath Ct NE63 . . . .**6** D3
Roseville St SR4 . . . .**102** B3
Rosewall Pl NE16 . . . .**69** A4
Rosewood NE12 . . . .**29** F3
Rosewood Ave NE3 . . . .**38** E6
Rosewood Cres
Newcastle-u-T NE6 . . . .**39** F1
Seaton Sluice NE26 . . . .**24** D4
Rosewood Gdns
Chester le S DH2 . . . .**88** B5
Gateshead NE9 . . . .**71** B5
Newcastle-u-T NE3 . . . .**37** F4
Rosewood Sq SR4 . . . .**85** A2
Rosewood Terr
Birtley DH3 . . . .**82** B5
Wallsend NE28 . . . .**41** A2
Roseworth Ave NE3 . . . .**38** D3
Roseworth Cl NE3 . . . .**38** D3
Roseworth Cres NE3 . . . .**38** D3
Roseworth Terr
Newcastle-u-T NE3 . . . .**38** C4
Whickham NE16 . . . .**69** D7
Roslin Pk NE22 . . . .**11** C1
Roslin Way NE23 . . . .**21** A3
Ross Ouston DH2 . . . .**82** A1
Ouston DH2 . . . .**81** F2
Ross Ave NE11 . . . .**54** F1
Ross Gr NE23 . . . .**21** F7
Ross Lea DH4 . . . .**90** A5
Ross St SR5 . . . .**75** C1
Ross Way
Newcastle-u-T NE3 . . . .**37** F8
Whitley Bay NE26 . . . .**31** E7
Rossdale 1 NE40 . . . .**51** F3
Rosse Cl NE37 . . . .**83** B8
Rossendale Pl NE12 . . . .**38** F6
Rosslyn Ave
Gateshead NE9 . . . .**71** A6
Newcastle-u-T NE3 . . . .**37** E5
Sunderland SR2 . . . .**92** F7
Rosslyn Mews SR4 . . . .**102** A2
Rosslyn Pl DH3 . . . .**82** D2

Rosslyn St SR4 . . . .**102** A2
Rosslyn Terr SR4 . . . .**102** A2
Rosyth Rd SR5 . . . .**74** E3
Rosyth Sq SR5 . . . .**74** E3
Rotary Parkway NE63 . . . .**6** B4
Rotary Way Blyth NE24 . . . . . .**17** F5
Hexham NE46 . . . .**45** C6
Rothay Pl NE5 . . . .**37** C2
Rothbury SR2 . . . .**92** D7
Rothbury Ave Blyth NE24 . . . .**17** B6
Gateshead NE10 . . . .**57** A1
Hebburn NE32 . . . .**58** A4
Rothbury Cl NE12 . . . .**38** B6
Rothbury Ct
Chester le S DH2 . . . .**88** A1
Killingworth NE12 . . . .**29** C4
Rothbury Gdns
Dunston NE11 . . . .**70** A5
Wallsend NE28 . . . .**40** F3
Widopen NE13 . . . .**28** C6
Rothbury Rd SR5 . . . .**74** D3
Rothbury Terr
Newcastle-u-T NE6 . . . .**56** C8
North Shields NE29 . . . .**41** D4
Rotherfield Cl NE23 . . . .**22** B7
Rotherfield Gdns 6 NE9 . . . .**71** A2
Rotherfield Rd SR5 . . . .**74** C3
Rotherfield Sq SR5 . . . .**74** C3
Rotherham Cl DH5 . . . .**94** D6
Rotherham Rd SR5 . . . .**74** C3
Rothesay DH2 . . . .**81** F1
Rothesay Terr NE22 . . . .**11** C2
Rothlea Gdns NE62 . . . .**11** A8
Rothley NE38 . . . .**83** F2
Rothley Ave Ashington NE63 . . .**6** D2
Newcastle-u-T NE5 . . . .**54** C7
Rothley Cl
Newcastle-u-T NE3 . . . .**38** D5
Ponteland NE20 . . . .**25** D7
Rothley Ct
Killingworth NE12 . . . .**29** D3
Sunderland SR5 . . . .**74** F4
Rothley Gdns NE30 . . . .**32** B1
Rothley Gr NE25 . . . .**23** C3
Rothley Terr DH8 . . . .**77** B1
Rothley Way NE26 . . . .**31** E7
Rothsay Terr NE64 . . . .**7** D3
Rothwell Rd
Newcastle-u-T NE3 . . . .**38** C5
Sunderland SR5 . . . .**74** C2
Roundhill NE32 . . . .**58** D1
Roundhill Ave NE5 . . . .**37** C2
Roundstone Cl NE7 . . . .**39** D4
Roundway The NE12 . . . .**39** B7
Row's Terr NE3 . . . .**38** E5
Rowan Ave NE38 . . . .**83** C1
Rowan Cl Bedlington NE22 . . .**10** F2
Sunderland SR4 . . . .**85** B5
Rowan Ct Blyth NE24 . . . .**17** D6
Burnopfield NE16 . . . .**79** B6
Longbenton NE12 . . . .**39** B8
10 South Shields NE34 . . . .**59** A4
Rowan Dr Hetton le H DH5 . . . .**94** F4
Newcastle-u-T NE3 . . . .**38** D5
Ponteland NE20 . . . .**25** E7
Rowan Gr
Cramlington NE23 . . . .**22** D5
Prudhoe NE42 . . . .**50** B2
Rowanberry Rd NE12 . . . .**39** B6
Rowans The NE9 . . . .**71** D2
Rowantree Rd NE6 . . . .**40** A1
Rowanwood Gdns NE11 . . . . . .**70** B5
Rowedge Wlk NE5 . . . .**37** A2
Rowell Cl SR2 . . . .**92** C6
Rowes Mews NE6 . . . .**56** C4
Rowland Burn Way NE39 . . . .**67** E2
Rowlands Gill Inf Sch
NE39 . . . .**67** F3
Rowlands Gill Jun Sch
NE39 . . . .**67** F3
Rowlandson Cres NE10 . . . . . .**71** D8
Rowlandson Terr
12 Gateshead NE10 . . . .**71** D8
9 Sunderland SR2 . . . .**86** E4
Rowley St NE24 . . . .**17** E7
Rowlington Ter NE63 . . . .**6** D2
Rowntree Way NE29 . . . .**42** A3
Rowsley Rd NE32 . . . .**58** C5
Roxburgh Cl NE21 . . . .**68** A8
Roxburgh Ho NE26 . . . .**32** A5
Roxburgh Pl 2 NE6 . . . .**56** B7
Roxburgh St SR6 . . . .**75** D2
Roxburgh Terr NE26 . . . .**32** A5
Roxby Gdns NE20 . . . .**99** B1
Royal Arc NE1 . . . .**99** B1
Royal Cres NE4 . . . .**54** E8
Royal Gram Sch NE2 . . . .**99** B3
Royal Ind Est NE32 . . . .**57** F8
Royal Quays Outlet Shopping
NE28 . . . .**41** E2
Royal Victoria Infmy NE2 . . . .**98** C3
Royalty The SR2 . . . .**102** B2
Roydon Ave SR2 . . . .**86** E3
Royle St SR2 . . . .**86** F2
Royston Terr NE6 . . . .**57** A4
Ruabon Cl NE23 . . . .**22** A3
Rubens Ave NE34 . . . .**59** D3
Ruby St DH4 . . . .**90** D2
Rudby Cl NE3 . . . .**38** D8
Rudchester Pl NE5 . . . .**36** F1
Ruddock Sq 6 NE6 . . . .**56** C4
Rudyard Ave SR2 . . . .**86** E3
Rudyerd Ct NE29 . . . .**42** B5
Rudyerd St
18 North Shields NE29 . . . .**42** A5
North Shields NE29 . . . .**42** B5

Rugby Gdns
Gateshead NE9 . . . .**71** C3
Wallsend NE28 . . . .**40** E3
Ruislip Pl NE23 . . . .**21** F3
Ruislip Rd SR4 . . . .**85** A5
Runcorn SR2 . . . .**92** C7
Runcorn Rd SR5 . . . .**74** C3
Runhead Est NE40 . . . .**52** D4
Runhead Gdns NE40 . . . .**52** D5
Runhead Terr NE40 . . . .**52** E5
Runnymede SR2 . . . .**92** D7
Runnymede Gdns NE17 . . . . . .**77** D7
Runnymede Rd
Ponteland NE20 . . . .**25** C5
Sunderland SR5 . . . .**74** D3
Whickham NE16 . . . .**69** A6
Runnymede Way
Newcastle-u-T NE3 . . . .**37** E4
Sunderland SR5 . . . .**74** D3
Runswick Ave NE12 . . . .**38** F6
Runswick Cl SR3 . . . .**92** C7
Runswick Dr SR7 . . . .**93** D1
Rupert Sq SR5 . . . .**74** E3
Rupert St SR6 . . . .**60** F1
Rupert Terr NE15 . . . .**52** F8
Rushall Pl NE12 . . . .**39** B6
Rushbury Ct NE27 . . . .**30** C5
Rushcliffe SR6 . . . .**75** D3
Rushford SR2 . . . .**92** D6
Rushie Ave NE15 . . . .**54** C5
Rushley Cres NE21 . . . .**53** C3
Rushsyde Cl NE16 . . . .**68** E5
Rushton Ave SR2 . . . .**86** E3
Rushyrig NE37 . . . .**83** A6
Ruskin Ave Ashington NE63 . . . .**6** F2
7 Dunston NE11 . . . .**54** F1
Easington Lane DH5 . . . .**97** D8
Longbenton NE12 . . . .**29** D1
Ruskin Cres NE34 . . . .**59** B3
Ruskin Dr
Newcastle-u-T NE7 . . . .**39** C3
West Boldon NE35 . . . .**74** A8
Ruskin Rd Birtley DH3 . . . .**82** C4
Gateshead N10,NE9 . . . .**71** B7
Whickham NE16 . . . .**69** A8
Russel Cl NE12 . . . .**38** F2
Russell Ave NE34 . . . .**60** A6
Russell Ct NE8 . . . .**100** C1
Russell Ho SR1 . . . .**103** B3
Russell Sq NE13 . . . .**28** B8
Russell St Jarrow NE32 . . . . . .**58** C7
8 North Shields NE29 . . . .**42** A5
7 South Shields NE33 . . . .**42** C3
Sunderland SR1 . . . .**103** B3
Washington NE37 . . . .**83** C8
Russell Terr
Bedlington NE22 . . . .**15** F8
Birtley DH3 . . . .**82** B6
Newcastle-u-T NE1,NE2 . . . . . .**99** C2
Rustic Terr NE64 . . . .**7** E5
Ruswarp Dr SR3 . . . .**92** B6
Ruth Ave NE21 . . . .**53** C2
Rutherford Ave 4 SR7 . . . . . .**92** F1
Rutherford Cl NE22 . . . .**10** E7
Rutherford Pl NE61 . . . .**8** F7
Rutherford Rd
Sunderland SR5 . . . .**74** B3
Washington NE37 . . . .**72** E2
Rutherford Sq SR5 . . . .**74** B3
Rutherford St Blyth NE24 . . . .**17** D7
Newcastle-u-T NE1 . . . .**98** C1
Wallsend NE28 . . . .**41** B3
Rutherglen Rd SR5 . . . .**74** E3
Rutherglen Sq SR5 . . . .**74** E3
Ruthven Ct NE7 . . . .**38** F7
Rutland Ave
New Silksworth SR3 . . . .**91** F7
Newcastle-u-T NE6 . . . .**57** A7
Rutland Pl
North Shields NE29 . . . .**41** F6
Washington NE37 . . . .**72** D2
Rutland Rd Hebburn NE31 . . . .**57** F3
Wallsend NE28 . . . .**40** A1
Rutland Sq DH3 . . . .**82** B5
Rutland St Ashington NE63 . . . .**6** C3
Hetton le H DH5 . . . .**94** F4
Sunderland SR4 . . . .**85** F7
Rutland Terr DH6 . . . .**97** E1
Ryal Cl Blyth NE24 . . . .**17** C2
Seaton Delaval NE25 . . . .**23** E3
Ryal Terr NE6 . . . .**56** F5
Ryal Wlk NE3 . . . .**37** D4
Ryall Ave NE13 . . . .**28** A4
Rydal NE10 . . . .**72** A8
Rydal Ave
Easington Lane DH5 . . . .**97** C8
Tynemouth NE30 . . . .**32** A2
Rydal Cl East Boldon NE36 . . .**74** C8
Killingworth NE12 . . . .**29** F3
Rydal Cres NE21 . . . .**68** B8
Rydal Gdns NE34 . . . .**59** E6
Rydal Mount
Newbiggin-by-t-S NE64 . . . .**7** C4
Sunderland SR5 . . . .**75** D1
Sunderland,Castletown SR5 . .**85** A3
Rydal Rd Chester le S DH2 . . .**88** C1
Newcastle-u-T,Gosforth
NE3 . . . .**38** D5
Newcastle-u-T,Lemington
NE15 . . . .**53** D8
Rydal St NE8 . . . .**101** B1
Rydal Terr NE13 . . . .**28** B4
Ryde Pl NE23 . . . .**22** B7
Ryde Terr NE11 . . . .**100** A1
Rye Cl NE15 . . . .**35** E1
Rye Hill
Newcastle-u-T NE4 . . . .**100** B4

Rye Hill *continued*
Newcastle-u-T NE4 . . . .**100** C4
Rye Terr NE46 . . . .**44** F5
Rye View SR2 . . . .**92** F7
Ryedale Sunderland SR6 . . . . .**75** F7
Wallsend NE28 . . . .**39** F5
Ryedale Cl NE63 . . . .**6** B2
Ryedale Ct 7 NE34 . . . .**59** A4
Ryedale Ho NE24 . . . .**16** F8
Ryehaugh NE20 . . . .**25** F6
Ryehill View DH5 . . . .**94** C5
Ryemount Rd SR2 . . . .**92** D7
Ryhope Engine Mus*
SR2 . . . .**92** E5
Ryhope Gdns NE9 . . . .**71** D4
Ryhope General Hospl
SR2 . . . .**92** F5
Ryhope Grange Ct SR2 . . . . . .**86** F1
Ryhope Inf Sch SR2 . . . .**92** F7
Ryhope Jun Sch SR2 . . . .**92** F7
Ryhope Rd Ryhope SR2 . . . . . .**93** A8
Sunderland SR2 . . . .**86** E3
Ryhope St
Houghton-le-S DH5 . . . .**94** F8
5 Sunderland SR2 . . . .**92** E7
Ryhope St S SR2 . . . .**92** F7
Ryhope Village CE Prim Sch
SR2 . . . .**92** F6
Ryton Com Inf Sch NE40 . . . . .**52** A5
Ryton Comp Sch NE40 . . . .**52** B5
Ryton Ct NE33 . . . .**42** D1
Ryton Hall Dr NE40 . . . .**52** C6
Ryton Ind Est NE21 . . . .**52** F5
Ryton Jun Sch NE40 . . . .**52** A5
Ryton Sq SR2 . . . .**86** E3
Ryton Terr
Newcastle-u-T NE6 . . . .**56** F4
Shiremoor NE27 . . . .**30** D1

S

Sackville Rd
Newcastle-u-T NE6 . . . .**39** C1
Sunderland SR3 . . . .**85** E3
Sacred Heart Lower Sch
NE4 . . . .**54** F6
Sacred Heart RC High Sch
NE4 . . . .**54** D7
Sacred Heart RC Mid Sch
NE4 . . . .**54** F7
Sacred Heart RC Prim Sch
Byermoor NE16 . . . .**79** D7
Newcastle-u-T NE4 . . . .**54** D7
Sacriston Gdns NE9 . . . .**71** C2
Saddleback NE37 . . . .**83** B7
Saffron Pl NE6 . . . .**57** A5
Saga Ct NE6 . . . .**39** F1
Sage Ct NE15 . . . .**53** C8
Sage Gateshead The
NE8 . . . .**101** C4
Saint Aidan's Ho NE29 . . . .**41** D8
Saint Cst SR3 . . . .**92** C7
Saint Wilfrid's RC Comp Sch
NE34 . . . .**59** D6
Saints Peter & Paul RC Prim
Sch NE33 . . . .**59** B6
St Acca's Ct NE46 . . . .**44** F5
St Agnes RC Prim Sch
NE40 . . . .**51** E4
St Agnes' Gdns NE40 . . . .**51** E4
St Agnes' Gdns N NE40 . . . . . .**51** E4
St Agnes' Gdns W NE40 . . . . . .**51** E4
St Agnes' Terr NE40 . . . .**51** E4
St Aidan's Ave
Sunderland SR2 . . . .**86** F2
Wallsend NE12 . . . .**30** C1
St Aidan's Cl NE29 . . . .**41** D8
St Aidan's Cres NE61 . . . .**9** A6
St Aidan's Ct NE30 . . . .**42** C7
St Aidan's Prim Sch
NE8 . . . .**100** C1
St Aidan's RC Comp Sch
SR2 . . . .**86** C4
St Aidan's RC Fst Sch
NE5 . . . .**6** D1
St Aidan's Rd
South Shields NE33 . . . .**42** D4
Wallsend NE28 . . . .**40** A1
St Aidan's Sq NE12 . . . .**30** C1
St Aidan's St NE8 . . . .**101** A1
St Aidan's Terr DH4 . . . .**90** E6
St Aidans Ct DH4 . . . .**90** E6
St Aidans Ct NE25 . . . .**31** A5
St Aidans Cres NE16 . . . .**71** C7
St Albans Cres NE10 . . . .**39** D2
St Alban's Pl
Gateshead NE10 . . . .**71** C7
Tynemouth NE30 . . . .**42** D7
St Alban's RC Prim Sch
NE10 . . . .**57** A1
St Alban's RC Sch NE6 . . . .**56** F7
St Alban's Terr NE8 . . . .**101** C1
St Albans Cl NE63 . . . .**7** A2
St Aldate's Ct SR4 . . . .**85** A2
St Aloysius RC Inf Sch
NE31 . . . .**57** E7
St Aloysius RC Jun Sch
NE31 . . . .**57** E7
St Aloysius View NE31 . . . .**57** D6
St Andrew's CE Fst Sch
NE15 . . . .**34** E2
St Andrew's Ct NE7 . . . .**39** C5
St Andrew's Dr NE9 . . . .**70** E3

St Andrew's La NE42 . . . .**49** D9
St Andrew's RC Fst Sch
NE24 . . . .**17** C7
St Andrew's Rd
Hexham NE46 . . . .**45** A5
Kip Hill DH9 . . . .**79** F7
St Andrew's St
Hebburn NE31 . . . .**57** C7
Newcastle-u-T NE1 . . . .**98** C1
St Andrew's Terr
Ashington NE63 . . . .**6** E1
3 Sunderland SR5 . . . .**75** E1
St Andrews DH4 . . . .**94** B8
St Andrews Ave NE37 . . . .**83** B8
St Andrews Cl NE25 . . . .**31** D5
St Andrews Ct 4 NE29 . . . .**41** F7
St Ann's Cl NE1 . . . .**56** A4
St Ann's Quay NE1 . . . .**99** C5
St Ann's St NE1 . . . .**99** C5
St Anne's Ct NE25 . . . .**31** E4
St Anne's RC Prim Sch
NE6 . . . .**71** B8
St Anselm Cres NE29 . . . .**41** C6
St Anselm Rd NE29 . . . .**41** C6
St Anthony's CE Prim Sch
NE6 . . . .**56** F4
St Anthony's Ct NE6 . . . .**56** F4
St Anthony's Ho NE6 . . . .**56** F4
St Anthony's RC Girls Sch
SR2 . . . .**102** C3
St Anthony's Rd NE6 . . . .**56** E4
St Anthony's Wlk NE6 . . . .**56** F4
St Asaph Cl NE12 . . . .**39** D6
St Augustine's RC Prim Sch
NE10 . . . .**72** A8
St Austell Cl NE15 . . . .**37** C6
St Austell Gdns NE9 . . . .**70** F1
St Barnabas DH4 . . . .**89** D8
St Barnabas Way SR2 . . . .**103** C3
St Bartholomew's CE Prim
Sch NE21 . . . .**29** D1
St Bartholomews CE Prim
Sch NE61 . . . .**2** D1
St Bede's NE36 . . . .**74** C7
St Bede's Cl DH5 . . . .**95** A4
St Bede's Dr NE8 . . . .**101** C4
St Bede's Ho NE9 . . . .**71** A7
St Bede's Pk SR2 . . . .**103** A3
St Bede's RC Fst Sch
NE22 . . . .**15** E8
St Bede's RC Prim Sch
Jarrow NE32 . . . .**58** C2
Newcastle-u-T NE15 . . . .**54** A2
South Shields NE33 . . . .**42** D2
Washington NE37 . . . .**72** C1
St Bede's Terr SR2 . . . .**103** A3
St Bedes Pl NE24 . . . .**17** E5
St Bedes Rd NE24 . . . .**17** E5
St Bedes Wlk NE27 . . . .**30** C4
St Benedict's RC Mid Sch
NE6 . . . .**6** A3
St Benet Biscop RC High Sch
NE22 . . . .**15** E8
St Benet's RC Prim Sch
DH2 . . . .**81** A2
St Benet's RC Prim Sch
SR6 . . . .**75** C3
St Bernadette's RC Prim Sch
NE28 . . . .**40** E3
St Buryan Cres NE5 . . . .**37** A2
St Catherine's Ct SR5 . . . .**74** D1
St Catherine's RC Prim Sch
NE2 . . . .**56** A5
St Catherines Gr NE2 . . . .**56** A4
St Cecilia's Cl SR2 . . . .**86** E4
St Chad's Cres SR3 . . . .**91** F6
St Chad's Rd SR3 . . . .**91** F6
St Chad's Villas 6 NE36 . . . . .**74** C7
St Charles' RC Prim Sch
NE3 . . . .**38** B1
St Christopher Way NE29 . . . . .**41** F4
St Christopher's Ho NE61 . . . . .**8** F7
St Christopher's Rd SR3 . . . . .**86** A3
St Christophers Cl NE63 . . . . . .**6** F1
St Clements Ct
Ashington NE63 . . . .**7** A1
3 Longbenton NE12 . . . .**39** B7
Newcastle-u-T NE3 . . . .**37** C4
Sunderland SR4 . . . .**85** C1
St Columba's Ct SR5 . . . .**75** C3
St Columba's RC Prim Sch
NE28 . . . .**40** E4
St Cuthbert Ave DH3 . . . .**88** B1
St Cuthbert's Ave NE34 . . . . . .**60** B5
St Cuthbert's Cl DH5 . . . .**95** A4
St Cuthbert's Ct
Gateshead NE8 . . . .**101** A2
Newcastle-u-T NE3 . . . .**38** A3
St Cuthbert's Dr NE10 . . . .**71** E6
St Cuthbert's Gn NE3 . . . .**37** F3
St Cuthbert's High Sch
NE15 . . . .**54** B6
St Cuthbert's La NE46 . . . .**45** A4
St Cuthbert's Pl NE8 . . . .**101** A1
St Cuthbert's RC Prim Sch
Newcastle-u-T NE5 . . . .**37** C2
North Shields NE29 . . . .**42** A6
Sunderland SR4 . . . .**85** B6
Walbottle NE15 . . . .**35** E1
St Cuthbert's Rd
Gateshead,Windmill Hills
NE8 . . . .**101** A1
New Herrington DH4 . . . .**90** A1
Newbottle DH4 . . . .**90** A1
Newcastle-u-T,Benwell NE5 . .**54** F5
Newcastle-u-T,Fenham NE5 . . .**54** F5

St Cuthbert's Rd continued
Sunniside NE16 ....80 B7
Wallsend NE28 ....40 E3
Wallsend,Holystone NE27 ...30 C1
St Cuthbert's Terr NE22 ..11 B1
St Cuthbert's Terr
Hexham NE46 ....45 A4
Sunderland SR4 ....102 B3
St Cuthbert's Wlk DH3 ..88 C3
St Cuthberts Cl
Hexham NE46 ....45 A4
Prudhoe NE42 ....50 C2
Wallsend NE27 ....30 C1
St Cuthberts Ct NE42 ....17 F7
St Cuthberts Lower Sch
NE15 ....54 C6
St Cuthberts Pk NE16 ...80 A8
St Cuthberts RC Prim Sch
DH3 ....88 D2
St Cuthberts Way
Blaydon NE21 ....53 D3
Wallsend NE27 ....30 C1
St David's Cl NE26 ......31 F8
St David's Way
Hedworth NE32 ....58 C1
Whitley Bay NE26 ....31 F8
St Ebba's Way DH8 ......76 E3
St Edmund Campion RC Sch
NE9 ....71 D4
St Edmund's Ct NE8 .....56 A1
St Edmund's Dr NE10 ....71 F7
St Edmund's Rd NE8 ....101 C1
St Etienne Ct 12 NE10 ...56 D1
St Gabriel's Ave
Newcastle-u-T NE6 ......39 B1
Sunderland SR4 ....85 F5
St George's Rd NE33,
NE34 ....59 E8
St George's Cl NE32 ....38 E2
St George's Cres NE29 ..41 F5
St George's Est NE34 ...83 C1
St George's Hospl NE61 ..4 A2
St George's Pl NE15 ....53 E5
St George's RC Prim Sch
NE15 ....53 D5
St George's Rd
Hexham NE46 ....45 A4
Newcastle-u-T NE15 ......53 E5
Tynemouth NE30 ....32 C3
St George's Terr
East Boldon NE36 ....74 D7
Newcastle-u-T,Lemington
NE15 ....53 E5
Newcastle-u-T,West Jesmond
NE2 ....38 E2
Sunderland SR6 ....75 F2
St George's Way SR2 ...103 A1
St Georges Cres NE25 ..31 F4
St Georges Ct NE10 .....72 B7
St Godric's Dr DH4 ......94 A2
St Gregory's Ct NE34 ...59 F5
St Gregory's RC Prim Sch
NE34 ....60 A7
St Helen's Cres NE9 ....70 E5
St Helen's La NE45 .....47 A6
St Helen's St NE45 .....46 F6
St Helens Terr NE9 .....70 F5
St Hilda Ind Est 4 NE33 ..42 C2
St Hilda St NE33 ....42 C2
St Hilda's Ave NE46 .....45 A4
St Hilda's Rd NE46 ......45 A4
St Ignatius Cl SR2 ......103 B1
St Ives Way NE5 ....37 C4
St James Bvld NE1,NE4 ..100 C4
St James Cl NE44 ....62 F7
St James Gate NE1 .....100 C4
St James Lodge 4 NE4 ..54 D5
St James RC Prim Sch
NE31 ....57 F4
St James Rd NE8 ....56 A2
St James Sq NE8 ....56 A2
St James St NE3 ....38 E5
St James Sta NE1 ....98 C1
St James Terr
Morpeth NE61 ....3 F1
Newcastle-u-T NE1 ....98 C2
Riding Mill NE44 ....63 A7
St James' Cres NE25 ....31 F4
St James' Gdns 6 NE15 ..54 D5
St James' Pk (Newcastle Utd
FC) NE1 ....98 C2
St James' Rd NE8 ....54 D5
St James' St NE1 ....98 C2
St James' Terr NE29 ....41 D3
St John & St Patrick's Church
Prim Sch SR1 ....103 C3
St John Bosco RC Prim Sch
SR5 ....54 A4
St John Boste RC Prim Sch
NE38 ....83 A5
St John St NE1 ....99 A1
St John the Baptist's RC
Prim Sch NE10 ....71 D8
St John Vianney RC Prim Sch
NE5 ....36 D1
St John's Ave NE31 .....57 D5
St John's Cl NE26 ......31 F8
St John's Gn NE22 ......11 D3
St John's Ct
Backworth NE27 ....30 C5
Newcastle-u-T NE4 ......54 E4
North Shields NE29 ......41 D3
St John's Gn NE33 ......42 D2
St John's Mall NE31 ....57 D5

St John's Pl
Bedlington NE22 ....11 D3
Birtley DH3 ....82 C4
Whitley Bay NE26 ....31 F8
St John's Rd NE22 ......11 D2
St John's Rd DH6 ....96 B5
St John's Rd NE4 ......54 E4
St John's St NE29 ......41 D3
St John's Terr
East Boldon NE36 ....74 E7
Jarrow NE32 ....39 A5
North Shields NE29 ......41 D3
8 Seaham SR7 ....92 E1
St John's W NE22 ....11 D3
St John's Wlk
Hebburn NE31 ....57 E5
Newcastle-u-T NE4 ......54 E4
North Shields NE29 ......41 D3
St Johns SR1 ....103 C4
St Johns Cl NE12 ....29 D1
St Johns Pl NE10 ....71 D8
St Johns Rd NE46 ....45 A3
St Johns Vale SR4 ......85 A4
St Joseph's Ct
8 Birtley DH3 ....82 C5
Hebburn NE31 ....57 D3
St Joseph's RC Comp Sch
NE31 ....57 D2
St Joseph's RC Inf Sch
DH3 ....82 C4
St Joseph's RC Jun Sch
DH3 ....82 C4
St Joseph's RC Mid Sch
NE46 ....44 F4
St Joseph's RC Prim Sch
Blaydon NE21 ....53 B3
Gateshead NE8 ....101 C2
Hedworth NE32 ....58 B1
Newcastle-u-T NE15 ......54 D4
North Shields NE29 ......41 E5
St Joseph's RC Prim Sch
NE39 ....67 B2
St Joseph's Washington RC
Sch NE38 ....83 D6
St Jude's Terr NE33 .....59 C8
St Julien Gdns
Newcastle-u-T NE7 ......39 D2
Wallsend NE28 ....41 B3
St Just Pl NE5 ....37 C4
St Keverne Sq NE5 .....37 C4
St Kitt's Cl NE26 ......31 F8
St Lawrence's RC Prim Sch
NE6 ....56 C6
St Lawrence Cl DH6 ....96 C5
St Lawrence Rd
High Pittington DH6 .....96 B5
Newcastle-u-T NE6 ......56 C4
St Lawrence Sq NE6 ....56 B5
St Leonard St SR7 .....86 F4
St Leonard's La NE61 ....3 B2
St Leonard's RC Prim Sch
SR3 ....92 B7
St Leonard's Wlk NE61 ..3 C2
St Lucia Cl
Sunderland SR3 ....103 B1
Whitley Bay NE26 ....31 E8
St Luke's Rd
North Shields NE29 ......41 D3
Sunderland SR4 ....85 D7
St Luke's Terr SR4 .....85 F7
St Lukes Cl NE31 ....57 D4
St Lukes Rd NE46 ......45 A4
St Margaret's Ave SR5 ..74 A1
St Margaret's Ct SR5 ...74 A1
St Margaret's Dr DH9 ...79 D4
St Margaret's Rd NE15 ..54 A4
St Margarets Ave NE12 ..39 D6
St Margarets Ct NE26 ...32 C4
St Mark's Cl 11 NE6 ....56 C7
St Mark's Cres SR4 ....102 B2
St Mark's Rd N SR4 ....102 A2
St Mark's RC Prim Sch
NE5 ....36 F4
St Mark's Rd SR4 ....102 B2
St Mark's Rd N SR4 ....102 A2
St Mark's Sq Morpeth NE61 ..3 E1
13 Newcastle-u-T NE6 ...56 C7
Sunderland SR4 ....102 B2
St Mark's Terr SR4 .....102 B2
St Mark's Way NE33 ....42 C1
St Marks Ct
Backworth NE27 ....30 E3
Newcastle-u-T NE5 ......36 F4
St Marks Rd NE46 ......45 A3
St Martin's Cl NE26 ....31 E7
St Martin's Ct NE26 ....31 E7
St Martin's Way NE26 ...31 E7
St Mary & St Thomas
Aquinas RC Prim Sch
NE21 ....53 A4
St Mary's Ave
South Shields NE34 ......59 F6
Whitley Bay NE26 ....31 F7
St Mary's Chare 9 NE46 ..45 B5
St Mary's Church (Mus)*
NE63 ....7 C6
St Mary's Coll NE4 .....54 E7
St Mary's College Flats
NE4 ....54 E7
St Mary's Ct
Gateshead NE8 ....101 C2
South Shields NE33 ......59 B7
St Mary's Dr Blyth NE24 ..17 B6
West Rainton DH4 ....94 A2

St Mary's Gn 4 NE16 ...69 B7
St Mary's Lodge NE26 ...31 F5
St Mary's or Bait Island*
NE26 ....24 G2
St Mary's Pl
Newcastle-u-T NE1 ......99 A2
Throckley NE15 ....35 E2
St Mary's Pl E NE1 .....99 A2
St Mary's RC Cath NE1 ..100 C4
St Mary's RC Comp Sch
NE7 ....39 A5
St Mary's RC Fst Sch
NE46 ....45 A4
St Mary's RC Prim Sch
Brockley Whins NE32 .....58 D3
Longbenton NE12 ....29 D1
Sunderland SR2 ....86 B4
Tynemouth NE30 ....32 A2
Whickham NE16 ....69 C7
St Mary's St NE1 ....99 A2
St Mary's Terr
East Boldon NE36 ....74 E7
Ryton NE40 ....52 B5
South Shields NE33 ......59 B7
St Mary's Training &
Enterprise Ctr NE4 .....98 B1
St Mary's Way SR1 .....103 A3
St Mary's Wynd
8 Hexham NE46 ....45 B5
Seaton Sluice NE26 .....24 E4
St Marys CE Prim Sch
NE33 ....59 B7
St Marys Cl DH2 ....88 B1
St Mathews La NE42 ....50 D2
St Matthew's RC Fst Sch
NE32 ....58 B2
St Matthew's Terr DH4 ..90 D4
St Matthews Rd NE46 ...44 F3
St Matthews View SR3 ..92 A7
St Michael's Ave
New Hartley NE25 ....23 D6
South Shields NE33 ......42 E1
St Michael's Ave N NE33 ..42 D1
St Michael's Mount 8
NE6 ....56 C5
St Michael's RC Prim Sch
DH5 ....94 D7
St Michael's Rd NE6 ....56 C5
St Michael's Way NE11 ..54 C1
St Michaels DH4 ....54 B8
St Michaels RC Prim Sch
NE4 ....100 A3
St Michaels Way SR1 ...102 C2
St Michaels Workshops 10
NE6 ....56 C5
St Nichola's Cath* NE1 ..99 B1
St Nicholas Ave
Newcastle-u-T,Gosforth
NE3 ....38 C4
Newcastle-u-T,South Gosforth
NE3 ....38 D4
Sunderland SR3 ....86 B3
St Nicholas Cl NE63 ....6 F5
St Nicholas Hospl NE3 ..38 A5
St Nicholas Rd
Hexham NE46 ....45 A4
West Boldon NE36 ....74 A7
St Nicholas View NE36 ..74 A7
St Nicholas' Church Yd
NE1 ....99 A1
St Nicholas' Sq 8 NE1 ..99 A1
St Nicholas' St NE1 ....101 A4
St Omers Rd NE11 ......56 E6
St Oswald's Ave NE6 ...56 E6
St Oswald's Gn NE6 ....56 E7
St Oswald's RC Prim Sch
NE9 ....71 C3
St Oswald's RC Prim Sch
Newcastle-u-T NE3 ......38 D7
Whiteleas NE34 ....59 D3
St Oswald's Rd
Hebburn NE31 ....57 F7
14 Hexham NE46 ....45 A4
Wallsend NE28 ....40 E4
St Oswald's Terr 8 DH4 ..90 B6
St Oswalds C of E Prim Sch
NE31 ....57 F7
St Oswalds Ct NE42 ....50 E3
St Oswin's Ave NE30 ...32 E3
St Oswin's Pl NE30 ....32 D7
St Oswin's St NE33 .....59 D7
St Patrick's Cl NE10 ...71 D8
St Patrick's RC Prim Sch
SR2 ....92 F6
St Patrick's Terr SR2* ..92 F6
St Patrick's Wlk NE10 ..71 D8
St Paul's CE Prim Sch
Newcastle-u-T NE4 ......100 B4
Ryhope SR2 ....92 F6
St Paul's Gdns NE25 ...32 A4
St Paul's RC Fst Sch
NE23 ....22 B5
St Paul's Rd NE32 .....39 A6
St Paul's Terr 6 SR2 ...92 F6
St Pauls Ct NE63 ....6 F5
St Pauls Ct NE8 ....100 C1
St Pauls Dr DH4 ....89 E8
St Pauls Monastery*
NE32 ....58 D7
St Pauls Rd NE46 ......44 F4
St Peter's Ave NE34 ...59 F7
St Peter's Ct NE6 ......56 C4
St Peter's Quayside E
NE6 ....56 D4

St Peter's Quayside W 9
NE6 ....56 C4
St Peter's RC Mid Sch
NE23 ....22 B4
St Peter's RC Prim Sch
NE9 ....71 A6
St Peter's Rd
Newcastle-u-T NE6 ......56 C5
Wallsend NE28 ....40 D3
St Peter's Sta SR5 .....103 A4
St Peter's View SR6 ....103 A4
St Peter's Wharf NE6 ..56 C4
St Peters' Way SR6 ....103 B4
St Philip Neri RC Prim Sch
NE11 ....70 A8
St Philips Cl NE4 ....98 B1
St Philips Way NE4 ....98 B1
St Robert of Newminster RC
Sch NE38 ....83 D2
St Robert's RC Fst Sch
NE61 ....8 F8
St Rollox St NE31 ......57 D5
St Ronan's Dr NE26 ....24 B7
St Ronan's Rd NE25 ...31 F4
St Ronans View NE9 ...71 A2
St Simon St NE34 ......59 A4
St Stephen's Cl NE29 ...23 B7
St Stephen's St NE6 ....56 A4
St Stephen's Way NE29 ..41 D3
St Stephens Cl DH4 ....89 E8
St Teresa's RC Prim Sch
NE6 ....56 B8
St Thomas Cl NE42 ....50 D2
St Thomas Mews NE42 ..50 D2
St Thomas More RC High Sch
NE29 ....41 D7
St Thomas More RC Sch
NE21 ....53 A3
St Thomas St 6 NE9 ...71 A5
St Thomas' Cres NE1 ..99 A2
St Thomas' Sq NE1 ....99 A2
St Thomas' St
Newcastle-u-T NE1 ......99 A2
Sunderland SR1 ....103 A3
St Thomas' Street Bsns Ctr
NE1 ....99 A2
St Thomas' Terr NE1 ...99 A2
St Vincent Cl NE8 .....56 A1
St Vincent St
Gateshead NE8 ....56 A1
South Shields NE33 ......42 E1
Sunderland SR2 ....103 B1
St Vincent's Pl NE26 ...31 F8
St Vincent's RC Sch NE6 ..56 A4
St Vincent's Way 1 NE26 ..31 F8
St Vincents Cl NE15 ...53 B8
St Vincents Ho NE10 ...42 D7
St Wilfred's RC Mid Sch
NE24 ....17 E2
St Wilfred's Rd NE46 ...47 A6
St Wilfrid's Cl 9 NE46 ..45 A4
St Wilfrid's RC Prim Sch
NE10 ....42 D7
St Wilfrid's Rd NE46 ...45 A4
Saker Pl 1 NE28 ....40 B1
Salcombe Ave NE32 ....58 D6
Salcombe Gdns NE9 ...70 F2
Salem Hill SR2 ....103 B1
Salem St Jarrow NE32 ..58 D7
South Shields NE33 ......42 C3
Sunderland SR2 ....103 B1
Salem St S SR2 ....103 B1
Salisbury Ave
10 Chester le S DH3 ....88 C2
Tynemouth NE29 ....42 A7
Salisbury Cl
7 Ashington NE63 ....6 F2
Cramlington NE23 ....21 E6
Salisbury Gdns NE2 ....56 A8
Salisbury Ho NE6 ......56 A6
Salisbury Pl NE33 .....42 E3
Salisbury St NE46 .....45 A4
Gateshead NE10 ....57 A1
Morpeth NE61 ....3 E1
South Shields NE33 ......42 D2
Sunderland SR1 ....103 B1
Sunderland,South Hylton
SR4 ....85 A7
Salisbury Way NE32 ...58 D6
Salkeld Gdns NE9 ......71 A8
Salkeld Rd NE9 ....71 A8
Sallyport Cres NE1 ....99 B1
Sallyport Ho NE1 ......99 B1
Salmon St NE33 ....42 D4
Saltburn Cl DH4 ....90 C1
Saltburn Gdns NE28 ...41 B3
Saltburn Rd SR6 ......88 A8
Saltburn Sq SR4 ....85 A5
Salter's La Haswell DH6 ..97 E6
Houghton-le-S SR3 ......91 F4
Seaham SR7 ....95 F6
Salterfen La SR2 ......93 A8
Salterfen Rd SR2 ....93 A8
Salters Cl NE3 ....38 E6
Salters Ct NE3 ....38 E6
Salters' La NE3,NE12 ...38 F7
Salters' Rd NE3 ....38 E6
Saltford NE9 ....71 A2
Saltmeadows Rd NE10,
NE8 ....56 B4
Saltwell Park Mansion Mus*
NE9 ....70 E6
Saltwell Pl NE8 ....70 D8
Saltwell Rd NE8 ....70 D7
Saltwell Rd S NE9 .....70 E4

Saltwell St NE8 ....70 D8
Saltwell View NE8 .....70 E7
Sam's Ct NE23 ....28 F8
Samson Cl NE12 ....29 C2
Sancroft Dr DH5 ....94 E7
Sand Point Rd SR6 ....75 F1
Sandalwood NE34 ......59 E3
Sandalwood Sq SR4 ...85 B2
Sanderling Cl NE40 ....52 D4
Sanderlings 3 NE28 ...40 B1
Sanders Gdns DH3 ....82 C5
Sanders' Meml Homes
DH2 ....88 C3
Sanderson Hospl NE3 ..38 B4
Sanderson Rd
Newcastle-u-T NE2 .....38 E2
Whitley Bay NE26 ....31 F5
Sanderson St NE4 .....54 F3
Sandfield Rd
Cambois NE22 ....12 B4
Tynemouth NE30 ....32 B3
Sandford Ave NE23 ....16 B1
Sandford Ct SR2 ......86 C3
Sandford Mews NE13 ..28 A5
Sandgate NE1 ....99 C1
Sandgrove SR6 ....60 A1
Sandhill NE1 ....101 B4
Sandhill View Sch SR3 ..85 D2
Sandhurst Ave NE30 ...32 C2
Sandiacres NE32 ......58 C1
Sandison Ct NE13 .....27 F6
Sandmere Pl NE15 ....54 A5
Sandmere Rd SR2 .....86 D1
Sandoe Gdns NE15 ...54 A5
Sandon Cl NE27 ......30 C5
Sandown NE25 ....31 D5
Sandown Ct NE25 .....23 D2
Sandown Ct NE28 .....41 A4
Sandown Gdns
Gateshead NE8 ....70 D8
New Silksworth SR3 ....91 F8
Wallsend NE28 ....40 F4
Sandpiper Cl Blyth NE24 ..17 F7
Ryton NE40 ....52 D4
Washington NE38 ....82 F2
Sandpiper Ct NE12 ....29 A7
Sandpiper Pl NE12 ....39 A7
Sandpiper Way NE63 ...6 D1
Sandray Cl DH3 ....82 D1
Sandridge NE64 ....7 F5
Sandringham Ave NE12 ..39 D6
Sandringham Cl NE25 ..31 B4
Sandringham Cres SR3 ..91 C6
Sandringham Ct
6 Longbenton NE12 ....39 A6
6 Gateshead NE10 .....71 C6
Sandringham Dr
Blyth NE24 ....17 D3
Whickham NE16 ....69 A7
Whitley Bay NE25 ....31 C4
Sandringham Gdns NE3 ..38 B3
Sandringham Mews 8
NE29 ....40 F4
Sandringham Rd
Newcastle-u-T,South Gosforth
NE3 ....38 E4
Newcastle-u-T,West Denton
NE5 ....36 D2
Sunderland SR6 ....75 D2
Sandringham Terr SR6 ..75 E2
Sandringham Way NE20 ..25 C4
Sands Ind Est The NE16 ..54 A1
Sandsay Cl SR1 ....92 D8
Sandstone Cl NE34 ....58 F3
Sandwell Dr DH4 ......89 F8
Sandwich Rd NE29 ....31 F1
Sandy Bank NE44 .....62 F7
Sandy Bay Cvn Pk NE63 ..12 C8
Sandy Chare SR6 .....75 E8
Sandy Cres NE6 ....56 E4
Sandy La Ashington NE63 ..7 B2
Brunswick Village NE13 ..27 E6
Gateshead NE9 ....71 D1
Sandy Lane Ind Area NE3 ..28 C4
Sandyford Ave NE42 ...50 F3
Sandyford Pk NE2 .....99 C4
Sandypath Ia NE16 ....79 A7
Sandysykes NE42 .....50 F3
Sans St SR1 ....103 B3
Sans St S SR1 ....103 B2
Sarabel Ave NE62 .....10 E7
Sargent Ave NE34 ....59 D2
Satley Gdns
Gateshead NE9 ....71 C2
Sunderland SR3 ....86 B2
Saunton Ct DH4 ....89 E8
Saville Lodge 3 NE33 ..42 D3
Saville Pl
Newcastle-u-T NE1 ......99 B2
Sunderland SR1 ....103 B3
Saville Row NE1 ......99 A2
Saville St
North Shields NE30 .....42 B5
4 South Shields NE33 ..42 A5
Saville St W NE29 .....42 A4
Savory Rd NE28 ....40 F3
Sawmill Cotts DH9 ....78 E1

Saxilby Dr NE3 . . . . .38 D8
Saxon Cl SR6 . . . . .59 E1
Saxon Cres SR3 . . . . .85 F3
Saxon Dr NE30 . . . . .32 C1
Saxon Way NE32 . . . . .58 C7
Saxondale Rd NE3 . . . . .37 E5
Saxton Gr NE7 . . . . .39 A4
Scafell DH3 . . . . .82 D1
Scafell Ct 22 SR3 . . . . .91 F6
Scafell Dr NE5 . . . . .37 D3
Scafell Gdns NE11 . . . . .70 A6
Scalby Cl NE3 . . . . .38 D8
Scales Cres NE42 . . . . .50 F2
Scarborough Ct
  Cramlington NE23 . . . . .22 B5
  Newcastle-u-T NE6 . . . . . . .56 D6
Scarborough Par NE31 . .58 A2
Scarborough Rd
  New Silksworth SR3 . . . . . . .91 F8
  Newcastle-u-T NE6 . . . . . . .56 D6
Sceptre Ct NE4 . . . . .100 A4
Sceptre Pl NE4 . . . . .98 A1
Sceptre St NE4 . . . . .98 A1
Schalksmuhle Rd NE22 . . .10 F1
Schimel St SR5 . . . . .75 B2
School App NE34 . . . . .60 A6
School Ave Dunston NE11 . .69 F8
                Guide Post NE62 . . . .10 F7
School Cl NE9 . . . . .71 D6
School La High Spen NE39 .67 A3
                Whickham NE16 . . . .69 C7
School Rd
  Bedlington NE22 . . . . .11 D3
  East Rainton DH5 . . . . .94 C4
School Row
  Hedley on t H NE43 . . . . . . .44 E4
  Prudhoe NE42 . . . . .50 E3
School St Birtley DH3 . . . . .82 C4
                Hebburn NE31 . . . . .57 F7
                Whickham NE16 . . .69 A7
School Terr DH4 . . . . .89 E1
School View DH5 . . . . .97 D8
Schoolhouse La NE16 . . . .79 E7
Scorer St NE29 . . . . .41 F5
Scorer's La DH3 . . . . .89 B1
Scot Terr NE17 . . . . .66 B1
Scot's Ho NE36 . . . . .73 B6
Scotby Gdns NE9 . . . . .71 B3
Scotland Ct NE21 . . . . .53 A1
Scotland Head NE21 . . . . . .68 A8
Scotland St SR2 . . . . .93 A6
Scotswood Rd NE11,NE4 . .54 B4
Scotswood View NE15 . . . .54 C2
Scott Ave NE23 . . . . .22 A5
Scott Ct NE46 . . . . .44 F2
Scott Ct NE34 . . . . .59 A3
Scott St
  East Hartford NE23 . . . . . . .16 B3
  Houghton-le-S DH4 . . . . . . .94 D8
Scott's Ave NE40 . . . . .51 F3
Scott's Ct NE10 . . . . .72 B6
Scott's Terr DH5 . . . . .95 A4
Scotts Life Ho NE2 . . . . . . .99 B3
Scoular Dr NE63 . . . . .7 A3
Scrogg Rd NE6 . . . . .56 F6
Scruton Ave SR3 . . . . .85 F3
Sea Banks NE30 . . . . .42 E8
Sea Crest Rd NE64 . . . . .7 E6
Sea La SR6 . . . . .75 E4
Sea Rd South Shields NE33 .42 E4
                Sunderland SR6 . . . .75 E4
Sea View Ashington NE63 . .12 A8
                Lynemouth NE61 . . . . .2 B3
                Ryhope SR2 . . . . . . .93 A6
Sea View Gdns SR6 . . . . . . .75 E3
Sea View La NE64 . . . . .7 E5
Sea View Pk
  Cramlington NE23 . . . . .22 D6
  Whitburn SR6 . . . . .75 D8
Sea View Rd SR2 . . . . .86 E3
Sea View Rd W SR2 . . . . . . .86 D2
Sea View St SR2 . . . . .86 F2
Sea View Villas NE23 . . . . .22 D6
Sea Way NE33 . . . . .42 E3
Sea Winnings Way
  South Shields NE33 . . . . . . .42 E2
  South Shields NE33 . . . . . . .42 F2
Seaburn Ave NE25 . . . . .23 D6
Seaburn Cl 1 SR6 . . . . .75 E4
Seaburn Dene Prim Sch
  SR6 . . . . .75 D5
Seaburn Dr 1 DH4 . . . . .94 B8
Seaburn Gdns
  Gateshead NE9 . . . . .71 D3
  Whitley Bay SR26 . . . . .75 E4
Seaburn Gr NE26 . . . . .24 C6
Seaburn Hill SR6 . . . . .75 E4
Seaburn Sta SR5 . . . . .75 C4
Seaburn Terr NE33 . . . . . . .75 F4
Seaburn View NE25 . . . . . . .23 D6
Seacombe Ave NE30 . . . . . .32 C3
Seacrest Apartments
  NE30 . . . . .32 C1
Seacrest Ave NE30 . . . . .32 C2
Seafield Rd NE30 . . . . .42 E7
Seafield Terr NE33 . . . . .42 E3
Seafield View NE30 . . . . . . .42 D8
Seafields SR6 . . . . .75 E5
Seaforth Rd SR3 . . . . .86 A3
Seaforth St NE24 . . . . .17 E8
Seaham Cl NE34 . . . . .60 B6
Seaham Gdns NE9 . . . . .71 C2
Seaham Grange Ind Est
  SR7 . . . . .92 E2

Seaham Rd
  Houghton-le-S DH5 . . . . . . .95 A8
  Ryhope SR2 . . . . .93 A6
Seaham Sch of Technology
  SR7 . . . . .93 A1
Seaham St SR3 . . . . .92 A7
Seal Terr 3 NE46 . . . . .45 A4
Seascale Pl NE9 . . . . .71 B4
Seatoller Ct 3 SR3 . . . . . . .91 F6
Seaton Ave
  Annitsford NE23 . . . . .22 B1
  Bedlington NE22 . . . . .11 B1
  Blyth NE24 . . . . .17 C4
  Houghton-le-S DH5 . . . . . . .95 A7
  Newbiggin-by-t-S NE64 . . . . .7 D4
Seaton Burn Coll NE13 . . . .28 C8
Seaton Cl NE10 . . . . .72 B6
Seaton Cres Holywell NE25 .23 F2
                Seaham SR7 . . . . . . .92 C1
                Whitley Bay NE25 . . .31 E5
Seaton Croft SR3 . . . . .29 C8
Seaton Delaval Fst Sch
  NE25 . . . . .23 F2
Seaton Delaval Hall*
  NE26 . . . . .24 A6
Seaton Gdns NE9 . . . . .71 C3
Seaton Hirst CE Mid Sch
  NE63 . . . . .7 A2
Seaton La SR7 . . . . .92 E1
Seaton Pl
  Brunswick Village NE13 . . . .28 A6
  Newcastle-u-T NE6 . . . . . . .56 E3
Seaton Rd Shiremoor NE27 .31 A4
                Sunderland SR3 . . . .85 D3
Seaton Sluice Fst Sch
  NE26 . . . . .24 D5
Seaton Sluice Mid Sch
  NE26 . . . . .24 B7
Seatonville Cres NE25 . . . .31 E3
Seatonville Gr NE25 . . . . . .31 E3
Seatonville Rd NE25 . . . . . .31 E3
Seaview Terr NE33 . . . . .42 E3
Second Ave Ashington NE63 .6 D4
                Blyth NE24 . . . . .17 D5
                Chester le S,Canada DH2 .88 B2
                Chester le S,South Pelaw
                DH2 . . . . .88 B8
                Dunston NE11 . . . . . .70 B6
                Morpeth NE61 . . . . . . .9 B7
                Newcastle-u-T NE6 . . .56 C7
                North Shields NE29 . .41 B4
Second Row Ellington NE61 .1 E4
                Linton NE61 . . . . .1 A3
Second St NE8 . . . . .101 A1
Secretan Way NE33 . . . . . . .42 C2
Sedbergh Rd NE30 . . . . .32 B2
Sedgefield Ct NE12 . . . . . . .29 D3
Sedgeletch Ind Est DH4 . . .90 A2
Sedgeletch Rd DH4 . . . . . . .90 A2
Sedgemoor NE12 . . . . .29 D4
Sedgemoor Ave NE15 . . . . .54 A4
Sedgewick Pl NE8 . . . . .101 B1
Sedley Rd NE28 . . . . .40 B1
Sedling Rd NE38 . . . . .83 B2
Sefton Ave NE6 . . . . .39 C1
Sefton Ct NE23 . . . . .16 C1
Sefton Sq SR3 . . . . .85 C2
Segedunum Cres NE28 . . . .40 E4
Segedunum Way NE28 . . . .40 F4
Segedunum Roman Fort Ctr*
  NE28 . . . . .40 C1
Seghill Fst Sch NE23 . . . . . .22 F1
Seine Ct NE32 . . . . .58 C6
Selborne Ave NE9 . . . . .70 E4
Selborne Gdns NE2 . . . . . . .56 A8
Selbourne Cl NE23 . . . . .21 E6
Selbourne St
  2 South Shields NE33 . . . . .42 D2
  Sunderland SR6 . . . . .75 E1
Selbourne Terr NE24 . . . . . .12 D3
Selby Cl NE23 . . . . .16 B1
Selby Ct 2 Jarrow NE32 . . .58 B7
                Newcastle-u-T NE6 . . .56 F4
Selby Gdns
  Newcastle-u-T NE6 . . . . . . .56 F8
  Wallsend NE28 . . . . .40 B3
Selby Sq SR3 . . . . .85 E3
Sele Ct 1 NE8 . . . . .101 A1
Sele Fst Sch The NE46 . . . .45 A5
Selina Pl SR6 . . . . .75 E1
Selkirk Cres DH3 . . . . .82 C6
Selkirk Gr NE23 . . . . .16 C1
Selkirk Sq SR3 . . . . .85 D3
Selkirk St NE32 . . . . .58 E3
Selkirk Way NE29 . . . . .41 C8
Selsdon Ave SR4 . . . . .85 A2
Selsey Ct NE10 . . . . .71 E6
Selwood Cl NE34 . . . . .59 F5
Selwyn Ave NE25 . . . . .31 D3
Selwyn Cl NE5 . . . . .37 D4
Senet Enterprise Workshops
  NE63 . . . . .6 D2
Serin Ho NE5 . . . . .37 A3
Serlby Cl NE37 . . . . .72 C1
Seton Ave NE34 . . . . .58 F4
Seton Wlk NE34 . . . . .58 F4
Setting Stones NE38 . . . . . .89 A8
Settlingstone Cl NE7 . . . . . .39 E3
Sevenoaks Dr SR4 . . . . .85 A2
Seventh Ave
  Ashington NE63 . . . . .6 E5
  Blyth NE24 . . . . .17 D6
  Chester le S DH2 . . . . .88 B4
  Gateshead NE11 . . . . .70 D4
  Morpeth NE61 . . . . .9 B7
  Newcastle-u-T NE6 . . . . . . .56 C7
Seventh Row NE63 . . . . .6 B4

Severn Ave NE31 . . . . .57 E3
Severn Ct 8 SR3 . . . . .91 F6
Severn Dr NE32 . . . . .58 C2
Severn Gdns NE8 . . . . .71 B8
Severn Hos NH37 . . . . .84 A8
Severn St NE17 . . . . .66 C1
Severs Terr NE5 . . . . .36 B6
Severus Rd NE4 . . . . .54 E7
Sextant Ho 6 NE24 . . . . . . .17 F8
Seymour Ct Ashington NE63 .7 B3
                Dunston NE11 . . . . .100 A1
Seymour Sq SR3 . . . . .85 E3
Seymour St
  Dunston NE11 . . . . .100 A1
  North Shields NE29 . . . . . . .42 A4
Seymour Terr
  Hetton le H DH5 . . . . .95 B1
  Ryton NE40 . . . . .52 A5
Sezze Bldg 6 NE46 . . . . . . .45 B4
Shadfen Cres NE61 . . . . .4 E3
Shadfen Park Rd NE30 . . . .32 A2
Shadon Way DH3 . . . . .82 E3
Shaftesbury Ave
  Jarrow NE32 . . . . .58 E5
  Ryhope SR2 . . . . .92 E7
  Whitley Bay NE26 . . . . .31 F6
Shaftesbury Cres
  Sunderland SR3 . . . . .85 F3
  Tynemouth NE30 . . . . .32 A3
Shaftesbury Gr NE6 . . . . . . .56 B7
Shaftesbury Ho NE33 . . . . .59 B6
Shaftesbury Wlk NE8 . . . .100 C2
Shafto Ct NE15 . . . . .54 B5
Shafto St
  Newcastle-u-T NE15 . . . . . .54 A5
  Wallsend NE28 . . . . .40 E3
Shaftoe Cl NE40 . . . . .51 F3
Shaftoe Cres NE46 . . . . .45 A5
Shaftoe Ct
  Killingworth NE12 . . . . .29 D3
  Newcastle-u-T NE3 . . . . . . .38 A7
Shaftoe Leazes NE46 . . . . .44 F4
Shaftoe Rd SR3 . . . . .85 D2
Shaftoe Sq SR3 . . . . .85 D2
Shaftoe Way NE13 . . . . .27 B7
Shakespeare Ave NE31 . . . .57 E6
Shakespeare St
  Houghton-le-S DH5 . . . . . . .94 E7
  Jarrow NE32 . . . . .58 B8
  Newcastle-u-T NE1 . . . . . . .99 A1
  18 South Shields NE33 . . . .42 D1
  Sunderland SR5 . . . . .75 B2
  Wallsend NE28 . . . . .40 F3
Shakespeare Terr SR2 . . .102 C1
Shalcombe Cl SR3 . . . . .92 A6
Shallcross SR2 . . . . .86 B4
Shallon Ct NE63 . . . . .6 C2
Shamrock St NE32 . . . . .72 F1
Shamrock Cl NE15 . . . . .53 C8
Shandon Way NE3 . . . . .37 C5
Shanklin Pl NE23 . . . . .21 E6
Shannon Cl SR5 . . . . .74 A1
Shannon St NE3 . . . . .37 C7
Shap Cl NE38 . . . . .83 D3
Shap Ct 2 SR3 . . . . .91 F6
Shap La NE5 . . . . .37 A4
Shap Rd NE30 . . . . .32 A2
Sharnford Cl NE27 . . . . .30 D5
Sharon Cl NE12 . . . . .29 B2
Sharpendon St NE31 . . . . . .57 E7
Sharperton Dr NE3 . . . . .28 A1
Sharpley Dr 5 SR7 . . . . . . .92 E1
Shaw Ave NE34 . . . . .59 B4
Shaw Gdns NE10 . . . . .72 B8
Shaw La DH8,HL47 . . . . .76 F4
Shawbrow Cl NE7 . . . . .39 E3
Shawdon Cl NE5 . . . . .37 B4
Shaws La Hexham NE46 . . .44 D4
                Hexham NE46 . . . . . .44 D5
Shaws Pk NE46 . . . . .44 E6
Shearlegs Rd NE8 . . . . .56 A3
Shearwater Ave NE12 . . . . .29 F8
Shearwater Cl NE5 . . . . .37 B4
Shearwater Ct NE5 . . . . .37 B4
Sheelin Ave DH2 . . . . .88 C1
Sheen Cl DH4 . . . . .94 A2
Sheen St NE3 . . . . .37 B5
Sheep Hill NE16 . . . . .79 B6
Sheepfolds N SR5 . . . . . . .103 A4
Sheepfolds Rd SR5 . . . . . .103 A4
Sheepwash Ave NE62 . . . . .11 B8
Sheepwash Bank NE62 . . . .10 E7
Sheepwash Rd NE61,NE62 .10 E7
Shefton Mus of Greek Art &
  Archaeology* NE1 . . . . . . .99 A2
Sheldon Cl NE12 . . . . .29 C1
Sheldon Gr
  Cramlington NE23 . . . . .16 B1
  Newcastle-u-T NE3 . . . . . . .38 A3
Sheldon Rd NE34 . . . . .42 F1
Sheldon St NE32 . . . . .58 B7
Sheldon Way NE23 . . . . .16 A1
Shelford Gdns NE15 . . . . . .53 E7
Shellbark DH4 . . . . .89 F6
Shelley Ave
  Easington Lane DH5 . . . . . .97 D8
  South Shields NE34 . . . . . . .60 B5
  Springwell NE9 . . . . .71 F1
  West Boldon NE35 . . . . .74 A8
Shelley Cres NE24 . . . . .17 C5
Shelley Dr NE8 . . . . .56 A2
Shelley Rd NE15 . . . . .53 A7
Shepherd St SR4 . . . . .102 A3
Shepherd's Ct NE46 . . . . . . .45 A6
Shepherd's Quay NE29 . . . .42 B4
Shepherds Way NE36 . . . . .73 D6
Sheppard Terr 1 SR5 . . . . .74 B1
Sheppey Ct SR3 . . . . .92 A6

Shepton Cotts NE16 . . . . . .69 C3
Sheraton NE10 . . . . .72 A5
Sheraton St NE2 . . . . .98 B4
Sherborne Ave NE29 . . . . . .41 D8
Sherburn Gr DH4 . . . . .90 C1
Sherburn Grange N NE32 . .58 A5
Sherburn Grange S NE32 . .58 A5
Sherburn Hill Prim Sch
  DH6 . . . . .96 D1
Sherburn Park Dr NE39 . . .67 F3
Sherburn Terr
  Gateshead NE9 . . . . .71 C2
  Hamsterley NE17 . . . . .76 F5
Sherburn Village Prim Sch
  DH6 . . . . .96 A2
Sherburn Way NE10 . . . . . .72 C7
Sherfield Dr NE7 . . . . .39 D2
Sheridan Gn NE38 . . . . .83 A1
Sheridan Rd NE34 . . . . .59 A3
Sheridan St 5 SR4 . . . . . . .85 F7
Sheriff's Highway NE9 . . . .71 A6
Sheriff's Moor Ave DH5 . . .97 C8
Sheriffs Cl NE10 . . . . .71 B8
Sheriffs Hall Villas 7 71
  NE9 . . . . .71 B7
Sheringham Ave NE29 . . . .41 D7
Sheringham Cl SR3 . . . . . . .92 A4
Sheringham Dr NE23 . . . . . .21 E6
Sheringham Ho NE38 . . . . .83 F4
Sheringham Ho 8 NE38 . . .83 F4
Sherringham Ave NE3 . . . . .37 E4
Sherwood NE27 . . . . .31 B2
Sherwood Cl
  Tynemouth NE27 . . . . .31 B2
  Washington NE38 . . . . .83 D5
Sherwood Ct 5 SR3 . . . . . .92 A6
Sherwood Pl NE3 . . . . .28 C2
Sherwood Terr NE28 . . . . . .40 A4
Shetland Ct 1 SR3 . . . . . . .92 A6
Shibdon Bank NE21 . . . . . .53 D2
Shibdon Bsns Pk NE21 . . .53 E3
Shibdon Cres NE21 . . . . . . .53 D2
Shibdon Cl NE21 . . . . .53 D2
Shibdon Park View NE21 . .53 D2
Shibdon Pond Nature
  Reserve* NE21 . . . . .53 E2
Shibdon Rd Blaydon NE21 .53 D3
                Blaydon NE21 . . . . . .53 E2
Shibdon Way NE21 . . . . . . .53 F2
Shield Ave NE16 . . . . .54 B1
Shield Ct Hexham NE46 . . .45 B3
                Newcastle-u-T NE2 . . .99 C3
Shield Gr NE33 . . . . .38 D6
Shield La 1 NE6 . . . . .56 C6
Shield St NE2 . . . . .99 C2
Shieldclose 2 NE37 . . . . . .83 A6
Shieldfield Gn NE2 . . . . . . .99 C2
Shieldfield Ho NE2 . . . . . . .99 C2
Shieldfield La NE2 . . . . .99 C2
Shields Pl DH5 . . . . .90 E1
Shields Rd
  Chester le S DH3 . . . . .88 D5
  Cleadon NE34 . . . . .60 A3
  Cleadon SR6 . . . . .60 A2
  Gateshead NE10 . . . . .72 F8
  Morpeth NE61 . . . . .9 B7
  Nedderton NE22 . . . . .15 C5
  Newcastle-u-T NE6 . . . . . . .56 C7
  Sunderland SR5,SR6 . . . . . .75 B5
  Whitley Bay NE25 . . . . .31 F3
Shields Rd W 5 NE6 . . . . .56 A6
Shillaw Pl NE23 . . . . .22 B3
Shilton Cl NE34 . . . . .60 B5
Shincliffe Ave SR5 . . . . .74 C2
Shincliffe Gdns NE9 . . . . . .71 D3
Shiney Row Prim Sch
  DH4 . . . . .90 B5
Shipcote La NE8 . . . . .72 A1
Shipcote Terr NE8 . . . . .70 F8
Shipley Art Gallery*
  NE8 . . . . .72 A1
Shipley Ave
  Newcastle-u-T NE4 . . . . . . .54 E6
  North Shields NE29 . . . . . . .41 C7
Shipley Ct NE8 . . . . .101 C1
Shipley Pl 18 NE6 . . . . .56 B6
Shipley Rd NE30 . . . . .42 C7
Shipley Rise 8 NE6 . . . . . . .56 C6
Shipley St 4 NE6 . . . . .53 C6
Shipley Wlk 22 NE6 . . . . . .56 B6
Shipton Cl NE35 . . . . .58 E1
Shire Farm Gr NE63 . . . . . . .6 A2
Shiremoor Prim Sch
  NE27 . . . . .30 E3
Shiremoor Sta NE27 . . . . . .30 F4
Shirlaw Cl NE5 . . . . .36 F3
Shirley Gdns SR3 . . . . .86 B3
Shirwood Ave NE16 . . . . . . .69 A5
Shop Row DH4 . . . . .90 C5
Shop Spouts NE21 . . . . .53 C3
Shopping Ctr The NE5 . . . .36 C2
Shore St SR6 . . . . .75 D1
Shoreham Sq SR3 . . . . .37 C2
Shoreham Sq SR3 . . . . .85 C2
Shorestone Ave NE30 . . . . .32 B3
Shoreswood Dr 3 SR3 . . . .92 B7
Short Row NE5 . . . . .36 B6
Shortridge St 1 NE33 . . . . .42 D3
Shortridge Terr NE2 . . . . . .38 F1
Shot Factory La NE4 . . . . .100 C3
Shotley Ave SR5 . . . . .75 B3
Shotley Ct NE63 . . . . .6 B2
Shotley Gdns NE9 . . . . .71 A7
Shotley Gr NE36 . . . . .74 B7
Shotton Ave NE24 . . . . .17 E6

Shotton La
  Cramlington NE23 . . . . .15 C2
  Shotton NE61,NE13 . . . . . . .20 F8
Shotton St NE23 . . . . .16 B3
Shotton Way NE10 . . . . .72 E6
Shrewsbury Cl NE12 . . . . . .39 D4
Shrewsbury Cres SR3 . . . . .85 F3
Shrewsbury Dr NE27 . . . . . .30 C5
Shrewsbury St NE11 . . . . . .69 F8
Shrewsbury Terr NE33 . . . .59 C2
Shrigley Cl NE38 . . . . .89 B8
Shrigley Gdns NE3 . . . . .37 F6
Shummard Cl NE4 . . . . .89 F8
Shunner Cl NE37 . . . . .83 A6
Sibthorpe St NE29 . . . . .42 B5
Side NE1 . . . . .101 B6
Side Cliff Rd SR6 . . . . .75 E3
Sidlaw Ave
  Chester le S DH2 . . . . .88 A3
  Tynemouth NE29 . . . . .31 F4
Sidlaw Ct NE63 . . . . .6 E1
Sidmouth Cl DH4 . . . . .90 C4
Sidmouth Rd
  Gateshead NE9 . . . . .70 F2
  North Shields NE29 . . . . . . .41 D7
Sidney Gr Gateshead NE9 .101 A4
                Newcastle-u-T NE4 . . .98 A2
Sidney St Blyth NE24 . . . . . .17 D7
                Boldon Colliery NE35 .73 F2
                North Shields NE29 . .42 A4
Silkey's La NE29 . . . . .41 F4
Silkstun Ct 8 SR3 . . . . .92 A6
Silksworth Cl NE4 . . . . .54 E7
Silksworth Gdns NE9 . . . . .71 C1
Silksworth Hall Dr SR3 . . .91 F7
Silksworth La
  New Silksworth SR3 . . . . . .91 F8
  Sunderland SR3 . . . . .85 F1
Silksworth Rd
  New Silksworth SR3 . . . . . .92 A4
  Sunderland SR3 . . . . .91 C1
Silksworth Row SR1 . . . . .102 C2
Silksworth Terr SR3 . . . . . .92 A4
Silkwood Cl NE23 . . . . .16 B1
Silkworth La 1 SR3 . . . . . . .92 A4
Silkworth Way SR3 . . . . . . .91 E1
Silloth Ave NE5 . . . . .54 A4
Silloth Dr NE37 . . . . .72 C1
Silloth Pl NE30 . . . . .32 B4
Silloth Rd SR3 . . . . .85 D3
Silvas Ct NE61 . . . . .4 A7
Silver Ct 3 NE9 . . . . .71 A4
Silver Fox Way
  Earsdon NE27 . . . . .31 A5
  Wallsend NE27 . . . . .40 F7
Silver Lonnen NE5 . . . . .54 B5
Silver St Sunderland SR1 . .103 C2
                Tynemouth NE30 . . . .42 A6
Silverbirch Ind Est NE12 . .29 F8
Silverbriar SR5 . . . . .74 F1
Silverdale SR3 . . . . .92 A6
Silverdale Ave Newcastle-u-T NE10 . .72 C2
Silverdale Dr NE21 . . . . . . .68 A8
Silverdale Rd NE23 . . . . . . .16 B1
Silverdale Sch NE28 . . . . . .41 A2
Silverdale Terr NE8 . . . . . . .70 F7
Silverdale Way
  Brockley Whins NE34 . . . . .58 F1
  Whickham NE16 . . . . .68 F6
Silverhill Dr NE5 . . . . .54 E8
Silverhill Sch The NE5 . . . .54 C1
Silverlink N The
  Shiremoor NE27 . . . . .30 E1
  Wallsend NE27 . . . . .40 F7
Silverlink Ret Pk NE28 . . . .41 A1
Silverlink The NE28 . . . . . . .41 A1
Silvermere Dr NE40 . . . . . . .52 D1
Silverstone NE12 . . . . .29 E1
Silverstone Rd NE37 . . . . . .83 E8
Silvertop Gdns NE40 . . . . . .52 A4
Silvertop Terr NE40 . . . . . . .52 A4
Silverwood Gdns NE11 . . . .70 E8
Simon Pl NE13 . . . . .28 B3
Simonburn NE38 . . . . .82 B1
Simonburn Ave
  Newcastle-u-T NE4 . . . . . . .54 E6
  North Shields NE29 . . . . . . .41 C7
Simonburn La 2 NE63 . . . . .6 F1
Simonside Prudhoe NE42 . .50 F3
                Seaton Sluice NE26 . .24 C8
Simonside Ave
  Stakeford NE62 . . . . .11 E8
  Wallsend NE28 . . . . .40 B4
Simonside Cl
  Morpeth NE61 . . . . .8 D2
  Seaton Sluice NE26 . . . . . .24 C8
Simonside Hall NE34 . . . . .58 F4
Simonside Ind Est NE32 . . .58 E6
Simonside Pl 16 NE9 . . . . .71 B1
Simonside Prim Sch
  Brockley Whins NE32 . . . . .58 D1
  Newcastle-u-T NE5 . . . . . . .36 F2
Simonside Rd
  Blaydon NE21 . . . . .53 C2
  Sunderland SR3 . . . . .85 C1
Simonside Terr
  Newbiggin-by-t-S NE64 . . . .7 F4
  Newcastle-u-T NE6 . . . . . . .56 C6
Simonside View
  Jarrow NE32 . . . . .58 F4
  Ponteland NE20 . . . . .25 D3
  19 Whickham NE16 . . . . . .69 A8
Simonside Way NE12 . . . . .29 F8
Simonside Wlk NE11 . . . . . .70 A7
Simpson Cl SR3 . . . . .92 B1
Simpson Ct NE63 . . . . .7 A2
Simpson St Blyth NE24 . . . .17 E8
                North Shields NE29 . .41 A5

Simpson St continued
Ryton NE40 ....52 E4
Sunderland SR4 ....102 B4
Tynemouth NE30 ....32 C4
Simpson Terr
Newcastle-u-T NE15 ....36 B1
Newcastle-u-T,Shieldfield
NE2 ....99 B2
Simpsons Meml Homes
NE40 ....52 A4
Sinclair Dr DH3 ....88 D8
Sinclair Gdns NE25 ....23 D3
Sinderby Cl NE3 ....38 D8
Sir Charles Parsons Sch
NE6 ....56 F7
Sir GB Hunter Meml Hospl
NE28 ....40 C2
Sir Godfrey Thomson Ct
NE10 ....71 C8
Siskin Ho NE12 ....39 E8
Sixth Ave Ashington NE63 ....6 E2
Blyth NE24 ....17 D6
Chester le S DH2 ....88 B3
Gateshead NE11 ....70 C4
Morpeth NE61 ....9 B7
Newcastle-u-T NE6 ....56 C7
Skaylock Dr NE38 ....83 A3
Skegness Par NE31 ....58 A2
Skelder Ave NE12 ....39 B6
Skelton Cl NE3 ....37 E8
Ski View SR3 ....91 F8
Skiddaw Dr SR6 ....75 C5
Skiddaw Pl NE9 ....71 B4
Skinnerburn Rd NE1,
NE4 ....100 C3
Skipper Cl NE11 ....70 B7
Skipsea View SR2 ....92 D7
Skipton Cl
Bedlington NE22 ....10 D2
Cramlington NE23 ....16 C1
Skipton Gn NE9 ....71 B2
Skirlaw Cl NE38 ....83 D4
Skye Cl 2 SR3 ....92 A6
Skye Gr NE32 ....58 E2
Slake Rd NE32 ....58 D8
Slaley NE38 ....83 E1
Slaley Cl NE10 ....72 C7
Slaley Ct Bedlington NE22 .....11 A1
4 Silksworth SR3 ....92 A6
Slatyford La NE5 ....54 A8
Sled La NE40,NE41 ....51 D3
Sleekburn Ave NE22 ....11 E3
Sleekburn Bsns Ctr NE22,
NE24 ....12 A6
Sleekburn Ho NE22 ....11 D2
Slingley Cl 4 SR7 ....92 E1
Slingsby Gdns NE7 ....39 D3
Slipway The NE10 ....57 A2
Sloane Ct NE2 ....99 B3
Smailes La NE39 ....67 C2
Smallholdings NE64 ....7 C6
Smeaton Ct 5 NE28 ....41 A1
Smeaton St 2 NE28 ....41 A1
Smith Gr SR2 ....92 E6
Smith St Ryhope SR2 ....92 F6
South Shields NE33 ....59 B8
Smith St S SR2 ....92 F6
Smith's Terr DH5 ....95 B1
Smithburn Rd NE10 ....71 C7
Smithy La NE11,NE9 ....70 F1
Smithy Sq NE23 ....22 B6
Smithy St NE33 ....42 C3
Smithyford NE9 ....71 A1
Smyrna Pl SR1 ....103 B2
Snipes Dene NE39 ....67 A6
Snowdon Gdns NE11 ....70 A6
Snowdon Gr NE36 ....74 E7
Snowdon Terr NE39 ....66 F5
Snowdrop Cl NE21 ....53 A2
Soane Gdns NE34 ....59 D3
Softley Pl NE15 ....53 F7
Solar Ho SR1 ....102 C2
Solingen Est NE24 ....17 F5
Solway Ave NE30 ....32 B2
Solway Rd NE31 ....57 F4
Solway Sq SR3 ....85 E3
Solway St NE6 ....56 C4
Somerford NE9 ....71 F2
Somersby Dr NE3 ....37 E5
Somerset Cl NE63 ....6 A4
Somerset Cotts 4 SR3 ....92 A8
Somerset Gdns NE28 ....40 A3
Somerset Gr NE29 ....41 D8
Somerset Pl NE4 ....98 A1
Somerset Rd
Hebburn NE31 ....57 F3
Sunderland SR3 ....85 D3
Somerset Sq SR3 ....85 D3
Somerset St SR3 ....92 A8
Someryl Ave NE12 ....38 F6
Sophy St SR5 ....75 B2
Sorley St SR4 ....102 A2
Sorrel Cl NE63 ....6 C2
Sorrel Gdns NE34 ....59 E3
Sorrell Cl NE4 ....54 D7
Soulby Ct NE3 ....38 E1
Sourmilk Hill La NE9 ....71 A6
Souter Lighthouse* SR6 ....60 F5
Souter Rd NE3 ....38 A5
Souter View SR6 ....60 F2
South App DH2 ....88 C4
South Ave Ryton NE40 ....52 C5
South Shields NE34 ....83 C8
Washington NE37 ....83 C8
Whickham NE16 ....69 B5
South Beach Fst Sch
NE24 ....17 E4

South Bend NE3 ....28 B1
South Bents Ave SR6 ....75 F6
South Benwell Prim Sch
NE4 ....54 E4
South Benwell Rd NE15 ....54 C4
South Burn Terr DH4 ....90 C6
South Burns DH3 ....88 C4
South Cl
Easington Lane DH5 ....97 D8
Ryton NE40 ....52 C4
South Shields NE34 ....59 F5
South Cliff SR6 ....75 F2
South Cres
Boldon Colliery NE35 ....73 F8
Great Lumley DH4 ....89 F1
Washington NE38 ....89 B8
South Croft NE12 ....39 E7
South Cross St NE3 ....38 C5
South Dene NE34 ....59 B6
South Dr Cleadon SR6 ....59 F1
Hebburn NE31 ....57 F4
Shotton NE13 ....20 E6
Woolsington NE13 ....37 A8
South Durham Ct SR1 ....103 B2
South East Farm NE15 ....50 D8
South Eldon St NE33 ....59 B8
South End Cleadon SR6 ....74 E8
High Pittington DI16 ....96 C5
South Farm
Nedderton NE22 ....15 B8
Ryhope SR2 ....93 A6
South Frederick St NE33 ......59 B7
South Front NE2 ....99 B4
South Gosforth Fst Sch
NE3 ....38 E4
South Gosforth Sta 3 NE3 ....38 E4
South Gr NE40 ....52 D4
South Grange Pk SR7 ....92 F2
South Hetton Ind Est
DH6 ....97 F7
South Hetton Prim Sch
DH6 ....97 F7
South Hetton Rd DH5,
DH6 ....97 D8
South Hill Cres SR2 ....102 B1
South Hill Rd NE8 ....101 A1
South Hylton Prim Sch
SR4 ....85 A6
South Hylton Sta SR4 ....85 B6
South La NE36 ....74 C7
South Lea Blaydon NE21 ....53 C1
Horsley NE15 ....50 C8
South Leigh DH9 ....79 D1
South Lodge Wood NE61 ....9 E4
South Magdalene DH8 ....77 B1
South Market St DH5 ....95 B4
South Nelson Ind Est
NE23 ....21 E8
South Nelson Rd NE23 ....21 E8
South Newsham Rd
NE24 ....17 D3
South Par
Choppington NE62 ....10 E6
Gateshead NE10 ....57 B2
Stocksfield NE43 ....64 A7
Whitley Bay NE26 ....31 B5
South Pelaw Inf Sch DH2 .....88 B5
South Preston Gr 1
NE29 ....42 A5
South Preston Terr 2
NE29 ....42 A5
South Rd Chopwell NE17 ......66 C1
Prudhoe NE42 ....50 D2
South Ridge
Annitsford NE23 ....7 B2
Newcastle-u-T NE3 ....38 B8
South Riggs NE22 ....15 F8
South Row NE8 ....56 A4
South Sherburn NE39 ....66 F4
South Shields Sta NE33 ....42 C3
South Shore Rd
Gateshead,East Gateshead
NE8 ....56 B3
Gateshead,Saltmeadows
NE8 ....56 A4
South Side Cresswell NE61 .....2 B7
Ashington NE63 ....7 B7
East Rainton DH5 ....94 C4
9 Fence Houses DH4 ....94 A8
South Stainmore NE62 ....10 F5
Gateshead NE8 ....101 C1
Hebburn NE31 ....57 F7
High Spen NE40 ....66 F4
Newbottle DH4 ....90 D3
Newcastle-u-T NE1 ....101 A4
Newcastle-u-T,Coxlodge
NE3 ....38 A5
Sherburn DH6 ....96 A1
Sunderland SR2 ....30 F4
Sunderland SR1 ....103 A3
West Rainton DH4 ....94 A2
South Street Prim Sch
NE8 ....101 C1
South Terr Chopwell NE17 .....77 B8
Morpeth NE61 ....3 F1
Sunderland SR5 ....75 B1
Wallsend NE28 ....40 E2
South Tyneside Coll
Seamanship Ctr NE33 ....42 C4
**South Tyneside General
Hospl** NE34 ....59 D5
South View
Annitsford NE23 ....22 B1
Ashington NE63 ....6 C4

South View continued
Birtley DH3 ....82 D4
Blyth NE24 ....17 C4
Cambois NE24 ....12 C6
Prudhoe NE42 ....77 A8
Crawcrook NE40 ....51 F4
Crawcrook,Clara Vale NE40 ....51 F7
Easington Lane DH5 ....97 D8
East Sleekburn NE22 ....11 F3
15 Gateshead NE10 ....71 D8
Guide Post NE62 ....10 E7
Hazlerigg NE13 ....28 D8
High Spen NE39 ....66 F3
Jarrow NE32 ....58 A6
Longbenton NE7 ....39 C5
Mickley Square NE43 ....49 E1
Newcastle-u-T NE5 ....53 E8
Pegswood NE61 ....4 F3
Prudhoe NE42 ....50 B2
Sherburn Hill DH6 ....96 D1
Shiney Row DH4 ....90 B6
16 Springwell NE9 ....71 F1
Washington NE38 ....75 D3
South View E NE39 ....67 C2
South View Gdns NE6 ....45 A4
South View Pl NE23 ....22 B6
South View Rd SR4 ....85 B5
South View Terr
Fence Houses DH4 ....94 B8
Medomsley NE16 ....69 B6
Medomsley,Swalwell NE16 ....69 B8
South View W
Newcastle-u-T NE5 ....56 A6
Rowlands Gill NE39 ....67 C2
South Wellfield Fst Sch
NE25 ....23 A4
South Woodbine St 1
NE33 ....42 D2
Southburn Cl DH4 ....94 C8
Southcliff NE26 ....32 C4
Southcote NE16 ....69 A5
Southcroft NE38 ....83 D1
Southdowns DH2 ....88 C2
Southend Ave NE24 ....17 C6
Southend Par NE31 ....58 A2
Southend Rd
Gateshead NE9 ....71 B5
Sunderland SR3 ....85 E2
Southend Terr NE9 ....71 B6
Southern Cl NE63 ....7 B3
Southern Rd NE6 ....56 F4
Southern Way NE40 ....52 C4
Southey St NE33 ....59 D8
Southfield Gdns NE16 ....69 C6
Southfield Gn NE16 ....69 C6
Southfield La NE39 ....77 F3
Southfield Rd
Longbenton NE12 ....39 D6
2 South Shields NE34 ....60 A8
Whickham NE16 ....69 C6
Southfield Terr
Newcastle-u-T NE6 ....57 A4
2 South Shields NE34 ....60 A8
Whickham NE16 ....69 C6
Southfields Ho 1 NE6 ....56 B6
Southfork NE15 ....53 C8
Southgarth E 2 NE33 ....59 E8
Southgate NE12 ....29 D3
Southgate Ct NE12 ....38 F6
Southgate Wood NE61 ....9 A5
Southhill Rd NE34 ....60 A6
Southlands
Gateshead NE9 ....71 C2
Hedworth NE32 ....58 D1
Hexham NE46 ....44 D4
Newcastle-u-T NE7 ....39 A2
Tynemouth NE30 ....32 B1
Southlands Mid Sch
NE30 ....32 B1
Southlands Sch NE30 ....32 A1
Southleigh NE26 ....32 B5
Southmayne Rd SR4 ....85 D4
Southmoor Com Sch SR7 .....86 E3
Southmoor Rd NE6 ....56 F7
Southport Par NE31 ....58 A2
Southridge Fst Sch NE25 .....31 D6
Southward Cl NE26 ....24 D5
Southward Ct NE26 ....24 D5
Southward Way NE25 ....23 E1
Southway Gateshead NE9 ......71 B6
Newcastle-u-T NE15 ....53 E7
Southwick Ind Est SR5 ....74 F7
Southwick Prim Sch SR5 ....75 A2
Southwick Rd SR5 ....75 A2
Southwold Gdns SR3 ....91 H6
Southwold Pl NE23 ....21 E6
Southwood Cres NE39 ....67 F2
Southwood Gdns NE3 ....37 F4
Sovereign Ct
Newcastle-u-T NE4 ....100 A4
Newcastle-u-T,Jesmond
NE2 ....99 C4
Sovereign Ho NE30 ....42 D7
Sovereign Pl NE4 ....100 A4
Spa Well Cl NE16 ....68 B8
Spa Well Dr SR5 ....74 C2
Spa Well Turn NE21 ....68 E7
Spalding Cl NE7 ....39 C4
Sparkwell Cl NE4 ....90 C4
Spartylea NE38 ....83 F1
Speculation Pl NE37 ....83 D8
Speedwell NE9 ....71 C5

Speedwell Ct NE63 ....6 B1
Spelter Works Rd SR2 ....86 F3
Spelvit La NE61 ....8 F7
Spen Burn NE39 ....67 A4
Spen La
Greenside NE39,NE40 ....66 F7
High Spen NE39 ....67 B3
Spen Rd NE39 ....66 F5
Spence Terr 1 NE29 ....41 F5
Spencer Ct NE24 ....12 B1
Spencer Dr NE61 ....4 E3
Spencer Gr NE16 ....69 A8
Spencer Rd NE24 ....12 B1
Spencer St Hebburn NE31 .....57 F7
Newcastle-u-T NE6 ....56 C8
20 North Shields NE29 ....42 A5
Spencer Terr NE15 ....36 B1
Spencers Bank 3 NE16 ....54 A1
Spenfield Rd NE5 ....37 D3
Spetchells NE42 ....50 D3
Spinney Terr NE6 ....56 F6
Spinney The
Annitsford NE23 ....22 C1
Killingworth NE12 ....29 E2
Morpeth NE61 ....9 A6
Newcastle-u-T NE7 ....39 A2
Washington NE38 ....83 D2
Spinneyside Gdns NE11 ....69 F7
Spire Rd NE37 ....83 F7
Spires La NE6 ....56 C6
Spital Cres NE64 ....7 D3
Spital La NE46 ....44 F7
Spital Rd NE64 ....7 D3
Spital St NE15 ....38 D5
Spital Villas NE15 ....33 A3
Spittal Terr NE46 ....45 A5
Split Crow Rd NE10,NE8 ....71 B8
Spohr Terr NE33 ....42 D2
Spoor St NE11 ....100 A1
Spoors Cotts NE16 ....69 A6
Spout La Washington NE37 ....83 D7
Washington,Concord NE37 ....83 D8
Washington,Washington Village
NE38 ....83 D6
Spoutwell La NE45 ....47 A5
Spring Cl DH8 ....76 E2
Spring Garden Cl SR1 ....103 B3
Spring Garden La NE4 ....98 B2
Spring Gardens Ct 12
NE4 ....42 A6
Spring Gardens Prim Sch
NE29 ....41 F6
Spring Gdns NE29 ....41 F5
Spring St NE4 ....98 B2
Spring Terr NE29 ....42 A6
Spring Ville NE22 ....11 F4
Springbank Ho NE2 ....56 A7
Springbank Rd
Newcastle-u-T NE2 ....56 A7
Sunderland SR3 ....85 D3
Springbank Sq SR3 ....85 D3
Springfeld NE10 ....71 F4
Springfell DH3 ....82 D3
Springfield
6 North Shields NE29 ....42 A6
Ovington NE42 ....49 D4
Springfield Ave NE7 ....71 C1
Springfield Cl NE42 ....49 D4
Springfield Gdns
Chester le S DH3 ....88 C5
Wallsend NE28 ....39 F3
Springfield Gr NE25 ....31 E3
Springfield Pl NE9 ....71 A6
Springfield Rd
Blaydon NE21 ....53 C1
Hexham NE46 ....45 A4
Newbottle DH4 ....90 D3
Newcastle-u-T NE5 ....37 D2
Springfield Terr 1 NE10 ......71 C7
Springhill Gdns NE15 ....54 D6
Springhill Wlk NE61 ....8 E7
Springhouse La DH8 ....76 E2
Springs The DH3 ....82 E3
Springsyde Cl NE16 ....68 E5
Springwell Ave
Gateshead NE9 ....71 C3
Jarrow NE32 ....58 C6
Newcastle-u-T NE6 ....56 E4
Springwell Cl NE21 ....53 D1
Springwell Dene Sch
SR3 ....85 E3
Springwell Rd
Gateshead NE9 ....71 C3
Jarrow NE32 ....58 B5
Springwell NE9 ....71 F1
Sunderland SR3,SR4 ....85 D3
Springwell Sta* NE9 ....71 F3
Springwell Terr
Gateshead NE9 ....71 E3
Hetton le H DH5 ....95 A2
17 Springwell NE9 ....71 F1
Springwell Village Prim Sch
NE9 ....71 F1
Springwood NE31 ....57 C7
Square Hos 4 NE10 ....71 C7
Square The
Guide Post NE62 ....10 F7
Ponteland NE20 ....26 C5
Riding Mill NE44 ....63 A8
3 Whickham NE16 ....69 B7
Squires Gdns NE10 ....71 D7
Stable Block NE45 ....47 C5
Stable La 2 NE8 ....71 A7
Stable La NE3 ....37 F8
Stables The DH4 ....90 F7

Stadium Ind Pk NE10 ....56 B3
**Stadium of Light (Sunderland
FC)** SR5 ....102 C4
Stadium of Light Sta
SR5,SR6 ....75 D1
Stadium Rd NE10 ....56 B3
Stadium Villas NE28 ....40 C2
Stadium Way SR5 ....102 C4
Stafford Gr Ryhope SR2 ....92 E6
Sunderland SR5 ....75 B1
Stafford St
Hetton le H DH5 ....94 F4
Sunderland SR1 ....103 C4
Stafford Villas 15 NE9 ....71 F1
Staffords La 1 SR6 ....75 F8
Stagshaw NE12 ....29 C5
Stagshaw Rd NE45 ....46 F6
Staindrop NE10 ....72 A5
Staines Rd NE6 ....56 D4
Stainthorpe Ct 1 NE46 ....45 B4
Stainton Dr NE10 ....71 D8
Stainton Gdns NE9 ....71 C2
Stainton Gr SR6 ....75 C5
Staith La NE21 ....53 A4
Staiths Ave NE12 ....39 C6
Staiths La NE61 ....4 A1
Staithes The
Dunston NE11 ....100 A2
Penshaw NE38 ....84 A3
Staithes St NE6 ....57 B6
Stakeford Cres NE62 ....11 B8
Stakeford Fst Sch NE62 ......11 C8
Stakeford La NE62 ....11 B4
Stakeford Rd NE22 ....11 C3
Stakeford Terr NE62 ....11 A7
Stalks Rd NE13 ....28 B6
Stamford NE12 ....29 D4
Stamford Ave
Seaton Delaval NE25 ....23 E1
Sunderland SR3 ....85 F3
Stamfordham Ave NE29 ....41 D5
Stamfordham Cl NE28 ....40 A2
Stamfordham Mews 7
NE5 ....37 D1
Stamfordham Rd
Newcastle-u-T NE5 ....36 C4
Ponteland NE5,NE15 ....35 D7
Stamp Exchange NE1 ....101 A4
Stampley Cl NE21 ....68 A8
Stamps La SR1 ....103 C3
Stancley Rd NE42 ....50 E2
Standfield Gdns NE10 ....72 C8
Stanelaw Way DH9 ....79 F1
Staneway NE10 ....71 E5
Stanfield Bsns Ctr SR2 ......103 C1
Stanfield Ct NE7 ....39 C7
Stang Wlk NE12 ....39 C7
Stanhope NE38 ....83 A5
Stanhope Cl DH4 ....94 D7
Stanhope Par NE31 ....59 D8
Stanhope Prim Sch NE33 ......59 C7
Stanhope Rd Jarrow NE32 .....58 D5
South Shields NE33 ....42 A2
Sunderland SR6 ....75 E4
Stanhope Se
Greenside NE40 ....51 F1
Newcastle-u-T NE4 ....98 B2
South Shields NE33 ....42 A2
Stanhope Way NE4 ....98 B2
Stanley Cres
Prudhoe NE42 ....50 E3
9 Whitley Bay NE26 ....32 B4
Stanley Gdns
Gateshead NE9 ....71 C2
Seghill NE23 ....22 F1
Stanley Gr
Bedlington NE22 ....11 D3
Newcastle-u-T NE7 ....39 B3
Stanley St Blyth NE24 ....17 F7
Houghton-le-S DH5 ....90 E1
Newcastle-u-T NE6 ....56 A4
North Shields NE29 ....42 A5
2 Sunderland SR5 ....74 B1
Wallsend NE28 ....40 A5
Stanley St W NE29 ....42 A5
Stanley Terr
Chester le S DH3 ....88 D2
Stanley DH9 ....90 B6
Stanmore Rd NE6 ....56 E6
Stannerford Rd NE40 ....51 F6
Stannington Ave NE6 ....56 B7
Stannington Fst Sch
NE61 ....14 B4
Stannington Gdns SR2 ....86 C2
Stannington Gr
6 Newcastle-u-T NE6 ....56 B7
Sunderland SR2 ....86 D2
Stannington Pl
1 Newcastle-u-T NE6 ....56 B7
Ponteland NE20 ....25 E8
Stannington Rd NE29 ....41 D5
Stannington Station Rd
NE61 ....14 D8
Stannington Vale NE61 ....14 D1
Stansfield St SR6 ....75 E1
Stanstead Cl SR5 ....85 A8
Stanton Ave Blyth NE24 ......17 F5
South Shields NE34 ....59 B6
Stanton Cl NE10 ....72 D7
Stanton Dr NE61 ....8 A2
Stanton Gr NE30 ....32 A1

Stanton Rd
Shiremoor NE27 .30 E3
Tynemouth NE30 .32 A1
Stanton St NE4 .98 A2
Stanway Dr NE7 .39 A3
Stanwick St NE30 .42 D8
Stanwix 1 NE28 .40 F4
Stapeley Ct 5 NE3 .37 D5
Stapeley View NE3 .37 D5
Staple Rd NE32 .58 C7
Stapleford Cl NE5 .37 B1
Stapylton Dr SR2 .86 B4
Star of the Sea RC Prim Sch NE25 .31 E2
Starbeck Ave NE2 .99 C3
Starbeck Mews NE2 .99 C3
Stardale Ave NE24 .17 A6
Stargate Gdns NE9 .71 C2
Stargate Ind Est NE40 .52 E3
Stargate La NE40 .52 E4
Starlight Cres NE25 .23 C3
Starling Wlk NE16 .69 C2
Station App Cleadon NE36 .74 E8
Gateshead NE11,NE9 .70 D3
Longbenton NE12 .39 D6
1 South Shields NE33 .42 C3
Station Ave DH5 .95 A3
Station Ave N DH4 .90 A1
Station Ave S DH4 .90 A1
Station Bank
Mickley Square NE43 .49 E2
Ryton NE40 .52 C6
Station Cl NE44 .62 F8
Station Cotts
Burnopfield NE39 .78 C6
Longhirst NE61 .5 B7
Morpeth NE61 .9 A7
Ponteland NE20 .25 E6
Seghill NE23 .23 A1
Station Field Rd DH9 .79 F1
Station First Sch The NE22 .11 D3
Station Ind Est NE42 .50 B3
Station La DH2,DH3 .82 B4
Station Mews 10 NE30 .42 D7
Station Rd Ashington NE63 .6 B4
Backworth NE27 .30 D3
Bedlington NE22 .11 C2
Boldon Colliery NE35 .58 E2
Chester le S DH3 .88 C3
Corbridge NE45 .46 F4
Cramlington NE23 .22 A7
Crawcrook NE41 .51 C5
Dudley NE23 .28 F8
East Boldon NE36 .74 D7
Gateshead,Bill Quay NE10 .57 B2
Gateshead,Low Fell NE9 .70 E5
Hebburn NE31 .57 D6
Heddon-on-t-W NE15 .35 A1
Hetton le H DH5 .95 A3
Hexham NE46 .45 C5
High Pittington DH6 .96 A6
Houghton-le-S DH4 .90 D1
Killingworth NE12 .29 B3
Longbenton NE12 .39 D7
Newburn NE15 .52 F7
Newcastle-u-T,Kenton Bankfoot NE13 .37 B6
Newcastle-u-T,South Gosforth NE3 .38 E5
Newcastle-u-T,Wincomblee NE6 .57 A5
North Shields NE29 .41 D4
Penshaw DH4 .89 E8
Prudhoe NE42 .50 C3
Rowlands Gill NE39 .67 F1
Ryhope SR2 .93 A6
Seghill NE23 .23 A1
Shiney Row DH4 .90 A6
South Shields NE33 .42 C2
Sunderland SR5,SR6 .75 D4
Tynemouth NE30 .32 C3
Wallsend NE28 .40 B2
Wallsend NE28 .40 C1
Wallsend,Willington Quay NE28 .41 A1
Washington NE38 .84 A4
Washington,Columbia NE38 .83 E4
Washington,Fatfield DH4, NE38 .83 E1
Whitley Bay NE26 .32 B4
Wylam NE41 .51 B5
Station Rd N
Hetton le H DH5 .95 A3
Longbenton NE12 .39 D8
Station Sq 1 NE26 .32 B4
Station St
4 Bedlington NE22 .11 D3
Blyth NE24 .17 E8
Haswell DH6 .97 F3
Jarrow NE32 .58 B7
Sunderland SR1 .103 A3
Station Terr
Choppington NE62 .10 F3
East Boldon NE36 .74 E7
Fence Houses DH4 .89 F1
Tynemouth NE30 .42 D7
10 Washington NE37 .83 E8
Station View DH5 .95 A3
Staveley Rd SR6 .75 C5
Stavordale Terr NE9 .71 A7
Staward Ave NE25 .23 D2
Staward Terr NE6 .56 F4
Staynebrigg NE10 .72 A6
Stead La NE22 .11 C1
Stead Lane Fst Sch NE22 .11 C1
Stead St NE28 .41 A3
Steadings The
Ashington NE63 .6 A2
Seaton Sluice NE26 .24 E4
Steadlands Sq NE22 .11 C1
Steads The NE61 .9 A6
Stedham Cl NE37 .72 E2
Steenbergs 8 NE1 .56 A6
Steep Hill SR3 .91 C7
Stella Bank NE21 .52 F5
Stella Hall Dr NE21 .53 A4
Stella La NE21 .53 A4
Stella Rd Blaydon NE21 .53 B4
Ryton NE21 .53 B4
Stephen Ct NE32 .58 C6
Stephen St Blyth NE24 .17 E8
East Hartford NE23 .16 B3
Newcastle-u-T NE6 .56 A6
Stephenson Bldg NE2 .99 C2
Stephenson Cl DH5 .95 B4
Stephenson Ct
North Shields NE30 .42 B5
Wylam NE41 .51 C6
Bedlington NE22 .11 A3
Stephenson Ho 15 NE46 .45 A5
Stephenson Ind Est
Killingworth NE12 .29 C2
Washington NE37 .72 E2
Stephenson Meml Prim Sch NE28 .41 A2
Stephenson Railway Mus* NE29 .41 A7
Stephenson Rd
Newcastle-u-T NE7 .39 B1
Washington NE37 .72 E2
Stephenson St
Gateshead NE8 .70 D8
North Shields NE30 .42 B5
1 Tynemouth NE30 .42 D7
Wallsend NE28 .41 B1
Stephenson Terr
Gateshead NE10 .71 D8
Newcastle-u-T NE15 .36 B1
Throckley NE15 .35 D2
Wylam NE41 .51 B6
Stephenson Way
Bedlington NE22 .11 A4
Blaydon NE21 .68 B8
Stephenson's La NE1 .101 A4
Stepney Bank NE1 .56 A6
Stepney La NE1 .99 C1
Stepney Rd 1 NE1,NE2 .56 A6
Sterling Cotts NE10 .71 C7
Sterling St SR4 .102 A2
Stevenson St DH4 .94 D8
Steward Cres NE34 .60 B6
Stewart Ave SR2 .92 E6
Stewart Dr NE36 .74 B7
Stewart St
New Silksworth SR3 .92 A7
Sunderland SR4 .102 B1
Stewartsfield NE39 .67 D1
Stileford NE10 .72 A7
Stillington Cl 4 SR2 .92 F5
Stirling Ave
Brockley Whins NE32 .58 E4
Rowlands Gill NE39 .67 E1
Stirling Cl NE38 .84 A4
Stirling Ct NE11 .70 E2
Stirling Dr
Bedlington NE22 .11 C2
Tynemouth NE29 .41 C8
Stirling La NE39 .67 F1
Stobart St SR5 .102 C4
Stobhill Villas NE61 .9 A7
Stockfold NE38 .83 E2
Stockholm Cl NE29 .41 B5
Stockley Ave SR5 .74 C2
Stockley Rd NE38 .83 F6
Stocksfield Ave NE5 .54 C7
Stocksfield Avenue Prim Sch NE5 .54 B7
Stocksfield Gdns NE9 .71 B2
Stocksfield Hall NE43 .64 A8
Stocksfield Sta NE43 .64 A7
Stockton Rd
North Shields NE29 .41 F3
Ryhope SR2,SR7 .92 F2
Sunderland SR2 .103 A1
Stockton Terr 8 SR2 .86 F2
Stockwell Gn NE6 .56 F8
Stoddart Ho NE2 .99 C2
Stoddart St
Newcastle-u-T NE1,NE2 .99 C2
South Shields NE34 .59 C6
Stoker Ave NE34 .58 F4
Stoker Terr NE39 .67 A3
Stokesley Gr NE7 .39 A3
Stokoe Dr NE63 .7 A3
Stone Cellar Rd NE37 .72 C2
Stone St NE10 .71 C6
Stonechat Cl 3 NE38 .82 F3
Stonechat Mount NE21 .53 A4
Stonechat Pl NE12 .39 A7
Stonecroft Gdns NE7 .39 D3
Stonecrop NE9 .71 C5
Stonecross NE63 .6 C2
Stonefold Cl NE5 .37 B3
Stonegate NE15 .33 D1
Stonehaugh Way NE20 .25 B2
Stonelaw Mid Sch NE23 .22 A4
Stoneleigh NE61 .9 E4
Stoneleigh Ave NE12 .39 A7
Stoneleigh Cl DH4 .90 C2
Stoneleigh Pl 1 NE12 .39 A6
Stonesdale DH4 .89 E8
Stonethwaite NE29 .41 E3
Stoney La Springwell NE9 .71 F1
Sunderland SR5 .75 A1
Stoneycroft E NE12 .29 E2
Stoneycroft W NE12 .29 E2
Stoneycroft Way SR7 .93 C1
Stoneygate Cl NE10 .56 E1
Stoneygate Gdns NE10 .56 E1
Stoneygate La NE10 .56 E1
Stoneyhurst Ave NE15 .54 B5
Stoneyhurst Rd NE3 .38 E4
Stoneyhurst Rd W NE3 .38 D4
Stoneylea Cl NE40 .51 E3
Stoneylea Rd NE5 .53 F8
Stoneywaites NE40 .66 E8
Stonybank Way NE43 .64 E8
Stonycroft NE37 .83 C7
Stonyflat Bank NE42 .50 E2
Store Bldgs NE35 .73 E8
Store Farm Rd NE64 .7 C5
Store St Blaydon NE21 .53 B1
Newcastle-u-T NE15 .53 C6
Store Terr DH5 .95 B1
Storey Cres NE64 .7 C5
Storey La NE21 .53 A4
Storey St NE23 .22 C5
Stormont Gn NE3 .37 F3
Stormont St NE29 .42 A5
Stothard St NE32 .58 C7
Stott's Pasture DH4 .90 A4
Stotts Rd NE6 .57 A8
Stowe Gdns NE61 .4 E4
Stowell Sq NE1 .98 C1
Stowell St NE1 .98 C1
Stowell Terr NE10 .71 E8
Straker Dr NE46 .44 E3
Straker St NE32 .58 D6
Straker Terr NE34 .59 C5
Strand The SR3 .91 E8
Strangford Ave 2 DH2 .88 B1
Stranton Terr SR6 .75 D2
Stratfield St SR4 .85 E7
Stratford Ave SR2 .86 E3
Stratford Cl
Cramlington NE23 .21 E7
Killingworth NE12 .29 E3
Stratford Gdns NE9 .70 F6
Stratford Gr NE6 .56 A7
Stratford Gr W NE6 .56 A7
Stratford Grove Terr NE6 .56 A7
Stratford Rd NE6 .56 A7
Stratford Villas NE6 .56 A7
Strathearn Way NE3 .37 F7
Strathmore Ave NE39 .67 E1
Strathmore Cres
Byermoor NE16 .79 D8
Newcastle-u-T NE4 .54 E6
Strathmore Rd
Gateshead N10,NE9 .71 B7
Newcastle-u-T NE3 .38 C7
Rowlands Gill NE39 .67 E1
Sunderland SR3 .85 E2
Strathmore Sq SR3 .85 E2
Stratton Cl SR2 .93 A8
Stratus Ct 12 SR3 .92 A6
Strawberry Ave NE23 .29 C5
Strawberry Cotts NE62 .11 B8
Strawberry Gdns NE28 .40 A4
Strawberry La NE1 .98 C1
Strawberry Pl NE1 .98 C2
Strawberry Terr NE13 .27 F4
Street Gate Pk NE16 .69 D3
Street The NE30 .42 B5
Stretford Ct NE9 .71 A1
Stretton Cl DH4 .94 A7
Stretton Way NE27 .30 C5
Stridingedge NE37 .83 B6
Stronsay Cl 2 SR2 .92 E8
Strothers Rd NE39 .66 F5
Strothers Terr NE39 .66 E4
Struan Terr NE36 .74 E7
Struddars Farm Ct NE21 .53 F2
Stuart Ct NE3 .37 C6
Stuart Gdns NE15 .35 D2
Stuart Terr NE10 .56 D1
Stubbs Ave NE16 .69 A8
Studdon Wlk NE3 .37 D5
Studland Cl NE29 .31 F1
Studley Gdns
2 Gateshead NE9 .70 F5
Whitley Bay NE25 .32 A4
Studley Terr NE4 .98 A3
Studley Villas NE12 .39 E7
Sturdee Gdns NE2 .38 E3
Styan Ave NE26 .32 B5
Styford Gdns NE15 .53 E7
Success Rd DH4 .90 B4
Sudbury Way NE23 .21 E6
Suddick St 2 SR5 .75 B1
Suez St NE30 .42 B6
Suffolk Cl NE63 .6 A4
Suffolk Gdns
South Shields NE34 .60 C7
Wallsend NE28 .40 E4
Suffolk Pl Birtley DH3 .82 D1
Gateshead NE8 .56 A4
Suffolk Rd NE31 .57 F3
Suffolk St Hetton le H DH5 .94 F4
Jarrow NE32 .58 B6
Sunderland SR2 .103 B1
Sugley Dr NE15 .53 D6
Sugley St NE15 .53 D6
Sugley Villas NE15 .53 D6
Sulgrave Ind Est NE37 .72 E1
Sulgrave Rd NE37 .72 F1
Sullivan Wlk NE31 .57 E5
Summer St NE10 .56 D1
Summerfield NE17 .77 A5
Summerfield Rd NE9 .70 F7
Summerhill Blaydon NE21 .53 B3
Hedworth NE32 .58 D1
Newcastle-u-T NE4 .100 A4
Sunderland SR2 .102 B2
Sunderland,Middle Herrington SR3 .91 B7
Summerhill Ave NE3 .28 D1
Summerhill Gr NE4 .98 B1
Summerhill Rd NE34 .60 A7
Summerhill St NE4 .98 B1
Summerhill Terr NE1 .100 C4
Summerhouse Farm DH5 .94 D5
Summerhouse La
Ashington,North Seaton NE63 .7 B3
Ashington,Woodbridge NE63 .7 B4
Summers St 7 NE24 .17 E8
Summerson St DH5 .95 B4
Summerson Way NE22 .11 D2
Sun St 3 NE16 .69 B2
Sun View Terr SR6 .59 E1
Sunbury Ave NE2 .38 E2
Sunderland Ent Pk SR5 .85 B8
Sunderland Eye Infmy SR2 .86 D3
Sunderland High Sch SR2 .103 A1
Sunderland High Sch Jun Sch SR2 .86 D4
Sunderland Highway NE37,NE38 .83 C6
Sunderland Mus & Winter Gdns* SR1 .103 A2
Sunderland Rd
Cleadon SR6 .75 B7
East Boldon NE36,SR5 .74 E6
Gateshead,Felling NE10 .71 E8
Gateshead,Heworth NE10 .71 F8
Gateshead,Wardley NE10 .72 C7
Newbottle DH4 .90 E4
South Shields NE33 .59 E8
South Shields,Harton NE34 .59 F6
Sunderland SR5 .75 A2
Sunderland Ret Pk SR6 .75 D1
Sunderland Royal Hospl SR4 .102 A2
Sunderland Ski Ctr* SR3 .85 F1
Sunderland St
Houghton-le-S DH5 .90 E1
2 Houghton-le-S,New Town DH4 .94 E8
Newcastle-u-T NE1 .100 C4
Sunderland SR1 .103 B3
Sunderland Sta SR1 .103 A2
Sunderland Tech Pk SR2 .102 C2
Sundew Rd NE9 .71 C4
Sundridge Dr NE10 .72 C7
Sunhill NE16 .69 B2
Sunholme Dr NE28 .40 A5
Sunlea Ave NE30 .32 C2
Sunnidale NE16 .68 E5
Sunnilaws NE34 .60 A3
Sunningdale
South Shields NE33 .42 E1
Whitley Bay NE25 .31 D5
Sunningdale Ave
Newcastle-u-T NE6 .57 A6
Wallsend NE28 .40 C2
Sunningdale Cl NE10 .71 D7
Sunningdale Dr NE37 .72 C2
Sunningdale Rd SR3 .85 E3
Sunningdale Sch SR3 .85 E2
Sunnirise NE34 .60 A4
Sunniside
North Shields NE29 .41 E5
Sunderland SR4 .85 A6
Sunniside Ct NE16 .69 B3
Sunniside Dr NE34 .60 A4
Sunniside Gdns
Gateshead NE9 .71 C2
Newcastle-u-T NE15 .54 B6
Sunniside La NE34,SR6 .60 B2
Sunniside Rd NE16 .69 B3
Sunniside Sta* NE16 .69 B1
Sunniside Terr SR6 .60 A2
Sunny Brae NE40 .66 F8
Sunnybank Ave NE15 .54 D5
Sunnybrow SR3 .91 F8
Sunnycrest Ave NE6 .56 F6
Sunnygill Terr NE40 .51 F2
Sunnyside NE23 .22 A6
Sunnyway NE5 .37 C2
Sunrise Ent Pk SR5 .85 A8
Sunrise La 1 DH4 .90 D1
Surrey Ave SR3 .92 A6
Surrey Cl NE63 .6 A4
Surrey Pl
Newcastle-u-T NE4 .98 A1
Penshaw DH4 .90 C6
Surrey Rd Hebburn NE31 .57 F3
North Shields NE29 .41 D6
Surrey St Hetton le H DH5 .94 F4
Jarrow NE32 .58 A6
Penshaw DH4 .90 C6
Surrey Terr DH3 .82 C1
Sussex Gdns NE28 .40 E3
Sussex Pl NE37 .72 D1
Sussex St 2 Blyth NE24 .17 F8
Jarrow NE32 .58 A6
3 New Silksworth SR3 .92 A8
Sutherland Ave
Newbiggin-by-t-S NE64 .7 D4
Newcastle-u-T NE4 .54 E7
Sutherland Ct NE34 .59 D2
Sutherland Dr SR4 .85 D4
Sutherland Grange DH4 .90 D6
Sutherland St
Gateshead NE8 .101 C1
Seaham SR7 .93 B1
Sunderland SR6 .75 D2
Sutton Cl DH4 .90 A6
Sutton Ct NE28 .39 F5
Sutton St NE6 .56 E7
Sutton Way NE34 .60 B5
Swainby Cl NE3 .38 D8
Swaledale Sunderland SR6 .75 F7
Wallsend NE28 .39 F5
Swaledale Ave NE24 .17 A7
Swaledale Cl DH5 .94 F1
Swaledale Cres DH4 .90 A8
Swaledale Ct NE24 .17 A7
Swaledale Gdns
Newcastle-u-T NE7 .39 B3
Sunderland SR4 .85 F5
Swallow Cl NE63 .11 E8
Swallow Ct NE12 .29 C4
Swallow Tail Ct NE34 .59 B5
Swallow Tail Dr NE11 .70 B7
Swallows The NE28 .40 E7
Swalwell Bank NE16 .69 A8
Swalwell Cl NE42 .50 C2
Swalwell Cty Prim Sch NE16 .69 B8
Swan Ave NE28 .40 D3
Swan Ct NE11 .100 A1
Swan Dr NE11 .100 A1
Swan Ind Est NE38 .83 F4
Swan Ind Est (South) NE38 .83 F3
Swan Rd
Newcastle-u-T NE6 .57 B4
Washington NE38 .83 F4
Swan St Gateshead NE8 .101 C3
Sunderland SR5 .75 C1
Swansfield NE61 .8 E7
Swanton Cl NE5 .37 B4
Swanway NE9 .71 B7
Swards Rd NE10 .71 E7
Swarland Ave NE7 .39 B5
Swarland Rd NE25 .23 D2
Swarth Cl NE37 .83 A6
Sweetbriar Cl NE61 .3 E2
Sweetbriar Way NE24 .17 C4
Sweethope Ave
Ashington NE63 .6 F2
Blyth NE24 .17 D8
Sweethope Dene NE61 .9 A6
Swiftdale Cl NE22 .10 F1
Swiftden Dr SR4 .85 A4
Swinbourne Gdns NE26 .31 F6
Swinbourne Terr NE32 .58 B3
Swinburn Rd NE25 .23 D2
Swinburne Pl Birtley DH3 .82 C3
Gateshead NE8 .101 C3
Newcastle-u-T NE4 .98 C1
Swinburne St
Gateshead NE8 .101 B3
Jarrow NE32 .58 E6
Swindale Cl NE21 .68 C8
Swindale Cotts NE41 .51 B6
Swindale Dr NE12 .29 C3
Swindon Rd SR3 .85 D3
Swindon Sq SR3 .85 E3
Swindon St NE31 .57 D6
Swindon Terr NE6 .39 B1
Swinhoe Gdns NE13 .28 B6
Swinhope NE38 .89 A8
Swinley Gdns NE15 .53 F6
Swinton Cl NE61 .9 B6
Swirle The NE1 .99 C1
Swirral Edge NE37 .83 C7
Swyntoft NE10 .72 B7
Sycamore DH2 .88 A5
Sycamore Ave Blyth NE24 .12 D1
Dinnington NE13 .27 C7
Guide Post NE62 .10 E7
Ponteland NE20 .25 D4
South Shields NE34 .59 F4
Washington NE38 .83 B1
Whitley Bay NE25 .31 F4
Sycamore Cl
Newcastle-u-T NE2 .38 F2
South Hetton DH6 .97 F7
Sycamore Dr SR5 .75 B3
Sycamore Gr
Gateshead NE10 .71 E8
Prudhoe NE42 .50 A2
Springwell NE9 .71 B1
Sycamore Pl NE12 .29 C4
Sycamore Rd
Blaydon NE21 .53 C2
Whitburn SR6 .60 F1
Sycamore St
Ashington NE63 .6 D3
Throckley NE15 .35 D3
Wallsend NE28 .40 C1
Sycamore Terr DH6 .97 F3
Sycamores The
Burnopfield NE16 .79 C5
Guide Post NE62 .10 E7
Newcastle-u-T NE4 .100 A3
Sunderland SR2 .86 E3
Sydenham Terr
14 South Shields NE33 .42 D3
Sunderland SR4 .102 A1
Sydney Ct NE8 .101 B3
Sydney Gdns NE34 .58 F3
Sydney Gr NE28 .40 A5
Sydney St DH4 .89 E2
Syke Rd NE16 .78 F5
Sylvan Cl NE61 .8 D7
Sylverton Gdns NE33 .42 F1
Symington Gdns SR3 .91 F8

Symon Terr NE17 . . . . . .77 B8
Synclen Ave NE45 . . . . . .47 A6
Synclen Gr NE45 . . . . . . .47 A6
Synclen Pl NE45 . . . . . . .47 A6
Synclen Terr NE45 . . . . . .47 A6
Syon St NE30 . . . . .42 D8
Syron NE16 . . . . .68 F7
Syston Cl DH4 . . . . .94 A7

T

Taberna Cl NE15 . . . . . . .34 E2
Tadcaster Rd SR3 . . . . . .85 C1
Tadema Rd NE33 . . . . . . .42 F2
Talbot Cl DH8 . . . . .83 D4
Talbot Cotts DH3 . . . . . . .82 C4
Talbot Gn NE5 . . . . .53 F8
Talbot Ho SR3 . . . . .35 F2
Talbot Rd
 South Shields NE34 . . . . .59 C6
 Sunderland SR6 . . . . . . .75 E3
Talbot Terr 12 DH3 . . . . . .82 C4
Talgarth NE38 . . . . .84 B5
Talisman View 6 NE9 . . . .71 A2
Talley Ct NE38 . . . . .21 A8
Tamar Ct 6 SR3 . . . . .91 F6
Tamar St DH5 . . . . .97 C8
Tamarisk Way NE9 . . . . . .71 C5
Tamerton Dr DH3 . . . . . . .82 D2
Tamerton St SR4 . . . . . . .85 F6
Tamworth Rd NE4 . . . . . . .98 A2
Tamworth Sq SR3 . . . . . . .85 C1
Tanbark DH4 . . . . .89 F6
Tanfield Gdns NE34 . . . . .60 B6
Tanfield Lea Ind Est DH9 .79 D2
Tanfield Lea Jun & Inf Sch
 DH9 . . . . .79 C1
Tanfield Lea South Ind Est
 DH9 . . . . .79 F1
Tanfield Pl NE9 . . . . .71 C2
Tanfield Rd
 Gateshead NE9 . . . . . . .71 C2
 Newcastle-u-T NE15 . . . .54 A6
 Sunderland SR3 . . . . . . .85 D1
Tanfield Rly* NE16 . . . . . .80 B6
Tanfield St SR4 . . . . .85 E7
Tangmere Cl NE23 . . . . . .22 C7
Tankerville Pl 3 NE2 . . . . .38 E1
Tankerville Terr NE2 . . . . .38 E1
Tanners Row 4 NE45 . . . .45 A5
Tanners' Bank NE30 . . . . .42 C6
Tantallon DH3 . . . . .82 D2
Tantallon Ct DH4 . . . . . . .89 D1
Tantobie Rd NE15 . . . . . . .54 A6
Tarlton Cres NE10 . . . . . . .71 C8
Tarn Dr SR2 . . . . .86 F1
Tarragon Way NE34 . . . . .59 E3
Tarrington Cl NE28 . . . . . .40 F5
Tarset Dr NE42 . . . . .50 D2
Tarset Pl NE3 . . . . .38 A6
Tarset Rd NE25 . . . . .31 B5
Tarset St NE1 . . . . .56 A5
Tasman Rd SR3 . . . . .91 C8
Tasmania Rd NE34 . . . . . .58 F3
Tate St 8 NE24 . . . . .17 F8
Tatham St SR1 . . . . .103 B2
Tatham Street Back
 SR1 . . . . .103 B2
Tattershall DH7 . . . . .86 B4
Taunton Ave Jarrow NE32 .58 E5
 Tynemouth NE29 . . . . . .31 D1
Taunton Cl NE28 . . . . .40 F5
Taunton Pl NE23 . . . . .22 B5
Taunton Rd SR3 . . . . .85 D2
Taunton Sq SR3 . . . . .85 D2
Tavistock Cl DH4 . . . . .90 A3
Tavistock Ho SR1 . . . . . .103 A2
Tavistock Pl Jarrow NE32 .58 D5
 Sunderland SR1 . . . . . .103 A2
Tavistock Rd NE2 . . . . . . .38 E2
Tavistock Sq SR3 . . . . . . .92 A8
Tavistock Wlk NE23 . . . . . .22 B8
Tay Rd SR3,SR4 . . . . .85 C1
Tay St Chopwell NE17 . . . .66 C1
 Easington Lane DH5 . . . .97 C8
Taylor Ave Ashington NE63 . .7 B3
 Rowlands Gill NE39 . . . . .67 F1
 Wideopen NE13 . . . . . . .28 C6
Taylor Gdns
 Gateshead NE10 . . . . . .57 A1
 Seaton Sluice NE26 . . . .24 D6
 10 Sunderland SR2 . . . . .86 E4
Taylor St Blyth NE24 . . . . .17 A8
 South Shields NE33 . . . .59 C6
Taylor Terr 8 NE27 . . . . . .30 E1
Taylor's Bldgs NE22 . . . . .11 D2
Taylors Ct 16 NE1 . . . . . . .99 A1
Taynton Gr NE23 . . . . .22 F2
Teal Ave NE24 . . . . .17 F4
Teal Cl Longbenton NE7 . . .39 C5
 8 Washington NE38 . . . . .42 F4
Team St NE8 . . . . .100 B1
Team Valley Bsns Ctr
 NE11 . . . . .70 D6
Team Valley Trad Est
 NE11 . . . . .70 D4
Teasdale Ho NE5 . . . . . . .37 A5
Teasdale St SR2 . . . . . .103 C1
Tebay Dr NE5 . . . . .53 F8
Tedco Bsns Ctr NE33 . . . . .4 F4
Tedco Bsns Wks 1 NE33 .42 C2
Teddington Cl NE3 . . . . . . .37 B3
Teddington Rd SR3 . . . . . .85 C2
Teddington Sq SR3 . . . . . .85 C2
Tedham Rd NE15 . . . . . . .53 C7
Tees Ct 18 Silksworth SR3 .91 F6
 South Shields NE34 . . . .59 C6

Tees Rd NE31 . . . . .57 E3
Tees St Chopwell NE17 . . . .66 C1
 Easington Lane DH5 . . . .97 D8
Tees Terr 9 NE37 . . . . . . .83 D8
Teesdale Ave DH4 . . . . . . .90 A8
Teesdale Gdns NE7 . . . . . .39 B3
Teesdale Gr NE12 . . . . . . .39 D8
Teesdale Pl 3 NE24 . . . . . .16 F8
Teindland Cl NE4 . . . . . . .54 E4
Tel-el-Kebir Rd SR2 . . . . . .86 E4
Telford Ct NE27 . . . . .30 C5
Telford Ct
 Morpeth,Loansdean NE61 . .8 F5
 North Shields NE28 . . . . .41 C2
Telford Rd SR3 . . . . .85 C1
Telford St Gateshead NE8 .70 D7
 North Shields NE28 . . . . .41 C2
Temperley Pl NE46 . . . . . .45 A4
Tempest St
 10 New Silksworth SR3 . . .92 A7
 Ryton NE21 . . . . .53 A4
Temple Ave NE4 . . . . .54 C4
Temple Bldgs 4 NE1 . . . . .98 C1
Temple Gn Gateshead NE8 .70 C8
 Sunderland SR3 . . . . . . .59 E5
Temple Park Inf Sch
 NE34 . . . . .59 D3
Temple Park Jun Sch
 NE34 . . . . .59 D3
Temple Park Rd NE34 . . .59 D6
Temple St
 Gateshead NE10 . . . . . .56 D1
 Newcastle-u-T NE1 . . . . .100 C4
 South Shields NE33 . . . .59 B7
Temple St W NE33 . . . . . .59 B7
Temple Town NE33 . . . . .59 B8
Ten Fields DH5 . . . . .95 A3
Tenbury Cres
 Longbenton NE12 . . . . . .39 C7
 Tynemouth NE29 . . . . . .31 E1
Tenby Rd SR3 . . . . .91 C8
Tenby Sq NE23 . . . . .22 C8
Tennant St Hebburn NE31 .57 D5
 3 South Shields NE34 . . . .59 A4
Tennyson Ave
 Hebburn NE31 . . . . .57 F6
 West Boldon NE35 . . . . . .74 B8
Tennyson Cres NE16 . . . .69 A8
Tennyson Ct
 Gateshead NE8 . . . . . . .56 A2
 Prudhoe NE42 . . . . .50 B1
Tennyson Gn NE3 . . . . . .37 F3
Tennyson St
 11 South Shields NE33 . . .42 D2
 8 Sunderland SR5 . . . . . .75 A2
Tennyson Terr NE29 . . . . .42 B4
Tenter Garth NE15 . . . . . .35 C2
Tenter Terr NE61 . . . . .9 A8
Tenth Ave Blyth NE24 . . . .17 E6
 Chester le S DH2 . . . . . .88 B3
 Gateshead NE11 . . . . . . .70 D2
 Morpeth NE61 . . . . .9 A6
 Newcastle-u-T NE6 . . . . . .56 C8
Tenth Ave W NE11 . . . . . .70 D2
Terra Ct NE24 . . . . .17 F4
Terrace Pl NE1 . . . . .98 C2
Terrace The
 6 Boldon Colliery NE35 . . .58 E1
 5 East Boldon NE36 . . . . .74 D7
 Longbenton NE12 . . . . . .39 C6
 Ovingham NE42 . . . . . . .50 A4
Terraces The NE38 . . . . . .83 E4
Terrier Cl NE22 . . . . .11 C1
Tesla St DH4 . . . . .90 D4
Tetford Pl NE12 . . . . .39 C6
Teviot NE38 . . . . .83 A1
Teviot St
 Easington Lane DH5 . . . .97 C8
 Gateshead NE8 . . . . . . .71 A8
Teviot Way NE32 . . . . . . .58 A5
Teviotdale Gdns NE7 . . . .39 B3
Tewkesbury NE12 . . . . . .29 D4
Tewkesbury Rd NE15 . . . .53 C7
Thackeray Rd SR3 . . . . . .85 D2
Thackeray St DH4 . . . . . .94 D8
Thames Ave NE32 . . . . . .58 C2
Thames Cres DH4 . . . . . .94 A8
Thames Gdns NE28 . . . . . .40 B1
Thames Rd Hebburn NE31 .57 F3
 Sunderland SR3 . . . . . . .85 C1
Thames St Chopwell NE17 .66 C1
 Easington Lane DH5 . . . .97 C8
 Gateshead NE8 . . . . . . .56 A1
Thanet Rd SR3 . . . . .85 D1
Tharsis Rd NE31 . . . . . . .57 D5
Thatcher Cl NE16 . . . . . . .69 A5
Theatre Pl 21 NE29 . . . . .42 A5
Thelma St SR4 . . . . .102 B1
Theme Rd SR3 . . . . .91 C8
Theresa Russell Ho NE6 . .56 C6
Theresa St NE21 . . . . . . .53 C3
Thetford NE38 . . . . .83 D4
Thieves Bank NE61 . . . . . .5 E1
Third Ave Ashington NE63 . .6 E3
 Blyth NE24 . . . . .17 D6
 Chester le S,Canada DH2 . .88 C3
 Chester le S,South Pelaw
 DH2 . . . . .88 B7
 Gateshead NE11 . . . . . . .70 D2
 Morpeth NE61 . . . . .9 A6
 Newcastle-u-T NE6 . . . . . .56 C6
 North Shields NE29 . . . . .41 B5
Third Row Ellington NE61 . .1 A4
 Linton NE61 . . . . .1 D3
Third St NE28 . . . . .40 D1
Thirkeld Pl DH4 . . . . .89 F8
Thirlington Cl NE5 . . . . . .37 B3
Thirlmere Birtley DH3 . . . .82 E2

Thirlmere *continued*
 Cleadon SR6 . . . . .60 A1
 Gateshead NE10 . . . . . . .72 A8
Thirlmere Ave
 Chester le S DH2 . . . . . .88 B1
 Easington Lane DH5 . . . .97 C8
 Tynemouth NE30 . . . . . .32 A2
Thirlmere Ct NE12 . . . . . .29 F3
Thirlmere Cres
 Blaydon NE21 . . . . .68 B8
 Penshaw DH4 . . . . .90 B6
Thirlmere Ct NE31 . . . . . .57 F4
Thirlmere Terr NE6 . . . . . .7 E4
Thirlmere Way Blyth NE24 .12 A1
 Newcastle-u-T NE5 . . . . .37 B1
Thirlmoor 9 NE37 . . . . . .83 A6
Thirlwall Ct NE12 . . . . . . .38 F6
Thirlwell Gr NE32 . . . . . . .58 B3
Thirlwell Rd NE8 . . . . . . .56 A3
Thirsk Rd SR3 . . . . .85 D2
Thirston Dr NE23 . . . . . . .22 C6
Thirston Pl NE29 . . . . . . .41 D7
Thirston Way NE3 . . . . . .37 F3
Thistle Ave NE40 . . . . . . .52 A4
Thistle Ct NE31 . . . . .57 D5
Thistle Ho SR3 . . . . .92 A5
Thistle Rd SR3 . . . . .85 C1
Thistlecroft DH5 . . . . . . .94 E7
Thistledon Ave NE16 . . . .68 F4
Thistley Cl NE6 . . . . .56 E4
Thistley Gn NE10 . . . . . . .57 B1
Thomas Bell Ho 8 NE34 . .59 A4
Thomas Bewick Sch NE5 .36 C2
Thomas Dr NE31 . . . . . . .57 D6
Thomas Ferguson Ct
 NE30 . . . . .42 C6
Thomas Hawksley Pk
 SR3 . . . . .86 A3
Thomas Hepburn Com Comp
 Sch NE10 . . . . .72 A7
Thomas Holliday Homes 10
 NE22 . . . . .11 D3
Thomas Horsley Ho NE15 .54 B5
Thomas St
 9 Chester le S DH3 . . . . .88 C2
 Gateshead NE9 . . . . . . .71 D1
 Hetton le H DH5 . . . . . . .95 A5
 Newcastle-u-T NE5 . . . . .36 F2
 Ryhope SR2 . . . . .92 F6
 South Shields NE33 . . . .42 C3
 8 Washington NE37 . . . . .83 E8
 Wickham NE16 . . . . .69 A7
Thomas St N Ryhope SR2 .92 F6
 Sunderland SR5 . . . . . . .75 A1
Thomas Taylor Cotts
 NE27 . . . . .30 C5
Thomas Walling Prim Sch
 NE5 . . . . .37 C2
Thompson Ave NE12 . . . .29 C4
Thompson Cres 7 SR5 . . .74 B1
Thompson Gdns NE28 . . . .40 B2
Thompson Pl NE10 . . . . . .71 D8
Thompson Rd SR5 . . . . . .75 B2
Thompson St
 9 Bedlington NE22 . . . . . .11 D3
 Blyth NE24 . . . . .12 D1
 Blyth NE24 . . . . .12 E1
Thompson Terr SR2 . . . . .93 A6
Thompson's Bldgs DH4 . . .90 C5
Thornbury Cl NE12 . . . . . .29 C4
Thornbury Dr NE25 . . . . . .31 C6
Thorn Cl NE13 . . . . .28 A5
Thorn Ho SR3 . . . . .92 A5
Thorn Tree Dr NE22 . . . . .10 F1
Thornbank Cl SR3 . . . . . .92 A4
Thornbeck Coll SR2 . . . . .12 C8
Thornborough Ho 18 NE6
 . . . . .56 C6
Thornbridge NE38 . . . . . .84 A5
Thornbury NE31 . . . . . . .53 B1
Thornbury Ave NE23 . . . . .23 A2
Thornbury Cl
 Boldon Colliery NE35 . . . .58 E1
 Newcastle-u-T NE15 . . . .53 F5
 Sunderland SR3 . . . . . . .85 D1
Thorn Cl NE13 . . . . .28 A5
Thorn Ho SR3 . . . . .92 A5
Thorn Tree Dr NE22 . . . . .10 F1
Thornbank Cl SR3 . . . . . .92 A4
Thornbeck Coll SR2 . . . . .12 C8
Thornborough Ho 18 NE6 .56 C6
Thornbridge NE38 . . . . . .84 A5
Thornbrough NE31 . . . . . .53 B1
Thornbury Ave NE23 . . . . .23 A2
Thornbury Cl
 Boldon Colliery NE35 . . . .58 E1
 Newcastle-u-T NE15 . . . .53 F5
 Sunderland SR3 . . . . . . .85 D1
Thornbury Dr NE25 . . . . . .31 C6
Thorndale Pl NE24 . . . . . .17 A8
Thorndale Rd
 Newcastle-u-T NE15 . . . .53 F5
 Sunderland SR3 . . . . . . .85 D1
Thorne Ave NE10 . . . . . . .72 B8
Thorne Brake NE10 . . . . .72 A7
Thorne Rd SR3 . . . . .85 C1
Thorne Sq SR3 . . . . .85 C1
Thorne Terr NE6 . . . . .56 E7
Thornehill Gdns NE16 . . . .11 A8
Thorney Close Prim Sch
 SR3 . . . . .85 C1
Thorney Close Rd SR3 . . .85 D1
Thorneyburn Ave NE25 . . .31 B5
Thorneyburn Cl DH4 . . . . .90 C2
Thorneyburn Way NE24 . . .17 C4
Thorneyford Pl NE20 . . . . .25 E7
Thorneyford Pl NE20 . . . . .25 E7
Thornfield Gr SR2 . . . . . . .86 E2
Thornfield Pl NE39 . . . . . .67 E3
Thornfield Rd NE3 . . . . . .38 B4
Thorngill NE37 . . . . .83 C6
Thornhaugh Ave NE16 . . . .68 F6
Thornhill Cl
 Gateshead NE11 . . . . . . .70 A8
 Seaton Delaval NE25 . . . .23 D2
Thornhill Cres SR2 . . . . .102 C2
Thornhill Gdns
 Burnopfield NE16 . . . . . .78 F5
 Sunderland SR2 . . . . . .102 C1

Thornhill Park Sch SR2 .102 C1
Thornhill Pk
 Ponteland NE20 . . . . . . .25 E7
 Sunderland SR2 . . . . . .102 C1
Thornhill Rd
 Longbenton NE12 . . . . . .39 D6
 Ponteland NE20 . . . . . . .25 E7
Thornhill Sch SR2 . . . . .102 C1
Thornhill St DH4 . . . . .94 D8
Thornhill Terr SR2 . . . . .102 C1
Thornholme Ave NE34 . . .60 B6
Thornholme Rd SR2 . . . .102 C1
Thornhope Cl NE38 . . . . .83 F6
Thornlea NE61 . . . . .9 E4
Thornlea Gdns NE9 . . . . .70 F6
Thornleigh Gdns SR6 . . . .60 A3
Thornleigh Rd NE2 . . . . . .38 E1
Thornley Ave
 Cramlington NE23 . . . . . .22 C6
 Gateshead NE10 . . . . . .72 B6
Thornley Cl NE16 . . . . . . .69 A4
Thornley La NE21,NE39 . . .68 A6
Thornley Rd NE5 . . . . . . .53 F8
Thornley Terr NE62 . . . . .11 C6
Thornley View NE39 . . . . .67 F2
Thornley Wood* NE21 . . . .68 B6
Thornton Ave NE33 . . . . .59 B7
 Penshaw DH4 . . . . .90 B7
Thornton Cotts NE40 . . . .52 C6
Thornton Cres NE21 . . . . .53 C3
Thornton Cl NE28 . . . . . .83 C5
Thornton Ho 10 NE1 . . . . .98 C1
Thornton St NE1 . . . . . . .98 C1
Thornton Terr NE12 . . . . .30 A1
Thorntree Ave NE13 . . . . .21 B1
Thorntree Cl NE25 . . . . . .31 B4
Thorntree Cotts NE13 . . . .21 B1
Thorntree Ct NE12 . . . . . .39 F8
Thorntree Dr
 Newcastle-u-T NE15 . . . .54 A7
 Whitley Bay NE25 . . . . . .31 C4
Thorntree Gdns NE63 . . . . .7 A2
Thorntree Mews SR3 . . . .85 C2
Thorntree Way NE24 . . . . .16 F7
Thorntree Wlk NE32 . . . . .58 D2
Thornwood Gdns NE11 . . .70 B6
Thornyford Ho NE4 . . . . . .98 B2
Thornygarth NE10 . . . . . .71 E7
Thoroton St NE24 . . . . . . .17 E8
Thorp Ave NE61 . . . . .4 A2
Thorp Cl NE24 . . . . .17 B5
Thorp Cotts NE40 . . . . . .52 A5
Thorpe Dr NE4 . . . . .98 A2
Thorpe St NE4 . . . . .98 A2
Thorpeness Rd SR3 . . . . .85 C1
Threap Gdns NE28 . . . . . .40 E4
Three Mile Ct NE3 . . . . . .38 C8
Three Rivers Ct NE36 . . . .74 A7
Threlkeld Gr SR6 . . . . . . .75 C5
Thrift St NE29 . . . . .42 A4
Thristley Gdns SR2 . . . . . .86 C3
Throckley Fst Sch NE15 . . .35 C2
Throckley Way NE34 . . . . .59 B5
Thropton Ave Blyth NE24 . .17 C5
 Newcastle-u-T NE7 . . . . .39 B5
Thropton Cl
 Chester le S DH2 . . . . . .88 A1
 Gateshead NE10 . . . . . . .72 C6
Thropton Cres NE3 . . . . . .38 B6
Thropton Pl NE29 . . . . . . .41 D7
Thropton Terr NE7 . . . . . .39 B2
Thrunton Ct 5 DH5 . . . . . .94 F8
Thrush Gr 2 SR5 . . . . . . .74 C1
Thurleston DH4 . . . . .90 C4
Thurlow Way DH5 . . . . . . .94 D6
Thursby DH3 . . . . .88 D1
Thursby Ave NE30 . . . . . .32 B2
Thursby Gdns NE9 . . . . . .71 B3
Thurso Cl SR3 . . . . .85 B1
Tiberius Cl 6 NE28 . . . . . .40 B1
Tidings The NE10 . . . . . . .57 B2
Tilbeck Sq SR3 . . . . .92 A5
Tilbury Cl DH4 . . . . .90 C5
Tilbury Gdns SR3 . . . . . . .91 D8
Tilbury Gr NE30 . . . . .32 A2
Tilbury Rd SR3 . . . . .91 C8
Tileshed La NE36 . . . . . . .59 D1
Till Ave NE21 . . . . .53 B2
Till Gr NE61 . . . . .1 E5
Till St 7 NE6 . . . . .56 B4
Tilley Cres NE42 . . . . .50 D3
Tilley Rd NE38 . . . . .83 C5
Tillmouth Ave NE25 . . . . . .23 E2
Tillmouth Gdns NE4 . . . . .54 C6
Tillmouth Park Rd NE15 . . .35 D1
Tilson Way NE7 . . . . .37 F6
Timber Beach Rd SR5 . . . .74 D1
Times Sq NE1 . . . . .100 C4
Timlin Gdns NE28 . . . . . . .41 B3
Timothy Duff Ct NE30 . . . .42 C6
Tindal Cl NE4 . . . . .98 B1
Tindal St NE4 . . . . .98 B1
Tindale Ave NE23 . . . . . . .22 C6
Tindale Dr NE16 . . . . .69 A6
Tinkler Terr DH3 . . . . .89 B1
Tinkler's Bank NE45 . . . . .46 F3
Tintagel Cl
 Cramlington NE23 . . . . . .22 B8
 Sunderland SR3 . . . . . . .85 B1
Tintern NE38 . . . . .83 C3
Tintern Cl DH4 . . . . .90 C2
Tintern Cres
 Newcastle-u-T NE6 . . . . . .56 B7
 Tynemouth NE29 . . . . . .41 D8
Tintern St SR4 . . . . .102 B2

Tiree Ct SR3 . . . . .92 A6
Tirril Pl NE5 . . . . .37 A1
Titan Ho 7 NE6 . . . . .57 A6
Titan Rd NE6 . . . . .57 A5
Titchfield Rd NE3 . . . . . . .83 C4
Titchfield Terr
 Ashington NE63 . . . . .6 D2
 Pegswood NE61 . . . . .4 F4
Tithe Cotts NE20 . . . . . . .25 E7
Titian Ave NE34 . . . . .59 C2
Titlington Gr NE31 . . . . . .57 D3
Tiverton Ave
 1 Newcastle-u-T NE4 . . . .54 E5
 Tynemouth NE29 . . . . . .31 C1
Tiverton Cl Newbottle DH4 .90 C4
 Wallsend NE28 . . . . .41 A5
Tiverton Gdns NE9 . . . . . .70 F3
Tiverton Pl NE23 . . . . . . .22 B8
Tiverton Sq SR3 . . . . .85 C1
Tivoli Bldgs DH4 . . . . .90 C6
Toberty Gdns NE10 . . . . . .72 B8
Todd's Nook NE4 . . . . . . .98 B1
Togstone Pl 4 NE5 . . . . . .37 C1
Toll Bar Ho SR2 . . . . .93 A8
Toll Bar Rd SR2 . . . . .92 E8
Toll Bridge Rd NE21 . . . . .53 F3
Tollerton Dr SR5 . . . . .74 A1
Tolls Ct SR5 . . . . .77 F5
Tolls Cl NE25 . . . . .31 C6
Tom Urwin Ho 11 SR3 . . . .92 A7
Tomlea Ave NE22 . . . . . . .11 D1
Tonbridge Ave NE29 . . . . .41 E4
Toner Ave NE31 . . . . .57 D4
Toner Avenue Prim Sch
 NE31 . . . . .57 D3
Topcliff SR6 . . . . .103 B4
Topcliffe Gn NE9 . . . . . . .71 B2
Toppings St NE35 . . . . . . .58 E1
Tor Mere Cl NE37 . . . . . . .83 A6
Torcross Way NE23 . . . . . .22 B8
Toronto Rd SR3 . . . . .85 D2
Toronto Sq SR3 . . . . .85 D2
Torquay Gdns NE9 . . . . . .70 F3
Torquay Par NE31 . . . . . . .58 A3
Torquay Rd SR3 . . . . .85 D2
Torrens Rd SR3 . . . . .85 D2
Torrington Cl DH4 . . . . . . .90 C4
Torver Cl NE13 . . . . .28 B5
Torver Cres SR6 . . . . .75 D5
Torver Pl NE9 . . . . .71 B4
Torver Way NE30 . . . . . . .31 F2
Tosson Cl NE23 . . . . .12 B1
Tosson Pl Ashington NE63 . .6 E3
 North Shields NE29 . . . . .41 D5
Tosson Terr NE6 . . . . .39 C1
Totnes Cl SR3 . . . . .85 B1
Totnes Dr NE23 . . . . .22 B8
Toward Rd
 Sunderland SR1,SR2 . . . .103 A2
 Sunderland SR2 . . . . . .103 B1
Tower Ct Dunston NE11 . . .100 A1
 Easington Lane DH5 . . . . .95 C1
Tower Gdns NE15 . . . . . . .54 C6
Tower Ho NE1 . . . . .99 C1
Tower Pl 1 SR2 . . . . .86 E4
Tower Rd NE37 . . . . .83 E7
Tower St
 Newcastle-u-T NE1 . . . . .99 B1
 Sunderland SR2 . . . . . .103 C1
Tower St W SR2 . . . . . . .103 B1
Tower View NE15 . . . . . . .54 C6
Towers Ave NE2 . . . . .38 E3
Towers Cl NE22 . . . . .16 A8
Towers Pl NE34 . . . . .58 E5
Towers The SR4 . . . . .85 B5
Town End Prim Sch SR3 . . .7 F4
Town Farm Field NE45 . . . .46 F6
Towne Gate The NE15 . . . .34 E2
Towneley Cotts NE40 . . . . .52 A4
Towneley Ct NE42 . . . . . . .50 E3
Towneley Terr NE39 . . . . .66 E4
Townend Ct NE34 . . . . . . .59 C5
Townfield Gdns NE15 . . . . .52 F8
Townley Fields NE39 . . . . .67 F2
Townley Rd NE39 . . . . . . .67 D2
Townsend Cres NE61 . . . . .8 D6
Townsend Rd SR3 . . . . . .85 D1
Townsend Sq SR3 . . . . . .91 C8
Townsville Ave NE25 . . . . .31 D3
Towton NE12 . . . . .29 D4
Toynbee NE38 . . . . .84 A5
Tracey Ave NE36 . . . . . . .74 B8
Trafalgar Ho 6 NE30 . . . . .42 D7
Trafalgar Rd NE37 . . . . . .72 F1
Trafalgar Sq SR1 . . . . . .103 C3
Trafalgar St NE1 . . . . .99 B1
Trafford NE9 . . . . .71 A1
Trafford Rd SR5 . . . . .75 A1
Trafford Wlk NE5 . . . . . . .36 C3
Trajan Ave NE33 . . . . . . .42 D4
Trajan St NE33 . . . . .42 D4
Trajan Wlk NE15 . . . . . . .34 D2
Transbritannia Ct NE21 . . .53 E4
Tranwell Cl
 Newcastle-u-T NE15 . . . .37 F8
 Pegswood NE61 . . . . .4 E3
Tranwell Cotts NE61 . . . . . .8 D4
Tranwell Ct NE61 . . . . .8 D4
Tranwell Dr NE25 . . . . . . .23 E2
Travers St DH4 . . . . .90 C6
Treby St SR4 . . . . .102 A3
Tredegar Cl NE5 . . . . .37 B4
Tree Ct 20 SR3 . . . . .91 F6
Tree Top Mews 7 NE28 . . .40 E5
Treecone Cl SR3 . . . . . . .92 A5

Treetops The NE32 . . . . .58 A4
Treherne Rd NE2 . . . . .38 D3
Trent Ave NE31 . . . . .57 E3
Trent Dr NE32 . . . . .58 C2
Trent Gdns NE8 . . . . .71 B8
Trent Rd SR3 . . . . .85 C1
Trent St Chopwell NE17 . . . . . .66 C1
 Easington Lane DH5 . . . . . . .97 C8
Trentham Ave NE7 . . . . .39 B5
Trentham Gdns NE61 . . . . . .4 F4
Trenton Ave NE38 . . . . .83 D6
Trevarren Dr SR2 . . . . .92 F7
Trevelyan Ave
 Bedlington NE22 . . . . .11 B1
 Blyth NE24 . . . . .17 C6
Trevelyan Cl SR3 . . . . .85 B1
Trevelyan Dr NE5 . . . . .37 A4
Trevethick St NE8 . . . . .70 D8
Trevone Pl NE23 . . . . .23 A2
Trevor Gr SR6 . . . . .75 A8
Trevor Terr NE30 . . . . .42 B7
Trewhitt Rd NE6 . . . . .56 C8
Trewit Rd NE16 . . . . .82 B5
Triangle Ho NE1 . . . . .98 C1
Tribune Pl NE9 . . . . .71 B6
Trident Rd SR3 . . . . .92 A7
Trimdon Gr NE9 . . . . .71 D3
Trimdon St SR4 . . . . .102 B3
Trimdon St W SR4 . . . . .102 B4
Trinity Bldgs NE30 . . . . .42 C5
Trinity Cl NE2 . . . . .42 A4
Trinity Ct Corbridge NE45 . . . .46 F6
 Gateshead NE8 . . . . .101 C3
  North Shields NE29 . . . . . . .42 A4
Trinity Ctyd NE6 . . . . .56 D4
Trinity Gr NE23 . . . . .23 A2
Trinity Maritime Mus*
 NE1 . . . . .101 B4
Trinity Pk DH4 . . . . .90 B5
Trinity Pl NE29 . . . . .42 A4
Trinity Sch (Deneview Site)
 NE3 . . . . .38 F4
Trinity Sch (Kenton Lodge
 Site) NE3 . . . . .38 F4
Trinity Sch (Oakfield Coll)
 NE6 . . . . .54 D6
Trinity Sq Gateshead NE8 . . .101 C3
 Sunderland SR1 . . . . .103 B3
Trinity St
 North Shields NE29 . . . . .42 A4
 Sunderland SR5 . . . . .74 F2
Trinity Terr
 Corbridge NE45 . . . . .46 F6
  North Shields NE29 . . . . . . .42 A4
Trinity Wlk NE33 . . . . .42 B1
Trojan Ave NE6 . . . . .56 E7
Tromso Cl NE29 . . . . .41 C5
Trool Ct SR3 . . . . .92 A5
Troon Cl NE37 . . . . .72 C2
Trotter Gr NE22 . . . . .11 C1
Trotter Terr SR2 . . . . .92 F6
Troutbeck Ave NE6 . . . . .56 F5
Troutbeck Gdns NE9 . . . . .71 A3
Troutbeck Rd SR6 . . . . .75 C5
Troutbeck Way NE34 . . . . .58 F3
Troutdale Pl NE12 . . . . .38 F6
Troves Cl NE4 . . . . .54 E4
Trowbridge Way NE3 . . . . .37 F5
Truro Gr NE29 . . . . .41 D8
Truro Rd SR3 . . . . .85 D1
Truro Way NE32 . . . . .58 C1
Tuart St DH3 . . . . .88 C3
Tudor Ave NE6 . . . . .41 E6
Tudor Ct NE20 . . . . .25 C4
Tudor Dr DH9 . . . . .79 D3
Tudor Gr SR3 . . . . .85 E3
Tudor Rd Chester le S DH3 . . .88 C2
 South Shields NE33 . . . . .42 C2
Tudor Way NE3 . . . . .37 B6
Tudor Wlk NE3 . . . . .37 C6
Tudor Wynd NE6 . . . . .39 D2
Tulip Cl NE21 . . . . .53 B2
Tulip Ct DH4 . . . . .90 B8
Tulip St Gateshead NE8 . . . . . .56 C1
 Prudhoe NE42 . . . . .50 B2
Tummel Ct SR3 . . . . .92 A6
Tumulus Ave NE6 . . . . .57 A8
Tunbridge Rd SR3 . . . . .85 D2
Tundry Way NE21 . . . . .53 F4
Tunis Rd SR3 . . . . .85 E2
Tunstall Ave
 Newcastle-u-T NE6 . . . . .56 D6
 South Shields NE34 . . . . .60 B6
Tunstall Bank SR2,SR3 . . . . . .92 D7
Tunstall Hill Cl SR2 . . . . .86 C2
Tunstall Hope Rd SR3 . . . . . . .92 B8
Tunstall Pk SR2 . . . . .86 C4
Tunstall Rd SR3 . . . . .86 B2
Tunstall Terr
 New Silksworth SR2 . . . . .92 B7
 Ryhope SR2 . . . . .92 F7
 Sunderland SR2 . . . . .102 C2
Tunstall Terr W SR2 . . . . .102 C2
Tunstall Vale SR2 . . . . .86 C4
Tunstall View SR3 . . . . .92 B8
Tunstall Village Gn SR3 . . . . . .92 C7
Tunstall Village Rd SR3 . . . . . .92 B7
Tunstall Villas SR3 . . . . .92 B7
Turbinia Gdns NE7 . . . . .39 E3
Turfside Gateshead NE10 . . . . .72 B7
 Hedworth NE32 . . . . .58 D1
Turn The NE61 . . . . .8 F5
Turnberry Ouston DH2 . . . . . . .81 F2
 South Shields NE33 . . . . .42 E1
 Whitley Bay NE25 . . . . .31 D5

Turnberry Cl NE37 . . . . .72 C2
Turnberry Ct NE10 . . . . .72 B7
Turnberry Way
 Cramlington NE23 . . . . .22 C6
 Newcastle-u-T NE3 . . . . .38 E6
Turnbull Ho SR5 . . . . .75 B1
Turnbull St SR1 . . . . .103 C4
Turnbull The NE1 . . . . .101 A4
Turner Ave NE34 . . . . .59 D2
Turner Cl NE40 . . . . .52 D4
Turner Cres NE3 . . . . .38 A5
Turner St NE27 . . . . .30 E1
Turners Way NE61 . . . . .8 D7
Turnham Rd SR3 . . . . .85 C1
Turnstile Mews SR6 . . . . . . .75 E2
Turnstone Dr NE38 . . . . .82 F3
Turret Rd NE15 . . . . .53 F7
Tuscan Rd SR3 . . . . .91 C8
Tweed Ave NE61 . . . . .1 E5
Tweed Cl SR2 . . . . .92 F8
Tweed Dr NE61 . . . . .9 E1
Tweed Gr NE15 . . . . .53 C2
Tweed St Ashington NE63 . . . . . .6 C4
 Chopwell NE17 . . . . .66 C1
 Easington Lane DH5 . . . . . . .97 C8
 Hebburn NE31 . . . . .57 E5
 Jarrow NE32 . . . . .58 A5
 Newcastle-u-T NE4 . . . . .54 F5
 Washington NE38 . . . . .83 F4
Tweedmouth Ct NE4 . . . . .38 E4
Tweedy St NE24 . . . . .17 A8
Tweedy Terr NE6 . . . . .56 F5
Tweedy's Bldgs NE40 . . . . . . .52 B5
Twelfth Ave Blyth NE24 . . . . . .17 D6
 Chester le S DH2 . . . . .88 B4
Twentieth Ave NE24 . . . . .17 C5
Twentyfifth Ave NE24 . . . . . . .17 D5
Twentysecond Ave NE24 . . . . .17 C5
Twentysixth Ave NE24 . . . . . . .17 C5
Twentythird Ave NE24 . . . . . . .17 C5
Twickenham Ct SR3 . . . . .92 F2
Twickenham Rd SR3 . . . . .85 C2
Twizell Ave NE21 . . . . .53 B2
Twizell Pl NE20 . . . . .25 E7
Twizell St NE24 . . . . .17 F6
Two Ball Lonnen NE4 . . . . .54 D8
Twyford Cl NE23 . . . . .22 B8
Tyldesley Sq SR3 . . . . .85 C1
Tyndal Gdns NE11 . . . . .54 F1
Tyne App NE32 . . . . .58 A8
Tyne Ct NE46 . . . . .45 A6
Tyne Dock Sta NE33 . . . . .59 B6
Tyne Gdns Ovingham NE42 . . .52 F4
 Ryton NE40 . . . . .52 E4
 Washington NE37 . . . . .72 D1
Tyne Gn NE46 . . . . .45 A6
Tyne Green Ctry Pk*
 NE46 . . . . .45 B6
Tyne Green Rd
 Hexham NE46 . . . . .45 A6
 Hexham NE46 . . . . .45 B6
Tyne Ho SR3 . . . . .91 F6
Tyne Main Rd NE10 . . . . .56 C2
Tyne Mills Ind Est NE46 . . . . . .45 C5
Tyne Point Ind Est NE32 . . . . .58 E5
Tyne Rd E NE8 . . . . .100 C2
Tyne Riverside Ctry Pk*
 Prudhoe NE42 . . . . .50 B3
 * Throckley NE15 . . . . .52 D8
Tyne St Ashington NE63 . . . . . . .6 C4
 Blaydon NE21 . . . . .53 B1
 Chopwell NE17 . . . . .66 B1
 Easington Lane DH5 . . . . . . .97 C8
 Gateshead,Bill Quay NE10 . . .57 A2
 Gateshead,Felling Shore
  NE10 . . . . .56 E2
 Gateshead,Pelaw NE10 . . . . .56 F2
 Jarrow NE32 . . . . .58 B8
 Newcastle-u-T NE1 . . . . .56 A5
  North Shields NE30 . . . . . . .42 B5
Tyne Terr NE34 . . . . .59 E3
Tyne Tunnel (Tynemouth)
 Trad Est NE29 . . . . .41 B5
Tyne Valley Gdns NE40 . . . . . .52 A5
Tyne View Blaydon NE21 . . . . .53 C1
 Crawcrook NE40 . . . . .51 F7
 Hebburn NE31 . . . . .57 C7
 Newcastle-u-T NE15 . . . . . . .53 D6
 Wylam NE41 . . . . .51 B6
Tyne View Ave NE16 . . . . .69 A8
Tyne View Com Prim Sch
 NE8 . . . . .100 C2
Tyne View Gdns NE10 . . . . . . .56 F1
Tyne View Pl NE8 . . . . .100 C1
Tyne View Terr
 North Shields NE28 . . . . .41 C1
 Prudhoe NE42 . . . . .50 D3
 Stocksfield NE43 . . . . .64 D7
Tyne Wlk NE15 . . . . .35 D1
Tynebank NE21 . . . . .53 B2
Tynedale Ave
 Wallsend NE28 . . . . .40 B4
 Whitley Bay NE26 . . . . .31 F6
Tynedale Cl NE41 . . . . .51 B6
Tynedale Cres DH4 . . . . .94 D8
Tynedale Dr NE24 . . . . .17 A8
Tynedale Dr NE24 . . . . .17 A7
Tynedale Gdns NE43 . . . . .64 D5
Tynedale Ho NE15 . . . . .54 B5
Tynedale Mews NE45 . . . . .46 F5
Tynedale Mid Sch NE34 . . . . . .17 A7
Tynedale Rd
 South Shields NE34 . . . . .59 F8
 Sunderland SR3 . . . . .85 C1
Tynedale Ret Pk NE46 . . . . . . .45 B5
Tynedale St DH5 . . . . .94 E1
Tynedale Terr
 Hexham NE46 . . . . .44 F4

Tynedale Terr continued
 Longbenton NE12 . . . . .39 D6
Tynegate Office Prec
 NE8 . . . . .101 C2
Tynell Wlk NE3 . . . . .37 B5
Tynemouth Castle*
 NE30 . . . . .42 E7
Tynemouth Cl NE6 . . . . .56 B6
Tynemouth Coll NE29 . . . . . . .41 F6
Tynemouth Ct NE6 . . . . .56 C7
Tynemouth Gr NE6 . . . . .56 C7
Tynemouth Pl NE30 . . . . . . .42 D7
Tynemouth Priory*
 NE30 . . . . .42 E7
Tynemouth Rd
 Jarrow NE32 . . . . .58 B2
 Newcastle-u-T NE6 . . . . .56 C7
 North Shields NE30 . . . . .42 C6
 Wallsend NE28 . . . . .41 A3
Tynemouth Sq SR3 . . . . .85 D1
Tynemouth Sta NE30 . . . . .42 D7
Tynemouth Terr NE30 . . . . . . .42 D7
Tynemouth Watch House
 (Mus)* NE30 . . . . .42 E7
Tynemouth Way NE6 . . . . . . .56 C7
Tyneside Rd NE4 . . . . .100 B3
Tynevale Ave NE21 . . . . .53 C1
Tynevale Terr
 Gateshead NE8 . . . . .100 C1
 Newcastle-u-T NE15 . . . . . . .53 C6
Tyneview Prim Sch NE6 . . . . . .57 A5
Tyneview Terr NE46 . . . . .45 C3
Tynewold Cl NE8 . . . . .100 C1
Tyzack Cres SR6 . . . . .75 D2

U

Uldale Ct NE3 . . . . .37 E7
Ullswater Ave
 Easington Lane DH5 . . . . . . .97 C8
 Hedworth NE32 . . . . .58 D3
Ullswater Cl NE24 . . . . .16 E8
Ullswater Cres NE21 . . . . .68 B8
Ullswater Dr NE12 . . . . .29 F3
Ullswater Gdns NE34 . . . . .59 D6
Ullswater Gr SR5 . . . . .75 C4
Ullswater Rd
 Chester le S DH2 . . . . .88 B1
 Newbiggin-by-t-S NE64 . . . . . .7 C3
Ullswater Terr DH6 . . . . .97 E8
Ullswater Way NE5 . . . . .54 B8
Ulverston Gdns NE9 . . . . .71 B4
Ulverstone Terr NE6 . . . . .56 E7
Umfraville Dene NE42 . . . . . . .50 D3
Underhill Dr NE62 . . . . .10 E6
Underhill Rd SR6 . . . . .59 F1
Underhill Terr NE9 . . . . .72 A1
Underwood NE10 . . . . .72 A6
Underwood Gr NE23 . . . . .16 A1
Union Alley NE33 . . . . .42 C3
Union Ct NE3 . . . . .38 C2
Union Hall Rd NE15 . . . . .53 D7
Union La SR1 . . . . .103 B3
Union Quay NE30 . . . . .42 C5
Union Rd
 Newcastle-u-T NE6 . . . . .56 C6
 North Shields NE30 . . . . .42 C6
Union St Blyth NE24 . . . . .17 F7
 Hetton le H DH5 . . . . .95 A4
 Jarrow NE32 . . . . .58 B8
 Newcastle-u-T NE2 . . . . .99 C2
 North Shields NE30 . . . . .42 B5
 South Shields NE33 . . . . .59 B6
 Sunderland SR1 . . . . .103 A3
 Sunderland,South Hylton
  SR4 . . . . .85 A6
 Wallsend NE28 . . . . .40 B2
Union Strs NE30 . . . . .42 B5
Unity Hall NE33 . . . . .42 B2
Unity Terr Cambois NE24 . . . . .12 D4
 Tantobie DH9 . . . . .79 B2
Univ of
 Newcastle-upon-Tyne
 NE1 . . . . .99 A3
Univ of Northumbria at
 Newcastle NE1 . . . . .99 B2
Univ of Sunderland Srl 102 C2
Univ of Sunderland Ashburne
 Ho (School of Arts,Design &
 Media) SR2 . . . . .102 A1
Univ of Sunderland Bede Twr
 SR2 . . . . .103 A1
Univ of Sunderland Benedict
 Bldg SR2 . . . . .103 A1
Univ of Sunderland Langham
 Twr SR2 . . . . .103 A1
Univ of Sunderland Liby
 Sunderland SR1 . . . . .102 C2
 Sunderland SR2 . . . . .103 A1
Univ of Sunderland Sir Tom
 Cowie Campus SR6 . . . . . . .103 B4
University Sta SR1 . . . . .102 C2
Uplands NE25 . . . . .31 D5
Uplands The Birtley DH3 . . . . . .82 D5
 Newcastle-u-T NE3 . . . . .37 F4
Uplands Way NE9 . . . . .71 F2
Upper Camden St 30
 NE30 . . . . .42 A6
Upper Crone St NE27 . . . . .30 F4
Upper Elsdon St NE29 . . . . .42 A4
Upper Fenwick Gr NE61 . . . . . . .4 A2
Upper Norfolk St NE30 . . . . . . .42 B6
Upper Pearson St NE30 . . . . . .42 B6
Upper Precinct The
 NE21 . . . . .53 D3
Upper Queen St NE30 . . . . . . .42 B6
Upton St NE8 . . . . .100 C1

Urban Gdns NE37 . . . . .83 D7
Urfa Terr NE33 . . . . .42 D4
Urswick Ct NE3 . . . . .37 B5
Urwin St DH5 . . . . .95 B3
Ushaw Rd NE31 . . . . .57 F6
Usher St SR5 . . . . .75 B1
Usk Ave NE32 . . . . .58 C3
Usworth Colliery Prim Sch
 NE37 . . . . .72 E1
Usworth Cotts SR5 . . . . .73 D3
Usworth Grange Prim Sch
 NE37 . . . . .72 F1
Usworth Hall NE37 . . . . .72 E2
Usworth Sch NE37 . . . . .72 D2
Usworth Station Rd
  Washington,Concord
 NE37 . . . . .83 E8
 Washington,Sulgrave NE37 . .83 F8
Uxbridge Terr NE10 . . . . . . .56 D1

V

Vale Ho NE2 . . . . .56 A8
Vale St Easington Lane DH5 . . .97 B8
 Sunderland SR4 . . . . .102 B1
Vale St E SR4 . . . . .102 B1
Vale Wlk NE2 . . . . .56 A8
Valebrooke SR2 . . . . .102 C1
Valebrooke Ave SR2 . . . . .102 C1
Valebrooke Gdns SR2 . . . . . .102 C1
Valehead NE25 . . . . .31 D5
Valentia Ave NE6 . . . . .56 E7
Valeria Ct NE28 . . . . .40 E6
Valerian Ave NE15 . . . . .34 F2
Valerian Ct NE63 . . . . .6 B1
Valeshead Ho NE28 . . . . . . .40 B2
Valeside NE15 . . . . .35 C2
Valley Cres NE21 . . . . .53 A2
Valley Ct SR2 . . . . .103 B1
Valley Dene NE17 . . . . .77 B7
Valley Dr Dunston NE11 . . . . . .69 F7
 Gateshead NE9 . . . . .70 F7
 Whickham NE16 . . . . .69 A8
Valley Forge NE38 . . . . .83 D6
Valley Gardens Mid Sch
 NE25 . . . . .31 D6
Valley Gdns
 Gateshead NE9 . . . . .71 A7
 Wallsend NE28 . . . . .40 D3
 Whitley Bay NE25 . . . . .31 D5
Valley Gn NE40 . . . . .51 F2
Valley La NE34 . . . . .60 C6
Valley Rd NE25 . . . . .23 C2
Valley Road Com Prim Sch
 SR2 . . . . .86 F4
Valley Shopping Village
 NE11 . . . . .70 D4
Valley View Birtley DH3 . . . . . .82 B6
 Burnopfield NE16 . . . . .78 F7
 Hetton le H DH5 . . . . .94 D1
 Hexham NE46 . . . . .45 A4
 Jarrow NE32 . . . . .58 B4
 Newcastle-u-T,Jesmond
  NE2 . . . . .38 F1
 Newcastle-u-T,Lemington
  NE15 . . . . .53 C7
 Prudhoe NE42 . . . . .50 E1
 Rowlands Gill NE39 . . . . .67 D2
 Washington NE38 . . . . .83 E1
Valley View Prim Sch
 NE32 . . . . .58 B4
Vallum Cl NE4 . . . . .98 B1
Vallum Pl NE9 . . . . .71 B6
Vallum Rd
 Newcastle-u-T NE6 . . . . .56 E6
 Throckley NE15 . . . . .35 E2
Vallum Way NE4 . . . . .54 D7
Vanburgh Ct NE25 . . . . .23 D2
Vanburgh Gdns NE61 . . . . .8 D7
Vance Bsns Pk NE11 . . . . .70 B7
Vance Ct NE21 . . . . .53 E4
Vancouver Dr NE7 . . . . .39 E4
Vane St SR3 . . . . .92 A7
Vane Terr SR2 . . . . .103 C1
Vanguard Ct SR3 . . . . .91 F6
Vardy Terr DH4 . . . . .90 E6
Vauxhall Rd NE6 . . . . .57 A8
Vedra St SR5 . . . . .75 B1
Velville Ct NE3 . . . . .37 B6
Venerable Bede CE Sec Sch
 SR2 . . . . .92 C7
Ventnor Ave NE4 . . . . .54 F7
Ventnor Cres NE9 . . . . .70 E5
Ventnor Gdns
 Gateshead NE9 . . . . .70 E6
 Whitley Bay NE26 . . . . .32 A6
Vera St NE40 . . . . .66 F8
Verdun Ave NE31 . . . . .57 D6
Vermont NE37 . . . . .83 D8
Vermont Ho NE37 . . . . .83 E8
Verne Rd NE29 . . . . .41 D6
Vernon Cl NE33 . . . . .59 B8
Vernon Dr NE25 . . . . .31 E4
Vernon Pl NE4 . . . . .7 E5
Vernon St NE37 . . . . .83 E8
Veryan Gdns SR3 . . . . .86 B3
Vespasian Ave NE33 . . . . .42 D4
Vespasian St NE33 . . . . .42 D4
Viador DH3 . . . . .88 D2
Viaduct St NE28 . . . . .40 E2
Vicarage Cl SR3 . . . . .91 F7
Vicarage La SR4 . . . . .85 A6
Vicarage Rd SR3 . . . . .92 A7
Vicarage Terr NE22 . . . . .16 A8
Vicaridge Cl DH5 . . . . .95 A4

Vicars' La NE7 . . . . .39 A5
Vicarsholme Cl SR3 . . . . .91 E5
Victor St
  Chester le S DH3 . . . . .88 C3
  Sunderland SR6 . . . . .75 E1
Victoria Ave
 Gateshead NE10 . . . . .71 C7
 Longbenton NE12 . . . . .39 D7
 Sunderland,Grangetown
  SR2 . . . . .86 E2
 Sunderland,South Hylton
  SR4 . . . . .85 B6
 Wallsend NE28 . . . . .40 B2
 Whitley Bay NE26 . . . . .32 B5
Victoria Ave W NE32 . . . . .86 E2
Victoria Bglws NE11 . . . . .100 A1
Victoria Bldgs SR1 . . . . .102 C2
Victoria Cl NE25 . . . . .23 D3
Victoria Cres
  North Shields NE30 . . . . . . .41 F5
 Tynemouth NE30 . . . . .32 C3
Victoria Ct
 Gateshead NE8 . . . . .100 C1
 Hebburn NE31 . . . . .57 D5
 Longbenton NE12 . . . . .29 C1
 Sunderland SR2 . . . . .102 C2
 Tynemouth NE30 . . . . .32 C3
Victoria Gr NE42 . . . . .50 E4
Victoria Ho NE8 . . . . .100 C1
Victoria Ind Est NE31 . . . . .57 C3
Victoria Mews Blyth NE24 . . . .17 D7
 Newcastle-u-T NE2 . . . . .56 A8
 Whickham NE16 . . . . .69 A7
 Whitley Bay NE26 . . . . .32 B5
Victoria Pl
  Chester le S DH3 . . . . .88 C2
 Sunderland SR1 . . . . .103 B2
  Washington NE37 . . . . .83 D8
 Whitley Bay NE25 . . . . .31 E4
Victoria Rd
 Gateshead NE8 . . . . .70 C8
 South Shields NE33 . . . . .42 C1
 Washington NE37 . . . . .83 D8
Victoria Rd E NE31 . . . . .57 F6
Victoria Rd W NE31 . . . . .57 D4
Victoria Sq
  Newcastle-u-T NE2 . . . . . . .71 D8
 Tynemouth NE2 . . . . .99 B3
Victoria St
 Crawcrook NE40 . . . . .51 F4
 East Boldon NE36 . . . . .74 C7
  Gateshead,Felling NE10 . . . .71 D8
 Gateshead,Wrekenton NE9 . .71 C3
 Hamsterley NE17 . . . . .77 B6
 Jarrow NE32 . . . . .58 A6
 Newbiggin-by-t-S NE64 . . . . . .7 A4
 Penshaw DH4 . . . . .90 C8
 Prudhoe NE42 . . . . .50 D2
 Rowlands Gill NE39 . . . . .67 C1
  Springwell NE9 . . . . .71 F1
  Throckley NE15 . . . . .35 D2
 Whitley Bay NE26 . . . . .32 B5
Victoria Villas NE22 . . . . .11 B1
Victory Cotts SR3 . . . . .22 A1
Victory Ho NE30 . . . . .42 D7
Victory St NE4 . . . . .85 E7
Victory St E DH5 . . . . .95 B4
Victory St W DH5 . . . . .95 B4
Victory Way SR3 . . . . .91 C5
Viewforth Dr SR5 . . . . .75 C3
Viewforth Gn NE5 . . . . .37 C1
Viewforth Rd SR2 . . . . .92 F5
Viewforth Terr SR5 . . . . .75 C3
Viewlands NE63 . . . . .6 D4
Vigo La Birtley DH3 . . . . .88 D8
 Washington NE38 . . . . .83 A1
 Washington NE38 . . . . .83 B1
Vigodale DH3 . . . . .82 E1
Viking Ind Est NE32 . . . . .58 A8
Viking Prec NE32 . . . . .58 B7
Villa Cl SR4 . . . . .85 F6
Villa Pl NE8 . . . . .101 B1
Villa View NE9 . . . . .71 A6
Village Ct NE26 . . . . .31 F5
Village Ctr
 Washington,Biddick NE38 . . .83 D4
 Washington,Donwell NE37 . . .72 B1
 Washington,Glebe NE38 . . . .83 D5
 Washington,Lambton NE38 . .83 B3
Village E NE40 . . . . .52 C6
Village Farm NE15 . . . . .34 A1
Village Hts NE8 . . . . .101 B2
Village La NE38 . . . . .83 D6
Village Pl NE6 . . . . .56 D5
Village Rd NE23 . . . . .22 C6
Village The SR2 . . . . .93 A6
Villas The Ryhope SR2 . . . . . . .92 F5
 Stannington NE61 . . . . .13 C7
Villette Brook St SR2 . . . . . .86 E4
Villette Path SR2 . . . . .86 E4
Villette Rd SR2 . . . . .86 E4
Villiers Pl DH3 . . . . .88 C4
Villiers St SR1 . . . . .103 B3
Villiers St S SR1 . . . . .103 B2
Vimy Ave NE31 . . . . .57 E6
Vindolanda NE28 . . . . .40 F4
Vindomora Rd NE17 . . . . .76 E4
Vindomora Roman Fort*
 DH8 . . . . .76 E4

Vindomora Villas DH8 .... 76 E4
Vine Cl NE8 .... 100 C1
Vine Ct NE46 .... 45 B4
Vine La NE1 .... 99 A2
Vine Pl
[6] Houghton-le-S DH4 .... 94 E8
Sunderland SR1 .... 102 C2
Vine St South Shields NE33 .... 59 C6
Wallsend NE28 .... 40 C1
Vine Terr NE46 .... 45 B4
Viola Cres DH2 .... 81 F2
Viola St NE37 .... 83 D8
Viola Terr NE16 .... 69 B7
Violet Cl NE4 .... 54 D4
Violet St
[6] Houghton-le-S DH4 .... 94 D8
Sunderland SR4 .... 102 B3
Sunderland,South Hylton SR4 .... 85 A6
Violet Terr DH4 .... 89 D3
Viscount Rd [4] SR3 .... 92 A7
Vivian Cres [1] DH2 .... 88 C2
Vivian Sq SR6 .... 75 D3
Voltage Terr DH4 .... 90 D4
Vulcan Pl Bedlington NE22 .... 16 A8
Sunderland SR6 .... 75 D1
Vulcan Terr NE12 .... 29 E1

W

Wade Ave NE15 .... 33 A7
Wadham Ct SR2 .... 92 E7
Wadham Terr NE34 .... 59 B5
Wadsley Sq SR2 .... 86 E3
Waggonway The NE42 .... 50 D3
Wagon Way NE28 .... 40 D1
Wagonway Rd NE31 .... 57 E7
Wagtail Cl NE21 .... 68 C8
Wakefield Ave NE34 .... 60 B5
Walbottle Campus Tech Coll NE15 .... 35 F2
Walbottle Hall Gdns NE15 .... 36 A1
Walbottle Rd
Newburn NE15 .... 52 F8
Walbottle NE15 .... 35 F1
Walbottle Village Fst Sch NE15 .... 35 F1
Walden Cl DH2 .... 81 D2
Waldo St NE29 .... 42 B5
Waldridge Cl NE37 .... 83 A6
Waldridge Gdns NE9 .... 71 D4
Waldridge La DH2 .... 88 A2
Waldridge Rd DH2 .... 88 B2
Waldron Sq SR2 .... 86 E3
Walker Ct [11] NE16 .... 69 A7
Walker Gate Hospl NE6 .... 39 E1
Walker Gate Ind Est NE6 .... 57 B6
Walker Gr NE6 .... 56 F8
Walker Park Cl NE6 .... 57 A4
Walker Park Gdns NE6 .... 57 A4
Walker Pl NE30 .... 42 C6
Walker Rd NE6 .... 56 E3
Walker Riverside Ind Pk NE6 .... 57 B4
Walker Riverside Pk* NE6 .... 56 F3
Walker Tech Coll NE6 .... 56 F6
Walker Terr NE8 .... 101 B2
Walker View NE10 .... 71 D8
Walkerburn NE23 .... 22 B3
Walkerdene Ho NE6 .... 57 B8
Walkergate Hospl NE6 .... 56 E8
Walkergate Prim Sch NE6 .... 56 E8
Walkergate Sta NE6 .... 56 E8
Walkers Bldgs [22] NE29 .... 42 A5
Wall Cl NE3 .... 38 A5
Wall St NE3 .... 38 A5
Wall Terr NE6 .... 56 E7
Wallace Ave NE16 .... 69 C8
Wallace Gdns NE9 .... 71 E3
Wallace St Dunston NE11 .... 100 A1
Houghton-le-S DH4 .... 94 D8
Newcastle-u-T NE2 .... 98 B4
Sunderland SR5 .... 75 C1
Wallace Terr NE40 .... 52 C6
Waller Terr DH5 .... 94 E7
Wallinfen NE10 .... 71 F5
Wallingford Ave SR2 .... 86 E2
Wallington Ave
Brunswick Village NE13 .... 28 A6
Tynemouth NE30 .... 32 A1
Wallington Cl NE22 .... 11 C2
Wallington Ct
Killingworth NE12 .... 29 C3
Newcastle-u-T NE3 .... 37 D7
Seaton Delaval NE25 .... 23 D3
Tynemouth NE30 .... 32 B1
Wallington Dr NE15 .... 53 E8
Wallington Gr [9] NE33 .... 42 D3
Wallington Rd NE63 .... 6 F2
Wallis St Penshaw DH4 .... 90 B8
[12] South Shields NE33 .... 42 C3
Wallridge Dr NE25 .... 23 E1
Wallsend Jubilee Prim Sch NE28 .... 40 A4
Wallsend Rd
North Shields NE29 .... 41 C3
North Shields NE29 .... 41 D4
Wallsend St Peter's CE Prim Sch NE28 .... 40 E2
Wallsend Sta NE28 .... 40 C1
Walmer Terr NE9 .... 71 D1
Walnut Gdns NE8 .... 70 C8
Walnut Pl NE3 .... 37 F3
Walpole Ct [1] SR4 .... 85 F6
Walpole St
Newcastle-u-T NE6 .... 56 E8
South Shields NE33 .... 42 C1
Walsh Ave NE31 .... 57 E7
Walsham Cl NE24 .... 17 B5
Walsingham NE38 .... 83 C4
Walter St
Brunswick Village NE13 .... 28 A6
Jarrow NE32 .... 58 B7
Walter Terr
Hetton le H DH5 .... 95 B1
Newcastle-u-T NE4 .... 98 A2
Walter Thomas St [3] SR5 .... 74 F2
Waltham NE38 .... 83 D4
Waltham Cl NE28 .... 39 F3
Waltham Pl [4] NE5 .... 37 B2
Walton Ave Blyth NE24 .... 17 C8
Tynemouth NE29 .... 41 F7
Walton Dr NE62 .... 10 F8
Walton La SR1 .... 103 B3
Walton Pk NE29 .... 41 F8
Walton Rd
Newcastle-u-T NE5 .... 37 A1
Washington NE38 .... 84 B5
Walton Terr DH8 .... 76 E4
Walwick Ave NE29 .... 41 D6
Walwick Rd NE25 .... 31 B5
Walworth Ave NE34 .... 60 C6
Walworth Gr NE32 .... 58 B3
Wandsworth Rd NE6 .... 56 B7
Wanless La NE46 .... 45 B4
Wanley St NE24 .... 17 E8
Wanlock Cl NE23 .... 22 C3
Wanny Rd NE22 .... 11 B1
Wansbeck NE38 .... 83 A1
Wansbeck Ave Blyth NE24 .... 17 E5
Stakeford NE62 .... 11 A8
Tynemouth NE30 .... 32 C2
Wansbeck Bsns Pk NE63 .... 6 B5
Wansbeck Cl Ellington NE61 .... 1 E5
Sunniside NE16 .... 69 A3
Wansbeck Cres NE61 .... 4 E3
Wansbeck Ct
Bedlington NE22 .... 16 A8
[19] Silksworth SR3 .... 91 F6
Wansbeck General Hospl NE63 .... 6 F4
Wansbeck Gr NE25 .... 23 D6
Wansbeck Ho NE15 .... 53 C6
Wansbeck Mews
Ashington NE63 .... 6 B4
South Shields NE34 .... 59 C5
Wansbeck Pl NE61 .... 3 E1
Wansbeck Rd
Ashington NE63 .... 6 B2
Dudley NE23 .... 28 F8
Jarrow NE32 .... 58 B5
Newcastle-u-T NE3 .... 38 A6
Wansbeck Rd S NE3 .... 38 A6
Wansbeck Riverside Pk* NE62,NE63 .... 5 F1
Wansbeck Road Sta NE3 .... 38 A6
Wansbeck Sq NE63 .... 6 C4
Wansbeck St
Ashington NE63 .... 12 A8
Chopwell NE17 .... 66 C1
Morpeth NE61 .... 9 A8
Wansbeck Terr NE62 .... 11 D7
Wansbeck View NE62 .... 11 B8
Wansdyke NE61 .... 3 D1
Wansfell Ave NE5 .... 37 D3
Wansford Ave NE5 .... 37 B1
Wansford Way
Whickham NE16 .... 68 F5
Whickham NE16 .... 69 A4
Wantage Ave NE29 .... 41 D4
Wantage St NE33 .... 59 D7
Wapping [1] NE24 .... 17 F8
Wapping St NE33 .... 42 B4
Warbeck Cl NE3 .... 37 B6
Warburton Cres NE9 .... 71 A8
Warcop Ct NE3 .... 37 E7
Ward Ct SR2 .... 103 B1
Warden Gr DH5 .... 94 F7
Warden Law La SR3 .... 91 F6
Wardenlaw NE10 .... 71 F5
Wardill Gdns NE9 .... 71 B7
Wardle Ave NE33 .... 42 E1
Wardle Dr NE23 .... 29 B8
Wardle Gdns NE10 .... 71 E7
Wardle St NE3 .... 38 E5
Wardle Terr NE40 .... 51 F4
Wardley Ct NE10 .... 72 D8
Wardley Dr NE10 .... 72 D7
Wardley La NE10,NE31 .... 57 C1
Wardley Prim Sch NE10 .... 72 B8
Wardroper Ho NE6 .... 57 A4
Warenford Cl NE23 .... 22 C4
Warenford Pl NE5 .... 54 C7
Warenmill Cl NE15 .... 53 B7
Warennes St [3] SR4 .... 85 C7
Warenton Pl NE29 .... 31 B1
Waring Ave NE26 .... 24 B7
Wark Ave
North Shields NE29 .... 41 C6
Shiremoor NE27 .... 30 F4
Wark Cres NE32 .... 58 B2
Wark Ct NE3 .... 38 E4
Wark St DH3 .... 88 C1
Warkdale Ave NE24 .... 17 A6
Warkworth Ave
Blyth NE24 .... 17 E5
South Shields NE34 .... 60 B7
Wallsend NE28 .... 40 C4
Whitley Bay NE26 .... 32 A5
Warkworth Cl NE38 .... 83 B4
Warkworth Cres
Ashington NE63 .... 6 C3
Warkworth Cres *continued*
Newburn NE15 .... 52 F7
Newcastle-u-T NE3 .... 38 B6
Warkworth Dr
Chester le S DH2 .... 88 A1
Ellington NE61 .... 1 E5
Pegswood NE61 .... 4 F3
Wideopen NE13 .... 28 C6
Warkworth Gdns NE10 .... 71 C8
Warkworth La NE61 .... 1 C6
Warkworth St
[3] Newcastle-u-T,Byker NE6 .... 56 C6
Newcastle-u-T,Lemington NE15 .... 53 C6
Warkworth Terr
Jarrow NE32 .... 58 B3
Tynemouth NE30 .... 42 D8
Warkworth Woods NE3 .... 28 B2
Warnham Ave SR2 .... 86 E2
Warnhead Rd NE22 .... 11 B1
Warren Ave NE6 .... 57 A8
Warren Cl DH4 .... 90 C4
Warren Ct NE63 .... 6 C2
Warren Sq SR1 .... 103 C4
Warrenmor NE10 .... 72 A7
Warrens Wlk NE21 .... 53 A1
Warrington Rd
Newcastle u-T,Elswick NE4 .... 100 A4
Newcastle-u-T,Fawdon NE3 .... 37 E6
Warton Terr NE6 .... 56 C8
Warwick Ave NE16 .... 69 B5
Warwick Cl Seghill NE23 .... 22 E1
Whickham NE16 .... 69 A5
Warwick Ct
Gateshead NE8 .... 101 C2
Newcastle-u-T NE3 .... 37 D7
Warwick Dr
Houghton-le-S DH5 .... 94 E7
Sunderland SR3 .... 91 C7
Washington NE37 .... 72 D2
Whickham NE16 .... 69 B5
Warwick Gr NE22 .... 10 D1
Warwick Hall Wlk NE7 .... 39 D3
Warwick Rd Hebburn NE31 .... 57 F3
Newcastle-u-T NE5 .... 53 E8
South Shields NE34 .... 59 D7
Wallsend NE28 .... 40 B1
Warwick St Blyth NE24 .... 17 C4
Gateshead NE8 .... 101 C2
Newcastle-u-T NE6 .... 56 A7
Sunderland SR5 .... 75 D1
Warwick Terr SR3 .... 92 A8
Warwick Terr W SR3 .... 92 A8
Wasdale Cl NE23 .... 22 C3
Wasdale Ct SR6 .... 75 C5
Wasdale Rd NE5 .... 54 B8
Washington 'F' Pit Mus* NE37 .... 83 C7
Washington Arts Ctr NE38 .... 83 D2
Washington Gdns NE9 .... 71 C3
Washington Highway
Penshaw DH4,NE38 .... 89 E8
Washington NE37,NE38 .... 83 B4
Washington Hospl The NE38 .... 88 E8
Washington Old Hall* NE38 .... 83 E6
Washington Rd SR5 .... 74 B2
Washington Sch NE37 .... 83 D7
Washington Service Area DH3,NE38 .... 82 E3
Washington St SR4 .... 85 F6
Washington Terr NE30 .... 42 C7
Washington Waterfowl & Wetlands Ctr* NE38 .... 84 C5
Washingwell Com Prim Sch NE16 .... 69 C6
Washingwell La NE16 .... 69 D6
Washingwell Pk NE16 .... 69 C6
Waskdale Cres NE21 .... 68 B8
Waskerley Cl NE16 .... 69 B3
Waskerley Gdns [3] NE9 .... 71 D3
Waskerley Rd NE38 .... 83 F5
Watch House Cl NE29 .... 42 A3
Watcombe Cl NE37 .... 72 F2
Water Row NE15 .... 52 E7
Water St NE4 .... 100 B3
Waterbeach Pl NE5 .... 37 B2
Waterbeck Cl NE23 .... 22 C3
Waterbury Cl SR5 .... 74 F3
Waterbury Rd NE3 .... 28 B1
Waterfield Rd NE22 .... 12 B4
Waterford Cl
East Rainton DH5 .... 94 D4
Seaton Sluice NE26 .... 24 D6
Waterford Cres [6] NE26 .... 32 B4
Waterford Gn NE63 .... 11 D8
Waterford Pk NE13 .... 27 F6
Watergate NE1 .... 101 B4
Waterloo Ct [5] NE37 .... 83 E8
Waterloo Pl
North Shields NE29 .... 42 A6
Sunderland SR1 .... 103 A2
Waterloo Rd Blyth NE24 .... 17 E7
Earsdon NE25 .... 31 A5
Washington NE37 .... 72 F3
Washington,Sulgrave NE37 .... 72 E1
Waterloo Sq [10] NE33 .... 42 C3
Waterloo St Blaydon NE21 .... 53 A1
Newcastle-u-T NE1 .... 100 C4
Waterloo Vale [8] NE33 .... 42 C3
Waterloo Wlk NE37 .... 83 E8
Waterlow Cl SR5 .... 74 F4
Watermark The NE11 .... 54 C3
Watermill NE40 .... 52 C5
Watermill La NE10 .... 71 E8
Watermill Pk NE10 .... 71 D7
Waterside NE61 .... 8 F8
Waterside Dr NE11 .... 54 E2
Waterside Pk NE31 .... 57 C6
Waterville Pl [16] NE29 .... 42 A5
Waterville Prim Sch NE29 .... 41 F4
Waterville Rd NE29 .... 41 E4
Waterville Terr [9] NE29 .... 42 A5
Waterworks Rd SR1 .... 102 C2
Waterworks The SR2 .... 92 E5
Watford Cl SR5 .... 74 F4
Watling Pl NE9 .... 71 B6
Watling St NE45 .... 46 F5
Watson Ave Dudley NE23 .... 29 A8
South Shields NE34 .... 60 B5
Watson Gdns NE28 .... 41 A3
Watson Pl NE34 .... 60 B5
Watson St
Burnopfield NE16 .... 79 B6
Gateshead NE8 .... 100 C1
High Spen NE39 .... 67 A5
Jarrow NE32 .... 58 C8
Watson Terr
Boldon Colliery NE35 .... 73 F7
[17] Morpeth NE61 .... 9 A8
Watt St NE8 .... 70 D7
Watt's La NE64 .... 7 E5
Watt's Rd NE26 .... 32 A6
Watts Moses Ho SR1 .... 103 C3
Wavendon Cres SR4 .... 85 E4
Waverdale Ave NE6 .... 57 A7
Waverdale Way NE33 .... 59 B7
Waverley Ave
Bedlington NE22 .... 11 B1
Bedlington NE22 .... 11 C2
Whitley Bay NE25 .... 31 F4
Waverley Cl NE21 .... 67 F8
Waverley Cres NE15 .... 53 D7
Waverley Ct NE22 .... 11 C2
Waverley Dr NE22 .... 11 C2
Waverley Lodge NE2 .... 99 C3
Waverley Pl NE64 .... 7 E5
Waverley Prim Sch NE15 .... 53 E6
Waverley Rd
Gateshead NE9 .... 71 B1
Newcastle-u-T NE4 .... 100 B4
Waverley Terr Dipton DH9 .... 78 E1
Sunderland SR4 .... 85 E7
Waverly Dr NE22 .... 11 D2
Waverton Cl NE23 .... 22 B3
Wawn St NE33 .... 59 D8
Wayfarer Rd SR5 .... 75 A1
Wayland Sq SR2 .... 86 E1
Wayman St SR5 .... 75 C1
Wayside
Newcastle-u-T NE15 .... 54 B5
South Shields NE34 .... 60 B6
Sunderland SR2 .... 86 B4
Wealcroft NE10 .... 71 F5
Wealcroft Ct NE10 .... 71 F5
Wealleans Cl NE63 .... 7 B3
Wear Ct NE34 .... 59 C5
Wear Lodge DH3 .... 88 C7
Wear Rd NE31 .... 57 E3
Wear St Chester le S DH3 .... 88 D2
Chopwell NE17 .... 66 B1
Fence Houses DH4 .... 94 A7
Hetton le H DH5 .... 95 A3
Jarrow NE32 .... 58 B7
Sunderland,Hendon SR1 .... 103 C2
Sunderland,Low Southwick SR5 .... 75 A1
Sunderland,South Hylton SR4 .... 85 A7
Wear Terr NE38 .... 83 E4
Wear View SR4 .... 85 B7
Weardale Ave Blyth NE24 .... 17 A8
Longbenton NE12 .... 39 D8
Newcastle-u-T NE6 .... 57 A6
Sunderland SR6 .... 75 E7
Wallsend NE28 .... 40 B4
Washington NE37 .... 83 C8
Weardale Cres DH4 .... 90 B7
Weardale St DH5 .... 94 E1
Weardale Terr DH3 .... 88 D2
Wearfield SR5 .... 74 F1
Wearhead Dr SR2,SR4 .... 102 B1
Wearmouth Ave SR5 .... 75 D2
Wearmouth Dr SR5 .... 75 D2
Wearmouth St SR6 .... 75 D1
Weathercock La NE9 .... 70 F5
Weatherside NE21 .... 53 B1
Webb Gdns NE10 .... 72 A8
Wedder Law NE23 .... 22 B3
Wedderburn Sq NE63 .... 6 C3
Wedgewood Cotts NE15 .... 53 D6
Wedmore Rd NE5 .... 36 D3
Weetman St NE33 .... 42 B1
Weetslade Cres NE23 .... 29 A7
Weetslade Rd NE23 .... 29 A7
Weetslade Terr NE23 .... 29 C5
Weetwood Rd NE23 .... 22 C4
Weidner Rd NE15,NE4 .... 54 D6
Welbeck Com Fst Sch NE63 .... 7 A2
Welbeck Gn NE6 .... 56 E5
Welbeck Prim Sch NE6 .... 56 D5
Welbeck Rd
Guide Post NE62 .... 10 E7
Newcastle-u-T NE6 .... 56 E5
Welbeck Terr
Ashington NE63 .... 6 D2
Pegswood NE61 .... 4 F4
Welburn Cl NE42 .... 50 C5
Welbury Way NE23 .... 22 B3
Weldon Ave SR2 .... 86 E2
Weldon Cres NE7 .... 39 B2
Weldon Pl NE29 .... 41 D8
Weldon Rd
East Cramlington NE23 .... 22 E5
Longbenton NE12 .... 39 B6
Weldon Terr DH3 .... 88 D2
Weldon Way NE3 .... 38 B6
Welfare Cres
Ashington NE63 .... 6 F3
Newbiggin-by-t-S NE64 .... 7 C4
Welfare Rd DH5 .... 95 A4
Welford Ave NE3 .... 38 A5
Well Bank NE45 .... 46 F5
Well Bank Rd NE37 .... 72 B1
Well Close Wlk NE16 .... 69 A6
Well Dean NE42 .... 50 D3
Well La Tynemouth NE27 .... 31 B2
Tynemouth NE27 .... 31 C2
Well Rd NE43 .... 64 B5
Well Ridge Cl NE25 .... 31 C6
Well Ridge Pk NE25 .... 31 C7
Well St SR4 .... 85 F7
Well Way NE61 .... 3 F1
Wellands Cl SR6 .... 60 E1
Wellands Ct SR6 .... 60 E1
Wellands Dr SR6 .... 60 E1
Wellands La SR6 .... 60 E1
Wellburn Rd NE37 .... 72 B1
Wellesley St NE32 .... 58 B5
Wellesley Terr NE4 .... 98 A1
Wellfield Cl NE15 .... 35 C1
Wellfield Ct NE40 .... 51 E3
Wellfield La NE5 .... 37 B2
Wellfield Mews SR2 .... 92 E5
Wellfield Mid Sch NE25 .... 31 B4
Wellfield Rd
Newcastle-u-T NE4 .... 54 D5
Newcastle-u-T NE4 .... 54 E5
Rowlands Gill NE39 .... 67 C2
Wellfield Terr
[3] Gateshead NE10 .... 71 C7
Newcastle-u-T NE10 .... 57 B1
Ryhope SR2 .... 92 E5
Wellgarth Rd NE37 .... 72 B1
Wellhead Dean Rd NE62 .... 5 F2
Wellhead Terr NE63 .... 6 A4
Wellhope NE38 .... 88 F8
Wellington Ave NE25 .... 31 A5
Wellington Ct
[2] Gateshead NE10 .... 71 C8
[6] Washington NE37 .... 83 E8
Wellington Dr NE33 .... 42 C4
Wellington La SR4 .... 102 B4
Wellington Rd
Dunston NE11 .... 54 E1
Dunston NE11 .... 54 F1
Stakeford NE62 .... 11 A7
Wellington Row DH4 .... 90 C5
Wellington St Blyth NE24 .... 17 F7
Gateshead NE8 .... 101 B3
Gateshead,Felling NE10 .... 71 C8
Hebburn NE31 .... 57 D5
High Pittington DH6 .... 96 B5
Newcastle-u-T NE4 .... 98 C1
Newcastle-u-T,Lemington NE15 .... 53 D6
[11] North Shields NE29 .... 42 A5
Wellington St E [10] NE24 .... 17 F8
Wellington St W [12] NE29 .... 42 A5
Wellington Wlk [2] NE37 .... 83 F8
Wellmere Rd SR2 .... 86 F1
Wells Cl NE12 .... 39 D4
Wells Gdns NE9 .... 70 F2
Wells Gr NE34 .... 60 A7
Wells St NE35 .... 58 E1
Wellshede NE10 .... 72 B7
Wellway NE32 .... 58 B2
Wellway Ct [8] NE61 .... 3 F1
Wellwood Gdns NE61 .... 4 A1
Welton Cl NE43 .... 64 D6
Welworth Way SR1 .... 102 C3
Welwyn Ave NE22 .... 11 D3
Welwyn Cl Sunderland SR5 .... 85 A8
Wallsend NE28 .... 39 F4
Wembley Ave NE25 .... 31 E4
Wembley Cl SR5 .... 74 F3
Wembley Gdns NE24 .... 12 B6
Wembley Rd SR5 .... 74 F3
Wembley Terr NE24 .... 12 C6
Wendover Cl SR5 .... 74 E4
Wendover Way SR5 .... 74 E4
Wenham Sq SR2 .... 86 B4
Wenlock NE38 .... 83 C4
Wenlock Dr NE29 .... 41 F8
Wenlock Pl [6] NE34 .... 59 A4
Wenlock Rd NE34 .... 59 A5
Wensley Cl
Newcastle-u-T NE5 .... 37 C4
Urpeth DH2 .... 81 F1
Wensley Ho [2] SR3 .... 91 F5
Wensleydale NE28 .... 39 F5
Wensleydale Ave
Penshaw DH4 .... 90 A7
Washington NE37 .... 83 C8
Wensleydale Dr NE12 .... 39 D8
Wensleydale Mid Sch NE24 .... 17 F6
Wensleydale Terr NE24 .... 17 F6
Wentworth NE33 .... 42 E1
Wentworth Cl NE10 .... 71 D7
Wentworth Ct NE20 .... 25 C4
Wentworth Dr NE37 .... 72 C2
Wentworth Gdns NE25 .... 31 C4
Wentworth Grange NE3 .... 38 D4

Wentworth Pl
Hexham NE46 ....45 B5
Newcastle-u-T NE4 ....100 B4
Wentworth Terr SR4 ....102 B3
Werhale Gn NE10 ......71 D8
Wesley Ct Blaydon NE21 ...53 D3
1 Gateshead,Felling NE10 ..71 C8
Wesley Dr NE12 ....30 B1
Wesley Gr NE40 ....51 E3
Wesley Mount NE40 ......51 E3
Wesley St
Gateshead,Low Fell NE9 ...70 F5
Newcastle-u-T NE2 ......99 C2
Prudhoe NE42 ....50 D2
15 South Shields NE33 ...42 C3
Wesley Terr
Chester le S DH3 ....88 C3
Dipton DH9 ....78 D1
Prudhoe NE42 ....50 D2
Sherburn Hill DH6 ......96 C1
Wesley Way
Longbenton NE12 ....30 B1
Throckley NE15 ....35 D2
Wessex Cl SR5 ....74 F4
Wessington Terr NE37 ...83 D7
Wessington Way
Sunderland SR5 ....74 E1
Sunderland,Castletown SR5 ..85 B8
West Acres Blaydon NE21 ..53 D2
Dinnington NE13 ....23 D6
West Ave Guide Post NE62 ..10 D7
Longbenton NE12 ....39 D6
Longbenton,Forest Hall
NE12 ....29 F1
Newcastle-u-T NE5 ......36 F2
Newcastle-u-T,Gosforth
NE3 ....38 C4
North Shields NE29 .....41 D5
Rowlands Gill NE39 .....67 D1
South Shields NE34 .....59 E6
Washington NE38 ....83 B1
Whitburn SR6 ....60 E1
Whitley Bay NE25 ....31 E5
West Bailey NE12 ....29 B3
West Boldon Prim Sch
NE36 ....74 A7
West Bridge St
Cambois NE24 ....12 D3
Penshaw DH4 ....89 E8
West Brunton Farm Cotts
NE13 ....27 D2
West Chirton (Middle) Ind
Est NE29 ....41 B7
West Chirton (South) Ind Est
NE29 ....41 C5
West Chirton North Ind Est
NE29 ....41 B7
West Clifton NE12 ....29 C4
West Copperas NE15 .....53 F7
West Cres Chopwell NE17 ..77 B7
Gateshead NE10 ....72 C8
West Ct NE24 ....17 C6
West Denton Cl NE15 ....53 D8
West Denton Prim Sch
NE5 ....36 D1
West Denton Rd NE15 ...53 D8
West Denton Ret Pk NE5 ..37 A2
West Denton Way NE5 ....36 E1
West Dr Blyth NE24 ......17 C4
Cleadon SR6 ....74 E8
West End NE26 ....24 D4
West End Terr 1 NE46 ...45 A4
West Farm Burdon SR3 ...92 B3
Medomsley DH8 ....77 C2
West Farm Ave NE12 ....39 A6
West Farm Ct
Cramlington NE23 ......22 B7
Killingworth NE12 ......29 E2
West Farm La DH8 ....77 C2
West Farm Rd
Cleadon SR6 ....75 B8
Newcastle-u-T NE6 ......56 E7
Wallsend NE28 ....40 F3
West Farm Wynd NE12 ..38 F6
West Ford Rd NE62 ......11 B8
West Gate Com Coll NE4 ..54 D6
West George Potts St 17
NE33 ....42 D1
West Gns 11 NE61 ....9 A8
West Gr SR4 ....98 C1
West Grange SR5 ....75 C3
West Hextol NE46 ....44 F4
West Hextol Cl NE46 ....44 F4
West High Horse Cl
NE39 ....68 A4
West Hill Morpeth NE61 ..8 E7
Sunderland SR4 ....85 E4
West Holborn NE33 ......42 B1
West Jesmond Ave NE2 ..38 E1
West Jesmond Prim Sch
NE2 ....38 E1
West Jesmond Sta NE2 ..38 E2
West La Blaydon NE21 ...68 A8
Byermoor NE16 ....68 C1
Chester le S DH3 ....88 C2
Killingworth NE12 ......29 D2
Medomsley NE17 ....77 B4
West Law Rd DH8 ....76 D1
West Lawn SR2 ....86 D4
West Lawrence St SR1 ..103 B2
West Lea Blaydon NE21 ...68 C8
New Herrington DH4 ....90 D6
West Market St NE61 ....2 B3
West Mdws NE5 ....36 D4

West Meadows Dr SR6 ...75 A8
West Meadows Rd SR6 ...75 B8
West Moff St 6 NE33 ...42 D1
West Monkseaton Sta
NE25 ....31 D4
West Moor Ct NE12 .....29 B1
West Moor Dr SR6 ......75 A7
West Moor Terr 1 SR4 ..85 E7
West Mount
Killingworth NE12 ......29 C3
Sunderland SR4 ....85 E5
West Par Hebburn NE31 ..57 D5
Newcastle-u-T NE4 .....100 B4
West Park Gdns NE21 ...53 C1
West Park Rd
Cleadon SR6 ....60 A1
Gateshead NE8,NE9 .....70 E7
South Shields NE33 .....59 C7
West Park View NE23 ...28 F8
West Pastures
Ashington NE63 ....6 B2
West Boldon NE36 ......73 C5
West Percy Rd NE29 ....41 F5
West Percy St NE29 .....42 A5
West Pk Dunston NE11 ...54 F1
Morpeth NE61 ....8 E7
Sunderland SR3 ....91 B6
West Quarter NE46 .....44 F5
West Quay Rd SR5 ......74 F1
West Rd Bedlington NE22 ..11 D2
Newcastle-u-T NE15,NE5 ..54 C6
Ponteland NE20 ....25 E6
Prudhoe NE42 ....50 B2
Tantobie DH9 ....79 A1
West Rig The NE12 ......37 E4
West Riggs NE22 ....15 F8
West Row DH4 ....82 E3
West Salisbury St 4
NE24 ....17 D8
West Sleekburn Ind Est
NE22 ....11 D6
West Sleekburn Mid Sch
NE62 ....11 F6
West Spencer Terr NE15 ..36 B1
West St 5 Birtley DH3 ...82 C4
Gateshead NE8 ....101 B3
Hebburn NE31 ....57 C6
High Spen NE39 ....66 F4
New Silksworth SR3 ....92 A8
Shiremoor NE27 ....30 D1
Sunderland SR3 ....102 C3
Wallsend NE28 ....40 A2
Whickham NE16 ....69 A7
West Stainton St 5
NE33 ....42 D1
West Stevenson St 5
NE33 ....42 D1
West Sunniside SR1 ....103 A3
West Terr Corbridge NE45 ..46 F6
Seaton Sluice NE26 ....24 D6
Stakeford NE62 ....11 C7
West Thorn Wlk NE16 ...69 A6
West Thorp NE5 ....36 F5
West Vallum NE15 ......54 C4
West View Ashington NE63 ..6 D3
Bedlington NE22 ....11 C3
Blaydon NE21 ....53 C3
Bournmoor DH4 ....89 E3
Burnopfield NE16 ......79 A6
Cambois NE24 ....12 C6
Chester le S DH3 ....88 C1
5 Longbenton NE12 .....39 D8
Morpeth NE61 ....3 C5
Newbiggin-by-t-S NE64 ..7 D3
Newbottle DH4 ....90 D2
Newcastle-u-T,Elswick NE4 ..54 F4
Newcastle-u-T,Lemington
NE15 ....53 C6
Pegswood NE61 ....4 E3
Penshaw DH4 ....90 B8
Ryhope SR2 ....92 E6
Seghill NE23 ....22 F1
Sherburn Hill DH6 ......96 C1
3 Sunderland,Castletown
SR5 ....74 B1
Standish,Monkwearmouth
SR6 ....75 D3
Wideopen NE13 ....28 B7
Wylam NE41 ....51 B6
West View Bldgs NE30 ...32 C3
West View Terr NE6 .....45 C3
West Walls NE1 ....98 C1
West Walpole St NE33 ...42 B1
West Way Dunston NE11 ..70 A7
South Shields NE33 .....59 B8
West Wear St SR1 ......103 A3
West Wylam Dr NE42 ...50 E3
West Wynd NE12 ....29 D3
Westacre Gdns NE5 .....54 C7
Westacres Ave NE16 ....69 B5
Westacres Cres NE15 ...54 C6
Westbourne Ave
Gateshead NE8 ....70 E8
3 Newcastle-u-T NE6 ...57 A6
Newcastle-u-T,Gosforth
NE3 ....38 C7
Stakeford NE62 ....6 A1
Westbourne Cotts 11
DH4 ....90 B6

Westbourne Dr DH4 .....90 B5
Westbourne Gdns 2
NE6 ....57 A6
Westbourne Gr NE46 ....44 F5
Westbourne Rd SR1 ....102 B2
Westbourne Terr
Seaton Delaval NE25 ...23 C3
2 Shiney Row DH4 .....90 A6
Westbrooke 8 SR2 ......86 D4
Westburn Gdns NE28 ...39 F4
Westburn Mews NE40 ...51 E3
Westburn Terr SR6 .....75 E2
Westbury Ave NE6 ......57 A8
Westbury Rd NE12 ......39 A5
Westbury St SR4 ....102 B3
Westcliffe Rd SR6 ......75 F4
Westcliffe Way NE34 ...58 F3
Westcott Ave NE33 .....42 E1
Westcott Rd NE34 .....59 C6
Westcott Terr DH4 .....90 C8
Westcroft SR6 ....60 E1
Westcroft Rd NE12 .....39 A6
Westcy St 1 SR3 ....91 F5
Westerdale Penshaw DH4 ..89 E8
Wallsend NE28 ....39 F4
Westerdale Pl NE6 .....57 B6
Westerham St SR3 .....74 F3
Westerhope Gdns 11
NE5 ....37 D1
Westerhope Prim Sch
NE5 ....36 E3
Westerhope Rd NE38 ...83 F5
Westerkirk NE23 ....22 C3
Western App
South Shields,High Shields
NE33 ....42 C1
South Shields,Tyne Dock
NE34 ....59 A6
Western App Ind Est 7
NE33 ....42 C2
Western Ave
Gateshead NE11 ....70 C4
Newcastle-u-T NE5 .....36 D1
Newcastle-u-T,Elswick NE4 ..54 E5
Prudhoe NE42 ....50 B2
Seaton Delaval NE25 ...23 C3
Western Com Prim Sch
NE28 ....40 A2
Western Ct 5 NE26 .....31 F8
Western Dr NE4 ....54 F5
Western Highway NE38 ..83 B2
Western Hill Ryhope SR2 ..92 E7
Sunderland SR2 ....102 B2
Western Terr Dudley NE23 ..28 F8
Washington NE37 ......83 D7
West Boldon NE36 .....74 B7
Western View NE11 .....71 C1
Western Way
Blaydon NE21 ....53 E2
Ponteland NE20 ....25 A2
Ryhope SR2 ....92 C4
Whitley Bay NE25 ......31 F8
Westernmoor NE37 .....82 F6
Westfield Dudley NE23 ..28 F8
Gateshead NE10 ....71 E6
Hedworth NE32 ....58 C1
Morpeth NE61 ....8 E7
Westfield Ave
Brunswick Village NE13 ..28 A6
Crawcrook NE40 ....51 F3
Newcastle-u-T NE3 .....38 C3
Whitley Bay NE25 ......31 D4
Westfield Cl NE46 ......44 F5
Westfield Cres
Crawcrook NE40 ....51 F3
Newbiggin-by-t-S NE64 ..7 D4
32 Springwell NE9 .....71 F1
Westfield Ct Jarrow NE32 ..58 B6
Sunderland SR4 ....85 E4
Wallsend NE28 ....57 B8
Westfield Dr NE3 ......38 C3
Westfield Gr
Newcastle-u-T NE3 .....38 B3
Sunderland SR4 ....85 E4
Westfield La NE40 ......52 B6
Westfield Lodge NE40 ...70 E4
Westfield Pk
Newcastle-u-T NE3 .....38 B3
Wallsend NE28 ....40 A2
Westfield Rd
Gateshead NE8 ....70 E8
Newcastle-u-T NE15 ...54 C5
Westfield Sch NE3 .....38 B3
Westfield Terr
Gateshead NE8 ....70 E8
Hexham NE46 ....44 F5
1 Springwell NE9 .....71 E1
Westgarth NE5 ....36 F4
Westgarth Terr 7 NE37 ..83 E8
Westgate NE61 ....8 D7
Westgate Ave SR3 .....92 A8
Westgate Cl NE25 ......31 C6
Westgate Ct NE4 ......98 B1
Westgate Gr SR3 ......92 B8
Westgate Hill Prim Sch
NE4 ....98 A1
Westgate Hill Terr NE4 ..98 B1
Westgate Rd NE1,NE4 ...98 B1
Westgreen NE62 ....10 F5
Westheath Ave SR2 ....86 E1
Westhills DH9 ....79 A2
Westholme Gdns NE15 ..54 D6
Westholme Terr 1 SR2 ..86 F2
Westhope SR6 ....60 A7

Westhope Rd NE34 ......60 A7
Westlands Hedworth NE32 ..58 D1
Newcastle-u-T NE5 .....36 C1
Newcastle-u-T,High Heaton
NE7 ....39 A2
Seaton Sluice NE26 ....24 C6
Sunderland SR4 ....85 F5
Tynemouth NE30 ....32 B1
Westlea NE23 ....15 D8
Westleigh Rd DH4 ......90 C3
Westley Ave NE26 ......24 F1
Westley Cl NE26 ....24 F1
Westline Ind Est DH2 ...82 B2
Westloch Rd NE23 .....22 B3
Westmacott St NE15 ...52 E8
Westminster Ave NE29 ..41 B8
Westminster Cl NE26 ...32 C4
Westminster Cres NE31 ..57 E2
Westminster Dr NE11 ...69 F6
Westminster St NE8 ....70 D8
Westminster Terr 4 SR2 ..86 F2
Westminster Way NE23 ..29 D4
Westmoor Dr NE12 .....29 C2
Westmoor Prim Sch
NE12 ....29 C2
Westmoor Rd SR4 .....85 D7
Westmoreland St NE28 ..40 C2
Westmorland Ave
Bedlington NE22 ....10 E1
Newbiggin-by-t-S NE64 ..7 D4
2 Wallsend NE28 ....41 B1
Westmorland Ct NE31 ..57 E2
Westmorland Gdns NE9 ..70 F5
Westmorland Ho NE9 ...70 E5
Westmorland La NE1 ..100 C4
Westmorland Rd
Newcastle-u-T NE4 ...100 C4
Newcastle-u-T,Elswick
NE1,NE4 ....100 A4
Westmorland Way NE23 ..22 A6
Westmorland Wlk NE4 ...54 E5
Westoe Ave NE33 ......42 E1
Westoe Crown Prim Sch
NE33 ....42 E2
Westoe Cty Inf Sch NE33 ..42 D1
Westoe Dr NE33 ....42 E1
Westoe Hall 1 NE33 ...59 E8
Westoe Rd NE33 ....42 E2
Westoe Village NE33 ...59 E8
Weston Ave NE16 ......68 F5
Westover Gdns NE9 ....70 F7
Westport Cl SR5 ....74 F4
Westray DH2 ....88 B1
Westray Cl SR2 ....92 C8
Westsyde NE20 ....25 B3
Westvale NE15 ....35 B2
Westward Ct NE5 ......36 B4
Westward Gn NE25 ....31 C4
Westward Pl NE38 .....83 E1
Westway Blaydon NE21 ..53 B2
Throckley NE15 ....35 D3
Newcastle-u-T NE15 ...35 D3
Westwell Ct NE3 ....38 F4
Westwood Ave NE6 ....57 A6
Westwood Cl NE16 .....79 B7
Westwood Gdns
Ashington NE62 ....5 F1
6 Gateshead NE9 ......71 D3
Newcastle-u-T NE3 .....37 E4
Westwood La NE17 ......7 B5
Westwood Rd NE3 .....28 C1
Westwood St SR4 ......85 F6
Westwood View
Chester le S DH3 ....88 C1
Crawcrook NE40 ....51 F3
Wetheral Gdns NE9 ....71 A3
Wetheral Terr NE6 .....56 F4
Wetherby Cl NE63 ......6 C2
Wetherby Gr NE8 ......70 D7
Wetherby Rd SR2 .....92 C8
Wettondale Ave NE24 ...17 A7
Weybourne Sq SR2 ....86 E2
Weyhill Ave NE5 ....41 D4
Weymouth Dr DH4 .....89 F5
Weymouth Gdns NE9 ...71 A2
Whaggs La NE16 ......69 B6
Whalebone La NE61 .....8 B4
Whalton Ave NE3 .....38 A6
Whalton Cl
Gateshead NE10 ......72 C7
Morpeth NE61 ....9 B5
Sherburn DH6 ....96 A1
Whalton Ct
Newcastle-u-T NE3 .....38 A6
South Shields NE34 ....59 E6
Wharfdale Pl NE6 ......57 B7
Wharfedale Penshaw DH4 ..90 A8
Wallsend NE28 ....39 F3
Wharfedale Ave NE37 ...83 C8
Wharfedale Dr NE33 ...59 C7
Wharfedale Gdns NE24 ..17 A8
Wharfedale Gn NE9 ....71 B1
Wharmlands Gn NE5 ...53 F7
Wharmlands Rd NE15 ...53 F7
Wharncliffe St 1 SR2 ..102 B2
Wharrier St NE6 ......56 F4
Wharrier Street Prim Sch
NE6 ....56 F4
Wharton Cl DH5 ....94 F4
Wharton St Blyth NE24 ..17 C5
South Shields NE33 ....42 D2
Wheatall Dr SR6 ....60 F4
Wheatear Cl 1 NE38 ...82 F3
Wheatfield Cl NE42 ....50 B5
Wheatfield Gr NE12 ...29 E2

Wheatfield Gr NE12 .....39 C7
Wheatfield Rd NE5 .....36 F3
Wheatfields NE25 ......23 B4
Wheatley Gdns NE36 ...74 A7
Wheatridge NE25 ......23 B4
Wheatsheaf Ct SR6 ....75 F1
Wheler St 3 DH4 ......90 D1
Whernside Cl 4 NE37 ..83 A6
Whernside Ct 24 SR3 ...91 F6
Whernside Pl NE23 ....22 B3
Whernside Wlk NE40 ...52 D4
Whetstone Bridge Rd
NE46 ....44 F4
Whetstone Gn NE46 ....44 F4
Whickham Ave 6 NE11 ..69 F8
Whickham Bank NE16 ...69 A7
Whickham Cl DH4 .....94 C8
Whickham Gdns 14 NE6 ..56 C5
Whickham Highway
NE11,NE16 ....69 E7
Whickham Ind Est NE16 ..69 C7
Whickham Lodge NE16 ..69 C7
Whickham Lodge Rise
NE16 ....69 C7
Whickham Parochial CE Prim
Sch NE16 ....68 F5
Whickham Pk NE16 ....69 A6
Whickham Rd NE31 ....57 E6
Whickham St NE6 .....69 A6
Whickham St E SR6 ....75 E1
Whickham View
Gateshead NE9 ....71 A4
Newcastle-u-T NE15 ...54 A6
Whickhope NE38 ....83 E2
Whinbank NE20 ....25 D2
Whinbrooke NE10 ......72 A6
Whinchat Ho NE28 .....40 D5
Whinfell NE37 ....83 B7
Whinfell Cl NE23 ......22 C3
Whinfell Ct 4 SR3 .....91 F6
Whinfield Ind Est NE39 ..67 C1
Whinfield Terr NE39 ...67 C1
Whinfield Way NE39 ...67 C1
Whinham Way NE61 ....9 B5
Whinlatter Gdns NE9 ...71 A4
Whinlater NE9 ....71 C4
Whinmoor Pl NE5 ......37 E1
Whinney Cl NE21 ......68 A8
Whinneyfield Rd NE6 ...56 F7
Whinny La Ebchester DH8 ..76 E1
Morpeth NE61 ....3 A8
Whinshaw NE10 ....71 F7
Whinstone Mews NE12 ..39 D6
Whinway NE37 ....83 B7
Whistler Gdns NE34 ...59 D3
Whitbeck Ct NE5 ......37 A1
Whitbeck Rd NE5 .....54 A8
Whitbourne Cl NE37 ...72 E2
Whitburn Bents Rd SR6 ..75 F7
Whitburn CE Sch SR6 ...75 F7
Whitburn Coastal Pk*
SR6 ....61 A4
Whitburn Gdns NE9 ....71 D3
Whitburn Hall SR6 .....75 F8
Whitburn Pl NE23 .....22 B3
Whitburn Rd Cleadon SR6 ..74 F8
Sunderland SR6 ....60 B1
Whitburn Rd E SR6 ....60 B1
Whitburn St SR6 ......103 A4
Whitburn Terr
East Boldon NE36 ......74 D7
Sunderland SR6 ....75 D4
Whitburn Village Prim Sch
SR6 ....75 E8
Whitby Ave Hexham NE46 ..44 F5
Sunderland SR6 ....75 E8
Whitby Cl NE8 ....101 C1
Whitby Cres NE12 .....39 C6
Whitby Dr NE38 ....83 D3
Whitby Gdns NE28 ....40 E4
Whitby St NE30 ....42 B6
Whitchester Ho NE4 ...98 B2
Whitchurch Cl
Boldon Colliery NE35 ...58 E1
Sunderland SR5 ....74 F4
Whitchurch Rd SR5 ....74 F4
Whitdale Ave NE24 ....17 A6
White Cross NE46 .....45 C4
White Gates Dr DH5 ...95 B2
White Hill Rd DH5 ....97 C8
White Horse View NE34 ..60 C6
White House Pl SR2 ...103 C2
White House Rd SR2 ...103 B2
White House Way NE10 ..71 E5
White Mere Com Prim Sch
NE10 ....72 C7
White Mere Gdns NE10 ..72 C7
White Oaks NE10 .....72 C7
White Rocks Gr SR6 ...60 F3
White Rose Way NE10 ..72 A7
White St NE6 ....57 B6
White-le-Head Gdns
DH9 ....79 A1
Whiteacres NE61 ....9 A7
Whitebark SR3 ....91 E4
Whitebeam Pl NE4 ....100 B3
Whitebridge Cl NE3 ...38 D7
Whitebridge Ct NE3 ...38 C7
Whitebridge Parkway
NE3 ....38 D8
Whitebridge Pk NE3 ...38 D8
Whitebridge Wlk NE3 ...38 D8
Whiteburn NE42 ....50 B1
Whitecliff Cl NE29 ....41 F8
Whitecroft Rd NE12 ...29 B2

Whitefield Cres
Pegswood NE61 . . . . .4 E3
Penshaw DH4 . . . . .90 A7
Whitefield Farm Cotts
NE61 . . . . .5 A2
Whitefield Gdns NE40 . . . . .66 F8
Whitefield Gr NE10 . . . . . . .71 D8
Whitefield Terr NE6 . . . . . . .39 D1
Whiteford Pl NE23 . . . . .23 A2
Whitefriars Way NE12 . . . .39 A6
Whitegate Cl NE11 . . . . .54 F2
Whitehall Rd
Gateshead NE8 . . . . .101 B1
Gateshead,Shipcote NE8 . . . . .70 D8
Walbottle NE15 . . . . .35 F2
Whitehall St NE33 . . . . .59 C6
Whitehall Terr ⑦ SR4 . . . . .85 F6
Whitehead St
South Shields NE33 . . . . .59 B7
South Shields,West Harton
NE33 . . . . .59 B6
Whitehill NE10 . . . . .71 F5
Whitehill Dr NE10 . . . . .71 F5
Whitehill Hall Gdns DH2 . .88 A4
Whitehill Rd NE23 . . . . .16 A1
Whitehouse Cres NE9 . . . . .71 E4
Whitehouse Farm Ctr*
NE61 . . . . .13 E8
Whitehouse La
Gateshead NE9 . . . . .71 E4
Tynemouth NE29 . . . . .41 D8
Whitehouse Mews NE4 . . . .40 C2
Whitehouse Prim Sch
NE29 . . . . .41 E8
Whitehouse Rd
Newcastle-u-T,Delaval
NE15 . . . . .54 C4
Newcastle-u-T,Old Benwell
NE15 . . . . .54 B4
Whitelades Cl NE38 . . . . . . .83 D6
Whitelaw Pl NE23 . . . . .22 C4
Whiteleas Way NE34 . . . . . .59 C3
Whiteleas Ct NE3 . . . . .37 E7
Whiteley Cl NE40 . . . . .52 A1
Whiteley Rd NE21 . . . . .53 E4
Whitemere Ct SR2 . . . . .86 E1
Whites Gdns NE31 . . . . .57 D6
Whiteside NE44 . . . . .62 F7
Whitethorn Cres NE5 . . . . .37 E2
Whitethroat Cl ⑥ NE38 . . .82 F3
Whitewell Cl NE40 . . . . .52 C5
Whitewell La NE40 . . . . .52 C5
Whitewell Rd NE21 . . . . .53 C2
Whitfield Dr NE12 . . . . .39 C6
Whitfield Rd
⑤ Longbenton NE12 . . . . . . .39 D8
Newcastle-u-T NE15 . . . . .53 F5
Seaton Delaval NE23 . . . . .23 B2
Whitfield Villas NE33 . . . . .59 B6
Whitgrave Rd NE5 . . . . .37 D3
Whithorn Ct NE24 . . . . .17 C7
Whitley Bay High Sch
NE26 . . . . .31 E6
Whitley Bay Sta NE25 . . . . .32 B4
Whitley Ct ⑦ NE9 . . . . .71 D3
Whitley Lodge Fst Sch
NE25 . . . . .31 E8
Whitley Terr
⑤ Bedlington NE22 . . . . .11 D3
Seaton Delaval NE25 . . . . .23 E2
Whitmore Rd NE21 . . . . .53 C3
Whitsun Ave NE22 . . . . .11 A1
Whitsun Gdns NE22 . . . . . . .11 A1
Whitsun Gr NE22 . . . . .11 A1
Whittington Cl
Ashington NE63 . . . . .6 A2
Cramlington NE30 . . . . .32 C2
Whittingham Ct NE8 . . . . .101 A1
Whittingham Rd
Newcastle-u-T NE5 . . . . .37 A4
Tynemouth NE30 . . . . .32 C1
Whittington Gr NE5 . . . . . . .54 C8
Whittleburn NE10 . . . . .71 F5
Whitton Ave NE24 . . . . .17 B5
Whitton Gr NE29 . . . . .41 D7
Whitton Pl
Newcastle-u-T NE7 . . . . .39 B4
Seaton Delaval NE25 . . . . .23 D3
Whitton Way NE3 . . . . .38 B6
Whitstall NE38 . . . . .83 F1
Whitstall Rd NE17 . . . . .66 A1
Whitstall Terr NE17 . . . . . . .66 A1
Whitwell Terr NE40 . . . . . . .52 C6
Whitworth Cl
Gateshead NE8 . . . . .70 D7
Newcastle-u-T NE6 . . . . .57 A5
Whitworth Pl NE6 . . . . .57 A5
Whitworth Rd NE37 . . . . . . .82 F7
Whorlton Grange Cotts
NE5 .36 A2
Whorlton La NE5 . . . . .36 D5
Whorlton Pl ❶ NE5 . . . . . . .36 E3
Whorlton Terr NE3 . . . . .36 B4
Whorral Bank NE61 . . . . . . .4 B2
Whyndyke NE10 . . . . .71 F5
Whytrigg Com Mid Sch
NE25 . . . . .23 C3
Whytrigg Cl NE25 . . . . .23 B3
Wickets The NE12 . . . . .38 D4
Wickham Ind Est NE16 . . . .54 A1
Wicklow Ct NE62 . . . . .11 D8
Widdrington Ave NE34 . . . .60 B8

Widdrington Gdns NE13 . .28 C6
Widdrington Rd NE21 . . . . .53 F4
Widdrington Terr
⑦ North Shields NE29 . . . . . .42 A5
Ryton NE21 . . . . .53 A4
Widnes Pl NE12 . . . . .39 C7
Wigeon Cl NE38 . . . . .83 A2
Wigham Terr NE16 . . . . .79 A4
Wigmore Ave NE6 . . . . .56 E4
Wilber Ct ⑨ SR4 . . . . .85 F7
Wilber St SR4 . . . . .85 F7
Wilberforce St
Jarrow NE32 . . . . .58 C7
Wallsend NE28 . . . . .57 B8
Wilberforce Wlk NE8 . . . .100 C2
Wilbury Pl NE5 . . . . .37 C2
Wildbriar NE38 . . . . .83 E2
Wilden Ct SR3 . . . . .86 B2
Wilden Rd NE38 . . . . .84 A3
Wildshaw Cl NE23 . . . . .22 C3
Wilfred St
Boldon Colliery NE35 . . . . . . .73 F8
Chester le St DH3 . . . . .88 C2
Newcastle-u-T NE6 . . . . .56 A6
Sunderland SR4 . . . . .85 E7
Wilfrid St DH3 . . . . .88 C2
Wilkes Cl NE5 . . . . .36 F2
Wilkinson Ave NE31 . . . . . .57 D3
Wilkinson Ct ❹ NE32 . . . . .58 B7
Wilkinson Terr SR2 . . . . . . .92 E6
Wilkwood Cl NE23 . . . . .22 C4
Willerby Dr NE3 . . . . .38 D8
William Allan Homes
NE22 . . . . .15 D8
William Armstrong Dr
NE4 .54 F3
William Cl NE12 . . . . .40 A8
William Doxford Ctr SR3 . .91 F6
William IV Yd NE8 . . . . . . .101 B4
William Morris Ave NE39 .67 B2
William Roberts Ct NE12 . .29 D1
William St Blyth NE24 . . . . .17 E6
Chester le S DH3 . . . . .88 C3
Chopwell NE17 . . . . .66 B1
Gateshead NE10 . . . . .56 D1
Hebburn NE31 . . . . .57 D7
Newcastle-u-T NE3 . . . . .38 E5
North Shields NE29 . . . . .42 A5
Pegswood NE61 . . . . .4 F3
⑤ South Shields NE33 . . . . . .42 C2
Sunderland SR1 . . . . .103 A3
⑨ Sunderland,South Hylton
SR4 .85 A6
⑨ Whickham NE16 . . . . .69 A7
William St W
Hebburn NE31 . . . . .57 D6
⑭ North Shields NE29 . . . . . .42 A5
William Terr NE31 . . . . .57 D7
William Whiteley Homes
NE40 . . . . .52 A1
Williams Pk NE12 . . . . .39 C6
Williams Terr SR2 . . . . .92 E6
Williamson Terr SR6 . . . . .103 A4
Willington Terr NE28 . . . . .40 E3
Willis St DH5 . . . . .95 A5
Willmore St SR4 . . . . .102 A2
Willoughby Dr NE16 . . . . . .31 E7
Willoughby Rd NE29 . . . . . .41 E6
Willoughby Way NE26 . . . .31 E7
Willow Ave Blyth NE24 . . . .12 D1
Dunston NE11 . . . . .69 F8
Newcastle-u-T NE4 . . . . .54 D8
Willow Bank Rd SR2 . . . . . .86 C3
Willow Cl Morpeth NE61 . . . .9 B8
Whickham NE16 . . . . .69 B6
Willow Cres Blyth NE24 . . .17 C4
Easington Lane DH5 . . . . .95 D1
Stakeford NE62 . . . . .11 B7
Willow Dyke NE45 . . . . .47 A6
Willow Gdns NE12 . . . . .29 C4
Willow Gn ⑦ SR2 . . . . .86 C4
Willow Gr Gateshead NE10 .71 E8
South Shields NE34 . . . . .59 F5
Wallsend NE28 . . . . .40 D1
Willow Grange NE32 . . . . . .58 A7
Willow Rd Blaydon NE21 . . .53 D2
Houghton-le-S DH4 . . . . .94 C8
Willow View NE16 . . . . .69 A6
Willow Way NE20 . . . . .25 E3
Willow's Ct ❶ NE38 . . . . . .83 F4
Willowbank Gdns NE12 . . .38 E4
Willowfield Ave NE3 . . . . . .37 F6
Willows Cl NE13 . . . . .28 A5
Willows The
Hebburn NE31 . . . . .57 E4
Hedworth NE32 . . . . .58 C1
Morpeth NE61 . . . . .9 A8
Seaton Burn NE13 . . . . .21 B1
Throckley NE15 . . . . .35 D1
Washington NE38 . . . . .84 A4
Willowvale DH2 . . . . .88 A5
Wills Mews NE17 . . . . .66 A1
Wills Oval NE7 . . . . .39 E2
Wilmington Cl NE3 . . . . .37 B6
Wilson Ave Birtley DH3 . . . .82 C5
Cambois NE62 . . . . .12 B3
Wilson Dr NE36 . . . . .74 B8
Wilson Gdns NE3 . . . . .38 B3
Wilson St Dunston NE11 . . .69 F8
South Shields NE33 . . . . .42 C1
Sunderland SR4 . . . . .85 F6
Wallsend NE28 . . . . .40 B2
Wilson St N SR5 . . . . .102 C4

Wilson Terr
❶ Longbenton NE12 . . . . . . .39 D8
New Silksworth SR3 . . . . .92 A8
Wilson's Ct ❹ NE1 . . . . .99 A1
Wilson's La NE9 . . . . .70 F5
Wilswary NE15 . . . . .35 C2
Wilton Ave NE6 . . . . .56 E4
Wilton Cl
Cramlington NE23 . . . . .22 C3
Whitley Bay NE25 . . . . .31 C5
Wilton Cotts ⑤ NE35 . . . . .58 E1
Wilton Dr NE25 . . . . .31 B5
Wilton Gdns N NE35 . . . . . .58 E1
Wilton Gdns S NE35 . . . . . .58 E1
Wilton Manse NE35 . . . . . . .31 B4
Wilton Sq SR2 . . . . .86 E1
Wiltshire Cl SR5 . . . . .74 E4
Wiltshire Dr NE28 . . . . .39 F4
Wiltshire Gdns NE28 . . . . . .40 A3
Wiltshire Pl NE37 . . . . .72 D2
Wiltshire Rd SR5 . . . . .74 E4
Wimbledon Cl SR5 . . . . . . .74 F3
Wimborne Cl NE35 . . . . . . .73 E8
Wimbourne Ave SR4 . . . . . .85 E4
Wimbourne Gn ❶ NE5 . . . .36 F3
Wimpole Cl NE37 . . . . .72 E2
Winslow Cl NE28 . . . . .39 F3
Winalot Ave SR2 . . . . .86 E2
Wincanton Pl NE29 . . . . . . .21 E4
Winchcombe Pl NE7 . . . . . .39 A4
Winchester Ave NE24 . . . . .17 E7
Winchester Cl ❻ NE63 . . . . .6 F2
Winchester St NE33 . . . . . . .42 D3
Winchester Terr NE4 . . . . . .98 B1
Winchester Way NE22 . . . .10 F2
Winchester Wlk NE13 . . . . .28 B6
Wincomblee Rd NE6 . . . . . .57 B4
Windburgh Dr NE23 . . . . . .22 B3
Windermere Birtley DH3 . . .82 D2
Cleadon SR6 . . . . .60 A1
Windermere Ave
Chester le S DH2 . . . . .88 C1
Easington Lane DH5 . . . . .97 C8
Gateshead NE10 . . . . .71 F8
Windermere Cl NE23 . . . . . .22 B2
Windermere Cres
Blaydon NE21 . . . . .68 B8
Hebburn NE31 . . . . .57 F4
Pelaw NE10 . . . . .58 D3
Pensham NE4 . . . . .90 C6
South Shields NE34 . . . . .59 E6
Windermere Dr NE12 . . . . . .29 C3
Windermere Gdns NE16 . . .69 C7
Windermere Rd
Newbiggin-by-t-S NE64 . . . . . .7 C3
Newcastle-u-T NE5 . . . . .54 C8
Windermere St
Gateshead NE8 . . . . .101 B1
Sunderland SR2 . . . . .86 F2
Windermere St W NE8 . . . .101 B1
Windermere Terr NE29 . . . .41 F6
Windhill Rd NE6 . . . . .56 F3
Winding The NE13 . . . . .27 B7
Windlass Ct NE34 . . . . .59 C5
Windlass La NE37 . . . . .83 A6
Windmill Ct NE2 . . . . .98 C4
Windmill Gr NE24 . . . . .17 A8
Windmill Hill Ellington NE61 .1 E5
Hexham NE46 . . . . .45 A5
South Shields NE33 . . . . .42 B1
Windmill Hill Cl NE61 . . . . .1 E6
Windmill Hills Prim Sch
NE8 . . . . .101 B2
Windmill Hts NE61 . . . . .1 E6
Windmill Ind Est NE23 . . . .15 C2
Windmill Sq SR5 . . . . .75 C4
Windmill Way
Gateshead NE8 . . . . .101 A2
Hebburn NE31 . . . . .57 E8
Morpeth NE61 . . . . .9 B8
Windshields Wlk NE15 . . . .35 C1

Windsor Ave
Gateshead NE8 . . . . .70 E8
Newcastle-u-T NE3 . . . . .38 C4
Whitley Bay NE26 . . . . .32 C4
Windsor Cl Wallsend NE28 . .41 A4
Whickham NE16 . . . . .69 A4
Windsor Cotts
Hebburn NE31 . . . . .57 F6
Houghton-le-S DH5 . . . . .94 F8
Newcastle-u-T NE5 . . . . .37 A3
Ovingham NE42 . . . . .50 B5
Whitley Bay NE26 . . . . .32 C6
Windsor Ct
Bedlington NE22 . . . . .15 F8
Corbridge NE45 . . . . .47 A6
Cramlington NE23 . . . . .16 A1
⑦ Gateshead NE10 . . . . .71 C8
Newcastle-u-T,Kingston Park
NE3 .37 E7
Newcastle-u-T,South Gosforth
NE3 .38 E5
Rowlands Gill NE39 . . . . .78 A8
Windsor Dr Blyth NE24 . . . .17 D3
Cleadon SR6 . . . . .59 F1
Houghton-le-S DH5 . . . . .94 F8
New Silksworth SR3 . . . . .92 A8
South Hetton DH6 . . . . .98 E1
Wallsend NE28 . . . . .41 A4
Windsor Fst Sch NE37 . . . . . .7 D3
Windsor Gdns
Bedlington NE22 . . . . .15 F8
Gateshead NE10 . . . . .71 C8
South Shields NE34 . . . . .59 E7
Whitley Bay NE26 . . . . .31 F6

Windsor Gdns W NE26 . . . .31 F6
Windsor Pk NE28 . . . . .39 F3
Windsor Pl
Longbenton NE27 . . . . .30 C1
Newcastle-u-T NE2 . . . . .99 B3
Ponteland NE20 . . . . .25 B4
Windsor Rd Birtley DH3 . . . .82 B6
Newbiggin-by-t-S NE64 . . . . . .7 D4
Springwell NE9 . . . . .72 A1
Whitley Bay NE25 . . . . .31 E5
Windsor St ❷ NE28 . . . . . . .40 B2
Windsor Terr
Choppington NE62 . . . . .10 F4
Corbridge NE45 . . . . .47 A6
Crawcrook NE40 . . . . .52 A4
Haswell DH6 . . . . .97 F2
Hexham NE46 . . . . .45 A4
Newcastle-u-T,South Gosforth
NE3 .38 E4
❶ Springwell NE9 . . . . .71 F1
Sunderland,East Herrington
SR3 .91 C6
⑧ Sunderland,Grangetown
SR2 .86 F2
Whitley Bay NE26 . . . . .32 C4
Windsor Villas NE23 . . . . . .11 A7
Windsor Way NF3 . . . . .37 D7
Windsor Wlk
Ashington NE63 . . . . .7 A2
Newcastle-u-T NE3 . . . . .37 D7
Windt St NE13 . . . . .28 A5
Windy Gyle NE63 . . . . .6 F4
Windy Nook Prim Sch
NE10 . . . . .71 D6
Windy Ridge NE10 . . . . .71 C7
Windy Ridge Villas NE10 . .71 C7
Wingate Cl
Houghton-le-S DH4 . . . . .94 D8
Newcastle-u-T NE15 . . . . .53 E6
Wingate Gdns NE9 . . . . .71 D3
Wingrove NE39 . . . . .67 D1
Wingrove Ave
Newcastle-u-T NE4 . . . . .54 F3
Sunderland SR6 . . . . .75 E3
Wingrove Gdns NE4 . . . . . . .54 F7
Wingrove Ho NE4 . . . . .54 F6
Wingrove Prim Sch NE4 . . .54 F6
Wingrove Rd NE4 . . . . .54 F7
Wingrove Terr ❶❶ NE9 . . . .71 F1
Winifred Gdns NE28 . . . . . . .40 C1
Winifred St SR6 . . . . .75 D5
Winifred Terr SR1 . . . . .86 D2
Winlaton West Lane Com
NE21 . . . . .68 A8
Winsford Ave ❹ NE29 . . . . .31 F1
Winshields NE23 . . . . .22 C4
Winship Cl NE34 . . . . .59 D3
Winship St NE24 . . . . .17 C4
Winskell Rd NE34 . . . . .59 A4
Winslade Cl SR3 . . . . .92 B8
Winslow Cl
Boldon Colliery NE35 . . . . . . .58 F2
Newcastle-u-T NE6 . . . . .57 A5
Sunderland SR5 . . . . .74 F4
Winslow Gdns NE9 . . . . .70 E5
Winslow Pl NE6 . . . . .57 A5
Winster NE38 . . . . .83 A1
Winster Pl NE23 . . . . .22 B3
Winston Cres SR4 . . . . .85 E4
Winston Ct NE9 . . . . .71 F1
Winston Gn DH4 . . . . .89 F8
Winston Way NE43 . . . . .64 B8
Winton Cl NE23 . . . . .23 A2
Winton Way NE3 . . . . .37 A2
Wirralshir NE10 . . . . .72 A6
Wiseton Ct NE7 . . . . .38 F5
Wishart Ho NE4 . . . . .54 E4
Wishart Terr NE39 . . . . .67 B1
Wishaw Cl NE23 . . . . .22 C3
Wishaw Rise NE15 . . . . .53 E7
Witham Gn NE32 . . . . .58 E3
Witham Rd NE31 . . . . .57 E3
Witherington Cl NE7 . . . . . .39 C4
Withernsea Gr SR2 . . . . .92 D7
Witherwack Prim Sch
SR5 .74 F4
Witney Cl SR5 . . . . .74 F4
Witney Way NE36 . . . . .74 B7
Witton Ave NE34 . . . . .60 A6
Witton Ct
Newcastle-u-T NE3 . . . . .37 E6
Sunderland SR3 . . . . .86 B2
Washington NE38 . . . . .83 B4
Witton Gdns
❶ Jarrow NE32 . . . . .58 A7
Jarrow NE32 . . . . .58 B3
Witton Gr DH4 . . . . .94 B8
Witton Rd Hebburn NE31 . . .57 F8
Shiremoor NE27 . . . . .30 F4
Wittonstone Ho NE3 . . . . . .38 A3
Woburn DH2 . . . . .88 B6
Woburn Cl
Cramlington NE23 . . . . .16 A1
Wallsend NE28 . . . . .39 F3
Woburn Dr
Bedlington NE22 . . . . .11 C2
Silksworth SR3 . . . . .92 A7
Woburn Way NE5 . . . . .37 A2
Wolmer Rd NE24 . . . . .17 F5
Wolseley Cl NE8 . . . . .70 E8
Wolseley Gdns NE2 . . . . . . .56 A8
Wolseley Terr SR4 . . . . .102 A1
Wolsey Ct NE34 . . . . .59 C6

Wolsingham Ct NE23 . . . . . .21 F7
Wolsingham Gdns ❺
NE9 .71 D3
Wolsingham Rd NE3 . . . . . . .38 B4
Wolsingham St NE4 . . . . . .100 A3
Wolsley Rd NE24 . . . . .17 C7
Wolveleigh Terr NE3 . . . . . .38 D5
Wolviston Grds NE9 . . . . . . .71 E3
Wood Fields NE20 . . . . .25 F6
Wood Gr NE15 . . . . .53 E7
Wood Ho ❽ SR3 . . . . .91 F5
Wood La NE22 . . . . .11 B1
Wood Lea DH5 . . . . .95 A7
Wood St Burnopfield NE16 . .79 A6
Dunston NE11 . . . . .69 F8
Sunderland SR4 . . . . .102 A3
Wood Terr
Gateshead NE10 . . . . .57 B2
High Spen NE39 . . . . .67 A2
Jarrow NE32 . . . . .58 A4
South Shields NE33 . . . . .59 D8
Washington NE37 . . . . .83 D8
Woodbine Ave
Newcastle-u-T NE3 . . . . .38 C4
Wallsend NE28 . . . . .40 B2
Woodbine Cl NE4 . . . . .54 F4
Woodbine Pl NE8 . . . . .52 B5
Woodbine Rd NE3 . . . . .38 C5
Woodbine St
Gateshead NE8 . . . . .101 B1
❷ South Shields NE33 . . . . .42 D3
Sunderland SR1 . . . . .103 C2
Woodbine Terr
Birtley DH3 . . . . .82 D4
Blyth NE24 . . . . .17 F6
Corbridge NE45 . . . . .47 A6
Gateshead,Bill Quay NE10 . . .57 A1
Gateshead,Felling NE10 . . . . .71 B8
Hexham NE46 . . . . .44 F5
Sunderland SR5 . . . . .85 F8
Woodbine Villas NE8 . . . . .101 B1
Woodbrook Ave NE5 . . . . . .54 A8
Woodburn NE10 . . . . .71 E5
Woodburn Ave NE4 . . . . . . .54 E8
Woodburn Cl
Blaydon NE21 . . . . .68 A8
Bournmoor DH4 . . . . .89 E2
Woodburn Dr
Burnside DH4 . . . . .90 C1
Whitley Bay NE26 . . . . .31 E7
Woodburn Gdns NE11 . . . . .70 A6
Woodburn Sq NE26 . . . . . . .31 E7
Woodburn St NE15 . . . . .53 C7
Woodburn Terr NE42 . . . . . .50 B2
Woodburn Way NE26 . . . . . .31 E6
Woodchurch Cl NE12 . . . . . .39 D4
Woodcliff Cl NE38 . . . . .23 B1
Woodcroft Cl NE23 . . . . .22 B1
Woodcroft Rd NE41 . . . . . . .51 A6
Woodend NE9 . . . . .25 D2
Woodend Way NE3 . . . . .37 D8
Woodford NE9 . . . . .70 F1
Woodford Cl SR5 . . . . .74 F4
Woodgate Gdns NE10 . . . . .57 B1
Woodgate La NE10 . . . . .57 B1
Woodhall Cl DH2 . . . . .81 E1
Woodhall Ct NE23 . . . . .23 C3
Woodhall Spa DH4 . . . . .90 A4
Woodhead Rd
Newcastle-u-T NE6 . . . . .56 F8
Prudhoe NE42 . . . . .50 A3
Woodhill Dr NE61 . . . . .8 E8
Woodhorn Colliery Mus*
NE63 .6 F5
Woodhorn Cotts NE64 . . . . .7 D5
Woodhorn Cres NE64 . . . . . .7 D5
Woodhorn Dr NE62 . . . . . . .10 F8
Woodhorn Farm NE64 . . . . .7 E6
Woodhorn La NE63 . . . . .7 B6
Woodhorn Mews NE64 . . . . .7 D6
Woodhorn Rd
Ashington NE63 . . . . .6 F4
Newbiggin-by-t-S NE64 . . . . . .7 D5
Woodhorn Villas NE63 . . . . .6 F4
Woodhouse Ct NE34 . . . . . .60 C7
Woodhouses La
Whickham,Fellside NE16 . . . .68 E6
Whickham,Swalwell NE16 . . .68 E6
Woodhurst Gr SR4 . . . . .85 A2
Woodkirk Cl NE23 . . . . .22 C3
Woodland Cres NE15 . . . . . .53 E6
Woodland Dr SR4 . . . . .85 E4
Woodland Grange NE37 . . .89 F1
Woodland Mews NE2 . . . . . .56 B3
Woodland Rise SR3 . . . . . . .91 F6
Woodland Terr
Penshaw DH4 . . . . .90 A8
Washington NE37 . . . . .83 E8
Woodland View DH4 . . . . . .94 A1
Woodlands
Burnopfield NE16 . . . . .79 B6
Chester le S DH3 . . . . .88 C4
Great Lumley DH4 . . . . .89 F1
Hexham NE46 . . . . .45 A6
Newcastle-u-T NE3 . . . . .38 C2
Pontland NE20 . . . . .25 D3
Seaham SR7 . . . . .92 F1
Tynemouth NE29 . . . . .41 E8
Washington NE38 . . . . .88 E8

Woodlands Cl
Earsdon NE25 . . . . .31 A5
High Spen NE39 . . . . .67 A3
Woodlands Ct
Kibblesworth NE11 . . . . . . .81 D6
Throckley NE15 . . . . .35 C2
Woodlands Dr SR6 . . . . . .75 A8
Woodlands Grange NE12 .29 E1
Woodlands Ho NE24 . . . . .17 B8
Woodlands Park Dr
NE21 . . . . .53 D2
Woodlands Park Villas
NE13 . . . . .28 C4
Woodlands Pk NE13 . . . . .28 C5
Woodlands Rd
Ashington NE63 . . . . .7 A2
Cleadon SR6 . . . . .75 A8
Newcastle-u-T NE15 . . . . . .53 D7
Rowlands Gill NE39 . . . . . . .67 D2
Woodlands Terr
Gateshead NE10 . . . . .71 C8
Longbenton NE12 . . . . .29 E1
⬛ South Shields NE33 . . . .42 D4
Woodlands The NE11 . . . .81 D6
Woodlands View SR6 . . . .75 A8
Woodlawn Sch NE25 . . . .31 D3
Woodlea Longbenton NE12 .29 D1
Newbiggin-by-t-S NE64 . . . . .7 E5
Woodlea Cl DH5 . . . . .95 A4
Woodlea Cres NE46 . . . . .45 C4
Woodlea Ct NE29 . . . . . . .41 E3
Woodlea Gdns NE3 . . . . .38 E6
Woodlea Prim Sch DH4 . .89 E1
Woodlea Rd NE39 . . . . . . .67 B2
Woodlea Sq NE29 . . . . . . .41 E3
Woodleigh Rd NE25 . . . . .31 E4
Woodleigh View NE5 . . . .37 E3
Woodman Cl NE61 . . . . . . .8 E7
Woodman St NE28 . . . . . .41 B3
Woodmans Way NE16 . . .68 F4
Woodpack Ave NE16 . . . . .68 F6
Woods Gn NE10 . . . . .57 C1
Woods Terr NE8 . . . . .101 C1
Woodside Bedlington NE22 .11 C1
Blyth NE24 . . . . .17 F6
Hexham NE46 . . . . .45 D4
Morpeth NE61 . . . . .8 D7
Ponteland NE20 . . . . .25 C2
Prudhoe NE42 . . . . .50 F2
Sunderland SR2 . . . . .102 C1
Sunderland,East Herrington
SR3 . . . . .91 C6
Woodside Ave
Corbridge NE45 . . . . .47 B6
Newcastle-u-T NE15 . . . . . .57 D7
Seaton Delaval NE25 . . . . . .23 D2
Throckley NE15 . . . . .35 E2

Woodside Cl NE40 . . . . . .52 C5
Woodside Cres NE12 . . . .39 E8
Woodside Ct NE12 . . . . . .39 E8
Woodside Gdns NE11 . . . .69 F7
Woodside Gr
Sunderland SR3 . . . . .91 C6
Tantobie DH9 . . . . .79 C3
Woodside La
Greenside NE40 . . . . .52 B3
Ryton NE40 . . . . .52 B4
Woodside Rd NE40 . . . . . .52 B5
Woodside Terr
Chopwell NE17 . . . . .77 B8
Sunderland SR3 . . . . .91 C6
Woodside Villas NE46 . . .45 D4
Woodside Way
Ryton NE40 . . . . .52 C5
South Shields NE33 . . . . . . .59 B7
Woodside Wlk NE39 . . . . .67 C1
Woodstock Ave SR2 . . . . .86 E2
Woodstock Rd
Gateshead NE8 . . . . .71 B2
Newcastle-u-T NE15 . . . . . .54 A5
Woodstone Terr DH4 . . . .89 D1
Woodthorne Rd NE2 . . . . .38 E3
Woodvale NE20 . . . . .25 C2
Woodvale Dr NE31 . . . . . .57 C4
Woodvale Gdns
Gateshead NE9 . . . . .71 C6
Newcastle-u-T NE15 . . . . . .53 E7
Wylam NE41 . . . . .51 B6
Woodvale Rd
Blaydon NE21 . . . . .53 D2
Killingworth NE12 . . . . .29 C4
Woodville Cres SR4 . . . . .85 E4
Woodville Ct SR4 . . . . . . .85 E4
Woodville Rd NE15 . . . . . .53 D8
Woodwynd NE10 . . . . .71 F6
Wooler Ave NE29 . . . . . . .41 D4
Wooler Cres NE8 . . . . .70 C8
Wooler Gn NE15 . . . . .53 B7
Wooler Sq Sunderland SR2 .86 E3
Wideopen NE13 . . . . .28 C7
Wooler Wlk NE32 . . . . . . .58 A4
Woolerton Dr
Gateshead N10,NE9 . . . . . .71 C6
Gateshead NE9 . . . . .71 B6
Newcastle-u-T NE15 . . . . . .53 E7
Wooley St NE28 . . . . .40 B1
Woolmer Ct NE7 . . . . .39 E3
Woolsington Ct NE22 . . . .10 F1
Woolsington Gdns NE13 . .36 F8
Woolsington Pk S NE13 . .36 F8
Woolsington Rd NE29 . . . .41 C7
Woolwich Cl SR5 . . . . .74 F4
Woolwich Rd SR5 . . . . . . .74 F4
Wooperton Gdns NE5 . . . .54 C7
Worcester Gn NE8 . . . . . .101 B2
Worcester St SR2 . . . . . .102 C1
Worcester Terr SR2 . . . . .102 C2

Worcester Way NE13 . . . .28 C5
Wordsworth Ave
Blyth NE24 . . . . .17 C6
Easington Lane DH5 . . . . . .97 D8
Hebburn NE31 . . . . .57 E6
Whickham NE16 . . . . .69 B8
Wordsworth Ave E DH5 . .94 E7
Wordsworth Ave W DH5 . .94 E7
Wordsworth Cres NE9 . . .71 F1
Wordsworth St NE8 . . . . .56 A2
Worley Ave NE9 . . . . .70 F4
Worley Cl NE4 . . . . .98 B1
Worley Mews NE9 . . . . . . .70 F4
Worley St NE4 . . . . .98 B1
Worley Terr DH9 . . . . .79 A1
Worm Hill Terr NE38 . . . . .83 E1
Worsdell St NE24 . . . . . . .12 E1
Worsley Cl NE28 . . . . .39 F4
Worswick St NE1 . . . . .99 B1
Worthing Cl NE28 . . . . . . .39 F3
Worthington Ct NE2 . . . . .99 C4
Wouldhave Ct NE33 . . . . .42 E3
Wouldhave St NE33 . . . . .42 E3
Wraith Terr SR2 . . . . .92 E6
Wraysbury Ct NE3 . . . . . . .37 D7
Wreay Wlk NE23 . . . . .22 C3
Wreigh St NE31 . . . . .57 D6
Wreken Gdns NE10 . . . . . .72 C8
Wrekenton Row NE9 . . . .71 C2
Wrekenton Sta* NE9 . . . . . .71 D2
Wren Cl NE38 . . . . .83 A3
Wren Gr ◼ SR5 . . . . .74 C1
Wretham Pl NE2 . . . . .99 C4
Wright Dr NE23 . . . . .29 A7
Wright St NE24 . . . . .17 D8
Wright Terr DH4 . . . . .90 A5
Wrightson St NE23 . . . . . .16 B3
Wroxham Ct
Newcastle-u-T NE5 . . . . . . .37 B4
Sunderland SR2 . . . . .86 E2
Wroxton NE38 . . . . .83 C3
Wuppertal Ct NE32 . . . . . .58 B6
Wych Elm Cl NE61 . . . . . . .1 D4
Wych Elm Cres NE7 . . . . .39 C3
Wychcroft Way NE5 . . . . .37 C2
Wycliffe Ave NE3 . . . . .37 F3
Wycliffe Rd SR4 . . . . .85 F4
Wydon Pk NE46 . . . . .45 A3
Wye Ave NE32 . . . . .58 C3
Wye Rd NE31 . . . . .57 E3
Wylam Ave NE25 . . . . .23 F2
Wylam Cl
South Shields NE34 . . . . . . .59 E5
Washington NE37 . . . . .72 E1
Wylam Fst Sch NE41 . . . . .51 B6
Wylam Gdns NE28 . . . . . .40 F4
Wylam Gr SR1 . . . . .103 B2
Wylam Mill NE41 . . . . .51 B6
Wylam Rd NE29 . . . . .41 F3
Wylam St NE32 . . . . .58 B7

Wylam Sta NE41 . . . . .51 C5
Wylam View NE21 . . . . . . .53 B2
Wylam Wood Rd NE41 . . .51 B5
Wynbury Rd NE9 . . . . .71 A5
Wyncote Ct NE7 . . . . .39 B2
Wynd The
Longbenton NE12 . . . . .29 F1
Newcastle-u-T NE3 . . . . . . .38 A4
Throckley NE15 . . . . .35 D1
Tynemouth NE30 . . . . .42 A8
Wynde The
Ponteland NE20 . . . . .25 D4
South Shields NE34 . . . . . . .59 D5
Wyndfall Way NE3 . . . . . .38 A3
Wyndham Ave NE3 . . . . . .37 F3
Wyndham Prim Sch NE3 .38 A3
Wyndham Way NE29 . . . .41 B8
Wynding The
Annitsford NE23 . . . . .22 B1
Bedlington NE22 . . . . .10 E1
Wyndley Cl NE16 . . . . .68 F5
Wyndley Ho NE3 . . . . .37 F3
Wyndley Pl NE3 . . . . .37 F3
Wyndrow Pl NE3 . . . . .37 F3
Wyndsail Pl NE3 . . . . .38 A3
Wyndtop Pl NE3 . . . . .38 A3
Wyndward Pl NE3 . . . . . . .38 A3
Wyndways Dr DH9 . . . . . .78 E1
Wynn Gdns NE10 . . . . . . .56 F1
Wynnstay Gdns DH2 . . . .88 A3
Wynyard Dr NE22 . . . . . . .11 C3
Wynyard Gdns NE9 . . . . .71 C2
Wynyard Sq SR2 . . . . .86 E2
Wynyard St Dunston NE11 .69 F8
Fence Houses DH4 . . . . . . .94 A8
New Silksworth SR3 . . . . . .92 A7
Wythburn Pl NE9 . . . . .71 B4
Wyvern Sq SR2 . . . . .86 E2

Y

Yardley Gr NE23 . . . . .22 A8
Yarmouth Dr NE23 . . . . . .22 A8
Yatesbury Ave NE5 . . . . . .37 B3
Yeadon Ct NE3 . . . . .37 C7
Yeavering Cl NE3 . . . . .38 B4
Yellow Leas Farm NE36 . .74 C7
Yelverton Cres NE6 . . . . . .56 F3
Yelverton Ct NE23 . . . . . . .22 A8
Yemeni Sch The NE33 . . .42 B1
Yeoman St NE29 . . . . .42 B5
Yeovil Cl NE23 . . . . .22 A8
Yetholm Ave DH2 . . . . . . .88 B2
Yetholm Pl NE5 . . . . .37 A4
Yetholm Rd NE8 . . . . .100 B1
Yetlington Dr NE3 . . . . . . .38 A4
Yew Tree Dr NE22 . . . . . . .10 F2
Yewburn Way NE12 . . . . . .29 C6
Yewcroft Ave NE15 . . . . . .54 A6

Yewdale Gdns NE9 . . . . . .71 A4
Yewtree Ave SR5 . . . . .74 F4
Yewtree Gdns NE6 . . . . . .40 A4
Yewtrees NE10 . . . . .71 E1
Yewvale Rd NE5 . . . . .37 D4
York Ave NE32 . . . . .58 B4
York Cl NE23 . . . . .22 A6
York Cres DH5 . . . . .94 F1
York Ct Chester le S DH3 . .88 D2
◼ Wallsend NE28 . . . . . . .40 B6
York Dr NE28 . . . . .40 B6
York Gr NE22 . . . . .10 D1
York Ho SR5 . . . . .74 A4
York Rd Birtley DH3 . . . . . .82 C6
Whitley Bay NE26 . . . . .32 B6
York St Blyth NE24 . . . . . . .17 E3
Gateshead NE10 . . . . .57 A1
Hetton le H DH5 . . . . .94 E1
Jarrow NE32 . . . . .58 A4
New Silksworth SR3 . . . . . .92 A6
Newcastle-u-T NE4 . . . . . . .98 B1
Sunderland SR1 . . . . .103 A4
York Terr Chester le S DH3 .88 D2
Gateshead NE10 . . . . .71 D4
York Way NE34 . . . . .60 A4
Yorkdale Pl NE6 . . . . .57 A4
Yorkwood NE31 . . . . .57 F4
Young Rd NE12 . . . . .29 F7
Younghall Cl NE40 . . . . . . .52 A4

Z

Zetland Dr NE25 . . . . .31 F2
Zetland Sq ◼ SR6 . . . . . . .75 E2
Zetland St SR6 . . . . .75 E2
Zion St SR1 . . . . .103 B1
Zion Terr Blaydon NE21 . . .53 E1
Sunderland SR5 . . . . .75 C1

Addresses

Name and Address	Telephone	Page	Grid reference

NG NH NJ NK

NM NN NO NP

NR NS NT NU

NX NY NZ

SC SD SE TA

SH SJ SK TF TG

SM SN SO SP TL TM

SR SS ST SU TQ TR

SW SX SY SZ TV

Any feature in this atlas can be given a unique reference to help you find the same feature on other Ordnance Survey maps of the area, or to help someone else locate you if they do not have a Street Atlas.

The grid squares in this atlas match the Ordnance Survey National Grid and are at 500 metre intervals. The small figures at the bottom and sides of every other grid line are the National Grid kilometre values (**00** to **99** km) and are repeated across the country every 100 km (see left).

To give a unique National Grid reference you need to locate where in the country you are. The country is divided into 100 km squares with each square given a unique two-letter reference. Use the administrative map to determine in which 100 km square a particular page of this atlas falls.

The bold letters and numbers between each grid line (**A** to **F**, **1** to **8**) are for use within a specific Street Atlas only, and when used with the page number, are a convenient way of referencing these grid squares.

Example The railway bridge over DARLEY GREEN RD in grid square B1

Step 1: Identify the two-letter reference, in this example the page is in **SP**

Eastings (read from left to right along the bottom) come before Northings (read from bottom to top). If you have trouble remembering say to yourself "Along the hall, THEN up the stairs"!

Step 2: Identify the 1 km square in which the railway bridge falls. Use the figures in the southwest corner of this square: Eastings **17**, Northings **74**. This gives a unique reference: **SP 17 74**, accurate to 1 km.

Step 3: To give a more precise reference accurate to 100 m you need to estimate how many tenths along and how many tenths up this 1 km square the feature is (to help with this the 1 km square is divided into four 500 m squares). This makes the bridge about **8** tenths along and about **1** tenth up from the southwest corner.

This gives a unique reference: **SP 178 741**, accurate to 100 m.

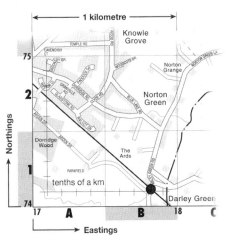